Employee Benefits

6th Edition

Burton T. Beam, Jr.
& John J. McFadden

**Real Estate
Education Company**®

This publication is designed to provide accurate and authoritative information in regard to the subject matter covered. It is sold with the understanding that the publisher is not engaged in rendering legal, accounting, or other professional service. If legal advice or other expert assistance is required, the services of a competent professional person should be sought.

Publisher: Evan Butterfield
Development Editor: Amanda Rahn
Development Editor: David Cirillo
Managing Editor: Ronald J. Liszkowski
Typesetting: Janet Schroeder
Art Manager: Lucy Jenkins

Published by Real Estate Education Company,®
a division of Dearborn Financial Publishing, Inc.®
155 North Wacker Drive
Chicago, IL 60606-1719
(312) 836-4400
http://www.REcampus.com

Printed in the United States of America.

00 01 02 10 9 8 7 6 5 4 3 2

Library of Congress Cataloging-in-Publication Data

Beam, Burton T.
    Employee benefits / Burton T. Beam, John J. McFadden—6th ed.
        p. cm.
    Includes bibliographical references (p.) and index.
    ISBN 0-7931-3960-0
    1. Employee fringe benefits—United States   2. Compensation management—United States
I. McFadden, John J.   II. Title.
HD4928.N62 U623 2000
658.3'25—dc21   00-059255

DEDICATION

To Betsy, Greg, Grant, and Gretchen
   B.T.B.

To Diana, Rhoda, and Susanna
   J.J. McF.

CONTENTS

v

PREFACE

Over the last two decades, few fields have changed as dramatically as that of employee benefits. Employers are spending an ever-increasing portion of total compensation dollars on benefit plans. Some of this increased spending is a result of new or expanded benefits being offered. However, a significant portion of the increase arises because the cost of certain benefits, such as medical expense coverage, has risen at a faster rate than wages. This spiraling cost has made employers increasingly concerned with containing benefit costs.

Legislation has also had a significant effect on employee benefit plans, causing employers to continually monitor and often to revise their plans. For example, the impact of the Employee Retirement Income Security Act of 1974 (ERISA) and subsequent legislation continually alter the area of pensions. The Age Discrimination in Employment Act resulted in benefits being provided to persons who previously had coverages terminated at a certain age, such as 65, and the Health Insurance Portability and Accountability Act of 1996 has greatly changed the area of medical expense insurance. In addition, the states continue to mandate the types of benefits that employees must be provided.

The federal tax treatment of employee benefit plans also has had a particularly significant impact on employee benefit plans. Certain types of plans, such as medical expense plans and qualified retirement plans, owe their popularity in large part to federal tax advantages. Cafeteria plans and Section 401(k) cash-or-deferred plans have become more widespread largely because of legislative clarification of their tax treatment. Since the tax benefits for employee benefit plans result in a substantial annual loss of federal tax revenues, Congress has imposed an elaborate and ever-changing scheme of regulation on these plans; in the last ten years, there have been eleven major tax law changes. The information in this text reflects current law through mid-2000.

This changing environment and the resultant need for up-to-date materials was one reason for the first edition of this book and has remained a major consideration in the latest edition. Since the last edition of the book was prepared, there have been significant changes affecting employee benefits.

Nowhere have the changes occurred any faster than in the area of medical expense coverage. Managed care plans have, by far, become the dominant method of providing medical expense coverage to employees. However, this has led to a consumer backlash and concern over the quality of care. There has been considerable reaction to this backlash at the state level and through voluntary changes adopted by managed care plans. Debate on the issue continues at the federal level. Employers have also reacted by increasingly requiring accreditation of managed care plans that they offer to their employees.

Within the managed care arena, there have also been significant changes as plans continue to evolve. Concerns about restrictions on the ability of patients to select their own providers have led to the continued growth of preferred-provider arrangements and point-of-service plans at the expense of HMOs.

All types of medical expense plans are more likely to provide an increasing array of benefits for alternatives to traditional medicine. In addition, carveouts for benefits, such as prescription drugs and disease management, continue to grow in use.

These changes are all reflected in a significant revision of the four chapters on medical expense benefits.

Some of the other changes for this edition include:

- Additional information about the role of the human resources department and their role in planning.
- New material on work/life benefits.
- Revision of material on the use of computers in benefit communication.
- New material on Medicare+Choice.
- Updating of material on the Age Discrimination in Employment Act and the Americans with Disability Act.
- Significant updating of material on accidental death and dismemberment coverage.
- Significant revision of material on long-term care insurance, group legal insurance, and voluntary benefits.
- Revision of material on cafeteria plan election changes.
- Significant revisions in the material on retirement planning resulting from 1998 tax law changes, including new rules for IRAs, new rules for qualified plan and IRA distributions, and new limits on plan benefits and contributions.
- Changes in retirement planning resulting from the trend toward plans attractive to younger employees, such as 401(k) and cash balance plans.

We have continued to use four other major guidelines in preparing this book. First, the book covers the broad spectrum of employee benefits, from social insurance programs to executive benefits. Second, the book is applicable to all sizes of employer groups, from the small employer using a multiple-employer trust to the large employer relying on alternative funding methods, including self-insurance. Third, the book explains the decisions involved in designing an employee benefit plan; it doesn't just describe the products available. Finally, we have tried to write a book that can be used not only in courses given by colleges and professional organizations but also as a reference resource for practitioners.

We have also tried to write a book that can be flexible for classroom use. If students have had other insurance courses, perhaps the material on social insurance could be eliminated. Depending on the length of the course and student backgrounds, the detailed material on group insurance taxation and rate making might be skipped or covered superficially. In the retirement plan part, Chapters 25, 26 and possibly 27 could also be omitted.

It was difficult to decide where we should place the chapter on employee benefit planning and management. On the one hand, readers should be aware of the importance of planning and management issues before they pursue the material further. On the other hand, they will probably better understand the issues after they are familiar with the benefit environment and the products and services that exist in this environment. We recommend that the principles of the chapter not be ignored after an initial reading. This is an important chapter that should be reviewed again after the remainder of the book is read.

The changing nature of employee benefits makes it essential to remain up-to-date. For this reason, we have included a list of additional resources, including Web sites. We particularly urge readers to become familiar with the loose-leaf services, periodicals and Web sites mentioned.

LEGAL REFERENCES IN THIS TEXT

In this text, legal authorities will be cited occasionally to help in finding further information about the subject, if the reader wishes. The term *the Code* will be used in referring to the Internal Revenue Code, and the Treasury Regulations will be cited as *the regulations*, with other citations given more fully. ERISA *Section 000* will be used to refer to the indicated section of the Employee Retirement Income Security Act of 1974.

No attempt is made to provide a complete citation of authorities for all of the propositions set forth. However, the general discussion in this text should be adequate to enable the interested reader to obtain citations of the necessary legal authorities from one of the loose-leaf qualified plan or tax services or one of the handbooks in the field of qualified plans. If accurate legal references are to be obtained, it is important to have thorough and up-to-date materials, because the legal authorities are voluminous and subject to very frequent change.

ACKNOWLEDGMENTS

As with any undertaking of this scope, we owe gratitude to the many persons who have been helpful in making this book a reality, from those persons who were immensely helpful in preparing the first edition to those who have offered valuable suggestions for its four revisions.

We would like to thank the following reviewers for their contributions to the sixth edition: Edwin W. Arnold, Auburn University-Montgomery, Peggy Anderson, Ph.D., Professor of HR Management, University of Wisconsin-Whitewater, and David W. Sommer, University of Georgia.

We owe a particular gratitude to Evelyn Rice for her hard work in helping us finish the instructor's manual for this edition.

Finally, we wish to acknowledge The American College, Bryn Mawr, Pennsylvania, for giving us permission to use the copyrighted material previously written by Burton T. Beam, Jr., and contained in *Group Benefits: Basic Concepts and Alternatives,* 8th edition (2000).

Burton T. Beam, Jr.
John J. McFadden

PART ONE

Introduction

CHAPTER 1

Introduction to Employee Benefits

OBJECTIVES

- Explain the meaning of the term *employee benefits*.

- Explain the significance of employee benefits in terms of both employer cost and benefits provided to employees.

- Identify the factors that have influenced the growth of group insurance and explain the significance of each factor.

- Identify the job opportunities available in the field of employee benefits.

In the early part of the century, very few employees received any compensation from their employers other than direct wages for time actually worked. Employees or their families were responsible for meeting the needs of old age, poor health, and death. Vacations, if allowed at all, were usually without pay.

The 1940s and 1950s witnessed the increasing use and acceptance of employee benefits as a form of compensation in addition to direct wages. During the last two decades, this growth has accelerated as new types of benefits have been added and existing benefits have expanded. Further, while employee benefits were once fairly standardized and free of government regulation, employers must now make more complex decisions regarding the benefits to be provided and the methods with which these benefits are funded.

DEFINITION OF EMPLOYEE BENEFITS

Before continuing, it is best to define exactly what is meant by *employee benefits*. The narrowest definition of the term includes only employer-provided benefits for death, accident, sickness, retirement, or unemployment. Even with this approach, there is disagreement on whether the definition should include those benefits that are financed by employer contributions but provided under social insurance programs, such as workers' compensation insurance, unemployment insurance, Social Security, and Medicare.[1] On the other hand, the broadest definition of employee benefits includes all benefits and services, other than wages for time worked, that are provided to employees in whole or in part by their employers.

This text uses a broad definition and defines employee benefits as including benefit plans for employees that arise from the following five categories of employer payments or costs[2]:

1. Legally required social insurance payments. These include employer contributions to the following programs:

   - Social Security
   - Medicare
   - Unemployment compensation insurance
   - Workers' compensation insurance
   - Temporary disability insurance

2. Payments for private insurance and retirement plans. These include the cost of establishing such plans, as well as contributions in the form of insurance premiums or payments through alternative funding arrange-

---

[1] The Social Security Administration uses a narrow definition in its studies of employee benefit plans. This definition includes only those benefits not underwritten or paid directly by the federal, state, or local governments.

[2] These categories are similar to those used by the Chamber of Commerce of the United States in its broad definition of employee benefits.

ments. Benefits are provided under these plans for personal loss exposures such as the following:

- Old age
- Dental expenses
- Death
- Legal expenses
- Disability income
- Property damage
- Medical expenses
- Liability judgments

3. Payments for time not worked. These include the following:

- Vacations and holidays
- Maternity leave
- Sick leave
- Sabbatical leaves
- Jury duty

4. Extra cash payments to employees. These are cash payments other than wages and bonuses based on performance. Benefits in this category include the following:

- Educational expense allowances
- Savings plans
- Moving expenses
- Christmas bonuses
- Current profit-sharing payments
- Suggestion awards

5. Cost of services to employees. These include items such as the following:

- Subsidized cafeterias
- Adoption assistance
- Recreation programs
- Wellness programs
- Clothing allowances
- Day care centers
- Financial counseling
- Transportation benefits
- Retirement counseling

Part Two of this book is devoted to the programs that constitute legally required social insurance payments. Group insurance benefits are discussed in Part Three, and retirement plans are covered in Part Five. The remaining categories of benefits are described in Part Four.

SIGNIFICANCE OF EMPLOYEE BENEFITS

The significance of employee benefits can best be shown by looking at some frequently quoted data of the U.S. Chamber of Commerce and the Bureau of Labor Statistics. These data come from periodic statistics of the two organizations and are generally updated every two years. It often takes a year or more to collect and tabulate these statistics, and the data shown are for the latest survey years available at the time this book was revised.

U.S. Chamber of Commerce

In a 1998 study of 619 companies, the United States Chamber of Commerce found that the average payment by employers for employee benefits was equal to 37.2 percent of payroll.[3] Of this figure, 8.4 percent of payroll went for the employer's share of legally required social insurance payments, 8.7 percent for payments to private retirement and savings plans, and 8.5 percent for medical and medically related benefits. The remaining 11.6 percent was for all other types of benefits, with paid vacations being the single most costly item in this category. The study showed substantial variations among business firms, with overall percentages ranging from less than 18 percent to more than 65 percent. Large variations were also shown by industry, with public utilities having the highest percentage (43.6) and communications having the lowest (23.9). Within specific industries, benefit percentages tend to be higher for firms with more than 100 employees than for firms with fewer than 100 employees, and nonmanufacturing firms have higher percentages than manufacturing firms. The percentages also tend to be somewhat higher for hourly employees than they are for salaried employees.

In addition to employer costs, employee payroll deductions for benefits amounted to 13.1 percent of payroll in 1998. The majority of this amount was for Social Security and Medicare taxes and contributions to retirement and savings plans.

The Chamber of Commerce study also shows that employees received an average of $14,655 in benefits in 1998. However, there was a significant range, with one-tenth of employees receiving more than $23,842 and one-tenth receiving $7,028 or less. These variations are the result of company, industry, geographic, and employee differences.

Bureau of Labor Statistics

The Bureau of Labor Statistics is part of the U.S. Department of Labor and maintains many databases for the department. The bureau periodically publishes detailed information on employee benefits in private organizations that have 100 or more employees. The latest survey of these medium- and large-sized

---

[3.]U.S. Chamber of Commerce, *The 1999 Employee Benefits Study.*

TABLE 1-1

Percentage of Full-Time Employees Participating in
Selected Employee Benefit Programs, Medium and Large Private Establishments*

Type of Program	All Employees	Professional, Technical, and Related Employees	Clerical and Sales Employees	Blue-Collar and Service Employees
Insurance				
Medical care	76%	79%	78%	74%
Dental care	59	64	59	56
Vision care	26	28	25	24
Life	87	94	91	81
Disability benefits				
Paid sick leave	56	73	73	38
Short-term disability coverage	55	54	52	58
Long-term disability coverage	43	62	52	28
Retirement				
Defined benefit plans	50	52	49	50
Defined contribution plans	57	70	63	46
Paid time off				
Holidays	89	89	91	88
Vacations	95	96	97	94
Personal leave	20	23	33	13
Funeral leave	81	84	85	76
Jury duty leave	87	92	89	83
Military leave	47	60	50	38
Family leave	2	3	3	1
Unpaid time off				
Family leave	93	95	96	91
Other benefits				
Severance pay	36	48	43	26
Supplemental unemployment benefits	5	2	2	7
Child care	10	14	10	7
Adoption assistance	10	16	12	6
Long-term care insurance	7	10	11	4
Wellness programs	36	44	36	32
Employee assistance	61	75	63	52
Fitness center	21	31	19	16
Job-related travel accident insurance	42	56	46	32
Subsidized commuting	6	10	7	3
Educational assistance				
Job-related	67	81	68	58
Nonjob-related	20	25	18	18
Section 125 cafeteria plans	52	70	62	36

*U.S. Department of Labor, Bureau of Labor Statistics, *Employee Benefits in Medium and Large Private Establishments, 1997.*

TABLE 1-2
Percentage of Full-Time Employees Participating in
Selected Employee Benefit Programs, Small Private Establishments*

Type of Program	All Employees	Professional, Technical, and Related Employees	Clerical and Sales Employees	Blue-Collar and Service Employees
Insurance				
Medical care	64%	76%	69%	56%
Dental care	31	40	35	24
Life	62	72	68	54
Disability benefits				
Paid sick leave	50	66	64	35
Short-term disability coverage	29	32	33	25
Long-term disability coverage	22	39	30	10
Retirement				
Defined benefit plans	15	12	16	15
Defined contribution plans	38	51	46	28
Paid time off				
Holidays	80	86	91	71
Vacations	86	90	95	79
Personal leave	14	21	18	8
Funeral leave	51	60	60	42
Jury duty leave	59	74	68	47
Military leave	18	25	23	12
Family leave	2	3	3	7
Other benefits				
Severance pay	15	23	19	9
Child care	2	4	2	1
Adoption assistance	1	3	2	1
Long-term care insurance	1	2	2	1
Wellness programs	8	11	9	5
Employee assistance	14	18	19	10
Fitness center	4	6	5	3
Job-related travel accident insurance	12	17	16	7
Subsidized commuting	1	3	2	1
Educational assistance				
Job-related	38	56	45	27
Nonjob-related	5	6	6	4
Section 125 cafeteria plans	23	31	29	16

*U.S. Department of Labor, Bureau of Labor Statistics, *Employee Benefits in Small Private Establishments, 1996.*

establishments covers 46 million full-time employees. Table 1-1 contains some of the survey results that show the prevalence of various types of employee benefits.

The bureau also conducts a periodic survey of small private establishments—those with fewer than 100 employees. Table 1-2 shows some results of the latest survey, which covers almost 40 million full-time employees.

Before viewing these statistics, note that they are for employees who *participate* in employee benefit programs. Some benefit plans are contributory, and not all employees elect to participate. Therefore, the number of employees who actually have a plan available to them is higher. One example of this is medical expense plans. Most employees of medium and large firms have a medical expense plan available to them. However, many employees elect not to participate in their own employer's plan, most commonly because they are covered as a dependent under a spouse's plan.

FACTORS INFLUENCING THE GROWTH OF EMPLOYEE BENEFITS

No one factor can be singled out as the reason for the substantial growth in employee benefits. Rather, this growth has resulted from a combination of factors, including industrialization, the influence of organized labor, wage controls, cost advantages, tax advantages, inflation, and legislation.

Industrialization

During the 19th century, the United States made the transition from an agrarian economy to one characterized by increasing industrialization and urbanization. The economic consequences of death, sickness, accidents, and old age became more significant as individuals began to depend more on monetary wages than on self-reliance and family ties to meet their basic needs. As a result, some employers began to provide retirement, death, and medical benefits to their employees. While benevolence may have influenced the decision to provide such benefits, the principal reason was probably the realization by employers that it was in their own best interest to do so. Not only did such benefits improve morale and productivity, they also reduced employee turnover and the expenses associated with it.

While some of the earlier benefits were paid directly by employers, the development of group insurance enabled these benefits to be funded by systematic payments to an insurance company. As group insurance became more common, employers were faced with adopting new or better plans to remain competitive in attracting and keeping employees. This competitiveness in employee benefits continues to exist.

Industrialization has also led to more benefits, such as Social Security, Medicare, unemployment insurance, and workers' compensation insurance, being provided by government.

Influence of Organized Labor

Since a Supreme Court ruling in 1949, there has been no question about the right of labor unions to negotiate legally for retirement and insurance plans. Although union pressures prior to that time had frequently resulted in the establishment or broadening of employee benefit plans, this ruling strengthened the influence of labor unions.

Labor unions have also influenced benefits for nonunion employees. Some employers provide generous benefit plans in an effort to discourage their employees from unionizing. In addition, employers with both union and nonunion employees often provide the same benefits for the nonunion employees as are stipulated in the union contracts.

Wage Controls

Employee benefit plans grew substantially during World War II and the Korean War when wage freezes were in effect. Although wages were frozen, no restrictions were imposed on employee benefits. Therefore, employee benefits became an important factor in attracting and retaining employees in labor markets characterized by little unemployment. When wage controls were instituted in the early 1970s, however, no unusual growth took place in employee benefit plans because the duration of the controls was relatively short and the unemployment rate was higher than in previous years.

Cost Advantages

Because of the economics associated with group underwriting and administration, benefits can usually be obtained at a lower cost through group arrangements than through separate contracts purchased by individual employees.

Tax Advantages

The Internal Revenue Code also provides favorable tax treatment to employer contributions for certain types of employee benefits. The employer may deduct the contributions as usual business expenses, and, within limits, employees will often have no taxable income that results from employer contributions on their behalf. In addition, payments received from some types of employee benefit plans may be received tax free by employees, even if provided by employer contributions. Benefits from other types of plans may not result in taxable income until payments are actually received. The extent of the favorable tax treatment applicable to specific benefits is discussed in detail in later chapters. Nevertheless, it should be noted here that the types of employee benefits with the most favorable tax treatment also tend to be the most prevalent.

Inflation

Inflation also affects employee benefits. When benefit levels are related to employees' wages, the level and cost of these benefits will increase as wages increase; when benefit levels are stated as fixed amounts, inflation results in employee pressure for increases. For most employers, the total cost of benefit programs has been increasing at a rate faster than wages, primarily because of the skyrocketing increase in the cost of providing medical expense benefits.

Legislation

Most states have traditionally limited the types of groups that are eligible for group insurance benefits. In addition, the types, and possibly the amounts, of coverage that could be written were also subject to restrictions. In recent years, the majority of these states have liberalized their laws and have allowed more group insurance coverage to be available to an increasing variety of groups.

The federal government and many states also have passed legislation mandating that certain benefits be included in group insurance contracts or that existing benefits be broadened. Examples include legislation requiring benefits for maternity, alcoholism, and drug abuse. These increased benefits have also increased the cost of providing group insurance coverage.

OPPORTUNITIES IN EMPLOYEE BENEFITS

A question often asked of the authors of this book is "What opportunities are there for me in employee benefits?" Employee benefits is a broad discipline that offers opportunities for persons with a wide diversity of backgrounds. Some of these are the following:

- Marketing majors. An important activity of any employee benefit provider is the marketing of its products and services to employers. These sales activities may be performed by commissioned agents of insurance companies, representatives of employee benefit consulting firms, and salaried employees of Blue Cross and Blue Shield plans or HMOs. Marketing departments of employee benefit providers also design and implement the sales activities of their firms.
- Human resources majors. Human resources departments frequently have the task of communicating benefits to employees, and in many firms they may also administer the employee benefit program.
- Finance majors. The employee benefit departments of many large employers are under the direction of the finance department. The finance department is often involved in the self-funding of benefits. Finance majors are also needed to determine investment strategies for the billions of dollars invested by retirement plans.

- Insurance majors. Many employee benefits are sold by insurance companies.
- Accounting majors. Accountants with public and private employers are often involved with employee benefit activities. Accountants in private practice frequently are in a position to advise clients about employee benefit decisions.
- Communication majors. As employee benefits become increasingly complex and expensive, employers are demanding better communication of benefits to employees. This communication may involve in-house personnel or materials prepared by employee benefit providers or consulting firms.
- Mathematics majors. The proper pricing of employee benefit products is an important function of the actuarial departments of employee benefit providers.
- Social science majors. Many job opportunities for social science majors involve interaction with people and the giving of advice about programs to meet their needs. Better advice can be given with an understanding of social insurance programs, wellness programs, employee-assistance programs, dependent-care assistance programs, and the like.
- Majors in medical fields. Today it is common for medical practitioners to be employed by benefit providers engaged in managed care activities. In fact, this is one of the growth areas for registered nurses.

The above list is merely meant as an example of the many opportunities available in the field of employee benefits. The providers of employee benefit products and services are diverse and, like any industry, need employees from a wide range of backgrounds.

STUDY QUESTIONS

1. Explain the different ways in which the term *employee benefits* may be defined.

2. The Chamber of Commerce of the United States estimates that the cost of employee benefit programs averages about 37.2 percent of payroll. What factors may account for a particular firm having a percentage-of-payroll figure that deviates from the average?

3. How has organized labor influenced the growth of employee benefit plans?

4. How does inflation affect the cost of employee benefit plans?

5. Briefly explain how favorable tax laws have contributed to the growth of many types of employee benefits.

CHAPTER 2

Employee Benefit Planning and Management

OBJECTIVES

- Explain the rationale for having employee-benefit-plan objectives and identify the forms such objectives might take.

- Identify the methods by which the benefit needs of employees may be determined.

- Analyze the provisions contained in employee benefit plans for controlling costs.

- Identify the objectives of an effective employee benefit communications program and describe the methods by which it might be implemented.

- Explain the rationale for benefit outsourcing and identify the decisions that must be made in the outsourcing process.

The significant growth in employee benefits requires increasingly complex decisions. Whether these decisions are made by employers providing benefits, unions negotiating for benefits, or employees selecting benefit options, the need for proper benefit planning is crucial. Employee benefit planning is a dynamic process that must continually be reviewed and modified if an overall benefit plan is to meet the changing needs of a changing environment.

If either a single type of employee benefit plan or an overall benefit plan is to be properly designed and managed, many questions must be asked. For example, should the plan reflect the wants of employees or the needs of employees as perceived by the employer? Should it have a probationary period for eligibility? Under what circumstances should the plan be self-insured? These questions are only subparts of six much broader issues:

1. What are the employer's objectives?
2. What types of benefits should be provided in the plan?
3. How should the plan be funded?
4. What provisions for controlling costs should be contained in the plan?
5. How should the plan be communicated to employees?
6. Should administrative functions be outsourced?

Unfortunately for those who like precise answers, plan design and management is an art rather than a science. However, decisions must be made. In some cases, the advantages and disadvantages of the various alternative answers to these questions must be weighed; in other cases, compromises must be made when the answers to two or more questions conflict.

Too often, the proper design of an employee benefit plan is viewed as a one-time decision rather than as an evolving process. However, benefit plans that were appropriate for yesterday's work force may not meet the needs of tomorrow's work force. As times and organizations change, employers' answers to the questions raised in this chapter may also have to change. For this reason, these issues must be frequently restudied to determine whether a group benefit plan is continuing to meet its desired purpose.

Because the question of funding is addressed in detail in Chapter 14, only the remaining questions will be discussed in this chapter.

One difficulty in writing a textbook of this nature is determining where to discuss the many issues and decisions that must be faced if proper planning is to take place. While some issues and decisions can easily be handled at the beginning of a textbook, many others are best discussed along with specific types of benefit plans. Still others are most meaningfully treated only after the basic coverages, provisions, and funding methods have been described. However, a treatment of the benefit-planning process seems appropriate in an introductory chapter to make readers aware that benefit planning is much more than a description of the many types of coverages and provisions that are the subject of most of this book. While this chapter is devoted entirely to planning and is the first and only place where certain issues are discussed, other planning issues are handled where appropriate throughout the book. Readers may wish to return to this chapter after they have completed the remainder of the book.

WHAT ARE THE EMPLOYER'S OBJECTIVES?

No benefit plan is properly designed unless it meets the employer's objectives. Unfortunately, these objectives may be unclear or nonexistent, particularly in small firms. However, most large corporations have—and *all* firms should have—specific written objectives that have been approved by the board of directors or by the owners of the firm. These objectives will vary for each individual organization, depending upon such factors as size, location, industry, the results of collective bargaining, and the philosophy of the employer. Without such objectives, it is difficult for the agent, broker, benefit consultant, or third-party administrator to make recommendations or for the firms's in-house benefit staff (often part of the human resources department) to make decisions.

Types of Objectives

Objectives for benefit plans can be general and part of a firm's overall compensation objective, that is, cash and employee benefits in the aggregate. This may be done to achieve a compensation package that is competitive within the firm's geographic area or industry. Such an average objective usually means that the firm wants both its wages and salaries and its employee benefits to be similar to what the competition is offering its employees. There is usually some, but not much, room for creativity in the design of a group benefit plan, unless the plans of the competition are quite diverse.

Some firms have separate objectives for cash compensation and employee benefits. For example, a growing firm may want its cash compensation to be competitive, but it may want its overall employee benefit plan to be above average in order to attract new employees. A difficulty with this type of objective for the plan designer is determining whether the firm wants all aspects of the employee benefit plan to be better than average or whether it would be willing to accept, for example, an average program of group insurance benefits but a better-than-average pension plan and more vacation time for its employees. Note that most objectives, even when they are very detailed, tend to apply to all employee benefits rather than to specific types.

It has become increasingly common for firms, particularly large firms, to maintain a lengthy and often detailed list of objectives for their employee benefit programs. The following are the objectives of one such firm:

■ To establish and maintain an employee benefit program that is based primarily on the employees' needs for leisure time and on protection against the risks of old age, loss of health, and loss of life

- To establish and maintain an employee benefit program that complements the efforts of employees on their own behalf
- To evaluate the employee benefit plan annually for its effect on employee morale and productivity, giving consideration to turnover, unfilled positions, attendance, employees' complaints, and employees' opinions
- To compare the employee benefit plan annually with that of other leading companies in the same field and to maintain a benefit plan with an overall level of benefits based on cost per employee that falls within the second quintile of these companies
- To maintain a level of benefits for nonunion employees that represents the same level of expenditures per employee as for union employees
- To determine annually the cost of new, changed, and existing programs as a percentage of salaries and wages and to maintain this percentage as much as possible
- To self-fund benefits to the extent that a long-run cost savings can be expected for the firm and catastrophic losses can be avoided
- To coordinate all benefits with social insurance programs to which the company makes payments
- To provide benefits on a noncontributory basis, except benefits for dependent coverage for which employees should pay a portion of the cost
- To maintain continual communications with all employees concerning benefit programs

Most lists of objectives contain few, if any, specific details regarding what provisions or what types of benefits should be contained in an employee benefit plan. Rather, they establish guidelines—instead of specific performance goals—within which management must operate. For example, the objectives listed above indicate this firm wants a plan that is understood and appreciated by employees and that is designed with employee opinion in mind. No mention, however, is made of how this is to be done. As will be seen later in this chapter, there may be alternative ways for this firm to achieve its objectives. Similarly, the objectives establish guidelines for the cost of providing benefits. Although the firm wants to have a better-than-average plan, it does not want to be a leader. There is a very specific statement about what the relationship between the cost of benefits for union and nonunion employees should be. However, nothing is mentioned to indicate that the benefits for the two groups must also be identical. If the two groups have different needs, different types and levels of benefits may be desired.

Three additional points about employer objectives should be made. First, as times change, benefit objectives may need revision.

Second, the frequent lack of specific guidelines in benefit objectives gives the in-house benefit staff great latitude to be creative, to come up with innovative solutions to benefit problems, and to respond to the changing benefit environment. Such creativity can often lead to success and financial reward.

However, a greater degree of freedom to be creative is also often accompanied by being the scapegoat when benefit decisions do not lead to the desired results.

Third, a firm's primary (and possibly only) objective may be to establish an overall employee benefit plan that channels as large a portion of the benefits as possible to the owner or owners. Although this is a poor objective for an overall plan, it is a reality that must be recognized, most commonly in small firms or in firms that have few owners. Large, publicly held corporations sometimes wish to provide better benefits for their executives than for other employees. These extra benefits are likely to be provided under separate executive compensation plans rather than under the benefit plan that applies to all employees.

Who Should Receive Benefits?

As part of establishing its objectives, an employer must determine its responsibilities to various categories of persons who might be eligible for coverage under the firm's overall benefit program. The list is much longer than one might initially think. It includes the following:

- Active full-time employees
- Dependents of active full-time employees
- Retired employees
- Dependents of retired employees
- Part-time employees
- Dependents of part-time employees
- Disabled employees
- Dependents of disabled employees
- Survivors of deceased employees
- Employees who have terminated employment
- Dependents of employees who have terminated employment
- Employees who are temporarily separated from employment (for example, employees on family leave)
- Dependents of employees who are temporarily separated from em-ployment

Obviously, most benefits are given to employees, and some benefits are given to their dependents, such as medical expense coverage. Whether other groups on the list receive any benefits depends on several factors. These include the attitude of the employer and the degree to which protection is available under other programs, such as Social Security. In addition, federal and state laws play a role. For example, some benefits must be continued because of family leave legislation. In addition, medical expense coverage must be continued in many cases as a result of COBRA. The extent to which benefits might be provided to each of these categories of persons are touched on throughout this book.

WHAT TYPES OF BENEFITS SHOULD BE PROVIDED IN THE PLAN?

A major decision for any employer is what types and levels of benefits to include in an overall employee benefit plan. For those few firms that do not have an employee benefit program, this decision involves choosing which benefits to offer initially. However, in most cases, the decision is ongoing and involves either the offering of new or improved benefits or the redesigning of all or a major portion of the benefit plan. An objective of most employee benefit plans is to meet the needs of employees. But what are these needs? If they vary for different groups of employees, should different benefit plans be established? Or should a single plan be designed in which employees are allowed to choose among alternative benefits?

Determining Needs

Every employer wants its employees to appreciate the benefits that are provided. However, employers are becoming increasingly aware that employee benefit programs are failing to achieve this desired level of appreciation. To some extent, this is due to the fact that as employee benefit plans have grown more comprehensive, employees have begun to take the benefits for granted. In addition, the growing consensus seems to be that the traditional methods of determining the types and levels of benefits to offer have lost much of their effectiveness. These include basing benefits on the following factors:

- *The employer's perception of the employees' needs.* This perception is largely based on the opinions of a firm's top management employees whose compensation is much higher than that of the average employee. Therefore, it is not surprising that many recent studies have shown that management's perception of employees' needs often differs from what the employees themselves feel they need.
- *What competitors are doing.* Too often, the emphasis is placed on having an employee benefit package that is virtually identical to that of the competition, even though the makeup of the work force may be different and the employees may have different needs.
- *Collectively bargained benefits.* Many employers pattern their benefit plans for salaried employees after their negotiated plans for union employees. Again, the needs of salaried employees may be substantially different and may call for a totally different plan.

■ *Tax laws and regulations*. Benefit plans are often designed to include those benefits that are best suited to the high tax brackets of top executives. The average employee who is in a modest tax bracket may actually have a preference for certain benefits even though they will result in currently taxable income.

In the last few years, two trends have taken place. First, employers have increasingly taken a marketing research approach to employee benefit planning. The employees' preferences for benefits are determined in a way similar to that in which consumers' demands for products are determined. For the most part, this approach has been used only for nonunion employees, because benefits for union employees are decided by collective bargaining. However, some employers and some unions use this procedure as a guide in their negotiations with union employees. Second, employers have increasingly turned to life-cycle and work/life approaches to benefit planning.

The Use of Marketing Research

A marketing research approach can be used for different purposes. Most often it is selected as a way to determine two things:

1. How funds should be allocated to new types of benefits
2. How funds should be used to improve current benefits

This can be for a one-time change in a firm's benefit plan or for changes that are implemented over time. In addition, a marketing research approach can help an employer determine what alternative provisions employees would prefer regarding a specific type of benefit. For example, a firm that allocates additional funds to a long-term disability plan could determine whether employees would prefer a shorter waiting period or an increase in the size of the monthly benefit.

Marketing research techniques must be used with caution. They can have a negative effect on employee morale unless the employer is committed to using their results in benefit decision making. Therefore, this approach should not be undertaken unless the employer intends to base expenditures for benefits on satisfying what employees perceive as their needs. In addition, employees must be made aware that changes in an overall benefit program will be subject to financial constraints and, possibly, trade-offs among benefits.

Although a variety of marketing research techniques can be used in benefit planning, those most commonly chosen fall into three major categories:

1. Personal interviews
2. Simplified questionnaires
3. Sophisticated research methods

Personal Interviews. Personal interviews with employees either alone or in small groups probably constitute the most effective marketing research technique for a small firm or for a benefit program that is limited to a small number of employees. On this scale, it is also the least expensive technique. An advantage of personal interviewing is that it can be used to collect the same type of information as do both simplified questionnaires and sophisticated research techniques. It is important in personal interviewing that the employees feel they can speak candidly. For this reason, it may be desirable to have the interviews conducted by someone outside the firm and to hold group interviews without the supervisor's presence.

Simplified Questionnaires. A simplified questionnaire often has two major parts: one determines benefit preferences, the other determines demographic data, such as age, sex, marital status, years of service, and salary range. The questionnaire is called *simplified* because employees are basically asked only to indicate and/or rank their preferences. However, the actual analysis of the data that are gathered may be a complex task, and unless a firm is small, it probably will require the use of a computer. It is important to use a clear, brief questionnaire that is not annoying to employees. Consequently, it is best that the questionnaire initially be given to only a few employees in order to test their reactions.

Figure 2-1 is a sample of a portion of a simplified questionnaire on benefit preferences. Note that the questionnaire is essentially a structured one and is not open-ended. Employees are requested only to rank their preferences, and they are not given the opportunity to state whether each benefit is important or whether it should be improved. They are also required to make their preferences known regarding possible trade-offs between benefits and pay. Even though the questionnaire is structured, employees are still given the opportunity to make general comments. Such a feature should be incorporated into any questionnaire as a way of letting employees know that their opinions will be heard. It also may result in useful, and sometimes surprising, information for the employer.

Sophisticated Research Methods. One difficulty with simplified questionnaires, and to some extent personal interviews, is that they fail to measure the intensity of employees' preferences. Consequently, some firms have used more sophisticated marketing research techniques in an attempt to measure the degree of importance that employees place on various benefit alternatives. These more sophisticated research techniques are typically used only when specific alternatives have been formulated by the employer. Therefore, they are often used as a follow-up to personal interviews and simplified questionnaires; they frequently also involve additional interviews and/or questionnaires.

FIGURE 2-1
Employee
Benefit
Questionnaire

1. In the right column below, rank the benefits from 1 to 7 in their importance to you and your family. Use 1 for the most important, 2 for the next important, etc.

BENEFIT	IMPORTANCE
Holidays	_____
Life Insurance	_____
Long-Term Disability Income	_____
Medical Expense Insurance	_____
Pension Plan	_____
Sick Pay	_____
Vacations	_____

2. To the list of benefits below, add the two benefits you would most like to see added by this company. In the right column, rank the benefits listed according to their need for improvement or adoption. Use 1 for the benefit you feel should have the highest priority for improvement or adoption, 2 for the next highest, etc.

BENEFIT	NEED FOR IMPROVEMENT OR ADOPTION
Holidays	_____
Life Insurance	_____
Long-Term Disability Income	_____
Medical Expense Insurance	_____
Pension Plan	_____
Sick Pay	_____
Vacations	_____

3. How would you prefer that additional funds for benefits be used? (check one)
    _____ Improve or add benefit programs
    _____ Reduce currently required employee contributions

4. Which of the following statements reflects your opinion? (check one)
    _____ More emphasis should be placed on improving wages and salaries and less on improving benefits.
    _____ More emphasis should be placed on improving benefits and less on improving wages and salaries.
    _____ The same emphasis as in the past should be placed on improving both benefits and wages and salaries.

5. Please use the back of this form to make any additional comments you feel will be of use to the company in its desire to improve the employee benefit programs.

FIGURE 2-2
Employee
Benefit
Questionnaire

EMPLOYEE BENEFIT QUESTIONNAIRE

The following benefit changes are being considered for adoption by this company in the next fiscal year. Although the company is committed to making improvements in its benefit package, financial considerations dictate that only some of these proposed changes can be adopted at that time. The first item on the list has been given a value of 100. Please rank the other items in their relative importance to you. For example, if item 2 is three times as important, it should be given a value of 300. If it is only half as important, it should be given a value of 50.

Proposed Change	Value
1. Increase annual dental maximum from $1,000 to $2,000.	$100
2. Eliminate employee contributions to long-term disability coverage.	
3. Increase life insurance coverage from $1\frac{1}{2}$ to 2 times base earnings.	
4. Add Columbus Day to the list of holidays.	
5. Increase the number of sick days from 10 to 12.	

Figure 2-2 illustrates one example of how preferences might be measured in a questionnaire.

Once the information is gathered, the firm must decide which benefits to adopt, based on employees' preferences and other cost and administrative considerations. For example, assume that the firm using the questionnaire is willing to spend up to $400 annually per employee to improve its benefit package. Also assume that the figures to the left represent the average importance of each proposed benefit to employees, as well as the expected annual cost per employee of providing each benefit.

Change	Average	Value
1	100	$100
2	310	200
3	140	100
4	240	200
5	190	250

It is clear that the employees feel the second proposed change, which has an annual cost of $200 per employee, is most important by a substantial margin. Therefore, it will most likely be adopted. However, it is difficult to determine what other benefit or benefits will be offered. The last proposed change will definitely not be made because only $200 per employee remains for additional benefit changes. The firm is therefore faced with two alternatives—either add Columbus Day as a holiday or increase both the life insurance coverage and the annual dental insurance maximum. Because the average importance of each alternative to employees is 240, and only one can be made within the cost constraint, the deciding factor will hinge on other considerations. The firm may look at the administrative aspects of each change or the effect of inflation on long-range costs. The firm may also analyze the data in terms of the demographic characteristics of employees. For example, long-time employees may have a slight preference for the insurance benefits, while younger employees would like the extra holiday. If the firm wishes to favor the older employees, it will change the insurance benefits; if morale is low among younger employees, it might decide to add the holiday instead.

It should be pointed out that these other considerations may also be the deciding factor for employers even when employee preferences are clear. However, if employees are led to believe that their preferences will be the primary consideration, other considerations should be weighed only when there are modest differences in employee preferences.

Life-Cycle Benefits

The design of employee benefit plans traditionally focused solely on providing active employees with protection against the financial consequences of illness, disability, retirement, and death. Over time, other types of benefits began to be offered, but plan design tended to focus on the employee's being part of a traditional family. Over the last two decades, the demographic makeup of the workforce has changed dramatically. As a result, many employers are frequently taking a life-cycle approach to benefit planning. While the traditional benefits are still part of the core of most overall employee benefit plans, employers are increasingly designing benefit plans with the realization that benefit needs may differ for males and females, and may differ when employees are single, when they have and raise children, when they care for elderly parents, and when they retire.

Intuition would lead one to believe that a life-cycle benefit plan would increase costs because it would tend to provide benefits that would be used by all categories of employees. To some extent this may be true. However, many employers who have taken this approach feel that additional costs are minimal and/or result in offsetting cost savings. For example, flexible work schedules that allow employees to better take care of dependents may cost little or nothing. Other benefits may result in significant cost savings due to less absenteeism and lower employee turnover. In addition, an employer may pass the majority of the cost of some benefits on to the employees who use them. For example, an employer may establish a day care center but charge a fee for its use to offset some of its operating costs. An employer may also make a voluntary long-term care insurance plan available on a payroll-deduction basis. Finally, employees may not automatically have all benefits; they might have to elect the benefits they want with a predetermined amount of employer funds under a cafeteria plan.

TABLE 2-1
Life-Cycle Benefits

Life-Cycle Stage	Desired Benefit
Young, unmarried workers	Extra vacation Fitness programs
Newlyweds	Marriage leave
Employees in childbearing years	Prenatal courses Parental leave Adoption assistance
Workers during child-rearing years	Day care centers Flexible work schedules
Employees dealing with divorce	Legal assistance
Workers in eldercare years	Long-term care insurance Support groups
Retirees	Medicare supplements Retiree job banks Preretirement counseling
Employees facing death of a family member	Grief counseling Funeral leave

Many of the benefits employees want at various stages in their lives are probably fairly obvious. However, many employers use questionnaires and personal interviews to determine these varying needs. One employer, in designing its life-cycle benefit plan, used the life-cycle stages shown in Table 2-1 and found the benefits indicated to be some of those of particular value to persons in that category.

Work/Life Benefits

Employers are increasingly taking a work/life approach to benefit planning. They have realized that employees, particularly in the tight labor market of recent years, are looking for employers that recognize that their employees have lives outside the office. Many of the benefits that appeal to this group of employees are those that have already been mentioned, such as flexible work schedules, child-care plans, eldercare benefits, family leave, and adoption assistance. All of these benefits have seen some growth in prevalence over the past decade.

Employers are also increasingly making on-site personal services available. Some of the more common services are ATMs and other banking activities, access to postal services, travel agencies, and dry-cleaning pickup. Less common are medical and dental clinics, pharmacies, convenience stores, automobile pickup and delivery for oil changes and state inspections, and take-home meals. In some cases, it's merely a matter of providing space for these types of service providers to rent; in other cases, some rental subsidy might be necessary. In a few cases, these services can be provided by the employer. For example, take-home meals might be prepared by the company cafeteria.

Different Plans

From an administrative standpoint, it is easiest for a firm to have a single employee benefit plan that applies to all employees. Nevertheless, some firms have different plans for different groups of employees. This most commonly occurs when the benefits for union employees are determined by collective bargaining. If the benefits for the union employees are provided through a negotiated trusteeship, a separate plan must be designed for the nonunion employees. The employer must then decide whether to play "follow the leader" and provide identical benefits to the nonunion employees or design a plan that reflects their different needs. When benefits are provided through a negotiated trusteeship, the employer is more likely to develop a different plan for nonunion employees than when the employer is required to provide benefits to union employees through group insurance or pension contracts that are purchased or self-funded by the employer. Under these circumstances, employers often find it simpler administratively to purchase a single contract that covers all employees. Different plans also typically exist for retired employees and other categories of people who are not active full-time employees or their dependents.

Even when unions are not involved, an employer still may decide to have different plans for different groups of employees. Usually one plan will be limited to hourly employees and another to salaried employees. In addition, a plan that offers supplemental benefits to top management also may be provided, but it will often be publicized only to those employees who are eligible for these benefits. Some firms that have employees located in different parts of the country also have found it desirable to provide somewhat different benefits at some or all locations in order to remain competitive locally.

Having different plans for different groups of employees is not without its disadvantages. Administrative costs are usually increased, communications with employees become more difficult, and resentment can occur if one group of employees feels its benefit plan is inferior to that of another group. To minimize this latter possibility, some firms have designed their plans so that an overall comparison is difficult. Each plan will have its own positive and negative features when a comparison is made with the plans for other groups of employees.

Different plans can also result by giving a choice to employees. For example, one group of employees may elect an HMO or PPO option, while another group may elect coverage under a traditional medical expense plan. A trend in recent years has been the growth of cafeteria plans. Because of their popularity, a separate chapter (see Chapter 17) is devoted to them.

WHAT PROVISIONS FOR CONTROLLING COSTS SHOULD BE CONTAINED IN THE PLAN?

Employers have always been concerned about the costs of providing employee benefits. Traditionally, this concern has led to plan provisions that transfer the costs to employees rather than reducing benefits. These include probationary periods, benefit limitations, and contributory financing. Many recent attempts to control costs have been primarily directed toward the rapidly increasing costs of medical care, and, for the most part, cost-containment provisions have been designed to reduce administrative and claim costs without transferring them to employees. Methods for controlling the costs of medical expenses are discussed in Chapters 9 through 14. The focus here is on provisions and activities that can be used with all types of benefit plans.

Probationary Periods

Probationary periods reduce costs to employers because any claims that are incurred by employees during this time must be borne by the employees. In addition, probationary periods reduce the adverse selection that would most likely exist without their use. Administrative costs are also minimized for those employees who terminate employment shortly after being hired. However, probationary periods do impose hardships on newer employees who incur claims but find themselves without benefits. (Employees can minimize these hardships by proper use of COBRA and temporary medical expense policies.) Primarily for competitive reasons in attracting employees, the use and length of probationary periods, particularly in medical expense plans, have been decreasing except in high turnover situations.

Benefit Limitations

Benefit limitations in the form of deductibles, coinsurance, maximum benefits, and exclusions for certain types of expenses are common in medical expense insurance. However, some of these techniques can also be used in other types of insurance. The following are some examples:

■ The limiting of benefits to a maximum percentage of income in disability income plans. In addition to reducing the amount of benefits paid by the employer, a maximum percentage also minimizes the possibility of feigned and unnecessarily prolonged disabilities.

■ The setting of maximum benefits under dental plans for expenses such as orthodontics. There is little doubt that the availability of benefits will encourage treatment of orthodontic conditions, particularly when the treatment is primarily sought for cosmetic reasons. There is also the feeling that dentists will encourage the treatment of relatively minor orthodontic conditions if a patient has coverage for orthodontics.

Contributory Financing

Many benefit plans require that each employee pay a portion of the costs for his or her own coverage. This may lower the employer's costs and/or may enable the employer to use these saved dollars to provide additional or improved benefits. There are several arguments both for and against contributory financing, but in many instances it is a moot point because the decision is determined by collective bargaining or competition.

When contributory financing is used for benefits other than pension plans, employees are generally able to voluntarily elect or decline coverage. To the extent that some employees decline coverage, the costs to the employer will be further lowered. However, this savings may be offset by the adverse selection that can result because of those who do elect coverage. Furthermore, having the option to decline coverage could mean that employees or their dependents will be without coverage should a loss occur. Finally, there tend to be more administrative costs associated with a contributory plan than with a noncontributory plan.

Advocates of a contributory plan feel that sharing in the cost will increase the employees' awareness and appreciation of both the plan and the contribution the employer is making. This can be countered by the argument that payroll deductions for benefits are a source of employee dissatisfaction because they may view the employer as "cheap" for not paying the entire cost of the plan.

Although there are no empirical studies to support the contention, it has been argued that employees are less likely to misuse medical and dental benefits under a contributory plan because they realize that such misuse will probably lead to an increase in their future contributions.

Contributory financing can be used to encourage desired employee behavior. Employees who elect a managed care plan in lieu of a traditional medical expense plan often have a smaller contribution toward the cost of their coverage or possibly no contribution at all. In many cases, this lower contribution is determined by the cost savings to the employer. For example, if the cost of coverage to an employer for an unmarried employee is $150 under an HMO and $200 under an indemnity plan, the employee who elects the indemnity plan will be required to pay $50 more per month than an employee who elects the HMO.

This alone will encourage many employees to elect the managed-care plan. Employers who want to encourage managed care because it tends to have lower annual cost increases might actually make the differential larger, perhaps $75.

Cost Containment

Recent attempts to control benefit costs have concentrated on either reducing the size of claims or minimizing the administrative costs associated with benefit plans. Rather than transfer the costs to employees, these techniques try to lower costs, or at least to lower the rate at which costs are increasing. Although employers are concerned primarily with their own costs, some of the advantages of this cost containment will affect the employees in the form of increased benefits or a lower rate of increase for out-of-pocket expenses.

Other than provisions or practices associated solely with medical expense plans, the following are some of the more common cost-containment techniques that are currently being used by employers:

- Alternative funding methods that lower administrative costs and improve cash flow (discussed in Chapter 14)
- Competitive bidding among insurance companies and third-party administrators that lowers administrative costs
- Wellness programs and employee-assistance plans that reduce future medical claims as well as minimize absences from work (discussed in Chapter 16)

Because many employers have coverage for dependents under their benefit plans, there is also an increasing awareness of the need to inform spouses of a firm's benefit programs. For example, spouses might be invited to benefit orientations.

HOW SHOULD THE PLAN BE COMMUNICATED TO EMPLOYEES?

Traditionally, employers placed a low priority on the communication of their benefit plans to employees. They took the attitude that employees appreciated any benefits that were given to them. The little information that was made available tended to be only the literature that had been prepared by the insurance companies providing the coverage. Over the last few years, this situation has changed dramatically. Employers are required by federal law to disclose a substantial amount of information to employees about their benefit plans. In addition, employers have come to realize that many employees take their benefit plans for granted, that they fail to realize the value of these benefits to themselves and their families, and that they are unaware of the employer's dollar outlay. Not only will effective communication solve this problem, it may also minimize the dissatisfaction that arises from misunderstandings about the benefit program, and it may reduce turnover to the extent that employees realize the true value of their benefits. Employers have also learned that effective communication is necessary to obtain employee support if cost-containment efforts are to be successful. Finally, benefit communication is increasingly important as employees are given more choice with regard to their own benefits. This is occurring as more employees have alternative medical expense plans, cafeteria plans and retirement plans that allow investment options.

Most benefit consultants feel an effective communications program should have four primary objectives.

1. To create an awareness of and an appreciation for the way current benefits improve the financial security of employees
2. To provide a high level of understanding about available benefits
3. To encourage the wise use of benefits
4. To comply with legal requirements

Effective Communication

Employees will obtain information about benefits in some manner. Without an effective communications program, an employee is likely to rely on the grapevine, which often provides incomplete and inaccurate information. Good communication rarely just happens. Rather, it requires that the employer set objectives in a manner similar to that used for benefit plan design. While any list of objectives is likely to include the clear and concise dissemination of information about current benefits, other objectives may change over time. For example, an employer may want to encourage employees to switch to a managed care plan.

Depending on the circumstance, communication may be ongoing or on a one-time basis. In either case, benefit consultants feel that it is important for employers to design communication materials that convey to employees that they and their needs are important to the firm, that the employer cares what employees think about benefits, and that the employer wants employees to understand their benefits. A successful long-run communications program also has a method for obtaining feedback that allows the employer to determine the effectiveness of the communications program. Steps can be taken to rectify inadequate information, and past experience can be of value in designing future communications.

Several factors can complicate the communication process. For example, an employer may have different benefit plans for different groups of employees and therefore may have to design alternative communication strategies. While it may be possible to have somewhat similar strategies, the sophistication levels of the different employee groups may call for entirely different approaches. A similar problem may occur if an employer has multiple locations.

In addition, employers must take the needs of non-English-speaking employees into consideration. Finally, communication strategies may vary for new employees and existing empolyees.

Whatever form a communications plan may take, communication specialists recommend that several basic factors be present:

- The communication should be written in a style that is clear and understandable. Legalese and benefit jargon should be avoided.
- The communication should make it clear what a benefit means to an employee. For example, if an employer is trying to encourage enrollment in a managed care plan, the lack of any deductibles and minimal (or no) copayments should be emphasized.
- The communication should explain why changes are being made. The effectiveness of the communication is likely to be lessened if an employer is not open and honest. Too many employers fail to realize that employees are smart enough to read between the lines of communications that are less than forthright.
- The communication should make use of graphics and examples. Too often communication that lacks these features is boring and therefore less effective.

Methods of Communication

The communication of benefit plans to employees is now regarded as a highly sophisticated task. No single method of communication is likely to accomplish all the desired objectives, so several methods should be combined. To meet these objectives, many employers hire communications experts who generally report to the person who is responsible for employee benefits. Other employers use the services of benefit-consulting firms, many of which have developed specialized units for advising their clients in this particular area. Benefit plans can be communicated to employees in audiovisual presentations, in face-to-face meetings, through printed materials, and, more recently, with computers.

Audiovisual Presentations

Audiovisual presentations are a very effective way to communicate benefit plans to new employees or to explain significant changes in existing benefit plans to current employees. It is much easier to require employees to view audiovisual presentations than to read printed materials. In addition, if properly done, audiovisual presentations can convey the employer's concern for the well-being of its employees, and they can explain proper benefit use more effectively than printed materials. In the past, many audiovisual presentations have been dull and sometimes uninformative. Recently, however, many employers have adopted more sophisticated communications methods, and they view these presentations, if not their entire communications program, as a way of advertising their employee benefit plans. In fact, some employers have actually hired advertising firms to design not only their audiovisual programs but other aspects of their communications program as well.

Meetings with Employees

Face-to-face meetings with employees can also be an effective way to explain employee benefit plans and to answer employees' questions. For small employers, this technique is generally used to present benefit plans to new employees or to explain the changes in existing plans. Large employers often combine meetings with audiovisual presentations. It is obvious that whoever conducts these meetings—be it the employer, agent, broker, consultant, or provider representative—must be truly knowledgeable about the plan. In addition, it is just as important that they be able to effectively communicate this knowledge to the employees.

The number of employees that attend a meeting may have an impact on its effectiveness. A large meeting may be satisfactory if its purpose is primarily to present information. However, a series of small meetings may be more manageable and appropriate if employees' opinions or questions are being solicited. These small meetings can be used in lieu of a large meeting or as follow-up meetings to a large group presentation. When employees must make decisions regarding their benefit plans, meetings with individual employees may also be necessary.

Group meetings can be used for purposes other than explaining new or changed benefit plans. They can be held periodically to reexplain benefits, to answer employees' questions, or to listen to employees' concerns and suggestions. In addition, every employer should have a procedure by which employees can have ready access to a knowledgeable person when they have any problems to discuss or questions to ask. Although this can often be accomplished by telephone, face-to-face meetings should be used when necessary.

The employer's attitude toward a group meeting can influence its effectiveness. Employers should not regard these meetings as necessary formalities; rather, they should view them as a way to communicate their concern about the security of their employees and the benefits with which they are provided. The success of face-to-face meetings may also be affected by when and where they are held. To achieve maximum employee interest and attention, the facilities should be comfortable and not overcrowded. In addition, meetings should be held during normal working hours, but not at the end of the working day, when many employees may be concerned with whether the meeting will end on time.

Printed Materials

Virtually every employer provides employees with some printed materials about its employee benefit plans. At a minimum, this material consists of group insurance certificates and the information that is required to be distributed under the disclosure provisions of the Employee Retirement Income Security Act (ERISA). The next most commonly provided source of information is the benefit handbook. If there is a typical benefit handbook, it can best be described as a reference book that summarizes the benefit plans that are available to all employees. In addition to describing group insurance benefits, it will include information about an organization's retirement plan, vacation policy, and possibly other benefits, such as educational assistance. Each plan will be described in terms of eligibility, benefits, and what employee contributions are required.

Traditionally, these benefit handbooks merely described each benefit plan separately; they did not discuss the relationship between the various benefit plans or what social insurance benefits might be available. Newer benefit handbooks are more likely to focus on the potential causes of lost income to an employee or his or her family. For example, rather than discuss short-term and long-term disability income plans separately, they will include a single section on disability income that describes how a short-term disability plan will initially pay benefits, and at what point it will be replaced by the long-term disability plan and Social Security.

Because of the general nature of benefit handbooks, many employers also give each employee a personalized benefit statement, usually on an annual basis. The most common form of personalized benefit statement specifies the plans for which the employee is eligible and what benefits are available to that particular employee (or his or her family) under each of these plans. (Note that such a statement will comply with the personal benefit statement that is required for qualified retirement plans.) Figure 2-3 shows a portion of one such statement. In addition, some employers feel that employees will better appreciate the value of their benefits if they are aware of the magnitude of the cost to the employer. Figure 2-4 is an example of one form that is used for reporting this information.

Other types of printed information, such as company newsletters, personal letters to employees at home, or notices in pay envelopes, may also be of value. This may be the simplest and least expensive way of announcing benefit changes that need little explanation, such as an increase in the annual dental plan maximum. In addition, they are an effective way to advertise or remind employees about the wellness programs that are available or what cost-containment provisions are included in their medical expense coverage. Experience has shown that without occasional reminders, the use of these programs and provisions by the employees will decrease.

Vendors of employee benefit products and services may also make printed materials available for distribution to employees.

FIGURE 2-3
Personal Statement of Benefits

Personal Statement of Benefits

This Personal Statement of Benefits lists the benefits that both protect you and your family now and provide security for your future. We know you will find this statement informative, and we hope it will be useful in your personal planning.

HEALTH-CARE BENEFITS
You have elected coverage for
❑   yourself   ❑   your family   ❑   You have not elected coverage.

The highlights of your Comprehensive Medical Plan are summarized in the following table. See your employee handbook for further details.

In-Hospital Benefits	Out-of-Hospital Benefits	Special Benefits
$100 deductible per person each calendar year (3-deductible maximum per family)		100% of outpatient emergency treatment of accidental injury (no deductible).
100% of covered expenses, including maternity care, after the deductible is met.	80% of first $3,000 of covered expenses, then 100% of remaining covered expenses.	100% of diagnostic X-ray and laboratory tests (deductible applies).
	50% of psychiatric treatment.	

OVERALL PLAN MAXIMUM: Unlimited

DISABILITY INCOME BENEFITS
Salary Continuation Plan
- Your full salary continues for _____ weeks, then ¾ of your salary continues for _____ weeks.

Long-Term Disability Income Plan
- If disabled over 26 weeks, you will receive _____ a month. This is 60% of your base pay and includes benefits under the corporation's plan and any Social Security benefits, other than family benefits, for which you are eligible.
- If you have eligible dependents, you can receive additional family benefits under Social Security up to _____ a month.
- If total long-term disability income from the above sources exceeds 80% of your base pay, disability benefits under the corporation's plan will be reduced to bring the total to the 70% level.

SURVIVOR'S BENEFITS
Group Life Insurance
- If you die from any cause, your survivors will receive _____ from the corporation's group life insurance plan.

FIGURE 2-3
Personal Statement of Benefits *(continued)*

Personal Statement of Benefits

Supplemental Life Insurance
- If you participate in the corporation's supplemental life insurance plan, your survivors will receive an additional _____ upon your death from any cause.

Travel Accident Insurance
- An additional benefit of _____ will be paid to your survivors if your death results from an accident while traveling on corporate business.

Social Security
- Social Security will provide a monthly income of up to _____ a month if you have an eligible spouse with 2 or more children.

Medical Coverage
- Dependent's coverage can continue on a contributory basis.

RETIREMENT BENEFITS
Normal Retirement
- At age 65, you will receive an estimated _____ a month from the corporation's retirement plan and Social Security. Additional Social Security benefits are payable for an eligible spouse age 62 or older.
- Your spouse will receive an estimated _____ a month from the corporation's retirement plan and Social Security if your spouse is age 65 or older at your death.
- If you leave the corporation before retirement, you will be eligible to receive a pension amounting to the vested portion of your accrued benefit. The pension is payable at age 65, but reduced benefits are available as early as age 55. Your current accrued benefit is approximately _____ a month. Your vested benefit is _____ a month.

Early Retirement
- You may retire as early as age 55 with five years' service and receive a reduced benefit. For example, at age 62, your retirement income from the corporation's plan and Social Security would be approximately _____.

Other Retirement Benefits
- Medical coverage continues after retirement and is coordinated with Medicare.
- Group life insurance coverage continues in the amount of $5,000.

Interactive Voice-Response Systems

Employers are increasingly turning to newer technologies to communicate and manage benefit plans. One of these technologies is the telephone and the use of interactive voice-response systems. At one extreme, a telephone system can be as simple as merely giving information to all employees about such

FIGURE 2-4
Benefit Statement Review

BENEFIT STATEMENT REVIEW
FOR
_____

Many of us forget that there is more to our paycheck than the amount we take home. The following are the "extras" that were provided in 20 ____ and their value as determined by the cost to your employer.

		Annual Value	Value per Hour
(1)	Social Security and Medicare (employer's contribution)	$_____	$_____
(2)	Worker's Compensation Insurance Premium	_____	_____
(3)	State Unemployment Insurance Premium	_____	_____
(4)	Paid Holidays	_____	_____
(5)	Vacation Days	_____	_____
(6)	Pension	_____	_____
(7)	Salary Continuation	_____	_____
(8)	Long-Term Disability Income Insurance	_____	_____
(9)	Life Insurance	_____	_____
(10)	Medical Expense Insurance (employer's contribution)	_____	_____
(11)	Others	_____	_____
	_____		
	_____		
		_____	_____
		_____	_____

The $_____ value of these sometimes forgotten benefits is equal to _____% of the $_____ you received as salary or wages in 20 ____. These benefits are provided to protect you and your family from certain financial risks and to help provide for your future retirement.

matters as times for employee meetings, enrollment deadlines, and plan changes. However, this use of the telephone requires all employees to have either a telephone or some alternative method to receive the information. From this point, telephone systems can get increasingly complex. At the next level, the system can allow employees, through a menu of options, to request general information and materials such as enrollment forms. Carried even further, the system can enable employees to obtain specific information about their own benefits, such as the amount of life insurance they have or the balance in their 401(k) account. Of course, if personal information is available, employees will need to be given a personal identification number to access the information. At the most complex extreme, telephones can be used to allow employees to make benefit elections and changes. For example, an employee may be able to change investment options for a 401(k) plan or to change from one medical expense plan to another during open enrollment periods.

There are both advantages and disadvantages to the use of telephone systems for benefit communication. Among the advantages:

- Employees can have 24-hour access.
- Employees can get quick and accurate responses.
- Employees can maintain a degree of anonymity by not having to disclose information to in-house personnel.
- Human resources personnel have more time to spend on issues other than routine phone inquiries.

However, there are also drawbacks and limitations, some of which can be overcome with proper planning and design:

- There is a lack of human interaction. This by itself will discourage some employees from using the telephone system if they can obtain the same information and perform the same transactions by calling someone personally. If the telephone system is the only way that employees can request certain information or initiate certain transactions, it is important that a new system be well publicized and possibly established in small increments. A well-designed system will be simple to use and not leave employees in an endless maze of pushing buttons. It will also give employees a method to reach a real person when they feel it is necessary to speak to one.
- Telephone systems can become increasingly expensive as they are expanded to allow employees a wider range of options. For some firms, the cost may outweigh the benefits.
- To the extent employees can make benefit changes and elections by merely pushing a button, there is the possibility of mistakes being made. Therefore it is necessary for the telephone response system to confirm all transactions over the phone and allow employees to enter needed corrections. In addition, a written confirmation should be sent to employees, possibly requiring the return of a signed copy of the confirmation.
- Telephone systems are not conducive to inputting data such as the name of a new dependent for purposes of obtaining medical expense coverage.

Computers

While telephone systems can be used effectively for obtaining information and simple benefit plan enrollments, computers enable employers to use technology to a much greater extent.

The majority of computer benefits systems are intranet-based over a local area network of company computers. These tend to have the advantage of speed and to minimize security concerns, whether they be perceived or real. Firms can also use Internet-based systems over a public network that is secured by password access. A major advantage of the Internet is that employees can be allowed access from home or while they are traveling. In addition, the Internet is often better for providing employees with links to other useful Web sites because, for security reasons, a firm may not wish to have other links with its intranet site. A few firms have benefit systems on both its intranet and the Internet. Computerized benefit systems can be on either employees' personal computers at their workstations or on computer terminals located at centralized stations. Employees may also be able to access these systems from their home computer or from other locations. By pressing the appropriate key, an employee can get a general description of the company's various plans. By inputting appropriate data (including an identification number), an employee may also be able to obtain information about his or her own particular situation. For example, an employee could determine a potential disability income or retirement benefit. An employee may also be able to obtain the answers to "what if" questions. For example, "If I contribute $100 per month to a 401(k) plan that is expected to earn 7 percent annually, how much will I have at age 65?" Or "If I elect these options under a cafeteria plan, will any additional employer dollars remain for other benefits, or will I have to make an additional contribution through a payroll deduction?"

Employers are increasingly using the computer to allow employees to make benefit selections. To have some verification in writing, a form is either printed on the spot for an employee to sign and return or generated in the personnel office, reviewed, and sent to the employee for signing. Computers also facilitate data input, such as the name of a new beneficiary for life insurance coverage or the name of a new spouse who is being added to an employee's medical expense coverage.

Computers can be used to educate employees as well as provide benefit information. For example, employees can be given information comparing the pros and cons of a managed care plan with those of a traditional indemnity plan. Employees can also be given information to help them in their overall personal financial planning, often through links to other Internet sites.

Finally, employers are beginning to use computers to disseminate legally required information, such as summary plan descriptions.

Many of the same advantages and disadvantages of using telephone systems also apply to the use of computers. A major drawback to a computerized benefit system has been cost in relation to return on investment. (However, this drawback is becoming less of an obstacle as more employees have computer access.) Moreover, the success of such a system requires a high level of technical competence at the human resources and management information systems levels. There must be an understanding that computer communications often need to be approached differently from printed communications. Finally, employees need to feel comfortable using computerized benefit systems. This is continuing to occur as employees become more computer-literate and intranet and Internet sites evolve.

SHOULD BENEFIT ADMINISTRATION BE OUTSOURCED?

Historically, most organizations have fully administered their benefit programs with their own employees. However, it has not been unusual for an organization to outsource some administrative functions to other parties. For example, third-party administrators have been used to administer self-funded medical expense plans, and actuaries have been used to perform some of the compliance functions for qualified retirement plans.

More recently there has been a significant increase in the outsourcing of employee benefit administration, with estimates indicating that between 40 and 50 percent of all employers currently use outsourcing to some degree. Surveys also indicate that another 15 to 20 percent of employers are actively exploring the use of outsourcing. In the last portion of this chapter, the reasons for outsourcing are identified. In addition, the types of functions commonly outsourced and the types of vendors used for outsourcing are described. Finally, the factors that must be considered when entering into a contract for outsourcing are discussed.

Reasons for Outsourcing

There are many reasons why an employer might decide to outsource benefit administration. The most common reason is that the organization lacks the technical and regulatory expertise to perform many of the necessary functions. For example, few employers have a staff with the expertise to perform actuarial calculations or utilization reviews. Functions of this nature are best left to firms that have a staff of specialists in these areas. Closely correlated with this reason is the desire of firms to seek more value for the dollars spent on benefits. While outsourcing costs money, it is often cheaper than performing the same functions in-house. Some of this savings is because of the high cost of the hardware and software that is increasingly needed. An outside vendor can spread this cost over many customers.

Better service to employees is also an often cited reason for outsourcing. Vendors frequently have toll-free numbers and a staff that specializes in specific benefit functions. Persons who answer telephones are typically trained to have the ability to handle 90 percent or more of the inquiries they receive. But more important, they have the ability to transfer the more complex calls to the appropriate person to handle the issue.

Another cited reason for outsourcing is that the organization should focus its attention on the firm's core activities. Outsourcing enables a firm to lower the size of the staff that administers its benefits or at least have the staff remain stable or grow more slowly in an era when benefit administration is becoming increasingly complex.

Functions Outsourced

Significant variations exist with respect to the benefit functions that are outsourced. Systems, staff, or both can be outsourced. *Systems outsourcing* refers to the use of an outsourcing organization's computer and other systems while retaining an in-house staff to perform administrative functions. *Staff outsourcing* refers to the outsourcing of people but the continued use of the organization's systems.

Outsourcing can also be classified as either partial or full. With *partial outsourcing,* an employer uses an outsourcing organization's personnel and/or staff for some benefit functions but continues other functions in-house. The term *full outsourcing* refers to those situations where most benefit functions are outsourced. Even with full outsourcing, some functions, such as financial management of benefit plans and benefit plan design, remain the responsibility of senior personnel at the firm.

Most employers use partial outsourcing. Among the most common functions to be outsourced are the following:

- COBRA administration
- Administration of medical and dental claims
- Utilization review
- Vision care programs
- Record keeping of defined-benefit pension plans
- Record keeping and administration of defined-contribution retirement plans
- Record keeping and administration of flexible spending accounts
- Preretirement planning
- Benefit communication

Vendors Used for Outsourcing

Many types of organizations operate as vendors for outsourcing. In addition, employers who outsource may use several vendors because vendors often specialize in a limited number of activities. In fact, some vendors are very specialized. For example, some vendors may specialize in only one type of benefit such as vision care.

The major providers of outsourcing services include benefit consulting firms, insurance companies, stock brokerage firms, mutual funds, and third-party administrators. Stock brokerage firms and mutual funds tend to be involved almost solely in functions relating to retirement plans. While the other vendors often engage in a wide variety of activities, they may also specialize in a limited number of outsourcing services. For example, benefit consulting firms frequently focus their activities on regulatory compliance, eligibility determination, and enrollment.

Recently a small number of large organizations have been marketing themselves as having the ability to provide complete outsourcing for an employer. The number of firms that do all their outsourcing with only one vendor is still very small but likely to grow.

The Decision To Outsource

The decision to outsource is not a simple task. An organization must determine what functions should be outsourced and what functions can best be performed in-house. Consideration also needs to be given to the firm's personnel. Outsourcing often involves working with computers and other systems. It is important that people with expertise in these areas be involved. In addition, the help of the internal benefit staff is vital. However, their assistance may be affected by the fact—either real or perceived—that outsourcing may result in the loss of their jobs.

Once a vendor has been selected to provide an outsourcing service, the process of changing vendors can be complex and expensive. Therefore a high degree of care should go into the vendor-selection process. There should also be contingency plans for changing vendors if that need arises.

A formal outsourcing process begins with a request for proposal (RFP) in which vendors are asked to bid to provide services. The RFP should clearly spell out the goals of outsourcing and identify the major responsibilities of the potential parties to an outsourcing contract.

The outsourcing contract itself needs to clearly establish responsibilities of both the vendor and the employer but yet be flexible enough to address situations that may arise in the future. Proper planning must be done with respect to data to make sure data important to the employer are not destroyed by the vendor—for example, while converting the data to the vendor's systems. It is also important for the employer to be able to retrieve data if the contract with the vendor terminates.

A good outsourcing contract (at least from the employer's standpoint) will contain performance guarantees. These guarantees may relate to factors such as timeliness, accuracy, productivity improvements, and employee complaints.

Because the primary purpose of outsourcing is to save money in the long run, it is also very important to address vendor compensation. The contract should not be so open-ended that unforeseen costs are automatically passed on to the employer. Even fixed-price contracts may prove to be expensive if a firm downsizes but the vendor gets the same compensation for servicing a smaller number of employers.

Some other issues that must be addressed include confidentiality and security of data, vendor responsibility for systems upgrades and employer responsibility to pay for them, insurance and/or bonding requirements, and procedures for resolving disputes among the parties.

STUDY QUESTIONS

1. Why is it important for an organization to have specific written objectives for its benefit plans?

2. Explain how the benefit objectives of an organization may vary in both length and specific details for realizing the objectives.

3. What are the various categories of persons for whom an employer might have responsibility to provide benefits?

4. Describe the traditional approaches for determining the benefit needs of employees and explain the drawbacks of each approach.

5. What is the potential negative impact of using a marketing research approach to determine the needs of employees?

6. a. What are the advantages of using personal interviews to determine employee needs?
   b. Why should these interviews be conducted without the presence of the employee's supervisor?

7. What advantages does a structured questionnaire for determining employee needs have over an open-ended questionnaire?

8. Some firms have different plans for different groups of employees.
   a. Under what circumstances are different benefits often used?
   b. What are the disadvantages of having different plans?

9. What is the purpose of life-cycle benefits?

10. a. Why are employers increasingly taking a work/life approach to benefit planning?
    b. What types of benefits might be provided under this approach?

11. Identify the potential advantages of requiring employees to pay a portion of the premiums for their own coverage.

12. What should be the objectives of an effective program for communicating benefit plans to employees?

13. What factors should be present in an effective communication plan?

14. Explain why some personalized benefit statements may be more effective techniques than benefit handbooks for communicating with employees.

15. Some firms now use interactive voice-response systems to communicate benefit plans to employees.
    a. How can such systems be used?
    b. What are their advantages and disadvantages?

16. What are some of the ways in which computers can be used to communicate employee benefit plans?

17. Why might an employer decide to outsource benefit administration?

18. What issues must be addressed in the process of outsourcing benefits?

PART TWO

Social Insurance

CHAPTER 3

Social Security and Medicare

- Identify the reasons why social insurance exists and describe the basic features of social insurance programs.

- Describe the financing of Social Security and Medicare benefits, including (1) the purpose and significant of the Social Security and Medicare trust funds and (2) the financial soundness of the programs.

- Explain the requirements necessary for benefit eligibility under Social Security and Medicare.

- Identify the types of benefits available under Social Security and Medicare.

- Explain how Medicare participants may elect coverage under a managed care plan.

- Explain the extent to which federal tax laws apply to Social Security contributions and benefits.

Social insurance programs in the United States fall into several categories. These include the following:

- Social Security
- Medicare
- Unemployment insurance
- Temporary disability insurance
- Workers' compensation insurance

Social Security and Medicare are described in this chapter; the remaining three programs are covered in the following chapter. Two other programs, which are not covered, are established by the Railroad Retirement Act and the Railroad Unemployment Insurance Act. These acts provide benefits to railroad workers that are similar to the benefits provided to other persons by Social Security and state unemployment insurance programs.

Social insurance programs are significant for several reasons. First, in the United States, nearly one quarter of the dollars employers spend on benefits for their employees is used to make legally required payments to social insurance programs. For employers with meager benefit plans, this proportion will be much higher and may even account for the majority of the total benefit package.

Second, the most significant insurance expense for most individuals is their contributions to Social Security and Medicare. For many persons, this contribution will exceed the combined cost of all other types of insurance purchased directly by the individual.

Third, these programs form the foundation on which employee benefit programs and individual insurance plans are built. Employers' medical expense, disability income, and retirement plans are often designed in light of the benefits already available to employees under social insurance programs. Some benefit plans apply to only those employees not adequately covered under comparable social insurance programs; other benefit plans may cover all employees but may provide reduced benefits in those areas where similar social insurance benefits are available. In addition, it is impossible to do a proper job of personal insurance planning without taking potential Social Security and Medicare benefits into consideration.

Many books have been devoted entirely to Social Security and Medicare. Because of space limitations, their treatment in this book is rather brief and is devoted primarily to a description of eligibility requirements, financing, and benefits. However, a few words should also be said about the reasons why Social Security, Medicare, and other social insurance programs exist and the general characteristics of such programs.

REASONS FOR SOCIAL INSURANCE

The existence and scope of social insurance programs are the result of several factors, probably the most significant of which is the need to solve the major social problems that affect a large portion of society. The industrialization of

American society and the decreasing self-sufficiency of families resulted in a greater dependence on monetary income to provide economic security. The widespread lack of such income during the Great Depression led to the passage of the Social Security Act as an attempt to provide economic security by attacking the sources of economic insecurity, including old age and unemployment.

A second reason for the existence of social insurance programs is the difficulty of privately insuring against certain types of losses. For example, the inability to predict future unemployment rates and the potential for catastrophic losses make the peril of unemployment virtually uninsurable in the private sector. In addition, broad medical expense coverage for the aged can be marketed commercially only at a price beyond the financial means of many retirees.

Finally, many Americans have come to expect the government to provide at least a degree of economic security against the consequences of premature death, old age, disability, and unemployment. As a result, social insurance programs enjoy widespread public acceptance.

CHARACTERISTICS OF SOCIAL INSURANCE

Even though there are variations in social insurance programs and exceptions to the rule always exist, social insurance programs tend to have the following distinguishing characteristics:

- Compulsory employment-related coverage
- Partial or total employer financing
- Benefits prescribed by law
- Benefits as a matter of right
- Emphasis on social adequacy

Compulsory Employment-Related Coverage

Most social insurance programs are compulsory and require that the persons covered be attached—either presently or by past service—to the labor force. If a social insurance program is to meet a social need through the redistribution of income, it must have widespread participation.

Partial or Total Employer Financing

While significant variations exist in social insurance programs, most require that the cost of the program be borne fully or at least partially by the employers of the covered persons. This is the basis for including these programs under the broad definition of *employee benefits*. The remaining cost of most social insurance programs is paid primarily by the persons covered under the programs. With the exception of Medicare and certain unemployment benefits, the general revenues of the federal government and state governments finance only a small portion of social insurance benefits.

Benefits Prescribed by Law

Although benefit amounts and the eligibility requirements for social insurance benefits are prescribed by law, benefits are not necessarily uniform for everyone. They may vary by such factors as wage level, length of covered employment, or family status. These factors are incorporated into the benefit formulas specified by law, and covered persons are unable to either increase or decrease their prescribed level of benefits.

Benefits as a Matter of Right

Social insurance benefits are paid as a matter of right under the presumption that a need for the benefits exists. This feature distinguishes social insurance programs from public assistance or welfare programs under which applicants, to qualify for benefits, must meet a needs test by demonstrating that their income or assets are below some specified level.

Emphasis on Social Adequacy

Benefits under social insurance programs are based more on social adequacy than on individual equity. Under the principle of social adequacy, benefits are designed to provide a minimum floor of income to all beneficiaries under the program, regardless of their economic status. Above this floor of benefits, persons are expected to provide additional resources from their own savings, employment, or private insurance programs. This emphasis on social adequacy also results in disproportionately large benefits in relation to contributions for some groups of beneficiaries. Under some programs, high-income persons, single persons or small families, and the young are subsidizing low-income persons, large families, and the retired.

If social insurance programs were based solely on individual equity, benefits would be actuarially related to contributions, just as they are under private insurance programs. While this degree of individual equity does not exist, there is some relationship between benefits and income levels (and thus contributions). Within certain maximum and minimum amounts, benefits are a function of a person's covered earnings under social insurance programs. However, the major emphasis is on social adequacy.

SOCIAL SECURITY AND MEDICARE

In a broad sense, the term *Social Security* can be used to refer to any of several programs resulting from the Social Security Act of 1935 and its frequent amendments over the years. The act established four programs aimed at providing economic security for the American society:

1. Old-age insurance
2. Unemployment insurance
3. Federal grants for assistance to certain needy groups: the aged, the blind, and children
4. Federal grants for maternal and child welfare, public health work, and vocational rehabilitation

The main focus in this chapter is on the old-age insurance program and the benefits that have been added to that program over the years. These additional benefits include survivors insurance (1939), disability insurance (1956), hospital insurance (1965), and supplementary medical insurance (1965). Taken together, these programs constitute the old-age, survivors, disability, and health insurance (OASDHI) program of the federal government. This program is often separated into two broad parts. The first part is the old-age, survivors and disability insurance (OASDI) program. Over the years, OASDI has become commonly referred to as *Social Security,* and this is the terminology that will be used in this book. The remainder of the OASDHI program is called *Medicare,* with hospital insurance being called *Part A* and supplemental medical insurance being called *Part B.*

The following discussion of Social Security and Medicare begins with a description of the extent of coverage under the programs and the way the programs are financed. It then focuses on the eligibility requirements and benefits under the various parts of the programs. Because of the many differences between Social Security and Medicare, the discussion largely treats each program separately. This is followed by a discussion of the adequacy of the funding of these programs. Finally, there is a description of the tax implications of Social Security and Medicare benefits and contributions.

Extent of Coverage

More than 90 percent of the workers in the United States are in covered employment under the Social Security program and more than 95 percent under the Medicare program. This means that these workers have wages (if they are employees) or self-employment income (if they are self-employed) on which Social Security and Medicare taxes must be paid. The following are the major categories of workers who are not covered under the programs or who are covered only if they have met specific conditions:

■ Civilian employees of the federal government who were employed by the government prior to 1984 and who are covered under the Civil Service Retirement System or certain other federal retirement programs. These workers are covered by government plans that provide benefits similar to those available under Social Security. Coverage for new civilian federal employees under the Social Security program was one of the most significant changes resulting from 1983 amendments to the Social Security Act. It should be noted, however, that *all* federal employees have been covered under Social Security for purposes of Medicare since 1983.

■ Railroad workers. Under the Railroad Retirement Act, employees of railroads have their own benefit system that is similar to Social Security. However, they are covered under Medicare. In addition, there are certain circumstances under which railroad workers receive benefits from the Social Security program even though their contributions were paid to the railroad program.

■ Some state and local government employees. Historically, employees covered under state and local government retirement plans have been covered under Social Security and Medicare only if a state entered into a voluntary agreement with the Social Security Administration. Under such an agreement, the state may either require that employees of local governments be covered or allow local governments to decide whether to include their employees. In addition, the state may elect to include all or only certain groups of employees. It is estimated that more than 80 percent of state and local government employees have Social Security and Medicare coverage as a result of such agreements. In addition, coverage under Medicare is compulsory for state and local employees hired after March 1986, and coverage under Social Security is compulsory for employees hired after July 1, 1991, if they do not participate in a public retirement system.

■ American citizens working abroad for foreign affiliates of U.S. employers, unless the U.S. employer owns at least a 10 percent interest in the foreign affiliate and has made arrangements with the secretary of the treasury for the payment of Social Security and Medicare taxes. However, Americans working abroad are covered under Social Security and Medicare if they are working directly for U.S. employers rather than for their foreign subsidiaries.

■ Ministers who elect out of coverage because of conscience or religious principles.

■ Workers in certain jobs, such as student nurses, newspaper carriers under age 18, and students working for the school at which they are regularly enrolled or doing domestic work for a local college club, fraternity, or sorority.

■ Certain family employment. This includes the employment of a child under age 18 by a parent. This exclusion, however, does not apply if the employment is for a corporation owned by a family member.

■ Certain workers who must satisfy special earnings requirements. For example, self-employed persons are not covered unless they have net annual earnings of $400 or more. In addition, certain agricultural workers must have annual cash wages of $150 or more, and domestic workers must earn $1,200 or more in cash wages in a calendar year.

Tax Rates and Wage Bases

Part B of Medicare is financed by a combination of monthly premiums paid by persons eligible for benefits and contributions from the federal government. Part A of Medicare and all the benefits of the Social Security program are financed through a system of payroll and self-employment taxes paid by all persons covered under the programs. In addition, employers of covered persons are also taxed. These taxes are often referred to as *FICA taxes* because they are imposed under the Federal Insurance Contributions Act.

In 2001, an employee and his or her employer each pay a tax of 7.65 percent on the first $80,400 of the employee's wages. Of this tax rate, 6.2 percent is for Social Security; 1.45 percent is for the hospital insurance portion of Medicare. The Medicare tax rate of 1.45 percent is also levied on all wages in excess of $80,400. The tax rates are currently scheduled to remain the same after 2001; however, the wage bases are adjusted annually for changes in the national level of wages. Therefore, if wage levels increase by 4 percent in a particular year, the wage base for the following year will also increase by 4 percent. The tax rate for the self-employed is 15.3 percent on the first $80,400 of self-employment income and 2.9 percent on the balance of any self-employment income. This is equal to the combined employee and employer rates.

Over the years, both the tax rates and wage bases have risen dramatically to finance increased benefit levels under Social Security and Medicare as well as new benefits that have been added to the program. Table 3-1 shows the magnitude of these increases for selected years.

The adequacy of the current funding structure to pay for Social Security and Medicare benefits continues to be a source of public concern and political debate. The issue is addressed in more detail after the programs are described.

SOCIAL SECURITY: ELIGIBILITY

To be eligible for benefits under Social Security, an individual must have credit for a minimum amount of work under the program. This credit is based on quarters of coverage. For 2001, a worker receives credit for one quarter of coverage for each $830 in annual earnings on which Social Security taxes are paid, up to a maximum of four quarters in any one calendar year, even if all wages are earned within one calendar quarter. Consequently, a worker paying Social Security taxes on as little as $3,320 (that is, $830 × 4) during the year will receive credit for the maximum four quarters. As in the case of the wage base, the amount of earnings necessary for a quarter of coverage is adjusted annually for changes in the national level of wages.

TABLE 3-1
Changes in Tax Rates and Wage Bases under Social Security and Medicare

Year	Wage Base	Tax Rate	Maximum Employee Tax
1950	$3,000	1.50%	$ 45.00
1970	7,800	4.80	374.40
1990	51,300	7.65	3,924.45
1991	first 53,400	7.65	
	next 71,600	1.45	5,123.30
1992	first 55,500	7.65	
	next 74,700	1.45	5,328.90
1993	first 57,600	7.65	
	next 77,400	1.45	5,528.70
1994	first 60,600	7.65	
	additional wages	1.45	‡
1995	first 61,200	7.65	
	additional wages	1.45	‡
1996	first 62,700	7.65	
	additional wages	1.45	‡
1997	first 65,400	7.65	
	additional wages	1.45	‡
1998	first 68,400	7.65	
	additional wages	1.45	‡
1999	first 72,600	7.65	
	additional wages	1.45	‡
2000	first 76,200	7.65	
	additional wages	1.45	‡
2001	first 80,400	7.65	
	additional wages	1.45	‡
2002 and after	*	†	

*Subject to automatic adjustment
†Same as 2000
‡No determinable maximum due to unlimited wage base for Medicare tax

Quarters of coverage are the basis for establishing an insured status under Social Security. The three types of insured status are *fully insured, currently insured,* and *disability insured.*

Fully Insured

A person is fully insured under Social Security if either of two tests is met. The first test requires credit for 40 quarters of coverage. Once a person acquires such credit, he or she is fully insured for life even if employment covered under Social Security ceases.

Under the second test, a person who has credit for a minimum of six quarters of coverage is fully insured if he or she has credit for at least as many quarters of coverage as there are years elapsing *after* 1950 (or *after* the year in which age 21 is reached, if later) and *before* the year in which he or she dies, becomes disabled, or reaches age 62, whichever occurs first. Therefore, a worker who reached age 21 in 1988 and who died in 2000 would need credit for only 11 quarters of coverage for his or her family to be eligible for survivors' benefits.

Currently Insured

If a worker is fully insured under Social Security, there is no additional significance to being currently insured. However, if a worker is not fully insured, certain survivors benefits are still available if a currently insured status exists. To be currently insured, it is only necessary that a worker have credit for at least 6 quarters of coverage out of the 13-quarter period ending with the quarter in which death occurs.

Disability Insured

To receive disability benefits under Social Security, it is necessary to be disability insured. At a minimum, a disability insured status requires that a worker (1) be fully insured and (2) have a minimum amount of work under Social Security within a recent time period. In connection with the latter requirement, workers aged 31 or older must have credit for at least 20 of the past 40 quarters ending with the quarter in which disability occurs; workers between the ages of 24 and 30, inclusively, must have credit for at least half the quarters of coverage from the time they turned 21 to the quarter in which disability begins; and workers under age 24 must have credit for 6 out of the past 12 quarters, ending with the quarter in which disability begins.

A special rule for the blind states that they are exempt from the recent-work rules and are considered disability insured as long as they are fully insured.

SOCIAL SECURITY: TYPES OF BENEFITS

As its name implies, the Social Security program provides three principal types of benefits:

1. Retirement (old-age) benefits
2. Survivors' benefits
3. Disability benefits

Retirement Benefits

A worker who is fully insured under Social Security is eligible to receive monthly retirement benefits as early as age 62. However, the election to receive benefits prior to the normal retirement age of 65 years results in a permanently reduced benefit.

In addition to the retired worker, the following dependents of persons receiving retirement benefits are also eligible for monthly benefits:

- A spouse aged 62 or older. However, benefits are permanently reduced if this benefit is elected prior to the spouse's reaching age 65. This benefit is also available to a divorced spouse under certain circumstances if the marriage lasted at least 10 years.
- A spouse of any age if the spouse is caring for at least one child of the retired worker who is (1) under age 16 or (2) disabled and entitled to a child's benefit as described below. This benefit is commonly referred to as a *mother's* or *father's benefit*.
- Dependent, unmarried children under age 18. This child's benefit will continue until age 19 as long as a child is a full-time student in elementary or secondary school. In addition, disabled children of any age are eligible for benefits as long as they were disabled before reaching age 22.

TABLE 3-2
Retirement Age for Nonreduced Benefits

Year of Birth	Normal Retirement Age
1937 and before	65 years
1938	65 years, 2 months
1939	65 years, 4 months
1940	65 years, 6 months
1941	65 years, 8 months
1942	65 years, 10 months
1943–54	66 years
1955	66 years, 2 months
1956	66 years, 4 months
1957	66 years, 6 months
1958	66 years, 8 months
1959	66 years, 10 months
1960 and later	67 years

It is important to note that retirement benefits as well as all other benefits under Social Security and Medicare are not automatically paid on eligibility but must be applied for.

Beginning in 2003, the normal retirement age for nonreduced benefits for workers and spouses will gradually increase until it reaches age 67 in 2027. This increase is shown in Table 3-2.

Survivors Benefits

All categories of survivors benefits are payable if a worker is fully insured at the time of death. However, three types of benefits are also payable if a worker is only currently insured. The first is a lump-sum death benefit of $255, payable in the following order of priority:

1. To a surviving spouse who was living with the deceased worker at the time of death
2. To a surviving spouse (other than a divorced spouse) who was not living with the deceased worker at the time of death if the surviving spouse is

eligible for or entitled to benefits based on the deceased wage earner's record for the month of death

3. To children who are eligible for or entitled to benefits based on the deceased wage earner's record for the month of death

If none of these categories of survivors exists, the benefit is not paid

There are two categories of persons who are eligible for income benefits as survivors if a deceased worker was either fully or currently insured at the time of death:

1. Dependent, unmarried children under the same conditions as previously described for retirement benefits

2. A spouse (including a divorced spouse) caring for a child or children under the same conditions as previously described for retirement benefits

The following categories of persons are also eligible for benefits, but only if the deceased worker was fully insured:

- A widow or widower aged 60 or older. However, benefits are reduced if taken prior to age 65. This benefit is also payable to a divorced spouse if the marriage lasted at least 10 years. In addition, the widow's or widower's benefit is payable to a disabled spouse at age 50 as long as the disability commenced no more than 7 years after (1) the worker's death or (2) the end of the year in which entitlement to a mother's or father's benefit ceased.
- A parent aged 62 or over who was a dependent of the deceased worker at the time of death.

Disability Benefits

A disabled worker under age 65 is eligible to receive benefits under Social Security as long as he or she is disability insured and meets the definition of disability under the law. The definition of disability is very rigid and requires a mental or physical impairment that prevents the worker from engaging in any substantial gainful employment. The disability must also have lasted (or be expected to last) at least 12 months or be expected to result in death. A more liberal definition of disability applies to blind workers who are aged 55 or older. They are considered disabled if they are unable to perform work that requires skills or abilities comparable to those required by the work they regularly performed before reaching age 55 or becoming blind, if later.

Disability benefits are subject to a waiting period and are payable beginning with the sixth full calendar month of disability. In addition to the benefit paid to a disabled worker, the other categories of benefits available are the same as those described under retirement benefits.

As previously mentioned, certain family members not otherwise eligible for Social Security benefits may be eligible if they are disabled. Disabled children are subject to the same definition of disability as workers. Disabled widows or widowers must be unable to engage in *any* gainful (rather than substantial gainful) employment.

Eligibility for Dual Benefits

In many cases, a person is eligible for more than one type of Social Security benefit. Probably the most common situation occurs when a person is eligible for both a spouse's benefit and a worker's retirement or disability benefit based on his or her own Social Security record. In this case and in any other case when a person is eligible for dual benefits, only an amount equal to the higher benefit is paid.

Termination of Benefits

Monthly benefits to any Social Security recipient cease on death of the recipient. When a retired or disabled worker dies, the family members' benefits that are based on the worker's retirement or disability benefits also cease, but the family members are then eligible for survivors benefits.

Disability benefits for a worker technically terminate at age 65 but are then replaced by comparable retirement benefits. In addition, any benefits payable because of disability cease if the definition of disability is no longer satisfied. However, the disability benefits will continue during a readjustment period that consists of the month of recovery and two additional months.

As long as children are not disabled, benefits usually terminate at age 18 but may continue until age 19 if the child is a full-time student in elementary or secondary school.

The benefits of a surviving spouse terminate on remarriage unless remarriage takes place at age 60 or later.

SOCIAL SECURITY: BENEFIT AMOUNTS

Calculating Benefits

With the exception of the $255 lump-sum death benefit, the amount of all Social Security benefits is based on a worker's primary insurance amount (PIA). The actual PIA calculation is complex and is done by the Social Security Administration when a beneficiary is eligible for benefits. It involves indexing past wages on which taxes were paid to current wage levels, eliminating some years with the lowest or no earnings, and averaging the indexed wages for the remaining years. The result is then put into a formula that is weighted in favor of lower-income workers.

The PIA is the amount a worker receives if he or she retires at age 65 or becomes disabled, and it is the amount on which benefits for family members are based. In 2001, the average PIA for a retired worker is just over $800. A worker who has continually earned the maximum income subject to Social Security taxes can expect a PIA of about $1,500 for retirement purposes and a PIA of between $1,500 and $1,700 for purposes of disability and survivors benefits. The higher PIA results for workers who are disabled or die at younger ages.

If a worker is retired or disabled, benefits are paid to family members, as shown in Table 3-3.

If the worker dies, survivors benefits are as shown in Table 3-4. However, the full benefits described in the table may not be payable because of a limitation imposed on the total benefits that may be paid to a family. This family maximum is again determined by a formula and is usually reached if three or more family members (including a retired or disabled worker) are eligible for benefits.

If the total amount of benefits payable to family members exceeds the family maximum, the worker's benefit (in the case of retirement and disability) is not affected, but the benefits of other family members are reduced proportionately. For example, assume a worker dies leaving a spouse under age 65 and three children who are each eligible for 75 percent of the worker's PIA of $1,200. If the family maximum is ignored, the benefits total $3,600 ($900 for each family member). However, the family maximum using the prescribed formula for 2001 is $2,160.80. Therefore, each family member has his or her benefit reduced to $540 (rounded to the next lower dollar). When the first child loses benefits at age 18, each of the other family members has his or her benefits increased to $720 (if any automatic increases in benefit amounts, including the family maximum, are ignored). When a second family member loses eligibility, the remaining two family members each receive the full benefit of $900 because the benefits received by the family now total less than the $2,160.80 calculated by the formula.

TABLE 3-3
Benefits for Family Members of a Disabled or Retired Worker

Family Member	Percentage of Worker's PIA
Spouse aged 65	50%
Spouse caring for disabled child or child under 16	50%
Child under 18 or disabled	50% each

TABLE 3-4
Benefits for Family Members of a Deceased Worker

Family Member	Percentage of Worker's PIA
Spouse aged 65	100%
Spouse caring for disabled child or child under 16	75%
Child under 18 or disabled	75% each
Dependent parent	82.5% for one, 75% for two

Other Factors Affecting Benefits

Special Minimum PIA

There is a minimum PIA for workers who have been covered under Social Security for at least 10 years but at very low wages. This PIA is used only if it is higher than a worker's PIA based on actual wages, which is usually not the case. The benefit is first determined by multiplying $11.50 times the number of years of coverage less 10, subject to a maximum of 20. This figure is then adjusted for the cumulative change in the consumer price index (CPI) since 1979. In 2001, a worker with 30 or more years of coverage under Social Security will have a minimum PIA at age 65 of just over $600.

Benefits Taken Early

If a worker elects to receive retirement benefits prior to age 65, benefits are permanently reduced by $5/9$ of 1 percent for every month that the early retirement precedes age 65. For example, for a worker who retires at age 62, the monthly benefit is only 80 percent of that worker's PIA. A spouse who elects retirement benefits prior to age 65 has benefits reduced by $25/36$ of 1 percent per month, and a widow or widower has benefits reduced by $19/40$ of 1 percent per month. In the latter case, benefits at age 60 are 71½ percent of the worker's PIA. If the widow or widower elects benefits at an earlier age because of disability, there is no further reduction.

Delayed Retirement

Workers who delay applying for benefits until after the normal retirement age (currently 65) are eligible for an increased benefit. Benefits are increased for each month of late retirement until age 70. For persons born in the years from 1917 to 1924, the increase is ¼ of 1 percent per month, which is equal to 3 percent for delaying application for benefit for one full year. To encourage later retirement, the monthly percentage gradually increases. Table 3-5 shows the percentage for each month of deferral as well as the maximum percentage increase that is available if retirement is postponed until age 70.

It should be pointed out that these increases apply to a worker's PIA as determined at the time a worker applies for retirement benefits. If a person continues to work during the period of delayed retirement and covered wages are sufficiently high, it is possible for a worker's PIA to be higher than it would have been at normal retirement age. Therefore, the increased monthly retirement benefit from working past normal retirement age may be greater than the percentages in the table.

Earnings Test

Through the 1999 tax year, benefits were reduced for Social Security beneficiaries under the age of 70 if they had wages that exceeded a specified level. For tax years beginning after 1999, Congress repealed this earnings test in and after the month in which a beneficiary attains the normal Social Security retirement age. As shown in Table 3-2, this age is currently 65 and is scheduled to increase. However, the earnings test still applies to beneficiaries under

TABLE 3-5
Increase for Delayed Retirement

Year of Birth	Monthly Percentage Increase	Maximum Percentage Increase
1917–24	1/4	15.00
1925–26	7/24	17.50
1927–28	1/3	20.00
1929–30	9/24	22.50
1931–32	5/12	25.00
1933–34	11/24	27.50
1935–36	1/2	30.00
1937	13/24	32.50
1938	13/24	31.42
1939	7/12	32.67
1940	7/12	31.50
1941	15/24	32.50
1942	15/24	31.25
1943–54	2/3	32.00
1955	2/3	30.67
1956	2/3	29.33
1957	2/3	28.00
1958	2/3	26.67
1959	2/3	25.33
1960 and later	2/3	24.00

age 65. They are allowed earnings of up to $10,680 in 2001, and this figure is subject to annual indexing for later years. If a beneficiary earns more than this amount, his or her Social Security benefit is reduced by $1 for each $2 dollars of excess earnings. Once the beneficiary reaches age 65, any amount can be earned without a Social Security reduction.

Any reduction in a retired worker's benefits resulting from excess earnings is charged against the entire benefits that are paid to a family and based on the worker's Social Security record. If large enough, this reduction may totally eliminate all benefits otherwise payable to the worker and family members. In contrast, excess earnings of family members are charged against their individual benefits only. For example, a widowed mother who holds a job outside the home may lose her mother's benefit, but any benefits received by her children are unaffected.

Cost-of-Living Adjustments

Social Security benefits are increased automatically each January as long as there has been an increase in the CPI for the one-year period ending in the third quarter of the prior year. The increase is the same as the increase in the CPI since the last cost-of-living adjustment, rounded to the nearest 0.1 percent.

There is one exception to this adjustment. In any year that the combined reserves of the Social Security trust funds drop below 20 percent of expected benefits, the cost-of-living adjustment is limited to the lesser of the increase in the CPI or the increase in national wages used to adjust the wage base for Social Security taxes. When benefit increases are based on wage levels, future cost-of-living increases can be larger than changes in the CPI to make up for the lower benefit increases in those years when the CPI was not used. However, this extra cost-of-living increase is made only in years when the reserve is equal to at least 32 percent of expected benefits.

Offset for Other Benefits

Disabled workers under age 65 who are also receiving workers' compensation benefits or disability benefits from certain other federal, state, or local disability programs have their Social Security benefits reduced to the extent that the total benefits received (including family benefits) exceed 80 percent of their average current earnings at the time of disability. In addition, the monthly benefit of a spouse or surviving spouse is reduced by two-thirds of any federal, state, or local government pension that is based on earnings not covered under Social Security on the last day of employment.

SOCIAL SECURITY: OBTAINING BENEFIT INFORMATION

In 1995, the Social Security Administration began sending an annual Earnings and Benefit Estimate Statement to each worker aged 60 and older. This statement, renamed the *Social Security Statement,* is now provided annually to all persons aged 25 or older who have employment covered under Social Security and are not currently entitled to monthly benefits. The statement enables an employee to verify his or her contributions to the Social Security and Medicare programs. It also contains an estimate of benefits that are available upon retirement, disability, or death.

The statement will help employees understand their total benefit package as well as enable any errors in earnings records to be corrected while information is readily available. As a general rule, requests for corrections must be made within 3 years, 3 months, and 15 days following the year in which wages were paid or self-employment income was earned. However, clerical or fraudulent errors can be corrected after that time.

MEDICARE: ELIGIBILITY

Part A, the hospital portion of Medicare, is available to any person aged 65 or older as long as the person is entitled to monthly retirement benefits under Social Security or the railroad retirement program. Civilian employees of the federal government aged 65 or older are also eligible. It is not necessary for these workers to actually be receiving retirement benefits, but they must be fully insured for purposes of retirement benefits. The following persons are also eligible for Part A of Medicare at no monthly cost:

- Persons aged 65 or older who are dependents of fully insured workers aged 62 or older.
- Survivors aged 65 or older who are eligible for Social Security survivors benefits.
- Disabled persons at any age who have been eligible to receive Social Security benefits for two years because of their disability. This includes workers under age 65, disabled widows and widowers aged 50 or over, and children 18 or older who were disabled prior to age 22.
- Workers who are either fully or currently insured and their spouses and dependent children with end-stage renal (kidney) disease who require renal dialysis or kidney transplants. Coverage begins either the first day of the third month after dialysis begins or earlier for admission to a hospital for kidney-transplant surgery.

Most persons aged 65 or over who do not meet the previously discussed eligibility requirements may voluntarily enroll in Medicare. However, they must pay a monthly Part A premium and also enroll in Part B. The monthly Part A premium may be as high as $300 in 2001, depending on the quarters of coverage a person earned under Social Security. The premium is adjusted annually to reflect the full cost of the benefits provided.

Any person eligible for Part A of Medicare is also eligible for Part B. A monthly premium must be paid for Part B. This premium, $50.00 in 2001, is adjusted annually and represents only about 25 percent of the cost of the benefits provided. The remaining cost of the program is financed from the general revenues of the federal government.

Persons receiving Social Security or railroad retirement benefits are automatically enrolled in Medicare if they are eligible. If they do not want Part B, they must reject it in writing. Other persons eligible for Medicare must apply for benefits. As a general rule, anyone who rejects Part B or who does not enroll when initially eligible may later apply for benefits during a general enrollment period that occurs between January 1 and March 31 of each year. However, the monthly premium is increased by 10 percent for each 12-month period during which the person was eligible but failed to enroll.

Medicare secondary rules, which are covered in detail in Chapter 12, make employer-provided medical expense coverage primary to Medicare for certain classes of individuals who are over 65, who are disabled, or who are suffering end-stage renal disease. These persons (and any other Medicare-eligible persons still covered as active employees under their employer's plans) may not wish to elect Medicare because it largely constitutes duplicate coverage. When their employer-provided coverage ends, these persons have a seven-month special enrollment period to elect Part B coverage, and the late enrollment penalty is waived.

Medicare is also secondary to benefits received by persons (1) entitled to veterans' or black-lung benefits, (2) covered by workers' compensation laws, or (3) whose medical expenses are paid under no-fault or liability insurance.

MEDICARE: PART A BENEFITS

Part A of Medicare provides benefits for expenses incurred in hospitals, skilled-nursing facilities and hospices. Some home health care benefits are also covered. For benefits to be paid, the facility or agency providing benefits must participate in the Medicare program. Virtually all hospitals are participants, as are most other facilities or agencies that meet the requirements of Medicare.

Part A of Medicare along with Part B provides a high level of benefits for medical expenses. However, as is described in the next few pages, deductibles and copayments may be higher than in prior group or individual coverage. In addition, certain benefits that were previously provided may be excluded or limited. For this reason, persons without supplemental retiree coverage from prior employment may wish to consider the purchase of a medigap policy in the individual marketplace.

Hospital Benefits

Part A pays for inpatient hospital services for up to 90 days in each benefit period (also referred to as a *spell of illness*). A benefit period begins the first time a Medicare recipient is hospitalized and ends only after the recipient has been out of a hospital or skilled-nursing facility for 60 consecutive days. A subsequent hospitalization then begins a new benefit period.

In each benefit period, covered hospital expenses are paid in full for 60 days, subject to an initial deductible of $792 in 2001. This deductible is adjusted annually to reflect increasing hospital costs. Benefits for an additional 30 days of hospitalization are also provided in each benefit period, but the patient must pay a daily copayment ($198 in 2001) equal to 25 percent of the initial deductible amount. In addition, each recipient also has a lifetime reserve of 60 additional days that may be used if the regular 90 days of benefits have been exhausted, but once a reserve day is used, it cannot be restored for use in future benefit periods. When using reserve days, patients must pay a daily copayment ($396 in 2001) equal to 50 percent of the initial deductible amount.

There is no limit on the number of benefit periods a person may have during his or her lifetime. However, there is a lifetime limit of 190 days of benefits for treatment in psychiatric hospitals.

Covered inpatient expenses include the following:

■ Room and board in semiprivate accommodations. Private rooms are covered only if required for medical reasons.

- Nursing services (except private-duty nurses).
- Use of regular hospital equipment, such as oxygen tents or wheelchairs.
- Drugs and biologicals ordinarily furnished by the hospital.
- Diagnostic or therapeutic items or services.
- Operating room costs.
- Blood transfusions after the first three pints of blood. Patients must pay for the first three pints of blood unless they get donors to replace the blood.

There is no coverage under Part A of Medicare for the services of physicians or surgeons.

Skilled-Nursing Facility Benefits

In many cases, a patient may no longer require continuous hospital care but may not be well enough to go home. Consequently, Part A provides benefits for care in a skilled-nursing facility if a physician certifies that skilled-nursing care or rehabilitative services are needed for a condition that was treated in a hospital within the past 30 days. In addition, the prior hospitalization must have lasted at least three days. Benefits are paid in full for 20 days in each benefit period and for an additional 80 days with a daily copayment ($98 in 2001) that is equal to 12.5 percent of the initial hospital deductible. Covered expenses are the same as those described for hospital benefits.

A skilled-nursing facility may be a separate facility for providing such care or a separate section of a hospital or nursing home. The facility must have at least one full-time registered nurse, and nursing services must be provided at all times. Every patient must be under the supervision of a physician, and a physician must always be available for emergency care.

One very important point should be made about skilled-nursing facility benefits: Custodial care is not provided under any part of the Medicare program unless skilled-nursing or rehabilitative services are also needed.

Home Health Care Benefits

If a patient can be treated at home for a medical condition, Medicare pays the full cost for an unlimited number of home visits by a home health agency. Such agencies specialize in providing nursing and other therapeutic services. To receive these benefits, a person must be confined at home and be treated under a home health plan set up by a physician. No prior hospitalization is required. The care needed must include skilled-nursing services, physical therapy, or speech therapy. In addition to these services, Medicare also pays for the cost of part-time home health aides, medical social services, occupational therapy, and medical supplies and equipment provided by the home health agency. There is no charge for these services other than a required 20 percent copayment for the cost of such durable medical equipment as iron lungs, oxygen tanks, and hospital beds. Medicare does not cover home services furnished primarily to assist people in activities of daily living such as housecleaning, preparing meals, shopping, dressing, or bathing.

If a person has only Part A of Medicare, all home health care services are covered under Part A. If a person has both Parts A and B, the first 100 visits that commence within 14 days of a hospital stay of at least three days are covered under Part A. All other home health visits are covered under Part B.

Hospice Benefits

Hospice benefits are available under Part A of Medicare for beneficiaries who are certified as being terminally ill persons with a life expectancy of six months or less. While a hospice is thought of as a facility for treating the terminally ill, Medicare benefits are available primarily for services provided by a Medicare-approved hospice to patients in their own homes. However, inpatient care can be provided if needed by the patient. In addition to including the types of benefits described for home health care, hospice benefits also include drugs, bereavement counseling, and inpatient respite care when family members need a break from caring for the ill person.

To qualify for hospice benefits, a Medicare recipient must elect such coverage in lieu of other Medicare benefits, except for the services of the attending physician or services and benefits that do not pertain to the terminal condition. There are modest copayments for some services.

The benefit period consists of two 90-day periods followed by an unlimited number of 60-day periods. These periods can be used consecutively or at intervals. A beneficiary may cancel the hospice coverage at any time (for example, to pursue chemotherapy treatments) and return to regular Medicare coverage. Any remaining days of the current hospice benefit period are lost forever, but the beneficiary can elect hospice benefits again. However, the beneficiary must be recertified as terminally ill at the beginning of each new benefit period.

Exclusions

There are some circumstances under which Part A of Medicare does not pay benefits. In addition, there are times when Medicare acts as the secondary payer of benefits. Exclusions under Part A include the following:

- Services outside the United States and its territories or possessions. There are a few exceptions to this rule for qualified Mexican and Canadian hospitals. Benefits are paid if an emergency occurs in the United States and the closest hospital is in one of these countries. In addition, persons living closer to a hospital in one of these countries than to a hospital in the United States may use the foreign hospital even if an emergency does not exist. Finally, there is coverage for Canadian hospitals if a person needs hospitalization while traveling the most direct route between Alaska and another state in the United States. However, this latter provision does not apply to persons vacationing in Canada.

- Elective luxury services, such as private rooms or televisions.
- Hospitalization for services not necessary for the treatment of an illness or injury, such as custodial care or elective cosmetic surgery.
- Services performed in a federal facility, such as a veterans' hospital.
- Services covered under workers' compensation.

Under the following circumstances, Medicare is the secondary payer of benefits:

- When primary coverage under an employer-provided medical expense plan is elected by (1) an employee or spouse aged 65 or older or (2) a disabled beneficiary.
- When medical care can be paid under any liability policy, including policies providing automobile no-fault benefits.
- In the first 30 months for end-stage renal disease when an employer-provided medical expense plan provides coverage. By law, employer plans cannot specifically exclude this coverage during this 30-month period.

Medicare pays only if complete coverage is not available from these sources and then only to the extent that benefits are less than would otherwise be payable under Medicare. These Medicare secondary rules are covered in more detail in Chapter 12.

MEDICARE: PART B BENEFITS

Benefits

Part B of Medicare provides benefits for most medical expenses not covered under Part A. These include the following:

- Physicians' and surgeons' fees. These fees may result from house calls, office visits, or services provided in a hospital or other institution. Under certain circumstances, benefits are also provided for the services of chiropractors, podiatrists, and optometrists.
- Diagnostic tests in a hospital or in a physician's office.
- Physical therapy in a physician's office, or as an outpatient of a hospital, skilled-nursing facility, or other approved clinic, rehabilitative agency, or public-health agency.
- Drugs and biologicals that cannot be self-administered.
- Radiation therapy.
- Medical supplies such as surgical dressings, splints, and casts.

- Rental of medical equipment such as oxygen tents, hospital beds, and wheelchairs.
- Prosthetic devices such as artificial heart valves or lenses after a cataract operation.
- Ambulance service if a patient's condition does not permit the use of other methods of transportation.
- Mammograms and Pap smears.
- Diabetes glucose monitoring and education.
- Colorectal cancer screening.
- Bone mass measurement.
- Prostate cancer screening.
- Pneumococcal vaccine and its administration.
- Home health care services as described for Part A when a person does not have Part A coverage or Part A benefits are not applicable.

As this book was being revised in late 2000, there were proposals by President Clinton and others to add prescription drug coverage to Medicare that would be partially financed by the large budget surpluses of recent years. In addition, there would be a relatively large increase in the Part B premium. Although the coverage would be subject to maximum annual limits and substantial copayments, the cost of this coverage would be significant because of the high use of expensive prescription drugs by the elderly.

Exclusions

Although the preceding list may appear to be comprehensive, there are numerous medical products and services not covered by Part B, some of which represent significant expenses for the elderly. They include the following:

- Most drugs and biologicals that can be self-administered, except drugs for osteoporosis, oral cancer treatment, and immune-suppressive therapy under specified circumstances
- Routine physical, eye, and hearing examinations, except those previously mentioned
- Routine foot care
- Immunizations, except pneumococcal vaccinations or immunization required because of an injury or immediate risk of infection
- Cosmetic surgery, unless it is needed because of an accidental injury or to improve the function of a malformed part of the body
- Dental care, unless it involves jaw or facial bone surgery or the setting of fractures
- Custodial care
- Eyeglasses, hearing aids, or orthopedic shoes

In addition, benefits are not provided to persons eligible for workers' compensation or to those treated in government hospitals. Benefits are provided only for services received in the United States, except for physicians' services and ambulance services rendered for a hospitalization that is covered in Mexico or Canada under Part A. Part B is also a secondary payer of benefits under the same circumstances described for Part A.

Amount of Benefits

With some exceptions, Part B pays 80 percent of the approved charges for covered medical expenses after the satisfaction of a $100 annual deductible. Annual maximums apply to outpatient psychiatric benefits ($450) and physical therapy in a therapist's office or at the patient's home ($400). A few charges are paid in full without any cost sharing. These include (1) home health services, (2) pneumococcal vaccine and its administration, (3) certain surgical procedures that are performed on an outpatient basis in lieu of hospitalization, (4) diagnostic preadmission tests performed on an outpatient basis within 7 days prior to hospitalization, (5) mammograms, and (6) Pap smears.

The approved charge for doctor's services covered by Medicare is based on a fee schedule issued by the Health Care Financing Administration. A patient is reimbursed for only 80 percent of the approved charges above the deductible—regardless of the doctor's actual charge. Most doctors and other suppliers of medical services accept an assignment of Medicare benefits and therefore are prohibited from charging a patient in excess of the fee schedule. They can, however, bill the patient for any portion of the approved charges that were not paid by Medicare because of the annual deductible and/or coinsurance. They can also bill for any services that are not covered by Medicare.

Doctors who do not accept assignment of Medicare benefits cannot charge a Medicare patient more than 115 percent of the approved fee for nonparticipating doctors. Because the approved fee for nonparticipating doctors is set at 95 percent of the fee paid for participating doctors, a doctor who does not accept assignment of Medicare benefits can charge a fee that is only 9.25 percent greater than if assignment had been accepted (115 percent × 95 percent = 109.25 percent). As a result, some doctors either do not see Medicare participants or limit the number of such patients that they treat.

The previous limitation on charges does not apply to providers of medical services other than doctors. Although a provider who does not accept assignment can charge any fee, Medicare pays only 80 percent of what the fee schedule shows has been approved. For example, assume the approved charge for medical equipment is $100 and the actual charge is $190. Medicare reimburses $80 (.80 × $100), and the balance is borne by the Medicare recipient.

MEDICARE+CHOICE

In 1985, Congress amended the Medicare program to allow a beneficiary to elect coverage under a health maintenance organization (HMO) as an alternative to the traditional Medicare program. At first, the number of persons electing this option was relatively small. Many of the elderly had not had HMO coverage during their working years and viewed such coverage with some skepticism. In addition, many HMOs continued to focus on expanding their traditional market of younger, healthier lives rather than entering a new and demographically different market. In addition, there were complex federal rules that had to be satisfied to enter the Medicare market.

The situation slowly changed as more HMOs got into the Medicare market and the public became more familiar with HMO coverage. In addition, as medical costs continued to rise, the election of an HMO option made more sense from a cost standpoint. As a result, HMO coverage for Medicare beneficiaries grew rapidly in the mid to late 1990s, and approximately one out of six beneficiaries now has such coverage.

Under the 1985 rules, an HMO is basically given 95 percent of what Medicare would expect to pay to provide benefits if a beneficiary electing HMO coverage had stayed in the traditional Medicare program. In turn, the HMO is expected to provide at least the same benefits as those that are available under Medicare. While an HMO can provide additional benefits and charge an extra premium, many HMOs have provided additional benefits such as prescription drugs without charging an additional premium. Such zero-premium plans have been very popular among Medicare beneficiaries. While they must continue to pay the Part B Medicare premium, these beneficiaries have been able to receive coverage that is broader than traditional Medicare and thus have no reason to purchase a supplemental medigap policy.

In 1999, Part C of Medicare (called *Medicare+Choice*) went into effect. It expands the choices available to most Medicare beneficiaries by allowing them to elect health care benefits through one of several alternatives to the traditional Parts A and B as long as the providers of these alternatives enter into contracts with the Health Care Financing Administration. However, beneficiaries must still pay the Part B premium.

The new Medicare+Choice plans include the following:

- HMOs as previously allowed
- Preferred-provider organizations (PPOs)
- Provider-sponsor organizations (PSOs), similar to HMOs but established by doctors and hospitals that have formed their own health plans
- Private fee-for-service plans
- Private contracts with physicians
- Medical savings accounts

These plans must provide all benefits available under Parts A and B. They may include additional benefits as part of the basic plan or for an additional fee.

Through 2001, beneficiaries may enroll in a Medicare+Choice plan or switch options (including reenrollment in parts A and B) at any time. In 2002, changes will be allowed only once during the first six months of the year. Beginning in 2003, an annual change will be allowed only during the first three months of the year.

Unfortunately, the initial reaction to Medicare+Choice has been less than overwhelming. As of early 2000, few new providers of alternative coverage have entered the marketplace. One reason for this is that the Medicare+Choice rules are extremely complex, and it is questionable if many of the potential providers can enter the market in a viable way. In addition, several HMOs that previously offered coverage have left the market for a variety of reasons; other HMOs no longer offer zero-premium plans or have increased premiums and/or reduced benefits. These changes stem from two factors. First, HMO costs have increased significantly in recent years, partially because of major increases in the cost of prescription drugs, which are a major source of medical expenses for the elderly. Second, the rate of growth of Medicare payments to HMOs has been reduced so that many HMOs are receiving increases that fail to match their increases in expenses.

At the time this book is being revised, there is considerable concern about the future of the Medicare+Choice program, and changes in reimbursement formulas and complex program rules are likely to be made.

ADEQUACY OF FINANCING

Social Security and Medicare are based on a system of funding that the Social Security Administration refers to as *partial advance funding*. Under this system, taxes are more than sufficient to pay current benefits and also provide some accumulation of assets for the payment of future benefits. Partial advance funding falls somewhere between *pay-as-you-go financing,* which was once the way Social Security and Medicare were financed, and *full advance funding*, as used by private insurance and retirement plans. Under pay-as-you-go financing, taxes are set at a level to produce just enough income to pay current benefits; under full advance funding, taxes are set at a level to fund all promised benefits from current service for those making current contributions.

All payroll taxes and other sources of funds for Social Security and Medicare are deposited into four trust funds: an old-age and survivors fund, a disability fund, and two Medicare funds. Benefits and administrative expenses are paid out of the appropriate trust fund from contributions to that fund and any interest earnings on accumulated assets. The trust funds have limited reserves to serve as emergency funds in periods when benefits exceed contributions, as in times of high unemployment. However, current reserves are relatively small and could pay benefits for only a limited time if contributions to a fund ceased. In addition, the reserves consist primarily of IOUs from the Treasury because the contributions have been "borrowed" to finance the government's deficit.

In the early 1980s, considerable concern arose over the potential inability of payroll taxes to pay promised benefits in the future. Through a series of changes, the most significant being the 1983 amendments to the Social Security Act, these problems appeared to have been solved for the Social Security program—at least in the short run. The changes approached the problem from two directions. On one hand, payroll tax rates were increased; on the other hand, some benefits were eliminated and future increases in other benefits were scaled back. However, the solutions of 1983 have not worked. Although the old-age and survivors fund will continue to grow for the time being and will be quite large by the time the current baby boomers retire, benefits will then begin to exceed income, and the fund will shrink as the percentage of retirees grows rapidly. Without further adjustments, the trust funds will have inadequate resources to pay claims in the foreseeable future. Current projections indicate that the Social Security trust funds will run out of money in 2037.

Because of an increasing number of persons aged 65 or older and medical costs that continue to grow at an alarming rate, there is also concern about the Medicare portion of the program. Estimates are that its trust funds will be depleted by about 2023. The seriousness of this problem was made clear by the fact that one of the earliest actions of the second Clinton administration was the passage of legislation to help maintain the solvency of the Medicare trust funds for a few additional years, primarily through encouraging additional enrollment in managed care plans and trimming projected payments to HMOs, hospitals, and doctors.

It is obvious that changes must be made—either now or later—in the Social Security and Medicare programs. Probably the most important step in finding a solution is to convince the public that changes in this very popular entitlement program must be made. Changes, of course, have significant political implications. While most members of Congress realize the need for reform, neither political party has been willing to compromise and take the necessary initiative and thus risk losing public support. The urgency of the problem also now seems somewhat less severe to them because of budget surpluses that resulted from the good economic conditions of the 1990s. Coupled as it is with some partisan politics at the end of the Clinton administration, some observers wonder if there will be any significant reform of either Social Security or Medicare in the near future. However, there seems to be bipartisan support for adding prescription drug coverage to Medicare, particularly if other Medicare issues can be addressed. As a result, other observers feel there is a reasonable possibility of some Medicare reform before the elections in 2000.

In the broadest sense, the solution lies in doing one or both of the following: increasing revenue into the trust funds or decreasing benefit costs. Possibilities for increasing revenue include the following:

- Increasing the Social Security and/or Medicare tax rate
- Increasing the wage base on which Social Security taxes are paid
- Using more general tax revenue to fund the programs
- Subjecting a greater portion of income benefits to taxation and depositing the increased tax revenue into the trust funds

■ Investing all or a portion of trust fund assets in higher-yielding investments than Treasury securities

Suggestions that have been made for decreasing benefit costs include the following:

■ Raising the normal retirement age beyond the planned increase to age 67
■ Raising the early retirement age beyond 62
■ Lowering the benefit formula so that future retirees will get somewhat reduced benefits
■ Lowering cost-of-living increases
■ Imposing a means test for benefits
■ Shifting more of the inflation risk to workers through the use of separate accounts for all or part of each worker's contributions, thus giving the worker some control over his or her account
■ Increasing the Medicare eligibility age beyond 65
■ Increasing Medicare deductibles and copayments
■ Increasing the Medicare Part B premium for everyone or possibly only for higher-income retirees
■ Lowering or slowing the growth of payments to Medicare providers
■ Encouraging or requiring Medicare beneficiaries to enroll in managed-care plans

Any single change will clearly offend one important group of voters or another. As a result, any ultimate solution will probably involve a combination of several of these changes so that everyone will bear a little of the pain.

EMPLOYER AND EMPLOYEE TAXATION

Deductibility of Premiums

Employer contributions to the Social Security and Medicare programs are tax deductible for federal income tax purposes. Any employee contributions are paid with after-tax dollars. Self-employed persons can deduct one-half of their Social Security tax as a business expense. In addition, Part B premiums are treated the same as other premiums for individual medical expense insurance and may be deductible as described in Chapter 12.

Taxation of Benefits

Benefits received in the form of monthly income under Social Security are partially subject to income taxation for some Social Security recipients. To determine the amount of Social Security benefits subject to taxation, it is necessary to calculate *modified adjusted gross income,* which is the sum of the following:

- The taxpayer's adjusted gross income (disregarding any foreign income and savings bond exclusions)
- The taxpayer's tax-exempt interest received or accrued during the year
- One-half of the Social Security benefits for the year

If the modified adjusted gross income is $25,000 or less for a single taxpayer ($32,000 or less for a married taxpayer filing jointly), Social Security benefits are not taxable. If the modified adjusted gross income is between the base amount and $34,000 ($44,000 for a married taxpayer filing jointly), up to 50 percent of the Social Security benefit is includable in taxable income. If the modified adjusted gross income exceeds $34,000 ($44,000 for a married taxpayer filing jointly), up to 85 percent of the Social Security benefit is includable in taxable income. The exact amount of the taxable Social Security benefit is determined by complex formulas that are beyond the scope of this discussion.

Medicare benefits and any lump-sum Social Security benefits are received tax free.

STUDY QUESTIONS

1. Why are social insurance programs necessary?

2. Describe the characteristics of social insurance programs.

3. How are the Social Security and Medicare programs financed?

4. As of this year, Nancy Westman, aged 37, had 28 quarters of coverage under Social Security. Twenty-four of these quarters were earned prior to the birth of her first child 11 years ago. Four quarters have been earned since she reentered the labor force one year ago.
   a. Is Nancy fully insured? Explain.
   b. Is Nancy currently insured? Explain.
   c. Is Nancy disability insured? Explain.

5. Describe the retirement benefits available under Social Security.

6. What categories of persons are eligible for Social Security survivors benefits?

7. a. What is the definition of disability under Social Security?
   b. What categories of persons may be eligible for disability benefits?

8. a. Explain the relationship between a worker's PIA and the benefits available for dependents and survivors.
   b. What happens if the total benefits for a family exceed the maximum family benefit?

9. Explain how a worker's retirement benefits under Social Security will be affected if that person elects early or delayed retirement.

10. Describe the earnings test applicable to the Social Security program.

11. Describe the automatic cost-of-living adjustment provision under Social Security as it relates to benefit amounts.

12. With respect to the hospital insurance portion of Medicare:
    a. Describe the types of benefits that are available.
    b. Explain the extent to which deductibles and copayments are requirements.
    c. Identify the major exclusions.

13. With respect to the supplementary medical insurance portion of Medicare:
    a. Describe the types of benefits that are available.
    b. Explain the extent to which copayments are requirements.
    c. Identify the major exclusions.

14. Describe the managed care options available under Medicare.

15. a. What is the purpose of the Social Security and Medicare trust funds?
    b. Identify possible actions that can better ensure the adequacy of these trust funds.

16. Explain the extent to which Social Security benefits are taxed to recipients.

CHAPTER 4

Other Social Insurance Programs

- Describe unemployment insurance programs with respect to objectives, eligibility requirements, benefits, and financing.

- Describe the nature of temporary disability insurance.

- Describe the typical workers' compensation program with respect to type of law, eligibility requirements, benefits, and financing.

- Explain the extent to which other social insurance benefits are subject to income taxation.

This chapter focuses on the three major social insurance programs other than Social Security and Medicare—unemployment insurance, workers' compensation insurance, and temporary disability laws. Unemployment insurance is a joint federal and state program, and workers' compensation insurance and temporary disability laws are solely under state control. Because the programs of each state are unique, the discussion in this chapter is general in nature. Readers should familiarize themselves with the programs in their own state and not assume that these programs will always conform to the generalizations that follow. Detailed information on a specific state's program can be obtained from the state agency that administers the program.

UNEMPLOYMENT INSURANCE

Prior to the passage of the Social Security Act in 1935, relatively few employees had any type of protection for income lost during periods of unemployment. The act stipulated that a payroll tax was to be levied on covered employers for the purpose of financing unemployment insurance programs that were to be established by the states under guidelines issued by the federal government. Essentially, the federal law levied a federal tax on certain employers in all states. If a state established an acceptable program of unemployment insurance, the state taxes used to finance its program could be offset against up to 90 percent of the federal tax. If a state failed to establish a program, the federal tax would still be levied, but no monies collected from the employers in that state would be returned for purposes of providing benefits to the unemployed there. Needless to say, all states quickly established unemployment insurance programs. These programs (along with a federal program for railroad workers) now cover more than 95 percent of all working persons, but major gaps in coverage exist for domestic workers, agricultural workers, and the self-employed.

There are several objectives of the current unemployment insurance program. The primary objective is to provide periodic cash income to workers during periods of involuntary unemployment. Benefits are generally paid as a matter of right, with no demonstration of need required. While federal legislation has extended benefits during times of high unemployment, the unemployment insurance program is basically designed for workers whose periods of unemployment are short-term; the long-term and hard-core unemployed must rely on other measures, such as public assistance and job-retraining programs, when unemployment insurance benefits are exhausted.

A second major objective of unemployment insurance is to help the unemployed find jobs. Workers must register at local unemployment offices, and unemployment benefits are received through these offices. Another important objective is to encourage employers to stabilize employment. As will be described later, this is accomplished through the use of experience rating in determining an employer's tax rate. Finally, unemployment insurance contributes to a stable labor supply by providing benefits so that skilled and experienced workers are not forced to seek other jobs during short-term layoffs and thereby remain available to return to work when called back.

Financing of Benefits

Unemployment insurance programs are financed primarily by unemployment taxes levied by both the federal and state governments. The federal tax is equal to 6.2 percent of the first $7,000 of wages for each worker, but this tax is reduced by up to 5.4 percentage points for taxes paid to state programs. The practical effect of this offset is that the federal tax is actually equal to .8 percent of covered payroll. A few states levy an unemployment payroll tax equal to only the maximum offset (5.4 percent on the first $7,000 of wages), but most states have a higher tax rate and/or levy their tax on a higher amount of earnings.

No state levies the same tax on all employers. Rather, states use a method of experience rating whereby all employers, except those in business for a short time or those with a small number of employees, pay a tax rate that reflects their actual experience, within limits. Thus, an employer who has laid off a large percentage of employees will have a higher tax rate than an employer whose employment record has been stable.

An employer with "good experience" will often pay a state tax of less than 1 percent of payroll and possibly as little as .1 percent. Other employers may pay a state tax as high as 9 percent or 10 percent. Regardless of the actual state tax paid, the employer will still pay the .8 percent federal tax.

The major argument for experience rating is that it provides a financial incentive for employers to stabilize employment. Those opposed to its use contend that many employers have little control over economic trends that affect employment. In addition, they argue that tax rates tend to rise in bad economic times and, in so doing, may actually thwart economic recovery.

The entire unemployment insurance tax is collected by individual states and deposited in the Federal Unemployment Insurance Trust Fund, which is administered by the secretary of the treasury. Each state has a separate account that is credited with its taxes and its share of investment earnings on assets in the fund. Unemployment benefits in the state are paid from this account. The federal share of the taxes received by the fund is deposited into separate accounts and is used for administering the federal portion of the program and for giving grants to the states to administer their individual programs. In addition, the federal funds are available for loans to states whose accounts have been depleted during times of high unemployment.

Eligibility for Benefits

In order to receive unemployment benefits, a worker must meet the following eligibility requirements:

- Have a prior attachment to the labor force
- Be able to work and be available for work
- Be actively seeking work
- Have satisfied any prescribed waiting period
- Be free of disqualification

Prior Attachment to the Labor Force

The right to benefits depends on the worker's attachment to the labor force within a prior *base period*. In most states, this base period is the 52 weeks or four quarters prior to the time of unemployment. During this base period, the worker must have earned a minimum amount of wages or worked a minimum period of time or both.

Able to Work and Available for Work

The right to benefits is also contingent on an unemployed worker's being both physically and mentally capable of working. The worker must also be available for work. Benefits may be denied if suitable work is refused or if substantial restrictions are placed on the type of work that will be accepted.

Actively Seeking Work

In addition to registering with a local unemployment office, most states require that a worker make a reasonable effort to seek work.

Waiting Period

Most unemployment programs have a one-week waiting period before benefits commence. Benefits are not paid retroactively for that time of unemployment.

Free of Disqualification

All states have provisions in their laws under which a worker may be disqualified from receiving benefits. This disqualification may take the form of (1) a total cancellation of benefit rights, (2) the postponement of benefits, or (3) a reduction in benefits. Common reasons for disqualification include the following:

- Voluntarily leaving a job without good cause.
- Discharge for misconduct.
- Refusal to accept suitable work.
- Involvement in a labor dispute.

■ Receipt of disqualifying income. This includes dismissal wages, workers' compensation benefits, benefits from an employer's pension plan, or primary insurance benefits under the Social Security program.

Benefits

The majority of states pay regular unemployment insurance benefits for a maximum of 26 weeks; the remaining states pay benefits for slightly longer periods. In most states, the amount of the weekly benefit is equal to a specified fraction of a worker's average wages for the calendar quarter of the base period during which the highest wages were earned. The typical fraction is $\frac{1}{26}$, which yields a benefit equal to 50 percent of average weekly earnings for that quarter. Other states determine benefits as a percentage of average weekly wages or annual wages during the base period. Some states also modify their benefit formulas to provide relatively higher benefits (as a percentage of past earnings) to lower-paid workers. Benefits in all states are subject to minimum and maximum amounts. Minimum weekly benefits typically fall within the range of $20 to $75, maximum benefits in the range of $200 to $375, and the average benefit in the range of $150 to $225. In addition, a few states currently provide additional benefits if there are dependents who receive regular support from the worker.

States also provide reduced benefits for partial unemployment. Such a condition occurs if a worker is employed less than full-time and has a weekly income less than his or her weekly benefit amount for total unemployment.

Since 1970, there has been a permanent federal-state program of extended unemployment benefits for workers whose regular benefits are exhausted during periods of high unemployment. The availability of these benefits is automatically triggered by a state's unemployment rate exceeding a specifed level. The benefits are financed equally by the federal government and the states involved, and they can be paid for up to 13 weeks, as long as the total of regular and extended benefits does not exceed 39 weeks. This program is operable when the *insured unemployment rate* in a state exceeds a specified level. The insured unemployment rate is the percentage of workers covered by unemployment insurance who are receiving regular benefits. Benefits can also be triggered if a state's *total unemployment rate* exceeds specified criteria. In this case, an additional 20 weeks of benefits can be paid.

In periods of severe unemployment, the federal government often enacts legislation to provide additional benefits that are financed with federal revenue. The last such program expired in 1994.

Problems and Issues

The current system of unemployment insurance has become increasingly subject to criticism, especially regarding the level of benefits. At current levels, the majority of employees would receive benefits that are less than half of their former wages. Because of maximum limits on the amounts of benefits, higher-income employees would receive proportionately smaller benefits than lower-paid employees.

In addition to the level of benefits, the percentage of persons receiving benefits at any point in time has dropped over the last two decades. Typically, fewer than 40 percent of the unemployed are receiving benefits. Some persons have benefits denied because of more stringent rules, particularly those dealing with initial benefit disqualification. Other persons exhaust the benefits that are available. Of course, there are those who argue that without disqualifications and limits on benefits, there would be little incentive for many of the unemployed to seek work.

Few employers provide any type of supplemental unemployment benefits. The plans that do exist are in highly unionized industries and result from collective bargaining. These plans are briefly discussed in the chapter on other nonretirement benefits.

There seems to be a feeling among economists that unemployment insurance programs today are less effective in dealing with unemployment issues than they were in the past. In theory, unemployment compensation insurance should be a counterbalance against recessions. In practice this is often not the case, perhaps because of the low percentage of persons receiving benefits. In addition, the degree of experience rating has declined over time, reducing the incentive for employers to retain employees in bad times rather than laying them off. It also has shifted an increasing burden for financing the program to employers in industries with stable employment.

TEMPORARY DISABILITY LAWS

At their inception, state unemployment insurance programs were usually designed to cover only unemployed persons who were both willing and able to work. Benefits were denied to anyone who was unable to work for any reason, including disability. Some states amended their unemployment insurance laws to provide coverage to the unemployed who subsequently became disabled. However, five states—California, Hawaii, New Jersey, New York, and Rhode Island—and Puerto Rico went one step farther by enacting temporary disability laws under which employees can collect disability income benefits regardless of whether their disability begins while they are employed or unemployed. While variations exist among the states, these laws (often referred to as *nonoccupational disability laws* because benefits are not provided for disabilities covered under workers' compensation laws) are generally patterned after the state unemployment insurance law and provide similar benefits.

In the six jurisdictions with temporary disability laws, most employers are required to provide coverage for their employees. In most jurisdictions, except Rhode Island, which has a monopolistic state fund, coverage may be obtained from either a competitive state fund or private insurance companies. Self-insurance is also generally permitted. Private coverage must provide at least the benefits prescribed under the law, but it may be more comprehensive. Depending on the jurisdiction, the cost of an employer's program may be borne entirely by employee contributions, entirely by employer contributions or by contributions from both parties.

Eligibility

Before an employee is eligible for benefits under a temporary disability law, the employee must satisfy (1) an earnings or employment requirement, (2) the definition of disability, and (3) a waiting period.

Earnings or Employment Requirement

Every jurisdiction requires that an employee must have worked for a specified time and/or have received a minimum amount of wages within some specific period prior to disability to qualify for benefits.

Definition of Disability

Most laws define disability as the inability of the worker to perform his or her regular or customary work because of a nonoccupational injury or illness including maternity. As with workers' compensation laws, certain types of disabilities are not covered. In most jurisdictions, these include disabilities caused by self-inflicted injuries or by illegal acts.

Waiting Period

The usual waiting period for benefits is seven days. However, in some jurisdictions the waiting period is waived if the employee is hospitalized.

Benefits

Benefits are a percentage, usually ranging from 50 percent to 66⅔ percent, of the employee's average weekly wage for some period prior to disability, subject to maximum and minimum amounts. Benefits are generally paid for at least 26 weeks if the employee remains disabled that long.

WORKERS' COMPENSATION LAWS

Prior to the passage of workers' compensation laws, it was difficult for employees to receive compensation for their work-related injuries or diseases. Group benefits were meager, and the Social Security program had not yet been enacted. The only recourse for employees was to sue their employer for damages. In addition to the time and expense of such actions (as well as the possibility of being fired), the probability of a worker's winning such a suit was small because of the three common-law defenses available to employers. Under the contributory negligence doctrine, a worker could not collect if his or her negligence had contributed in any way to the injury. Under the fellow-servant doctrine, the worker could not collect if the injury had resulted from the negligence of a fellow worker. And finally, under the assumption-of-risk doctrine, a worker could not recover damages if he or she had knowingly assumed the risks inherent in the trade.

To help solve the problem of uncompensated injuries, workers' compensation laws were enacted to require that employers provide employee benefits for losses resulting from work-related accidents or diseases. These laws are based on the principle of liability without fault. Essentially, an employer is absolutely liable for providing the benefits prescribed by the workers' compensation laws, regardless of whether the employer would be considered legally liable in the absence of these laws. However, benefits, with the possible exception of medical expense benefits, are subject to statutory maximums.

All states have workers' compensation laws. In addition, the federal government has enacted several similar laws. The Federal Employees Compensation Act provides benefits for the employees of the federal government and the District of Columbia. Railroad employees and seamen aboard ships are covered under the Federal Employer's Liability Act, and stevedores, longshoremen, and workers who repair ships are covered under the U.S. Longshore and Harbor Workers' Act.

Type of Law

Most workers' compensation laws are compulsory for all employers covered under the law. A few states have elective laws, but the majority of employers do elect coverage. If they do not, their employees are not entitled to workers' compensation benefits and must sue for damages resulting from occupational accidents or diseases. However, the employers lose their right to the three common-law defenses previously described.

Financing of Benefits

Most states allow employers to comply with the workers' compensation law by purchasing coverage from insurance companies. Several of these states also have competitive state funds from which coverage may be obtained, but these funds usually provide benefits for fewer employers than insurance companies do. Six states have monopolistic state funds that are the only source for obtaining coverage under the law.

Almost all states, including some with monopolistic state funds, allow employers to self-insure their workers' compensation exposure. These employers must generally post a bond or other security and receive the approval of the agency administering the law. While the number of firms using self-insurance for workers' compensation is small, these firms account for approximately one-half the employees covered under such laws.

In virtually all cases, the full cost of providing workers' compensation benefits must be borne by the employer. Obviously, if an employer self-insures benefits, the ultimate cost will include the benefits paid plus any administrative expenses.

Employers who purchase coverage pay a premium that is calculated as a rate per $100 of payroll and that is based on the occupations of their workers. For example, rates for office workers may be as low as $.10, and rates for workers in a few hazardous occupations may exceed $50. Most states also require that, when their total workers' compensation premiums exceed a specified amount, employers be subject to experience rating; that is, employers' premiums become a function of benefits paid for past injuries to their workers. To the extent that safety costs are offset or eliminated by savings in workers' compensation premiums, experience-rating laws encourage employers to take an active role in correcting conditions that may cause injuries.

Covered Occupations

Although it is estimated that about 90 percent of workers in the United States are covered by workers' compensation laws, the percentage varies among the states from less than 70 percent to more than 95 percent. Many laws exclude certain agricultural, domestic, and casual employees. Some laws also exclude employers with a small number of employees. Furthermore, coverage for employees of state and local governments is not universal.

Eligibility

Before an employee can be eligible for benefits under a workers' compensation law, he or she must work in an occupation covered by that law and be disabled or killed by a covered injury or illness. The typical workers' compensation law provides coverage for *accidental occupational injuries (including death) arising out of and in the course of employment.* In all states, this includes injuries arising out of accidents, which are generally defined as sudden and unexpected events that are definite in time and place. Most workers' compensation laws exclude self-inflicted injuries and accidents resulting from an employee's intoxication or willful disregard of safety rules.

Every state has some coverage for illnesses resulting from occupational diseases. While the trend is toward full coverage for occupational diseases, some states cover only those diseases that are specifically listed in the law.

Benefits

Workers' compensation laws typically provide four types of benefits:

1. Medical care
2. Disability income
3. Death benefits
4. Rehabilitative services

Medical Care

Benefits for medical expenses are usually provided without any limitations on time or amount. In addition, they are not subject to a waiting period.

Disability Income

For an employee to collect disability income benefits under workers' compensation laws, his or her injuries must result in one of the following four categories of disability:

1. Temporary total. The employee cannot perform any of the duties of his or her regular job. However, full recovery is expected. Most workers' compensation claims involve this type of disability.
2. Permanent total. The employee will never be able to perform any of the duties of his or her regular job or any other job. Several states also list in their laws certain disabilities (such as loss of both eyes or both arms) that result in an employee's automatically being considered permanently and totally disabled even though future employment might be possible.
3. Temporary partial. The employee can perform only some of the duties of his or her regular job but is neither totally nor permanently disabled. For example, an employee with a sprained back might be able to work part-time.
4. Permanent partial. The employee has a permanent injury, such as the loss of an eye, but may be able to perform his or her regular job or may be retrained for another job.

Most workers' compensation laws have a waiting period for disability income benefits that varies from two to seven days. However, benefits are frequently paid retroactively to the date of the injury if an employee is disabled for a specified period of time or is confined to a hospital.

Disability income benefits under workers' compensation laws are a function of an employee's average weekly wage over some time period, commonly the 13 weeks immediately preceding the disability. For total disabilities, benefits are a percentage (usually 66⅔ percent) of the employee's average weekly wage, subject to maximum and minimum amounts that vary substantially by state. Benefits for temporary total disabilities continue until an employee returns to work; benefits for permanent total disabilities usually continue for life but have a limited duration (such as ten years) in a few states.

Benefits for partial disabilities are calculated as a percentage of the difference between the employee's wages before and after the disability. In most states, the duration of these benefits is subject to a statutory maximum. Several states also provide lump-sum payments to employees whose permanent partial disabilities involve the loss (or loss of use) of an eye, an arm, or other body member. These benefits, which are determined by a schedule in the law, may be in lieu of or in addition to periodic disability income benefits.

Death Benefits

Most workers' compensation laws provide two types of death benefits:

1. Burial allowances
2. Cash income payments to survivors

Burial allowances are a flat amount in each state and vary from $300 to $5,000 with benefits of $1,000 and $1,500 being common.

Cash income payments to survivors, like disability income benefits, are a function of the worker's average wage prior to the injury resulting in death. Benefits are usually paid only to a surviving spouse and children under age 18. In some states, benefits are paid until the spouse dies or remarries and all children have reached age 18. In other states, benefits are paid for a maximum time, such as ten years, or until a maximum dollar amount has been paid, such as $50,000.

Rehabilitation Benefits

All states have provisions in their workers' compensation laws for rehabilitative services for disabled workers. Benefits are included for medical rehabilitation as well as for vocational rehabilitation, including training, counseling, and job placement.

A difficulty faced in providing vocational rehabilitation is that employers are reluctant to hire workers with permanent physical impairments because a subsequent work-related injury may result in their total disability and thus an increased workers' compensation premium. For example, a worker who lost an arm in a previous work-related accident would probably be totally and permanently disabled if the other arm was lost in a later accident. Consequently, most states have established second-injury funds. If a worker is disabled by a second injury, the employer is responsible only for providing benefits equal to those that would have been provided to a worker who had not suffered the first injury. Any remaining benefits are provided by the second-injury fund.

Problems and Issues

As with unemployment insurance, there are problems and issues associated with workers' compensation insurance. These involve the extent of coverage, the size of benefit payments and increasing costs. One often-discussed issue is whether a system of 24-hour coverage would be an improvement.

Extent of Coverage

Labor unions have been particularly critical of workers' compensation insurance because of its incomplete coverage of workers. State laws do not cover all workers because of elective laws, numerical exemptions and exclusions, or less-than-full coverage for certain groups, such as agricultural, domestic, and casual workers. It is estimated that, nationally, between 10 percent and 15 percent of workers are without coverage and that this figure is as high as 30 percent in some states.

Adequacy of Benefits

Benefits have been criticized as inadequate because they seldom exceed two-thirds of a worker's earnings prior to injury, and most states do not adjust income benefits for inflation. However, some lower-paid workers may have little incentive to return to work because benefits may actually exceed their prior take-home pay. This results from relatively high minimum benefits and the fact that workers' compensation benefits are not subject to Social Security and Medicare taxes or personal income taxes. In terms of the replacement of lost income, the situation is worse for higher-paid employees because of the maximum dollar limits on benefits.

Increasing Costs

A major concern of employers is the soaring cost of workers' compensation coverage. Estimates are that costs have tripled over the past decade. This increase is the result of a combination of several factors, including the following:

- Soaring increases in the cost of medical care.
- Increased benefits. Most states have increased benefits faster than average wages have increased. One interesting result of higher benefit levels is that they tend to result in an increased number of claims filed and an increase in the duration of claims.
- Expansion of coverage to additional workplace injuries and diseases, such as mental stress.
- Increased litigation. Estimates are that approximately one-quarter of workers' compensation costs are associated with attorneys' fees and other legal costs.

These increasing costs have resulted in large underwriting losses for many insurance companies, leading in turn to higher premiums and more stringent underwriting. As underwriting has tightened, more employers have been forced into the substandard insurance market, where costs are even higher. These higher costs are ultimately passed on to consumers and increase inflationary pressures. Some firms, particularly small ones, are also finding their financial survival threatened by these high costs.

At the state level, there always seems to be talk of workers' compensation reform. However, labor equates reform with increased benefits, and employers equate it with lower costs. As a result, fundamental changes often do not occur.

The Concept of 24-Hour Coverage

When workers' compensation laws were first passed, most employees did not have employer-provided benefits for medical expenses or disability income. Today both types of benefits are common. As a result, it has been suggested that the old systems are obsolete and that the concept of 24-hour coverage should be adopted. Under this concept, employees would have a single benefit plan that would respond to injuries whether they occurred on or off the job. This concept could be applied to medical expense coverage only or to medical expense coverage and some or all types of disability income coverage. Arguments in favor of 24-hour coverage include the following:

■ The financial needs of employees are the same regardless of whether an injury or illness is work-related.
■ It is often impossible to determine whether an injury or illness is work-related.
■ Medical costs would be better managed because cost-containment techniques used in group insurance could also be used for work-related claims.
■ The current system is fragmented and may contain both gaps and overlapping benefits. A single comprehensive system may be able to provide better benefits at a lower cost.

Naturally, there are also arguments against 24-hour coverage:

■ The principle of liability without fault would be violated if employees were required to assume deductibles, copayments, or a percentage of work-related claims.
■ Smaller firms that have few employee benefits could not afford 24-hour coverage and might be forced out of business.
■ The strong emphasis on loss control that is associated with workers' compensation insurance might be jeopardized if the program were merged with traditional group insurance programs.

The concept of 24-hour coverage continues to receive a considerable amount of attention. It is an integral part of some proposals for reforms to the nation's health care system. In addition, some states now allow 24-hour coverage to be written for medical expenses, with the employer purchasing a workers' compensation policy to provide benefits other than medical expenses.

FEDERAL TAXATION

Unemployment insurance benefits are included in a recipient's gross income. However, workers' compensation benefits are received free of income taxation.

Benefits received under temporary disability laws must be included in gross income. However, disabled persons with gross incomes below a specified level may be eligible for a federal tax credit. In those jurisdictions where benefits can also be received by unemployed persons, any benefits paid to unemployed persons are considered unemployment insurance benefits and are taxed accordingly.

STUDY QUESTIONS

1. What are the objectives of unemployment insurance?

2. Explain how unemployment insurance benefits are financed.

3. What requirements must be satisfied before a worker is eligible for unemployment insurance benefits?

4. For the extended benefits program of unemployment compensation, explain
   a. the circumstances under which benefits are made available.
   b. the method by which benefits are financed.

5. Why are unemployment benefits viewed by some as being inadequate?

6. How did the passage of workers' compensation laws alter the traditional system of common law with respect to employee injuries?

7. What are the usual eligibility requirements for receiving workers' compensation benefits?

8. Briefly describe the types and amounts of benefits available under workers' compensation laws.

9. Why are workers' compensation benefits viewed by some as being inadequate?

10. What has caused the increase in the cost of providing workers' compensation benefits.

11. What are the pros and cons of 24-hour coverage?

PART THREE

Group Insurance

CHAPTER 5

The Group Insurance Environment

OBJECTIVES

■ Identify the characteristics that distinguish group insurance from individual insurance.

■ Identify the factors that are of concern to group underwriters and explain the significance of each factor.

■ Describe the major aspects of state regulation applying to group insurance.

■ Identify the types of groups eligible for coverage under the laws of most states and explain the significant characteristics and regulations pertaining to each.

■ Explain the provisions of the Age Discrimination in Employment Act.

■ Explain how employee benefit plans are affected by the provision of the Pregnancy Discrimination Act.

■ Explain how the passage of the Americans with Disabilities Act affects employee benefit plans.

The term *group insurance,* like the term *employee benefits,* can have different meanings to different persons. Most employees view group insurance in a very broad sense as any arrangement under which an employer makes benefits available to employees for life insurance, disability income, medical and dental expenses, legal expenses, and property and liability insurance. To employees, it usually makes little difference whether a benefit plan is funded with a traditional insurance contract or through some type of alternative arrangement; it still is group insurance.

Even though the broad meaning of group insurance is used in this book, it is important to make a distinction between group insurance plans that are funded with traditional insurance contracts and those that use alternative funding methods. Although alternative funding methods, including total self-funding, are becoming more common, the majority of group insurance is still fully insured through insurance contracts. This chapter begins with a discussion of these traditional arrangements. Alternative funding methods are described in detail in Chapter 14. It should also be emphasized at this point that although much of the discussion in following chapters centers on the provisions found in insurance contracts, similar provisions must also be contained in group insurance plans that are funded in other ways.

The character of group insurance has been greatly influenced by the numerous laws and regulations that state governments and the federal government have imposed. These laws and regulations are discussed in the remainder of the chapter. The major impact of state regulation has been felt through the insurance laws governing insurance companies and the products they sell. Traditionally, these laws have affected only those benefit plans funded with insurance contracts. However, as a growing number of employers are turning toward self-funding of benefits, there has been increasing interest on the part of state regulatory officials to extend these laws to plans using alternative funding methods. The federal laws affecting group insurance, on the other hand, have generally been directed toward any benefit plans that are established by employers for their employees, regardless of the funding method used.

CHARACTERISTICS OF TRADITIONAL GROUP INSURANCE

Traditionally, group insurance has been characterized by a group contract, experience rating of larger groups, and group underwriting. Perhaps the best way to define group insurance is to compare its characteristics with those of individual insurance, which is underwritten on an individual basis.

Group Contract

In contrast to most individual insurance contracts, the group insurance contract provides coverage to a number of persons under a single contract issued to someone other than the persons insured. The contract, referred to as a *master contract,* provides benefits to a group of individuals who have a specific relationship with the policyholder. Most commonly, group contracts cover individuals who are full-time employees, and the policyholder is either their employer or a trust established to provide benefits for the employees. Although the employees are not actual parties to the master contract, they can legally enforce their rights. Consequently, employees are often referred to as *third-party beneficiaries* of the insurance contract.

Employees covered under the contract receive *certificates of insurance* as evidence of their coverage. A certificate is merely a description of the coverage provided and is not part of the master contract. In general, a certificate of insurance is not even considered to be a contract and usually contains a disclaimer to that effect. However, some courts have held the contrary to be true when the provisions of the certificate, or even the explanatory booklet of a group insurance plan, vary materially from the master contract.

In individual insurance, the coverage of the insured normally begins with the inception of the insurance contract and ceases with its termination. However, in group insurance, individual members of the group may become eligible for coverage long after the inception of the group contract, or they may lose their eligibility status long before the contract terminates.

Experience Rating

A second distinguishing characteristic of traditional group insurance is the use of experience rating. If a group is sufficiently large, the actual experience of that particular group will be a factor in determining the premium the policyholder will be charged. The experience of an insurance company will also be reflected in the dividends and future premiums associated with individual insurance. However, such experience will be determined on a class basis and will apply to all insured in that class. This is also true for group insurance contracts when the group's membership is small. The use of experience rating is discussed in Chapter 15.

Group Underwriting

The applicant for individual insurance must generally show evidence of insurability. For group insurance, on the other hand, individual members of the group are usually not required to show any evidence of insurability when initially eligible for coverage. This is not to say that there is no underwriting, but rather that underwriting is focused on the characteristics of the group instead of on the insurability of individual members of the group. As with individual insurance, the underwriter must appraise the applicant, decide on the conditions of the group's acceptability, and establish a rating basis.

The purpose of group insurance underwriting is twofold:

1. To minimize the problem of *adverse selection* (those who are most likely to have claims are also those who are most likely to seek insurance)
2. To minimize the administrative costs associated with group insurance

Because of group underwriting, coverage can be provided through group insurance at a lower cost than through individual insurance.

Underwriting considerations peculiar to specific types of group insurance are discussed in appropriate sections of later chapters. However, there are certain general underwriting considerations applicable to all or most types of group insurance that affect the contractual provisions contained in group insurance contracts as well as insurance company practices pertaining to group insurance. These general underwriting considerations include the following:

- The reason for the existence of the group
- The stability of the group
- The persistency of the group
- The method of determining benefits
- The provisions for determining eligibility
- The source and method of premium payments
- The administrative aspects of the group insurance plan
- The prior experience of the plan
- The size of the group
- The composition of the group
- The industry represented by the group
- The geographic location of the group

Reason for Existence

Probably the most fundamental group underwriting principle is that a group must have been formed for some purpose other than to obtain insurance for its members. Such a rule protects the group insurance company against the adverse selection that would likely exist if poor risks were to form a group just to obtain insurance. Groups based on an employer-employee relationship present little difficulty with respect to this rule.

Stability

Ideally, an underwriter would like to see a reasonable but steady flow of persons through a group. A higher-than-average turnover rate results in increased administrative costs for the insurance company as well as for the employer. If turnover exists among recently hired employees, these costs can be minimized by requiring employees to wait a period of time before becoming eligible for coverage. However, such a *probationary period* does leave newly hired employees without protection if their previous group insurance coverage has terminated.

A lower-than-average turnover rate often results in an increasing average age for the members of a group. To the extent that a plan's premium is a function of the mortality (death rates) and the morbidity (sickness and disability rates) of the group, such an increase in average age will result in an increasing premium rate for that group insurance plan. This may cause the better risks to drop out of a plan, if they are required to contribute to its cost, and may ultimately force the employer to terminate the plan because of its increasing cost.

Persistency

An underwriter is concerned with the length of time a group insurance contract will remain on the insurance company's books. Initial acquisition expenses, often including higher first-year commissions, frequently cause an insurance company to lose money during the first year the group insurance contract is in force. Only through the renewal of the contract for a period of time, often three or four years, can these acquisition expenses be recovered. For this reason, firms with a history of frequently changing insurance companies or those with financial difficulty are often avoided.

Determination of Benefits

In most types of group insurance, the underwriter requires that benefit levels for individual members of the group be determined in some manner that precludes individual selection by either the employees or the employer. If employees could choose their own benefit levels, there would be a tendency for the poorer risks to select greater amounts of coverage than the better risks would select. Similarly, adverse selection could also exist if the employer were able to choose a separate benefit level for each individual member of the group. As a result, this underwriting rule has led to benefit levels that are either identical for all employees or determined by a benefit formula that bases benefit levels on some specific criterion, such as position or salary.

Benefits based on salary or position may still lead to adverse selection because disproportionately larger benefits are provided to the owner or top executives who may have been involved in determining the benefit formula. Consequently, most insurance companies have rules for determining the maximum benefit that may be provided for any individual employee without evidence of insurability. Additional coverage either is not provided or is subject to individual evidence of insurability.

The general level of benefits for all employees is also of interest to the underwriter. For example, benefit levels that are too high may encourage overutilization and malingering, while benefit levels that are unusually low may lead to low participation if a plan is voluntary.

Determination of Eligibility

The underwriter is also concerned with the eligibility provisions that are contained in the group insurance plan. Many group insurance plans contain probationary periods that must be satisfied before an employee is eligible for coverage. In addition to minimizing administrative costs, a probationary period also discourages persons with known medical conditions from seeking employment primarily because of a firm's group insurance benefits. This latter problem is also addressed by the requirement that an employee be actively at work before coverage commences or, particularly with major medical coverage, by limiting coverage for preexisting conditions to the extent allowed by federal and state laws.

Most group insurance plans normally limit eligibility to full-time employees because, from an underwriting standpoint, the coverage of part-time employees may not be desirable. In addition to having a high turnover rate, some part-time employees may be seeking employment primarily to obtain group insurance benefits. Similar problems exist with seasonal and temporary employees and, consequently, eligibility is often restricted to permanent employees.

Premium Payments

Group insurance plans may be contributory or noncontributory. Members of *contributory plans* pay a portion, or possibly all, of the cost of their own coverage. When employees pay the entire portion, the plans are often referred to as *fully contributory* or *employee-pay-all plans*. Under *noncontributory plans*, the policyholder pays the entire cost. Because all eligible employees are usually covered, noncontributory plans are desirable from an underwriting standpoint because adverse selection is minimized. In fact, most insurance companies and the laws of many states require 100 percent participation of eligible employees under noncontributory plans. In addition, the absence of employee solicitation, payroll deductions, and underwriting of late entrants into the plan results in administrative savings to both the policyholder and the insurance company, thus favoring the noncontributory approach to the financing of group insurance benefits.

Most state laws prohibit an employer from requiring an employee to participate in a contributory plan. The insurance company is then faced with the possibility of adverse selection because those who elect coverage will tend to be the poorer risks. From a practical standpoint, 100 percent participation in a contributory plan would be unrealistic because, for many reasons, some employees neither desire nor even need the coverage provided under the plan. However, insurance companies require that a minimum percentage of the eligible members elect to participate before the contract is issued. The common requirement is 75 percent, although a lower percentage is often acceptable for large groups and a higher percentage may be required for small groups. A 75 percent minimum requirement is also often a statutory requirement for group life insurance and sometimes for group health insurance.

A key issue in contributory plans is how to treat employees who did not elect to participate when first eligible but who later desire coverage or who dropped coverage and want it reinstated. Unfortunately, this desire for coverage may arise when these employees or their dependents have medical conditions that will lead to claims once coverage is provided. To control this adverse selection, insurance companies commonly require individual evidence of insurability by these employees or their dependents before coverage will be made available. However, there are two exceptions: First, some plans have short, periodic open enrollment periods during which the evidence-of-insurability requirement is lessened or waived. Second, the Health Insurance Portability and Accountability Act (discussed in detail in later chapters) effectively eliminates the use of evidence of insurability for medical expense plans, but not for other types of group insurance.

Insurance companies frequently require that the employer pay a portion of the premium under a group insurance plan. This is also a statutory requirement for group life insurance in most states and occasionally for group health insurance. Many group insurance plans set an average contribution rate for all employees, which in turn leads to the subsidizing of some employees by other employees, particularly in those types of insurance where the frequency of claims increases with age. Without a requirement for employer contributions, younger employees might actually find coverage at a lower cost in the individual market, thereby leaving the group with only the older employees. Even when group insurance already has a cost advantage over individual insurance, its attractiveness to employees is enhanced by employer contributions. With constantly increasing health care costs, employer contributions help cushion rate increases to employees and thus minimize participation problems as contributions are raised. In addition, underwriters feel that the lack of employer contributions may lead to a lack of employer interest in the plan and, consequently, to poor cooperation with the insurance company and poor plan administration.

Administration

To minimize the expenses associated with group insurance, the underwriter often requires that the employer carry out certain administrative functions. These commonly include communicating the plan to the employees, handling enrollment procedures, collecting employee contributions on a payroll-deduction basis, and keeping certain types of records. In addition, employers are often involved in the claims process. Underwriters are concerned not only with the employer's ability to carry out these functions but also with the employer's willingness to cooperate with the insurance company.

Prior Experience

For most insurance companies, a large portion of newly written group insurance consists of business that was previously written by other insurance companies. Therefore, it is important for the underwriter to ascertain the reason for the transfer. If the transferred business is a result of dissatisfaction with the service provided by the prior insurance company, the underwriter must determine whether the insurance company can provide the type and level of service desired. Because an employer is most likely to shop for new coverage when faced with a rate increase, the underwriter must evaluate whether the rate increase was due to excessive claims experience. Often, particularly with larger groups, excessive claims experience in the past is an indication of the same type of experience in the future. Occasionally, however, the prior experience may be due to circumstances that will not continue in the future, such as a catastrophe or large medical bills for an employee who has died, totally recovered, or terminated employment.

Past excessive claims experience may not result in coverage denial for a new applicant, but it will probably result in a higher rate. As an alternative, changes in the benefit or eligibility provisions of the plan might eliminate a previous source of adverse claims experience.

The underwriter must determine the new insurance company's responsibility for existing claims. Some states prohibit a new insurance company from denying (by using a preexisting-conditions clause) the continuing claims of persons who were covered under a prior group insurance plan if these claims would otherwise be covered under the new contract. The rationale for this "no-loss, no-gain" legislation is that claims should be paid neither more liberally nor less liberally than if no transfer had taken place. Even in states that have no such regulation, an employer may still wish to provide employees with continuing protection. In either case, the underwriter must evaluate these continuing claims as well as any liability of the previous insurance company for their payment.

Finally, the underwriter must be reasonably certain that the employer will not present a persistency problem by changing insurance companies again in the near future.

Size

The size of a group is a significant factor in the underwriting process. With large groups, prior group insurance experience can usually be used as a factor in determining the premium, and considerable flexibility also exists with both rating and plan design. In addition, adjustments for adverse claims experience can be made at future renewal dates under the experience-rating process.

The situation is different for small groups. In many cases, coverage is being written for the first time. Administrative expenses tend to be high in relation to the premium. There is also an increased possibility that the owner or major stockholder might be interested in coverage primarily because he or she, or a family member, has a medical problem that will result in large immediate claims. As a result, contractual provisions and the benefits available tend to be standardized to control administrative costs. Also, because past experience for small groups is not necessarily a realistic indicator of future experience, most insurance companies use pooled rates under which a uniform rate is applied to all groups that have a specific coverage. Because excessive claims experience for a particular group is not charged to that group at renewal, more restrictive underwriting practices relating to adverse selection are used. These include less liberal contractual provisions and, in some cases, individual underwriting of group members.

Composition

The age, sex, and income of employees in a group will affect the experience of the group. As employees age, the mortality rate increases. Excluding maternity claims, both the frequency and duration of medical and disability claims also increase with age.

At all ages, the death rate is lower for females than for males. However, the opposite is true for medical expenses and disability claims. Even if maternity claims are disregarded, women as a group tend to be hospitalized and disabled more frequently and require medical and surgical treatment more often than men.

Employees with high income levels tend to incur higher-than-average medical and dental expenses. This is partly because practitioners sometimes base charges on a patient's ability to pay. In addition, persons with higher incomes are more likely to seek specialized care or care in more affluent areas, where the charges of practitioners are generally higher. On the other hand, low-income employees can also pose difficulties. Turnover rates tend to be higher, and there is often difficulty in getting and retaining proper levels of participation in contributory plans.

Adjustments often can be made for all of these factors when determining the proper rate to charge the policyholder. Some states, however, require the use of unisex rates, in which case the mix of employees by sex becomes an underwriting consideration. Also, major problems can arise in contributory plans: to the extent that higher costs for a group with a less-than-average mix of employees are passed on to these employees, a lower participation rate may result.

Industry

The nature of the industry represented by a group is also a significant factor in the underwriting process. In addition to different occupational hazards among industries, employees in some industries have higher-than-average health insurance claims that cannot be directly attributed to their jobs. Therefore, insurance companies commonly make adjustments in their life and health insurance rates based on the occupations of the employees covered as well as the industries in which they work.

In addition to occupational hazards, the underwriter must weigh other factors as well. Certain industries are characterized by a lack of stability and persistency and thus may be considered undesirable risks. The underwriter must also be concerned with what impact changes in the economy will have on a particular industry.

Geographic Location

The size and frequency of health insurance claims varies considerably among geographic regions and must be considered in determining a group insurance rate. For example, medical expenses tend to be higher in the Northeast than in the South, and higher in large urban areas than in rural areas. Certain geographic regions also tend to have a higher frequency of disability claims.

A group with geographically scattered employees also poses more administrative problems and probably results in greater administrative expense than a group in a single location. In addition, the underwriter must determine whether the insurance company has the proper facilities to service policyholders at their various locations.

STATE REGULATION

Even though the U.S. Supreme Court has declared insurance to be commerce and thus subject to federal regulation when conducted on an interstate basis, Congress gave the states substantial regulatory authority by the passage of the McCarran-Ferguson Act (Public Law 15) in 1945. This act exempts insurance from certain federal regulations to the extent that individual states actually regulate insurance. In addition, it provides that most other federal laws are not applicable to insurance unless they are specifically directed at the business of insurance.

As a result of the McCarran-Ferguson Act, a substantial body of laws and regulations has been enacted in every state. While no two states have identical laws and regulations, there have been attempts to encourage uniformity among the states. The most significant influence in this regard has been the National Association of Insurance Commissioners (NAIC), which is composed of state regulatory officials. Because the NAIC has as one of its goals the promotion of uniformity in legislation and administrative rules affecting insurance, it has developed numerous model laws. Although states are not bound to adopt these model laws, many states have enacted them.

Some of the more significant state laws and regulations affecting group insurance include those pertaining to the types of groups eligible for coverage, contractual provisions, benefit limitations, and taxation. Moreover, because many employers have employees in several states, the extent of the regulatory jurisdiction of each state is a question of some concern.

Eligible Groups

Most states do not allow group insurance contracts to be written unless a minimum number of persons are insured under the contract. This requirement, which may vary by type of coverage and type of group, is most common in group life insurance, where the minimum number required for plans established by individual employers is generally ten persons. A few states have either a lower minimum or no such requirement. A higher minimum, often 100 persons, may be imposed on other plans, such as those established by trusts, labor unions, or creditors. Only about half the states impose any minimum number requirement on group health insurance contracts. Where one exists, it usually is either five or ten persons.

Most states also have insurance laws concerning the types of groups for which insurance companies may write group insurance. Most of these laws specify that a group insurance contract cannot be delivered to a policyholder in the state unless the group meets certain statutory eligibility requirements for its type of group. In some states these eligibility requirements even vary by type of coverage. While the categories of eligible groups may vary, at least four types of groups involving employees are acceptable in virtually all states:

1. Individual employer groups
2. Negotiated trusteeships
3. Trade associations
4. Labor union groups

Other types of groups, including multiple-employer trusts, are also acceptable in some states. Some states have no insurance laws regarding the types or sizes of groups for which insurance companies may write group insurance. Rather, eligibility is determined on a contract-by-contract basis by the underwriting standards of the insurance company.

Individual Employer Groups

The most common type of eligible group is the individual employer group— a corporation, partnership, or sole proprietorship. Many state laws are very specific about what constitutes an employee for group insurance purposes. In addition to those usually considered to be employees of a firm, coverage can generally be written for retired employees and employees of subsidiary and affiliated firms as well. Furthermore, individual proprietors or partners usually are eligible for coverage as long as they are actively engaged in and devote a substantial part of their time to the conduct of the organization. Similarly, directors of a corporation may be eligible for coverage if they are also employees of the corporation.

Negotiated Trusteeships (Taft-Hartley Trusts)

Negotiated trusteeships are formed as a result of collective bargaining over benefits between a union and the employers of the union members. Generally, the union employees are in the same industry or a related one. For the most part, these industries, such as trucking or construction, are characterized by frequent movement of union members among employers. The Taft-Hartley Act prohibits employers from paying funds directly to a labor union for the purpose of providing group insurance coverage to members. Payments must be made to a trust fund established for the purpose of providing benefits to employees. The trustees of the fund must consist of equal numbers of representatives from both the employers and the union. The trustees can elect to either self-fund benefits or purchase insurance contracts with themselves as policyowner. Because eligible employees include only members of the collective bargaining unit (which may include some nonunion members), benefits for other employees must be provided in some other manner.

Negotiated trusteeships differ from other types of groups in how benefits are financed and how eligibility for benefits is determined. Contributions are often made by employers based on the number of hours worked by the employees covered under the collective bargaining agreement, regardless of whether these employees are eligible for benefits. Eligibility for benefits during a given time period usually is based only on some minimum number of hours worked during a previous time period. For example, a union member might receive coverage during a calendar quarter (even while unemployed) if he or she worked at least 300 hours in the previous calendar quarter. This situation, where the employees for whom contributions are made may differ from those eligible for benefits, presents a unique problem for the underwriter. Rates must be adequate to build up the contingency reserves necessary to pay benefits in periods of heavy layoffs during which a large portion of contributions ceases but eligibility for benefits continues.

While negotiated trusteeships normally provide benefits for the employees of several employers, they can also be established for the employees of a single employer. However, situations involving collective bargaining with a single employer will usually result in the employer's being required to purchase a group insurance contract and provide benefits. Although benefits and eligibility are specified in the bargaining agreement, the employer is the policyholder and the group is an individual employer group rather than a negotiated trusteeship. This approach also enables the employer to provide benefits for employees not represented by the bargaining unit under the same contract.

Trade Associations

A trade association, for eligibility purposes, is an association of employers that has been formed for reasons other than obtaining insurance. In most cases, these employers are in the same industry or type of business. Many such associations contain a large number of employers who do not have the minimum number of employees necessary to qualify for an individual employer group insurance contract. While in some states the master contract is issued directly to the trade association, in most states it is necessary that a trust be established. Through payment of premiums to the association or the trust, individual employers may provide coverage for their employees.

Both adverse selection and administrative costs tend to be greater in trade association groups than in many other types of groups. Therefore, most underwriters and state laws require that a minimum percentage of the employers belonging to the association, such as 50 percent, participate in the plan and that a minimum number of employees, possibly as high as 500, be covered. In addition, individual underwriting or strict provisions regarding preexisting conditions may be used, and employer contributions are usually required. To ensure adequate enrollment, the underwriter must determine whether the association has the resources as well as the desire to promote the plan enthusiastically and to administer it properly.

Labor Union Groups

Labor unions may establish group insurance plans to provide benefits for their members, with the master contract issued to the union. In addition to the prohibition by the Taft-Hartley Act of employer payments to labor unions for insurance premiums, state laws generally prohibit plans in which union members pay the entire cost from their own pockets. Consequently, the premiums come solely from union funds or partially from union funds and partially from members' contributions. Labor union groups account for a relatively small amount of group insurance, most of which is life insurance.

Multiple-Employer Welfare Arrangements

The final type of eligible group designed to provide benefits for employees is the multiple-employer welfare arrangement (MEWA). MEWAs are a common but often controversial method of marketing group benefits to employers who have a small number of employees. MEWAs are legal entities (1) sponsored by an insurance company, an independent administrator, or some other person or organization and (2) organized to provide group benefits to the employees of more than one employer. Each MEWA must have an administrator that is either an insurance company or a professional administrator. MEWAs may be organized as trusts, in which case there must be a trustee that may be an individual but is usually a corporate trustee, such as a commercial bank.

MEWAs are generally established to provide group benefits to employers within a specific industry, such as construction, agriculture, or banking. However, employers are not required to belong to an association. MEWAs may provide either a single type of insurance (such as life insurance) or a wide range of coverages (for example, life, medical expense, and disability income insurance). In some cases, alternative forms of the same coverage (such as comprehensive health insurance or basic health insurance) are available.

An employer desiring to obtain insurance coverage for its employees from a MEWA must subscribe and become a member of the MEWA. The employer is issued a joinder agreement, which spells out the relationship between the MEWA and the employer and specifies the coverage to which the employer has subscribed. It is not necessary for an employer to subscribe to all coverages offered by a MEWA.

A MEWA may either provide benefits on a self-funded basis or fund benefits with a contract purchased from an insurance company. In the latter case, the MEWA, rather than the subscribing employers, is the master insurance contract holder. In either case, the employees of subscribing employers receive benefit descriptions (certificates of insurance in insured MEWAs) in a manner similar to the usual group insurance arrangement.

In addition to the methods of funding benefits, MEWAs can also be categorized according to how they are administered, that is, whether by an insurance company or by a third-party administrator. It is generally agreed that there are three types of MEWAs. Unfortunately, the terminology used to describe the three types is not uniform and is often misleading. In this text, the following terminology and definitions will be used:

- *Fully insured multiple-employer trust (MET).* Benefits are insured and the MET is administered by an insurance company. (All MEWAs were once referred to as METs. In 1982, however, the Employee Retirement Income Security Act [ERISA], which is discussed later in this chapter, was amended to clarify the regulation of such arrangements. The act used the term *multiple-employer welfare arrangement* rather than the term *multiple-employer trust.* Over time, MEWA has become the accepted overall terminology, but most insurance companies continue to use MET to describe fully insured MEWAs as a way to distinguish them from the more controversial self-funded MEWAs.)
- *Insured, third-party-administered MEWA.* Benefits are insured and the MEWA is administered by a third party.
- *Self-funded MEWA.* Benefits are self-funded and the MEWA is administered by a third party.

Fully Insured METs. Fully insured METs are established and administered by insurance companies, with a commercial bank usually acting as trustee. Coverage under such METs is normally marketed by the sales force of the insurer involved and may be made available to other licensed insurance agents or brokers. It should be noted that a trust purchases coverage from the insurance company, and what is being marketed to employers is the availability of insurance through participation in the trust, not an insurance contract from the insurance company.

Fully insured METs were developed to provide group insurance to small employer groups. A single insurance company may have one MET or several, with each designed for a different industry (such as construction or manufacturing). Through METs, insurance companies have provided group insurance at a cost lower than the cost of a direct sale to the employer or to individual employees. Regulatory restrictions regarding minimum group size are overcome because the employees of many small employers are insured under a single group contract issued to the trust. Costs are also minimized because each type of coverage offered by the trust tends to be standardized for all employers using the trust.

In addition, underwriting standards have been developed to minimize the problems of adverse selection and the higher administrative costs associated with providing coverage to small groups of employees. While these standards vary among companies, the following are some common examples:

- More stringent participation requirements, such as 100 percent, for employers with fewer than five employees.
- A requirement that life insurance coverage be purchased. This tends to be a profitable and stable form of coverage for insurance companies. In some cases, the more life insurance coverage purchased, the more comprehensive the medical expense benefits made available.
- Limitations on the period of time for which rates are guaranteed, rarely more than six months.
- Probationary periods, often two or three months, for new employees.
- Restrictive provisions for preexisting conditions.
- Limitations on the amounts of life insurance coverage available on a simplified or guaranteed-issue basis (e.g., $20,000 for four or fewer employees; $40,000 for five or more). Additional coverage may be available, but individual evidence of insurability is required.
- Limitations on the amount of long-term disability insurance coverage that will be issued, such as 50 percent or 60 percent of income, subject to a $1,500 monthly maximum.
- Ineligible groups. Most METs have a lengthy list of ineligible groups, including those characterized by excessive claims experience or high turnover rates.

Because it is generally accepted under insurance regulatory law that an insurance contract is subject to regulation by the state in which the contract was delivered, many insurers have established METs where they consider the regulatory climate to be favorable. This has allowed an insurance company, in effect, to offer a nationally standardized contract to small employers (through subscribing to the trust) rather than different contracts that comply with the regulatory requirements in each subscriber's state. However, some states require that METs make their coverage conform to applicable state law when an employer from that state becomes a subscriber.

During the 1980s, the importance of METs (and insured, third-party-administered MEWAs) decreased somewhat. Some insurers, primarily because of difficulties in providing medical expense coverage to small employers, left the group insurance business. Health maintenance organizations (HMOs) increasingly and successfully sought business from smaller employers. In addition, many employers—particularly those with 25 to 100 employees—started to use self-funding. Nevertheless, in many parts of the country METs remain a major source of group insurance coverage for small employers.

Insured, Third-Party-Administered MEWAs. Insured, third-party-administered MEWAs are similar to fully insured METs in that benefits are provided through an insurance contract issued to a trust. However, these MEWAs are administered by some person or organization other than an insurance company.

The impetus for the establishment of an insured, third-party-administered MEWA comes from either the insurance company or the administrator. An insurance company desiring to enter the MEWA field may feel it lacks the expertise or resources to administer MEWAs properly at a competitive cost. Consequently, it seeks out third-party administrators to provide many of the necessary administrative functions. The third-party administrators under such arrangements are normally organizations specializing in either the administration of various types of insurance programs or solely the management of MEWAs. In addition to general administrative duties, the third-party administrator (subject to the insurance company's rules) may be involved in any or all of the following functions associated with MEWAs: underwriting, claims administration, benefit design, or marketing.

Third-party administrators desiring to enter the MEWA field or hoping to increase their share of MEWA business may seek out insurance companies to provide insurance coverages for the MEWAs they wish to establish. Some of these administrators specialize in the administration of insurance programs; others are insurance agents or brokers who desire a product over which they can have marketing control.

Unfortunately, the experience of insured, third-party-administered MEWAs has not always been satisfactory. There were several instances of mismanagement that caused some of these MEWAs to cease operations. In certain cases, eagerness to enter the field resulted in inadequate rates or lax underwriting; in other situations, administrators were more interested in management fees and sales commissions than in making a profit for the insurance company. While such occurrences tarnished the image of insured, third-party-administered MEWAs, many did operate successfully and were managed by capable administrators. Two factors have minimized the aforementioned difficulties in recent years. First, insurance companies, aware of past experiences, are cautious as they enter the field, giving particular regard to the selection of their administrators. Second, some states have passed legislation aimed at regulating administrators of MEWAs and other insurance arrangements.

Self-Funded MEWAs. Self-funded MEWAs are normally established and marketed by the persons or organizations that will administer them. The MEWA does not purchase an insurance contract, except possibly for stop-loss coverage; instead, benefits are self-funded with premiums paid by subscribing employers. While many self-funded MEWAs operated successfully and were well administered, others went bankrupt and left participants with unpaid claims. (Under an insured MEWA, the insurer would have been responsible for paying claims even if the MEWA failed.) Again, administrators often did not charge enough to establish proper reserves for future benefits, or they were more concerned with generating management fees and sales commissions than in properly managing the MEWA. In some cases, outright fraud was involved.

For several years, state insurance departments tried to obtain the power to shut down mismanaged MEWAs, but the administrators of these plans argued that ERISA exempted them from state regulation. Finally, in 1982, Congress enacted legislation that provides for state regulation of self-funded MEWAs. Self-funded MEWAs can apply for ERISA certification, but even if it is granted, the MEWA is still subject to state rules governing reserves and contributions. In addition, while ERISA certification is pending, a MEWA has to meet all state insurance regulations or the state can force it to cease operations. State regulation also applies if a MEWA either fails to apply for certification or is denied certification.

Initially, the overall effect of the 1982 legislation was to greatly reduce the number of self-funded MEWAs. However, two major factors caused a subsequent increase in the number of these MEWAs. First, many insurers abandoned the small-group market or became increasingly strict in their underwriting. As a result, self-funded MEWAs became the only alternative for some employers. Second, MEWAs frequently wrote coverage at a cost significantly below the cost of alternative coverage, often because of inadequate actuarial calculations regarding the size of future claims and the need for establishing adequate reserves.

Unfortunately, the resurgence of self-funded MEWAs was accompanied by many bankruptcies and unpaid claims. The General Accounting Office estimates that between 1988 and 1991, almost 200 self-funded MEWAs failed and left nearly 400,000 employees with $132 million in unpaid claims. There seems to be little doubt that many states have been unsuccessful in adequately regulating self-funded MEWAs. Even when appropriate laws exist, many MEWAs simply ignore them. A state insurance department finds out about an errant MEWA only when a complaint is received, and by then the MEWA may be in serious financial difficulty or out of business.

Contractual Provisions in Group Insurance

Through its insurance laws, every state provides for the regulation of contractual provisions. In many instances, certain contractual provisions must be included in group insurance policies. These mandatory provisions may be altered only if they result in more favorable treatment of the policyholder. Such provisions tend to be most uniform from state to state in the area of group life insurance, primarily because of the widespread adoption of the NAIC model bill pertaining to group life insurance standard provisions. As a result of state regulation, coupled with industry practices, the provisions of most group life and health insurance policies are relatively uniform from company to company. In most instances, an insurance company's policy forms can be used in all states. However, riders may be necessary to bring certain provisions into compliance with the regulations of some states.

Traditionally, the regulation of contractual provisions has focused on provisions pertaining to such factors as the grace period, conversion, and incontestability rather than on factors pertaining to the types or levels of benefits. These latter provisions have been a matter between the policyholder and the insurance company. However, in recent years this has changed in many states. In some states, certain benefits—such as well-baby care and treatment for alcoholism or drug abuse—must be included in any group insurance contract; in other states, they must be offered to group policyholders as optional benefits. Still other state laws and regulations specify minimum levels for certain benefits if those benefits are included.

It is interesting to note that, with few exceptions, the regulation of contractual provisions affects only those employee benefit plans funded with insurance contracts. This is because provisions of ERISA seem to exempt employee benefit plans from most types of state regulation. However, there are exceptions to this exemption; these include insurance regulation and therefore the provisions in insurance contracts. As a result of this ERISA exemption, states have few laws and regulations applying to the provisions of uninsured benefit plans. However, ERISA does not exempt uninsured plans from state regulation in such areas as age and sex discrimination, and laws pertaining to these areas commonly apply to all benefit plans. A few states are also trying to mandate other types of benefits for uninsured plans, and ultimately the issue will probably have to be settled by Congress or the Supreme Court.

Benefit Limitations

Statutory limitations may be imposed on the level of benefits that can be provided under group insurance contracts issued to certain types of eligible groups. With the exception of group life insurance, these limitations rarely apply in situations involving an employer-employee relationship. In the past, most states limited the amount of group life insurance that could be provided by an employer to an employee. Today, only Texas still has such a restriction, but its limit is so high that the limit has little practical effect. However, several states limit the amount of coverage that can be provided under contracts issued to groups other than individual employer groups. In addition, some states limit the amount of life insurance coverage that may be provided for dependents.

Taxation

Every state levies a premium tax on out-of-state insurance companies licensed to do business in its state, and most states tax the premiums of insurance companies domiciled in their state. These taxes, which are applicable to premiums written within a state, average about 2 percent.

The imposition of the premium tax has placed insurance companies at a competitive disadvantage with alternative methods of providing benefits. Premiums paid to HMOs are not subject to the tax, nor are premiums paid to Blue Cross and Blue Shield plans in some states. In addition, the elimination of this tax is one cost saving under self-funded plans. Because the trend toward self-funding of benefits by large corporations has resulted in the loss of substantial premium tax revenue to the states, there have been suggestions that all premiums paid to any type of organization or fund for the purpose of providing insurance benefits to employees be subject to the premium tax.

Where state income taxation exists, the tax implications of group insurance premiums and benefits to both employers and employees are generally similar to those of the federal government. Employers may deduct any premiums paid as business expenses, and employees have certain exemptions from taxation with respect to both premiums paid on their behalf and benefits attributable to employer-paid premiums.

Regulatory Jurisdiction

A group insurance contract will often insure individuals living in more than one state—a situation that raises the question of which state or states have regulatory jurisdiction over the contract. The issue is a crucial one because factors such as minimum enrollment percentages, maximum amounts of life insurance, and required contract provisions vary among the states.

Few problems usually arise if the insured group qualifies as an eligible group in all the states where insured individuals reside. Individual employer groups, negotiated trusteeships, and labor union groups fall into this category. Under the *doctrine of comity,* by which states recognize within their own territory the laws of other states, it is generally accepted that the state in which the group insurance contract is delivered to the policyholder has governing jurisdiction. Therefore, the contract must conform only to the laws and regulations of this one state, even though certificates of insurance may be delivered in other states. However, a few states have statutes that prohibit insurance issued in other states from covering residents of their state unless the contract conforms to their laws and regulations. While these statutes are effective with respect to insurance companies licensed within the state (that is, admitted companies), their effectiveness with respect to nonadmitted companies is questionable, because states lack regulatory jurisdiction over these companies.

This does not mean that the policyholder may arbitrarily seek out a situs (place of delivery) that is most desirable from a regulatory standpoint. Unless the place of delivery has a significant relationship to the insurance transaction, other states may seek to exercise their regulatory authority. Therefore, it has become common practice that an acceptable situs must be at least one of the following:

- The state where the policyholder is incorporated (or the trust is created if the policyholder is a trust)
- The state where the policyholder's principal office is located
- The state where the greatest number of insured individuals are employed
- Any state where an employer or labor union that is a party to a trust is located

While a policyholder may have a choice of situs if these locations differ, most insurers are reluctant to issue a group contract in any state unless a corporate officer or trustee who can execute acceptance of the contract is located in that state and unless the principal functions related to the administration of the group contract will be performed there.

The issue of regulatory jurisdiction is more complex for those types of groups that are not considered to be eligible groups in all states. METs are a typical example. If the state has no regulation to the contrary and if the insured group would be eligible for group insurance in other states, the situation is the same as previously described. In addition, most other states will accept the doctrine of comity and not interfere with the regulatory jurisdiction of the state where the contract is delivered. However, some states either prohibit coverage from being issued or require that it conform with the state's laws and regulations other than those pertaining to eligible groups.

FEDERAL REGULATION

Many aspects of federal regulation have affected the establishment and character of group insurance, especially the following, which are covered in some detail in this book:

- The Age Discrimination in Employment Act
- The Pregnancy Discrimination Act
- The Employee Retirement Income Security Act
- The Americans with Disabilities Act
- The Social Security Act
- The Internal Revenue Code
- The Health Maintenance Organization Act
- The Consolidated Omnibus Budget Reconciliation Act (COBRA)
- The Health Insurance Portability and Accountability Act
- The Newborns' and Mothers' Health Protection Act
- The Women's Health and Cancer Rights Act
- The Mental Health Parity Act
- The Family and Medical Leave Act

This chapter focuses on the first four acts listed, since these have had a similar influence on most types of group insurance. Nondiscrimination rules are also discussed.

The Social Security Act was discussed in detail in Chapter 3, and discussions in later chapters consider the integration of group disability income and group medical expense benefits with the benefits provided under the act.

The income tax implications of the Internal Revenue Code, which may vary for different types of group insurance coverage, are described in those chapters pertaining to each type of coverage.

The next six acts affect medical expense coverage and are described at various places in the four later chapters on group medical expense coverage.

Finally the Family and Medical Leave Act is covered along with the discussion of family leave in Chapter 16.

The Age Discrimination in Employment Act

The Age Discrimination in Employment Act applies to employers with 20 or more employees and affects employees aged 40 and older. With some exceptions, such as individuals in executive or high policymaking positions, compulsory retirement is no longer allowed. Employee benefits, which traditionally ceased or were severely limited at age 65, must be continued for older workers. However, some reductions in benefits are allowed. While the *federal* act does not prohibit such discrimination in benefits for employees under age 40 or for all employees of firms that employ fewer than 20 persons, some *states* may prohibit such discrimination under their own laws or regulations.

The act permits a reduction in the level of some benefits for older workers so that the cost of providing benefits for older workers is no greater than the cost of providing them for younger workers. However, the most expensive benefit—medical expense coverage—cannot be reduced. The following discussion is limited to reductions after age 65, by far the most common age for reducing benefits, even though reductions can start at an earlier age if they are justified on a cost basis. It should be emphasized that these restrictions apply to benefits for active employees only; there are no requirements under the act that any benefits be continued for retired workers.

When participation in an employee benefit plan is voluntary, an employer can generally require larger employee contributions instead of reducing benefits for older employees, as long as the proportion of the premiums paid by older employees does not increase with age. Thus, if an employer pays 50 percent of the cost of benefits for younger employees, it must pay at least 50 percent of the cost for older employees. If employees pay the entire cost of a benefit, older employees may be required to pay the full cost of their coverage to the extent that this is a condition of participation in the plan. However, this provision does not apply to medical expense benefits. Employees over age 65 cannot be required to pay any more for their coverage than is paid by employees under age 65.

In cases where benefits are reduced, two approaches are permitted: a benefit-by-benefit approach or a benefit-package approach. Under the more common *benefit-by-benefit* approach, each employee benefit may be reduced to a lesser amount as long as each reduction can be justified on a cost basis. Under a *benefit-package approach,* the overall benefit package may be altered. Some benefits may be eliminated or reduced to a lesser amount than can be justified on a cost basis, as long as other existing benefits are not reduced or the benefit package is increased by adding new benefits for older workers. The only cost restriction is that the cost of the revised benefit package may be no less than if a benefit-by-benefit reduction had been used. The act also places two other restrictions on the benefit-package approach by prohibiting any reduction in medical expense benefits or retirement benefits.

In reducing a benefit, an employer must use data that approximately reflect the actual cost of the benefit to the employer over a reasonable period of years. Unfortunately, such data either have not been kept by employers or are not statistically valid. Consequently, the reductions that have taken place have been based on estimates provided by insurance companies and consulting actuaries. This approach appears to be satisfactory to the Equal Employment Opportunity Commission (EEOC), which enforces the act's provisions. The act allows reductions to take place on a yearly basis or to be based on age brackets of up to five years. Any cost comparisons must be made with the preceding age bracket. For example, if five-year age brackets are used, the cost of providing benefits to employees between the ages of 65 and 69 must be compared with the cost of providing the same benefits to employees between the ages of 60 and 64.

While reductions in group insurance benefits for older employees are permissible, they are not required. Some employers make no reductions for older employees, but most employers reduce life insurance benefits at age 65 and long-term disability benefits at age 60 or 65.

Group Term Life Insurance Benefits

Based on mortality statistics, most insurance companies feel that group term life insurance benefits can be reduced to the percentages of the amount of coverage provided immediately prior to age 65, shown in Figure 5.1.

Therefore, if employees normally receive $40,000 of group term life insurance, those employees between the ages of 65 and 69 can receive only $26,000, employees between the ages of 70 and 74 can receive $18,000, and so forth. Similarly, if employees normally receive coverage equal to 200 percent of salary, this may be reduced to 130 percent of salary at age 65, with additional reductions at later ages.

Reductions may also be made on an annual basis. If an annual reduction is used, it appears that a reduction of up to 11 percent of the previous year's coverage can be actuarially justified, starting at age 65 and continuing through age 69. Starting at age 70, the reduction should be 9 percent.

FIGURE 5-1	
Age	**Percentage**
65–69	65
70–74	45
75–79	30
Over 79	20

In a plan with employee contributions, the employer may either reduce benefits as described above and charge the employee the same premium as those employees in the previous age bracket or continue full coverage and require that the employee pay an actuarially increased contribution.

Group Disability Income Benefits

The Age Discrimination in Employment Act allows reductions in insured short-term disability income plans, but no reductions are allowed in uninsured sick-leave plans. While disability statistics for those aged 65 and older are limited, some insurance companies feel a benefit reduction of approximately 20 percent is appropriate for employees between the ages of 65 and 69, with additional decreases of 20 percent of the previous benefit for each consecutive five-year period. However the laws of the few states that require that short-term disability income benefits be provided allow neither a reduction in benefits nor an increase in any contribution rate for older employees.

Under the act, two methods are allowed for reducing long-term disability income benefits for those employees who become disabled at older ages. Either the level of benefits may be reduced without altering benefit eligibility or duration or the benefit duration may be reduced without altering the level of benefits. These reductions again must be justified on a cost basis. Unfortunately, no rough guidelines can be given because any possible reductions will vary considerably, depending on the eligibility requirements and the duration of benefits under a long-term disability plan.

Group Medical Expense Benefits

The Age Discrimination in Employment Act requires that employers offer *all* employees over age 65 (and any employees' spouses who are also over age 65) the same medical coverage they provide for younger employees (and their spouses). Consequently, benefits cannot be reduced for older employees because of increasing cost to the employer. In addition, older employees cannot be required to contribute more than younger employees.

The employer's plan is the primary payer of benefits, with Medicare assuming the secondary-payer role. However, employees may reject the employer's plan and elect Medicare as the primary payer of benefits, but federal regulations prevent an employer from offering a health plan or option designed to induce such a rejection. This effectively prohibits an employer from paying the Part B premium or offering any type of supplemental plan to employees who elect Medicare as primary. (However, supplemental and carve-out plans can be used for retirees.) Therefore, most employees elect to remain with the employer's plan unless it requires large employee contributions. When Medicare is secondary, the employer may pay the Part B premium for those employees who elect Medicare, but the employer has no legal responsibility to do so.

The Pregnancy Discrimination Act

At one time, pregnancy usually was treated differently from other medical conditions under both individual and group insurance policies. However, the Pregnancy Discrimination Act (a 1978 amendment to the Civil Rights Act) requires that women affected by pregnancy, childbirth, or related medical conditions be treated the same for employment-related purposes (including receipt of benefits under an employee benefit plan) as other persons who are not so affected but who are similar in their ability to work. The act applies only to the benefit plans (both insured and self-funded) of those employers who have 15 or more employees. While employers with fewer employees are not subject to the provisions of the act, they may be subject to comparable or more stringent state laws. Similarly, because the act applies only to employee benefit plans, pregnancy may be treated differently from other medical conditions under insurance policies that are not part of an employee benefit plan.

While the act itself is brief, enforcement falls under the jurisdiction of the EEOC, which has detailed guidelines for interpreting the act. The highlights of these guidelines are as follows:

- If an employer provides any type of disability income or sick-leave plan for employees, the employer must provide coverage for pregnancy and its related medical conditions on the same basis as for other disabilities. For example, an employer cannot limit disability income benefits for pregnancies to a shorter period than that applicable to other disabilities.
- If an employer provides medical expense benefits for employees, the employer must provide coverage for the pregnancy-related conditions of employees (regardless of marital status) on the same basis as for all other medical conditions.
- If an employer provides medical expense benefits for dependents, the employer must provide equal coverage for the medical expenses (including those arising from pregnancy-related conditions) of spouses of both male and female employees. The guidelines also allow an employer to exclude pregnancy-related benefits for female dependents other than spouses as long as such an exclusion applies equally to the nonspouse dependents of both male and female employees.
- Extended medical expense benefits after termination of employment must apply equally to pregnancy-related medical conditions and other medical conditions. Thus, if pregnancy commencing during employment is covered until delivery, even if the employee is not disabled, a similar nondisability extension of benefits must apply to all other medical conditions.
- Medical expense benefits relating to abortions may be excluded from coverage except when the life of the woman is endangered. However, complications from an abortion must be covered. In addition, abortions must be treated like any other medical condition with respect to sick leave and other fringe benefit plans.

The Employee Retirement Income Security Act (ERISA)

ERISA was enacted to protect the interests of participants in employee benefit plans as well as the interests of the beneficiaries. While all sections of the act—often referred to as the *Pension Reform Act*—generally apply to retirement plans, certain sections pertaining to fiduciary responsibility and reporting and disclosure also apply to employee welfare benefit plans, including most traditional group insurance plans. ERISA defines a welfare benefit plan as any plan, fund, or program established or maintained by an employer (or an employee organization) for the purpose of providing for its participants or their beneficiaries, through the purchase of insurance or otherwise, any of the following:

- Medical, surgical, or hospital care or benefits
- Benefits in the event of sickness, accident, disability, death, or unemployment
- Vacation benefits
- Apprenticeship or other training programs
- Day care centers
- Scholarship funds
- Prepaid legal services
- Any benefit described in Section 302(c) of the Labor Management Relations Act of 1947, such as holiday pay and severance pay

Because of its greater impact on retirement plans, the complete discussion of ERISA is contained in Part Five. The provisions of most relevance to employee welfare benefit plans—fiduciary responsibilities and reporting and disclosure requirements—are found in Chapter 26.

The Americans with Disabilities Act

The Americans with Disabilities Act (ADA), which deals with employment, public services, public accommodations, and telecommunications, is the most far-reaching legislation ever enacted in this country to make it possible for disabled persons to join the mainstream of everyday life.

At the time the act went into effect in 1992, it was estimated that almost 45 million Americans are disabled, and nearly $300 billion of government resources were devoted annually to this group. Fifteen million of the disabled were of working age, but only about 30 percent of these were in the workforce, compared with 80 percent of the nondisabled.

As with any social legislation, the act provides benefits, including a better quality of life, for many disabled persons and annual savings in the form of decreased government payments to the disabled. However, there are also costs, many of which are borne by employers and some of which take the form of increased expenditures for employee benefits.

Title I of the ADA, which pertains to employment, makes it unlawful for employers with 15 or more employees to discriminate on the basis of disability against a qualified individual with respect to any term, condition, or privilege of employment. This includes employee benefits.

Congress gave the responsibility for enforcing Title I to the EEOC, which has numerous regulations and a lengthy technical assistance manual to help qualified individuals understand their rights and to facilitate and encourage employer compliance.

While the act has resulted in significant improvements in public accommodations and the availability of telecommunications for the disabled, the percentage of disabled in the workforce has increased only slightly. However, it should be noted that many employers hired the disabled before ADA. Although intuition might suggest that the disabled would be more likely than other employees to have conditions requiring ongoing medical care, many employers who have made an effort to hire the disabled have not found this to be the case. In fact, some employers feel that the disabled make excellent workers and actually save them money. With jobs more difficult to obtain for the disabled, there is the feeling that the disabled are less likely to switch employers (thus minimizing costs to train new employees) and may actually work harder to keep the jobs they have. Whether this situation will continue as more severely disabled persons enter the workforce and have more opportunities to change jobs is an unanswered question.

Effect on Employment Practices

The ADA defines a disabled person as one who has a physical or mental impairment that substantially limits one or more major life activities, such as caring for oneself, performing manual tasks, walking, seeing, hearing, speaking, breathing, and learning. The EEOC specifically mentions the following as being disabilities: epilepsy, cancer, diabetes, arthritis, hearing and vision loss, AIDS, and emotional illness. A person is impaired even if the condition is corrected, as in the case of a person who is hearing-impaired and wears a hearing aid. The ADA does exclude from the definition of disability persons who are currently engaged in the illegal use of drugs. However, anyone who has successfully completed a supervised rehabilitation program or is currently in such a program is subject to the act's protection as long as he or she is not currently abusing drugs.

The act does not set quotas or require that the disabled be hired. It does, however, provide that a person cannot be discriminated against if he or she is able to perform the essential functions of a job with or without *reasonable accommodation,* which includes making existing facilities that employees use readily accessible and usable by individuals with disabilities. Reasonable accommodation may be as simple as rearranging furniture or changing the height of a work space to accommodate a wheelchair. (There are estimates that a significant percentage of the disabled can be accommodated with expenditures of $100 or less for each disabled person.) Reasonable accommodations do not include changes that would cause undue hardship for an employer. The act defines *undue hardship* as a significant difficulty or expense by the employer in light of such factors as the cost of the accommodation, the employer's financial resources, and the impact on other employees. With one exception, reasonable accommodation is for specific individuals for an individual job; it need not be made just because a disabled person may someday apply for work. The exception is that an employer must make facilities for *applying* for a job accessible to the handicapped and provide employment information that is usable by persons who are hearing-impaired or vision-impaired.

As a general rule, the ADA prohibits medical examinations or inquiries into a person's disability status prior to an offer of employment. Many questions that were previously asked of prospective employees are no longer allowed. For example, an employer cannot ask about prior illnesses or injuries, sick days used at a previous employer, prescription drugs taken, or the like.

The portion of the ADA pertaining to employment practices is lengthy and complex, and a more detailed discussion is beyond the scope of this book. However, it should be noted that this part of the act continues to be a source of many lawsuits and complaints to the EEOC. The vast majority of these lawsuits and complaints pertain to issues of hiring, termination of employment, and the failure to make reasonable accommodations. Employee benefits, on the other hand, have been a less significant issue.

Effect on Employee Benefits

The ADA was less precise with respect to employee benefits, and the original technical assistance manual was vague. However, the situation was significantly clarified in June 1993, when the EEOC issued interim enforcement guidance for EEOC investigators to use when investigating ADA claims pertaining to health insurance.

The ADA specifically allows the development and administration of benefit plans in accordance with accepted principles of risk assessment. The EEOC guidelines state that the purpose of the act is not to disrupt the current regulatory climate for self-insured employers or the current nature of insurance underwriting. Furthermore, its purpose is not to alter current industry practices in sales, underwriting, pricing, administrative and other services, claims, and related activities. The act allows these activities based on classification of risks as regulated by the states, unless these activities are being used as a subterfuge to evade the purpose of the ADA.

The 1993 guidelines stipulate that employees with disabilities be accorded equal access to whatever health insurance coverage the employer provides to other employees. Coverage for dependents is also subject to ADA rules, but the scope of coverage for dependents can be different from the scope of coverage that applies to employees. In addition, the guidelines state that decisions about the employment of a person cannot be based on concerns about the effect of the person's disability on the employer's health insurance plan.

The EEOC guidelines recognize that certain coverage limitations are acceptable. For example, a lower level of benefits than is provided for physical conditions is permissible for mental and nervous conditions. Even though such a limitation may have a greater impact on certain persons with disabilities, the limitation is not considered discriminatory because it applies to the treatment of many dissimilar conditions and affects individuals both with and without disabilities. Similarly, a lower level of benefits for eye care is singled out as acceptable. However, there have been a number of lawsuits on the issue of whether different benefits for mental and physical disabilities violates the ADA. The EEOC now feels that such disparities are a violation, but the courts that have heard these lawsuits have not agreed with this position.

The guidelines allow blanket preexisting-condition clauses that exclude from coverage the treatment of conditions that predate an individual's eligibility for benefits under a plan. The exclusion of experimental drugs or treatment and elective surgery is also permissible. The guidelines allow coverage limits for procedures that are not exclusively, or nearly exclusively, utilized for the treatment of a specific disability. This category includes, for example, limits on the number of blood transfusions or X-rays, even though such limits may adversely affect persons with certain disabilities.

However, disability-based provisions are not allowed. These include the exclusion or limitation of benefits for (1) a specific disability, such as deafness, AIDS or schizophrenia; (2) a discrete group of disabilities, such as cancer, muscular dystrophy, or kidney disease; and (3) disability in general.

If the EEOC determines that a health plan violates the ADA, the burden of proving otherwise is on the employer. However, the guidelines contain the following "noninclusive list of potential business/insurance justifications" that an employer can use to prove that a plan provision that has been challenged by the EEOC is not a violation of the ADA (Note that the quoted words are taken directly from the guidelines. While examples used in the guidelines answer some questions about the exact meaning of the words, their precise meaning is open to interpretation until clarified by regulation or the courts.):

- The employer may prove that "it has not engaged in the disability-based disparate treatment alleged." For example, if it is alleged that a benefit cap for a particular catastrophic disability is discriminatory, the employer may prove that its health insurance plan actually treats all similarly catastrophic conditions in the same way.
- The employer may prove that "the disparate treatment is justified by legitimate actuarial data, or by actual or reasonably anticipated experience, and that conditions with comparable actuarial data and/or experience are treated in the same fashion."
- The employer may prove that "the disparate treatment is necessary to ensure that the challenged health insurance plan satisfies the commonly accepted or legally required standards for the fiscal soundness of such an insurance plan." For example, the employer may prove that it limited cov-

erage for the treatment of a discrete group of disabilities because continued unlimited coverage would have been so expensive as to cause the health insurance plan to become financially insolvent, and there was no nondisability-based health insurance plan alternative that would have avoided insolvency.

■ The employer may prove that "the challenged insurance practice or activity is necessary to prevent the occurrence of an unacceptable change either in the coverage of the health insurance plan, or in the premiums charged for the health insurance plan." An unacceptable change is a drastic increase in premium payments (or in copayments or deductibles) or a drastic alteration to the scope of coverage or level of benefits provided that would (1) make the health insurance plan effectively unavailable to a significant number of other employees, (2) make the health insurance plan so unattractive as to result in significant adverse selection, or (3) make the health insurance plan so unattractive that the employer could not compete in recruiting and maintaining qualified workers due to the superiority of health insurance plans offered by other employers in the community.

■ "If coverage for a disability-specific treatment is denied, the employer may prove by reliable scientific evidence that the disability-specific treatment does not cure the condition; slow the degeneration, deterioration or harm attributable to the condition; alleviate the symptoms of the condition; or maintain the current health status of disabled individuals who receive the treatment."

Nondiscrimination Rules

For many years, nondiscrimination rules have applied to employee benefit plans that provide retirement benefits. The purpose of these rules is to deny favorable tax treatment to plans that do not provide equitable benefits to a large cross section of employees. In effect, the owners and executives of a business cannot receive tax-favored benefits if a plan is designed primarily for them. Nondiscrimination rules in recent years have slowly been applied to various other types of employee benefit plans, but these rules, each of which is complex, have not been uniform.

Congress attempted to eliminate this lack of uniformity by adding Section 89 to the Internal Revenue Code as part of the Tax Reform Act of 1986. This code section was extremely far-reaching and complex, and it would have been very costly both for the government to implement and for employers to comply with. As a result, Section 89 was repealed in 1989, and all the old nondiscrimination rules it replaced were reinstated. These rules are discussed where appropriate throughout this book.

STUDY QUESTIONS

1. What general characteristics distinguish group insurance from individual insurance?

2. a. What factors do underwriters take into consideration when evaluating group benefit proposals?
   b. What is the significance of each factor?

3. a. How do negotiated trusteeships (Taft-Hartley trusts) differ from other types of groups with respect to financing of benefits and determination of eligibility?
   b. How do labor union groups differ from negotiated trusteeships?

4. Providing group insurance coverage to small groups of employees through trade association plans or MEWAs presents unique problems with respect to adverse selection and high administrative costs. Explain how insurance company underwriting standards have been modified to confront these problems.

5. Describe the alternative ways in which MEWAs may be funded and administered.

6. Explain the extent to which states regulate the provisions found in group insurance contracts.

7. How do state premium taxes put insurance companies at a competitive disadvantage with alternative methods of providing benefits?

8. The Felton Corporation is incorporated in the state of Pennsylvania where it was established. However, its principal office is now located in Wilmington, Delaware, where all administrative functions are performed. While it has some employees in these two states, the majority of its work force of 500 are employed in New Jersey. The corporation has been told by its benefit consultant that most insurance companies will deliver the group insurance contracts for its employees in any of these three states.
   a. Is the agent correct? Explain.
   b. From a practical standpoint, why might the corporation prefer a situs other than the state where its administrative functions are performed?

9. Describe the general approaches that are acceptable for reducing benefits under the Age Discrimination in Employment Act.

10. Explain the extent to which reductions in group term life insurance and group disability income insurance appear justified (using a benefit-by-benefit approach) under the Age Discrimination in Employment Act.

11. The medical expense plan of the Mallory Corporation provides benefits for pregnancy-related conditions to married female employees but excludes such coverage

for unmarried female employees and unmarried female dependents of employees. Abortions are excluded unless the life of the mother is in danger. In addition, the corporation limits benefits under its short-term disability insurance plan to a maximum of six weeks for pregnancy-related conditions. Assuming the Mallory Corporation is subject to the pregnancy provisions of the Pregnancy Discrimination Act, do these plans conform to the requirements of the act? Explain.

12. a. What employers must comply with Title I of the Americans with Disabilities Act?
    b. What type of discrimination is prohibited by the ADA?

13. Under what circumstances must an employer make reasonable accommodations for a disabled person under the Americans with Disabilities Act?

14. To what extent does the Americans with Disabilities Act allow medical expense plans to contain (a) coverage limitations and (b) preexisting-conditions provisions?

Group Life Insurance: Term Coverage

Traditionally, most group life insurance plans were designed to provide coverage during an employee's working years, with coverage usually ceasing upon termination of employment for any reason. Today, the majority of employees are provided with coverage that will continue, often at a reduced amount, when termination is a result of retirement. Group term life insurance, which provides preretirement coverage, is described in this chapter. The methods and contracts used to provide coverage after retirement are discussed in the following chapter.

The oldest and most common form of group life insurance is group term insurance. Coverage consists primarily of yearly renewable term insurance that provides death benefits only, with no buildup of cash values. The group insurance marketplace, with its widespread use of yearly renewable term coverage, contrasts with the individual marketplace, in which term insurance accounts for slightly more than one-third of coverage in force. This is primarily due to increasing annual premiums, which become prohibitive for many insureds at older ages. In group life insurance plans, the overall premium, in addition to other factors, is a function of the age distribution of the group's members. While the premium for any individual employee increases with age, the flow of younger workers into the plan and the retirement of older workers tend to result in a relatively stable age distribution and, thus, an average group insurance rate that remains constant or rises only slightly.

The following discussion of group term life insurance focuses largely on common contract provisions, other coverages that are often added to the basic contract, and relevant federal tax laws.

CONTRACT PROVISIONS

The provisions contained in group term life insurance contracts are more uniform than those found in other types of group insurance. Much of this uniformity is a result of the adoption by most states of the Group Life Insurance Standard Provisions Model Bill developed by the National Association of Insurance Commissioners (NAIC). This bill, coupled with the insurance industry's attempts at uniformity, has resulted in provisions that are virtually identical among insurance companies. While the following contract provisions represent the norm and are consistent with the practices of most insurance companies, some states may require slightly different provisions, and some companies may vary their contract provisions. In addition, negotiations between a policyholder and an insurance company may result in the modification of contract provisions.

Benefit Schedules

The purpose of the benefit schedule is twofold. It classifies the employees who are eligible for coverage, and it specifies the amount of life insurance that will be provided to the members of each class, thus minimizing adverse selection because the amount of coverage for individual employees is predetermined. A benefit schedule can be as simple as providing a single amount of life insurance for all employees or as complex as providing different amounts of insurance for different classes of employees. For individual employer groups, the most common benefit schedules are those in which the amount of life insurance is based on either earnings or position.

Earnings Schedules

Most group term life insurance plans use an earnings schedule under which the amount of life insurance is determined as a multiple (or percentage) of each each employee's earnings. For example, the amount of life insurance for each employee may be twice (200 percent of) the employee's annual earnings. Most plans use a multiple between one and two, but higher and lower multiples are occasionally used. The amount of insurance is often rounded to the next higher $1,000 and for underwriting purposes may be subject to a maximum benefit, such as $200,000. For purposes of the benefit schedule, an employee's earnings usually consist of base salary only and do not include additional compensation like overtime pay or bonuses.

An alternative to using a flat percentage of earnings is to use an actual schedule of earnings such as the one in Table 6-1. This type of schedule may be designed so that all employees receive an amount of coverage that is approximately equal to the same multiple of annual earnings or, as in this example, larger multiples with higher earnings. Benefit schedules usually provide for a change in the amount of an employee's coverage when the employee moves into a different classification, even if this does not occur on the policy anniversary date. For example, the schedule in Table 6-1 indicates that the amount of coverage for an employee earning $28,000 would increase from $40,000 to $75,000 if the employee received a $4,000 raise. Some schedules, however, specify that adjustments in amounts of coverage will be made only annually or on monthly premium due dates.

TABLE 6-1
Earnings Schedule

Annual Earnings	Amount of Life Insurance
Less than $20,000	$ 20,000
$20,000 to $29,999	40,000
$30,000 to $39,999	75,000
$40,000 to $49,999	100,000
$50,000 and over	150,000

Position Schedules

Position schedules are similar to earnings schedules except that, as Table 6-2 shows, the amount of life insurance is based on an employee's position within the firm rather than on the employee's annual earnings.

Because individuals in high positions are often involved in designing the benefit schedule, underwriters are concerned that the benefits for these individuals be reasonable in relation to the overall plan benefits. Position schedules may also pose problems in meeting nondiscrimination rules if excessively large amounts of coverage are provided to persons in high positions.

Even though position schedules are often used when annual earnings can be easily determined, they are particularly useful when it is difficult to determine an employee's annual income. This is the situation when income is materially affected by such factors as commissions earned, number of hours worked, or bonuses that are based on either the employee's performance or the firm's profits.

TABLE 6-2
Position Schedule

Position	Amount of Life Insurance
President	$300,000
Vice presidents	150,000
Managers	90,000
Salespersons	60,000
Other employees	30,000

Flat-Benefit Schedules

Under flat-benefit schedules, the same amount of life insurance is provided for all employees regardless of salary or position. This type of benefit schedule is commonly used in group insurance plans covering hourly paid employees, particularly when benefits are negotiated with a union. In most cases, the amount of life insurance under a flat-benefit schedule is relatively small, such as $10,000 or $20,000. When an employer desires to provide only a minimum amount of life insurance for all employees, a flat-benefit schedule is often used.

Combination Benefit Schedules

It is not unusual for employers to have benefit schedules that incorporate elements from several of the various types previously discussed. While there are numerous possible combinations, a common benefit schedule of this type provides salaried employees with an amount of insurance that is determined by a multiple of their annual earnings and hourly employees with a flat amount of life insurance.

Reduction in Benefits

It is common for a group life insurance plan to provide for a reduction in benefits for active employees who reach a certain age, commonly 65 to 70. Such a reduction, which is due to the high cost of providing benefits for older employees, is specified in the benefit schedule of a plan. Any reduction in the amount of life insurance for active employees is subject to the provisions of the Age Discrimination in Employment Act, which are discussed in Chapter 5.

Benefit reductions fall into three categories: (1) a reduction to a flat amount of insurance; (2) a percentage reduction, such as to 65 percent of the amount of insurance that was previously provided; or (3) a gradual reduction over a period of years (for example, a 10 percent reduction in coverage each year until a minimum benefit amount is reached).

Eligibility

Group insurance contracts are very precise in their definition of what constitutes an eligible person for coverage purposes. In general, an employee must be in a covered classification, work full-time, and be actively at work. In addition, any requirements concerning probationary periods, insurability, or premium contributions must be satisfied.

Covered Classifications

All group insurance contracts specify that an employee must fall into one of the classifications contained in the benefit schedule. While these classifications may be broad enough to include all employees of the organization, they may also be so limited as to exclude many employees from coverage. In some cases, these excluded employees may have coverage through a negotiated trusteeship or under other group insurance contracts provided by the employer; in other cases, they may have no coverage because the employer wishes to limit benefits to certain groups of employees. No employee may be in more than one classification, and the responsibility for determining the appropriate classification for each employee falls on the policyholder.

Full-Time Employment

Most group insurance contracts limit eligibility to full-time employees. A full-time employee is generally defined as one who works no fewer than the number of hours in the normal work week established by the employer, which must be at least 30 hours. Subject to insurance company underwriting practices, an employer can provide coverage for part-time employees. When this is done, *part-time* is generally defined as less than *full-time* but more than some minimum number of hours per week. Part-time employees may be subject to more stringent eligibility requirements. For example, full-time hourly paid employees may be provided with $20,000 of life insurance immediately on employment, while part-time employees may be provided with only $10,000 of life insurance and may be subject to a probationary period.

Actively-at-Work Provision

Most group insurance contracts contain an actively-at-work provision, whereby an employee is not eligible for coverage if absent from work because of sickness, injury, or other reasons on the otherwise effective date of coverage under the contract. Coverage will commence when the employee returns to work. This provision is often waived for employers with a large number of employees when coverage is transferred from one insurance company to another and the employees involved have been insured under the previous insurance company's contract.

Probationary Periods

Group insurance contracts may contain probationary periods that must be satisfied before an employee is eligible for coverage. When a probationary period exists, it rarely exceeds six months, and an employee is eligible for coverage on either the first day after the probationary period or on the first day of the month following the end of the probationary period.

Insurability

While most group insurance contracts are issued without individual evidence of insurability, in some instances underwriting practices require evidence of insurability. This commonly occurs when an employee fails to elect coverage under a contributory plan and later wants coverage or when an employee is eligible for a large amount of coverage. In these cases, an employee is not eligible for coverage until he or she has submitted the proper evidence of insurability and the insurance company has determined that the evidence is satisfactory.

Premium Contribution

If a group insurance plan is contributory, an employee is not eligible for coverage until the policyholder has been given the proper authorization for payroll deductions. If this is done before the employee otherwise becomes eligible, coverage commences on the eligibility date. During a period of 31 days following the eligibility date, coverage begins when the policyholder receives the employee's authorization. If the authorization is not received within the 31 days, the employee must furnish evidence of insurability at his or her own expense to obtain coverage. Evidence of insurability is also required if an employee drops coverage under a contributory plan and wishes to regain coverage at a future date.

Beneficiary Designation

With few exceptions, an insured person has the right to name the beneficiary under his or her group life insurance coverage. The exceptions include dependent life insurance, where the employee is the beneficiary. In addition, the laws and regulations of some states prohibit naming the employer as beneficiary. Unless a beneficiary designation has been made irrevocable, an employee has the right to change the designated beneficiary at any time. While all insurance contracts require that the insurance company be notified of any beneficiary change in writing, the effective date of the change may vary, depending on contract provisions. Some contracts specify that a change will be effective on the date it is received by the insurance company; others make it effective on the date the change was requested by the employee.

Under individual life insurance policies, death benefits are paid to an insured person's estate if no beneficiary has been named or if all beneficiaries have died before the insured. Some group term life insurance contracts contain an identical provision; others stipulate that the death benefits will be paid through a *successive beneficiary provision*. Under the successive beneficiary provision, the proceeds are paid, at the option of the insurance company, to any one or more of the following survivors of the insured person: spouse, children, parents, brothers and sisters, or executor of the employee's estate. In most cases, insurance companies will pay the proceeds to the person or persons in the first category that includes eligible survivors.

Settlement Options

Group term life insurance contracts covering employees provide that death benefits be payable in a lump sum unless an optional mode of settlement has been selected. Each employee insured under the contract has the right to select and change any available mode of settlement during his or her lifetime. If no optional mode of settlement is in force at the employee's death, the beneficiary generally has the right to elect any of the available options. The most common provision in group term insurance contracts is that the available modes of settlement are those customarily offered by the insurance company at the time the selection is made. The available options are not generally specified in the contract, but information about them is usually given to the group policyholder. In addition, many insurance companies have brochures that describe either all or the most common options available to employees. Any guarantees associated with these options will be those that are in effect when the option is selected.

In addition to a lump-sum option, most insurance companies offer all the following options and possibly other options as well:

- An interest option. The proceeds are left on deposit with the insurance company, and the interest on the proceeds is paid to the beneficiary. The beneficiary can usually withdraw the proceeds at any time.
- An installment option for a fixed period. The proceeds are paid in equal installments for a specified period of time. The amount of any periodic installment is a function of the time period and the amount of the death proceeds.
- An installment option for a fixed amount. The proceeds are paid in equal installments of a specified amount until the proceeds plus any interest earnings are exhausted.
- A life income option. The proceeds are payable in installments during the lifetime of the beneficiary. A choice of guarantee periods is usually available during which a secondary beneficiary or the beneficiary's estate will continue to receive benefits even if the beneficiary dies. The amount of any

periodic installment is a function of the age and sex of the beneficiary, the period for which payments are guaranteed, and the amount of the death proceeds.

Premiums

Group insurance contracts stipulate that it is the responsibility of the policyholder to pay all premiums to the insurance company, even if the group insurance plan is contributory. Any required contributions from employees are incorporated into the employer's group insurance plan, but they are not part of the insurance contract and therefore do not constitute an obligation to the insurance company by the employees. Rather, these contributions represent an obligation to the employer by the employees and are commonly paid by payroll deduction. Subject to certain limitations, any employee contributions are determined by the employer or as a result of labor negotiations. Most states require that the employer pay at least a portion of the premium for group term life insurance (but not for other group insurance coverage), and a few states impose limitations on the amounts that may be paid by any employee.

Premiums are payable in advance to the insurance company or any authorized agent for the time period specified in the contract. In most cases, premiums are payable monthly but may be paid less frequently. The rates used to determine the premium for any policyholder are guaranteed for a certain length of time, usually one year. The periodic premium is determined by applying these rates to the amount of life insurance in force. Consequently, the premium actually payable will change each month as the total amount of life insurance in force under the group insurance plan varies. A detailed explanation of premium computations is contained in the discussion on group insurance rate making in Chapter 15.

Group insurance contracts state that any dividends or experience refunds are payable to the policyholder in cash or may be used at the policyholder's option to reduce any premium due. To the extent that these exceed the policyholder's share of the premium, they must be used for the employees' benefit. This is usually accomplished by reducing employee contributions or increasing benefits.

Claims

The provision concerning death claims under group life insurance policies is very simple. It states that the amount of insurance under the contract is payable when the insurance company receives written proof of death. No time period is specified in which a claim must be filed. However, most companies require that the policyholder and the beneficiary complete a brief form before a claim is processed.

Assignment

For many years, the owners of individual life insurance policies have been able to transfer any or all of their rights under the insurance contract to another party. Such assignments have been commonly used to avoid federal estate taxation by removing the proceeds of an insurance contract from the insured's estate at death. Historically, assignments have not been permitted under group life insurance contracts, often because of state laws and regulations prohibiting them. In recent years, most states have eliminated such prohibitions; consequently, many insurance companies have modified their contracts to permit assignments, or they will waive the prohibition upon request. Essentially, an assignment is valid as long as it is permitted by and conforms with state law and the group insurance contract. Insurance companies generally require any assignment to be in writing and to be filed with the company.

Grace Period

Group life insurance contracts allow for a grace period (almost always 31 days) during which a policyholder may pay any overdue premium without interest. If the premium is not paid, the contract will lapse at the end of the grace period unless the policyholder has notified the insurance company that an earlier termination should take place. Even if the policy is allowed to lapse or is terminated during the grace period, the policyholder is legally liable for the payment of any premium due during the portion of the grace period when the contract was still in force.

Entire Contract

The entire-contract clause states that the insurance policy, the policyholder's application that is attached to the policy, and any individual (unattached) applications of any insured persons constitute the entire insurance contract. All statements made in these applications are considered to be representations rather than warranties, and no other statements made by the policyholder or by any insureds can be used by the insurance company as the basis for contesting coverage. When compared with the application for individual life insurance, the policyholder's application that is attached to a group insurance contract may be relatively short. Often, most of the information needed by the insurance company is contained in a preliminary application that is not part of the insurance contract. When a group insurance contract is delivered to the policyowner, it is common practice to have the policyholder sign a final "acceptance application," which in effect states that the coverage as applied for has been delivered. Consequently, a greater burden is placed on the insurance company to verify the statements made by the policyholder in the preliminary application.

The entire-contract clause also stipulates that no agent has any authority to waive or amend any provisions of the insurance contract and that a waiver of or amendment to the contract is valid only if certain specified corporate officers of the insurance company have signed it.

Incontestability

Like individual life insurance contracts, group insurance contracts contain an incontestability provision. Except for the nonpayment of premiums, the validity of the contract cannot be contested after it has been in force for a specified period, generally either one or two years. During this time, the insurance company can contest the contract on the basis of policyholder statements in the application attached to the contract that are considered to be material misrepresentations. Statements made by any insured person can be used as the basis for denying claims during this period only if such statements relate to the individual's insurability. In addition, the statements must have been made in a written application signed by the individual, and a copy of the application must have been furnished to either the individual or his or her beneficiary. It should be pointed out that the incontestability clause does not concern most covered persons because evidence of insurability is not usually required and, thus, no statements about individual insurability tend to be made.

Misstatement of Age

If the age of any person covered under a group term life insurance policy is misstated, the benefit payable is the amount that is specified under the benefit schedule. However, the premium is adjusted to reflect the true age of the individual. This is in contrast to individual life insurance contracts, where benefits are adjusted to the amount that the premium paid would have purchased at the true age of the individual. Under a group insurance contract, the responsibility for paying any additional premium or the right to receive a refund belongs to the policyholder and not to the individual employee whose age is misstated, even if the plan is contributory. If the misstated age has affected the employee's contribution, this is a matter to be resolved between the employer and the employee.

Termination

All group insurance contracts stipulate the conditions under which either the insurance company or the policyholder may terminate the contract. The circumstances under which the coverage for a particular insured person will terminate are also specified.

A group term life insurance contract can be terminated for nonpayment of the premium at the end of the grace period. Insurance companies may also terminate coverage for an individual employer group on any premium due date if certain conditions exist and notice of termination has been given to the policyholder at least 31 days in advance. These conditions include the failure to maintain a stated minimum number of participants in the plan and, in contributory plans, the failure to maintain a stated minimum percentage participation. The policyholder may also terminate the contract at any time by giving the insurance company 31 days' advance written notice. Moreover, the policyholder has the right to request an amendment of the contract at any time by notifying the insurance company.

The coverage for any insured person terminates automatically (subject to any provisions for a continuation or conversion of coverage) when any of the following circumstances exist:

- The employee terminates employment.
- The employee ceases to be eligible (for example, if the employee no longer satisfies the full-time work requirement or no longer falls into a covered classification).
- The policyholder or the insurance company terminates the master contract.
- Any required contribution by the employee has not been made (generally because the employee has notified the policyholder to cease the required payroll deduction).

Temporary Interruption of Employment

Most group term life insurance contracts provide that the employer (but not individual employees) may elect to continue coverage on employees during temporary interruptions of active full-time employment. These may arise from leaves of absence, layoffs, or the inability to work because of illness or injury. The employer must continue paying the premium, and the coverage may be continued only for a relatively short period of time, such as three months, unless the time period is extended by mutual agreement between the employer and the insurance company.

Continuation of Coverage for Disabled Employees

Most group term life insurance contracts make some provision for the continuation of coverage on employees whose active employment has terminated due to disability. By far the most common provision in use today is the *waiver-of-premium provision* (sometimes called an *extended death benefit*). Under this provision, life insurance coverage is continued without the payment of premiums as long as the employee is totally disabled, even if the master contract is terminated. However, certain requirements must be met:

- The disability must commence while the employee is insured under the master contract.
- The disability must begin prior to a specified age, commonly age 60.

- The employee must be totally disabled. *Total disability* is normally defined as the employee's complete inability to engage in any gainful occupation for which he or she is or becomes qualified by reason of education, training, or experience.
- The disability must have lasted continuously for a specified time, often six or nine months.
- The employee must file a claim within a prescribed period (normally 12 months) and must submit annual evidence of continuing disability.

If an employee no longer meets the definition of disability and returns to work, the employee may again be insured under the group insurance contract on a premium-paying basis as long as the employee meets the contract's eligibility requirements. If for any reason the employee is not eligible for insurance under the group insurance contract, he or she can exercise the conversion privilege, discussed in the following section.

A small but growing trend is for disabled employees to continue as eligible employees under a group insurance contract, with the employer paying the periodic cost of their coverage just as if they were active employees. At the termination of the contract, the insurance company has no responsibility to continue coverage unless a disabled employee is eligible, elects to convert coverage, and pays any required premiums. However, depending on the provisions of the group insurance plan, the employer may have a legal responsibility to continue coverage on disabled employees in some manner.

Conversion

All group term life insurance contracts covering employees contain a conversion privilege that gives any employee whose group coverage ceases the right to convert to an individual insurance policy. The terms of the conversion privilege vary, depending on the reason for termination of coverage under the group contract. The most generous conversion rights are available to those employees who either have terminated employment or no longer fall into one of the eligible classifications still covered by the master contract. These employees have the right to purchase an individual life insurance policy from the insurance company without evidence of insurability, but it is often one without accidental death or dismemberment or other supplementary benefits. However, this right is subject to the following conditions:

- The employee must apply for conversion within 31 days after termination of employment or membership in an eligible classification. During this 31-day period, the employee's death benefit is equal to the amount of life insurance that is available under the conversion privilege, even if the employee does not apply for conversion. Disability and supplementary benefits are not extended during this period unless they are also subject to conversion.

The premium for the individual policy must accompany the conversion application, and coverage is effective at the end of the conversion period.

- The individual policy selected by the employee generally may be any form, except term insurance, that the insurance company customarily issues at the age and amount applied for. Some insurance companies also make term insurance coverage available, and a few states require that employees be allowed to purchase term insurance coverage for a limited time (such as one year), after which an employee must convert to a cash-value form of coverage.

- The face amount of the individual policy may not exceed the amount of life insurance that terminated under the group insurance contract.

- The premium for the individual policy is determined using the insurance company's current rate applicable to the type and amount of the individual policy for the employee's attained age on the date of conversion and for the class of risk to which the employee belongs. Although no extra premium may be charged for reasons of health, an extra premium may be charged for any other hazards considered in an insurance company's rate structure, such as occupation or avocation.

It is estimated that only 1 percent to 2 percent of eligible employees actually take advantage of the conversion privilege. Several reasons account for this. Many employees obtain coverage with new employers; others are discouraged by the high cost of the permanent insurance to which they must convert. Still others, if they are insurable at standard rates, may find coverage at a lower cost with other insurers and be able to purchase supplementary coverage (such as disability benefits) that are not available under conversion policies. In addition, insurance companies have not actively encouraged group conversions because those who convert tend to be the poorer risks. Finally, because some employers are faced with conversion charges as a result of experience rating (see Chapter 15), they are also unlikely to encourage conversion.

There is a more restrictive conversion privilege if an employee's coverage is terminated because the master contract is terminated for all employees or is amended to eliminate eligible classifications. Under these circumstances, the employee is given a conversion right only if he or she was insured under the contract for a period of time (generally five years) immediately preceding the date on which coverage was terminated. In addition, the amount of insurance that can be converted is limited to the lesser of (1) $2,000 or (2) the amount of the employee's life insurance under the contract at the date of termination.

Portability of Term Coverage

A few, but an increasing number of, insurers issue contracts with a portability provision that allows employees whose coverage terminates to continue coverage at group rates in much the same manner as is found in voluntary employee-pay-all plans. The rates are age-based and will continue to increase as an insured person ages. Depending on the insurance company, the experience of this class of business may or may not be charged back to the former employer when future renewal rates are determined.

Accelerated Benefits

Over the last several years, many insurers have introduced an accelerated benefits provision in their individual life insurance products. Under such a provision, an insured is entitled to receive a portion of his or her death benefit while still living if one or more of the following events apply: (1) the diagnosis of a terminal illness that is expected to result in death within 6 to 12 months; (2) the occurrence of a specified catastrophic illness, such as AIDS, a stroke, or Alzheimer's Disease; or (3) the incurring of nursing home and possibly other long-term care expenses. The categories of triggering events and the specific definitions of each vary among insurers.

What becomes popular in the individual marketplace often starts to show up in the group insurance marketplace. Such is the case with accelerated benefits, which are now offered by most group insurers. In fact, many group insurers make accelerated death benefits a part of their standard group term coverage unless an employer does not want the benefit provided.

Most group insurers allow accelerated benefits for terminal illnesses only. Some insurers use a life expectancy of 6 months or less; most use a life expectancy of 12 months or less. In either case, a doctor must certify the life expectancy.

The amount of the accelerated benefit is expressed as a percentage of the basic life insurance coverage and may range from 25 percent to 100 percent. In addition, most insurers limit the maximum benefit to a specified dollar amount that may vary from $25,000 to $250,000. Any amount not accelerated is paid to the beneficiary upon the insured's death.

There are no limitations on how the accelerated benefit can be used. It might be used to pay medical expenses and nursing home care not covered by other insurance, or it could even be used to prepay funeral expenses.

Although some insurers make no charge for the inclusion of an accelerated death benefit, most do levy some type of charge. In some cases, this may be a higher premium levied on the policyowner. In other cases, any accelerated death benefit paid will be reduced by an amount equal to the interest that could have been earned on the money over the next 6 to 12 months. Finally, a few insurers levy a modest transaction charge when an accelerated death benefit is taken.

ADDED COVERAGES

Group term life insurance contracts often provide additional insurance benefits. Historically, these have been added through the use of riders, but many insurers now incorporate some or all of these benefits into their basic term insurance contracts. The most common types of these benefits, which are also forms of group term insurance, are (1) supplemental life insurance, (2) accidental death and dismemberment insurance, and (3) dependent life insurance. These added benefits may be provided for all employees insured under the basic group term contract or may be limited to certain classes of employees. With the exception of dependent life insurance, these coverages may also be written as separate contracts.

Supplemental Life Insurance

The majority of group life insurance plans enable all or certain classes of employees to purchase additional amounts of life insurance. Generally, the employer provides a basic amount of life insurance to all eligible employees on a noncontributory basis. This is commonly a flat amount of coverage or a multiple of annual earnings. The supplemental coverage is contributory and may be either incorporated into the basic group life insurance contract or contained in a separate contract. The latter method tends to be more common when the supplemental coverage is available only to a select group of employees. The employee may pay the entire cost of the supplemental coverage; however, state laws that require employer contributions or insurance company underwriting practices often result in the employer's paying a portion of the cost. It is not unusual for there to be two sets of rates—one for smokers and another for nonsmokers.

The amount of supplemental coverage available is specified in a benefit schedule. Under some plans, an employee must purchase the full amount of coverage; under other plans, an employee may purchase a portion of the coverage. Tables 6-3 and 6-4 are two examples of benefit schedules for a basic-plus-supplemental life insurance plan.

Giving employees the right to choose their benefit amounts leads to adverse selection. As a result, more stringent underwriting requirements are usually associated with supplemental coverage. These often include requiring individual evidence of insurability, except possibly when the additional amount of coverage is modest. In addition, higher rates may be charged for supplemental insurance than for basic coverage.

TABLE 6-3
Benefit Schedule (Flat Amount)

Type of Coverage	Amount of Life Insurance
Basic insurance	$25,000
Supplemental insurance	50,000

TABLE 6-4
Benefit Schedule (Multiple of Annual Earnings)

Type of Coverage	Amount of Life Insurance
Basic insurance	1 times salary
Supplemental insurance	1/2, 1, 1 1/2, or 2 times salary, subject to a maximum (including basic insurance) of $250,000

Accidental Death and Dismemberment Insurance

Many group life insurance contracts contain an accidental death and dismemberment (AD&D) provision that supplies additional benefits if an employee dies accidentally or suffers certain types of injuries. Traditionally, this group coverage was available only as a rider to a group life insurance contract. Now, however, it is common to find these benefits in separate group insurance contracts in which coverage is usually contributory on the part of employees. Such contracts are referred to as *voluntary accidental death and dismemberment insurance.* There are also separate contracts, called *carve-outs,* that employers can purchase to replace the employer-paid coverage available from their group life insurance carrier. These contracts are used because of more favorable provisions and/or cost savings.

Traditional Coverage

Under the traditional form of accidental death and dismemberment insurance, an employee eligible for group life insurance coverage (and electing the life insurance coverage if it is contributory) automatically receives accidental death and dismemberment coverage if the employer has added it or purchased an AD&D carve-out. A few plans impose a probationary period, such as six months, before coverage begins. Under the typical accidental death and dismemberment rider, the insurance company pays an additional amount of insurance that is equal to the amount of coverage under the basic group life insurance contract (referred to as the *principal sum*) if an employee dies as a result of accidental bodily injuries while he or she is covered under the policy. It is specified that death must occur within a certain time, often 90 days, following the date that injuries are sustained, but some courts have ruled this time period to be invalid and have required insurance companies to pay claims when longer periods have been involved. In addition to an accidental death benefit, the benefit schedule shown in Table 6-5 is provided for certain specific types of injuries.

TABLE 6-5
Position Schedule Based on Type of Injury

Type of Injury	Benefit Amount
Loss of (including loss of use of):	
Both hands or both feet	The principal sum
The sight of both eyes	The principal sum
One hand and sight of one eye	The principal sum
One foot and sight of one eye	The principal sum
One foot and one hand	The principal sum
One hand	One-half the principal sum
One foot	One-half the principal sum
The sight of one eye	One-half the principal sum

TABLE 6-6
Position Schedule Based on Type of Loss

Type of Loss	Benefit Amount
Death while traveling on business when occupying, boarding, alighting from, or struck by any motor vehicle, airplane, or other conveyance, including company-owned or personally owned vehicles	3 times the principal sum
Death at all other times	2 times the principal sum
Dismemberment	Up to the principal sum (as shown in Table 6-5)

In some cases, the accidental death and dismemberment rider is written to provide the same benefits for any accident covered under the contract. However, it is not unusual to have a higher level of benefits for accidents that occur while the employee is traveling on business for the employer. These larger travel benefits may apply to death benefits only. They may also be limited to accidents that occur, for example, when the employee is occupying (or entering or alighting from or struck by) a public conveyance and possibly a company-owned or personally owned vehicle. Table 6-6 is an example of a benefit schedule reflecting some of these variations.

Death benefits are paid in accordance with the beneficiary provision of the group life insurance contract, and dismemberment benefits are paid to the employee. Coverage is usually written to cover both occupational and nonoccupational accidents. However, when employees are in hazardous occupations, coverage may apply only to nonoccupational accidents, in which case employees would still have workers' compensation coverage for any occupational accidents.

Some insurers also pay an additional benefit if an insured suffers a covered loss as the result of an automobile accident, as long as the insured is wearing a properly fastened seat belt and is not under the influence of alcohol. Other insurers may include additional educational benefits for dependent children. For competitive reasons, some insurers make a number of additional benefits available for purchase by the employer to cover an employee who is injured or killed in a covered accident. Some additional benefits include the following:

■ A benefit to help cover the costs an employer incurs to make worksite adaptations necessitated by the Americans with Disabilities Act to accommodate a disabled employee
■ A benefit to return an injured employee or the body of a deceased employee home if death or disability occurs elsewhere

- Rehabilitation benefits for an injured employee
- Monthly income benefits for an employee who is permanently disabled
- Monthly income benefits for an employee who becomes a paraplegic or quadriplegic, and
- Monthly income benefits for an employee who is in a coma

Coverage is usually not subject to a conversion privilege. However, an increasing number of insurers are allowing conversion, but possibly only up to specified limits that are lower than the former group coverage. When life insurance coverage continues after retirement, accidental death and dismemberment benefits normally cease. As with life insurance coverage, however, this coverage may be continued during temporary periods of unemployment. In contrast to the group term insurance policy to which it is attached, group accidental death and dismemberment insurance contains some exclusions. These include losses resulting from the following:

- Suicide at any time (It is interesting to note that, except for a few multiple-employer trusts, group term insurance does not contain a suicide provision.)
- Disease or bodily or mental infirmity or medical or surgical treatment thereof
- Ptomaines or any infection other than one occurring simultaneously with and through an accidental cut or wound
- War
- Travel or flight in any type of aircraft as a pilot, student pilot, or officer or member of the crew (There is a trend toward eliminating this exclusion, particularly when coverage is written on large groups)

Voluntary Coverage

The provisions of voluntary group accidental death and dismemberment insurance are practically identical to those in a group life insurance contract with an accidental death and dismemberment insurance rider. However, there are a few differences. Voluntary plans usually require that the employee pay the entire cost of coverage, and they virtually always provide both occupational and nonoccupational coverage. Subject to limitations, the employee may select the amount of coverage desired, and the maximum amount of coverage available tends to be larger than when coverage is provided through a rider. For example, one plan allows coverage to be purchased at the following levels: $50,000, $75,000, $100,000, $200,000, $300,000, or $500,000, as long as the amount selected does not exceed ten times annual salary. The amount of coverage often decreases after age 65 or 70, just as the amount of traditional coverage decreases when it is a function of a life insurance benefit that is decreased at older ages.

Yet another difference is the frequent use in voluntary plans of a common accident provision, whereby the amount payable by the insurance company is limited to a stipulated maximum for all employees killed or injured in any single accident. If this exceeds the sum of the benefits otherwise payable for each employee, benefits are prorated.

A final difference is that some plans allow an employee to purchase coverage on dependents. For example, under one plan the coverage on a spouse is equal to 40 percent of the coverage on the employee, and coverage on each child is 10 percent of the employee's coverage. When dependent coverage is purchased, some insurers make a variety of optional benefits available. Some of these include the following:

- Education benefits for children enrolled in a university, college, or trade school following an employee's death
- Additional dismemberment benefits for children who periodically need to be refitted with prosthetic devices as they grow
- Day care expense coverage for children if the day care is necessitated by the death of a parent
- Benefits to pay the cost of a family's COBRA coverage after the death of an employee
- An additional benefit to the children if both parents are killed in the same accident

Dependent Life Insurance

Some group life insurance contracts provide insurance coverage on the lives of employees' dependents. Dependent life insurance has been viewed as a method of giving the employee resources to meet the funeral and burial expenses associated with a dependent's death. Consequently, the employee is automatically the beneficiary. The employee also elects and pays for this coverage if it is contributory. Coverage for dependents is almost always limited to employees who are themselves covered under the group contract; even if an employee's coverage is contributory, the employee must elect coverage for himself or herself in order to be eligible to elect dependent coverage.

For purposes of dependent life insurance coverage, dependents are usually defined as an employee's spouse who is not legally separated from the employee and an employee's unmarried dependent children (including stepchildren and adopted children) who are older than 14 days of age and younger than some specified age, commonly 19 or 21. To prevent adverse selection, an employee usually cannot select coverage for individual dependents. A few policies do allow an employee to elect coverage for the spouse only or for children only. If dependent coverage is selected, all dependents fitting the definition are insured. When dependent coverage is in effect for an employee, any new eligible dependents are automatically insured.

The amount of coverage for each dependent is usually quite modest. Some states limit the maximum amount of life insurance that can be written, and a few states actually prohibit writing any coverage on dependents. Employer contributions used to purchase more than $2,000 of coverage for each dependent are recognized as income to the employee for purposes of federal taxation. However, amounts in excess of $2,000 may be purchased with employee contributions without adverse tax consequences. In some cases, the same amount of coverage is provided for all dependents; in other cases, a larger amount is provided for the spouse than for the children. It is also not unusual for the amount of coverage for children to be less until the children attain some specified age, such as six months. Tables 6-7 and 6-8 are examples of benefit schedules under dependent coverage.

A single premium applies to the dependent coverage for each employee and is unrelated to the number of dependents. In some cases, the premium may vary, depending on the age of the employee (but not the dependents), but more commonly it is the same amount for all employees regardless of age. Dependent coverage usually contains a conversion privilege that applies only to the coverage on the spouse. However, some states require that the conversion privilege apply to the coverage on all dependents. Assignment is almost never permitted, and no waiver of premium is available if a dependent becomes disabled. However, if the basic life insurance contract contains a waiver-of-premium provision applicable to the employee, the employee's disability sometimes will result in a waiver of premium for the dependent coverage. A provision similar to the actively-at-work provision pertaining to employees is often included for dependents. It specifies that dependents are not covered when otherwise eligible if they are confined in a hospital (except for newborn children, who are covered after 14 days). Coverage commences when the dependent is discharged from the hospital.

TABLE 6-7
Benefit Schedule (Same Amounts for All Dependents)

Class	Amount of Insurance
Each dependent	$2,000

TABLE 6-8
Benefit Schedule for Dependents (Varied Amounts)

Class	Amount of Insurance
Spouse	50% of the employee's insured amount, subject to a maximum of $5,000
Dependent children: at least 14 days old but less than 6 months of age	$ 500
6 months of age or older	$1,000

TAXATION

A discussion of group term insurance is incomplete without an explanation of the tax laws affecting its use. While discussions of these laws are often limited to federal income and estate taxation, federal gift taxation and taxation by the states should also be considered.

Federal Taxation

The growth of group term life insurance has been greatly influenced by the favorable tax treatment afforded it under federal tax laws. This section is devoted to the effects of these tax laws on basic group term insurance and on coverages that may be added to a basic group term life insurance contract.

Deductibility of Premiums

In general, employer contributions for an employee's group term life insurance coverage are fully deductible by the employer under Code Section 162 as an ordinary and necessary business expense as long as the employee's overall compensation is reasonable. The reasonableness of compensation (which includes wages, salary, and other fringe benefits) is usually only a potential issue for the owners of small businesses or the stockholder-employees of closely held corporations. For income tax purposes, a firm may not deduct any compensation that the Internal Revenue Service (IRS) determines to be unreasonable. In addition, the Internal Revenue Code does not allow a firm to take an income tax deduction for contributions (1) that are made on behalf of sole proprietors or partners under any circumstances or (2) that are made on behalf of stockholders unless they are providing substantive services to the corporation. Finally, no deduction is allowed under Code Section 264 if the employer is named as beneficiary.

Contributions by any individual employee are considered payments for personal life insurance and are not deductible for income tax purposes by that employee. Thus, the amount of any payroll deductions authorized by an employee for group term insurance purposes is included in the employee's taxable income.

Employees' Income Tax Liability

In the absence of tax laws to the contrary, the amount of any compensation for which an employer receives an income tax deduction (including the payment of group insurance premiums) represents taxable income to the employee. However, Section 79 of the Internal Revenue Code gives favorable tax treatment to employer contributions for life insurance that qualifies as group term insurance.

Section 79 Requirements. To qualify as group term insurance under Section 79, life insurance must meet the following conditions:

- It must provide a death benefit excludable from federal income taxation.
- It must be given to a group of employees, defined to include all employees of an employer. If all employees are not covered, membership must be determined on the basis of age, marital status, or factors relating to employment.

- It must be provided under a policy carried directly or indirectly by the employer. A policy is defined to include a master contract or a group of individual policies. The term *carried indirectly* refers to those situations when the employer is not the policyholder but rather provides coverage to employees through master contracts issued to organizations such as negotiated trusteeships or multiple-employer welfare arrangements.
- The plan must be arranged to preclude individual selection of coverage amounts. However, it is acceptable to have alternative benefit schedules based on the amount an employee elects to contribute. Supplemental plans that give an employee a choice, such as either 1, 1½, or 2 times salary, are considered to fall within this category. An employee can be allowed to reject coverage in excess of $50,000 if he or she does not want any imputed income.

All life insurance that qualifies under Section 79 as group term insurance is considered to be a single plan of insurance, regardless of the number of insurance contracts used. For example, an employer might provide coverage for union employees under a negotiated trusteeship, coverage for other employees under an individual employer group insurance contract, and additional coverage for top executives under a group of individual life insurance policies. Under Section 79, these all constitute a single plan. This plan must be provided for at least ten full-time employees at some time during the calendar year. For purposes of meeting the "ten-life" requirement, employees who have not satisfied any required waiting periods may be counted as participants. Employees who have elected not to participate are also counted as participants—but only if they would not have been required to contribute to the cost of other benefits besides group term insurance if they had participated. As is described later, a plan with fewer than ten full-time employees may still qualify for favorable tax treatment under Section 79 if it meets more restrictive requirements.

Exceptions to Section 79. Even when all the previous requirements are met, there are some situations in which Section 79 does not apply. In some cases, different sections of the Internal Revenue Code provide alternative tax treatment. For example, when group term insurance is issued to the trustees of a qualified pension plan and is used to provide a death benefit under the plan, the full amount of any life insurance paid for by employer contributions results in taxable income to the employee, as discussed in Chapter 21.

There are three situations in which employer contributions for group term insurance do not result in taxable income to an employee, regardless of the amount of insurance: (1) if an employee has terminated employment because of disability, (2) if a qualified charity (as determined by the Internal Revenue Code) has been named as beneficiary for the entire year, or (3) if the employer has been named as beneficiary for the entire year.

Coverage for retired employees is subject to Section 79, and these persons are treated in the same manner as active employees. Thus, they have taxable income in any year in which the amount of coverage received exceeds $50,000.

However, a grandfather clause to this rule stipulates that it does not apply to group term life insurance plans (or to comparable successor plans or plans of successor employers) in existence on January 1, 1984, for covered employees who (1) retired before 1984 or (2) were at least 55 years of age before 1984 and were employed by the employer any time during 1983. There is one exception to this grandfather clause; it does not apply to persons (either key or nonkey employees) retiring after 1986 if a plan is discriminatory.

General Tax Rules. Under Section 79, the cost of the first $50,000 of coverage is not taxed to the employee. Because all group term insurance provided by an employer that qualifies under Section 79 is considered to be one plan, this exclusion applies only once to each employee. For example, an employee who has $10,000 of coverage that is provided to all employees under one policy and $75,000 of coverage provided to executives under a separate insurance policy would have a single $50,000 exclusion. The cost of coverage in excess of $50,000, minus any employee contributions for the entire amount of coverage, represents taxable income to the employee. For purposes of Section 79, the cost of this excess coverage is determined by a government table called the *Uniform Premium Table I* (see Table 6-9). This table was revised in 1999 with significantly lower costs.

To calculate the cost of an employee's coverage for one month of protection under a group term insurance plan, the Uniform Premium Table I cost shown for the employee's age bracket (based on the employee's attained age at the end of the tax year) is multiplied by the number of thousands in excess of 50 of group term insurance on the employee. For example, if an employee aged 57 (whose Table I monthly cost is $.43 per $1,000 of coverage) is provided with $150,000 of group term insurance, the employee's monthly cost (assuming no employee contributions) is calculated as follows:

TABLE 6-9
Uniform Premium Table I

Age	Cost per Month per $1,000 of Coverage
24 and under	$ .05
25–29	.06
30–34	.08
35–39	.09
40–44	.10
45–49	.15
50–54	.23
55–59	.43
60–64	.66
65–69	1.27
70 and over	2.06

Coverage provided	$150,000
Minus Section 79 exclusion	–50,000
Amount subject to taxation	$100,000

Monthly cost = $.43 ÷ $1,000 × $100,000 = $43

The monthly costs are then totaled to obtain an annual cost. Assuming no change in the amount of coverage during the year, the annual cost is $43 × 12, or $516. Any employee contributions for the entire amount of coverage are deducted from the annual cost to determine the taxable income that an employee must report. If an employee contributes $.25 per month ($3 per year) per $1,000 of coverage, the employee's total annual contribution for $150,000 of coverage is $450. This reduces the amount reportable as taxable income from $516 to $66. Note that if the employee contribution is $.30 rather than $.25 per month, the annual employee contribution in this example is $540. Because $540 exceeds the Table I cost, there is no imputed income.

One final point is worthy of attention. The use of Uniform Premium Table I results in favorable tax treatment for the cost of group term insurance when the monthly costs in the table are lower than the actual cost of coverage in the marketplace. However, group term insurance coverage can often be purchased at a lower cost than Table I rates. There are some who argue that in these instances the actual cost of coverage can be used in place of the Table I cost for determining an employee's taxable income. From the standpoint of logic and consistency with the tax laws, this view makes sense. However, the regulations for Section 79 are very specific: Only Table I costs are to be used.

Nondiscrimination Rules. Any plan that qualifies as group term insurance under Section 79 is subject to nondiscrimination rules, and the $50,000 exclusion will not be available to key employees if a plan is discriminatory, defined as a plan that favors key employees in either eligibility or benefits. In addition, the value of the full amount of coverage for key employees, less their own contribution, will be considered taxable income, based on the greater of actual or Table I costs. (The actual cost of discriminatory coverage is determined by a complex process that is not covered in this book. See Internal Revenue Code Reg. 1.79-4T.)

A key employee of a firm is defined as any person who at any time during the current plan year or the preceding four plan years is any of the following:

- An officer of the firm who earns from the firm more than 50 percent of the Internal Revenue Code limit on the amount of benefits payable by a defined-benefit plan. This amount (50 percent of $135,000, or $67,500, for 2000) is indexed annually. For purposes of this rule, the number of employees treated as officers is the greater of three employees or 10 percent of the firm's employees, subject to a maximum of 50. In applying the rule the following employees can be excluded: persons who work part time, persons who are under age 21, and persons with less than six months of service with the firm.
- One of the ten employees owning the largest interest in the firm and having an annual compensation from the firm of more than $30,000.
- An individual who owns more than 5 percent of the firm.
- An individual who owns more than 1 percent of the firm and who earns over $150,000 per year.

Note that the definition of key employee includes not only active employees but also retired employees who were key employees at the time of retirement or separation from service.

Eligibility requirements are not discriminatory if (1) at least 70 percent of all employees are eligible, (2) at least 85 percent of all employees who are participants are not key employees, (3) participants constitute a classification that the IRS determines is nondiscriminatory, or (4) the group term insurance plan is part of a cafeteria plan and Section 125 requirements are satisfied. For purposes of the 70 percent test, employees with less than three years' service, part-time employees, and seasonal employees may be excluded. Employees covered by collective-bargaining agreements may also be excluded if plan benefits were the subject of good-faith bargaining.

Benefits are not discriminatory if neither the type nor amount of benefits discriminates in favor of key employees. It is permissible to base benefits on a uniform percentage of salary.

Groups with Fewer than Ten Full-Time Employees. A group insurance plan that covers fewer than ten employees must satisfy an additional set of requirements before it is eligible for favorable tax treatment under Section 79. These rules predate the general nondiscrimination rules previously described, and it was assumed that the "under-ten" rules would be abolished when the new rules were adopted. However, that was not done, so smaller groups are subject to two separate and somewhat overlapping sets of rules. Again, note that Section 79 applies to an employer's overall plan of group insurance, not to separate group insurance contracts. For example, an employer providing group insurance coverage for its 50 hourly employees under one group insurance contract and for its six executives under a separate contract is considered to have a single plan covering 56 employees and thus is exempt from the "under-ten" requirements. While the stated purpose of the "under-ten" requirements is to preclude selection of coverage by individual employees, their effect is to prevent the group insurance plan from discriminating in favor of the owners or stockholder-employees of small businesses.

With some exceptions, plans covering fewer than ten employees must provide coverage for all full-time employees. For purposes of this requirement, employees who are not customarily employed for more than 20 hours in any one week or five months in any calendar year are considered part-time employees. It is permissible to exclude full-time employees from coverage under the following circumstances:

- The employee has reached age 65.
- The employee has not satisfied the plan's probationary period, which may not exceed six months.
- The employee has elected not to participate in the plan, but only if the employee would not have been required to contribute to the cost of other benefits besides group term life insurance if he or she had participated.

■ The employee has not satisfied the evidence of insurability required under the plan. An employee's eligibility for insurance (or the amount of insurance on the employee's life) may be subject to evidence of insurability. However, this evidence of insurability must be determined solely on the basis of a medical questionnaire completed by the employee and not by a medical examination.

The amount of coverage must be a flat amount, a uniform percentage of compensation, or an amount based on different employee classifications. These employee classifications, which are referred to as *coverage brackets* in Section 79, may be determined in the manner described earlier in this chapter in the section on benefit schedules. The amount of coverage for each employee in any classification may be no greater than 2½ times the amount of coverage provided to each employee in the next lower classification. In addition, each employee in the lowest classification must be provided with an amount of coverage that is equal to at least 10 percent of the amount for each employee in the highest classification. There must also be a reasonable expectation that there will be at least one employee in each classification. The benefit schedule shown in Table 6-10 is unacceptable for two reasons. First, the amount of coverage provided for the hourly employees is only 5 percent of the amount of coverage provided for the president. Second, the amount of coverage for the supervisor is more than 2½ times the amount of coverage provided for the hourly employees. The benefit schedule in Table 6-11, however, is acceptable.

TABLE 6-10
Unacceptable Benefit Schedule

Classification	Amount of Coverage
President	$100,000
Supervisor	40,000
Hourly employee	5,000

TABLE 6-11
Acceptable Benefit Schedule

Classification	Amount of Insurance
President	$100,000
Supervisor	40,000
Hourly employee	20,000

If a group insurance plan that covers fewer than ten employees does not qualify for favorable tax treatment under Section 79, any premiums paid by the employer for such coverage represent taxable income to the employees. The employer, however, still receives an income tax deduction for any premiums paid on behalf of the employees as long as overall compensation is reasonable.

Taxation of Proceeds

In most instances, Code Section 101 provides that the death proceeds under a group term insurance contract do not result in any taxable income to the beneficiary if they are paid in a lump sum. If the proceeds are payable in installments over more than one taxable year, only the interest earnings attributable to the proceeds are included in the beneficiary's income for tax purposes.

Under certain circumstances, the proceeds are not exempt from income taxation if the coverage was transferred (either in whole or in part) for a valuable consideration. Such a situation arises when the stockholder-employees of a corporation name each other as beneficiaries under their group term insurance coverage as a method of funding a buy-sell agreement. The mutual agreement to name each other as beneficiaries is the valuable consideration. Under these circumstances, any proceeds paid to a beneficiary constitute ordinary income to the extent that the proceeds exceed the beneficiary's tax basis, as determined by the Internal Revenue Code.

In many cases, benefits paid by an employer to employees or their beneficiaries from the firm's assets receive the same tax treatment as benefits provided under an insurance contract. This is not true for death benefits. If they are provided other than through an insurance contract, the amount of the proceeds represents taxable income to the beneficiary. For this reason, employers are less likely to use alternative funding arrangements for death benefits than for disability and medical expense benefits.

Under Code Section 2042, the proceeds of a group term insurance contract, even if paid to a named beneficiary, are included in an employee's gross estate for federal estate tax purposes as long as the employee possessed incidents of ownership in the coverage at the time of death. However, no estate tax is levied on any amounts, including life insurance proceeds, left to a surviving spouse. In addition, taxable estates of $675,000 or less are generally free of estate taxation regardless of the beneficiary.

When an estate would otherwise be subject to estate taxation, an employee may remove the proceeds of group term insurance from his or her taxable estate by absolutely assigning all incidents of ownership to another person, usually the beneficiary of the coverage. Incidents of ownership include the right to change the beneficiary, to terminate coverage, to assign coverage or, to exercise the conversion privilege. For this favorable treatment, however, the Internal Revenue Code requires that such an assignment be permissible under both the group term insurance master contract and the laws of the state having jurisdiction. The absolute assignment is usually in the form of a gift, which is not without its own tax implications. The amount of insurance is considered a gift made each year by the employee to the person to whom the absolute assignment was granted. Consequently, if the value of the gift is of sufficient size, federal gift taxes are payable.

The assignment of group term life insurance also results in the inclusion of some values in the employee's estate. If the employee dies within three years of making the assignment, the full amount of the proceeds are included in the employee's estate. If death occurs more than three years after the assignment is made, only the premiums paid within the three years prior to death are included in the employee's taxable estate. In the past, a problem arose if the employer changed group insurance carriers, thus requiring the employee to make a new assignment and again be subject to the three-year time limit. However, the IRS now considers this type of situation to be a continuation of the original assignment as long as the amount and provisions of the new coverage are essentially the same as those of the old coverage.

As of 1997, the tax treatment of accelerated death benefits was added to the Internal Revenue Code. If certain requirements are satisfied, benefits paid to persons who are either terminally or chronically ill will receive favorable tax treatment. Benefits received because of a terminal illness are treated as income-tax-free death benefits as long as a physician has certified that the insured has an illness or physical condition that can reasonably be expected to result in death within 24 months or less after the date of certification. If a group contract provides accelerated death benefits to other categories of individuals, benefits can also be received with favorable tax treatment if a person is chronically ill and the coverage qualifies as a long-term care insurance contract. The definition of *chronically ill* and the conditions to qualify as a long-term care insurance contract are discussed when group long-term care insurance is covered in a later chapter.

Treatment of Added Coverages

Supplemental life insurance can be written as either a separate contract or as part of the contract providing basic group term life insurance coverage. If it is a separate contract and if the supplemental group life insurance meets the conditions of qualifying as group term insurance under Section 79, the amount of coverage provided is added to all other group term insurance for purposes of calculating the Uniform Premium Table I cost. Any premiums the employee pays for the supplemental coverage are included in the deduction used to determine the final taxable income. In all other ways, supplemental life insurance is treated the same as group term insurance.

Many separate supplemental contracts are noncontributory, and the cost for each employee's coverage does not exceed the Table I cost. In this case, the supplemental contract does not qualify as group term life insurance under Section 79. As a result, the value of the coverage is not included in an employee's income.

When supplemental life insurance coverage is written in conjunction with a basic group life insurance plan, employers have the option of treating the supplemental coverage as a separate policy of insurance as long as the premiums are properly allocated among the two portions of the coverage. There is no advantage in treating the supplemental coverage as a separate policy if it would still qualify by itself as group term insurance under Section 79. However, this election minimizes taxable income to employees if the cost of the supplemental coverage is paid totally by the employees and all employees are charged rates at or below Table I rates.

Premiums paid for accidental death and dismemberment insurance are considered to be health insurance premiums rather than group term insurance premiums. However, as are group term life insurance premiums, these are deductible by the employer as an ordinary and necessary business expense. Benefits paid to an employee under the dismemberment portion of the coverage are treated as benefits received under a health insurance contract and are free of income taxation. Death benefits received under the coverage are treated like death benefits received under group term life insurance.

Employer contributions for dependent life insurance coverage are fully deductible by the employer as an ordinary and necessary business expense if the employee's overall compensation is reasonable. Employer contributions do not result in taxable income to an employee as long as the value of the benefit is *de minimis*. This means that the value is so small that it is administratively impractical for the employer to account for the cost on a per-person basis. Dependent coverage of $2,000 or less on any person falls into this category. If more than $2,000 of coverage is provided for any dependent from employer contributions, the cost of the entire amount of coverage for that dependent (as determined by Uniform Premium Table I rates) is considered taxable income to the employee.

Death benefits are free of income taxation and are not included in the dependent's taxable estate for estate tax purposes.

State Taxation

In most instances, state tax laws affecting group term insurance are similar to the federal laws. However, two major differences exist: In most states, the payment of group term insurance premiums by the employer does not result in any taxable income to the employee, even if the amount of coverage exceeds $50,000. In addition, death proceeds receive favorable tax treatment under the estate and inheritance tax laws of most states. Generally, the proceeds are at least partially, if not totally, exempt from such taxation.

STUDY QUESTIONS

1. Describe the following types of benefit schedules:
   a. Earnings schedules
   b. Position schedules
   c. Flat-benefit schedules

2. What are the criteria that generally must be satisfied before an employee is eligible for group term insurance coverage?

3. a. Under what circumstances is the assignment of group life insurance coverage valid?
   b. What requirements do insurance companies impose on assignments of group life insurance coverage?

4. The owner of the Midtown Garage decided to amend his group insurance contract to provide coverage for part-time employees. His agent said such a change presented no problem and wrote the owner a letter stating that the change had been

made. Two weeks later, the agent called and informed the owner that the insurance company had refused to amend the contract. Can the insurance company overrule its agent? Explain.

5. Describe the methods for continuing group term life insurance coverage for disabled employees.

6. Because of severe business difficulties, the Newtown Manufacturing Company permanently laid off 20 percent of its employees last March. All had been employed by the company for less than three years. In June, salaries and fringe benefits were reduced for the remaining employees. This included amending the company's group term insurance contract to eliminate all eligible classifications except those pertaining to four executives. Explain the extent, if any, to which the following groups of employees would have had the right to convert any coverage that was terminated under the plan:
   a. Employees who were laid off in March.
   b. Employees whose coverage was terminated in June.

7. What is the purpose of an accelerated death benefit?

8. How have insurance companies handled the problem of adverse selection associated with supplemental life insurance?

9. How may the amount of an accidental death benefit vary depending on when and how an employee dies?

10. How does dependent life insurance differ from group term life insurance for employees with respect to
   a. Conversion privilege?
   b. Ability to assign benefits?
   c. Availability of a waiver-of-premium provision?

11. What requirements must be met in order for life insurance to qualify as group term insurance under Code Section 79?

12. a. Last year, Sarah Robbins, aged 32, was provided with $75,000 of group term insurance by her employer for the entire year. Sarah is not a key employee, and the employer paid the entire premium. Using Table I, calculate the amount of Federal taxable income Sarah had because of this coverage.
   b. What if Sarah had contributed $3 per month for her coverage?

13. a. To what extent are group life insurance proceeds included in an employee's gross estate for federal estate tax purposes?
   b. What are the potential tax implications for an employee if an absolute assignment is used to remove life insurance proceeds from his or her estate?

Group Life Insurance: Lifetime Coverage

Group term life insurance plans were traditionally designed to provide employees with preretirement life insurance coverage. At retirement, an employee was faced with the decision of whether to let coverage terminate or to convert to an individual policy at an extremely high premium rate. In recent years, however, an increasing number of group life insurance plans have been designed to provide postretirement as well as preretirement life insurance coverage. In some cases, this has been accomplished by continuing group term insurance coverage, often at a reduced amount, after retirement. In other cases, this has been achieved by means of life insurance that provides permanent benefits funded during employees' working years.

The popularity of various approaches for providing postretirement life insurance coverage has changed over time, primarily because of changes in tax laws. Older and once popular products such as group paid-up insurance and group ordinary insurance are no longer written. Newer products like group universal life insurance and group variable universal life insurance have come on the scene and grown in popularity. This chapter discusses four approaches that are currently used:

1. Continuation of group term insurance
2. Group universal life insurance
3. Group variable universal life insurance
4. Group term carve-outs

CONTINUATION OF GROUP TERM INSURANCE

Most postretirement life insurance coverage consists of the continuation of group term insurance. This requires the employer to make important decisions regarding the amount of coverage to be continued and the method of paying for the continued coverage. Although the full amount of coverage prior to retirement may be continued, the high cost of group term life insurance coverage for older employees frequently results in a reduction in the amount of coverage. In some cases, employees are given a flat amount of coverage (such as $2,000 or $5,000); in other cases, employees are given a percentage (such as 50 percent) of the amount of coverage they had on the date of retirement.

Current Revenue Funding

The cost of providing postretirement life insurance is usually paid from current revenue, with each periodic premium the insurance company receives based on the lives of all employees covered, both active and retired. Because retired employees have no salaries or wages from which payroll deductions can be made, most postretirement life insurance coverage is noncontributory.

The tax implications of providing postretirement group term insurance on a current-revenue basis are the same for both the employer and the employee as those discussed in Chapter 6.

Retired-Lives Reserve To Continue Coverage

In the late 1970s and early 1980s, increasing interest was shown in pre-funding the cost of postretirement group term insurance coverage through retired-lives-reserve arrangements. Much of this interest stemmed from Internal Revenue Service Section 79 regulations that made previously popular products less attractive. The concept was not new; retired-lives reserves, while not extensively used prior to that time, had been in existence for many years, primarily for very large employers. However, the trend in the 1970s was to establish them for smaller employers because the tax laws allowed the plans to be designed so that they often provided significant benefits to the firm's owners or key employees. Because the Tax Reform Act of 1984 imposed more stringent requirements on retired-lives reserves and because of the availability of newer products for postretirement coverage, there is little interest in establishing new plans. Nevertheless, plans still exist, primarily in heavily unionized industries and usually for employers with 2,000 to 5,000 employees. In addition, other plans still exist for employees and retirees previously covered under them, but other arrangements are used for newer employees.

A retired-lives reserve is best defined as a fund established during employees' working years to pay all or a part of the cost of their group term insurance after retirement. The fund may be established and maintained through a trust or with an insurance company. If properly designed, a retired lives reserve (1) will enable an employer to make currently tax-deductible contributions to the fund during employees' working years and (2) will not result in any taxable income to employees before retirement. However, current deductions may be taken only for prefunding coverage that will be received tax free by retired employees under Section 79. This amount is generally $50,000 but may be higher for certain employees, subject to a grandfather clause. In addition, contributions on behalf of key employees cannot be deducted if the plan is discriminatory under Section 79.

At retirement, the assets of the fund can be used to pay the cost of maintaining the postretirement coverage. If assets are withdrawn from a trust, there is the possibility of the fund's being inadequate in the long run because of higher premiums and/or shorter life expectancies than anticipated. However, insurance company products typically assume the adverse mortality risk and guarantee that the fund will be adequate to maintain the promised benefits as long as the prescribed contributions have been deposited with the insurer.

As long as an employee has no rights in a retired-lives reserve except to receive postretirement group term insurance coverage until his or her death, the employee will incur no income taxation as a result of either employer contributions to the reserve or investment earnings on the reserve. In addition, up to $50,000 can be received income-tax free by beneficiaries.

In those instances where death benefits are paid directly from trust assets, the tax consequences to the employee are the same as if death benefits were provided through group term insurance contracts, except that death proceeds will represent taxable income to the beneficiary.

GROUP UNIVERSAL LIFE INSURANCE

Beginning in the mid-1980s, many large writers of group insurance started to sell group universal life insurance, a trend that was greeted with much interest by insurers, employers, and even employees. This interest seems to stem primarily from the following five factors:

1. The success of universal life insurance in the individual marketplace.
2. Tax legislation that made employer-provided term life insurance in excess of $50,000 taxable after retirement.
3. The clarification of the tax treatment of universal life insurance. For the first few years after the introduction of universal life insurance, there was concern that the Internal Revenue Service (IRS) would not grant it the same favorable tax treatment that was granted to traditional cash-value life insurance policies. There was speculation that the interest paid on the cash value might become subject to taxation and also that the death benefit would be considered taxable income for the beneficiary. For the most part these fears were laid to rest by tax legislation, as long as a universal life insurance policy meets certain prescribed guidelines. Therefore, the cash value of a universal life insurance policy accumulates tax free, and death benefits are free of income taxation.
4. The desire of employers to contain employee benefit costs. Little needs to be said about the attempts of employers to minimize the costs of their employee benefit plans. Group universal life insurance plans can make life insurance available to employees with little cost to the employer.
5. Less favorable tax treatment for formerly popular products for prefunding postretirement life insurance, such as retired-lives reserves.

Group universal life insurance products are being marketed primarily as supplemental life insurance plans, either to replace existing supplemental group term life insurance plans or as additional supplemental plans. Some insurers are promoting them as a way of providing the basic life insurance plan of an employee. Marketing efforts tout group universal life insurance as having the following advantages to the employer:

- No direct costs other than those associated with payroll deductions and possibly enrollment, because the entire premium cost is borne by the employee. In this sense, group universal life insurance plans are much like the payroll-deduction–funded plans described in Chapter 13.
- No Employee Retirement Income Security Act (ERISA) filing and reporting requirement as long as the master contract is issued to a trust and as long as there are no employer contributions for the cost of coverage. The current products are marketed through multiple-employer trusts, with the trust being the policyholder.

■ The ability of employees to continue coverage into retirement, alleviating pressure for the employer to provide postretirement life insurance benefits.

The following advantages are being claimed for employees:

■ The availability of a popular life insurance product at group rates
■ The opportunity to continue insurance coverage after retirement, possibly without any postretirement contributions
■ Flexibility in designing coverage to best meet the needs of the individual employee

The current plans being marketed are still evolving, and differences do exist among the plans being offered by competing insurance companies. Because of the flexibility given to policyholders, the administrative aspects of a group universal plan are formidable, and most insurers originally designed their plans only for employers with a large number of employees, usually at least 1,000. However, some insurers that write the product now make it available for as few as 50 employees or less.

Skeptics, including employees of some insurance companies offering group universal life coverage, wonder if the administrative problems can be handled so that coverage can be offered at a cost significantly lower than what is found in the individual marketplace. In raising this question, skeptics point out the administrative problems and costs that have arisen when universal life insurance has been included in payroll-deduction individual insurance plans. In addition, the highly competitive market for individual universal life insurance has resulted in rates with extremely low margins for contributions to surplus. These drawbacks, coupled with the lack of employer contributions, make savings to employees through the group insurance approach less likely than for many other types of insurance. Other critics point out that the popularity of universal life insurance in the individual marketplace decreased as interest rates have dropped over the last few years. Nevertheless, plans that are installed are usually well received by employees, and participation generally meets or exceeds expectations.

In 1998, universal life insurance accounted for about 6.5 percent of group life insurance certificates in force, up from 2 percent in 1995.[1]

General Nature

Group universal life insurance is a flexible-premium policy that, unlike traditional cash-value life insurance, divides the term insurance protection and the cash-value accumulation into separate and distinct components. The employee is required to pay a specified initial premium, from which a charge is subtracted for one month's mortality. This mortality charge in effect is used to purchase the required amount of term insurance (often referred to as *pure in-*

[1.] American Council of Life Insurance, *Life Insurance Fact Book,* 1999.

surance or the amount at risk) at a cost based on the insured's current age. Under some policies, an additional deduction is made for expenses. The balance of the initial premium becomes the initial cash value of the policy, which, when credited with interest, becomes the cash value at the end of the period. The process continues in succeeding periods. New premiums are added to the cash value, charges are made for expenses and mortality, and interest is credited to the remaining cash value. Employees receive periodic disclosure statements showing all charges made for the period, as well as any interest earnings.

Group universal life insurance offers an employee considerable flexibility to meet several life-cycle financial needs with a single type of insurance coverage. The death benefit can be increased because of marriage, the birth of a child or an increase in income. The death benefit can be reduced later when the need for life insurance decreases. Cash withdrawals can be made for the down payment on a home or to pay college tuition. Premium payments can be reduced during those periods when a young family has pressing financial needs. As financial circumstances improve, premiums can be increased so that an adequate retirement fund can be accumulated. The usual settlement options found in traditional cash-value life insurance are available, so an employee can periodically elect to liquidate the cash accumulation as a source of retirement income.

Types of Group Universal Products

Two approaches have been used in designing group universal life insurance products. Under the first approach, there is a single group insurance plan. An employee who wants only term insurance can pay a premium equal to the mortality and expense charges so that there is no accumulation of cash values. Naturally, an employee who wants to accumulate cash values must pay a larger premium.

Under the second approach, there are actually two group insurance plans— a term insurance plan and a universal life insurance plan. An employee who wants only term insurance contributes to the term insurance plan, and an employee who wants only universal life insurance contributes to the universal life insurance plan. With this approach, an employee purchasing universal life insurance must make premium payments that are sufficient to generate a cash-value accumulation. Initially, the employee may be required to make minimum premium payments, such as two or three times the cost of the term insurance. If an employee who has only the term insurance coverage later wants to switch to universal life insurance coverage, his or her group term insurance certificate is canceled, and the employee is issued a new certificate under the universal life insurance plan. An employee can also withdraw his or her cash accumulation under the universal life insurance plan and switch to the term insurance plan or can even have coverage under both plans. Typically, an employee is eligible to purchase a maximum aggregate amount of coverage under the two plans. For example, if this amount is three times annual salary, the employee can purchase term insurance equal to two times salary and universal life insurance that has a term insurance amount equal to one times salary.

Underwriting

Insurance companies that write group universal life insurance have underwriting standards concerning group size, the amounts of coverage available, and insurability.

Currently, most group universal life insurance products are limited primarily to employers who have at least 100 or 200 employees. However, a few insurers write coverage for even smaller groups. Some insurance companies also have an employee percentage-participation requirement, such as 20 percent or 25 percent, that must be satisfied before a group can be installed. Other insurance companies feel their marketing approach is designed so that adequate participation will result and, therefore, have no participation requirements.

Employees can generally elect amounts of pure insurance equal to varying multiples of their salaries, which typically start at one-half or one and range as high as three or five. There may be a minimum amount of coverage that must be purchased, such as $10,000. The maximum multiple an insurance company will offer is influenced by factors such as the size of the group, the amount of insurance provided under the employer's basic employer-pay-all group term insurance plan, and the percentage participation in the plan. In general, the rules regarding the amounts of coverage are the same as those that have been traditionally applied to supplemental group term life insurance plans. The initial premium, which is a function of an employee's age and death benefit, is frequently designed to accumulate a cash value at age 65 equal to approximately 20 percent of the total death benefit.

Other approaches for determining the death benefit may be used, depending on insurance company practices and employer desires. Under some plans, employees may elect specific amounts of insurance, such as $25,000, $50,000, or $100,000. Again, an employee's age and the death benefit selected determine the premium. Some plans allow an employee to select the premium he or she wants to pay. The amount of the premium and the employee's age then automatically determine the amount of the death benefit.

The extent to which evidence of insurability is required of individual employees is also similar to that found under most supplemental group term life insurance plans. When an employee is initially eligible, coverage is usually issued on a guaranteed basis up to specified limits, which again are influenced by the size of the group, the amount of coverage provided under the employer's basic group term insurance plan and the degree of participation in the plan. If an employee chooses a larger death benefit, simplified underwriting is used up to a second amount, after which regular underwriting is used. Guaranteed issue is often unavailable for small groups; underwriting on the basis of a simplified questionnaire is used up to a specific amount of death benefit, after which regular underwriting is used.

With some exceptions, future increases in the amount of pure insurance are subject to evidence of insurability. These exceptions include additional amounts resulting from salary increases, as long as the total amount of coverage remains within the guaranteed issue limit. A few insurance companies also allow additional purchases without evidence of insurability when certain events occur, such as marriage or the birth of a child.

The Death Benefit

The policyholder under an individual group universal life insurance policy typically has a choice of two death benefit options. Option A provides a level death benefit in the early policy years. As the cash value increases, the amount of pure insurance decreases so that the total amount paid to a beneficiary upon the insured's death remains constant. Without any provision to the contrary, the cash value would eventually approach the amount of the total death benefit. To prevent this from occurring, and also to keep the policy from failing to qualify as a life insurance policy under existing tax regulations, the amount of pure insurance does not decrease further once the cash value reaches a predetermined level. Thereafter, the total death benefit increases unless the cash value decreases. Figure 7-1 graphically demonstrates option A. Note

FIGURE 7-1
Universal Life Insurance—Death Benefit Option A

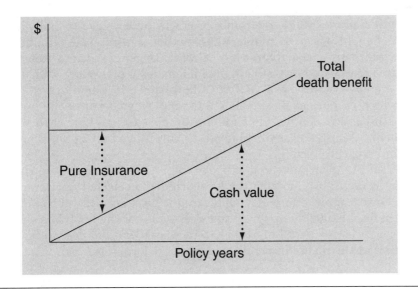

FIGURE 7-2
Universal Life Insurance—Death Benefit Option B

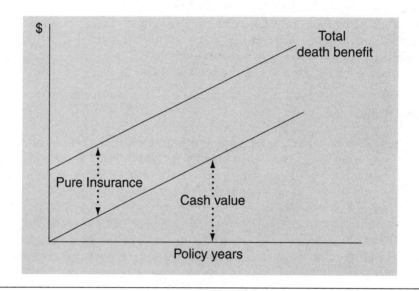

that this and the following figure are for illustrative purposes only. The actual death benefit for a particular individual will vary by such factors as the amount of interest credited, premiums paid, loans, and withdrawals.

Under option B, the amount of pure insurance is constant, and the death benefit increases each period by the change in the policy cash value. This is shown graphically in Figure 7-2.

With group universal life insurance products, an employee usually has only one death benefit option available, and whether it is option A or option B depends on which one the employer has selected. In general, there seems to be a feeling that the availability of both options makes a plan more difficult to explain to employees and more costly to administer. Most employers select option B, which is more easily marketed to employees because the increasing total death benefit is a visible sign of any increase in their cash value, or "investment." As a result, several insurers now make only option B available with their group products.

Universal life insurance products give the insured the right to increase or decrease the death benefit from the level originally selected as circumstances change. For example, the policyholder might have initially selected a pure death benefit of $100,000 under option B. Because of the birth of a child, this amount might be increased to $150,000. Increases, but not decreases, typically require that the insured provide evidence of insurability.

Mortality Charges

Most products have a guaranteed mortality charge for three years, after which the mortality charge is based on the experience of each particular group. As with experience rating in general, the credibility given to a group's actual experience is greater for larger groups. Most insurance companies guarantee that any future increases in the mortality charge will not exceed a stated maximum.

The products designed for small groups typically use pooled rates that apply to all groups insured through a particular trust. Therefore, the mortality charge for any employer will vary not with the employer's overall experience but rather with the overall experience of the trust.

Expense Charges

Among group life insurance products, probably the greatest variation occurs in expense charges levied. Typically, a percentage of each premium, such as 2 percent, is deducted for expenses. In addition, there is a flat monthly charge, normally ranging from $1 to $3, to maintain the accumulation account. Some insurance companies levy this charge against all certificate holders, even those who are contributing only enough to have the pure insurance coverage. Other insurance companies levy the charge only against those accounts that have a positive cash-value accumulation. A few insurance companies also load their mortality charges for expenses. Finally, many companies levy a transaction charge, such as $25, that often applies to withdrawals in early policy years. A transaction charge may also apply to policy loans and additional lump-sum contributions. In evaluating the expense charges of different insurers, one should remember that an insurer with a lower-than-average charge may be subtly compensating for this charge by having a higher mortality charge or crediting a lower interest rate to cash-value accumulations than would otherwise be paid.

Interest Rates

Insurance companies guarantee that the initial interest rate applied to cash-value accumulations will remain in effect for a minimum period of time, usually one year. After that time, the rate is typically adjusted quarterly or semiannually but cannot be below some contractual minimum such as 4 percent or $4\frac{1}{2}$ percent. The interest rate credited is usually determined on a discretionary basis but is influenced by the insurance company's investment income and competitive factors. However, some insurers stipulate that it be linked to some money market instrument, such as three-month Treasury bills. In general, the same interest rate is credited to all groups that an insurance company has underwritten.

Premium Adjustments

Employees are allowed considerable flexibility in the amount and timing of premium payments. Premiums can be raised or lowered and even suspended. In the latter case, the contract will terminate if an employee's cash-value accumulation is inadequate to pay current mortality and expense charges. Of course, premium payments could be reinstated to prevent this from happening. Additional lump-sum contributions may also be made to the accumulation account.

Two restrictions are placed on premium adjustments. First, the premium payment cannot be such that the size of the cash-value accumulation becomes so large in relationship to the pure insurance that an employee's coverage fails to qualify as a policy of insurance under IRS regulations. Second, because changes in premium payments through payroll deductions are costly to administer, many employers limit the frequency with which adjustments are allowed.

Loans and Withdrawals

Employees are allowed to make loans and withdrawals from their accumulated cash values, but for administrative reasons the frequency of loans and withdrawals may be limited. There are also minimum loan and withdrawal amounts, such as $250 or $500. In addition, an employee is usually required to leave a minimum balance in the cash-value account sufficient to pay mortality and expense charges for some time period, possibly as long as one year. If an option A death benefit is in effect, the amount of the pure insurance is increased by the amount of the loan or withdrawal so that the total death benefit remains the same. With an option B death benefit, the amount of the total death benefit is decreased.

The interest rate charged on policy loans is usually pegged to some index, such as Moody's composite bond yield index. In addition, the interest rate applied to an amount of the cash value equal to the policy loan is reduced. This reduced interest rate may be the guaranteed policy minimum or may also be based on some index; for example, the rate may be 2 percent less than Moody's composite bond yield.

An employee can withdraw his or her entire cash-value accumulation and terminate coverage. Total withdrawals are subject to a surrender charge during early policy years. The charge decreases with policy duration and is usually in addition to any transaction charge that might also be levied.

Dependent Coverage

Most products allow an employee to purchase a rider that provides term insurance coverage on his or her spouse and children. For example, one insurance company allows an employee to elect spousal coverage of $10,000 to

$50,000 in $10,000 increments and coverage on children in the amount of either $5,000 or $10,000. Other insurers make varying amounts available.

Some insurance companies allow separate universal life insurance coverage to be elected, but usually only for the spouse. In such cases, the coverage is provided under a separate group insurance certificate rather than a rider.

Accidental Death and Waiver of Premium

A group universal life insurance plan may provide accidental death benefits and a disability waiver of premium. These benefits are not optional for each employee; rather they are part of the coverage only if the employer has elected to include them in the plan. When a waiver of premium is included, all that is waived in case of disability is the portion of the premium necessary to pay the cost of the pure insurance protection for the employee and any dependents.

Employee Options at Retirement and Termination

Several options are available to the retiring employee. First, the employee can continue the group insurance coverage as if an active employee. However, if premium payments are continued, the employee is billed by the insurance company, probably on a quarterly basis. Because of the direct billing, the employee may be subject to a higher monthly expense charge. Second, the employee can terminate the coverage and completely withdraw his or her accumulated cash value. Third, the employee can elect one of the policy settlement options for the liquidation of cash value in the form of annuity income. Finally, some insurers allow the retiring employee to decrease the amount of pure insurance so that the cash value is adequate to keep the policy in force without any more premium payments. In effect, the employee then has a paid-up policy.

The same options are generally available to an employee who terminates employment prior to retirement. In contrast to most other types of group insurance arrangements, the continuation of coverage does not involve a conversion and the accompanying conversion charge; rather, the employee usually remains in the same group. This ability to continue group coverage after termination of employment is commonly referred to as *portability*. If former employees who continue coverage have higher mortality rates, this is reflected in the mortality charge for the entire group. However, at least one insurer places terminated employees into a separate group consisting of terminated employees from all plans. These persons are subject to a mortality charge based solely on the experience of this group. Thus, any higher mortality due to adverse selection is not shared by the actively working employees.

If the employer terminates the group insurance arrangement, some insurance companies keep the group coverage in force on a direct-bill basis, even if the coverage has been replaced with another insurer. Other insurance companies continue the group coverage only if the employer has not replaced the plan. If replacement occurs, the insurance company terminates the pure insurance amount and either gives the cash value to participants or transfers it to the trustee of the new plan.

Enrollment and Administration

Variations exist in the method by which employees are enrolled in group universal life insurance plans. Some early plans used agents who were compensated in the form of commissions or fees, but several insurance companies have dropped this practice. The actual enrollment is typically done by the employer with materials the insurance company provides. However, salaried or commissioned representatives of the insurer usually meet with the employees in group meetings to explain the plan.

The employer's main administrative function is to process the payroll deductions associated with a plan. As previously mentioned, employee flexibility may be somewhat limited to minimize the costs of numerous changes in payroll deductions.

The insurance company or a third-party administrator performs other administrative functions, including providing employees with annual statements about their transactions and cash-value accumulation under the plan. Toll-free telephone lines are often maintained to provide information and advice to employees.

Taxation

Group universal life insurance products are not designed to be policies of insurance under Section 79. In addition, each employee pays the full cost of his or her coverage. Therefore, the tax treatment is the same to employees as if they had purchased a universal life insurance policy in the individual insurance marketplace.

GROUP VARIABLE UNIVERSAL LIFE INSURANCE

In the mid-1990s, most major insurers that wrote group universal life insurance introduced a variable product, which has the same basic characteristics that were previously described for group universal life with one major difference—employees have a series of investment accounts to which they may allocate their net premiums. Once an employee elects the initial allocation, all future net premiums are allocated in the same proportion unless the employee makes a written request for a change. With the one exception described below, there are no minimum guarantees, and the full investment risk rests solely with the employee.

Group variable universal life insurance plans may offer up to 20 or more differing types of investment funds. These typically include at least one and possibly more of the following: growth funds, bond funds, money market funds, index funds, international stock funds, mortgage securities funds, and small company stock funds. Employers can choose the investment options that will be made available to employees. For ease of administration and communication, this number is often in the range of four to six.

Many group variable universal life insurance products also have an account that has a minimum interest-rate guarantee. An employee who is selecting a 100 percent allocation to this account in effect has the equivalent of coverage under a group universal life insurance contract rather than a variable contract. This feature leads some observers to predict that if the variable product should gain more widespread acceptance, there will be little need for insurers to maintain both a group universal life product and a group variable universal life product. However, group universal life insurance currently accounts for less than one-half of 1 percent of new group life insurance certificates issued.[2]

GROUP TERM CARVE-OUTS

Prior to 1984, employees had no taxable income if they were provided with postretirement coverage under a group term life insurance plan. After that time, coverage in excess of $50,000 became subject to the imputed income rules of Section 79, based on Table I cost, which are relatively high at older ages. As a result, employers increasingly turned to group term carve-outs. While carve-outs can be used for any employee with more than $50,000 of group term coverage, they typically apply only to shareholders and key executives.

Bonus Plans

In the simplest sense, a carve-out works like this: The employer decides which employees are to be covered under the carve-out plan and limits coverage for these employees under its group term plan to the $50,000 that can be received tax free. The employer then gives any premium savings to each "carved-out" employee in the form of a bonus, which is fully deductible to the employer as long as the employee's overall compensation is reasonable. The bonus amounts are either paid directly to an insurance company for individual coverage on the lives of the participants in the carve-out plan or, in some cases, provided to the employees as compensation to pay life insurance premiums. In most cases, the coverage purchased under the carve-out plan is some form of permanent life insurance protection that provides paid-up coverage at retirement. Traditional whole life insurance, universal life insurance, variable universal life insurance, and variable life insurance are all viable alternatives.

[2.]Ibid.

At retirement, the employee can either keep the coverage in force (possibly at a reduced paid-up amount) or surrender the policy for its cash value.

The popularity of carve-out plans lies in the fact that a comparable or greater amount of life insurance coverage can often be provided to participants at a lower cost than if the participants had received all their coverage under the group term life insurance plan. Because the carve-out plan does not qualify as a plan of insurance under Section 79, each participant has taxable income in the amount of the bonus. However, this income is offset by the absence of any imputed income from Table I.

In reality, carve-out plans are more complex. In many cases, the cost of permanent coverage for an employee may actually be greater than the cost of group term coverage during the working years. However, this high cost is often more than compensated for by the cash value at retirement and the absence of imputed income after retirement. Under some carve-out plans, participants must pay this increased premium cost with after-tax dollars. Under other plans, the employer increases the bonus amount. In effect, the employer is now paying more than if the carve-out plan did not exist, but this arrangement is often acceptable to the employer as a way of providing shareholders and key executives with a benefit that is not available to other employees. In many plans, the bonus is also increased to compensate the employee for any additional income taxes that must be paid because of the carve-out plan. Such an arrangement is commonly referred to as a *zero-tax approach*.

A carve-out plan can pose a potential problem if there are rated or uninsurable employees, but the problem is ameliorated if the plan has enough participants that the insurance company will use simplified underwriting or grant concessions on impaired risks. Any employee who is still uninsurable can be continued in the group term plan.

Other Types of Carve-Out Plans

While a bonus arrangement is the most common type of carve-out plan, other alternatives are available. Some carve-out plans are designed as death-benefit-only plans, under which the employer agrees only to pay a death benefit to the employee's beneficiary out of corporate assets. The employer often funds the plan with corporate-owned life insurance on the employee's life. With this approach, the employee has no taxable income, but death benefits will result in taxable income to the beneficiary. In addition, the employer is unable to deduct the premiums as a business expense but does receive the death proceeds tax free.

Some firms also use split-dollar life insurance in carve-out plans. The most common approach is to use a collateral assignment arrangement, under which the employer pays most of the premium and the employee collaterally assigns a portion of the cash value and death benefit to the employer equal to the employer's premium payments. At retirement (or any other predetermined time), the employee withdraws the cash value necessary to repay the employer, who then removes the collateral assignment. At that time, the employee has full control of the policy, and the remaining cash value can be used to keep coverage in force. Many split-dollar arrangements are also used to provide nonqualified retirement benefits to key employees as a supplement to the benefits under the employer's qualified retirement plan.

Determining the Best Plan

In many instances, carve-out plans are the most cost-effective approach for providing benefits to key employees. The best plan depends on the overall benefit objectives of employer. A proper analysis of alternatives involves a complex consideration of many factors, including the employer's tax bracket, the effect on the employer's financial statements, the employee's tax bracket, premium costs, and the time value of money.

STUDY QUESTIONS

1. Why is postretirement life insurance coverage usually noncontributory?

2. Describe the nature of retired-lives reserves.

3. What are the tax implications of retired-lives reserves?

4. What circumstances have sparked the current interest in group universal life insurance?

5. What are the advantages of group universal life insurance for (a) the employer and (b) employees?

6. What underwriting requirements are often found in group universal life insurance products with respect to
   a. group size?
   b. amounts of coverage available?
   c. insurability?

7. Briefly describe the typical group universal life insurance product with respect to
   a. guarantees of mortality charges.
   b. types of expense charges.
   c. interest rates applied.
   d. premium flexibility.
   e. loans and withdrawals.
   f. dependent coverage.
   g. waiver of premiums for accidental death.

8. What options are available under group universal life insurance plans to employees who retire or terminate employment?

9. Why is group universal life insurance not treated as group term life insurance for tax purposes?

10. How do group variable universal life insurance products differ from group universal life insurance products?

11. Briefly describe the types of group term carve-out plans.

12. What factors should be considered in designing a group term carve-out plan?

Group Disability Income Coverage

- Describe the characteristics of sick-leave plans.

- Describe the characteristics of short-term group disability income insurance.

- Describe the characteristics of long-term group disability income insurance.

- Explain the tax implications of group disability income premiums and benefits for both the employer and the employees.

The purpose of disability income coverage is to partially (and sometimes totally) replace the income of employees who are unable to work because of sickness or accident. While employers expect employees to miss a few days of work from time to time, there is often a tendency to underestimate both the frequency and severity of disabilities that last for longer periods. At all working ages, the probability of being disabled for at least 90 consecutive days is much greater than the chance of dying. One out of every three employees will have a disability that lasts at least 90 days during his or her working years, and one out of every ten employees can expect to be permanently disabled prior to age 65.

In terms of its financial impact on the family, long-term disability is more severe than death. In both cases, income ceases. In the case of long-term disability, however, family expenses—instead of decreasing because of one less family member—may actually increase because of the cost of providing care for the disabled person.

Employers are less likely to provide employees with disability income benefits than with either life insurance or medical expense benefits. It is difficult to estimate the exact extent of disability coverage because often benefits are not insured and workers are sometimes covered under overlapping plans. However, a reasonable estimate would be that at least 75 percent of all employees have some form of short-term employer-provided protection, but only about 40 percent have protection for long-term disabilities. This does not mean that almost all employees have some sort of disability income coverage, because many employees have both short-term and long-term protection and thus are included in both estimates. These estimates are also somewhat misleading because most employees have long-term disability income coverage under Social Security as well as coverage for certain types of disabilities under other government programs.

Group disability income protection consists of two distinct products:

1. Short-term disability income plans, which provide benefits for a limited period of time, usually six months or less. Benefits may be provided under uninsured plans or under insured plans, often referred to as *accident and sickness insurance* or *weekly indemnity benefits.*
2. Long-term disability income plans, which provide extended benefits (possibly for life) after an employee has been disabled for a period of time, frequently six months.

Two important tasks in designing and underwriting insured group disability income plans are to coordinate these products with each other (if both a short-term and a long-term plan are provided for employees) and to coordinate them with other benefits to which employees might be entitled under social insurance programs or uninsured sick-leave plans. A lack of coordination can lead to such a generous level of benefits for employees that absences from work because of disability might be either falsified or unnecessarily prolonged.

SICK-LEAVE PLANS

Employers use two approaches to provide short-term disability benefits to employees: sick-leave plans and short-term disability income insurance plans. Sick-leave plans, often called *salary continuation plans,* are uninsured and generally fully replace lost income for a limited period of time, starting on the first day of disability. In contrast, short-term disability income insurance plans (which are covered in the next section of this chapter) usually provide benefits that replace only a portion of an employee's lost income and often contain a waiting period before benefits start, particularly for sickness. While it is impossible to obtain precise statistics, surveys indicate that about half the employees with short-term coverage obtain benefits under sick-leave plans, about one-quarter under insured plans, and about one-quarter under plans that combine the two approaches.

Traditionally, many sick-leave plans were informal, with the availability, amount, and duration of benefits for an employee being at the employer's discretion. Although some plans used by small firms or for a limited number of executives still operate this way, informal plans are generally inappropriate. There is a possibility that the Internal Revenue Service (IRS) will consider benefit payments to be either a gift or a dividend and therefore not tax deductible by the employer. In addition, an informal plan increases the likelihood of suits brought by persons who do not receive benefits. As a result, the vast majority of sick-leave plans are now formalized and have specific written rules concerning eligibility and benefits.

Eligibility

Almost all sick-leave plans are limited to permanent full-time employees, but benefits may also be provided for permanent part-time employees. Most plans require that an employee satisfy a short probationary period (commonly one to three months) before being eligible for benefits. Sick-leave plans may also be limited to certain classes of employees, such as top management or nonunion employees. The latter is common when the union employees are covered under a collectively bargained, but insured, plan.

Benefits

Most sick-leave plans are designed to provide benefits equal to 100 percent of an employee's regular pay. Some plans, however, provide a reduced level of benefits after an initial period of full pay.

Several approaches are used in determining the duration of benefits. The most traditional approach credits eligible employees with a certain amount of sick leave each year, such as ten days. The majority of plans using this approach allow employees to accumulate unused sick leave up to some maximum amount, which rarely exceeds six months (sometimes specified as 180 days or

TABLE 8-1
Benefit Schedule Based on Months of Service

Length of Service	Amount of Sick-Leave*
Less than 3 months	None
3 or more months	1 day at full pay for each month of service (retroactive to date of employment)

*Maximum unused sick leave: 130 days

TABLE 8-2
Benefit Schedule Based on Length of Service

Length of Service	Maximum Days of Sick-Leave Per Year
Less than 3 months	0
3 months to 1 year	5
2 years	10
3 years	15
5 years	20
7 years	25
10 years	30

26 weeks). A variation of this approach is to credit employees with an amount of sick leave, such as one day, for each month of service. Table 8-1 is an example of a benefit schedule that uses this variation.

Another approach, illustrated in Table 8-2, bases the duration of benefits on an employee's length of service.

An alternative to this approach provides benefits for a uniform length of time to all employees, except possibly those with short periods of service. However, benefits are reduced to a level less than full pay after some period of time that is related to an employee's length of service. Table 8-3 is an illustration of this increasingly common approach.

In some instances, an employee is not eligible for sick-leave benefits if he or she is eligible for benefits under social insurance plans, such as workers' compensation. However, most sick-leave plans are coordinated with social insurance programs. For example, if an employee is entitled to 100 percent of pay and receives 60 percent of pay as a workers' compensation benefit, the salary sick-leave will pay the remaining 40 percent.

A problem for the employer is how to verify an employee's disability. In general, the employee's word is accepted for disabilities that last a week or less. Most sick-leave plans have a provision that benefits for longer periods will be paid only if the employee is under the care of a physician, who certifies that the employee is unable to work.

INSURED DISABILITY INCOME PLANS

As mentioned, insured disability income plans consist of two distinct products: short-term coverage and long-term coverage. In many respects, the contractual provisions of both short-term and long-term disability income contracts are the same or very similar. In other respects—notably, the eligibility requirements, the definition of disability, and the amount and duration of benefits—there are significant differences.

Eligibility

The eligibility requirements in group disability income insurance contracts are similar to those found in group term insurance contracts. In addition to being in a covered classification, an employee must usually work full-time and be actively at work before coverage commences. Any requirements concerning probationary periods, insurability, and premium contributions must also be satisfied.

Short-term and long-term disability income insurance plans frequently differ in both the classes of employees who are eligible for coverage and the length of the probationary period. Employers are more likely to provide short-term benefits to a wider range of employees, and it is not unusual for short-term plans to cover all full-time employees. However, these plans may be a result of collective bargaining and apply only to union employees. In this situation, other employees frequently have short-term disability benefits under uninsured sick-leave plans.

Long-term disability plans often limit benefits to salaried employees. Claims experience has traditionally been less favorable for hourly paid employees for a number of reasons. Claims of hourly paid employees tend to be more frequent, particularly in recessionary times when the possibility of temporary layoffs or terminations increases. Such claims also tend to be of longer duration, possibly because of the likelihood that these employees hold repetitive and nonchallenging jobs. Some long-term plans also exclude employees below a certain salary level because this category of employees, like hourly paid employees, is considered to have a reasonable level of benefits under Social Security.

Long-term disability income plans tend to have longer probationary periods than do short-term disability income plans. While the majority of short-term disability plans (as well as group term insurance plans and medical expense plans) either have no probationary period or have a probationary period of three months or less, it is common for long-term disability plans to have probationary periods ranging from three months to one year. While short-term plans only require that an employee be actively at work on the date he or she is otherwise eligible for coverage, long-term plans sometimes require that the employee be on the job for an extended period (such as 30 days) without illness or injury before coverage becomes effective.

TABLE 8-3
Benefit Schedule With Varied Coverage Based on Months of Service

| | Weeks of Sick-leave per Disability | | |
Length of Service	100% of Pay	50% of Pay	Total Weeks
Less than 6 months	0	0	0
6 months to 1 year	2	0	2
1 year	4	22	26
2 years	8	18	26
3 years	12	14	26
4 years	16	10	26
5 years	20	6	26
6 years or more	26	0	26

Definition of Disability

Benefits are paid under disability income insurance contracts only if the employee meets the definition of disability as specified in the contract. Virtually all short-term disability income insurance contracts define disability as *the total and continuous inability of the employee to perform each and every duty of his or her regular occupation.* A small minority of contracts use a more restrictive definition, requiring that an employee be unable to engage in any occupation for compensation. Partial disabilities are usually not covered, but a few newer plans do provide benefits. In addition, the majority of short-term contracts limit coverage to nonoccupational disabilities, because employees have workers' compensation benefits for occupational disabilities. This limitation tends to be most common when benefits under the short-term contract are comparable to or lesser in amount than those under the workers' compensation law. In those cases where workers' compensation benefits are relatively low and the employer desires to provide additional benefits, coverage may be written for both occupational and nonoccupational disabilities.

A few long-term disability income contracts use the same liberal definition of disability that is commonly used in short-term contracts. However, the term *material duties* often replaces the term *each and every duty*. Some other contracts define disability as *the total and continuous inability of the employee to engage in any and every gainful occupation for which he or she is qualified or shall reasonably become qualified by reason of training, education, or experience.* However, most of long-term disability contracts use a dual definition that combines these two. Under a dual definition, benefits are paid for some period of time (usually 24 or 36 months) as long as an employee is unable to perform his or her regular occupation. After that time, benefits are paid only if the employee is unable to engage in any occupation for which he or she is qualified by reason of training, education, or experience. The purpose of this combined definition is to require and encourage a disabled employee who becomes able after a period of time to adjust his or her lifestyle and earn a livelihood in another occupation.

A more recent definition of disability found in some long-term contracts contains an occupation test and an earnings test. Under the occupation test, a person is totally disabled if he or she meets the definition of disability as described in the previous paragraph. However, if the occupation test is not satisfied, a person is still considered disabled as long as an earnings test is satisfied. This means that the person's income has dropped by a stated percentage, such as 50 percent, because of injury or sickness. This newer definition makes a group insurance contract similar to an individual disability income policy that provides residual benefits.

The definition of disability in long-term contracts may differ from that found in short-term contracts in several other respects. Long-term contracts are somewhat more likely to provide benefits for partial disabilities. Generally, these benefits are provided in a manner similar to that described in Chapter 4 for workers' compensation insurance. However, the amount and duration of such benefits may be limited when compared with those for total disabilities, and the receipt of benefits is usually contingent upon a prior period of disability. In addition, most long-term contracts provide coverage for both occupational and nonoccupational disabilities. Finally, short-term contracts usually have the same definition of disability for all classes of employees. Some long-term contracts use different definitions for different classes of employees—one for most employees and a more liberal definition for executives or salaried employees.

Exclusions

Under certain circumstances, disability income benefits are not paid even if an employee satisfies the definition of disability. Common exclusions under both short-term and long-term disability income contracts specify that no benefits will be paid under the following circumstances:

- For any period during which the employee is not under the care of a physician.
- For any disability caused by an intentionally self-inflicted injury.
- Unless the period of disability commenced while the employee was covered under the contract. (For example, an employee who previously elected not to participate under a contributory plan cannot obtain coverage for an existing disability by deciding to pay the required premium.)
- If the employee is engaged in any occupation for remuneration. This exclusion applies in those situations when an employee is totally disabled with respect to his or her regular job but is engaged in other employment that can be performed despite the employee's condition.

Until the Pregnancy Discrimination Act, it was common for disabilities resulting from pregnancy to be excluded. Such an exclusion is now illegal under federal law if an employer has 15 or more employees. Employers with fewer than 15 employees may still exclude pregnancy disabilities unless they are subject to state laws to the contrary.

Additional exclusions are often found in long-term contracts. These commonly deny benefits for disabilities resulting from the following:

- War, whether declared or undeclared.
- Participation in an assault or felony. Note that some insurers have recently expanded this exclusion to include the commission of any crime.
- Mental disease, alcoholism, or drug addiction. However, some contracts provide benefits if an employee is confined in a hospital or institution specializing in the care and treatment of such disorders; other contracts provide benefits but limit their duration (such as for 24 months per disability).
- Preexisting conditions.

The exclusion for preexisting conditions is designed to counter the adverse selection and potentially large claims that could occur if an employer established a group disability income plan or if an employee elected to participate in the plan because of some known condition that is likely to result in disability. While variations exist, a common provision for preexisting conditions excludes coverage for any disability that commences during the first 12 months an employee is covered under the contract if the employee received treatment or medical advice for the disabling condition both (1) prior to the date the employee became eligible for coverage and (2) within 90 consecutive days prior to the commencement of the disability.

When coverage is transferred from one insurance company to another, it is not unusual, particularly in the case of large employers, for the new insurance company to waive the limitation for preexisting conditions for those employees who were insured under the previous contract. This is often referred to as *prior coverage credit* or a no-loss, no-gain provision. In some instances, the provision is modified so that benefits are limited to those that would have been provided under the previous contract, possibly for a specified duration, such as one year. Note that a transfer of coverage has no effect on the responsibility of the prior insurance company to continue paying benefits for claims that have already occurred, except in rare cases where some arrangement is made for the new contract to provide benefits.

Benefits

A discussion of the benefits under disability income contracts is more complex than a discussion of the benefits under group life insurance contracts. A similarity exists in that there are benefit schedules that classify employees and specify the amount of disability income to be provided. However, the relationship between an employee's earnings and the employee's potential benefits is more important in disability income insurance than in group life insurance. In addition, disability benefits are subject to several provisions not found in group life insurance contracts. These pertain to the length of time that benefits will be paid and the coordination of benefits with other available types of disability income.

Benefit Schedules

As in group life insurance, there is a variety of benefit schedules found in group disability income contracts. Benefits may be available to all employees or limited to specific groups of employees. In addition, benefits may be expressed as either flat-dollar amounts, varying dollar amounts by classification, or a percentage of earnings.

A major difficulty in disability insurance is determining the appropriate level of benefits to provide. Absenteeism is encouraged and the incentive to return to work is diminished if a disabled employee is given a level of income that is comparable to his or her regular earnings. In general, disability income plans are designed to provide a level of benefits that replaces between 50 percent and 70 percent of an employee's gross income. While this may appear to represent a substantial reduction of regular earnings, it should be remembered that a disabled employee does not have the usual expenses associated with working, such as transportation costs. In addition, disability income benefits are not subject to Social Security taxation after a period of time and, depending on the source and amount, may be free of income taxation. Despite the logic in providing a reduced level of income, some short-term disability income plans provide employees with 100 percent of their predisability earnings. In most cases this level of benefits is either a result of collective bargaining or an effort by employers to provide nonunion employees with a level of benefits that is comparable to that of union employees.

Many short-term disability income plans and the majority of long-term plans base benefits on a single percentage of regular earnings (excluding bonuses and overtime). This percentage varies widely for short-term plans, and benefits as low as 50 percent or as high as 100 percent are not unusual. However, many insurers are reluctant to underwrite plans that provide benefits higher than 70 percent of earnings. In some instances, short-term plans, like sick-leave plans, may use different percentages, such as 100 percent of earnings for four weeks and 70 percent of earnings for the remaining benefit period. The length of time for which the higher level of benefits is provided may also be a function of the length of an employee's service.

Long-term plans typically provide benefits that range from 50 percent to 70 percent of earnings, with 60 percent and 66⅔ percent being the most prevalent. Some plans also use a sliding scale, such as 66⅔ percent of the first $4,000 of monthly earnings and 40 percent of earnings in excess of $4,000.

It is common for plans that determine benefits as a percentage of earnings to also place a maximum dollar amount on the benefit that will be provided, regardless of earnings. For example, a short-term plan covering hourly employees may have a benefit equal to 70 percent of earnings that might be subject to a maximum of $250 per week. Similarly, a long-term plan may provide benefits equal to 66⅔ percent of earnings, but might be subject to a monthly maximum that varies from $1,000 for some small groups to $4,000 or $5,000 (and sometimes higher) for large groups. The purpose of such a maximum is to prevent the absolute benefit from being so high that an employee, by adjusting his or her lifestyle, could live comfortably on the disability income benefit and thus have no financial incentive to return to work.

Other types of benefit schedules are found in short-term disability income plans, particularly when these plans are designed for hourly paid employees. If the weekly earnings of most employees fall within a narrow range, the benefit might be expressed as a flat-dollar amount. For example, if all employees earn between $300 and $400 per week, a benefit of $225 per week might be used. If earnings vary widely, a benefit schedule such as the one shown in Table 8-4 might be used.

A similar approach is occasionally used in long-term disability income plans, as shown in the Table 8-5 benefit schedule for salaried employees earning in excess of $18,000 per year.

Period of Benefits

To determine the period for which disability income benefits will be paid, it is necessary to determine when benefits will begin and how long they will be paid. In both respects, there are differences between short-term and long-term plans.

TABLE 8-4
Benefit Schedule for Short-Term Disability

Weekly Earnings	Weekly Benefit
$301 to $340	$220
$341 to $380	250
$381 to $420	280
$421 to $460	310
Over $460	340

TABLE 8-5
Benefit Schedule for Long-Term Disability

Monthly Earnings	Monthly Benefit
$1,500 to $2,500	$1,200
$2,501 to $3,500	1,500
$3,501 to $4,500	2,400
$4,501 to $5,500	3,000
Over $5,500	4,000

Short-Term Plans. Short-term disability income contracts commonly contain a waiting period (referred to in such contracts as an *elimination period*). The waiting period is the length of time for which an employee covered under the contract must be disabled before benefits begin. In the typical short-term contract, there is no waiting period for disabilities resulting from accidents, but a waiting period ranging from one to seven days consecutive is used for disabilities resulting from sicknesses. However, in some plans there is a single waiting period that applies to disabilities from either accidents or sicknesses; in a few plans there are no waiting periods for either cause. Waiting periods longer than seven days are occasionally used, particularly when there is a sick-leave plan to provide benefits during the initial portion of a disability. In addition to lowering the cost of a disability income plan, the waiting period discourages unwarranted absences from work because of sickness. In a few cases, benefits are paid retroactively to the date of disability if the disability lasts for a predetermined period of time. However, it is generally felt that retroactive benefits cause employees to prolong their return to work in order to receive benefits for the full period of their disability.

Once an employee begins to receive benefit payments under a short-term disability contract, the benefits continue until the end of the benefit period specified in the contract if the employee remains disabled for that length of time. Although short-term contracts may provide benefits for up to two years (with long-term contracts providing benefits for periods in excess of two years), it is unusual for benefits to continue for more than one year. In fact, the majority of short-term contracts stipulate that benefits will be paid for either 13 or 26 weeks, with the latter period being most prevalent. It is also common for short-term plans to be described in terms of their elimination period and their duration of benefits. For example, a "1-8-26" plan pays benefits for a maximum of 26 weeks beginning with the first day of disability in the case of an accident and with the eighth day of disability in the case of sickness.

In a few cases, the maximum period of benefits applies to a specified duration of time (such as any consecutive 12 months) regardless of the number of separate disabilities. However, in most plans both the maximum benefit period and the elimination period apply to each separate disability. Moreover, successive periods of disability caused by the same accident or the same or related sickness are generally considered to be a single disability unless they are separated by a period (normally two weeks) of continuous resumption of active employment. This provision prevents an employee from briefly returning to work in order to obtain a second maximum period of benefits for the same disability.

Even though a reduction in short-term disability income benefits for older employees can probably be justified on a cost basis, few plans have incorporated such a reduction.

Long-Term Plans. While waiting periods in long-term disability income plans may be as short as 30 days or as long as one year or more, the vast majority of plans contain elimination periods ranging from three to six months, with six months most common. In many cases, the length of the waiting period corresponds to the length of time benefits are paid under a firm's short-term disability income plan or sick-leave plan. In contrast to short-term plans, there is no difference between the waiting periods for sicknesses and accidents.

Long-term disability income benefits may be paid for as short a period as two years or as long as the lifetime of the disabled employee. In a few cases, the length of the benefit period may differ, depending on whether the disability was a result of an accident or a sickness. At one time, it was common for long-term disability income benefits to cease at age 65. However, this is no longer permissible under the Age Discrimination in Employment Act. Several different approaches are now used for older employees. In a few cases, benefits are paid until age 70 for any disability that occurred before that age. For disabilities occurring at age 70 or later, benefits are paid for a reduced duration. A more common approach is to use a graded benefit period and provide benefits to age 65 for employees who are disabled prior to a specified age. Employees disabled after the specified age are given benefits for a limited time, as shown in Table 8-6.

A similar approach uses a sliding level of benefit durations after a certain age. For example, a plan may provide that employees disabled prior to age 60 receive benefits until age 65. The schedule shown in Table 8-7 might then be used for employees who are disabled at age 60 or older.

As in short-term disability income plans, provisions are made in long-term plans for successive disabilities. The majority of contracts stipulate that successive periods of disability that are separated by less than some period (usually varying from three to six months) of continuous, active full-time employment are considered a single disability, unless the subsequent disability (1) arises from an unrelated cause and (2) begins after the employee has returned to work.

TABLE 8-6
Graded Benefit Periods for Long-Term Disability

Age at Commencement of Disability	Benefit Duration
59 and younger	To age 65
60–64	5 years
65–69	To age 70
70–74	1 year
75 and older	6 months

TABLE 8-7
Benefit Periods for Long-Term Disability (Age 60 or Older)

Age at Commencement of Disability	Benefit Duration (in Years)
60	5
61	4
62	3½
63	3
64	2½
65	2
66	2
67	1
68	1
69	1

Coordination with Other Benefits

To minimize the possibility that an employee will receive total benefits higher than his or her predisability earnings, disability income plans commonly stipulate that benefits be integrated with other sources of disability income. The effect of this integration is to reduce (either totally or partially) the benefits payable under the disability income contract to the extent that certain other benefits are available. In general, the insurance laws or regulations of most states allow such reductions to be made as a result of benefits from social insurance programs and group insurance or retirement plans provided by the employer, but not as a result of benefits from individual disability income contracts unless they were purchased by the employer. Employers and employees often resent the fact that disability income benefits that they have paid for may be reduced. However, such reductions are considered in determining the rates charged for disability income insurance. In effect, the employer is purchasing a contract that is only a supplement to these other available sources of disability income rather than being penalized because these resources are available.

For various reasons, including the limited duration of benefits and the desire for simplified operating procedures, integration with other benefits is less likely to exist in short-term plans than in long-term plans. If a short-term plan covers only nonoccupational disabilities, there is no need for integration with workers' compensation benefits; and unless benefits are provided for disabilities lasting longer than five months, there is no need to integrate benefits with Social Security. In general, benefits under short-term plans are integrated with (1) workers' compensation benefits, if the plan covers occupational disabilities; (2) temporary disability laws, if they are applicable; and (3) Social Security benefits, if the maximum benefit period is longer than five months.

Some insurance companies sell long-term disability income coverage without any provision for coordination with other disability income benefits. However, the availability and potential magnitude of other benefits are an underwriting factor in determining the maximum amount of coverage that will be written. Long-term disability income benefits are usually integrated with benefits provided under the following:

- Social Security
- Workers' compensation laws
- Temporary disability laws
- Other insurance plans for which the employer makes a contribution or payroll deduction
- Pension plans for which the employer has made a contribution or payroll deduction to the extent that the employee elects to receive retirement benefits because of disability
- Sick-leave plans
- Earnings from employment, either with the employer or from other sources

The integration with Social Security may be based solely on the benefit a disabled worker receives for himself or herself (referred to as the *employee's primary insurance amount*). It may also be based on the employee's total family benefit if the employee has eligible dependents.

Two basic approaches to integration are used: a full-integration approach and a dual-percentage approach. Under the *full-integration approach,* long-term disability income benefits are reduced to the extent that any benefits subject to integration are received. For example, assume that an employee earning $2,500 per month is entitled to a disability income benefit of 60 percent, or $1,500 per month. In addition, suppose the employee is entitled to a disability benefit of $900 under Social Security, as well as additional family benefits of $450 (a total of $1,350). If the long-term disability income benefit plan provides for integration with total family benefits, the employee receives $1,500 ($1,350 from Social Security and the remaining $150 from the long-term plan). However, if full integration is provided only with respect to the primary insurance amount (in other words, the $450 of family benefits is not considered), the employee receives $1,950 ($1,350 from Social Security and $600 from the long-term disability plan).

Under the *dual-percentage approach,* two percentages are used: one that is applicable to benefits that will be provided under the long-term plan when there are no other benefits subject to integration, and another higher percentage that is applicable to total benefits payable from the long-term plan and other sources subject to integration. For example, an insured plan might provide benefits equal to 60 percent of earnings in the absence of other benefits subject to integration. If there are benefits subject to integration, benefits under the insured plan will be reduced by the amount that the sum of the benefits under the long-term disability plan and the benefits subject to integration exceed another percentage, such as 70 percent. Using these percentages and the previous example, 70 percent of earnings is $1,750. Because the long-term disability benefit and all the Social Security benefits total $2,850 ($1,500 + $900 + $450), the long-term disability benefit will be reduced by $1,100 if the plan provides for integration with total family benefits. Therefore the employee will receive a total benefit of $1,750 ($1,350 from Social Security and $400 from the long-term plan).

It is possible for integration with other benefits to totally eliminate a long-term disability benefit. To prevent this from happening, many plans provide (and some states require) that a minimum benefit, such as $50 or $100 per month, be paid. Most plans also contain a provision freezing the amount of any Social Security offset at the initial level that was established when the claim began. For example, assume an employee is entitled to receive $1,000 per month in disability income benefits under a long-term plan that contains a provision for full integration with Social Security. If the employee initially receives $400 from the long-term plan and $600 from Social Security, the $400 will continue to be paid under a provision that freezes the offset even if Social Security benefits are increased. If a 5 percent increase is later granted in Social Security benefits, the employee will receive a total benefit of $1,030. Without such a provision, the intended effect of increases in Social Security benefits would be erased by equivalent reductions in other disability income benefits provided to the employee. Such reductions would be regarded by some regulators as being contrary to public policy and, thus, a reason for requiring insured plans to contain a freeze in the amount of the Social Security offset.

As a general rule, both the insured and the insurer will benefit if the insured is able to collect Social Security benefits for a disability. The insured will have an increased overall benefit, and the insurer will have a substantially lower claim to pay. Consequently insurers are often willing to provide assistance to claimants by helping them with the filing of Social Security claims and the appealing of decisions denying claims.

Supplemental Benefits

It is becoming increasingly common to find group long-term disability income plans that provide employees with a base of employer-paid benefits and allow each covered employee to purchase additional coverage at his or her own expense. For example, a plan may have basic benefits of 50 percent of earnings and an option for an employee to increase this amount to 55 percent, 66⅔ percent or 70 percent of earnings. These supplemental or "buy-up" plans are growing in popularity as employers try to control benefit costs by shifting a greater burden of the cost to employees.

Some plans are also designed to "carve out" benefits for certain employees, often key executives. For example, an employer might design one plan to cover most of its employees, but top executives might be covered with another group plan that provides enhanced benefits in the form of a larger percentage of earnings and a more liberal definition of disability. Another variation of a carve-out plan provides the executives with a lower benefit percentage than other employees but provides supplemental benefits in the form of individual disability income policies. In addition to more favorable policy provisions, such a carve-out plan might offer better rate guarantees and an overall higher benefit than a group plan could offer. Furthermore, the portability of an individual policy might be attractive to executives, if not to the employer.

Other Contract Provisions

Many provisions in group disability income contracts are similar to those in group term insurance contracts and will not be discussed further in this chapter. These provisions pertain to incontestability, a grace period, the entire-contract clause, and the payment of premiums. The provisions that will be discussed either are unique to group disability income benefit contracts or differ in certain respects from similar provisions found in group term insurance contracts.

Claims

The provisions concerning claims under both short-term and long-term disability income contracts are essentially the same. The insurance company must be notified within a relatively short time period—20 or 30 days (or as soon as is reasonably possible)—after the disability for which benefits are being claimed begins. A formal proof of loss must then be filed with the insurance company, usually within 90 days after the commencement of the disability or after the end of the week, month, or other time period for which benefits are payable. The proof of loss normally consists of a statement by the employee concerning the disability, a statement by the attending physician, and a statement by the employer indicating the date and reason that active employment ceased. Provisions require periodic reports from the attending physician or permit the insurance company to request such reports at reasonable intervals. The insurance company also has the right to have the employee examined by a physician of its own choice (and at its own expense) at reasonable time periods during the duration of the claim.

Payment of Benefits

The insurance company is not obligated to make benefit payments until a proof of loss has been filed. Although benefits are usually payable to the employee, a facility-of-payment provision is included to allow payments to a guardian if the employee is physically, mentally, or otherwise incapable of giving a valid release for any payment received. Benefits may be assigned to another party if such an assignment is permissible under state law and the insurance contract.

Rehabilitation

As an incentive to encourage disabled employees to return to active employment as soon as possible, but perhaps at a lower-paying job, most insurance companies include a rehabilitation provision in their long-term disability income contracts. This provision permits the employee to enter a trial work period of one or two years in rehabilitative employment. During this time, disability benefits continue but are reduced by some percentage (varying from 50 percent to 80 percent) of the earnings from rehabilitative employment. For example, with a 50 percent reduction, an employee who is otherwise entitled to a disability benefit of $1,500 per month has this benefit reduced by only $600 if he or she earns $1,200 at the new job. If the trial work period indicates that the employee is unable to perform the rehabilitative employment, the original long-term benefits are continued and the employee is not required to satisfy a new waiting period.

While there are seldom other provisions in long-term disability income contracts that require the insurance company to aid in the rehabilitation of disabled employees, it has become increasingly common for insurance companies to provide benefits for rehabilitation when they feel that the cost of these benefits could be offset by a shortened disability period. These benefits may be in the form of physical therapy, job training, adaptive aids that enable a disabled person to perform job functions, or even the financing of a business venture.

In the past, the decision to seek rehabilitation was left to the disabled person. Some insurers now require that the person undertake rehabilitation or have benefits reduced or stopped.

The rehabilitation of disabled workers is continuing to grow in importance among companies. In fact, rehabilitative services are often used as a selling feature for an insurance company's product. More and more companies are taking a proactive role in managing disability claims by employing skilled professionals (such as physicians and nurses) and by intervening earlier in the claims process. Because early intervention is undoubtedly a key factor in getting disabled employees back to work sooner, many benefit consultants see an advantage in an employer's using the same company for a firm's short-term and long-term disability income plans. This approach enables the insurer's rehabilitation staff to become involved when a claim is filed under the short-term plan rather than waiting until the elimination period for long-term benefits has been met.

In addition to providing rehabilitation benefits, insurance companies are monitoring claims data more closely; in doing so, they can better advise employers where action can be taken to reduce the number of future claims.

Termination

For the most part, the provisions in disability income contracts concerning either the termination of the master contract or an employee's coverage are the same as those found in group life insurance. However, there is one notable exception: a conversion privilege is rarely included, based on the theory that the termination of employment also terminates an employee's income and, thus, the need for disability income protection. If a conversion privilege is available, an extra charge is made for the coverage.

One other situation should be mentioned. When an employee meets the definition of total disability under a disability income contract, the employee is considered to have terminated employment by reason of ceasing to be an active, full-time employee. Without some provision to the contrary, an employee who resumes work is then required to resatisfy any eligibility requirements, including a new probationary period. Therefore, most group disability income contracts allow the employer to consider disabled employees as not having terminated employment for insurance purposes. The employer may continue coverage as long as it is done on a nondiscriminatory basis and as long as the required premiums are paid. In short-term contracts, coverage is generally continued by the payment of premiums on the same basis as for active employees. However, it is common for long-term contracts to contain a waiver-of-premium provision. This waiver normally begins at the time benefit payments start, not at the beginning of the waiting period.

It should be noted that the only practical effect of continuing coverage on a disabled employee is to guarantee that the employee will again be eligible for disability income benefits after he or she has returned to active employment.

The continuation of coverage (or termination of coverage) has no effect on future disability income benefits for an employee who is currently disabled and, therefore, entitled to receive benefits.

Additional Benefits

Several types of additional benefits are occasionally found under long-term disability income contracts. The most common are a cost-of-living adjustment (COLA), a pension supplement, and a survivors' benefit.

Some disability income plans have COLAs, so that inflation does not erode the purchasing power of disability income benefits being received. Under the typical COLA formula, benefits increase annually along with changes in the Consumer Price Index.

Many firms make provisions in their pension plan for treating disabled employees as if they were still working and accruing pension benefits. Such a provision requires that contributions on behalf of disabled employees be made to the pension plan, usually from the employer's current revenues. However, some disability income contracts stipulate that the contributions necessary to fund a disabled employee's accruing pension benefits will be paid from the disability income contract.

It should also be noted that some pension plans provide disability income benefits by allowing disabled employees to begin receiving retirement benefits when they are totally and permanently disabled. It is common, however, to limit these early retirement benefits to employees who have satisfied some minimum period of service or who have reached some minimum age. In recent years, the feeling among employee benefit consultants seems to be that it is preferable to have separate retirement and disability income plans.

Some long-term contracts provide a benefit to survivors in the form of continued payments after the death of a disabled employee. In effect, the disability income payments are continued, possibly at a reduced amount, for periods ranging up to 24 months, with 3 to 6 months being most common. Payments are generally made only to eligible survivors—commonly the spouse and unmarried children under age 21.

While even less common, other types of additional benefits may also be found. Examples include child-care payments for disabled employees who can work on a part-time basis, spousal disability benefits payable to the employee, and benefits to pay premiums for medical expense coverage.

FEDERAL TAXATION

As with group life insurance, employer contributions for an employee's disability income insurance are fully deductible to the employer as an ordinary and necessary business expense under Code Section 162 if the employee's overall compensation is reasonable. Sick-leave payments are similarly tax deductible. Contributions by an individual employee are considered payments for personal disability income insurance and are not tax deductible.

Income Tax Liability of Employees

In contrast to group life insurance, for which employer contributions may result in some taxable income to an employee, Code Section 106 provides that employer contributions for disability income insurance result in no taxable income to an employee. However, the payment of benefits under an insured plan or sick-leave plan may or may not result in the receipt of taxable income. To make this determination, it is necessary to look at whether the plan is fully contributory, noncontributory, or partially contributory.

Fully Contributory Plan

Under a fully contributory plan, the entire cost is paid by employee contributions and benefits are received free of income taxation.

Noncontributory Plan

Under a noncontributory plan, the entire cost is paid by the employer and benefits are included in an employee's gross income. However, the Internal Revenue Code provides a tax credit to persons who are permanently and totally disabled. A tax credit is subtracted from an individual's federal income tax liability, not deducted from gross income. For purposes of this tax credit, the IRS uses the Social Security definition of disability; that is, an employee must be unable to engage in any kind of gainful work because of a medically determinable physical condition that has lasted or is expected to last at least 12 months or is expected to result in death.

The maximum credit is $750 for a single person, $1,125 for a married person filing jointly, and $562.50 for a married person filing separately. The credit cannot exceed the taxable disability benefit actually received. The maximum credit is reduced if a single individual has an adjusted gross income (including the disability benefit) over $7,500, if a married person filing jointly has an adjusted gross income over $10,000, or if a married person filing separately has an adjusted gross income over $5,000. The reduction is equal to $7\frac{1}{2}$ percent of any income over the limit. In addition, the credit is reduced by 15 percent of any tax-free income received as a pension, annuity, or disability benefit from certain government programs, including benefits from Social Security. Because disability income plans are usually integrated with Social Security, the tax credit available to most persons who receive disability benefits from employer plans is substantially reduced or eliminated altogether.

Partially Contributory Plan

Under a partially contributory plan, benefits attributable to employee contributions are received free of income taxation. Benefits attributable to employer contributions are includable in gross income, but employees are eligible for the tax credit described previously.

The portion of the benefits attributable to employer contributions (and thus subject to income taxation) is based on the ratio of the employer's contributions to the total employer-employee contributions for an employee who has been under the plan for some period of time. For example, if the employer paid 75 percent of the cost of the plan, 75 percent of the benefits would be considered attributable to employer contributions and 25 percent to employee contributions. The time period used to calculate this percentage varies, depending on the type of disability income plan and the length of time that the plan has been in existence. Under group insurance policies, the time period used is the three policy years ending prior to the beginning of the calendar year in which the employee is disabled. If coverage has been in effect for a shorter time, IRS regulations specify the appropriate time period to use. Similar provisions pertain to contributory sick-leave plans, the major exception being that the time period is based on calendar years rather than policy years. If benefits are provided under individual disability income insurance policies, the proportion is determined on the basis of the premiums paid for the current policy year.

Tax Withholding and Social Security Taxes

Benefits paid directly to an employee by an employer under a sick-leave plan are treated like any other wages for purposes of tax withholding. Disability income benefits paid by a third party (such as an insurance company or a trust) are subject to the withholding tax rules and regulations only if the employee requests that taxes be withheld. In both cases, benefits that are attributable to employer contributions are subject to Social Security and Medicare taxes. However, taxes are payable only during the last calendar month in which the employee worked and the six months that follow.

STATE TAXATION

For income tax purposes, some states consider an individual's taxable income to be the figure shown on the individual's federal income tax return, and those states treat disability income and sick-leave benefits as the federal government does. While considerable variations exist in other states, disability income and sick-leave benefits are generally treated more favorably than under the federal tax laws and are often totally exempt from state income taxation.

STUDY QUESTIONS

1. Why is it important to coordinate insured group disability income plans with other sources of disability income benefits?

2. Describe the approaches used to determine the duration of benefits under sick-leave plans.

3. Why are long-term disability income plans less likely to cover all employees than are short-term disability income plans?

4. What is the rationale for providing disability benefits that are less than an employee's earnings prior to disability?

5. Compare insured short-term and long-term disability income contracts with respect to
   a. definition of disability.
   b. coverage for partial disabilities.
   c. coverage for nonoccupational disabilities.

6. Compare insured short-term and long-term disability income contracts with respect to
   a. exclusions.
   b. waiting (elimination) period.
   c. duration of benefits.
   d. extent to which benefits are usually reduced for older employees.
   e. extent to which benefits are usually coordinated with other disability income benefits.

7. Lindsay Grant, who earns $1,600 per month, is covered under a group long-term disability income plan that provides benefits equal to 60 percent of predisability earnings. If disabled, she will also receive Social Security disability benefits of $780: $520 as her primary insurance amount and an additional $260 as a family benefit. If the group plan contains an integration provision that reduces benefits to the extent that the long-term disability income benefit and the primary insurance amount exceed 75 percent of earnings, how much will Lindsay receive from each source if she is disabled?

8. Describe the rehabilitation provision often found in long-term disability income contracts.

9. Explain how long-term disability income contracts are sometimes modified to provide
   a. a pension supplement.
   b. survivor benefits.

10. Under the federal income tax laws, to what extent are employer contributions for disability income insurance
    a. deductible to the employer?
    b. taxable as income to an employee?

CHAPTER 9

Group Medical Expense Benefits: The Changing Environment

OBJECTIVES

- Describe the development of medical expense coverage.

- Explain the reasons for the increasing cost of health care.

- Identify the measures used by employers to contain health care costs.

- Describe the role of the states in health care reform.

- Identify the questions that must be addressed in designing a national health insurance program.

- Describe the basic approaches that have been proposed for a national health insurance program.

- Explain how the Health Insurance Portability and Accountability Act affects the availability of medical expense coverage.

Medical expense insurance is the most significant type of group insurance in terms of both the number of persons covered and the dollar outlay. With the exception of employers with a very small number of employees, virtually all employers offer some type of medical expense plan. In almost all cases, coverage identical to that offered for employees is also available for eligible dependents. In the absence of employee contributions, the cost of providing medical coverage for employees is several times greater for most employers than the combined cost of providing life insurance and disability income insurance.

Group medical expense contracts are not as standardized as group life insurance and group disability income insurance. Coverage may be provided through Blue Cross and Blue Shield plans, health maintenance organizations (HMOs), and preferred-provider organizations (PPOs) as well as insurance companies. In addition, a large and increasing percentage of the benefits is provided under plans that are partially or totally self-funded (self-insured). An overall medical expense plan may be limited to specific types of medical expenses, or it may be broad enough to cover almost all medical expenses. Even when broad coverage is available, benefits may be provided under either a single contract or a combination of contracts. Furthermore, in contrast to other types of group insurance, benefits may be in the form of services rather than cash payments. Finally, the skyrocketing cost of providing medical expense benefits over a long period of time has led to changes in coverage and plan design aimed at controlling these costs. Many of these changes have resulted in more similarities among the providers of medical expense coverage than existed in the past.

Over the past decade, two major issues—affordability and accessibility of medical care—have led to profound changes in the health care industry. Not only has there been a continued shift to managed care plans but the entire character of the health care industry has changed. Where once there was a distinction between the providers of care (such as doctors and hospitals) and the organizations that financed the care (such as insurers, the Blues, and HMOs), this distinction is becoming blurred. Physicians and hospitals are establishing HMOs and PPOs. Physicians may be employees of managed care plans. Some Blue Cross Associations are merging with hospitals. There are those who feel that in the not-too-distant future most Americans will receive their medical expense coverage from one of a small number of large organizations that both provide medical care and finance the cost of that care.

The issues surrounding medical care have also become a concern of government. Many states have enacted programs to make coverage available to the uninsured, including those who work for employers with a small number of employees. At the federal level, lively debate over health care has occurred and is likely to continue.

This chapter, the first of four chapters devoted to group medical expense coverage, discusses the following topics:

- A brief history of the development of medical expense coverage
- An overview of the trend toward cost containment and managed care

- State initiatives to make medical expense coverage more available
- A discussion of national health insurance—the extent to which it already exists and proposals to expand its scope

Chapter 10 is devoted to traditional medical expense plans, while managed care approaches are discussed in Chapter 11. Common provisions of medical expense plans and the tax treatment of medical expense premiums and benefits are covered in Chapter 12.

DEVELOPMENT OF MEDICAL EXPENSE COVERAGE

To understand the wide array of medical expense plans available today, it is appropriate to understand their historic development. There is further discussion of each type of plan in later chapters.

Until the 1930s, medical expenses were borne primarily by ill or injured persons or their families. It was not unusual, however, for hospitals and physicians to provide care on a charity basis if the patient lacked the resources to pay. What have been described as the earliest "health insurance" plans were in reality disability income coverage. However, at that time medical costs were relatively low, and the continuation of income was often the difference between a person's ability to pay medical bills and the need to rely on charity.

Birth of the Blues

The Great Depression saw the development of the first organizations that would later be called *Blue Cross*. These organizations, which were initially controlled by hospitals, were designed to provide first-dollar coverage for hospital expenses, but with a limited duration of benefits. In the late 1930s, physicians followed the hospitals' approach and established Blue Shield plans. Through the 1940s, the Blues were the predominant providers of medical expense coverage.

Early HMOs

Although it is often thought that health maintenance organizations were a product of the 1970s, some HMOs were among the earliest providers of medical expense coverage. What is usually considered to be the first HMO, the Ross-Loos Clinic, was founded in Los Angeles in 1929. Other HMOs, such as the Kaiser Plans, had their beginnings in the 1930s. However, HMOs remained only a small player in the marketplace for medical expense coverage until the past two decades.

Early Efforts of Insurance Companies

Insurance companies, seeing the success of Blue Cross, entered the market for hospital insurance in the 1930s and later added coverage for surgical expenses and physicians' expenses. However, insurance companies were only modestly successful in competing with the Blues until a new product was introduced in 1949—major medical insurance. As a result, by the mid-1950s insurance companies surpassed the Blues in premium volume and number of persons covered.

The 1960s—Era of Government Involvement

The number of persons covered by medical expense insurance plans grew rapidly during the 1950s and 1960s. Much of this growth was in employer-sponsored plans as a result of a 1949 Supreme Court ruling that employee benefits were subject to collective bargaining.

While the types of products available underwent little change during this period, there were two major developments in the mid-1960s. For the first time, the federal government became a major player in providing medical expense coverage by creating national health insurance programs for the elderly and the poor. Medicare provides benefits for persons aged 65 and older. The financing of the benefits under this program comes from three sources: government revenue, premiums of Medicare beneficiaries, and the FICA taxes paid by most working persons and their employers.

The second program—Medicaid—provides medical benefits for certain classes of low-income individuals and families. There is little doubt that both Medicare and Medicaid provide benefits to major segments of the population with large numbers of persons who would otherwise be unable to receive adequate medical care. However, the effect of so many additional persons with coverage beginning at the same time created shortages of medical facilities and professionals. This increased demand for medical care is one reason for the high rate of inflation for health care costs that soon developed.

The 1970s—First Reactions to Spiraling Costs

In 1950, expenditures for health care equaled 4.4 percent of GNP; they increased to 5.4 percent in 1960 and 7.3 percent in 1970. When these spiraling costs received the attention of employers and the federal government, large employers started turning to the self-funding of medical expense benefits. In addition to improved cash flow, savings were achieved by the avoidance of state-mandated benefits and state premium taxes. The passage of ERISA in 1974 thwarted initial state attempts to bring self-funded plans under their insurance regulations. This federal legislation freed self-funded plans from state regulation and hastened the growth of this financing technique.

The 1970s also saw the first large-scale debate over national insurance. As in the mid-1990s, the majority of the members of Congress supported one of the many plans that were introduced, but opinions were diverse and little common ground was found. However, one significant piece of legislation was passed—the Health Maintenance Organization Act of 1973. This legislation sought to encourage the growth of HMOs by providing funding for their development costs and mandating that certain employers make these plans available to employees. There is little doubt that the growth of HMOs is a result of this legislation.

The 1980s and 1990s—Continued Change

Attempts to rein in the cost of medical care in the 1970s seemed to have little effect. By 1980, expenditures for health care reached 9.2 percent of GNP. This figure was 12.2 percent by 1990, and nearly 14 percent by the end of the decade. In addition, about 14 percent of the population, including many employed persons and their families, remained uninsured.

Reactions to these statistics came from many sources. Many state governments adopted programs to make coverage more available and affordable to the uninsured. At the federal level, there were suggestions that the entire health care system needed an overhaul. While the initial national health insurance proposal by the Clinton administration was dead, there was still continued support by members of Congress for changes in the nation's approach to providing and financing health care. Significant federal legislation was enacted in 1996, but little new and significant legislation was enacted after that.

The many efforts by employers to contain costs included the following:

- Growth in the self-funding of benefits. Much of this growth came from small- and medium-sized employers.
- Cost-shifting to employees. It became increasingly common for employers to raise deductibles and require that employees pay a larger portion of their medical expense coverage.
- Increased use of managed care plans that are alternatives to HMOs, such as PPOs and point-of-service plans. These approaches often overcame the reluctance of some employees to participate in managed care plans.
- Requiring or encouraging managed care plans. Some employers dropped traditional medical expense plans and offered managed care alternatives only. A more prevalent approach was to offer employees a financial incentive to join managed care plans.

Many of these reactions are reflected in changing statistics about the extent of varying types of medical expense coverage; unfortunately, precise statistics are difficult to obtain. For example, many Blue Cross and Blue Shield associations and HMOs report only the total number of persons covered and make no distinction between individual coverage and group coverage. Many persons receive portions of their coverage from different types of providers, such as hospital coverage from a Blue Cross plan and other medical expense coverages from an insurance company under a supplemental major medical contract. In addition, self-funded plans may operate as HMOs, purchase stop-loss coverage, and/or utilize PPOs.

Even though precise statistics cannot be obtained, there is no doubt that a significant change took place in the 1990s. In 1980, approximately 90 percent of all insured workers were covered under "traditional" medical expense plans, and 5 percent were covered under HMOs. Under a *traditional* plan, if a worker or family member was sick, he or she had complete freedom in choosing a doctor or a hospital. Medical bills were paid by the plan, and no attempts were made to control costs or the utilization of services. It is estimated that between 10 and 15 percent of the employees under these traditional plans were in plans that were totally self-funded by the employer; the remainder of the employees were split fairly evenly between plans written by insurance companies and the Blues.

By the end of the 1990s, the figures had changed dramatically, with the majority of employees covered under plans that controlled costs and the access to medical care. Close to 85 percent of employees were enrolled in managed care plans—HMOs, PPOs, or point-of-service plans, often owned by insurance companies or the Blues. Of the remaining employees, few were in traditional plans. Many were still with insurance companies and the Blues, but under traditional plans that had been redesigned to incorporate varying degrees of managed care.

One important change is hidden in these statistics—the increasing trend toward self-funding of medical expenses by employers. It is estimated that over 50 percent of all workers are covered under plans that are totally or substantially self-funded. Self-funding is more prevalent as the number of employees increases, with between 80 and 90 percent of persons who work for employers with more than 20,000 employees being covered under self-funded plans. However, employers with as few as 25 to 50 employees also use self-funding. It should be noted that the way benefits are provided under a self-funded plan can vary—the employer may design the plan to provide benefits on an indemnity basis or as an HMO or PPO.

Despite the difficulty in obtaining precise statistics, the data collected by the Health Insurance Association of America[1] show that enrollment in medical expense plans that can be characterized as traditional indemnity plans dropped from more than 70 percent to 14 percent since 1990. During the same time period, the number of enrollees in plans that use PPOs increased significantly to 34 percent. Point-of-service plans and HMOs grew more slowly and now account for about 30 percent and 22 percent, respectively, of the number of enrollees.

---

[1] Health Insurance Association of America, *Source Book of Health Insurance Data, 1999–2000.*

Into the New Millennium

Just as in past decades, the health care system will continue to evolve in the first decade of the new millennium. What the changes will be is only speculation, but a few observations can be made about the current environment:

- Renewal rates in 2000 for employer-provided medical expense plans are increasing at the highest percentage since the early 1990s, and these high percentage increases are predicted to continue in the foreseeable future.
- Surveys indicate that the vast majority of Americans are satisfied with their own health care plans. The relatively low degree of dissatisfaction, however, is higher for plans with the greatest degree of managed care.
- Despite satisfaction with their own coverage, surveys also indicate that Americans are becoming less satisfied with and less confident about the health care system.
- There is a growing backlash against managed care, particularly HMOs. Two observations can be made about this trend. First, many persons appear to have based their opinions on media reports and stories from friends, not on their own experiences. In this regard, opinions about managed care and Congress tend to be somewhat similar, with a high percentage of negative attitudes, although most persons give high ratings to their own managed care plans and their own Congresspersons. Second, this backlash has gotten the attention of Congress and the states. Some legislation has resulted at the state level. However, managed care plans are also becoming increasingly flexible and consumer-friendly, possibly to prevent further legislation aimed at managed care reform. Managed care reform is discussed in Chapter 11.
- There was little federal health care legislation during Clinton's second term, at least partially due to a Congressional majority of a different political party from the President. While there seems to be bipartisan agreement that there are some problems with the current system, there is bipartisan disagreement about what should be done. Whether this situation will change as a result of the 2000 election is unclear at the time this book is being revised.

COST CONTAINMENT AND MANAGED CARE

Between 1970 and the early 1990s, the average annual increases in the cost of medical care were approximately twice the average annual increases in the consumer price index. No single factor accounts for these increases. Rather, it was a combination of the following reasons:

■ Technological advances. In the last few years, many exciting technological advances have taken place. Numerous lives are now being saved by such techniques as CAT scans, MRIs, fetal monitoring, and organ transplants. As miraculous as many of these techniques are, they are also very expensive. Technological advances can also prolong the life of the terminally ill and increase associated medical expenses.

■ Increasing malpractice suits. The providers of care are much more likely to be sued than in the past, and malpractice awards have outpaced the general rate of inflation. This development has resulted in higher malpractice insurance premiums, a cost that is ultimately passed on to consumers. The increase in malpractice suits has also led to an increase in defensive medicine, with routine tests likely to be performed more often.

■ Increases in third-party payments. A growing portion of the country's health care expenditures is now paid by private health insurers or the government. Patients and providers of health care often have no financial incentives to economize on the use of health care service.

■ Underutilization of medical facilities. Currently, the United States has an overabundance of hospital beds, and a surplus of physicians is also beginning to develop. Empty hospital beds are expensive to maintain, and an oversupply of physicians tends to drive up the average costs of medical procedures so that physicians' average income does not drop.

■ Design of medical expense plans. Many medical expense plans now provide first-dollar coverage for many health care costs. There is often little incentive for patients to avoid the most expensive forms of treatment.

■ AIDS. The continuing increase in the number of AIDS cases over the past 10 years has resulted in increasing costs to employers. Costs in excess of $100,000 for an employee with AIDS are not unusual.

■ An aging population. The incidence of illness increases with age. Current demographics indicate that this trend will be a source of cost increases for several years to come.

During the period from 1994 to 1996, several factors caused the cost of medical expense coverage to remain uncharacteristically stable, particularly for managed care plans. Many providers of medical services and medical expense plans were reluctant to raise costs while the Clinton health care proposal was being debated. In addition, managed care plans were holding down premiums while actively increasing enrollments.

However, the late 1990s started to see significant increases in health care costs, particularly because of skyrocketing costs for prescription drugs. There is a feeling among benefit consultants that expanding managed care plans have saturated the market to the point that savings resulting from additional employees moving to managed care plans will be modest. There is also an interesting trend occurring among medical providers. The large number of mergers of hospitals and other providers of medical services in many parts of the country may in fact shift the balance of bargaining power to these providers from managed care plans and other buyers of medical services. In addition, costs will increase somewhat because of federal and state legislation that continues to mandate benefits.

Increasing health care costs have become the concern of almost everyone — government, labor, employers, and consumers. In this introduction to cost containment, many of the measures employers use are enumerated. Some of the following measures are discussed in more detail throughout the next three chapters (with others discussed later in the book):

- Benefit plan design
- Alternative providers
- Alternative funding methods
- Claims review
- Health education and preventive care
- Encouragement of external cost-control systems
- Managed care

Benefit Plan Design

Numerous design features of a medical expense plan can control costs. These have traditionally been in the form of contractual provisions that shift costs to employees. The following are examples:

- Deductibles
- Coinsurance
- Exclusions and limitations
- Maximum benefits

In recent years, design features have been aimed at reducing costs rather than shifting them. In fact, benefit plans are often designed to provide a higher level of benefits if less costly alternatives are used. Examples of these cost-containment features include the following:

- Preadmission testing
- Second surgical opinions
- Coordination of benefits
- The use of alternatives to hospitals (such as skilled-nursing facilities, home health care, hospice care, birthing centers and ambulatory care centers)
- The use of medical savings accounts

Alternative Providers

The use of HMOs and PPOs has been popular for some years as a cost-containment method. These methods have now been joined by point-of-service plans. Each is described in more detail in Chapter 11.

Alternative Funding Methods

Employers are increasingly turning to funding methods that are alternatives to the traditional insurance company plan or Blue Cross–Blue Shield plan. Chapter 14 is devoted to a discussion of these techniques.

Claims Review

There is no doubt that claims review can generate substantial cost savings. In general, this review is done not by the employer but by the provider of medical expense benefits, a third-party administrator, or some independent outside organization. At a minimum, claims should be reviewed for patient eligibility, eligibility of the services provided, duplicate policies, and charges that are in excess of the usual, customary, and reasonable amounts. Many medical expense plans routinely audit hospital bills, particularly those that exceed some stipulated amount, such as $5,000 or $10,000. They check for errors in such items as length of stay, services performed, and billed charges. Many insurance companies have found that each dollar spent on this type of review results in two or three dollars of savings.

A newer trend in claims review is utilization review or case management, which may be done on a prospective basis, a concurrent basis, a retrospective basis, or a combination of the three. A *prospective review* involves analyzing a case to see what type of treatment is necessary. Hospital preadmission authorization, second surgical opinions, and predetermination of dental benefits fall into this category. However, when a patient is hospitalized, concurrent review can lead to shorter stays and the use of less expensive facilities. *Concurrent review* is normally carried out by a registered nurse and typically begins with precertification of a hospital stay for an initial specified length of time. The nurse then works with the patient's physician to monitor the length of stay and to determine whether other alternatives to hospitalization—such as hospice or home health care—can be used. Many providers of medical expense benefits pay for these alternative forms of treatment even if they are not specifically covered under the medical expense plan, as long as their cost is lower than the cost of continued hospitalization.

A *retrospective review* involves an analysis of care after the fact to determine if it was appropriate. Such a review may lead to a denial of claims, but its purpose is often to monitor trends so that future actions can be taken in high-cost areas. For example, a retrospective review may lead to the establishment of a concurrent review program for a hospital with excessive lengths of stay.

Health and Preventive Care

There is little doubt that persons who lead healthy lifestyles tend to have fewer medical bills, particularly at younger ages. It is also evident that healthier employees save an employer money by taking fewer sick days and having fewer disability claims. For these reasons, employers are increasingly establishing wellness programs and employee-assistance plans, both of which are discussed in Chapter 16. With increasing health awareness among the general population, the existence of these programs has a positive side effect—the improvement of employee morale.

Encouragement of External Cost-Control Systems

While a certain degree of cost containment is within the control of employers, the proper control of costs is an ongoing process that requires participation by consumers (both employers and individuals), government, and the providers of health care services. Many agencies and committees of the Department of Health and Human Services carry out these activities at the federal level. This government department has the primary responsibility for identifying health care needs, monitoring resources, establishing priorities, recommending courses of action, and overseeing laws that pertain to health care.

At the state and local level, many employers are active in coalitions whose purpose is to control costs and improve the quality of health care. These groups—which may also involve unions, providers of health care, insurance companies, and regulators—are often the catalyst for legislation, such as laws authorizing PPOs and establishing hospital budget-review programs. Some coalitions act as purchasing groups to negotiate lower-cost coverage for members. For example, one midwestern coalition consists of several large corporations and offers a uniform health plan to the 50,000 employees of its members. The plan is self-funded by the coalition and utilizes the services of about 1,000 primary care physicians and 4,000 specialists. Another coalition, an example of a different approach, represents over 10,000 companies with fewer than 150 employees each. The coalition negotiates with providers of medical expense coverage and offers its members a choice of about a dozen different group plans. The annual increase in cost to coalition members has been significantly less than the annual increase in cost for other companies in the area that do not belong to the coalition.

Managed Care

The current buzzword with respect to cost containment is *managed care*. In a general sense, the term can be defined to include any medical expense plan that attempts to contain costs by controlling the behavior of participants. However, in practice the term is used by many persons to mean different things. At one extreme are traditional indemnity plans that require second opinions and/or hospital precertification. At the other extreme are HMOs and PPOs that limit a participant's choice of medical providers, negotiate provider fees, and use case management.

Managed care plans have evolved over the last few years. Today, it is generally felt that a true managed care plan should have five basic characteristics:

1. *Controlled access to providers.* It is difficult to control costs if participants have unrestricted access to physicians and hospitals. Managed care plans attempt to encourage or force participants to use predetermined providers. Because a major portion of medical expenses results from referrals to specialists, managed care plans tend to use primary care physicians as gatekeepers to determine the necessity and appropriateness of specialty care. By limiting the number of providers, managed care plans are better able to control costs by negotiating provider fees.

2. *Comprehensive case management.* Successful managed care plans perform utilization review at all levels. This involves reviewing a case to determine the type of treatment necessary, monitoring ongoing care, and reviewing the appropriateness and success of treatment after it has been given.

3. *Preventive care.* Managed care plans encourage preventive care and the attainment of healthier lifestyles.

4. *Risk sharing.* Managed care plans are most successful if providers share in the financial consequences of medical decisions. Newer managed care plans have contractual guarantees to encourage cost-effective care. For example, a physician who minimizes diagnostic tests may receive a bonus. Ideally, such an arrangement will eliminate unnecessary tests, not discourage tests that should be performed.

5. *High-quality care.* A managed care plan is not well received and selected by participants if there is a perception of inferior or inconvenient medical care. In the past, too little attention was paid to this aspect of cost containment. Newer managed care plans not only select providers more carefully but also monitor the quality of care on a continuing basis.

There seems to be a reasonable consensus among employers and benefit specialists that there is a negative correlation between benefit costs and the degree of managed care—that is, the greater the degree of managed care, the lower the cost. For example, studies generally rank benefit plans in the following order (from highest to lowest) with respect to annual benefit costs:

- Traditional insurance company and Blue Cross and Blue Shield plans without case management
- Traditional insurance company and Blue Cross and Blue Shield plans with case management
- PPOs
- Point-of-service plans
- Independent practice association HMOs
- Closed-panel HMOs

It is interesting to note that the degree of managed care increases as one goes down the list. There also seems to be a high correlation between annual benefit costs and the rate of cost increases. For example, the cost of traditional benefit plans has been increasing recently at an annual rate in excess of the annual increase in cost for closed-panel HMOs.

STATE REFORMS

Often overlooked in the debate over national health insurance is the role of the states in health care reform. Since 1989, almost all states have passed some type of legislation to make medical expense coverage more available and less costly to certain segments of the population. Some of this legislation was passed before the initial national health insurance proposal of the Clinton administration, and it is interesting to note that some of the administration's ideas reflected practices already instituted in some states. Other states continued to pass their own reforms as the debate over national health insurance continued at the national level during most of the first Clinton administration. The potential importance of state actions should not be overlooked. There has been and continues to be considerable support in Congress for having the states, rather than the federal government, take the initiative in health care reform.

State reforms fall into two categories. One category is laws and regulations aimed at uninsured individuals other than employees. These are not discussed in this book. The other category is those laws and regulations that constitute what is commonly referred to as *small-group reform*. It is in these groups of fewer than 25 or 50 employees that the majority of employees without employer-sponsored coverage is found. Most states have passed National Association of Insurance Commissioners (NAIC) model legislation, and a few states have gone even farther with other types of legislation. Unfortunately, the results seem to be somewhat mixed. Some states report modest results, but the national percentage of employees with medical coverage under small-employer plans has remained static. In addition, several insurers no longer choose to write business for small groups because of the limitations imposed by the legislation. While coverage is still more readily available, the legislation does not make it more affordable. Some small employers cannot afford to pay a significant share of the cost for their employees, and the employee share under contributory plans is often in excess of what employees can or are willing to pay.

NAIC Model

The most common approach to state reform has been the adoption of one of the versions of the NAIC Small Employer Health Insurance Availability Model Act. The stated purpose and intent of the model act are "to promote the availability of health insurance to small employers regardless of their health status or claims experience, to prevent abusive rating practices, to require disclosure of rating practices to purchasers, to establish rules regarding renewability of coverage, to establish limitations on the use of preexisting-conditions exclusions, to provide for development of basic and standard health benefit plans to be offered to all small employers, to provide for establishment of a reinsurance program, and to improve the overall fairness and efficiency of the small-group health insurance market." While some provisions of the model act may result in lower costs for certain employers, the main emphasis of the model act is on the availability of coverage, not on the employer's or employees' ability to afford the coverage.

Although the following discussion focuses on the provisions of the NAIC model act, it is important to remember that states often adopt model acts with variations. Some of the more significant variations are described.

Plans Subject to the Act

The model act defines a *small employer* as one who had 25 or fewer employees working on at least 50 percent of the days during the previous calendar quarter. Several states extend their legislation to employers with as many as 50 employees and/or exclude groups of one or two employees.

The model act applies to most medical expense products provided by insurance companies, HMOs, and prepaid service plans. Certain types of coverage are specifically excluded from the act's provisions: dental insurance, vision insurance, Medicare supplements, long-term care insurance, and disability income insurance. In addition, payroll deduction plans of individual medical expense insurance under which the employer pays no portion of the cost may or may not be subject to a specific state's legislation.

The small-group legislation does not force the providers of medical expense coverage to operate in the small-employer market. However, if a provider of coverage does sell medical expense coverage to small employers, the provisions of the legislation must be followed.

Benefit Provisions

The model act establishes a committee representing providers of medical expense coverage, employers, employees, health care practitioners, and agents to recommend the form and level of coverage to be made available to small employers. The committee must recommend a basic plan and a more comprehensive standard plan and make decisions regarding benefit levels, cost-sharing levels, exclusions, and limitations. In designing the basic plan, the committee can ignore any state mandates for benefits unless the small-group legislation specifically requires them.

Preexisting-conditions provisions are allowed, but with limitations. A medical condition can be treated as preexisting if it was treated (or if a prudent person would have sought treatment) within a specified prior period, which cannot exceed 6 months. Coverage for preexisting conditions cannot be excluded for more than 12 months following the effective date of coverage. Preexisting conditions must be covered as any other medical conditions if a person had benefits for the medical condition under a prior medical expense plan for at least 90 continuous days prior to the effective date of the new coverage.

One unfortunate and probably unintended side effect of the small-group legislation is that the policies that must be made available in many states are very precisely prescribed, making it impossible for insurance companies to use the same policies in multiple states. The expense of designing and refiling policies for many states, coupled with rate controls and the inability to underwrite for medical conditions, has resulted in several insurers leaving the small-group market.

Underwriting

With few exceptions, coverage must be written for all small employers. An insurance company or other provider of medical expense coverage is permitted to have requirements for minimum participation and minimum employer contributions as long as these requirements are the same for all similarly sized groups. These requirements cannot be increased after an employer has been accepted for coverage.

Coverage must be made available to all employees and their dependents. However, persons who did not enroll when initially eligible can be denied coverage for up to 18 months or have coverage excluded for preexisting conditions for up to 18 months.

Rates and Renewability

The model act prescribes a procedure for determining an "index rate" to be charged by each provider of medical expense coverage. Under certain circumstances, such as the use of more than one type of marketing system, the provider can use different rates for different classes of business to reflect substantial differences in expected claims experience or administrative costs.

However, the index rate for any class of business cannot be more than 20 percent higher than the index rate for any other class of business.

Although the act allows rate differences among groups because of variations in age, sex, industry, geographic area, family composition, and group size, far fewer refinements are allowed than would be the case without this legislation. Some states have adopted more restrictive legislation and require community rating.

At annual renewals, rates can be changed because of changes in the index rate, changes in the mix of employees, and possibly group experience. In the latter case, the size of the adjustment is limited to a modest amount. The provider of medical expense coverage must renew all policies subject to certain exceptions, such as nonpayment of premium or the failure to meet any minimum participation requirement. The provider may also elect not to renew all policies for small employers in a state. However, proper notification (usually 180 days) must be given to the insurance commissioner and all employers.

Relation to New Federal Legislation

The Health Insurance Portability and Accountability Act (HIPAA) contains provisions that are similar to many provisions of the NAIC model act. State law continues to apply to insured medical expense plans unless it interferes with the new federal legislation. Provisions of the state law supersede the federal legislation if they are more generous toward insured individuals. For example, the maximum allowable length of preexisting-conditions periods may be shorter in some states than under the federal legislation.

Other State Reforms

Other reforms passed by the states include the following:

- Tort reform. Several states have passed legislation to control medical malpractice suits. This legislation ranges from limiting recovery for noneconomic loss to mandatory arbitration.
- Claim administration reform. A few states now require the use of standardized claim forms, including a uniform system of coding diagnoses and procedures.
- The establishment of health insurance purchasing cooperatives (HIPCs). Several states have laws that establish HIPCs, entities that act as brokers between the purchasers and providers of medical expense coverage. They negotiate alternative plans of coverage on the basis of price and quality. Those eligible to use the HIPC, which may vary from all purchasers to small employers only, may elect one of the available plans directly from the HIPC. With some HIPCs, an employer deals directly with the cooperative without using agents or brokers. In one state, however, an employer

can purchase coverage through an agent or broker or deal directly with the cooperative and receive a discount equal to the commission that would be paid to an agent or broker. An unexpected result of this arrangement is that almost 70 percent of the employers have elected to use an agent or broker. Clearly, these employers feel that the services agents and brokers provided are worth the extra cost.

A few states have considered the adoption of even more radical reforms to the health care market, such as the adoption of single-payer plans, which are discussed in the next section of this chapter.

NATIONAL HEALTH INSURANCE

Few issues in recent years have gotten as much attention as the debate over national health insurance. With health care expenditures taking nearly one out of every six dollars spent in this country and about 14 percent of the population without adequate coverage for medical expenses, the magnitude of the problem cannot be overemphasized. There are no easy solutions to the problems of increasing costs and the lack of coverage for everyone. Health care is an emotional issue, and any reform will be complex and affect almost all Americans to varying degrees.

The following discussion of national health insurance does not give any precise answers or solutions. Rather it addresses many aspects of the issue, describes some approaches suggested for solving current problems, and attempts to predict what seems most feasible in the short term. The major goal of this discussion is to provide readers with a better framework for following—and perhaps participating in—the debate that will undoubtedly continue for some time.

Some Basic Questions

The issue of national health insurance is best addressed by having an understanding of its many dimensions. This discussion is organized around several questions, not all of which have precise or easy answers.

Don't We Already Have National Health Insurance?

The answer is "yes," for many Americans. Unlike most other industrialized countries, however, the United States does not have a system of national health insurance that covers everyone. Although national health insurance does exist in the form of Medicare, Medicaid, certain veterans' benefits, and coverage of military personnel and their families, each of these programs attempts to address the issue of health insurance for a specific group and each takes a different approach.

Some people would say that most other Americans are also covered under a national health insurance program. While the role of the federal government is probably not extensive enough for most persons to agree with this observation, the federal government does in fact have an influence on the design of employer-provided medical expense plans of almost all but the smallest employers. This influence comes from numerous pieces of federal legislation, such as ERISA, COBRA, the Family and Medical Leave Act, the Age Discrimination in Employment Act, the Americans with Disabilities Act, and HIPAA.

Many Americans have a tendency to feel that the federal government should have no role in health care reform. But approximately 50 percent of all medical care expenditures are for persons who are either employees of the federal government or covered under the national health insurance programs previously mentioned. Therefore, the government and the taxpayers who fund its activities have a direct stake in controlling the cost of medical care. (However, it is easy for many observers to become a bit cynical when they compare their own medical expense plan with the generous plan available to members of Congress.)

What Is the Objective of National Health Insurance?

It is difficult to determine exactly what a national health insurance program should accomplish. Alternative proposals either have different objectives or place varying degrees of emphasis on a combination of objectives. There are two primary concerns with the current health care system—rapidly increasing costs and the lack of coverage for a large segment of the population. Some programs are essentially a proposed solution to only one of these concerns; other proposals address both concerns in varying degrees. It would be much easier to find a solution if there was consensus on the scope of the actual problem.

Unfortunately, the two problems are not independent, and solving one problem may actually exacerbate the other. For example, making broad coverage available to everyone might so increase the demand for medical treatment that costs would go up because of a shortage of medical providers. This situation occurred after the passage of Medicare. In addition, efforts to control costs could lead to rationing of medical care so that some types of care would be available only to the more affluent segment of the population who could afford some type of supplemental insurance protection.

Do Americans Want Reform?

This is a difficult question to answer. During the health care debate over the last few years, numerous polls were taken. There seemed to be overwhelming agreement among the American people that the health care system is broken and needs fixing. Some proponents of national health insurance inferred from this opinion that there was support for radical reform.

As the debate continued and more polls about the underlying mood of the public were conducted, a different picture began to emerge. Most Americans were happy with their own medical expense coverage. They were also aware of rapidly rising costs, but those in managed care plans had been less significantly affected by them. In fact, as many employees elected managed care options, they actually saw their out-of-pocket medical expenses decrease. Although the public was not in favor of changes that would affect their relationships with providers of medical care, a surprisingly large percentage of the public was aware that reform carried a financial cost, and within limits many Americans were willing to foot the bill.

These further surveys also indicated that the major concern of Americans was the lack of security surrounding their own medical expense coverage, particularly if they became unemployed or changed jobs. There was fear that the loss of employment would put them in the category of uninsured. Even if coverage could be continued under COBRA, its high cost would make it unaffordable. Considerable concern was also expressed over the lack of coverage when changing jobs because of preexisting-conditions provisions in the new employer's coverage. While Congress is often considered out of touch with the electorate, these, in fact, were significant issues addressed by recent major health insurance legislation.

One final observation about these surveys: They showed that the majority of Americans do not want another program as bureaucratic as they view Medicare to be.

Is the Goal Universal Coverage or Universal Access?

Some national health insurance programs call for universal coverage, which means that all Americans would be covered. Unfortunately the cost of universal coverage would be very expensive, and it is questionable whether such a program could be accomplished voluntarily. As long as some people are in a position of voluntarily electing coverage, there are those who would be unwilling to pay the price, even if it was subsidized. Therefore, universal coverage probably requires a program similar to Medicare and accompanying tax revenue to support the program. With the majority of the public wanting a nongovernment program of health insurance, many other national health insurance proposals focus on universal access and realize that a goal of slightly less than universal coverage is all that is realistically attainable. But even this goal will require subsidies for some segments of the population.

Who Should Pay the Cost?

A majority of the uninsured have inadequate resources to pay the cost of voluntary coverage, even if it were suddenly available. As a result, there will be some need to subsidize the cost of coverage if the number of uninsured is going to be reduced substantially. Who pays? The alternatives are many, but they can largely be summed up in one word—*taxes*. There have been numerous suggestions about the form of these taxes, but in all cases they will fall on some or all taxpayers. These alternatives include general tax revenue, additional Social Security taxes, and taxes on cigarettes because smoking is the source of many medical problems.

Sometimes overlooked is the fact that many of the uninsured do receive medical treatment. Even though uninsured persons may be unable to pay, treatment by hospitals and physicians is usually not denied for serious illnesses or injuries. However, when the hospital or physician writes off a large portion of these bills as uncollectible, the cost is in effect being passed on to those who do pay their bills (usually through insurance) in the form of higher charges than would otherwise be made. In theory, the cost to many individuals or employers will decrease if a larger portion of the population has the resources to pay their own expenses. This is used as the rationale for taxing employers or individuals to pay the cost of providing protection for the uninsured.

What Benefits Should Be Available?

One of the major debates in designing a national health insurance program involves the scope of the benefits that will be included. At one extreme in the debate are those who feel the government should guarantee only a minimum level of health care. Private medical expense insurance or personal resources would be necessary to obtain broader benefits. At the other extreme are those who feel that a comprehensive level of health care should be available to all Americans. This group views complete health care protection as a basic right that belongs to everyone regardless of income.

The current system of health insurance falls somewhere between these two extremes, and this is probably where any ultimate solution will be found. Most Americans do not have coverage for long-term care, and many have limitations on such benefits as mental health and substance abuse. Some medical expense plans limit coverage for prescription drugs. Such limitations exist not because employers see no value in these benefits but because realistic cost constraints dictate the benefits that are provided. Employers cannot afford a medical expense plan that will do everything for everyone, and it is questionable whether Americans are willing to pay the cost of a national health insurance program that has such a lofty goal.

Another issue is whether a uniform package of benefits should be available nationwide. Under some proposals, benefits would be determined on a state-by-state basis, while under other proposals, a national benefit standard would be established. These proposals typically call for the abolishment of state benefit mandates.

Does Cost Containment Harm Quality?

While there are undoubtedly inefficiencies in the health care system, many of these inefficiencies have been addressed in recent years. For example, hospitals, faced with limits on Medicare and Medicaid reimbursements, have been forced to operate in a more cost-effective manner. However, future efforts to control costs will probably need to be more severe and may come with a high price. Americans arguably have the best and most innovative health care system in the world. Can this quality be continued if prices are controlled? Or will it continue only for those who have additional resources to pay? Control of costs, if taken beyond a certain point, will lead to the situation that exists in most countries with national health insurance programs—rationing of medical care. Questions like the following will then need to be answered: Should organ transplants be limited to persons under age 50? Should very expensive health care continue to be provided to premature babies who have a less than 25 percent chance of survival? To what extent should medical treatment be provided to persons with AIDS and other terminal illnesses? Will controls on the cost of prescription drugs eliminate the resources needed to develop the next generation of medicines?

Are Employer Mandates the Proper Approach?

National health care proposals differ with respect to the employer's role in making coverage available to its employees. Some proposals would require virtually all employers to make coverage available to employees (including part-time employees) and their dependents and to pay a portion of the cost. Under all such proposals, there are additional programs for the unemployed and subsidies to some employers for whom the cost exceeds a certain limit. However, small employers would be hit hard by most of these proposals and have lobbied against employer mandates. There is considerable support for the argument that the cost of employer mandates would force some small employers out of business.

One major argument for employer mandates is that the alternative is a government-run program with its accompanying bureaucracy.

What Is the Role of Medicare and Medicaid?

Many differences exist over the role of Medicare and Medicaid in health care reform. Although some argue for a single system to cover all Americans, opponents argue that the Medicare and Medicaid programs serve specific groups and are working reasonably well. Why alter the part of the system that is already closest to the concept of universal coverage?

It is interesting to note that national health insurance proposals are much more likely to fold Medicaid recipients into a new program than they are to include Medicare recipients. This fact reflects the reality that tinkering with Medicare can have grave consequences because of the high voter turnout of the elderly.

What Are the Political Realities?

The possibility of any national health insurance program depends on whether Congress can design a program that receives broad-based support. Although Republicans are unlikely to offer solutions that are as far-reaching as the initial Clinton administration's proposal and that will offend as many segments of society, public clamor for change will undoubtedly lead to continued reform of the current health care system, modest though it may be. Clearly any change will be designed to appeal to a different class of constituents. While the initial Clinton administration's proposal appealed to such groups as organized labor, the Republicans are much more likely to be influenced by the concerns of small businesses. However, no program will be successful and politically palatable unless it receives support from many diverse groups, including employers, insurers, hospitals, physicians, drug companies, and the general public.

Possible Approaches

One difficulty for the author of any textbook is the extent to which current proposals should be covered in detail. In a debate like the one occurring over health insurance, new proposals are continually replacing old ones, and those that are around for any length of time undergo revision. For this reason, the discussion is general and describes the following generic approaches that are being discussed:

- Managed competition plans
- Single-payer plans
- Medical savings accounts
- Reform on a state-by-state basis
- Modest reform of the current system

It is important to remember that the use of any one of these approaches does not dictate a specific national health insurance plan. Within each approach, there is wide latitude to address many of the issues discussed in the previous pages.

Managed Competition Plans

The term *managed competition* received considerable attention because it was the approach taken by the Clinton administration in designing its initial national health insurance proposal. However, the term and the concept have been discussed since the 1970s. The basic philosophy behind the idea of managed competition is that competition for medical expense insurance should be based on price rather than on the risk characteristics of those needing coverage. A managed competition plan would create a new type of organization—often referred to as an *HIPC* or a *health insurance purchasing cooperative.* (Note that some states have now adopted HIPCs, as was discussed earlier in this chapter.) An HIPC would act as a purchasing agent and negotiate with insurance companies, HMOs, and other providers of medical expense coverage to offer a menu of different insurance plans to employers and individuals who subscribe to the HIPC. In addition to price, subscribers would be given information on each plan's quality of care.

Under most managed care proposals, HIPCs would be established under state regulation, would operate in a specified geographic region, and would not compete with each other. Some proposals require all employers to be subscribers to the HIPC in their area, which would be the only source for providing coverage to employees. To varying degrees, however, most managed competition proposals allow larger employers to establish their own HIPCs for self-funding benefits.

Most managed care proposals also establish standards for what are often called *approved* or *accountable health plans* (AHPs). These AHPs are the only medical providers that can deal with an HIPC, which would require each AHP to offer a standard set of benefit packages. HMOs are in a position to do this, but other providers would need to form alliances, such as an insurance company forming an AHP with a network of hospitals and physicians.

All employers (and also unemployed and self-employed persons) would be eligible for coverage from the HIPC, and there would be no preexisting-conditions provisions for employees. Some proposals use community rating, which would establish a set price per covered person for the plan selected. Other proposals would adjust rates by such factors as age or sex.

While individual proposals for national health insurance may vary, there is nothing in the basic idea of managed competition that dictates any specific benefit package, level of employer contribution to the cost of the coverage for employees, or government price controls.

The critics of managed competition are many. It involves a fundamental change in the delivery of health care and has been opposed by many physicians who fear that their ability to treat patients will come under government control. Insurance agents have been particularly vocal because their role would be virtually eliminated. However, there would still be a modest role for benefit consultants to advise employers on the selection of alternative plans under the HIPC. HIPCs are also unappealing to persons who are not already in managed care plans and wish to retain control over their choice of medical practitioners. Employers that operate in many regions would also be required to deal with several HIPCs.

Managed competition has also been criticized for creating another level of health care bureaucracy by the formation of HIPCs and the additional regulation that would be needed. It has been suggested that this might also negate the effect of any cost-saving features of the approach.

Single-Payer Plans

Several proposals for national health insurance can be categorized as single-payer plans, which is the approach taken in Canada and many European countries. Under a single-payer plan, everyone is automatically covered by a single program run by the government, and the same benefit package is provided to everyone. Some proposals have a totally federal program; other proposals call for each state to administer the program for its residents, but under specific federal guidelines.

Single-payer plans eliminate the employer's role in providing medical expense benefits to employees. The agent's role is also eliminated unless the plan benefits are at a level where there is a market for supplemental insurance. However, most proposals call for very comprehensive coverage with few if any copayments.

Most proposals for a single-payer plan call for the financing of the program through taxes rather than premiums. While the taxes could take a variety of forms, a Social Security type of payroll tax on both employers and employees is most commonly mentioned.

In some respects, a single-payer plan can be viewed as a Medicare-type program that covers everyone. The single-payer approach, however, goes farther and calls for more government control of medical care. A national health care budget would be established, and reimbursement schedules to providers would be determined at the state or federal level within the constraints of this budget. In addition, the budget would result in the government's exercising controls over the types of treatment available for specific conditions and the extent to which monies would be spent on new technology and medical facilities. In effect, a single-payer plan rejects market forces as the allocator of medical resources and implies that there would be some rationing of medical care under government guidelines.

Although the broad nature of a single-payer plan would result in additional costs because of increased demand for health care, these costs would be offset by efficiencies associated with the approach. For example, the claim process would be dramatically streamlined, and marketing costs would be virtually eliminated. Furthermore, the widespread availability of medical care would probably lead to more preventive care, which would minimize the need for more expensive treatments in the future.

Much of the support for a single-payer approach to the health care problem arises from the perception that Americans have of the Canadian health care system. There is no doubt that Canadians overwhelmingly believe they have a good system, but just as in the United States, the system is becoming a subject of national debate. Costs are lower than in the United States, but they are increasing at a rapid rate. Moreover, there is rationing of care, which can lead to lengthy waits to schedule surgeries. As a result, some Canadians come to the United States for treatment that privately insured Americans can receive on demand. These facts, coupled with the American public's concern over bigger government and its bureaucracy, make the adoption of a single-payer approach unlikely.

Medical Savings Accounts

Unlike the two previous approaches to national health insurance, the use of medical savings accounts (MSAs) is seldom proposed as the sole method of providing medical expense coverage. Instead, their use is an option that would be available to employers. Depending on the proposal, employers might use this approach for all employees or let employees choose an MSA in lieu of another form of medical expense coverage.

An MSA is an alternative to a medical expense plan and has few copayments. Instead, an employee gets a comprehensive medical plan with virtually total coverage for medical expenses to the extent that they exceed a high deductible, such as $2,000. The employer then contributes part of the savings in premium to an MSA, which is often an interest-bearing account. An employee can draw from the account to pay medical expenses not covered by the medical expense plan, such as charges for routine office visits or the cost of eyeglasses. At the end of the year, any monies in the MSA might either be left in the MSA to pay future unreimbursed medical expenses or be paid to the employee.

The rationale for an MSA is that significant cost savings can occur for two primary reasons. First, the expensive cost of administering small claims is largely eliminated, as demonstrated by the fact that a major medical policy with a $2,500 deductible can often be purchased for about one-half the cost of a policy with a $250 deductible. Second, employees now have a direct financial incentive to avoid unnecessary care and to seek out the most cost-effective form of treatment.

A few employers have used MSAs for some time with positive results. Costs have in fact been lowered or risen less rapidly than would otherwise be expected. Reactions of employees have generally been favorable, but there has been one major drawback—contributions to an MSA have constituted taxable income to employees. However, as described in Chapter 10, this issue has been addressed by recent legislation.

As with almost any approach to cost containment, MSAs have their critics. It is argued that MSAs may make sense when used with traditional indemnity plans, but long-term health care reform should focus on managed care. Proponents counter that the concept could also work with HMOs or PPOs. Another argument against MSAs is that employees will minimize treatment for minor medical expenses and preventive care that would have been covered under a plan without an MSA. This avoidance of medical care, contend the critics, may lead to major expenses that could have been avoided or minimized with earlier treatment. A final criticism of MSAs is that they do not focus on the problem of the uninsured. In rebuttal, proponents argue that any technique that lowers costs for employers will encourage some additional small employers to provide coverage that would have previously been unaffordable.

State Reform

There is increasing support in Congress for the idea that national health insurance should take the form of a series of state programs rather than a single federal program. This support comes from many new members of Congress who are more amenable to having the states rather than the federal government solve some of the nation's problems. Support also comes from some state governors. Some other members of Congress, who might otherwise prefer a federal solution, feel that reform at the state level is preferable to partisan debate at the national level with little chance of any real reform.

To give the states flexibility in health care reform, it will be necessary for the states to be free of such constraints as ERISA. Without an ERISA preemption, states will be unable to apply reform to employees who are in self-funded plans. Employers who self-fund benefits, particularly those who have been successful with cost containment, will be reluctant to support such a change in federal law because it may ultimately result in increased costs, particularly if a state adopts some type of community rating. Self-funded employers that operate in many states would also be burdened by having to comply with each state's mandates.

An interesting paradox has developed in Congress. While Republican control has increased interest in letting the states solve problems, there is also increased sympathy for the wishes of business. As a result, support for an ERISA preemption seems less likely than in the past.

Reform of the Current System

The 1994 elections, which resulted in a more conservative Congress, effectively ended any hopes of the Clinton administration for a major comprehensive restructuring of the nation's health care system. Despite very divergent views in Washington, however, 1996 saw the most far-reaching federal legislation to affect medical expense insurance in many years. It was clear to all sides that the public strongly supported certain changes, and these changes were enacted with bipartisan support. In addition, each side seemed willing to give the other side a little bit of what it wanted. While the overall result is not a basic restructuring of the health care system, it clearly represents significant reform and change.

The primary piece of health care legislation in 1996 was HIPAA. Although a detailed discussion of many of the act's provisions appears in the appropriate sections of later chapters, these provisions can be summarized as follows:

- Increased availability of medical expense coverage, discussed in the next section of this chapter
- A trial program of tax-favored MSAs, discussed in Chapter 10
- Increased portability of medical expense coverage, discussed in Chapter 12
- Expansion of eligibility for COBRA benefits, discussed in Chapter 12

- Increased tax deductibility of medical expense premiums for the self-employed, discussed in Chapter 12
- Favorable income tax treatment for long-term care insurance, discussed in Chapter 13

HIPAA was not the only 1996 legislation to affect group medical expense coverage. The Mental Health Parity Act requires that many employers provide increased benefits for mental illnesses. In addition, the Newborns' and Mothers' Health Protection Act may increase the length of inpatient benefits for childbirth in many cases. The effect of each act on medical expense plans is discussed in Chapter 10.

For the foreseeable future, it appears that changes to the health care system will continue on a piecemeal approach to address specific issues and problems. For example, at the time this book is being revised, there is proposed legislation to make medical expense benefits available to more children. It is interesting to note that many recent state health care reforms (such as the establishment of HIPCs and small-group legislation) and many provisions of HIPAA and other federal legislation incorporate aspects of the original Clinton proposal for national health insurance.

Increased Availability of Medical Expense Coverage

HIPAA contains several provisions designed to help both employees and employers obtain coverage more easily. Portions of the act that deal with pre-existing conditions are covered in Chapter 12 when the issue of eligibility is discussed. The discussion in this chapter focuses on the plans covered by the act and portions of the act that address nondiscrimination rules, special enrollment periods, renewability and small groups.

Covered Plans

The act applies to group health plans that cover two or more employees, whether insured or self-funded. However, there is a long list of excepted benefits to which the act does not apply. The following are excepted benefits in all circumstances:

- Coverage for accidents, including accidental death and dismemberment
- Disability income insurance
- Liability insurance
- Coverage issued as a supplement to liability insurance
- Workers' compensation or similar insurance
- Automobile medical payments insurance
- Credit-only insurance, such as mortgage insurance
- Coverage for on-site medical clinics

In addition, certain other benefits are excepted benefits under specified circumstances:

■ Limited vision or dental benefits, long-term care insurance, nursing home insurance, home health care insurance, and insurance for community-based care if these benefits are offered separately rather than as an integral part of a medical expense plan

■ Coverage for a specific disease or illness or for hospital or other fixed indemnity insurance if the benefits (1) are provided under a corporate policy and certificate or contract of insurance and (2) are not coordinated with other coverage under a medical expense plan

■ Medicare supplement insurance or other similar supplemental coverage if the policy is offered as a separate insurance policy rather than as a continuation of coverage under a plan that also covers active employees

■ Flexible spending accounts (FSAs) under cafeteria plans, as long as (1) the employee has other coverage available under a group health plan of the employer and (2) the maximum payment under the FSA for the year does not exceed the greater of two times the employee's salary reduction or the amount of the employee's salary reduction plus $500 (Virtually all FSAs, which are discussed in Chapter 17, meet these requirements.)

With one exception, all employers—including the federal government—must comply with the act's provisions. State and local government plans can elect to be excluded from most of HIPAA's provisions.

Nondiscrimination Rules

The act prohibits the use of any of the following health-related factors as a reason to exclude an employee or dependent from coverage under a group health plan or to charge the individual or dependent a higher premium:

■ Health status
■ Medical condition, including both physical and mental condition
■ Claims experience
■ Receipt of health care
■ Medical history
■ Genetic information
■ Evidence of insurability, including conditions caused by domestic violence
■ Disability

It is important to note that these factors relate to coverage for specific individuals under a plan. The overall plan itself (except for plans in the small-group market, as explained later) can still be subject to traditional underwriting standards. In addition, group health plans are not required to offer any specific benefits and can limit benefit levels as long as they do not discriminate on the basis of these health-related factors. The act does not restrict the amount an insurance company or other provider of health care coverage can charge an employer for coverage. The act does allow an employer or provider of medical expense coverage to establish premium discounts or to modify co-payments or deductibles for persons who participate in programs of health promotion or disease prevention.

Special Enrollment Periods

For various reasons, employees and their dependents may elect not to en-roll in an employer's plan when they are initially eligible for coverage. For ex-ample, a new employee may have coverage under a spouse's plan. The act requires that employers allow these employees and dependents to enroll in the employer's plan under any one of several specified circumstances as long as the employee had previously stated in writing that the original declination was because there was other coverage. However, the requirement of a written declination does not apply unless the employer requires it and notifies the em-ployee that it is a requirement for future coverage. The following are the cir-cumstances for special enrollment:

- The other coverage was lost because of loss of eligibility under the other plan. This loss of eligibility can result from such circumstances as divorce, the spouse's termination of employment, or the spouse's death.
- The other coverage was lost because employer contributions for the cover-age terminated.
- The other coverage was COBRA coverage that is exhausted. (COBRA is discussed in detail in Chapter 12.)

The employee has 30 days following the loss of coverage to request enroll-ment in the employer's plan.

In addition, new dependents (including children placed for adoption) are also eligible for coverage under special enrollment rules. The employee must enroll the dependent within 30 days of his or her gaining dependent status. Coverage for a new spouse must become effective no later than the first month beginning after the employee's request. Coverage for children must go into ef-fect as of the date of birth, adoption, or placement for adoption.

Guaranteed Renewability

All group health insurers must renew existing health insurance coverage unless one of the following circumstances exists:

- The plan sponsor failed to pay premiums or the issuer of health insurance coverage failed to receive timely premiums.
- The plan sponsor performed an act of fraud or made an intentional mis-representation of material fact under the terms of the coverage.

- The plan sponsor failed to comply with a material plan provision relating to employer contribution or group participation rules, as long as these rules are permitted under applicable state or federal law. For example, an employer might fail to maintain a minimum required percentage of participation under a plan.
- There is no covered employee who lives or works in the service area of a network plan, such as an HMO.
- The employer is no longer a member of the association that sponsors a plan.
- The issuer of coverage ceases to offer coverage in a particular market. The issuer must notify each plan sponsor, participant, and beneficiary at least 90 days prior to the discontinuation of coverage, and the issuer must offer each plan sponsor the option to purchase other health insurance coverage currently being offered by the issuer to a group health plan in the market. If the issuer exits the market entirely, the period of notice is 180 days, and the issuer cannot reenter the market and sell health insurance coverage for at least five years.

Similar rules require that multi-employer plans and multiple-employer welfare arrangements renew coverage for employers. It also establishes guaranteed-issue rules for the individual marketplace.

Guaranteed Issue for Small-Group Plans

With some exceptions, the act requires that insurers, HMOs, and other providers of health care coverage that operate in the small-group market to accept all small employers—defined as employers with 2 to 50 employees—that apply for coverage. In addition, all employees of small employers and their dependents must be accepted for coverage as long as they enroll during the period in which they are first eligible. This rule is in line with the small-group legislation of many states. Some states have similar rules for groups as small as one employee, and some stipulate an upper limit of 25 above which the small-group legislation does not apply.

Exceptions to this guaranteed-issue requirement are allowed if a provider of coverage in the small-group market has inadequate network or financial capacity or if applicants are not in a plan's service area.

Minimum participation or employer contribution requirements are acceptable as long as they are permitted under applicable state law.

Interrelationship of State and Federal Legislation

For the most part, the new federal legislation does not preempt state laws pertaining to group health insurance (which might be more stringent than HIPAA), except in those situations where any state standard or requirement would prevent the application of the federal law. To prevent any preemption, many states have had to make some modifications to their laws and regulations. (As explained in Chapter 12, the situation is different for the rules pertaining to preexisting conditions.)

The act permits a state to enforce the act's provisions with respect to insurance companies and other medical expense providers. However, the federal government can take over enforcement if a state does not perform its duties. In that case, enforcement is by the secretary of health and human services. The secretary of labor has enforcement power for the act's provisions as they apply to group health plans themselves, including the act's portability provisions. When there is federal enforcement, the penalty for noncompliance can be up to $100 per day for each individual with respect to whom a plan or issuer is in noncompliance.

STUDY QUESTIONS

1. a. How did the federal government become a major player in providing medical expense coverage during the 1960s?
   b. What effect did this have on health care costs?

2. How was medical expense coverage affected by legislation in the 1970s?

3. Describe the efforts that employers have used in recent years to control the cost of medical expense coverage.

4. What are some of the reasons for the significant increases in the cost of health care?

5. What are the major components of health care cost containment?

6. What characteristics should be contained in a managed care plan?

7. Describe the provisions of the NAIC Small Employer Health Insurance Availability Model Act.

8. In addition to making coverage more available and affordable for small employers, what other types of health care reform are being adopted by the states?

9. What are the two primary objectives of national health insurance?

10. Why is the goal of universal coverage probably unobtainable?

11. What is the rationale for taxing employers and individuals to pay the cost of providing medical expense coverage for the uninsured?

12. What are the arguments for and against managed competition as an approach for designing a national health insurance program?

13. a. How does a single-payer plan affect the role of the employer and the agent in providing medical expense coverage?

    b. What effects would a single-payer plan likely have on costs for medical care and medical expense insurance?

14. a. What is the rationale for medical savings accounts?

    b. What are the criticisms of the use of medical savings accounts?

15. a. What are the arguments for giving an ERISA preemption to the states?

    b. Why are certain groups opposed to such preemptions?

16. What types of provisions are contained in the Health Insurance Portability and Accountability Act (HIPAA)?

17. What health-related factors does HIPAA prohibit as a reason to exclude an employee from coverage under a group health plan or to charge an individual or dependent a higher premium?

18. Describe the circumstances under which HIPAA requires a group health plan to have special enrollment periods.

19. Under what circumstance does HIPAA allow an insurer to not renew a group health plan?

20. What is the relationship between HIPAA and state laws?

Group Medical Expense Benefits: Traditional Plans

OBJECTIVES

■ Compare the characteristics of medical expense plans offered by Blue Cross and Blue Shield plans and by insurance companies.

■ Describe the benefits and exclusions contained in each of the following basic medical expense coverages:
1. Hospital expense benefits
2. Surgical expense benefits
3. Physicians' visits expense benefits

■ Describe the approaches used to provide major medical coverage.

■ Describe the characteristics of major medical insurance.

■ Describe the types of managed care provisions used in traditional medical expense insurance plans.

■ Describe the characteristics and tax treatment of medical savings accounts.

Prior to the mid-1970s, most employees were covered by what are commonly referred to as *traditional,* or *indemnity, plans.* Medical expenses were incurred, patients had considerable freedom in choosing the providers of medical care, and claims were paid with virtually no attempts to control costs. As was pointed out in the previous chapter, some employees are still covered under plans that are largely traditional in nature. However, these plans have evolved. While they are still far from what might be called *managed care plans,* these plans contain provisions designed to control costs, influence the behavior of persons needing medical care, and provide preventive care.

This chapter begins with a brief discussion of the providers of traditional medical expense coverage. It continues by first analyzing plans that provide basic coverage and then discussing major medical coverage. The chapter next reviews some managed care techniques that might be found in traditional plans. Other techniques are described where appropriate throughout the chapter. This is followed by a brief discussion of coverage for alternative medicine.

The chapter concludes with a discussion of medical savings accounts (MSAs). The rationale for including their coverage in this chapter is that most MSAs being established are used in conjunction with traditional major medical plans that have a high deductible.

Before proceeding further, two comments need to be made about the importance of this chapter. First, interest in traditional plans will undoubtedly vary by the state in which a reader resides. It was pointed out in the previous chapter that only about 14 percent of employees and their families are covered under traditional plans. However, this percentage varies significantly by state. For example, HMO enrollments are small (10 percent or less) in about 20 percent of the states—mostly states with small and heavily rural populations. In these states, most employees and their families are covered by traditional plans or PPOs, which can be viewed as traditional major medical plans that have adopted a wide range of managed care characteristics. In another 20 percent of the states—typically populous and urban states—40 to 55 percent of employees and their families are covered by HMOs and almost all of the remaining employees and families are covered by other forms of managed care.

Second, the discussion of medical expense plans in this and the following chapter largely follows the historical development of medical expense plans. Much of the terminology and coverage of legislation introduced here also applies to the managed care approaches to medical care that are discussed in the following chapter.

PROVIDERS OF TRADITIONAL COVERAGE

Providers of traditional coverage include Blue Cross–Blue Shield plans, insurance companies, and employers using self-funded arrangements, which are discussed in more detail in Chapter 14. While the plans described in this chapter are characteristic of those offered by the Blues and insurance companies, self-funded plans must be properly designed to be effective. Such plans have "borrowed" liberally from insured plans and contain similar—if not identical—provisions.

Blue Cross–Blue Shield Plans

Prior to the Great Depression, "health" insurance contracts provided by insurance companies were primarily designed to give income benefits to persons who were disabled by accidents and, to a limited degree, illnesses. It was generally accepted that individuals should pay their own medical expenses from their savings. During the depression, however, the savings of many individuals disappeared, unemployment was severe, and most insurance companies ceased writing disability income contracts. Faced with financial difficulties arising from the inability of many patients to pay their bills, many hospitals established plans for the prepayment of hospital expenses. By paying a monthly fee to the hospital, a *subscriber* (the term used to describe persons covered by such plans) was entitled to a limited number of days of hospitalization per year. The early plans were limited to a single hospital, but by the mid-1930s many plans had become communitywide or statewide operations, offering subscribers the choice of using any participating hospital. Much of this expansion resulted from actions by the American Hospital Association to promote and control this type of plan. In the late 1930s, the American Hospital Association adopted the Blue Cross name and emblem and permitted them to be used only by plans that met standards established by the association. As a general rule, only one plan within a geographic area was allowed to use the Blue Cross name. Eventually, the Blue Cross activities of the American Hospital Association were transferred to a separate national organization, the Blue Cross Association.

The success of the early Blue Cross plans and the inability of physicians to collect bills for their services during the depression resulted in the development of Blue Shield plans, established by local medical associations to prepay physicians' charges. The evolution of Blue Shield plans paralleled that of Blue Cross plans, with the American Medical Association acting similarly to the American Hospital Association. Eventually, the role of the American Medical Association was transferred to the National Association of Blue Shield Plans, which then became the national coordinating body.

To a large extent, the persons covered by Blue Shield plans were the same ones whose hospital charges were covered by Blue Cross plans, and in many geographic regions this overlapping led to a close working relationship between the two. For many years in some areas of the country one plan administered the other. However, this administration was typically on a fee-for-administration basis, with the two plans being separate legal entities. In recent years, there has been a consolidation of most Blue Cross and Blue Shield plans. Usually, this consolidation has taken the form of a complete merger; in a few cases the consolidation has been only partial. These partial consolidations have resulted in Blue Cross–Blue Shield plans that operate under a single staff but with separate governing boards.

There has been consolidation at the national level also. In 1978, the staffs of the two national organizations were merged, and a new organization—the Blue Cross and Blue Shield Associations—was formed to act on matters of mutual interest to both Blue Cross plans and Blue Shield plans. It was governed by members of the boards from both the Blue Cross Association and the National Association of Blue Shield Plans. In 1982, a complete merger took place, with the resulting organization called the *Blue Cross and Blue Shield Association*.

As of late 2000, there were 50 plans in existence. Most jointly wrote Blue Cross and Blue Shield coverage, but there were a few separate Blue Cross plans and Blue Shield plans. Although most states are served by a single Blue Cross–Blue Shield plan, in a few states there is more than one plan, each operating within a specific geographic region. In a few instances, plans may cover more than one state. Only in a few cases is there any overlapping of the geographic areas served by individual plans.

Each local Blue Cross, Blue Shield, or Blue Cross–Blue Shield plan is a legally separate entity operated by a governing board, which establishes specific practices for the plan in accordance with the broad standards of the national Blue Cross and Blue Shield Association. Consequently, individual plans may differ substantially from one another. The boards of these plans used to be dominated by the providers of coverage, but now the boards of most plans are dominated by "nonproviders," including representatives of consumer organizations, foundations, labor unions, businesses, and the general public.

Traditionally, Blue Cross and Blue Shield plans have been nonprofit corporations and acted as insurers of last resort in most states. This meant that they wrote coverage on almost anyone at competitive rates. For this, the Blues tended to receive favorable tax treatment. However, as insurance companies and HMOs expanded their market share, they tended to take the better business and leave the Blues with coverage of an increasing number of unhealthy lives. As a result, the Blues have become more restrictive in their underwriting practices. In addition, a few of the Blues have changed to for-profit status in order to raise the capital necessary to compete more effectively with other types of providers of medical expense coverage. Many of the Blues also own subsidiaries that are run to make a profit.

Insurance Companies

For many years, Blue Cross and Blue Shield plans were the predominant providers of medical expense coverage; insurance companies were much slower to enter the market and took a different approach. Rather than emphasizing basic first-dollar coverage for hospital or physicians' charges, most insurers chose to write major medical coverage with deductibles and coinsurance. By the mid-1950s, insurance companies surpassed the Blues in premium volume for medical expense coverage.

Like other types of insurance, medical expense coverage is written by both stock and mutual insurance companies. While some coverage is written by insurers that specialize in the medical expense market, much of the premium volume for group coverage is written by large life insurance companies. It is interesting to note that medical expense coverage is also a line of insurance sometimes written by property-casualty insurance companies.

Comparison of the Blues and Insurance Companies

Perhaps the best way to describe the characteristics of Blue Cross–Blue Shield plans and insurance company plans is to compare their characteristics. Traditionally, the similarities between the Blues and insurance companies were overshadowed by their differences. Over time, however, intense competition has often caused one type of provider to adopt the more popular but differing practices of the other. As a result, insurance companies and the Blues are becoming increasingly similar, in spite of their many distinctly different characteristics.

The following comparison of the Blues and insurance companies focuses on their operation with respect to traditional medical expense insurance coverage. It is followed by a brief treatment of how both types of organizations have expanded into managed care.

Regulation and Taxation

In a few states, Blue Cross–Blue Shield plans are regulated under the same laws that apply to insurance companies. However, in most states the Blues are nonprofit organizations and are regulated under special legislation. Typically, this regulation is carried out by the same body that regulates insurance companies. However, in some respects the Blues receive preferential treatment over insurance companies, probably the most significant example being their exemption from premium taxation and income taxation by many states. Because premium taxes (usually about 2 percent of premiums) are passed on to consumers, this gives the Blues a cost advantage. In many other respects, however, the Blues are subject to more stringent regulation than insurance companies. For example, in most states their rates are subject to regulatory approval. With recent trends toward consumerism, this approval has become more burdensome and expensive.

In addition, the Blues are also accorded favorable tax treatment under the federal income tax laws. Prior to the Tax Reform Act of 1986, the Blues (except for the few plans that were incorporated as insurance companies) were exempt from federal income taxation. The tax act eliminated this complete exemption. Because of various deductions that can be taken, however, the average effective tax rate for the Blues is significantly below the average tax rate for insurance companies.

Form of Benefits

Traditionally, the Blues offered benefits in the form of services, while insurance companies offered benefits on an indemnity (or reimbursement) basis. Under the service-benefit concept, benefits are expressed in terms of the services that are provided by the hospitals or physicians participating in the plan rather than in terms of dollar maximums. For example, a Blue Cross plan might provide up to 90 days of hospitalization per year in semiprivate accommodations. In contrast, an insurance company might provide reimbursement for hospital charges subject to both dollar and duration limits, such as $400 per day for 90 days. In both cases, however, any charges in excess of the benefits must be borne by the covered person.

Blue Cross–Blue Shield plans involve two separate types of contractual relationships: a plan promises to provide specified services to a subscriber for whom a premium has been paid, and it has contracts with providers of services whereby the providers are reimbursed for the cost of services rendered to subscribers. In general, subscribers are not billed for the cost of covered services or required to file claim forms. Rather, this cost is negotiated between the plan and the providers. This type of arrangement generally requires that subscribers receive their services from providers participating in the plan; however, most hospitals and physicians are participants. If nonparticipating providers can be used (such as for emergencies), benefits are usually paid on an indemnity basis, as is done by insurance companies.

In contrast, an insurance company that writes traditional medical expense coverage agrees only to reimburse a covered person for medical expenses up to the limits specified in the insurance contract. There is no contractual relationship between the providers of medical services and the insurance company. Thus, covered persons must file the appropriate claim forms. While covered persons have a legal obligation to pay their medical bills, the insurance company's obligation (unless benefits are assigned) is only to reimburse the covered person, not to actually pay the providers. However, most hospitals and many other providers require that any potential insurance benefits be assigned to them by a patient before they will render services. In effect, such an assignment requires the insurance company to pay benefits directly to the provider on behalf of the covered person.

In the past, insurance companies incorporated maximum daily room and board limits into their contracts that did not cover medical expenses in full. However, to compete with the Blues, many insurance companies now frequently write contracts that provide full reimbursement for certain medical expenses. Even though a covered person may see little difference in the benefits received from either type of provider, the traditional distinction still exists: The Blues are providing services, whereas insurance companies are providing reimbursement for the cost of services.

Types of Benefits

Over the years the Blues specialized in providing basic medical benefits, with Blue Cross providing coverage for hospital expenses and Blue Shield providing coverage for surgical expenses and physicians' visits. Major medical benefits were rarely available. However, competition from insurance companies and increased cooperation between Blue Cross and Blue Shield have resulted in the Blues now offering virtually the same coverages as insurance companies. It is interesting to note that as the Blues have expanded the scope of benefits offered, they have frequently included deductible and coinsurance provisions similar to those used by insurance companies. When there is a deductible, a covered person is required to pay expenses up to some limit (such as $100 per year or per illness) out of his or her own pocket before benefits are paid. When coinsurance is used, a covered person is required to pay a percentage (such as 20 percent) of some or all expenses, the remaining portion being covered under the medical expense plan.

The advantage many insurance companies have had over the Blues has been their ability to offer a wide variety of group benefits, including life insurance coverage and disability income coverage. Until a few years ago, most states had laws and regulations that prevented the Blues from offering any coverage other than medical expense benefits, but because of recent changes in these laws and regulations, the Blues can now offer a wider range of group benefits to their subscribers. While competition between the Blues and insurance companies over writing these other benefits is increasing, the Blues currently write relatively little coverage other than medical expense benefits.

Reimbursement of Providers

The method by which the Blues reimburse the providers often results in their having a competitive advantage over insurance companies. Most Blue Cross plans pay participating hospitals on a per diem basis for each day a subscriber is hospitalized. Periodic negotiations with Blue Cross determine the amount of this payment (which includes room-and-board charges as well as other covered charges) for each hospital. For example, if the per diem amount is $600, the hospital will receive $600 for each day a subscriber is hospitalized, regardless of what the actual charges might be. While this per diem amount is adequate on the average, the hospital will "lose money" on some patients but "make money" on others.

In addition to the administrative simplicity of this method of reimbursement, the per diem amount is often less than the average daily hospital charges. Frequently, it is determined by excluding such hospital costs as bad debts, charity care, and nursing school costs. These costs are used in determining charges for patients who are not Blue Cross subscribers or members of managed care plans that have entered into similar arrangements. Therefore, Blue Cross subscribers, in effect, receive a discount on the charges made to some other patients, including those whose benefits are provided by insurance companies under many traditional medical expense plans. However, insurance companies often also reimburse hospitals on a per diem basis under their managed care plans.

Under some Blue Shield plans, physicians may also be reimbursed at less than their actual charges, as is discussed later in this chapter.

National Coverage

While Blue Cross–Blue Shield plans operate in precise geographic regions, many insurance companies have historically operated on a national basis. In the era of traditional medical expense plans, the Blues had a more difficult time competing with insurance companies for the group insurance business of employers whose employees were located in areas served by several different Blue Cross–Blue Shield plans. Today, the situation has changed. It is more difficult for insurance companies to operate on a national basis because of differences in the state regulation of medical expense insurance. In addition, in this era of managed care, a national presence requires the ability to set up provider networks everywhere. As a result, many insurance companies have withdrawn from the medical expense market or do not sell products in all states. The Blues, on the other hand, have developed procedures on a cooperative basis among themselves for providing coverage to "national accounts." For example, an employer can arrange a medical expense plan that allows any employee to have coverage through the HMO or PPO of the Blue Cross–Blue Shield organization that operates in the area where the employee resides.

Flexibility

There seems to be a feeling among benefit consultants that insurance companies have a greater degree of flexibility than Blue Cross–Blue Shield in modifying their group contracts to meet employers' needs and desires. Blue Cross–Blue Shield contracts have traditionally been quite standardized, with few, if any, variations allowed. One major reason for this rigidity is that changes in the benefits promised to subscribers also have an effect on the contracts between the Blues and the providers. However, with employers increasingly wanting new approaches to medical expense benefits, often for cost-containment reasons, many Blue Cross–Blue Shield plans have taken a more flexible approach. Many variations exist among plans, and some have been very innovative in meeting the demands of the marketplace, even going as far as to administer benefit plans that are self-funded by employers.

Rating

In their early years, the Blues used only a "community-rating" approach in determining what premium rates to charge. Under this approach, each plan used the same rate structure for all subscribers, regardless of their past or potential loss experience and regardless of whether coverage was written on an individual or a group basis. Usually, the only variations in the rate structure resulted from variations in coverage: whether it was for an individual, a couple without children, or a family. The philosophy behind the community-rating approach was that coverage should be available to the widest range of persons possible at an affordable cost. Charging lower premium rates to segments of the community with better-than-average loss experience was thought to result in higher and possibly unaffordable premium rates for other segments of the community.

Community rating placed Blue Cross and Blue Shield plans at a competitive disadvantage when insurance companies began to aggressively market group medical expense insurance and use experience rating, which allowed them to charge certain employer groups much lower premiums than those charged by the Blues. As a result, by the mid-1950s insurance companies surpassed the Blues in the number of persons covered. Faced with the growing dilemma that rate increases necessary to compensate for the loss of better-than-average business tended to drive even more business to the insurance companies, the Blues initiated the use of experience rating for groups. Today, there is little difference in this regard between these two major providers with respect to group business. However, the Blues still use community rating in pricing products for smaller employers and for the individual marketplace.

Marketing

The Blues tend to have lower acquisition expenses than insurance companies, and most coverage is marketed by salaried employees. However, more than half of the plans also market coverage through agents and/or brokers in addition to their own sales forces. In general, the commissions paid to agents or brokers are below the commissions paid by insurance companies.

The Blues and Insurance Companies in Today's Environment

Today, the Blues and insurance companies have moved far beyond writing only traditional medical expense plans and are major players in the managed care marketplace. Together they write the majority of PPO coverage and a significant portion of HMO coverage.

Most of the Blues now have their own HMOs, PPOs, and point-of-service plans. In fact, national statistics show that slightly more than one-third of Blue Cross–Blue Shield subscribers are covered under PPOs, and this is the fastest-growing market segment. About one-third of their subscribers are covered under traditional plans, and a little less than one-third are covered under HMOs. As the Blues have expanded into broader markets, many of them have changed their names and do not use Blue Cross or Blue Shield in the new names.

Similarly, insurance companies have expanded their offerings. Most insurers that write traditional medical expense coverage also offer PPO products. Some insurers have actually gotten out of the market for traditional products and only offer PPOs. A relatively small number of insurers have gotten into the HMO market—sometimes through mergers with existing HMOs—but these insurers account for about 20 percent of HMO coverage written. Insurance companies also offer a wide array of products and services for use with self-funded plans.

BASIC MEDICAL EXPENSE COVERAGES

Historically, medical expense coverage consisted of separate benefits for hospital expenses, surgical expenses, and physicians' visits. Coverage was limited, and many types of medical expenses were not covered. In this environment, two developments took place: (1) basic coverages for other types of medical expenses were developed (2) and a vast majority of employers began to provide more extensive benefits to employees than had previously been available through the commonly written basic coverages. While this broader coverage is often provided through a single comprehensive contract, many employees who have medical expense benefits under traditional plans are still covered under medical expense plans that consist of selected basic coverages supplemented by a major medical contract. This is particularly true for large employers, while small employers are much more likely to use a single major medical contract. Basic plans consist of three traditional coverages:

1. Hospital expense benefits
2. Surgical expense benefits
3. Physicians' visits expense benefits

In addition, other types of medical expense coverage can be written as a basic benefit. While many of these basic coverages can be written separately, it is common for them to be incorporated into a single contract.

Hospital Expense Benefits

Hospital expense coverage provides benefits for charges incurred in a hospital by a covered person (that is, the employee or his or her dependents) who is an inpatient or, in some circumstances, an outpatient. Every medical expense contract discussed in this book defines what is meant by a hospital. While the actual wording may vary among insurance companies and in some states, the following definition is typical:

The term *hospital* means (1) an institution that is accredited as a hospital under the hospital accreditation program of the Joint Commission on Accreditation of Healthcare Organizations or (2) any other institution that is legally operated under the supervision of a staff of physicians and with 24-hour-a-day nursing service. In no event should the term *hospital* include a convalescent nursing home or include any institution or part thereof that (1) is used principally as a convalescent facility, rest facility, nursing facility, or facility for the aged; or (2) furnishes primarily domiciliary or custodial care, including training in the routines of daily living; or (3) is operated primarily as a school.

Inpatient Benefits

Hospital inpatient benefits fall into two categories: coverage for room-and-board charges and coverage for "other charges."

Room and Board. Coverage for room-and-board charges includes the cost of the hospital room, meals, and the services normally provided to all inpatients, including routine nursing care. Separate charges for such items as telephones and televisions are usually not covered. Benefits are normally provided for a specific number of days for each separate hospital confinement, a time period that may vary from 31 days to 365 days. Some contracts provide coverage for an unlimited number of days. For purposes of this time period, as well as for other benefits, most contracts stipulate that successive periods of hospital confinement are treated as a single hospital confinement unless they (1) arise from entirely unrelated causes or (2) are separated by the employee's return to continuous full-time active employment for some specified period of time, such as two weeks. For dependents, this latter requirement is replaced by one specifying that they must completely recover or remain out of the hospital for a certain period of time, such as 3 months.

The amount of the daily room-and-board benefit may be expressed in one of two ways: either a flat-dollar maximum or the cost of semiprivate accommodations. Under the first approach, benefits are provided for actual room-and-board charges up to a maximum daily amount, such as $500.

The majority of hospital expense contracts cover actual room-and-board charges up to the cost of semiprivate accommodations (that is, two-person rooms). The cost of a private room may be covered in full if it is medically necessary, and a few insurance plans provide additional coverage, usually a fixed daily dollar amount, for elective private room occupancy. Many hospital expense contracts include additional room-and-board benefits for confinement in an intensive care unit.

Other Charges. Coverage for "other charges" (often referred to as *miscellaneous charges, ancillary charges,* or *hospital extras*) provides benefits for certain services and supplies ordered by a physician during a covered person's hospital confinement, such as drugs, operating room charges, laboratory services, and X-rays. With a few exceptions, only the hospital portion of these charges is covered; any associated charges for such professional services as physicians' fees are not covered. The exceptions often include charges for ambulance services and anesthesia if anethesia is not covered as part of surgical expense benefits.

The amount of the benefit for other charges is usually expressed in one of the following three ways:

1. Full coverage up to a dollar maximum. This approach is most commonly found in contracts when the daily room-and-board benefit is also subject to a dollar limit. In most cases, this maximum is some multiple (often 20) of the daily room-and-board benefit. For example, a contract with a daily room-and-board benefit of $750 might have a $15,000 maximum for other charges.
2. Full coverage up to a dollar maximum (again, often expressed as a multiple of the room-and-board benefit) and partial coverage for a limited amount of additional expenses.
3. Full payment subject only to the duration for which room-and-board benefits are payable.

When coverage for ambulance services is provided, it is common to limit the benefit to a dollar maximum, such as $50 per hospital confinement. A few plans have a mileage limit in lieu of a dollar limit.

Preadmission Certification. As a method of controlling costs, most medical expense plans have adopted utilization review programs. One aspect of these programs, which were discussed in the previous chapter, is preadmission certification. Such a program requires that a covered person or his or her physician obtain prior authorization for any nonemergency hospitalization. Authorization usually must also be obtained within 24 to 48 hours of admissions for emergencies.

The initial reviewer, typically a registered nurse, determines whether hospitalization or some type of alternative care is most appropriate and what the appropriate length of stay for the medical condition should be. If the preapproved length of stay is insufficient, the patient's physician must obtain prior approval for any extension.

Most plans reduce benefits if the preadmission certification procedure is not followed. Probably the most common reduction is to pay only 50 percent of the benefit that would otherwise be paid. If a patient enters the hospital after a preadmission certification has been denied, many plans do not pay for any hospital expenses, whereas other plans provide a reduced level of benefits.

Outpatient Benefits

Although hospital expense contracts did not originally cover outpatient expenses, today it is common to find coverage for such expenses arising from the following:

- Surgery. The purpose of this benefit is to provide comparable coverage and thus lower hospital utilization when surgical procedures can be performed on an outpatient basis. It should be noted that this benefit covers only hospital charges or charges of outpatient surgical centers (such as the use of operating room facilities), not the surgeon's fee.
- Preadmission testing. The first day or two of hospital confinement, particularly for surgical procedures, were historically devoted to necessary diagnostic tests and X-rays. This benefit requires the performance of these procedures on an outpatient basis prior to hospitalization and covers the costs as if the person were an inpatient. For benefits to be paid, these procedures must generally be (1) performed after a hospital confinement for surgery has been scheduled, (2) ordered by the same physician who ordered the hospital confinement, (3) performed in the hospital where the confinement will take place, and (4) accepted by the hospital in lieu of the same tests that would normally be performed during confinement. Benefits are paid even if the preadmission testing leads to a cancellation of the scheduled confinement.
- Emergency room treatment. Hospital expense contracts commonly provide coverage for emergency room treatment of accidental injuries within some specified time period (varying from 24 to 72 hours) after an accident. In a few cases, similar benefits are also provided for sudden and serious illnesses. It should be noted that any emergency room charges incurred immediately prior to hospitalization are considered inpatient expenses.

Exclusions

While variations exist among the providers of hospital coverage (some of which result from state legislation), most hospital expense contracts do not usually cover expenses resulting from the following:

- Occupational injury or disease to the extent that benefits are provided by workers' compensation laws or similar legislation.
- Cosmetic surgery, unless such surgery is to correct a condition resulting from an accidental injury incurred while the covered person is insured under the contract or coverage of such surgery is mandated by the Women's Health and Cancer Rights Act.
- Most physical examinations (including diagnostic tests and X-rays), unless such examinations are necessary for the treatment of an injury or illness.
- Convalescent, custodial or rest care.
- Private-duty nursing.
- Services furnished by or on behalf of government agencies, unless there is a requirement for either the patient or the patient's medical expense plan to pay for the services. Under federal law, medical expense plans must

generally pay benefits to the government for care in Department of Veterans Affairs (VA) or military hospitals on the same basis as they pay for care received elsewhere. However, if a plan does not pay charges in full because of deductibles, coinsurance, or plan limitations, the patient is not responsible for the balance. The exceptions to the law—meaning that the plan is not responsible for payment—include treatment in VA hospitals for service-connected disabilities and treatment of active-duty members of the armed services in military hospitals.

Mental Illness, Alcoholism, and Drug Addiction. In the absence of state mandates to the contrary, some hospital expense contracts either exclude (or provide limited benefits for) expenses arising from mental illness, alcoholism, and/or drug addiction. Benefit plans that cover more than 50 employees and that have benefit limitations pertaining to mental illness must be in compliance with the Mental Health Parity Act, which is discussed in more detail later in this chapter under the section on major medical coverage.

Maternity. Until the passage of the Pregnancy Discrimination Act, it was not unusual to exclude maternity-related expenses from hospital expense contracts. However, the act requires that benefit plans of employers with 15 or more employees treat pregnancy, childbirth, and related conditions the same as any other illness. (See the discussion in Chapter 5.)

In the absence of state laws to the contrary, pregnancy may be and is sometimes excluded under group insurance contracts written for employers with fewer than 15 employees. If these employers wish to provide such coverage, it can usually be added as an optional benefit. In some cases, pregnancy is treated like any other illness covered under the contract. In other cases, benefits are determined in accordance with a schedule that most commonly provides an all-inclusive benefit for hospital, surgical, and certain other expenses associated with delivery. Regular physician visits and diagnostic tests may or may not be covered. Table 10-1 is an example of a maternity schedule.

A variation of this schedule that is often used by Blue Cross–Blue Shield plans provides a surgical benefit (possibly including visits prior to delivery) but covers hospital expenses on a semiprivate room basis.

An expense associated with maternity is the nursery charge for a newborn infant, which in most cases is equal to at least 50 percent of a hospital's normal room-and-board charge. This expense is not part of a maternity benefit, and a few hospital expense contracts do not cover the expense if the infant is healthy (since the contract covers only expenses associated with accidents and illnesses). However, many contracts do cover nursery charges, and a number of states require that they be covered.

TABLE 10-1

Type of Pregnancy	Benefit
Normal Delivery	$2,000
Cesarean	4,000
Miscarriage	1,000

Since 1998, group health plans have been subject to the provisions of the Newborns' and Mothers' Health Protection Act. This federal act is very broad and, with one exception, applies to all employers regardless of size and to self-funded plans as well as those written by health insurers and managed care plans. The exception is for plans subject to similar state legislation, which exist in more than half the states. The impetus for such legislation at both the state and federal levels arose over consumer backlash from the practice of an increasing number of HMOs and insurance companies limiting maternity benefits to 24 hours after a normal vaginal birth and 48 hours after a cesarean section. The act affects maternity benefits if they are provided. It does not mandate that such benefits be included in benefit plans. Of course, many employers are subject to other state and federal laws that do mandate maternity benefits.

The act prohibits a group health plan or insurer from restricting hospital benefits to less than 48 hours for both the mother and the newborn following a normal vaginal delivery and 96 hours following a cesarean section. In addition, a plan cannot require that a provider obtain authorization from the plan or insurer for a stay that is within these minimums. While a new mother, in consultation with her physician, might agree to a shorter stay, a plan or insurer cannot offer a monetary or nonmonetary incentive to the mother for this purpose. For example, follow-up visits from a home health nurse cannot be provided to mothers and children who are discharged early unless these visits are also provided to mothers and children who stayed in the hospital for the full period specified in the act. In addition, the plan or insurer cannot limit provider reimbursement because care was provided within the minimum limits or make incentives available to providers to render care inconsistent with the minimum requirements.

If a plan has deductibles or other benefit restrictions, these cannot be greater during the 48- or 96-hour period than those imposed on any preceding portion of the hospital stay prior to the birth.

Effect of Women's Health and Cancer Rights Act. The Women's Health and Cancer Rights Act amended ERISA and applies to group health plans as well as to individual medical expense insurance. Under the provisions of the federal act, any benefit plan or policy that provides medical and surgical benefits for mastectomy must also provide coverage for the following:

- Reconstruction of the breast on which the mastectomy has been performed
- Surgery and reconstruction of the other breast to produce a symmetrical appearance
- Prostheses and physical complications of all stages of mastectomy, including lymphedema

Prior to the act's taking effect, such coverage often was not available because of exclusions, particularly exclusions that applied to cosmetic surgery. Such coverage can be subject to deductibles and coinsurance provisions as long as it is consistent with those provided for other procedures under the plan or policy. Plan participants must be notified of the existence of these benefits on an annual basis.

Deductibles and Coinsurance

It is common for deductibles and coinsurance to apply to major medical expense coverage. In contrast, hospital expenses under basic hospital expense coverage (and benefits under other basic medical expense coverages as well) usually are not subject to deductibles or coinsurance. Rather, any limitations that exist are most likely to be in the form of maximum amounts that will be paid. It should be noted, however, that deductibles and coinsurance are more likely to be used for basic coverages than was once the case.

Surgical Expense Benefits

Surgical expense coverage provides benefits for physicians' charges associated with surgical procedures. While one tends to think of a surgical procedure as involving cutting, insurance contracts typically define the term broadly to include such procedures as suturing, electrocauterization, removal of a stone or foreign body by endoscopic means, and the treatment of fractures or dislocations.

Even though surgical expense coverage is frequently sold in connection with hospital expense coverage, surgical expense coverage normally provides benefits for surgery performed not only for patients in the hospital (either as inpatients or outpatients) but also for outpatients in a free-standing (that is, separate from a hospital) ambulatory surgical center and in a physician's office. To discourage unnecessary hospitalization, some surgical expense benefit contracts actually provide larger benefits if a procedure is performed as outpatient surgery.

Outpatient surgery also results in charges for medical supplies, nurses and the use of facilities. As mentioned, these charges are often covered if surgery is performed on an outpatient basis in a hospital or outpatient surgical facility.

Benefits

Surgical expense coverage traditionally provided benefits only for the fee of the primary surgeon. However, newer contracts often provide separate benefits for assistant surgeons and anesthesiologists as well. Because both hospital expense coverage and surgical expense coverage often cover anesthesia, it is important that an overall medical expense plan be properly designed to make sure this benefit is neither omitted nor overlapping. The major difficulty in this regard occurs when different providers are used for the hospital and surgical benefits.

In providing basic surgical expense benefits, some insurance companies and some Blue Shield plans use a surgical fee schedule in which charges are paid up to the maximum amounts specified in the schedule of surgical procedures in the master contract. However, the majority of surgical expense plans follow the approach used in major medical contracts and provide benefits to the extent that surgical charges are reasonable and customary. Unfortunately, the precise meaning of these terms in insurance contracts is vague, and each company determines what it considers reasonable and customary. In general, *reasonable-and-customary charges* (sometimes referred to as *usual, customary, and reasonable charges* or *prevailing charges*) are considered to be those that fall within the range of fees normally charged for a given procedure by physicians of similar training and experience within a geographic region.

The usual practice of insurance companies is to pay charges in full as long as they do not exceed some percentile (usually ranging from the 85th to the 95th) of the range of charges for a specific surgical procedure within a certain geographic region. For example, if an insurance company uses the 90th percentile and if for a certain procedure 90 percent of the charges are $300 or less, this is the maximum amount that is paid. The covered person is required to absorb any additional charges if he or she uses a more expensive physician. Through the use of computers, insurance companies now have statistics that categorize expenses by geographic regions that are as small as the ZIP codes of medical-care providers. Thus, while $300 may be the maximum reasonable-and-customary amount in one part of a metropolitan area, $350 may be considered reasonable and customary in another part of the same metropolitan area.

Blue Shield plans often use a somewhat modified approach in determining the maximum amount that is paid. Each year, physicians file their charges for the coming year with the Blue Shield plan, and during that year the plan pays charges in full up to some percentile of these filed charges. Under some plans, the physicians agree not to charge Blue Shield patients amounts in excess of their filed fees. Participating physicians in other Blue Shield plans agree to accept any Blue Shield payment as payment in full, particularly for employees with an income level below a certain amount, such as $10,000 for an individual and $15,000 for a family.

Second Surgical Opinions

In an attempt to control medical costs by eliminating unnecessary surgery, many medical expense plans, both traditional and managed care, provide benefits for second surgical opinions. While such opinions undoubtedly cause some patients to decide against surgery, it is still unclear whether the cost savings of second surgical opinions are illusory. For example, surgery may still be required at a later date, or long-term costs for alternative treatment may be incurred.

A voluntary approach for obtaining second surgical opinions is often used. If a physician or surgeon recommends surgery, a covered person can seek a second opinion and the cost is borne by the medical expense plan. In some instances the benefit is limited to a specific maximum, but in most cases the costs of the second opinion, including X-rays and diagnostic tests, are paid in full. Some plans also pay for a third opinion if the first two opinions disagree. When there are divergent opinions, the final choice is up to the patient, and the plan's regular benefits are usually paid for any resulting surgery. As an incentive to encourage second opinions, some plans actually provide larger benefits for a covered person who has obtained a second opinion, even if it does not agree with the first opinion.

In the last few years, it has become increasingly common for medical expense plans to require mandatory second opinions, which may apply to any elective and nonemergency surgery but frequently apply only to a specified list of procedures. In most cases, a surgeon selected by the insurance company or other provider of benefits must give the second opinion. If conflicting opinions arise, a third opinion may be obtained. The costs of the second and third opinions are paid in full. In contrast to voluntary provisions, mandatory provisions generally specify that benefits are paid at a reduced level if surgery is performed either without a second opinion or contrary to the final opinion.

The trend toward mandatory second opinions has had an interesting result. Because many employers felt money was being saved under their voluntary programs, wouldn't it be logical to save more money by making the program mandatory? Unfortunately, the opposite situation has often been the case: people who voluntarily seek a second opinion are frequently looking for an alternative to surgery, while those who obtain a second opinion only because it is required are more likely to accept surgery as the best alternative. Employers have also found that a second opinion by a surgeon is still likely to call for surgery. As a result, there seems to be a growing feeling that the cost of mandatory second opinions may exceed any decrease in surgical benefits paid. Consequently, some employers have returned to voluntary programs or stopped providing coverage for second opinions altogether.

Exclusions

As with hospital expense coverage and virtually all other types of medical expense coverage, exclusions exist under basic surgical expense contracts for occupational injuries or disease, certain services provided by government agencies, and cosmetic surgery. All surgical expense contracts have an exclusion for certain types of dental surgery. However, the extent of the exclusion varies and care must be taken to properly integrate any dental coverage with other basic coverages. At one extreme, some contracts exclude virtually any procedures associated with the teeth or disease of the surrounding tissue or bone structure. At the other extreme, a more common exclusion eliminates coverage for most dental procedures but does provide surgical benefits if a covered person is hospitalized for the removal of impacted teeth or for surgery of the gums or bone structure surrounding the teeth. It is interesting to note that although benefits for oral surgery may not be paid even if a covered person is hospitalized, the hospital expenses are often covered under hospital expense contracts.

Physicians' Visits Expense Benefits

Physicians' visits expense coverage (often referred to as *medical expense coverage* or *regular medical expense coverage*) provides benefits for fees of attending physicians other than surgeons (because the charges of the latter are paid under surgical expense benefits coverage). Benefits are usually provided only for physicians' visits while a covered person is hospitalized, although coverage may also include office and home visits.

In-Hospital Coverage

In-hospital coverage is designed to provide benefits for physicians' charges when a covered person is hospitalized as an inpatient. Three general approaches determine the amount and duration of benefits. Under one approach, physicians' fees are paid on a reasonable-and-customary basis, up to a specific number of visits per hospitalization. Under the second approach, benefits are limited to a daily maximum that is expressed as a dollar amount (such as $50). The third approach expresses the total benefit as a lump-sum amount equal to the daily benefit times the number of days hospitalized. For example, if the daily benefit is $40 and the covered person is hospitalized for 10 days, physicians' charges would be paid in full up to $400, regardless of the charges incurred on any specific day or the number of visits made by the physician.

Three additional types of benefits are sometimes included when in-hospital coverage is provided:

1. Coverage for physicians' visits when a covered person is in an intensive care unit. If benefits are paid on a reasonable-and-customary basis, these charges are covered in the same manner. Under plans with a daily maximum, the maximum may be increased to reflect the more expensive charges normally associated with intensive care.
2. Coverage for consultation services. Although most plans cover only the charges of attending physicians, some plans provide benefits for the consultation services of other physicians. This benefit may be subject to a dollar maximum or paid on a reasonable-and-customary basis.
3. Coverage for physicians' visits in other types of medical care facilities, such as extended care centers. This benefit is most commonly provided when room-and-board charges for these alternative facilities are also covered.

In-Hospital and Out-of-Hospital Coverage

In addition to the benefits previously described, coverage for physicians' visits may also include physicians' charges incurred in a physician's office or in a covered person's home. This broader coverage is usually not written as a separate and distinct benefit but rather as a single overall coverage for all types of physicians' visits. Benefits may be paid on a reasonable-and-customary basis or be subject to a dollar maximum per visit. In the latter case, it is not unusual to have two different dollar maximums: one for hospital visits and home visits and a lesser one for office visits. Benefits are subject to some overall maximum limit, which may be expressed as either a dollar amount (such as $1,000) or a specified number of visits (such as 60). This limit may be applied on an annual basis or for any single illness or injury. Most plans contain a waiting period, commonly ranging from one to five visits, before benefits for home and office visits are paid. However, this waiting period is often waived in the case of an accident.

Some plans also provide coverage for well-baby care, which includes benefits for inoculations and physicians' examinations (both in and out of the hospital) of healthy infants for a limited period of time, such as three months after birth. In addition, coverage sometimes includes benefits for hospital nursery charges. Some states require that medical expense contracts cover these benefits for newborns only until the infant is discharged from the hospital.

Exclusions

Most of the exclusions mentioned previously in connection with surgical expense coverage also apply to physicians' visits expense coverage. In addition to these exclusions, there are usually no benefits for physical examinations, eye examinations, or dentistry. Fees charged when a physician did not actually see a patient (such as for a telephone consultation) are often excluded. Finally, charges made by a physician who is a salaried staff member of a hospital are frequently not covered.

Other Basic Benefits

Over the years, numerous other types of basic coverage were developed to broaden the benefits provided by hospital, surgical, and physicians' visits coverages. The need for these coverages as separate benefits diminished as most employees with the traditional basic coverages also became covered by supplemental major medical plans that included these coverages. However, other basic coverages continued (and occasionally still continue) to be written—often as a result of collective bargaining negotiations—because this approach allowed the benefits to be provided on a first-dollar basis without deductibles and coinsurance.

FIGURE 10-1

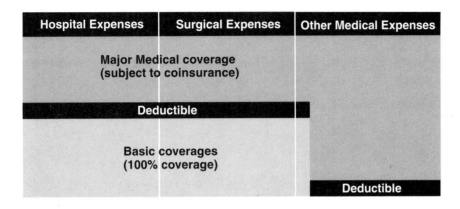

Examples of these types of coverages, all of which are discussed later in this book with respect to major medical plans and managed care carve-outs, include extended care facility, home health care, hospice, birthing center, prescription drug, and vision care benefits.

MAJOR MEDICAL COVERAGE

Most employees have some type of major medical expense coverage that protects against catastrophic medical expenses, with few exclusions or limitations. However, employees must often pay part of the cost of these medical expenses because of deductibles and coinsurance provisions.

Types of Major Medical Coverage

There are two general types of plans for providing major medical coverage—supplemental (or superimposed) plans and comprehensive plans. *Supplemental plans* coordinate major medical coverage with various basic medical expense coverages. Figure 10-1 shows one example of such a plan.

Subject to its own limitations and exclusions, a supplemental major medical plan covers the following expenses:

- Expenses not within the scope of the basic coverages. For example, benefits for office visits to a physician may be included if the basic coverages provide benefits only for in-hospital visits.
- Expenses no longer covered under the basic coverages because those benefits have been exhausted. For example, if the basic coverages provide room-and-board benefits in full, but only for a maximum of 60 days, the

FIGURE 10-2

Hospital Expenses	Surgical Expenses	Other Medical Expenses
	Major Medical coverage (subject to coinsurance)	
	Deductible	

major medical plan covers the cost of room and board beginning on the 61st day.

■ Expenses specifically excluded under the basic coverages. For example, if the basic coverages exclude hospital charges for the treatment of alcoholism, the major medical coverage may provide benefits. However, expenses that are excluded under the basic coverages are often excluded under the major medical plan.

In the *comprehensive* type of major medical coverage, a single major medical contract covers all medical expenses, as illustrated in Figure 10-2. In this example, once the deductible is satisfied, most medical expenses are covered subject to a coinsurance provision. Although Figure 10-2 shows a comprehensive major medical plan in its purest form, most comprehensive medical expense contracts contain modifications of the deductibles and/or coinsurance provisions for certain expenses, often resulting in payment of 100 percent of reasonable and customary charges. These variations are discussed later in this chapter.

Supplemental versus Comprehensive

At first glance, it might appear that the simplicity of a comprehensive major medical plan makes it preferable to a supplemental plan. However, supplemental plans continue to cover a large percentage of employees insured under traditional medical expense plans, even though most newly written plans are of the comprehensive type. The reasons for choosing separate coverages include the employer's desire to (1) use more than one provider of coverage, (2) offer first-dollar coverage, or (3) use different contribution rates for the basic and supplemental coverages. There are also disadvantages to using supplemental plans, including more difficult administration and communication.

More than One Provider of Coverage

Sometimes the provider of a supplemental major medical plan is different from the provider of the underlying basic coverages. For example, Blue Cross or Blue Shield may provide the basic coverages and an insurance company may provide the supplemental coverage. In the past, only a few of the Blues offered major medical coverage because (1) some of them felt such coverage was not within the scope of their traditional benefit structure, (2) some states legally prohibited it and (3) some Blues experienced administrative difficulties with effectively and efficiently coordinating these broader benefits. Although most Blue Cross–Blue Shield plans now offer major medical coverage (sometimes referred to as *extended benefits*), insurance companies are still the largest providers of major medical benefits.

The most common type of supplemental plan is the one shown in Figure 10-1, but occasionally a major medical plan is designed to supplement only a basic Blue Cross plan.

First-Dollar Coverage

Under the traditional comprehensive major medical plan, a deductible and coinsurance apply to all covered expenses. However, because of competition or labor negotiations, employers frequently offer their employees *first-dollar coverage* for certain medical expenses. With first-dollar coverage, there is no deductible and usually no coinsurance provision, and the basic medical expense plan consists only of those benefits provided on a first-dollar basis. Because first-dollar coverage has been characteristic of the Blues, they are frequently used as the providers of basic coverages. Therefore, to compete with them, most insurance companies now offer comprehensive major medical plans that are modified to provide similar first-dollar coverage.

It should be emphasized that, all other things being equal, first-dollar coverage increases the cost of a medical expense plan. Employers have become increasingly concerned with the cost of providing medical expense coverage and are less likely than in the past to provide first-dollar coverage.

Different Contribution Rates

A few employers still maintain separate basic medical and major medical expense plans because different employer contributions are made for each plan. The most common arrangement under these circumstances has the employer paying the entire cost of the basic coverages for the employee (and possibly his or her dependents) and the employee paying a portion, if not all, of the costs of the major medical coverage. However, most employers have a single plan even when the contribution rates for the basic and major medical coverages differ.

Administration and Communication

Most employers want to have benefit plans that minimize administrative problems and that can be easily communicated to employees. In both respects, comprehensive plans have the advantage. With supplemental plans, the employer must often deal with two providers of coverage, so two plans must be properly coordinated so that no undesired gaps in coverage exist. In addition, the processing of claims becomes more burdensome for both the employer and the employees. The complexity of medical expense plans in general makes them difficult to communicate to employees, and the task becomes even more challenging when two plans are used.

Even when a single provider supplies both the basic medical expense plan and a supplemental major medical plan, the same problems may exist. The employer must often negotiate the plans with separate divisions of the provider's organization, and separate claims forms and claims departments are frequently used.

Characteristics of Major Medical Coverage

The distinguishing features of major medical expense plans—either supplemental or comprehensive—include a broad range of covered expenses, deductibles, coinsurance, and high overall maximum benefits.

Covered Expenses

Major medical plans give broad coverage for necessary expenses incurred for medical services and supplies that a physician has ordered or prescribed. These services and supplies, which are specified in the contract, generally include the following:

- Hospital room and board. Traditionally, coverage has not been provided either for confinements in extended-care facilities or for home health care. However, major medical plans now often include such coverage. Some plans also provide benefits for room and board in alternative facilities, such as birthing centers. These types of facilities and the benefits for them are covered later in this chapter.
- Other hospital charges.
- Charges of outpatient surgical centers.
- Anesthetics and their administration.
- Services of doctors of medicine or osteopathy.
- Professional services of a registered nurse. The services of a nurse midwife, nurse practitioner and nurse anesthetist may also be covered.
- Services of certain other types of providers. Most states mandate that the services of certain types of providers other than physicians and nurses

must be covered as long as the service is a covered benefit and the provider is operating within the scope of his or her license. The list of providers varies from state to state and may include one or more of the following: acupuncturists, audiologists, chiropractors, dentists, marriage and family therapists, dietitians, optometrists, physical therapists, physicians' assistants, podiatrists, psychologists, social workers, and speech pathologists.

- Prescription drugs. This benefit, as discussed in Chapter 11, is often carved out and provided through a separate prescription drug program.
- Physical and speech therapy.
- Diagnostic X-ray and laboratory services.
- Radiation therapy.
- Blood and blood plasma.
- Artificial limbs and organs.
- Pacemakers.
- Casts, splints, trusses, braces, and crutches.
- Rental of wheelchairs, hospital beds, and iron lungs.
- Ambulance services.

The expenses of dental care may also be included as a major medical benefit. However, dental benefits (discussed in Chapter 13) are usually provided under a separate dental expense plan.

Even though coverage is broad, major medical contracts contain certain exclusions and limitations.

Exclusions. This list of exclusions varies, but exclusions found in most major medical contracts include charges arising from the following:

- Occupational injuries or diseases, to the extent that benefits are provided by workers' compensation laws or similar legislation.
- Services furnished by or on behalf of government agencies, unless there is a requirement for the patient or the patient's medical expense plan to pay.
- Care provided by family members or when no charge would be made for the care received in the absence of the insurance contract.
- Cosmetic surgery, except as required by the Women's Health and Cancer Rights Act, unless such surgery is to correct a condition resulting from either an accidental injury or a birth defect (if the parent has dependent coverage when the child is born).
- Most physical examinations, unless such examinations are necessary for the treatment of an injury or illness. While most major medical plans contain this exclusion, it should be noted that some plans (as discussed later in this chapter) do provide coverage for some forms of preventive medicine, which might involve specific types of physical examinations.
- Experimental or investigational drugs and treatment.

- Convalescent, custodial, or rest care.
- Dental care except for (1) treatment required because of injury to natural teeth and (2) hospital and surgical charges associated with hospital confinement for dental surgery. This exclusion is not included if dental coverage is provided under the major medical contract.
- Eye refraction, or the purchase or fitting of eyeglasses or hearing aids. Like the dental care exclusion, this exclusion is not included if the major medical coverage provides benefits for vision and hearing care. These benefits, however, are most likely to be provided under a separate plan. Separate vision care plans are discussed in Chapter 11.
- Expenses either paid or eligible for payment under Medicare or other federal, state, or local medical expense programs.
- Benefits provided by any other benefit program to which the employer makes a contribution. This includes any benefits provided under basic medical expense plans if a supplementary major medical plan is used.

To minimize the problem of adverse selection, most major medical plans also contain an exclusion for preexisting conditions. However, this exclusion applies only for a limited time, after which the condition is no longer considered preexisting and is covered in full, subject to any other contract limitations or exclusions. It is interesting to note that a preexisting-conditions clause is common in major medical contracts, but it is rarely found in basic medical expense contracts.

A *preexisting condition* is typically defined as any illness or injury for which a covered person received medical care during the three-month period prior to the person's effective date of coverage. Usually, the condition is no longer considered preexisting after the earlier of (1) a period of three consecutive months during which no medical care is received for the condition or (2) 12 months of coverage under the contract by the individual.

The use of preexisting-conditions provisions in group medical expense plans was affected by the passage of the Health Insurance Portability and Accountability Act (HIPAA), but the traditional time periods that apply to such conditions are within the act's guidelines. However, the act does limit the use of preexisting-conditions provisions with respect to newborn or adopted children. In addition, preexisting-conditions provisions cannot apply to pregnancy. The topic of preexisting conditions is discussed in more detail in Chapter 12.

Some insurance companies provide limited coverage rather than excluding coverage for preexisting conditions. During the time a condition is considered preexisting, benefits may be paid subject to limitations, such as a 50 percent coinsurance provision or a calendar-year maximum of $1,000. It is also not unusual, particularly with large employers, for the preexisting-conditions clause to be waived for persons who are eligible for coverage on the date a master contract becomes effective. However, future employees will be subject to the provision.

Finally, there are certain types of medical expenses that may or may not be excluded. While these exclusions are not found in most major medical contracts, they are found in many. Examples include charges arising from the following:

- Treatment for weight reduction and morbid obesity
- Treatment of injuries resulting from attempted suicide or self-inflicted injury
- Sexual transformation or sexual dysfunction
- Procedures to restore or enhance fertility, reversal of sterilizations, artificial insemination, or in vitro fertilization
- Treatment of injuries incurred while committing a felony

Limitations. Major medical plans also contain "internal limits" for certain types of medical expenses. Although the expenses are covered, the amounts that are paid under the contract are limited. Benefits are very rarely paid for charges that exceed what is reasonable and customary. In addition, limitations are often placed on the following expenses:

- Hospital room and board. Benefits are generally limited to the charge for semiprivate accommodations, unless other accommodations are medically necessary. In some cases a flat-dollar maximum is placed on the daily semiprivate accommodation rate.
- Extended-care facilities, home health care benefits, and hospice benefits (if provided). Benefits for extended-care facilities are often subject to a dollar limit per day for room-and-board charges as well as a time limit on the number of days that coverage is provided. Similarly, home health care benefits are often subject to a maximum daily benefit and limited to a certain number of visits within a specific time period. Hospice benefits are usually limited to a specified maximum amount.
- Dental care, vision and hearing care, and physical examinations. When these are covered under major medical contracts, benefits are frequently subject to schedules and annual limitations.
- Ambulance service, such as $250 per trip.
- Rental or purchase of durable equipment, such as $5,000.

Some plans also have limits on outpatient prescription drugs, such as $2,500 per year per person.

Treatment of Mental Illness, Alcoholism, and Drug Addiction. It is common for major medical plans to provide limited benefits for treatment of mental and nervous disorders, alcoholism, and drug addiction. Unless state laws require that such conditions be treated like any other medical condition, inpatient coverage is often limited to a specific number of days each year (commonly 30 or

60). Outpatient benefits, which are even more limited, are usually subject to 50 percent coinsurance and to a specific dollar limit per visit. One unfortunate effect of more stringent limitations on outpatient care is that it encourages many persons to seek inpatient treatment, which is significantly more expensive but no more effective in the eyes of many medical experts. As a result, some plans have started to carve out coverage from the major medical plan. Benefits are then coordinated by a managed care plan that specializes in mental health and/or substance abuse problems. These plans are discussed in Chapter 11.

It has been common for major medical plans to impose an annual maximum (such as $1,000) and/or an overall maximum lifetime limit (such as $25,000) on benefits for mental and nervous disorders, alcoholism, and drug addiction. Under federal legislation, such limitations are no longer allowed for mental health benefits in many employee benefit plans.

At the time of the 1996 debate over HIPAA, there was considerable disagreement over the issue of requiring mental illness to be treated as any other illness for purposes of medical expense coverage. With estimates that complete parity would raise the cost of providing medical expense benefits by 4 to 10 percent (depending on whose estimate one believed), Congress left the issue unresolved. The debate continued after the passage of the previously mentioned act and resulted in the passage of another act the following month—the Mental Health Parity Act. Because of cost considerations, however, its provisions are limited, and the use of the term *parity* is probably a misnomer.

The provisions of the act apply only to employers that have more than 50 employees. The act prohibits a group health plan, insurance company, or HMO from setting annual or lifetime dollar limits on mental health benefits that are less than the limits applying to other medical and surgical benefits. If there are no such dollar limitations for substantially all other (meaning two-thirds or more) medical and surgical benefits under a plan, there can be none for mental health benefits. If substantially all benefits are subject to an annual or lifetime limit, the parity requirements can be satisfied by either having separate dollar limits that are equal for mental health benefits and other medical and surgical benefits or applying a uniform dollar limit to all benefits in the aggregate. If a plan has different limits for different categories of benefits, the act calls for the use of a weighted average of all the limits to be used for the mental health limitations.

Besides imposing no limitations on benefits for alcoholism or drug addiction, the act is noteworthy for other things it does not do. It does not require that employers make any benefits available for mental illness, and it does not impose any other restrictions on mental health benefits. Employers can still impose limitations, such as an annual maximum on number of visits or days of coverage and different cost-sharing provisions for mental health benefits than those that apply to other medical and surgical benefits.

Congressional advocates of the act estimate that overall medical costs to employers should not increase by more than .4 percent. Any employer who can prove that the act's provisions increase its group health plan costs by more than 1 percent is exempt from the act. This exemption is available only if the employer has complied with the act for six months and uses a prescribed formula for measuring the cost increase.

The act is subject to a sunset provision of September 30, 2001. As of that date, any benefits required by the act can be eliminated unless Congress extends the date or removes the sunset provision prior to that time.

Deductibles

A *deductible* is the initial amount of covered medical expenses an individual must pay before he or she receives benefits under a major medical plan. For example, if a plan has an annual deductible of $200, the covered person is responsible for the first $200 of medical expenses incurred each year. Covered expenses in excess of $200 are then paid by the major medical plan, subject to any limitations or coinsurance. In addition to the different types of deductibles, there are variations in (1) the amounts of the deductible, (2) the frequency with which it must be satisfied, and (3) the expenses to which it applies.

Types of Deductibles. Probably the simplest form of deductible is the *initial deductible* commonly used in comprehensive major medical plans (see Figure 10-2). Essentially, a covered person must satisfy this deductible before the plan pays any insurance benefits.

Most supplemental medical expense plans use a *corridor deductible* (see Figure 10-1), under which no benefits are paid by the major medical plan until an individual has incurred a specific amount of covered expenses above those paid under his or her basic coverages. For example, assume an individual incurs $4,000 of covered medical expenses, $2,500 of which are paid by the basic coverages. If the supplemental major medical plan has a $200 corridor deductible, the plan pays $1,300 of the expenses, subject to any limitations or coinsurance. This is determined as follows:

Covered expenses	$4,000
Minus expenses covered under basic protection	−2,500
	$1,500
Minus deductible	− 200
	$1,300

In those situations when no benefits are paid under the basic coverages, the corridor deductible operates as if it were an initial deductible.

Deductible Amounts. Deductible amounts for any covered person under group benefit plans tend to be relatively small. Most deductibles are fixed-dollar amounts that apply separately to each person and usually fall within the range of $100 to $250. A few major medical expense plans contain deductibles that are based on a percentage of an employee's salary (such as 1 or 2 percent), possibly subject to a maximum annual limit (such as $250).

In most major medical expense plans, the deductible must be satisfied only once during any given time period (usually a calendar year), regardless of the number of causes from which medical expenses arise. This type of deductible is often referred to as an *all-causes deductible*. A few plans have *per-cause deductibles* (also referred to as *per-disability deductibles*), under which the deductible amount must be satisfied for each separate accident or illness before major medical benefits are paid.

Deductibles apply to each covered individual, including the dependents of an employee. To minimize the family's burden of satisfying several deductibles, most major medical expense plans also contain a *family deductible*. Once the family deductible is satisfied, future covered medical expenses of all family members are paid just as if each member of the family had satisfied his or her individual deductible.

Two basic types of family deductibles are found in major medical expense plans. The most common type waives any deductible requirements for other family members once a certain number of family members (generally two or three) have satisfied their individual deductibles. Two important points should be noted: First, major medical benefits are paid for each individual family member once his or her individual deductible is satisfied, even though the family deductible has not been met. Second, the waiver of any deductible requirements that results from the satisfaction of the family deductible does not apply to medical expenses incurred prior to the date the deductible is satisfied. For example, assume a family deductible is satisfied when each of three family members incurs $200 in covered medical expenses. If a fourth family member has had $60 in medical expenses up to that point, future medical expenses for that person will be paid under the major medical coverage. The $60, however, is not covered. In effect, the satisfaction of the family deductible freezes the deductible for each family member at the lesser of the individual deductible or the amount of medical expenses incurred up to that time.

Another approach taken in some major medical plans is to have a fixed-dollar amount for the family deductible (such as $500). In addition, each family member has to meet an individual deductible (such as $200). Major medical benefits are paid for any given family member once his or her deductible is satisfied, and future deductible requirements for all family members are waived once the family maximum has been reached. Although the same expenses can satisfy both the family deductible and an individual deductible, any amount that is applied toward the family deductible cannot exceed the individual deductible. For example, if a family has deductibles of $200 for an individual and $500 for the family and if one family member incurs $1,000 in covered medical expenses, the $800 exceeding the individual deductible is paid under the major medical plan, subject to any limitations and coinsurance. The $200 used to satisfy the individual deductible, but no more, can also be applied to the family deductible. The family deductible will not be completely satisfied until other family members incur another $300 in covered expenses (but no more than $200 from any one family member).

Most major medical expense contracts contain a *common accident provision,* whereby if two or more members of the same family are injured in the same accident, the covered medical expenses for all family members are at most subject to a single deductible, usually equal to the individual deductible amount. This deductible establishes the maximum amount of medical expenses an employee must bear for his or her family before major medical benefits are paid. Sometimes the employee may actually bear a smaller portion of the medical expenses if the amount satisfies the family or individual deductibles. For example, if each of three family members incurs $300 of medical expenses in an accident under a plan that contains a $200 deductible, at least $700 of these expenses are covered under the major medical coverage. If due to previous medical expenses only $40 is needed to satisfy the family deductible, then $860 of these expenses are covered under the major medical plan.

Deductible Frequency. An all-causes deductible usually applies to medical expenses incurred within a 12-month period, typically a calendar year (January 1 to December 31). Under such a *calendar-year deductible,* expenses incurred from January 1 apply toward the deductible. Once it has been satisfied, the balance of any covered expenses incurred during the year are then paid by the major medical plan, subject to limitations and coinsurance.

Many plans with a calendar-year deductible also have a carryover provision that allows any expenses (1) applied to the deductible and (2) incurred during the last three months of the year to also be applied to the deductible for the following year. For example, assume an individual satisfies only $150 of a $200 deductible prior to October 1. If less than $50 of covered expenses are incurred in the last three months of the year, the deductible is not totally satisfied for the year, but this amount can be applied to the deductible for the following year. If $50 or more of covered expenses are incurred in this three-month period, not only is the deductible satisfied for the year but this amount ($50) can also be applied to the deductible for the following year. No carryover is allowed if the deductible for the year is satisfied prior to the last three months of the year.

With a per-cause deductible, a different approach normally is taken. Medical expenses used to satisfy the deductible for each illness or accident must be incurred within a specified *accumulation* period. Although the accumulation period can be a calendar year or some other 12-month period, most accumulation periods consist of any consecutive two-month, three-month or six-month period. Once the deductible for an accumulation period has been met, benefits are paid for a *benefit period,* which usually begins when the deductible is satisfied, but sometimes begins on the date the first expense toward the deductible is incurred. (In the latter case, expenses used to satisfy the deductible are not paid by the major medical plan.) The benefit period typically lasts until the earlier of (1) two years or (2) the end of some time period (usually 60 or 90 days) in which covered medical expenses from that cause are less than a small but specified dollar amount (such as $25 or $50). Once the benefit period ends, an individual must again satisfy the deductible before a new benefit period begins.

Expenses to Which the Deductible Applies. Most major medical plans have a single deductible that applies to all medical expenses. However, some plans have two (or more) deductibles that apply separately to different categories of medical expenses. While many variations exist, the most common plan of this type has a small deductible (such as $50) that applies to those expenses over which individuals have the least control (for example, hospital charges, surgical charges, and charges resulting from accidents). A larger deductible (such as $100) applies to all other medical expenses.

In some major medical plans, the deductible does not apply to certain expenses, in effect giving the covered person first-dollar coverage for these charges. Insurance companies sometimes write comprehensive major medical expense plans without any deductible for hospital and/or surgical expenses as their way of competing with the first-dollar coverage offered by the Blues. In addition, these expenses may be paid in full but possibly up to certain maximums. Above these maximums, coinsurance applies.

Coinsurance

Major medical expense plans contain a coinsurance provision, whereby the plan pays only a specified percentage (in most cases, 80 percent) of the covered expenses that exceed the deductible. The term *coinsurance* as used in this book refers to the percentage of covered expenses paid by a medical expense plan. Thus, a plan with 80 percent coinsurance, sometimes referred to as an 80/20 plan, pays 80 percent of covered expenses while a person who receives benefits under the plan must pay the remaining 20 percent. In some plans, a percentage participation, such as 20 percent, is specified. As commonly used, a *percentage participation* refers to the percentage of covered medical expenses that is not paid by a medical expense plan and that must be paid by a person receiving benefits. Note that percentage participation is sometimes referred to as a *copayment,* but that terminology usually implies a fixed-dollar amount that an insured must pay for a covered service. To make the matter even more confusing, some insurers refer to the percentage participation, rather than their portion of the benefit payment, as *coinsurance.*

If a comprehensive major medical expense plan has a $200 calendar-year deductible and an 80 percent coinsurance provision that applies to all expenses, an individual who incurs $1,200 of covered medical expenses during the year (assuming no limitations) will receive an $800 reimbursement, calculated as follows:

Covered expenses	$1,200
Minus deductible	– 200
	$1,000
Times coinsurance percentage	× .80
	$ 800

The individual will have to pay the remaining $400 from his or her own pocket (that is, the deductible plus 20 percent of those expenses exceeding the deductible). It has been argued that having such provisions is a financial incentive for employees to control their use of medical care because they must bear a portion of the cost of any expenses incurred.

Just as deductibles vary, so do coinsurance provisions. Sometimes different coinsurance percentages apply to different categories of medical expenses. For example, outpatient psychiatric charges may be subject to 50 percent coinsurance, while other covered medical expenses are subject to 80 percent coinsurance. In addition, certain medical expenses may be subject to 100 percent coinsurance (and usually no deductible), which, in effect, means that the expenses are paid in full, subject to any limitations. Such full coverage is most likely to exist (1) for those expenses over which an individual has little control, (2) when there is a desire to provide first-dollar coverage for certain expenses, or (3) when there is a desire to encourage the use of the most cost-effective treatment (such as outpatient surgery, preadmission testing, or birthing centers).

Figures 10-3 through 10-6 illustrate some possible modifications that could be made in both the deductible and coinsurance provisions of a comprehensive major medical expense plan.

FIGURE 10-3

FIGURE 10-4

Hospital Expenses	Surgical Expenses	Other Medical Expenses

Major medical coverage (100% coverage)

Major medical coverage (subject to coinsurance)

Deductible

Figure 10-3 illustrates a medical expense plan that has hospital expenses, surgical expenses, and certain other expenses paid in full up to specified limits. This type of modification results in a plan similar to a Blue Cross–Blue Shield plan that has supplemental major medical coverage but no corridor deductible. Figure 10-4 shows a similar plan that is designed to provide first-dollar coverage for hospital expenses only. Figures 10-5 and 10-6 illustrate two other possible variations. In figure 10-5, most medical expenses are paid in full, but a few are subject to a deductible and coinsurance. In Figure 10-6, all

FIGURE 10-5

Hospital Expenses	Surgical Expenses	Other Medical Expenses

Major medical coverage (100% coverage)

Major medical coverage (subject to coinsurance)

Deductible

FIGURE 10-6

Hospital Expenses	Surgical Expenses	Other Medical Expenses
	Major medical coverage (subject to coinsurance)	
Major medical coverage (100% coverage)		
	Deductible	

expenses are subject to the deductible, above which some expenses are covered in full up to specified limits.

In the case of catastrophic medical expenses, the coinsurance provision could result in an individual having to assume a large dollar amount of his or her own medical expenses. Consequently, many major medical expense plans place a limit (often called a *stop-loss* or *coinsurance limit* or *cap*) on the amount of out-of-pocket expenses that a covered person must bear during any time period. It is sometimes specified that the coinsurance provision only applies to a limited amount of expenses and that expenses over this limit are paid in full. For example, the plan may have a $200 deductible, an 80 percent coinsurance provision that applies to the next $3,000 of covered expenses, and full coverage for any remaining covered expenses. Therefore, the most an individual will pay out of pocket in any year is the $200 deductible and 20 percent of $3,000 (for a total of $800). Occasionally, this type of plan is modified to allow a gradual increase in the coinsurance percentage, such as 80 percent of the first $2,000 of covered expenses above the deductible, 90 percent of the next $2,000, and 100 percent of the remainder.

Another way of limiting out-of-pocket expenses is to state the maximum dollar amount that any individual (or a family) must bear during a specific period. Once this limit is reached, by paying either deductibles or a percentage of medical expenses, additional expenses are paid in full. For example, under a plan with a $200 deductible and an 80 percent coinsurance provision, a limit of $1,000 is met if total medical expenses reach $4,200. Of this amount, the individual is responsible for the $200 deductible and 20 percent of the remaining $4,000 (for a total of $1,000). Any medical expenses in excess of $4,200 are paid in full.

Maximum Benefits

The maximum benefits that will be paid for any covered person under a major medical contract may be determined in one of two ways. Although the use of a *lifetime maximum* is most common, a few contracts contain a *per-cause maximum*. In both instances, the benefit maximum applies separately to each employee and each dependent covered under the contract.

Lifetime Maximum. When a lifetime maximum is used, the specified overall maximum applies to all medical expenses paid (after the application of deductibles and coinsurance) during the entire period an individual is covered under the contract. It is no longer common to find benefit maximums of less than $1 million, and most benefit maximums fall within the range of $1 million to $2 million. Higher maximum benefits (such as $5 million) or even an unlimited maximum benefit are sometimes available, but their availability is much less common with traditional major medical contracts than it is with PPO products.

The lifetime maximum is reduced by the amount of any benefits paid. For example, an individual with a $200 calendar-year deductible, an 80 percent coinsurance provision, and a $100,000 lifetime maximum who incurs $4,000 of medical expenses in his or her first year of coverage (assuming it corresponds with the calendar year) receives benefits of $3,040 (that is, 80 percent of $3,800). This reduces the remaining lifetime benefit to $96,960.

Until recently, it was common to have one or more provisions in major medical contracts that restored (either partially or totally) the lifetime maximum to its original level. In some cases, this restoration required showing evidence of insurability or having no claims for a period of time. This type of provision has largely been dropped because it appears to be in conflict with state and federal regulations that prohibit the basing of benefits on health status.

A few plans still have an automatic annual restoration of a small amount of benefits, varying from $1,000 to $5,000 per year. Such a restoration was of significant value a few years ago when lifetime maximums were much lower. However, there is little practical value in such a restoration with today's maximum lifetime benefits of $1 million or more. As a result, this type of provision has also been dropped by the majority of plans.

In addition to the overall lifetime maximum, *internal maximums* are sometimes found in major medical contracts. For example, a plan may have a $1 million overall lifetime maximum, but a $10,000 lifetime maximum for benefits relating to alcoholism and drug addiction. In other words, only $10,000 of the $1 million will be paid for expenses relating to these conditions. Such a limitation was once also common for mental and nervous disorders, but the provisions of the Mental Health Parity Act prohibit this type of maximum for many employee benefit plans. A few plans do contain calendar-year or per-disability internal maximums.

Per-Cause Maximum. A few plans contain maximum limits for each cause of medical expenses, but in general this type of maximum limit is used only when the deductible is also applied on a per-cause basis. While coverage terminates for any cause for which the maximum benefits have been paid, it remains in force for medical expenses arising from other causes.

MANAGED CARE PROVISIONS IN TRADITIONAL PLANS

Historically, traditional medical expense plans contained few provision aimed at managing the care of covered persons, but this situation continues to evolve. A few managed care provisions that were described earlier in this chapter, such as hospital precertification and second opinions, have been around for many years. It has also been common for some time to see benefits provided for treatment in facilities other than hospitals. These types of facilities and the benefits for them are discussed below.

Other managed care provisions and practices that may be found in traditional plans include the following:

- Preapproval of visits to specialists.
- Increased benefits for preventive care.
- Carve-outs of benefits that can be provided cost effectively under arrangements that employ various degrees of managed care. Examples include prescription drugs, mental illness, substance abuse, and maternity management. These types of carve-outs are discussed in Chapter 11.

Some traditional major medical plans actually make wide use of managed care techniques; the primary factor that prevents them from being called *managed care plans* is that there are few restrictions on access to providers.

Alternative Facilities for Treatment

Many traditional medical expense plans provide coverage for treatment in facilities that are alternatives to hospitals. Initially, this coverage was provided primarily to the extent that it reduced hospital benefits that were otherwise covered. While this is still the primary effect of this coverage, it is often an integral part of medical expense plans, and benefits are provided even if they might not have been covered under a plan limited solely to treatment received in hospitals. The following types of coverage are discussed:

- Extended-care-facility benefits
- Home health care benefits
- Hospice benefits
- Birthing centers

Extended-Care-Facility Benefits

Many hospital patients recover to a point where they no longer require the full level of medical care provided by a hospital, but they cannot be discharged because they still require a period of convalescence under supervised medical care. Extended-care facilities (often called *convalescent nursing homes* or *skilled-nursing facilities*) have been established in many areas to provide this type of care. To the extent that patients can be treated in these facilities (which are often adjacent to hospitals), daily room-and-board charges can be reduced—often substantially.

Extended-care-facility coverage provides benefits to the person who is an inpatient in an extended-care facility, which is typically defined as an institution that furnishes room and board and 24-hour-a-day skilled-nursing care under the supervision of a physician or a registered professional nurse. It does not include facilities that are designed as a place for rest or domiciliary care for the aged. In addition, facilities for the treatment of drug abuse and alcoholism are often excluded from the definition.

To receive benefits, the following conditions must usually be satisfied:

- The confinement must be recommended by a physician.
- Twenty-four-hour-a-day nursing care must be needed.
- The confinement must commence within (1) 14 days after termination of a specified period of hospital confinement (generally three days) for which room-and-board benefits were payable or (2) 14 days of a previous confinement in an extended-care facility for which benefits were payable. A few but an increasing number of contracts include benefits for situations where extended-care facilities are used in lieu of hospitalization.
- The confinement must be for the same or a related condition for which the covered person was hospitalized.

Benefits are provided in much the same manner as under hospital expense coverage. If hospital expense benefits are paid on a semiprivate accommodation basis, extended-care-facility benefits are generally paid on the same basis. If hospital expense benefits are subject to a daily dollar maximum, extended-care-facility benefits are usually likewise subject to a daily dollar maximum, most typically equal to 50 percent of the daily hospital benefit. The maximum length of time for which extended-care-facility benefits are paid may be independent of the period of time for which a person is hospitalized, in which case a maximum of 60 days' coverage is fairly common. Alternatively, the benefit period may be related to the number of unused hospital days. The most common approach in this instance is to allow two days in an extended-care facility for each unused hospital day. For example, if a hospital expense plan provides benefits for a maximum period of 90 days and if a covered person is hospitalized for 50 days, the 40 unused hospital days can be exchanged for 80 days of benefits in an extended-care facility. Other charges incurred in an extended-care facility may be treated in one of several ways. They may be covered in full, subject to a separate dollar limit, or treated as part of the maximum benefit payable for other charges under hospital expense coverage.

Home Health Care Benefits

Home health care coverage is similar to extended-care-facility benefits but designed for those situations when the necessary part-time nursing care ordered by a physician following hospitalization can be provided in the patient's home. Coverage is for (1) nursing care (usually limited to a maximum of two hours per day) under the supervision of a registered nurse; (2) physical, occupational and speech therapy; and (3) medical supplies and equipment, such as wheelchairs and hospital beds.

In most cases, the benefits payable are equal to a percentage, frequently 80 percent, of reasonable-and-customary charges. Benefit payments are limited to either a maximum number of visits (such as 60 per calendar year) or to a period of time (such as 90 days after benefits commence). In the latter case, the time period may be a function of the unused hospital days, such as three days of home visits for each unused hospital day.

Hospice Benefits

Hospices for the treatment of terminally ill persons are a recent development in the area of medical care. Hospice care does not attempt to cure medical conditions but rather is devoted to easing the physical and psychological pain associated with death. In addition to providing services for the dying patient, a hospice may also offer counseling to family members. While a hospice is usually thought of as a separate facility, this type of care can also be provided on an outpatient basis in the dying person's home. Where hospice care is available, the cost of treating terminally ill patients is usually much less than the cost of traditional hospitalization. Hospice benefits may be subject to a specified maximum benefit, such as $5,000.

Birthing Centers

Another recent development in medical care is birthing centers, separate from hospitals. The cost of using birthing centers is considerably less than using hospitals. Deliveries are performed by nurse-midwives, and mothers and babies are released shortly after birth. Benefits may be paid as if the mother had used a hospital and obstetrician but are frequently paid in full as an incentive to use these lower-cost facilities.

Preapproval of Visits to Specialists

Many persons elect to bypass primary care physicians, such as family physicians and pediatricians, and use specialists and the emergency room as their primary access to medical care; this results in additional costs but does not improve medical outcomes, in the opinion of much of the medical community. To counter this practice, some traditional medical expense plans require that a visit to a specialist be preceded by a visit to a primary care physician. It is not necessary for the primary care physician to actually certify that a trip to a specialist is necessary, only that he or she has been told that the patient plans to make such a visit. The rationale for this procedure is that the primary care physician may convince the patient that he or she is able to treat the condition and that a specialist is unnecessary, at least at that time. If a specialist is needed, the primary care physician is also in a better position to recommend the right type of specialist and to coordinate health care for persons seeing multiple specialists.

Failure to use the primary care physician as a quasi gatekeeper will result in a reduction in benefits. Usually, benefits will still be paid, but at a lower level.

Benefits for Preventive Care

Most traditional medical expense plans provide at least a few benefits for preventive care. Probably the most frequently found benefits, because of state mandates for group insurance contracts, are well-baby care, childhood immunizations, and mammograms. Plans may also go as far as providing routine physicals for children at specified ages and, perhaps, for all covered persons, typically subject to an annual maximum benefit, such as $150 or $200. However, coverage for routine adult physicals is much more likely to be covered under managed care plans.

COVERAGE FOR ALTERNATIVE MEDICINE

During the 1990s, the use of alternative medicine increased dramatically, with estimates that over half of the population has used one or more of these types of services. In addition, the majority of physicians have recommended alternative medical techniques, particularly for treatment of neck and back problems, anxiety, depression, and headaches. Examples of alternative medicine services include the following:

- Acupuncture
- Biofeedback
- Chiropractic treatment
- Herbal medicine
- Homeopathy
- Hypnosis
- Massage therapy
- Meditation
- Relaxation
- Therapeutic touch

■ Vitamin therapy
■ Yoga

The attractiveness of these programs has increased over the past few years for a number of reasons. Patients appreciate the rapport they develop with their alternative medicine practitioners, and this is indicated by a higher degree of satisfaction with these practitioners than with their physicians. Patients also like the fact that alternative medicine practitioners are more likely than traditional medical practitioners to actively involve patients in the development of treatment plans. As a result, patients are more likely to follow plans of alternative medicine than they are to follow conventional medical treatment plans. Finally, complications from treatment are less likely than from conventional medical treatment, possibly because of the less-invasive nature of alternative medicine.

Insurers and plan administrators have typically been leery of adding benefits for alternative medicine because they fear increases in claims costs. This will obviously occur if alternative medicine is used in addition to traditional medical treatment. However, it is often used as a replacement for traditional medical treatment. If successful, costs might decrease. There is also concern over the qualifications and training of many of the persons who provide alternative medicine.

Many insurance contracts and managed care plans provide limited benefits for chiropractic treatment, and a smaller number cover acupuncture, sometimes as a result of state mandates. However, benefits are often subject to limitations. Some providers of medical benefits will add other types of alternative medicine to their insurance contracts or managed care plans if the employer is willing to pay an increased premium. Employers may be willing to pay this cost as a response to employee interest or to differentiate their medical expense plan from those of other employers. Results of surveys vary, but it appears that over half of employers have benefit plans that cover chiropractic services, about 20 percent have plans that cover acupuncture, and about 10 percent have plans that cover some other forms of alternative medicine.

To control costs, coverage of alternative medicine is subject to a variety of controls. These include one or more of the following:

■ Annual or lifetime dollar limits
■ Limits on the number of annual visits
■ A requirement that treatment is for specified medical conditions
■ A requirement for a referral from a primary care physician

MEDICAL SAVINGS ACCOUNTS

The concept of medical savings accounts (MSAs) as a method of reforming the nation's health care system was briefly discussed in Chapter 9. The use of MSAs has increased as a result of HIPAA. The act provides favorable tax treatment for MSAs established under a pilot project that began on January 1, 1997, as long as prescribed rules are satisfied. The project, which runs through the end of 2000, allows the establishment of up to approximately 750,000 MSAs. However, as of late 1999, fewer than 100,000 had been purchased. At the end of the four-year trial period, no more tax-favored MSAs can be established unless Congress expands the program, but existing MSAs can generally continue in force after that time under the current rules. During this four-year period, the act calls for two studies to assist Congress in making its decision regarding MSAs. First, the Treasury Department will assess MSA participation and its effect on tax revenue. Second, the General Accounting Office will assess the effect of MSAs on the small-group market by looking at such factors as the effect of MSAs on health care costs and the use of preventive care.

The following discussion is limited to MSAs that receive favorable tax treatment. It should be noted that many MSAs, which existed on a non–tax-favored basis prior to 1997, have been revised to meet the act's requirements and receive favorable tax status.

General Nature

An MSA is a personal savings account from which unreimbursed medical expenses, including deductibles and copayments, can be paid. Coverage can be limited to an individual or include dependents. The MSA must be in the form of a tax-exempt trust or custodial account established in conjunction with a high-deductible health (that is, medical expense) plan. An MSA is established with a qualified trustee or custodian in much the same way that an IRA is established. Any insurance company or bank (as well as certain other financial institutions) can be a trustee or custodian, as can any other person or entity already approved by the IRS as a trustee or custodian for IRAs. While there are some similarities between MSAs and IRAs, there are also differences. As a result, an IRA cannot be used as an MSA, and an IRA and MSA cannot be combined into a single account.

Even though employers can sponsor MSAs, these accounts are established for the benefit of individuals and are portable. If an employee changes employers or leaves the workforce, the MSA remains with the individual.

Eligibility for an MSA

Two types of individuals are eligible to establish MSAs:

1. An employee (or spouse) of a small employer that maintains an individual or family high-deductible health plan covering that individual. These persons will establish their MSAs under an employer-sponsored plan.

2. A self-employed person (or spouse) maintaining an individual or family high-deductible health plan covering that individual. These persons will need to seek out a custodian or trustee for their MSAs.

A *small employer* is defined as an employer who has an average of 50 or fewer employees (including employees of controlled-group members and predecessor employers) on business days during either of the two preceding calendar years. In the case of a new employer, the number of employees is based on an estimate of the reasonably expected employment for the current year. After the initial qualification as a small employer is satisfied, an employer can continue to make contributions to employees' MSAs, and employees can continue to establish MSAs until the first year following the year in which the employer has more than 200 employees. At that time, participating employees may take over contributions to their accounts, but no employer contributions can be made and nonparticipating employees may not start new accounts.

A *high-deductible health plan,* for purposes of MSA participation, is a plan that has the following deductibles and annual out-of-pocket limitations (These amounts are for 2000 and subject to inflation adjustments.):

■ In the case of individual coverage, the deductible must be at least $1,550 and cannot exceed $2,350. The maximum annual out-of-pocket expenses cannot exceed $3,100.

■ In the case of family coverage, the deductible must be at least $3,100 and cannot exceed $4,650. The maximum annual out-of-pocket expenses cannot exceed $5,700.

A high-deductible plan can be written by an insurance company or a managed care organization such as an HMO. Currently, the high-deductible plans are being written primarily by insurance companies in the form of traditional major medical products but possibly with the requirement that covered persons use preferred-provider networks. No HMOs have yet established high-deductible plans.

A high-deductible plan can be part of a cafeteria plan, but the MSA must be established outside the cafeteria plan.

With some exceptions, a person who is covered under a high-deductible health plan is denied eligibility for an MSA if he or she is covered under another health plan that does not meet the definition of a high-deductible plan but that provides any benefits that are covered under the high-deductible health plan. The exceptions include coverage for accident, disability, dental care, vision care, and long-term care as well as liability insurance, insurance for a specific disease or illness, and insurance paying a fixed amount per period of hospitalization.

Contributions

Either the account holder of an MSA or the account holder's employer, but not both, may make a contribution to an MSA. If the employer makes a contribution, even one below the allowable limit, the account holder may not make a contribution. Contributions must be in the form of cash.

Contributions by an employer are tax deductible to the employer and are not included in an employee's gross income or subject to Social Security and other employment taxes. Employee contributions are deductible in computing adjusted gross income. As with IRAs, individuals' contributions must generally be made by April 15 of the year following the year for which the contributions are made.

The amount of the annual deductible contribution to an employee's account is limited to 65 percent of the deductible for the health coverage if the MSA is for an individual. The figure is 75 percent if an MSA covers a family. If each person in a married couple has an MSA and if one or both of the MSAs provide family coverage, the aggregate deductible contribution is equal to 75 percent of the deductible for the family coverage with the lowest deductible. The deductible contribution is split equally between the two persons in the couple unless they agree to a different division.

The actual MSA contribution that can be deducted is limited to $\frac{1}{12}$ of the annual amount, as described in the previous paragraph, times the number of months that an individual is eligible for MSA participation. For example, assume that the deductible under an individual's health plan is $1,800. The maximum annual contribution to the MSA is then 65 percent of this amount, which is $1,170, and the monthly amount is $97.50. If the individual is covered under a high-deductible plan for only the first eight months of the year, then the annual deductible contribution is eight times $97.50, or $780. Note, however, that there are no requirements that contributions be made on a monthly basis or at any particular time. In this example, the full $1,170 could have been made early in the year. The excess over $780 would then be an excess contribution.

An excess contribution occurs to the extent that contributions to an MSA exceed the deductible limits or are made for an ineligible person. Any excess contribution made by the employer is included in the employee's gross income. In addition, account holders are subject to a 6 percent excise tax on excess contributions for each year these contributions are in an account. This excise tax can be avoided if the excess amount and any net income attributable to the excess amount are removed from the MSA prior to the last day prescribed by law, including extensions, for filing the account holder's income tax return. The net income attributable to the excess contributions is included in the account holder's gross income for the tax year in which the distribution is made.

An employer that makes contributions to MSAs is subject to a comparability rule that requires the employer to make comparable contributions for all employees who have MSAs. However, full-time employees and part-time employees (those working fewer than 30 hours per week) are treated separately.

The comparability rule requires that the employer contribute either the same dollar amount for each employee or the same percentage of each employee's deductible under the health plan. Failure to comply with this rule subjects the employer to an excise tax equal to 35 percent of the aggregate amount contributed to MSAs during the period when the comparability rule was not satisfied.

Growth of MSA Accounts

Unused MSA balances carry over from year to year, and there is no prescribed period in which they must be withdrawn. Earnings on amounts in an MSA are not subject to taxation as they accrue.

Distributions

An individual can take distributions from an MSA at any time. The amount of the distribution can be any part or all of the account balance. Subject to some exceptions, distributions of both contributions and earnings are excludible from an account holder's gross income if used to pay medical expenses of the account holder and the account holder's family, as long as these expenses are not paid by other sources of insurance. For the most part, the eligible medical expenses are the same ones that would be deductible, ignoring the 7.5 percent of adjusted gross income limitation, if the account holder itemized his or her tax deductions. However, tax-free withdrawals are not permitted for the purchase of insurance other than long-term care insurance, COBRA continuation coverage, or health coverage while an individual receives unemployment compensation. In addition, in any year a contribution is made to an MSA, tax-free withdrawals can be made to pay the medical expenses of only those persons who were eligible for coverage under an MSA at the time the expenses were incurred. For example, MSA contributions cannot be withdrawn tax free to pay the unreimbursed medical expenses of an account holder's spouse who is covered under a health plan of his or her employer that is not a high-deductible plan.

Distributions for reasons other than paying eligible medical expenses are included in an account holder's gross income and are subject to a 15 percent penalty tax unless certain circumstances exist. The penalty tax is not levied if the distribution is made after the account holder turns 65 or because of the account holder's death or disability. In addition, the penalty tax does not apply to funds rolled over to a new MSA as long as the rollover is done within 60 days. Transfers of MSA accounts as a result of divorce are also tax free.

Estate Tax Treatment

Upon death, the remaining balance in an MSA is includable in the account holder's gross estate for estate tax purposes. If the beneficiary of the account is a surviving spouse, the MSA belongs to the spouse and he or she can deduct the account balance in determining the account holder's gross estate. The surviving spouse can then use the MSA for his or her medical expenses. If the beneficiary is anyone else, or if no beneficiary is named, the MSA ceases to exist.

STUDY QUESTIONS

1. Compare Blue Cross and Blue Shield organizations with private insurance companies with respect to each of the following features:
   a. Regulation and taxation
   b. Form of benefits provided
   c. Types of benefits provided
   d. Reimbursement of providers
   e. Rating
   f. Marketing

2. Describe the coverage that may be contained in a hospital expense contract for the following:
   a. Room and board
   b. Other inpatient charges
   c. Outpatient expenses

3. a. What is the purpose of hospital preadmission certification?
   b. What are the possible penalties if the preadmission process is not followed?

4. How are benefit limitations under medical expense contracts usually expressed?

5. Explain how most insurance companies determine whether a surgical fee is reasonable and customary.

6. Explain how surgical benefits may be affected by the following:
   a. Voluntary provisions
   b. Mandatory provisions for second surgical opinions

7. Describe the approaches used to determine the amount and duration of benefits for physicians' visits when each of the following is provided:
   a. In-hospital coverage only
   b. Both in-hospital and out-of-hospital coverage

8. Why has hospice care become a topic of interest among employers?

9. How does a supplemental major medical contract broaden the benefits provided under the basic medical expense coverage?

10. What types of exclusions are commonly found in major medical contracts?

11. What types of internal limitations are usually placed on the benefits provided under major medical contracts?

12. Describe the types of deductibles found in major medical contracts.

13. Describe the methods used to place a limit on the amount of out-of-pocket medical expenses that must be borne by an individual under the coinsurance provision of a major medical contract.

14. Explain how medical expense plans use each of the following to control medical expenses:
    a. Alternative facilities for treatment
    b. Preapproval of visits to specialists
    c. Benefits for preventive care

15. Why have benefits for alternative medicine become attractive in recent years?

16. Describe the general nature of medical savings accounts.

17. What types of individuals are eligible to establish medical savings accounts?

18. What is the income tax treatment of contributions to and distributions from medical savings accounts?

CHAPTER 11

Group Medical Expense Benefits: Managed Care Plans

OBJECTIVES

- Explain how managed care plans differ from traditional medical expense plans.

- Describe the recent developments that pertain to the quality of care provided by managed care organizations.

- Describe the characteristics of health maintenance organizations, and explain the effect of the Health Maintenance Organization Act of 1973.

- Describe the characteristics of preferred-provider organizations.

- Describe the characteristics of point-of-service plans.

- Explain the reasons for the use of multiple-option plans.

- Explain the nature of benefit carve-outs.

T he concept of managed care was introduced in Chapter 9. This chapter is devoted primarily to an analysis of the types of managed care plans that are available—health maintenance organizations (HMOs), preferred-provider organizations (PPOs), and point-of-service (POS) plans. This is followed by a discussion of benefit carve-outs, which often use managed care arrangements. The chapter begins with a discussion of some of the differences between traditional medical expense plans and managed care plans and why a person might select managed care in general or a particular managed care plan.

Before proceeding further, it is important to note that managed care is not only growing in use, but it is also very different today from what it was just a few years ago.

DIFFERENCES FROM TRADITIONAL PLANS

It was pointed out in Chapter 9 that a true managed care plan should have five main characteristics:

1. Controlled access to providers
2. Comprehensive case management
3. Preventive care
4. Risk sharing
5. High-quality care

The major characteristic of managed care plans that differentiates them from traditional medical expense plans is probably the limitations on the choice of medical care providers that may be used. The question arises as to whether these choice limitations lead to a different quality of care. Despite these apparent or perceived differences, more than three-quarters of the population is now in some type of managed care plan, and the majority seem reasonably satisfied with the arrangement. In the past few years, much of the growth in managed care has come from employers with fewer than 50 employees. Unlike larger employers, who usually give employees a choice between one or more managed care plans and a traditional indemnity plan, small employers are more likely to offer a single managed care plan rather than any options.

Despite the relatively high level of satisfaction, there has been some recent consumer backlash against managed care that has led to plan changes and legislation, particularly at the state level.

Limited Choice of Medical Providers

Managed care plans attempt to eliminate the unrestricted use of medical care providers by either requiring or encouraging participants to use preapproved providers. The earliest managed care plans, which were HMOs, usually provided no coverage for treatment outside the managed care network, discouraging enrollment because many Americans valued the choice that had traditionally been available when medical treatment was needed.

The concept of managed care received considerable attention in the late 1960s and early 1970s, culminating in the passage of the Health Maintenance Organization Act of 1973. The act resulted in modest growth of HMO plans, but the real growth that came later for managed care was encouraged by several developments that gave employees more choice in selecting providers of medical care. One of these changes was more flexibility under HMO plans. For example, many of the early HMOs assigned a primary physician to a new member. Gradually, new forms of HMOs developed, and existing HMOs were modified to allow members to select a primary care physician from a list of primary care providers.

At the same time, the traditional insurance industry was entering managed care, primarily through the marketing of PPO products, which allowed more flexibility than most HMOs with respect to selection of specialists. In addition, benefits were usually available for treatment received outside a managed care setting, though at a reduced payment level.

The popularity of PPO products with both employers and employees forced the HMOs to adopt even more flexibility. This they did through the establishment of POS plans, which covered nonnetwork treatment. The typical POS plan is more flexible than a typical HMO but more restrictive than a typical PPO product. However, the variations in all three types of plans today are so significant that it is sometimes difficult to determine exactly what is typical.

Survey statistics of the percentage of managed care participants in each type of plan vary, depending on who conducts the survey. However, results of these surveys are similar and indicate that about 40 percent of managed care participants are enrolled in PPOs, 35 percent are enrolled in traditional HMOs, and 25 percent are enrolled in POS plans. All of the surveys show that the percentage for PPOs has recently been increasing. While the percentages for both HMOs and POS plans have declined somewhat, each of these types of managed care plans have continued to have growth in absolute enrollment as more employees leave traditional insured plans and move to managed care.

Quality of Care

A difficult question to answer is whether persons covered by managed care plans receive the same quality of care as persons covered under traditional medical expense plans. If the sole objective of a managed care plan is to offer coverage at the lowest possible cost, there may be a decline in the quality of care. However, some type of quality assurance program is one aspect of any managed care plan. If properly administered, this type of program can weed out providers who give substandard and unnecessary care. In this regard, managed care plans may be more progressive than the medical field as a whole.

The results of numerous surveys and studies on the quality of medical care plans have been mixed. Some studies show that persons in managed care

plans are less likely than persons in traditional medical expense plans to receive treatment for a serious medical condition from specialists, and they are
also likely to have fewer diagnostic tests. There are those who argue that family physicians can treat a wide variety of illnesses and avoid unnecessary diagnostic tests and referrals to specialists. On the other hand, an opposing
argument contends that the decline in the use of specialists and frequency of
diagnostic tests is also a clear indication that there is a decline in the level of
medical care. Other studies show that persons in managed care plans are
much more likely than the rest of the population to receive preventive care
and early diagnosis and treatment of potentially serious conditions such as
high blood pressure and diabetes. In addition, managed care plans are viewed
as having been successful in coordinating care when it is necessary for a person to see several different types of specialists. There is no doubt that there
are some small provider networks with a limited choice of specialists, but
most networks are relatively large or allow persons to select treatment outside
the network. There are also many managed care plans that do refer patients
to highly regarded physicians and hospitals or have these providers as part of
their networks.

In evaluating the quality of medical care, it is also interesting to look at
surveys of participants in the various types of medical expense plans. Most
persons in traditional medical expense plans are convinced they receive better
care because of their unlimited ability to choose providers of medical care as
needed. While surveys of participants in managed care plans usually show a
high degree of satisfaction with the medical care received, there are some concerns that have resulted in recent plan changes and legislative actions and interest.

Two recent developments relate to the quality of care provided by managed
care organizations—an increased interest in accreditation and a consumer
backlash against some aspects of managed care. This backlash has led to the
introduction or passage of laws in many states aimed at solving consumer and
provider concerns about access to care, quality of care, and choice.

Accreditation

As managed care matures and becomes more widespread, there is an increasing focus by government, employers, and consumers on quality. This has
led many employers, particularly large employers, to require that managed
care organizations for their employees meet some type of accreditation standards. Accreditation does more than just provide consumers with information
about health plans. The process, which may cost a managed care organization
several thousand dollars, compares it with what are considered benchmark
standards of quality care. The organization knows where it stands in relation
to its competitors and also what must be done to become accredited or to
achieve a higher level of accreditation.

The leading organization for accrediting appears to be the National Committee for Quality Assurance (NCQA), an independent, not-for-profit organization that has been accrediting HMOs and POS plans since 1991 and plans to start accrediting PPOs. (It also accredits managed behavioral health care organizations, credentials-verification organizations, and physician organizations.) Unlike some accrediting organizations, NCQA makes detailed information available to the general public. The NCQA accredits managed care organizations by evaluating the following five areas of performance (the percentage weighting of each area in the overall accreditation decision is also indicated):

1. *Access and service.* Do health plan members have access to the care and service they need? For example, are physicians in the health plan free to discuss all treatment options available? Do patients report problems getting needed care? How well does the health plan follow up on grievances? (40 percent)
2. *Qualified providers.* Does the health plan assess each physician's qualifications and what health plan members say about their providers? For example, does the health plan regularly check the licenses and training of physicians? How do health plan members rate their personal physician or nurse? (20 percent)
3. *Staying healthy.* Does the health plan help people maintain good health and avoid illness? Does it give its physicians guidelines about how to provide appropriate preventive health services? Are members receiving tests and screenings as appropriate? (15 percent)
4. *Living with illness.* How well does the health plan care for people with chronic conditions? Does the plan have programs in place to assist patients in managing chronic conditions such as asthma? Do diabetics, who are at risk for blindness, receive eye exams as needed? (15 percent)
5. *Getting better.* How well does the health plan care for people when they become sick? How does the health plan evaluate new medical procedures, drugs, and devices to ensure that patients have access to safe and effective care? (10 percent)

From this information, the NCQA gives health plans one of the following accreditation outcomes:

- Excellent
- Commendable
- Accredited
- Provisional
- Denied

The NCQA has also developed a set of performance measures that are designed to enable purchasers and consumers to have necessary information to reliably compare the performance of managed care plans. These measures are commonly referred to as the *Health Plan Employer Data and Information Set,* or *HEDIS*. The current version (which tends to change almost annually) has more than 50 measures that fall into the following categories:

- Effectiveness of care
- Access/availability of care
- Satisfaction with the experience of care
- Health plan stability
- Use of services
- Cost of care
- Informed health care choices
- Health plan descriptive information

Examples of a few of the measures that HEDIS reports, which then can be compared with suggested norms, are the following:

- Percentage of adolescents receiving immunizations
- Percentage of patients receiving beta-blocker treatment following a heart attack
- Percentage of patients receiving appropriate treatment for asthma
- Percentage of women receiving counseling at the onset of menopause

There are also other bodies that accredit various types of health care organizations, including managed care plans, and make their data available to consumers. The Joint Commission on Accreditation of Healthcare Organizations (JCAHO) has accredited hospitals for many years. It also accredits health care networks (including PPOs), home care organizations, long-term care facilities, behavioral health care organizations, ambulatory care organizations, and clinical laboratories.

Another major accrediting organization is the American Health Care Commission/URAC, commonly referred to just as URAC. URAC focuses on accrediting specific aspects of managed care, such as utilization review. Managed care organizations, such as HMOs and PPOs, can have their own utilization review activities accredited if prescribed standards are met. In addition, URAC accredits the activities of organizations that specialize solely in utilization review and that sell their services to managed care plans that do not have their own utilization review staffs. URAC also accredits organizations with respect to the following: case management standards, health call center standards, health network standards, health plan standards and network credentialing standards.

Reactions to Consumer and Provider Concerns

As previously mentioned, the majority of employers and employees are reasonably satisfied with managed care plans but have increasing concerns. However, the satisfaction of physicians and other providers is much more negative, primarily because of decreased control over medical decisions for their patients and a loss of income. As a result, there has been what the media describe as a "backlash against managed care." In some ways, this terminology is inaccurate. First, some of the public's concerns, such as the lack of mental health parity and the lack of coverage for certain preventive medical screenings, apply to the entire health care system. Second, while some of the concerns are aimed at all types of managed care plans, many are aimed solely at practices of HMOs.

This backlash has had several results:

- States continue to enact legislation that addresses many of the concerns.
- Managed care organizations voluntarily modify their practices in light of legislative activity and competitive forces.
- The federal government continues to grapple with consumer legislation.

State Reform

State legislatures in recent years have passed several types of laws aimed at managed care reform. Many of these laws, which have been passed by from 12 to almost all states, include the following:

- Antigag-clause rules
- Grievance, review, and appeal procedures
- Any-willing-provider laws
- Mandatory POS options
- Continuity of care
- Provider protection
- Emergency room coverage
- Mental health parity
- Diabetes health benefits
- Minimum stays for certain procedures
- Plastic surgery mandates
- Direct access to providers

A smaller number of states have passed other types of reform legislation.

It should be noted that some of these changes tend to bring managed care plans closer to traditional indemnity plans in terms of both coverage and cost.

Antigag-Clause Rules. Most states have passed legislation preventing managed care organizations from including provisions in their contracts that prevent physicians from discussing with patients treatment options that may not be covered under their health plans or from referring very ill patients for specialized care by providers outside the plan.

Grievance, Review, and Appeal Procedures. A concern of many consumers over the years has been that managed care plans did not have adequate procedures to receive complaints or appeals about denials of coverage or to make decisions in a timely fashion. As a result, all states have passed some type of legislation that requires managed care plans to follow specified grievance, review, and appeal procedures. At a minimum, this legislation requires that enrollees be informed of the procedures, usually in writing. There is often a specific time period in which a plan must respond to a grievance, particularly when emergency care is needed. Some states have gone farther and require an independent external review process if an enrollee is dissatisfied after going through the plan's grievance and appeal process. The decision of the independent review organization is usually binding on the parties, but it is nonbinding in a few states.

Any-Willing-Provider Laws. There has been some concern, particularly by physicians, that managed care organizations exclude or expel physicians for providing care and/or tests that the physician, but not the managed care organization, feels is necessary. As a result, several states have passed "any willing provider" laws. These laws require that HMOs and other networks of medical care providers accept any provider who is willing to agree to the plan's basic terms and fees. This legislation has been opposed by managed care plans on the basis that it will prevent them from negotiating for the best possible terms with highly qualified and efficient providers.

Mandatory POS Options. As is discussed later, closed-panel HMOs have traditionally required that enrollees seek treatment from network providers. Several states have recently adopted legislation that requires that managed care organizations permit enrollees to seek treatment from nonnetwork providers by paying a portion, but not all, of the expenses incurred with these providers. In effect, such legislation turns a traditional HMO into a POS plan. (POS plans are discussed later in this chapter.) In some states, this legislation applies only to HMOs with a minimum number of members, such as 10,000. In other states, a POS option must be made available to employer groups above a certain size, such as 25 employees.

Continuity of Care. One drawback to receiving care through a managed-care plan is that continuity of care may be lost if the provider ceases to be a part of the provider network, for whatever reason. Several states have recently addressed this issue through legislation. For example, one state requires that the managed care plan continue to pay for care for as long as 60 days, if such a continuation is appropriate. Many of the state laws deal primarily with pregnant patients and may, for example, require coverage to be continued until birth or shortly thereafter for any woman who is in the third trimester of a pregnancy at the time of her obstetrician's departure from the network.

Provider Protection. Most states now require that managed care plans disclose their criteria for selecting medical care providers, give these providers advance notice of contract termination, and provide them with procedures for contesting the termination. One purpose of this legislation is to address the concern that providers who give quality care might lose their provider contract if this care was more expensive or extensive than that the managed care plan deemed necessary.

Emergency Room Coverage. Managed care organizations have been criticized for often refusing to pay for emergency room care, claiming that emergency room treatment was unnecessary. For example, some plans do not pay if a person who goes to an emergency room with chest pains is found to have indigestion rather than a heart attack. The majority of states now require that a plan pay emergency room charges whenever a prudent layperson considers a situation to be an emergency. In addition, care cannot be delayed to get plan authorization for treatment.

Mental Health Parity. Some states have passed mental health parity laws that go beyond the federal law in that they require either complete parity for benefits arising from physical illnesses and mental illnesses or complete parity for physical illnesses and certain severe mental illnesses, such as schizophrenia, depression, or bipolar disorder. These types of laws apply to benefits provided under both traditional insurance contracts and managed care contracts.

Diabetes Health Benefits. Many states require that insurance contracts or managed care plans pay for certain education, equipment, and supplies required by diabetics. With proper care, diabetics can often avoid many serious complications of the disease, such as blindness, amputations, strokes, heart disease, and kidney disease. It is interesting to note one difference between the passage of the laws for mental health parity and diabetes health benefits. The push for mental health parity was partially a result of some managed care plans providing more restrictive benefits than many traditional major medical contracts. On the other hand, the diabetes legislation was probably encouraged by the publicity and success of practices adopted by some managed care plans that were not used in traditional major medical contracts.

Minimum Stays for Certain Procedures. As a result of concerns that some HMOs were compromising proper health care by forcing new mothers and their babies to leave the hospital too soon, most states adopted laws requiring minimum stays for mothers and newborns following deliveries. As a rule, these are for the same periods of time now required by the federal legislation. Most states also mandate that coverage be provided for minimum stays following surgery for breast cancer. For example, several states mandate coverage for stays of 48 hours for mastectomies and 24 hours for lymph node dissections.

Plastic Surgery Mandates. As a result of publicity over several cases where HMOs denied coverage for reconstructive surgery (for example, to deformed children), several states enacted legislation to require all health insurance contracts or health plans to provide coverage for certain types of reconstructive surgery. This legislation may apply to the repair of birth defects only or to a broader list of situations in which reconstruction might be needed as a result of mastectomies, trauma, infections, tumors, or disease.

Direct Access to Providers. Most states have passed laws to allow women covered under managed care plans to have direct access to an obstetrician/gynecologist without obtaining approval or a referral from their health plan. A few states require direct access to other types of providers, such as dermatologists.

Other Legislation. Other types of legislation have been introduced in several states, but the number of states adopting the legislation has been small to date. The following are examples:

- Allowing managed care organizations to be sued for medical malpractice if their denial of medically necessary treatment results in harm or injury to a patient. Under a typical state law, a managed care plan cannot be sued for medical malpractice because it is not considered to be practicing medicine.
- Requiring that patients and/or state regulators be informed of financial incentives offered to providers.
- Granting patients access to all prescription drugs approved by the government for sale.
- Making health care plans disclose their policies for covering experimental treatments.
- Improving state monitoring of managed care plans by requiring that these plans report the status of patient grievances to the states.

Voluntary Reform by Managed Care Organizations

Many managed care reforms have been initiated voluntarily by managed care organizations. Some reforms are probably a result of the natural evolving of a new form of financing and providing health care. Other changes have occurred because of competition among managed care organizations for market share. However, most of the reforms probably are reactions to legislation that is proposed or passed by the states. After a few states pass a certain type of managed care legislation, there is often a tendency for managed care organizations nationwide to revise their plans to address the concerns that resulted in the legislation. There then may be little need for other states to adopt similar legislation, and, in fact, managed care bills introduced in state legislatures are often not enacted if the legislature learns that the managed care industry has already resolved the problem.

The threat of legislation, at either the state or federal level, is a major impetus for voluntary changes by managed care plans, just as it is for other types of businesses. Such voluntary reform may dampen the likelihood that more restrictive government regulation will result.

Federal Reform

Congress has addressed some health care concerns with the passage of such legislation as the following acts, which are discussed earlier in this book: the Mental Health Parity Act, the Newborns' and Mothers' Health Protection Act, and the Women's Health and Cancer Rights Act.

At the time this book is being revised in late 2000, there are numerous bills in Congress that would add significant federal legislation to the health care environment. Sometimes referred to as a *patient's bill of rights,* this type of legislation seems to have bipartisan support. However, there are differences of opinion as to what should be done, and these often vary by political party. The following discussion addresses a few of these issues.

There is disagreement whether the legislation should apply to all health insurance plans or to self-funded plans only. For the most part, ERISA exempts self-funded benefit plans from state regulation; therefore, the types of state reforms previously described apply only to "insured" plans in the sense that they apply to insurance contracts and managed care plans over which the states have legislative control. There are arguments that federal legislation should apply only to self-funded plans because the states are already regulating the plans that are not self-funded. There are other arguments that federal legislation should apply to all health insurance plans because of a lack of legislation in some states and less-stringent regulation in many states.

Much of the proposed federal regulation is in fact broader than that found in most states, and even the Congressional Budget Office agrees that a federal bill would increase the cost of health care plans. Unfortunately, increased health plan costs lead to an increase in employers and employees being unable to afford coverage. This has resulted in a debate over what should be the proper balance between availability and cost.

There is also disagreement over the issue of health plan and employer liability. Some proposed legislation would allow employees to sue health plans and their employers if they are injured by a delay or denial of benefits. There are concerns that this type of legislation would benefit trial lawyers more than consumers. In addition, there are concerns that the potential liability might result in many employers terminating health care plans and giving employees pay increases with which they would have to arrange their own health insurance coverage. Such a result would undoubtedly increase the number of uninsureds because some employees would find other uses for the money. Some bills do not impose liability on employers; rather, they provide a process of external review over medical decisions of managed care plans.

If there is no federal legislation prior to the 2000 elections, health care reform is an issue that the new president will certainly face. Readers should follow legislative developments and their potential effect on health care plans.

REASONS FOR USE OF MANAGED CARE

There are many reasons why employees elect coverage under a managed care plan. First, it may be the only plan the employer provides, although most employers allow a choice of benefit plans. In those situations, the following factors have been identified as reasons why a managed care plan, in general, or a particular managed care plan might be selected:

- The reputation of the managed care plan. To some extent, this is a function of the managed care plan's experience. In areas where managed care plans have been established for many years, a larger percentage of employees participate. Employees are also concerned with perceived quality of care and are less likely to choose a plan known for frequent coverage denials and difficulty in obtaining referrals to specialists.

- The extent to which employees have established relationships with physicians. Employees are reluctant to elect a managed care option if it requires that they give up a physician with whom they are satisfied. In some cases, of course, this physician also may participate in the managed care plan. In general, new employees are more likely to elect a managed care option if they are new residents of the area or are just entering the labor force.

- Costs. Managed care plans are obviously more attractive to employers when they offer a less expensive alternative to coverage under insurance company plans. As a rule, managed care plans are less expensive, and any employee share of the premium is lower. Even when the premium cost is comparable, there is often broader coverage and no deductibles or percentage participation. If employees view a managed care alternative as being less expensive in the long run, their participation is greater.

In the early days of the growth of managed care, employers were concerned primarily with cost savings when they adopted managed care plans. In a more mature managed care marketplace, employers are concerned with the same factors when they change plans as are employees: reputation, availability of providers, and cost. Throughout most of the late 1990s, the economy was booming, labor markets were tight, and employers faced relatively modest premium increases from year to year. As a result, employers were much more likely than in the past to modify managed care plans or to adopt new plans that were less restrictive, and therefore somewhat more expensive, in their management of care. With greater premium increases as the new millennium begins, some benefit consultants feel that this trend may reverse itself, particularly if there is an economic downturn.

HEALTH MAINTENANCE ORGANIZATIONS

HMOs are generally regarded as organized systems of health care that provide a comprehensive array of medical services on a prepaid basis to voluntarily enrolled persons living within a specified geographic region. HMOs act like insurance companies and the Blues in that they finance health care. However, unlike insurance companies and the Blues, they also deliver medical services.

Even though the term *health maintenance organization* is relatively new, the concept of the HMO is not. For many years, *prepaid group practice plans* (as they were called) operated successfully in many parts of the country. However, growth was relatively slow until the passage of the Health Maintenance Organization Act of 1973. This act resulted from a belief on the part of the federal government that HMOs were a viable alternative method of financing and delivering health care and thus should be encouraged. In fact, the act also resulted in many employers being required to offer their employees the option of coverage by an HMO instead of by a more traditional medical expense plan. There are approximately 600 HMOs in existence, with the 25 largest plans enrolling nearly half of all HMO participants. In addition, a large majority of HMO subscribers are in plans that belong to one of about 50 chains of HMOs.

Characteristics of HMOs

HMOs have several characteristics that distinguish them from traditional medical expense contracts offered by insurance companies and the Blues.

Comprehensive Care

HMOs offer their subscribers a comprehensive package of health care services, generally including benefits for outpatient services as well as for hospitalization. Subscribers usually get many of these services at no cost except the periodically required premium (referred to as a *capitation payment*). However, in some cases, a copayment may be imposed for certain services, such as $5 or $10 per physician's visit or per drug prescription. HMOs emphasize preventive care and provide such services as routine physicals and immunizations. The cost of such preventive care was historically not covered under the contracts of insurance companies or the Blues, even when major medical coverage was provided. Today, however, as a result of legislation and consumer demand, these plans also provide some preventive care and immunization but to a lesser degree than HMOs.

Delivery of Medical Services

HMOs provide for the delivery of medical services, which in some cases are performed by salaried physicians and other personnel employed by the HMO. Although this approach is in contrast to the usual fee-for-service delivery system of medical care, some HMOs do contract with providers on a fee-for-service basis.

Subscribers are required to obtain their care from providers of medical services who are affiliated with the HMO. Because HMOs often operate in a geographic region no larger than one state or a single metropolitan area, this requirement may result in limited coverage for subscribers if treatment is received elsewhere. Most HMOs do have "out-of-area coverage," but only in the case of medical emergencies.

HMOs emphasize treatment by primary care physicians to the greatest extent possible. These practitioners provide a gatekeeper function and historically have controlled access to specialists. The traditional HMO covers benefits provided by a specialist only if the primary care physician recommends the specialist. This specialist may be a fellow employee in a group-practice plan or a physician who has a contract with the HMO. The subscriber has little or no say regarding the specialist selected, which has been one of the more controversial aspects of HMOs and one that has discouraged larger enrollment. In response to consumer concerns, many HMOs now make the process of seeing a specialist easier. Referrals can often be made by nurses in physicians' offices or by staff members of the HMO whom subscribers can contact by telephone. Some HMOs, referred to as *direct-access* or *self-referral HMOs,* allow subscribers to see network specialists without going through a gatekeeper. However, the specialist may have to contact the HMO for authorization before proceeding with tests or treatment. A variation of an HMO, called a *POS plan,* allows even more choice. This type of managed care plan is discussed later in this chapter.

Cost Control

A major emphasis of HMOs is the control of medical expenses. By providing and encouraging preventive care, HMOs attempt to detect and treat medical conditions at an early stage, thereby avoiding expensive medical treatment in the future. HMOs have also attempted to provide treatment on an outpatient basis whenever possible. Because insurance companies and the Blues have provided more comprehensive coverage for a hospitalized person in the past, less expensive outpatient treatments were often not performed. Emphasizing outpatient treatment and preventive medicine has resulted in a lower hospitalization rate for HMO subscribers than for the population as a whole, although some of this decreased hospitalization rate over the years appears to be a result of younger and healthier employees having been more likely to elect HMO coverage. This increased emphasis on outpatient treatment has resulted in HMOs often providing better coverage than other types of plans for mental health, alcoholism, or drug addiction if the treatment is received outside a hospital setting. However, if hospitalization is needed, HMOs often have more limited benefits than other types of plans.

HMOs practice a greater degree of utilization review and control than do other types of health plans. In addition to the usual types of prospective review, such as hospital preadmission certification or second surgical opinions, other techniques are often used, such as controlled access to specialists by gatekeepers and preauthorization for certain outpatient procedures. Note that the burden for obtaining preadmission certification or preauthorization for medical procedures lies with the plan physician, not the plan member. This is in contrast to traditional medical expense plans and nonnetwork PPO coverage, where that responsibility is on the plan member.

HMOs are more likely than other types of health plans to conduct a high degree of concurrent review while patients are hospitalized. In addition, HMOs closely monitor the practice patterns of physicians. If a physician, for example, orders a higher-than-average number of diagnostic tests or admits more patients to hospitals than do other physicians, the HMO reviews the situation with the physician to determine whether proper practice standards are being followed. If they are not, the HMO may help the physician adopt better standards. It should be noted that physicians sometimes are not aware of all alternatives to hospitalization or that the medical community has changed its standards regarding the effectiveness and frequency of some diagnostic tests. Working with the physician may result in an effective change in practice patterns or, in the most extreme cases, the termination of the physician from the plan. HMOs that monitor practice patterns closely may also contact physicians who do not seem to be ordering enough diagnostic tests or who provide lower-than-usual amounts of preventive care.

HMOs also tightly control payments to physicians and other providers of medical services. In some cases, these providers are employees of the HMO. In other cases, their compensation is controlled by capitation or other arrangements by which the providers share some of the risk that costs will exceed certain levels. These techniques are discussed later in this chapter.

Sponsorship of HMOs

Traditionally, most HMOs operated as nonprofit organizations and had the majority of subscribers until a few years ago. The majority of new HMOs are profit making, and almost two-thirds of subscribers are covered under this type of organization. While many subscribers are covered by HMOs that have been sponsored by consumer groups, a sizable and increasing portion is covered by plans sponsored by insurance companies or the Blues. Sponsorship also may come from physicians, hospitals, labor unions, or private investors. Some recently established HMOs have been formed by physician-hospital organizations (PHOs). A PHO is a legal entity that is formed by one or more physicians' groups and hospitals. It negotiates, contracts, and markets the services of the physicians and the hospitals. PHOs may form their own HMOs or they may contract with existing HMOs or other types of managed care organizations.

The issue of whether insurance companies and the Blues should be involved with HMOs was once a source of disagreement within the industry. Some insurance companies viewed HMOs as competitors with the potential of putting them out of the health insurance business. Other insurance companies viewed them as a viable alternative method of financing and delivering health care that can be offered to employers as one of the products in their portfolio.

Over time, the latter viewpoint prevailed. In addition to actually sponsoring and owning HMOs, some insurance companies are actively involved with them in a variety of ways. These include the following:

- Consulting on such matters as plan design and administration.
- Administrative services, such as actuarial advice, claims monitoring, accounting, and computer services.
- Marketing assistance, such as designing sales literature. In a few cases, the agents of insurance companies have been used to market HMOs. This has been done in conjunction with the marketing of the insurance company's hospitalization plan when the HMO does not provide hospitalization coverage to its subscribers.
- Providing hospitalization coverage. HMOs that do not control their own hospital facilities may provide this benefit by purchasing coverage for their subscribers.
- Providing emergency out-of-area coverage. An insurance company operating on a national basis may be better equipped to administer these claims than an HMO.
- Providing financial support in a variety of ways, including reinsurance if an HMO experiences greater-than-expected demand for services and agreements to bail out financially troubled HMOs.

Types of HMOs

There are several types of HMOs. The earliest plans can best be described as *closed-panel plans,* under which subscribers must use physicians employed by the plan or by an organization with which it contracts. With most closed-panel plans having several general practitioners, subscribers usually can select their physician from among those accepting new patients and make medical appointments just as if the physician was in private practice. However, there is frequently little choice among specialists because a plan may have a contract with only one physician or a limited number of physicians in a given specialty.

The number of closed-panel plans is relatively small, but they account for almost 20 percent of all HMO subscribers. The three different types of closed-panel plans—staff-model HMOs, group-model HMOs, and network-model HMOs—are discussed in more detail below.

Many newer HMOs have been formed as individual practice associations (IPAs), which can be described as *open-panel plans*. This type of plan has more flexibility with respect to subscribers choosing physicians and the ability of physicians to participate in the plan. About 45 percent of HMO subscribers are in IPAs.

Most of the remaining subscribers to HMOs receive their coverage in a variety of ways under *mixed-model plans*. Some subscribers are also in open-ended HMOs, which are discussed later in this chapter as POS plans.

Staff-Model HMO

Under a staff-model HMO, the HMO owns its own facilities and hires its own physicians. It may own hospitals, laboratories, or pharmacies or it may contract for these services. The HMO may also have contracts with specialists to treat subscribers if it is not large enough to justify hiring its own specialists in a given medical field.

Employees of staff-model HMOs are paid a salary and possibly an incentive bonus. A staff-model HMO offers a great degree of control over costs because it controls the salaries of the physicians who might find themselves unemployed if the HMO is unprofitable or if they do not provide care within the cost and utilization parameters of the HMO.

Despite the potential for cost savings in staff-model HMOs, few have actually been established, primarily because of high start-up costs and high fixed costs once they are operating.

Group-Model HMO

The most common type of closed-panel plan is the group-model HMO. Under this arrangement, physicians (and other medical personnel) are employees of another legal entity that has a contractual relationship with the HMO to provide medical services for its subscribers. In most cases, this is an exclusive arrangement, and the provider's physicians only treat subscribers of the HMO. These physicians also typically operate out of one or more common facilities.

Under a group-model plan, the HMO may contract with a single provider of medical services or with different providers for different types of services (for example, one contract for physicians' services and another for hospital services). The HMO often pays for services on a capitation basis, which means that the provider of services gets a predetermined fee per year for each subscriber and must provide any and all covered services for this capitation fee. The fee is independent of how the provider compensates its own employees. Under this arrangement, the provider shares the risk in that it loses money if utilization is higher than expected or increases its profit if utilization is lower than expected. Therefore, the provider has a very real incentive to control costs.

Network-Model HMO

A network-model HMO differs from a group-model HMO in that it contracts with two or more independent groups of physicians to provide medical services to its subscribers. Physician groups that enter into this type of arrangement often treat non-HMO patients on a fee-for-service basis.

Individual Practice Associations

In IPAs, participating physicians practice individually or in small groups at their own offices. In most cases, these physicians accept both non-HMO patients, on a traditional fee-for-service basis, and HMO subscribers. IPAs are often referred to as *open-panel plans* because subscribers choose from a list of participating physicians. The number of physicians participating in this type of HMO is frequently larger than the number participating in group practice plans and may include several physicians within a given specialty. In some geographic areas, most physicians may participate; in other geographic areas, only a relatively small percentage of physicians may participate. Because most of the newer HMOs are IPAs, the percentage of HMO subscribers served by these plans continue to grow.

Several methods may be used to compensate physicians participating in an IPA. The most common is a fee schedule based on the services provided to subscribers. To encourage physicians to be cost effective, it is common for plans to have a provision for reducing payments to physicians if the experience of the plan is worse than expected. On the other hand, the physicians may receive a bonus if the experience of the plan is better than expected. Particularly with respect to general practitioners, some IPA plans pay each physician a flat annual amount for each subscriber who has elected to use him or her. For this annual payment, the physician must see these subscribers as often as necessary during the year.

It is unusual for IPAs to own their own hospitals. Instead, they enter into contracts with local hospitals to provide the necessary services for their subscribers.

Mixed-Model HMOs

An increasing number of HMOs are now operating as mixed-model plans, which means that the organization of the plan is a combination of two or more of the approaches previously described. Such a combination generally occurs as a plan continues to grow. For example, a plan might have been established as a staff-model HMO, and at a later time the HMO decided to expand its capacity or geographic region by adding additional physicians under an IPA arrangement. Some mixed models have also resulted from the merger of two plans that each used a different organizational form.

Extent of HMO Use

It is estimated that more than 60 million employees and dependents are covered under HMOs, with the enrollment varying considerably by geographic region. For example, two states (California and Massachusetts) have more than 50 percent of their population enrolled in HMOs, while several other states have enrollments of 5 percent or less. There are also significant variations by metropolitan area, with approximately two-thirds of all enrollees living in 30 metropolitan areas. In several metropolitan areas, the majority of persons are covered by HMOs.

Except in rare instances, employees covered by HMO plans have elected this form of coverage as an alternative to their employer's insurance company plan or Blue Cross–Blue Shield plan. Although state law may require certain employers to offer an HMO option, other employers voluntarily offer it. The administrative details of such an option may be burdensome and expensive for small employers, but they seem to pose few problems for large employers with specialized employee benefit staffs. In many cases, the financial consequences to the employer of such an option are insignificant because the employer makes the same contribution on an employee's behalf regardless of which plan is selected. Until recently, the general attitude of employers toward HMOs seems to have been somewhat ambivalent: Some employers had been in favor of them, others against, and the majority indifferent. However, according to several recent studies, most employers feel that HMOs have been a very effective technique for controlling benefit costs.

Where there is a choice of medical expense plans, most employees do not elect an HMO option unless there is a financial incentive to do so. However, studies have revealed that employees who have elected HMOs are for the most part satisfied with their choice and are unlikely to switch back to an insurance company plan or Blue Cross–Blue Shield plan as long as the HMO option remains available.

Health Maintenance Organization Act of 1973

The Health Maintenance Organization Act of 1973 has had a significant influence on both the interest in and the growth of HMOs. The act introduced the concept of the *federally qualified HMO*. For several years after the act's passage, most HMOs were formed to take advantage of this federal qualification, which entitled them to federal grants for feasibility studies and development (including grants to solicit subscribers) and federal loans (or loan guarantees) to assist them in covering initial operating deficits. In addition, many employers were required to make federally qualified HMOs available to their employees until late 1995. Federal qualification also exempted federally qualified HMOs from restrictive laws in many states that had effectively prevented the establishment of HMOs in those states. Such state laws have now essentially disappeared.

The need now for a federal HMO law is debatable. Most states have similar legislation. While newer HMOs may forgo federal qualification, the majority of older HMOs still retain that status. It is felt that this grants them a "seal of approval" from the federal government. In addition, many employers will deal only with federally qualified HMOs. However, this practice is changing as employers are increasingly requiring some type of accreditation (either solely or as an alternative to federal qualification) as their measure of quality. Finally, federal qualification continues to be one way that HMOs can satisfy certain qualifications necessary to provide coverage for Medicare recipients. Today, about two-thirds of HMO subscribers are covered by federally qualified plans.

It should be pointed out that an HMO may have more than one line of business, with some lines being federally qualified and other lines not being federally qualified.

Requirements for Federal Qualification

To become federally qualified, an HMO must meet certain requirements (set forth in the act) to the satisfaction of the secretary of health and human services. In return for a periodic prepaid fee, an HMO must provide the following basic benefits to its subscribers at no cost or with nominal copayments:

■ Physicians' services, including consultant and referral services, up to 10 percent of which may be provided by physicians who are not affiliated with the HMO
■ Inpatient and outpatient hospital services
■ Medically necessary emergency health services
■ Short-term (up to 20 visits) outpatient mental health services
■ Medical treatment and referral services for alcohol or drug abuse or addiction
■ Diagnostic laboratory services and diagnostic and therapeutic radiologic services
■ Home health services
■ Preventive health services such as immunizations, well-baby care, periodic physical examinations, and family-planning services
■ Medical social services, including education in methods of personal health maintenance and in the use of health services

The HMO also may provide the following supplemental benefits, either as part of its standard benefit package or as optional benefits for which an additional fee may be charged:

■ Services of intermediate- and long-term care facilities
■ Vision care
■ Dental care
■ Additional mental health services

- Rehabilitative services
- Prescription drugs

In addition to the benefits that either are required or may be included, an HMO must meet the following other requirements with respect to its operations:

- A fiscally sound operation, including provisions against the risk of insolvency
- Annual open enrollment periods
- An ongoing quality assurance program

Prior to 1988, the HMO act required that HMOs determine their rates on the basis of community rating for all employer groups. This provision of the act decreased the attractiveness of HMOs to employers whose employees had lower-than-average benefit claims. A 1988 amendment to the act permits HMOs to establish advance rates based on an employer's past and projected claims experience if a group has 100 or more employees. Experience rating can also be used for groups of fewer than 100 employees, but the advance rate cannot be more than 10 percent higher than the HMO's community rates. In contrast to the usual practice of experience rating (see Chapter 15), HMOs are *not* allowed to make retrospective rate adjustments if claims turn out to be higher or lower than expected.

Open Enrollment Periods

Once an HMO option is made available, an employer must provide for a group enrollment period of at least ten working days each year in which eligible employees may transfer between any available health insurance plans without the application of waiting periods, exclusions, or limitations based on health status. During this open enrollment period and at least 30 days prior to it, an employer must allow any participating HMOs to have fair and reasonable access to eligible employees for purposes of presenting and explaining their programs.

A problem may arise if an HMO ceases operations because of financial difficulties. Unfortunately, this has occurred in some cases, even among HMOs that have met the standards for federal qualification. Unless the cessation of HMO coverage coincides with an open enrollment period, these employees may not be able to join or rejoin their employer's insurance company plan or Blue Cross–Blue Shield plan without showing evidence of insurability. However, under these circumstances, many insurance companies and Blue Cross–Blue Shield plans include provisions in their contracts for coverage without evidence of insurability for these employees. In fact, many HMOs also have a similar provision in case other plans available to employees cease operations for any reason.

Contributions

Employers who voluntarily offer federally qualified HMOs are required to make nondiscriminatory contributions to the HMOs. Under regulations issued in 1996 by the Health Care Financing Administration, the following five employer contribution practices are considered nondiscriminatory:

1. The employer may contribute the same amount it contributes to non-HMO alternatives
2. The employer's contributions may vary by class of enrollee on the basis of attributes, such as age, sex, and family status that are reasonable predictors of utilization, experience, costs, or risks. For each enrollee in a class, the employer would contribute the same amount, regardless of the plan that an employee chooses
3. If the employer requires employee contributions, the employee contribution rate to the HMO plan cannot be greater than 50 percent of the contribution rate to the most popular non-HMO plan
4. The employer may pay the same percentage of the cost of all available health plans
5. The employer and an HMO may negotiate a payment schedule that is mutually acceptable as long as it meets the basic criteria for nondiscrimination against employees who enroll in HMOs.

State Regulation

HMOs are heavily regulated by the states. All states have numerous laws that are enforced by various state officials, often including both the insurance and public health commissioners. In many cases, the state legislation largely duplicates the federal HMO act.

Almost all states have adopted the NAIC Health Maintenance Organization Model Act, which focuses substantially on issues relating to licensing of HMOs and the maintenance of their financial solvency. However, it also addresses numerous other issues, such as the types of activities in which HMOs can engage, the requirement of a quality assurance program, standards for materials given to subscribers, grievance procedures, enrollment periods, and coordination-of-benefits provisions.

HMO Coverage as an Alternative to Major Medical

Most HMOs provide broad protection for medical expenses. In fact, federally qualified HMOs often give more comprehensive protection than most major medical plans because in addition to covering such items as routine examinations and immunizations, they tend to require fewer out-of-pocket expenses by the members. HMOs that meet the requirements for federal qualification are allowed to use copayments for services (1) if the copayment for any single service does not exceed 50 percent of the cost for that service and (2) if the total of all copayments does not exceed more than 20 percent of the cost of supplying all basic health services. In practice, copayments (if used at all) are usually substantially below these permissible limits. In addition, no subscriber is required to copay more than 50 percent of the annual subscriber fee that would have been charged if coverage had been written without any copayments.

Table 11-1 on the following pages compares the major medical plan and two HMOs that are offered to the employees of one organization. All three plans are reasonably representative of their respective plan type.

PREFERRED-PROVIDER ORGANIZATIONS

A concept that continues to receive considerable attention from employers and insurance companies is the preferred-provider organization. A few PPOs have existed on a small scale for many years, but since the early 1980s PPOs have grown steadily in number and in membership. Today, PPOs provide coverage for medical expenses to more Americans than do HMOs, primarily because of the flexibility of covered persons to choose their own medical providers.

What Is a PPO?

The term *PPO* tends to be used in two ways. One way is to apply it to health care providers that contract with employers, insurance companies, union trust funds, third-party administrators, or others to provide medical care services at a reduced fee. Using this definition, a PPO may be organized by the providers themselves or by other organizations such as insurance companies, the Blues, HMOs, or employers. Like HMOs, they may take the form of group practices or separate individual practices. They may provide a broad array of medical services, including physicians' services, hospital care, laboratory costs, and home health care, or they may be limited to only hospitalization or physicians' services. Some of these types of organizations are very specialized and provide specific services such as dental care, mental health benefits, substance abuse services, maternity care, or prescription drugs. In this book, these providers are referred to not as *PPOs* but as *preferred providers* or *network providers*.

The second use of the term *PPO,* and the one generally assumed when the term is used throughout this book, is to apply it to benefit plans that contract with preferred providers to obtain lower-cost care for plan members. PPOs typically differ from HMOs in several respects. First, the preferred providers are generally paid on a fee-for-service basis as their services are used. However, fees are usually subject to a schedule that is the same for all similar providers within the PPO, and providers may have an incentive to control utilization through bonus arrangements. Second, employees and their dependents are not required to use the practitioners or facilities that contract with

TABLE 11-1
A Comparison: Insured Plan Versus HMOs

	INSURED COMPREHENSIVE MAJOR MEDICAL EXPENSE PLAN	GROUP-MODEL HMO	INDIVIDUAL PRACTICE ASSOCIATION HMO
Choice of Physician	Member may select any licensed physician or surgeon.	Member selects a personal physician from the medical group, who coordinates and directs all health care needs, including referrals to specialists.	Members select a personal primary care physician from among the health plan physicians.
Where Primary Care and Specialty Care Are Available	Care is provided in physician's office or outpatient facility.	Care is provided at four multispecialty centers.	Care is provided in participating private physicians' offices.
Choice of Hospitals	Member may select any accredited hospital—choice depends on where physician has admitting privileges.	Selection is from participating hospitals.	Selection is from participating hospitals.
Annual Deductible and Coinsurance	There is a $200 deductible. The plan pays 100% of expenses for hospitalization, but it does have 80% coinsurance for other covered services. The coinsurance provision is subject to a $3,000 out-of-pocket limit.	There is no deductible and 100% coinsurance (except small copayments for home visits and outpatient mental health).	There is no deductible and 100% coinsurance (except small copayments for home visits, outpatient mental health, and a deductible for prescription drugs).
Maximum Benefit	$1 million lifetime maximum	No overall maximum limit	No overall maximum limit
Preventive Care			
Routine physicals	Not covered	Covered in full	Covered in full
Well-baby care	Covered in full	Covered in full	Covered in full
Pap smears	Routine exams not covered	Covered in full	Covered in full
Immunizations	Not covered	Covered in full	Covered in full
Eye exams	Not covered	Covered in full, including written prescriptions for lenses	Paid in full for children up to age 18
Hearing exams	Not covered	Covered in full	Covered in full
Health education	Available through some physicians' offices	Periodic classes held on diet, prenatal care, physical fitness, etc.	Covered in full through participating hospital programs
Physician Care			
Surgery	Covered at 80% after satisfying deductible	Covered in full	Covered in full
Inpatient visits	Covered at 80% after deductible	Covered in full	Covered in full
Office and home	Covered at 80% after deductible	Covered in full after a $5 copayment per visit	Covered in full after a $10 copayment per visit
X-rays and lab	Covered at 80% after deductible	Covered in full	Covered in full

TABLE 11-1 (continued)
A Comparison: Insured Plan Versus HMOs

	INSURED COMPREHENSIVE MAJOR MEDICAL EXPENSE PLAN	GROUP-MODEL HMO	INDIVIDUAL PRACTICE ASSOCIATED HMO
Hospital Services			
Room and board	Covered in full for unlimited days in semiprivate room after satisfying deductible	Covered in full for unlimited days in semiprivate room	Covered in full for unlimited days in semiprivate room
Supplies, tests, medication, etc.	Covered in full for covered benefit days	Covered in full	Covered in full
Private-duty nurse	Covered in full while hospitalized (outpatient licensed practical nurse services covered at 50% up to $250 per year)	Covered in full	Covered in full
Emergency Care	Covered in full for care received in hospital outpatient department within 24 hours of an accident	Covered in full for around-the-clock emergency care by plan physicians and in participating hospitals. Emergency care by non-plan physicians or hospitals is also covered when obtaining plan care is not reasonable because of distance and urgency.	Covered in full for around-the-clock emergency care by participating physicians and in participating hospitals. Emergency care by nonparticipating physicians or hospitals is also covered when obtaining plan care is not reasonable because of distance and urgency.
Ambulance service	Covered in full for local transportation after satisfying deductible	Covered in full	Covered in full
Maternity Care			
Hospital	Covered in full after deductible	Covered in full	Covered in full
Physician	Covered at 80% after deductible	Covered in full	Covered in full
Mental Health Care			
Hospital	Covered as regular hospitalization, i.e., 365-day/lifetime limitation	Covered in full for 45 days per year	Covered in full for 30 days during 12-month period
Inpatient physician	Covered as regular inpatient physician care	Covered in full for 45 days per year	Covered in full for 30 days during 12-month period
Outpatient physician	Covered at 50% up to $30 per visit	Covered for 30 visits per year; first 3 visits covered in full, member pays $20 per visit for next 27 visits	Covered for 20 visits per period; first 3 visits covered in full, member pays 25% of regular fee for next 7 visits, member pays 50% of regular fee for next 10 visits
Alcohol and drug addiction	Covered like other mental health services	No special limits; covered as other medical and mental health services	After detoxification treatment, covered as for mental health problems

TABLE 11-1 (continued)
A Comparison: Insured Plan Versus HMOs

	INSURED COMPREHENSIVE MAJOR MEDICAL EXPENSE PLAN	GROUP-MODEL HMO	INDIVIDUAL PRACTICE ASSOCIATED HMO
Dental Care Hospital	Covered for hospital costs when confinement is necessary for dental care	Covered for hospital costs when confinement is necessary for dental care	Covered for hospital costs when confinement is necessary for dental care
Dentist or dental surgeon	Covered for treatment of accidental injury to natural teeth	Covered for treatment of accidental injury to natural teeth and certain oral surgical procedures (e.g., impacted wisdom teeth)	Covered for treatment of diseases and injuries to the jaw and removal of impacted wisdom teeth
Outpatient Medication Prescription drugs	Covered at 80% after deductible, if related to treatment of nonoccupational illness or injury	Covered subject to a $10 copayment per prescription for generic drugs, $15 for brand-name formulary drugs and $25 for nonformulary drugs	Covered subject to a $5 copayment per prescription for generic drugs and $10 copayment for nongeneric drugs. Prior authorization required for certain high-cost drugs
Injections	Covered at 80% after deductible, if related to treatment of nonoccupational illness or injury	Covered in full	Covered in full
Prescribed Home Health Services	Covered at 80% after deductible	Covered in full	Covered in full
Allergy Care	Covered at 80% after deductible	Covered in full	Covered in full
Eligibility	Spouse and unmarried dependent children to age 19 or age 23 if a full-time student	Spouse and unmarried dependent children to age 19 or 23 if a full-time student	Spouse and unmarried dependent children through age 19 or 23 if a full-time student
Conversion	Conversion to individual coverage available	Conversion to nongroup coverage available	Conversion to individual enrollment available at same benefit level

the PPO; rather, a choice can be made each time medical care is needed, and benefits are also paid for care provided by nonnetwork providers. However, employees are offered incentives to use network providers; they include lower or reduced deductibles and copayments as well as increased benefits such as preventive health care. Third, most PPOs do not use a primary care physician as a gatekeeper; employees do not need referrals to see specialists.

Employers were disappointed with some of the early PPOs. While discounts were received, they seemed to have little effect on benefit costs because discounts were from higher-than-average fees, or providers were more likely to perform diagnostic tests or prolong hospital stays to generate additional fees to compensate for the discounts. Needless to say, these PPOs seldom lasted long. The successful PPOs today emphasize quality care and utilization review. In selecting physicians and hospitals, PPOs look not only at the type of care provided but also at the provider's cost effectiveness. In this era of fierce competition among medical care providers, these physicians and hospitals are often willing to accept discounts in hopes of increasing patient volume. It is also important for a PPO to monitor and control utilization on an ongoing basis and to deal with groups of preferred providers that monitor their own costs and utilization. As a general rule, however, PPOs do not monitor their preferred providers as closely as HMOs do.

Variations

Over time, PPOs have continued to evolve. A few PPOs compensate providers on a capitation basis, while a few others perform a gatekeeper function. If a specialist is not recommended by a subscriber's primary care physician, benefits may be reduced. With these changes, it is sometimes difficult to determine the exact form of a managed care organization. However, those that operate as traditional HMOs generally provide medical expense coverage at a slightly lower cost than those that operate as traditional PPOs, but there are wide variations among HMOs as well as among PPOs. Therefore, a careful analysis of quality of care, cost, and financial stability is necessary before a particular HMO or PPO is selected.

Another variation of the PPO is the exclusive-provider organization, or EPO. The primary difference is that an EPO does not provide coverage outside the preferred-provider network, except in those infrequent cases when the network does not contain an appropriate specialist. This aspect of an EPO makes it very similar to an HMO. The number of EPOs is small.

Sponsorship

Most of the early PPOs were established by insurance companies to provide products to compete with HMOs. In the 1990s, the number of PPOs grew significantly to about 1,100, with about 60 percent still owned by insurance companies. Another 10 percent are owned by HMOs to give them another product in their health plan portfolios to offer employers. The remaining 30 percent have a variety of ownership forms, including the Blues, third-party administrators, private investors, and groups of physicians and/or hospitals.

Benefit Structure

The basic benefit structure of a PPO is very similar to that of the traditional comprehensive major medical contract, which is discussed in Chapter 10. The most significant difference is that there is a higher level of benefits for care received from network providers than there is for care received from nonnetwork providers. Many PPOs have extensive networks of preferred providers, particularly in the geographic areas in which they operate, and there is little reason to seek care outside the network. Some of these PPOs also have reciprocity agreements elsewhere with networks of other PPOs and hospitals (called *centers of excellence*) that have excellent outcomes and reputations for certain types of medical procedures, such as cancer treatment, organ transplants. or burn treatment. Under these agreements, benefits are paid as if care was received from network providers. Other PPOs have more limited networks, and the need and desire for treatment from nonnetwork providers is greater. Table 11-2 shows excerpts of the benefit structure from an actual PPO.

The level of benefits under PPOs may vary because of differences in deductibles, coinsurance, maximum lifetime benefits, and precertification rules. There may also be a few additional benefits that are available only if care is received from a network provider. Finally, the procedures for filing claims also differ. The major purpose of these differences is to encourage an employee or dependent to receive care from preferred providers who have agreed to charge the plan a discounted fee.

Deductibles

A PPO may have annual deductibles that apply separately to network and nonnetwork charges. For examples, these might be $100 and $250, respectively. However, many PPOs have no deductible for network charges. As mentioned in Chapter 10, deductibles may be waived for some medical services, such as emergency or preventive care.

Coinsurance

Most PPOs use coinsurance percentages that are 20 percent (and occasionally 30 percent) lower when care is received from nonnetwork providers. The most frequently found provision applies 90 percent coinsurance to network charges and 70 percent coinsurance to nonnetwork charges. Coinsurance provisions of 100/80, 90/80, and 100/70 are also frequently used. As with deductibles, the percentage participation may be waived for certain medical services. In addition, different stop-loss limits or coinsurance caps, such as $1,000 and $3,000, may apply to network and nonnetwork charges.

While PPOs typically have higher coinsurance percentages for network charges than do traditional major medical plans, a covered person may be responsible for modest copayments in some circumstance. For example, there might be a copayment of $5, $10, or $15 for each visit to a primary care physician.

TABLE 11-2
Selected Benefits Under a PPO

	NETWORK BENEFIT	NONNETWORK BENEFIT
Deductible	None	$250 per person per year. Family deductible equals 2 times the individual deductible. The deductible does not apply to emergency care, pediatric immunizations, routine gynecological examinations, Pap smears, and routine mammograms.
Coinsurance	100% for most services	80% for most services
Out-of-Pocket Limit	None	$1,000
Lifetime Maximum	Unlimited	$1 million per covered person
Hospital Services	100%	80%
Emergency Room	100% with $25 copayment	100% with $25 copayment
Surgical Services	100%	80%
Outpatient Diagnostic Services	100%	80%
Cardiac Rehabilitation Therapy (limit 18 sessions per benefit period)	100% with $15 copayment per session	80%
Psychiatric Services		
Inpatient	100% for 30 days per benefit period	80% for 20 days per benefit period
Outpatient	100% for 9 visits with $10 copayment; $20 copayment for visits 10–30; no coverage for more than 30 visits	50% for up to 20 visits per benefit period
Outpatient Diabetic Education	100%	80%
Primary Care Service	100% with $10 copayment per visit	80%
Prescription Drugs	100% with $10 copayment for generic drugs and $15 for nongeneric drugs	50%

In evaluating PPOs, it is important to determine the basis the PPO uses to apply the coinsurance percentage. For example, assume a plan uses 80 percent coinsurance for nonnetwork charges and that a charge of $100 is incurred for a medical procedure from a nonnetwork provider. Most PPOs first determine whether this charge is usual, customary, and reasonable. If it is, the plan pays $80. If the plan determines that the usual, customary, and reasonable charge is $90, it will be 80 percent of that amount, or $72. However, some plans apply the coinsurance percentage to what is often referred to as *allowable charges*. In most cases, this is the amount that is paid to network providers for the same procedure. In some cases, network discounts are quite large and, for example, the allowable charge in this example might be only $60. For a nonnetwork charge, the plan pays 80 percent of this amount, or $48. Thus the insured has an out-of-pocket expense of $52. Needless to say, few employees and their families are going to seek nonnetwork care under this type of plan. For this reason, plans that pay nonnetwork charges on this basis are sometimes referred to as *phantom PPOs*.

Maximum Benefits

While there are variations, most PPOs have a lifetime maximum of $1 million for nonnetwork benefits. The lifetime maximum for network benefits is seldom less that $2 million and may even be unlimited.

Precertification Rules

PPOs often have precertification requirements for many types of hospitalizations, outpatient procedures, and medical supplies. For network benefits, the person responsible for obtaining the needed certification is the network provider, and the covered person is not penalized if the network provider fails to obtain the proper precertification. (This becomes an issue between the PPO and the provider.) However, this responsibility shifts to the employee or family member for nonnetwork services. If precertification is not obtained when required, there usually is a reduction in benefits. For example, what was once 80 percent coinsurance might shrink to 60 percent.

Additional Network Benefits

For the most part, PPOs pay benefits for the same medical procedures, whether they are performed by a network or a nonnetwork provider. However, a few procedures may be covered only if they are received from network providers. For example, routine physical exams may be covered only in the network. In addition, there might be coverage for more outpatient psychiatric visits if a network provider is used.

Claims

No claim forms are required for network services. The covered person merely pays any required copayment, and the provider of medical services does the paperwork needed to receive the additional amounts payable by the plan. Just as in traditional major medical plans, it is the ultimate responsibility of the covered person to file the claims forms necessary to receive benefits for non-network care. Of course, the provider may do much of the paperwork and accept an assignment of benefits.

Regulation

PPOs have been subject to much less stringent regulation than HMOs with respect to their managed care activities. In fact, until recently, they were largely unregulated. As a result, the NAIC passed the Preferred Provider Arrangements Model Act, which has now been adopted by more than half the states. The act is relatively brief and establishes only a minimal regulatory framework. The act requires that PPOs incorporate cost-containment mechanisms, such as utilization review, to determine whether a service is medically necessary. Covered persons must be given reasonable access to medical services. The act also allows PPOs to provide incentives for persons to use the preferred-provider network and to place limitations on the number and types of providers with whom they contract.

It should be noted that most PPO contracts also meet the definition of insurance and are subject to the same regulation by state insurance departments as traditional insurance contracts with respect to contract provisions and benefit mandates.

POINT-OF-SERVICE PLANS

A newer and fast-growing type of managed care arrangement is the POS plan. A *POS plan* is a hybrid arrangement that combines aspects of a traditional HMO and a PPO. With a POS plan, participants in the plan elect, at the time medical treatment is needed, whether to receive treatment within the plan's tightly managed network, usually an HMO, or outside the network. Expenses received outside the network are reimbursed in the same manner as described earlier for nonnetwork services under PPO plans.

There are two basic types of POS plans: the open-ended HMO and the gatekeeper PPO. An *open-ended HMO* is by far the most common form and is the HMO industry's response to the demand for more consumer flexibility in the choice of providers, even though it increases costs somewhat. It essentially consists of traditional HMO coverage with an endorsement for nonnetwork coverage. It can take the basic form of any of the HMOs previously described. However, at any time a subscriber can elect to go outside the HMO network of medical care providers.

It can be argued that any PPO is actually a POS plan. However, the normal usage of the term *POS* implies a higher degree of managed care than is found in most PPOs. A *gatekeeper PPO* requires that the PPO participant elect a primary care physician in the manner of an HMO participant. This physician acts as a gatekeeper to control utilization and refer members to specialists within the PPO network. However, any time that care is needed a covered person can elect to go outside the network. This type of PPO has generally been formed by a traditional PPO or insurance company that does not own an HMO.

Under some POS plans, a covered person can go outside the plan's network without informing the plan of this fact. In other POS plans, the person must notify the gatekeeper that such treatment will be sought. Even though the gatekeeper has no power to prevent the nonnetwork treatment, the gatekeeper may be able to convince the person that proper treatment is available within the network. Furthermore, the gatekeeper can better manage future medical care by being aware of all medical treatment that a person is receiving.

MULTIPLE-OPTION PLANS

Until recently, an employer who wanted to make an HMO or POS option available to employees had to enter into a separate contractual arrangement with an HMO. Unless a PPO was sponsored by the insurance company or Blue Cross–Blue Shield plan of an employer, a similar contractual arrangement was also required. Several insurance companies and Blue Cross–Blue Shield plans are now providing all these options under a single medical expense contract. For example, one insurer markets a so-called quadruple-option plan that gives employees the choice of a traditional major medical contract, a PPO, an HMO, or a POS plan. In most cases, the HMOs and PPOs used in such arrangements have been formed or purchased by the insurance company or Blue Cross–Blue Shield plan, but occasionally a contractual relationship has been established with an existing HMO or PPO. HMOs, in addition to offering POS options, also frequently offer PPO products to employers as part of a multiple-option plan.

These plans offer certain advantages to the employer. First, administration is easier because all elements of the plan are purchased from a single provider. Second, costs may be lower because the entire plan, including the HMO, may be subject to experience rating. Because federally qualified HMOs cannot fully use experience rating (particularly on a retrospective basis), only nonfederally qualified HMOs are often used in multiple-option plans.

COMPARISON OF TYPICAL MEDICAL EXPENSE PLANS

The various types of medical expense plans and how they differ have been discussed throughout the last two chapters. While variations within each type of plan exist, some generalizations can be made. These are summarized in Table 11-3. The degree of managed care increases as one moves from left to

TABLE 11-3
Comparison of Health Insurance Plans

	TRADITIONAL MAJOR MEDICAL CONTRACTS	PPOS	POS PLANS	HMOS
Provider Choice	Unlimited	Unlimited in network, but benefits are greater if network provider is used	Unlimited in network, but benefits are greater if network provider is used	Network of providers must be used; care from nonnetwork providers covered only in emergencies
Use of Gatekeeper	None	None	Used for care of network specialists	Used for access to specialists
Out-of-Pocket Costs	Deductibles and percentage participation	Deductibles and percentage participation, but lower if network providers used; may have small co-payment for network services	Small copayments for network services; deductibles and percentage participation for nonnetwork services	Small copayments for some services
Utilization Review	Traditionally little, but a few techniques are likely to be used now	More than traditional plans, but less than HMOs; network provider may be subject to some controls	Like HMOs for network services; like PPOs for nonnetwork services	Highest degree of review, including financial incentives and disincentives for providers
Preventive Care	Little covered other than that required by law	Usually, more coverage than traditional major medical plan but less than HMOs and POS plans	Covered	Covered
Responsibility for Claims Filings	Covered person	Plan provider for network services; the covered person for nonnetwork services	Plan provider for network services; the covered person for nonnetwork services	Plan providers

right in the table. However, the cost of the plans, on the average, decreases as the degree of managed care increases. In addition, a higher degree of managed care is generally associated with lower annual premium increases by a plan.

BENEFIT CARVE-OUTS

The use of benefit carve-outs by medical expense plans has grown in popularity in recent years, often as a method of cost containment through the use of managed care techniques. In addition, many medical expense plans have come to realize that they cannot always provide as high a quality of care as a well-managed specialty provider. Carve-outs for prescription drugs, vision care, dental care, and behavioral health have been common for a number of years. Increasingly, carve-outs are being used to better manage a wide variety of medical conditions such as pregnancy, asthma, and diabetes. The final section of this chapter is devoted to a discussion of the nature of such carve-outs, the reasons for their use, possible concerns and a few of the more common types of carve-out arrangements.

Nature

A benefit carve-out can best be defined as coverage under a medical expense plan for a health care service that has been singled out for individual management by a party other than the employer or the employer's primary health plan provider. Some types of carve-outs predate managed care as it is now known. For example, many employees have long been covered under separate prescription drug plans. However, the early emphasis under these plans was on discounts with preferred providers of prescription drugs. Today, prescription drug plans and other types of carve-outs use a wider variety of managed care techniques.

An employer can purchase a medical expense plan to provide benefits to its employees for most types of medical care and then enter into a separate contract with another provider for the carved-out benefit. However, in most cases, it is the insurance company, Blue Cross–Blues Shield plan, HMO, or PPO that enters into the carve-out arrangement with a "subcontractor" that manages the benefits. From the standpoint of employers and employees, the benefit is part of the provider's plan.

It should be pointed out that the vendors who provide carve-outs often act as managed care plans for a single medical expense benefit and take on the characteristics of HMOs or PPOs. They also have learned over time that their type of specialty care should sometimes be accompanied by a unique benefit structure. This is one reason why mental health and prescription drug benefits are often subject to different deductibles, copayments, or benefit limitation than those used for most types of medical expenses.

Reasons for Use

There are several reasons for using benefit carve-outs. These include the following:

- The carve-out can save money. A good carve-out vendor should be able to provide products and services in a cost-effective manner and pass along savings from these efficiencies.
- The carve-out may result in a shifting of financial risk and a better ability to budget. It is often difficult for a benefit plan to control costs. One way of doing this is to select a carve-out vendor that is paid on a capitated basis. This shifts much of the financial risk of higher-than-average claims to the carve-out vendor.
- The carve-out vendor may be better able to build a network of specialists. For some diseases or medical conditions, even very large HMOs or PPOs have too few claims to justify establishing their own in-plan network. The carve-out vendor may also be able to provide better outcomes data because of its size and expertise.
- The carve-out vendor may increase employer and employee satisfaction by lowering plan costs, providing high-quality care through the use of well-regarded specialists, and providing easier access to medical products and services.

Possible Concerns

A carve-out arrangement must be entered into with care. Today, there are many vendors that claim they can properly perform the required tasks, but benefit plans sometimes find themselves less than satisfied. Therefore, a proper evaluation of potential vendors is of utmost importance. Some of the questions that need to be answered include the following:

- How does the carve-out vendor credential providers?
- Is the carve-out vendor financially able to deliver what it promises?
- Does the carve-out vendor have the management expertise to deliver what it promises?
- Why is the carve-out vendor in business? Carve-out arrangements are often marketed by providers of medical products and services, and this may result in their having the expertise to run a high-quality operation. On the other hand, it is important to distinguish these arrangements from those whose primary goal is to increase sales of the provider's products and services.
- Will the carve-out vendor keep a patient's primary care physician informed about the patient's treatment? This information is essential if the primary care physician is to properly do his or her job of coordinating patient care.

Types of Carve-Outs

There are numerous types of benefit carve-outs. The following are discussed in this chapter:

- Prescription drugs
- Vision benefits
- Behavioral health
- Disease management
- Maternity management

Prescription Drugs

The cost of prescription drugs is approaching 15 percent of all medical expense claims, and the percentage continues to grow. This increase results from several factors. One is the availability and prescribing of high-priced new pharmaceutical products. Another factor is increased use arising from several sources: the aging population, which uses more prescription drugs, and the shift from inpatient to outpatient treatment, resulting in more intensive pharmaceutical treatments. Finally, new drugs have been found for many previously untreatable conditions. As a result, prescription drug benefits are often carved out in an attempt to control costs.

While separate prescription drug plans have existed for many years, the initial focus was on obtaining lower costs through discounts with participating pharmacies and mail-order suppliers of drugs. However, the situation changed significantly in the early 1980s when pharmacy benefit managers (PBMs) appeared in the marketplace. It is estimated that over 75 percent of prescription drugs are provided through PBMs, and that fewer than 10 large PBMs cover more than 80 percent of the health plan participants who received drugs in this manner. PBMs may be affiliated with pharmaceutical companies or health care providers such as insurance companies. They may also be independently owned.

Pharmacy Benefit Managers. PBMs administer prescription drug plans on behalf of self-funded employers, HMOs, PPOs, insurance companies, Blue Cross–Blue Shield plans, and third-party administrators. The on-line capabilities of PBMs enable them to offer considerable flexibility in designing a prescription drug program for a specific employer or benefit plan provider.

In addition to developing networks for the dispensing of prescription drugs, PBMs typically also do the following:

- Drug utilization review. This practice compares information gathered from a patient's medical and prescription drug records to determine such factors as overutilization, underutilization, drug-to-drug interactions, improper drugs for pregnant patients, early refills, and therapeutic duplication.

- Physician profiling and education. For example, physicians whose prescribing patterns lie outside acceptable variations from established benchmarks can be identified and counseled.
- Pharmacy profiling and education. For example, pharmacies that recommend large amounts of brand-name drugs might be contacted about making more use of generic substitutions.
- Patient profiling and education. For example, patients treated for hypertension can be identified and sent educational materials on their condition. This material focuses on the risks associated with the condition, safety issues associated with drug treatment, and the importance of complying with prescribed drug regimens. Patients who fail to refill needed medication can also be identified and contacted.

PBMs are also increasingly developing disease management programs that focus on diagnostic aids identification, treatment guidelines, education, and outcomes measurement for specific diseases. PBMs may also be involved in the overall case management of a patient.

PBMs have been leaders in the integration of formularies into prescription drug plans. A formulary is a list of preferred medications for a specific medical condition developed by a committee of pharmacists and physicians. This list is provided to physicians with the hopes that it will positively affect their prescribing behavior. A formulary, for example, will let physicians know of approved uses of new drugs on the market, appropriate uses for existing drugs, and appropriate times to use generic and therapeutic substitutions. A therapeutic substitution is a drug with a therapeutic effect similar to that of the prescribed drug. Unlike generic substitution, which can often be made by patients or pharmacists, a physician's permission is needed for a therapeutic substitution.

Many prescription drug plans do not have a price differential for a patient if formulary drugs are not prescribed. However, PBMs will offer plans that either cover formulary drugs only or provide a financial incentive for patients to use them.

Nature of Plans. The typical prescription drug plan covers the cost of drugs (except those dispensed in a hospital or in an extended-care facility) that are required by either state or federal law to be dispensed by prescription. Drugs for which prescriptions are not required by law are usually not covered even if a physician orders them on a prescription form. One frequent exception to this general rule is injectable insulin, which is generally covered despite the fact that in many states it is a nonprescription drug. No coverage is provided for charges to administer drugs or the cost of the therapeutic devices or appliances such as bandages or hypodermic needles. It is also common to exclude benefits for a quantity of drugs in excess of a specified amount. In some plans, this quantity is expressed as the amount normally prescribed by physicians; in other plans, it is expressed as a supply for a certain time period, often 34 days. However, refills are considered new prescriptions.

Contraceptive drugs may be covered or excluded. Some prescription drug plans take a middle approach by covering these drugs only when they are prescribed for treating some medical condition rather than for preventing conception. Drugs for treatment of infertility or sexual dysfunction, such as Viagra, may or may not be covered.

Drug plans are increasingly requiring precertification for the use of certain expensive drugs.

Most prescription drug plans have a copayment that must be paid by a covered person for any prescriptions filled. In most cases, this is a flat amount that usually varies from $5 to $10 per prescription. Some plans have two copayments—one for generic drugs and a higher one for brand-name drugs. It is also becoming increasingly common to see a three-tier structure, such as a $5 copayment for generic drugs, $10 for brand-name formulary drugs, and $15 for brand-name nonformulary drugs. Some plans also provide financial incentives for prescriptions to be filled by mail-order pharmacies or on the Internet. A few plans have quarterly, semiannual, or annual spending caps. For example, benefits might be limited to $500 per person per quarter or $3,000 per year per family.

Two basic methods are used to provide prescription drug coverage: a reimbursement approach and a service approach. Under plans using a *reimbursement approach,* a covered individual personally pays the cost of prescription drugs. The person may be able to use any pharmacy he or she chooses or may be required to use a participating pharmacy. A claim for reimbursement is then filed with the provider of benefits, either by the employee or electronically by the pharmacy. Reimbursement (subject to any copayments) is made to the covered person on the basis of either billed charges or reasonable-and-customary charges.

While coverage for prescription drugs under major medical plans is often on a reimbursement basis, the majority of prescription drug plans use a *service approach.* Under this approach, drugs are provided to covered persons by participating pharmacies upon receipt of prescriptions, proper identification (usually a card issued by the plan), and any required copayments. The pharmacy then bills the provider of coverage (usually electronically) for the remaining cost of any prescription filled. This provider may be a PBM, a Blue Cross–Blue Shield association, an HMO, an insurance company or, a third-party administrator acting on behalf of either an insurance company or an employer with a self-insured plan. Because of the specialization that can be used in handling many small claims and the need to establish a system of participating pharmacies, most insurance companies, except for a few large ones, use PBMs for their prescription drug plans.

Under virtually all service plans, the provider of coverage or the third-party administrator negotiates a contract with participating pharmacies to provide the drugs at a reduced cost, usually equal to the wholesale cost of the drug plus a flat dispensing fee, such as $3 for each prescription. Prescriptions filled at nonparticipating pharmacies are often covered but handled on a reimbursement basis. In addition, reimbursement in these cases is typically less than the cost of the prescription. In some cases, the plan will pay up to the amount that would have been paid to a participating pharmacy. In other cases, benefits may be limited to some percentage (for example, 75 percent) of the cost of a prescription purchased at a nonparticipating pharmacy, minus any copayment.

Vision Benefits

Carve-out vision benefits may be provided by insurance companies, Blue Cross–Blue Shield plans, plans of state optometric associations patterned after Blue Shield, closed-panel HMO-type plans established by local providers of vision services, vision care PPOs, or third-party administrators.

More than half of the persons covered under employer-provided medical expense plans have some type of vision coverage, and the majority of this coverage is provided under some type of carve-out arrangement. Despite concerns with rising benefit costs in recent years, vision care is one type of benefit that employers continue to add. Routine eye exams can result in better overall health care because certain other types of health problems—such as high blood pressure, diabetes, and kidney problems—are first discovered during the course of such exams. Proper vision correction can also result in fewer accidents and greater productivity by minimizing eyestrain and headaches.

Benefits are occasionally provided on a reasonable-and-customary basis or are subject to a flat benefit per year that may be applied to any covered expenses. Normally, however, a benefit schedule will be used that specifies the type and amounts of benefits and the frequency with which they will be provided. Table 11-4 is an example of one such schedule. If the plan is written by a provider of vision services, it is common for a discount, such as 20 percent, to be available for costs incurred with the provider that are not covered by the schedule of benefits. Under some plans, most benefits are provided on a service basis rather than being subject to a maximum benefit. However, these plans usually cover only the cost of basic frames, which the covered persons can upgrade at an additional expense.

Exclusions commonly exist for any extra charge for plastic lenses or the cost of safety lenses or prescription sunglasses. Benefits are generally provided for eye examinations by either an optometrist or an ophthalmologist, and larger benefits are sometimes provided if the latter is used. Vision care plans do not

TABLE 11-4
Vision Benefit Schedule

Type of Benefit	Maximum Amount
Any 12-Month Period	
Eye examination	$ 45
Lenses, pair	
Single vision	45
Bifocal	75
Trifocal	125
Lenticular	200
Contact (when medically necessary)	300
Contact (when not medically necessary)	125
Any 24-Month Period	
Frames	60

pay benefits for eye surgery or treatment of eye diseases because these are covered under the regular coverage of a medical expense plan.

Behavioral Health

The providing of behavioral health benefits has always been an area of difficulty for medical expense plans. There is less uniformity in treatment standards for mental health, alcoholism, and drug addiction than for most other medical conditions. This, and the difficulty of monitoring treatment, has often led to unnecessary, expensive, and dangerous treatment by less-than-scrupulous providers of behavioral health care. Historically, benefit plans addressed these problems by having very limited benefit levels. But even these benefit levels still had a tendency to encourage more expensive inpatient care over outpatient treatment, which in most cases appears to be as clinically effective. In addition, there was little follow-up care after treatment. With rapidly increasing costs for behavioral health, employers and providers of benefit plans are increasingly carving out this benefit by contracting with vendors that use managed care techniques. However, even with the use of carve-outs, benefit plans still continue to limit behavioral health benefits to a level significantly below that for other medical conditions.

Characteristics of a successful behavioral health program, whether it be a carve-out arrangement or not, should include the following:

- The use of case management to design and coordinate treatment plans and to monitor the need for follow-up care.
- A mechanism for referring a patient to the program. In many cases, this is through a gatekeeper who is a primary care physician. However, there is also increasing coordination of behavioral health programs with employee-assistance programs, which are discussed in Chapter 16.
- The development of a provider network that specializes in behavioral health. In addition to physicians, the network will include psychologists and therapists. It will also include alternatives to hospital treatment, such as residential centers, halfway houses, and structured outpatient programs. Benefits may or may not be provided if nonnetwork treatment is sought. If it is covered, there is usually a lower benefit level than for network treatment.
- Patient access to care on a 24-hour basis. Persons who have behavioral health problems often need immediate crisis intervention. Of course, the availability of such care needs to be well communicated to patients.

Disease Management

Traditionally, medical expense plans have focused on the treatment of sickness rather than prevention and education. Even though this philosophy changed with managed care, there has often been less-than-complete attention paid to controlling chronic conditions that can lead to frequent and often expensive medical intervention. The list of chronic conditions is lengthy; a few of the conditions on this list are asthma, diabetes, heart disease, high blood pressure, arthritis, allergies, back pain, and multiple sclerosis. Many chronic conditions are high maintenance, and most are not curable. However, with proper control, hospitalization for the condition and related complications can be reduced. In addition, the patient's longevity and quality of life can be increased. As managed care has evolved, the concept of disease management has taken on increasing importance, sometimes through the use of carve-outs for certain chronic conditions. The two most commonly carved-out chronic conditions are probably diabetes and asthma.

Traditional case management begins with an episode of illness, whereas disease management begins prior to it. Disease management programs attempt to identify persons with chronic conditions as early as possible so that proper treatment can minimize future spells of illness. In this regard, it is important to work with primary care physicians so that they can steer patients toward the disease management program.

Disease management programs have a network of providers who deliver the needed care and prevention. These include physicians as well as nurses who provide patient counseling and education and who may even make home visits. Education about a chronic condition is crucial in that a disease management program is much more effective if a patient understands how to manage his or her lifestyle in light of the condition. It is also important for a disease management program to involve pharmacists, because patients with chronic diseases are often on maintenance drugs, the effectiveness of which can be influenced by prescription drugs that might be prescribed for other illnesses. A disease management program also has procedures for reacting to emergencies and providing ambulatory care following a hospitalization.

Maternity Management

The identification of high-risk pregnancies and proper medical treatment can result in significant cost savings to a benefit plan. For example, the expenses associated with premature birth can amount to several hundred thousand dollars. As a result, many plans have begun to incorporate maternity management, which focuses on low-frequency, high-cost claims, in contrast to many cost-containment efforts. Although there is a cost in providing this coverage, this cost will usually be more than offset if only one large claim is avoided. Some providers of medical expense plans provide maternity management with their own staff, while others carve out the benefit.

A maternity-management provision requires a patient or her primary care physician to notify the maternity management program within some prescribed time period after confirmation of pregnancy. Failure to obtain this precertification may result in a reduction of benefits. A case manager, usually a registered nurse, works closely with the expectant mother and her physician throughout the pregnancy to see that a complete assessment of the mother's health is made so that unfavorable risk factors can be monitored. Individualized maternity education is provided through brochures and telephone contact. This education focuses on such aspects of prenatal care as nutrition, alcohol use, and smoking.

STUDY QUESTIONS

1. How do managed care plans attempt to eliminate the unrestricted use of medical care providers?

2. What are the purposes of accreditation of managed care organization?

3. What types of legislation are states adopting to address consumer and providers concerns about managed care?

4. What characteristics distinguish HMOs from insurance companies?

5. Explain how HMOs may vary with respect to each of the following:
   a. Choice of medical providers
   b. Reimbursement of physicians

6. How does an IPA differ from a closed-panel HMO?

7. a. Why might an HMO seek federal qualification?
   b. What provisions are contained in the Health Maintenance Organization Act of 1973 with respect to
      i. required benefit?
      ii. open enrollment periods?
      iii. the level of employer contributions?

8. Explain how PPOs differ from HMOs.

9. What must a successful PPO do in addition to seeking discounts from preferred providers?

10. Describe the benefit structure of PPOs.

11. To what extent are PPOs and HMOs subject to state regulation?

12. How do POS plans differ from PPOs?

13. What advantages do multiple-option plans have for employers?

14. a. What are the reasons for benefit carve-outs?
    b. What are the concerns about benefit carve-out vendors?

Group Medical Expense Benefits: Plan Provisions and Taxation

■ Identify and explain the five following contract provisions common to the various types of medical expense coverage:
1. Eligibility
2. Coordination of benefits
3. The relationship with Medicare
4. Termination of coverage
5. Claims

■ Explain how the Health Insurance Portability and Accountability Act limits the use of preexisting-conditions provisions and provides for group-to-individual portability of medical expense coverage.

■ Explain the tax implications of group medical expense premiums and benefits for the employer and employees.

T his chapter is devoted primarily to a discussion of many of the major provisions in medical expense plans, whether the plan benefits are self-funded or provided through a traditional insurance contract, HMO, or PPO. While these provisions may stand alone as part of the employer's plan, most of them are incorporated into the contracts of the providers that fund the plan's benefits. To a large extent, these provisions are similar—if not identical—to those discussed in Chapter 6 for group term life insurance. However, certain provisions are either unique to medical expense plans or different from those found in other types of group benefits. These provisions pertain to eligibility, coordination of benefits, the effect of Medicare, termination (including postretirement benefits), and claims. Several of the provisions have changed in recent years as a result of the passage of the Health Insurance Portability and Accountability Act (HIPAA) in 1996.

The last portion of the chapter describes the tax treatment of medical expense benefits. One unusual characteristic of this tax treatment is the difference in the way that insured benefits and self-funded benefits are treated.

ELIGIBILITY

The eligibility requirements for medical expense coverage are essentially the same as those discussed earlier for group term insurance—an employee must usually be in a covered classification, must satisfy any probationary period, and must be a full-time employee. Coverage is rarely made available to part-time employees. In addition, medical expense contracts often contain an actively-at-work provision. This provision may be waived, particularly for larger employers for whom adverse selection tends to be less of a problem than for smaller groups because any adverse selection for a large group is reflected in future premiums through the experience-rating process.

Eligibility requirements may vary somewhat if an employer changes providers for a plan's benefits. Note that the following discussion refers to the employer's plan with benefits paid by the previous provider as the "old plan" and the employer's plan with benefits paid by the new provider as the "new plan." In actuality, the employer still has the same medical expense plan. It has only been modified with the use of a new provider and, possibly, a different level of benefits. This is a material modification to a group health plan, and ERISA requires that participants be notified of this change by a summary of material modification. The ERISA rules are covered in Chapter 5.

Even though it has been adopted by only a few states, most providers follow the procedures established by the National Association of Insurance Commissioners (NAIC) Group Coverage Discontinuance and Replacement Model Regulation for medical expense coverage (and possibly other group coverages). This regulation stipulates that coverage be provided (but possibly limited) under a new plan to anyone who (1) was covered under the old plan at the date it was discontinued and (2) is in an eligible classification of the new plan. Employees actively at work on the date coverage is transferred are automatically covered under the new plan and are exempt from any probationary periods. If the new plan contains a preexisting-conditions provision, benefits applicable to an individual's preexisting conditions are limited to the lesser of (1) the maximum benefits of the new plan (ignoring the preexisting conditions) or (2) the maximum benefits of the old plan.

Employers often negotiate with the provider of benefits to ensure that for employees who are covered under the old plan but who are not actively at work on the date coverage is discontinued (such as an employee disabled by illness or injury or employees suffering temporary interruptions of employment) are included in the new plan. However, their benefits are frequently limited to the old plan's level until they meet the new plan's actively-at-work requirement.

Two final points should be made concerning the transfer of coverage. First, the new plan will not pay benefits for expenses covered by the old plan under an extension-of-benefits provision (discussed later); second, when applying any deductibles or probationary periods under the new plan, credit is often given for the satisfaction (or partial satisfaction) of the same or similar provisions during the last three months of the old plan. For example, assume that coverage is transferred in the middle of a calendar year and the new plan contains the same $200-a-year calendar deductible as the old plan. If an employee has already satisfied the deductible under the old plan, no new deductible is required for the remainder of the calendar year, provided that (1) the expenses used to satisfy the deductible under the old plan satisfy the deductible under the new plan and (2) the expenses were incurred during the last three months of the old plan. If only $140 of the $200 was incurred during those last three months, an additional $60 deductible is required under the new plan for the remainder of the calendar year.

Dependent Eligibility

Typically, the same medical expense benefits that are provided for an eligible employee are also available for that employee's dependents. Conversely, however, dependent coverage is rarely available unless the employee also has coverage. As long as any necessary payroll deductions have been authorized, dependent coverage is typically effective on the same date as the employee's coverage. If coverage under a contributory plan is not elected within 31 days after dependents are eligible, future coverage is available only during an open enrollment period or when satisfactory evidence of insurability is provided. However, if an employee was previously without dependents (and therefore had no dependent coverage), any newly acquired dependents (by birth, marriage, or adoption) are eligible for coverage as of the date they gain dependent status.

The term *dependents* most commonly refers to an employee's spouse who is not legally separated from the employee and any unmarried dependent children (including stepchildren and adopted children) under the age of 19. However, coverage is usually provided for children to age 23 if they are full-time students. In addition, coverage may also continue (and is required to be continued in some states) for children who are incapable of earning their own living because of a physical or mental infirmity. Such children are considered dependents as long as this condition exists, but periodic proof of the condition may be required. If an employee has dependent coverage, all newly acquired dependents (by birth, marriage, or adoption) are automatically covered.

Some persons that meet the definition of a dependent may be ineligible for coverage because they are in the armed forces or they are eligible for coverage under the same plan as the employees themselves. This latter restriction, however, may not apply to a spouse unless the spouse is actually covered under the plan. Some plans also exclude coverage for any dependents residing outside the United States or Canada.

Medical expense plans may contain a "nonconfinement" provision for dependents, which is similar to the actively-at-work provision for employees. Under this provision, a dependent is not covered if he or she is confined for medical care or treatment in a hospital or at home at the time of eligibility. Coverage, however, becomes effective when the dependent is released from such confinement. Until the passage of HIPAA, a nonconfinement provision was commonly found in medical expense plans. However, many legal and benefit experts feel that such a provision violates HIPAA, because it involves the use of health status as a basis for eligibility. In addition, some states do not allow the provision in insured contracts. As a result, many providers no longer include a nonconfinement provision, and an employee's dependents are eligible for coverage at the same time the employee is eligible.

When coverage is transferred, dependents are treated the same as employees, except that any actively-at-work provision may be replaced by a nonconfinement provision.

Federal Rules for Children's Coverage

Until the passage of the Omnibus Budget Reconciliation Act of 1993 (OBRA '93), provisions regarding eligibility were determined by the employer, provider underwriting practices, and/or any applicable state laws. OBRA '93 brought the federal government into the picture with a series of rules designed to better guarantee that benefits are available to children. Some of these rules pertain to eligibility.

Coverage for Adopted Children

One rule is in the form of an amendment to ERISA. If a work-related group medical expense plan provides coverage for dependent children of participants or beneficiaries, it must provide benefits for adopted children or children placed for adoption under the same terms and conditions that apply to natural children. For purposes of this change, a *child* is defined as a person under the age of 18 at the time of adoption or placement for adoption. Placement for adoption occurs at the time in the adoption process when the plan participant or beneficiary assumes and retains the legal duty for the total or partial support of a child to be adopted.

In addition to providing coverage, a plan cannot restrict benefits because of a preexisting condition at the time coverage is effective as long as the adoption or placement for adoption occurs while the parent is eligible for plan participation.

Medical Child Support Orders

Two other rules have as their goal the shifting of Medicaid cost from the government to the private sector by requiring employer-provided benefit plans to pick up more of the cost of providing medical expense benefits to the children of divorced and separated parents. The first of these rules amended ERISA by requiring employer-sponsored medical expense plans to recognize qualified medical child support orders by providing benefits for a participant's children in accordance with the requirements of such an order.

The act defines a *medical child support order* as a court judgment, decree, or order that (1) provides for child support with respect to the child of a group plan participant or provides benefit coverage to such a child, is ordered under state domestic relations law, and relates to benefits under the plan or (2) enforces a state medical support law enacted under the new Medicaid rules discussed below. The support order then becomes *qualified* if two additional requirements are met. First, the order must create or recognize the right of the child to receive benefits to which the plan participant or other beneficiary is entitled under a group plan. Second, the order must include such information as the name and last known mailing address of the plan participant and the child, a reasonable description of the coverage to be provided the period for which coverage must be provided and each plan to which the order applies. However, a qualified order cannot require a plan to offer any benefit that is not already available under the plan unless the benefits are necessary to meet the requirements of a state medical child support law established under the Social Security Act.

When a plan administrator receives a medical child support order, the administrator must promptly notify the participant and each child named under the order and inform them of the plan's procedure for determining if the order is a qualified medical child support order. Under the act, all group plans must establish reasonable written procedures for determining whether these orders are qualified.

Changes in Medicaid Rules

Under the final rule that is discussed, states were encouraged (under threat of losing some Medicaid reimbursement) to adopt a series of laws relating to medical child support. One of these laws prohibits plan administrators from denying enrollment of a child under a parent's insurance plan on the grounds that (1) the child was born out of wedlock, (2) the child is not claimed as a dependent on the parent's federal income tax return, or (3) the child does not reside with the parent or in the insurer's service area. In addition, a second law provides that if a court orders a parent to provide medical support, the parent's plan must enroll the child without regard to any enrollment restrictions. If the parent fails to enroll the child, enrollment can be made by the child's other parent or by the state Medicaid agency. The employer is required to withhold from the parent's compensation any payments that the parent must make toward the cost of coverage.

Portability

Some of the most significant parts of HIPAA are the provisions dealing with "portability" of medical expense coverage. These provisions are not for the purpose of allowing an employee to take specific insurance from one job to another. Rather, they put limitations on preexisting-conditions exclusions and allow an employee to use evidence of prior insurance coverage to reduce or eliminate the length of any preexisting-conditions exclusion when the employee moves to another medical expense plan. These provisions should minimize job lock for employees by eliminating the fear that medical expense coverage will be lost if an employee changes jobs.

The portability provisions apply to almost all group health insurance plans (either insured or self-funded) as long as they have at least two active participants on the first day of the plan year. Note that the same definition of *group health plan* mentioned in the initial discussion of HIPAA in Chapter 9 applies to the portability provisions.

Limitations on Preexisting Conditions

Restrictions for preexisting conditions are limited to a maximum of 12 months (18 months for late enrollees). In addition, the period for preexisting conditions must be reduced for prior creditable coverage as defined below. It should be noted that there is nothing in the act that prohibits an employer from imposing a probationary period before a new employee is eligible to enroll in a medical expense plan. (Note: HIPAA refers to the probationary period as a *waiting period*. However, the term *probationary* is consistent with the terminology used in this book and is therefore used in this discussion.) However, any probationary period must be applied uniformly without regard to the health status of potential plan participants or beneficiaries. In addition, the probationary period must run concurrently with any preexisting-conditions period. For example, an employee might be subject to a preexisting-conditions period of seven months because of prior coverage. If the employer's plan had a three-month probationary period for enrollment, the length of the preexisting-conditions period after enrollment could be only four months. An HMO is also permitted to have an affiliation period of up to two months (three months for late enrollees) if the HMO does not impose a preexisting-conditions provision and if the affiliation period is applied without regard to health status-related factors.

Under the act, a *preexisting condition* is defined as a mental or physical condition for which medical advice, diagnosis, care, or treatment was recommended or received within the six-month period ending on the enrollment date. No preexisting-conditions exclusions can apply to pregnancy or to newborn children or, if under age 18, to newly adopted children or children newly placed for adoption, as long as they become covered for creditable coverage within 30 days of birth, adoption, or placement. In addition, the use of genetic information as a preexisting condition is prohibited unless there is a diagnosis of a preexisting medical condition related to the information.

The 12-month limitation for preexisting conditions applies if an employee enrolls when he or she is initially eligible for coverage. It also applies in the case of special enrollment periods (discussed in Chapter 9) that are required by the act for employees and dependents who lose other coverage and for new dependents. Anyone who does not enroll in an employer's plan during the first period he or she is eligible or during a special enrollment period is a late enrollee and can be subject to a preexisting-conditions period of 18 months.

Creditable Coverage

The act defines *creditable coverage* as coverage under an individual policy, an employer-provided group plan (either insured or self-funded), an HMO, Medicare, Medicaid, or various public plans, regardless of whether the coverage is provided to a person as an individual, an employee, or a dependent. However, coverage is not creditable if there has been a break in coverage of 63 days or more.

In determining the length of a person's preexisting-conditions period, the period of prior creditable coverage must be subtracted. Assume, for example, that an employer's plan has a preexisting-conditions period of 12 months. If a new employee has 12 months or more of creditable coverage, the preexisting-conditions period is satisfied. If the period of creditable coverage is only seven months, then the preexisting-conditions period runs five more months. Note, however, that if the employee has been without coverage for at least 63 days between jobs, the full preexisting-conditions period applies.

Employers have two ways in which they can apply creditable coverage: on a blanket basis to all categories of medical expense coverage or on a benefit-specific basis. For example, if an employee had prior coverage that excluded prescription drugs, this particular coverage could be subject to the full preexisting-conditions period, while the period for other benefits would be reduced because creditable coverage had applied to them. For administrative ease, an employer usually picks the first method.

The act requires that an employer automatically give persons losing group coverage a certificate that specifies the period of creditable coverage under the plan they are leaving, including any period of coverage under the Consolidated Omnibus Budget Reconciliation Act of 1985 (COBRA). In addition, the employer must provide the certificate to anyone who requests it within 24 months after coverage ceases. If an individual is eligible for COBRA coverage, the certificate must be provided no later than the time when a COBRA election notice must be provided. In other cases, the employer must provide the certificate within a "reasonable" time. This certificate of creditable coverage must include the following information:

- The date the certificate was issued
- The name of the health plan that provided the coverage
- The name and identification number of individual(s) whose coverage has ceased
- The name, address, and telephone number of the administrator responsible for the certificate
- A statement that the individual(s) had at least 18 months of creditable coverage or the date any probationary period began and the date coverage began
- The date coverage ended

One certificate may include coverage for the employee and all dependents, or the employer may issue separate certificates for each person.

Sample certificates of creditable coverage are readily available, including blank ones that can be downloaded from the Internet. This has led to a high incidence of fraudulent certificates. As a result, many plans contact the prior employer to verify the accuracy of any certificates they are given.

State Options

The act's provisions on portability generally override state laws. However, state laws that provide greater portability are not overridden. For example, a look-back period of less than six months might be required, or the maximum preexisting-conditions period could be less than 12 months.

Benefits for Domestic Partners

In the mid-1980s, the plans of a few employers began to define the term *dependent* broadly enough to include unmarried domestic partners. For example, one plan covers unmarried couples as long as they live together, show financial interdependence and joint responsibility for each other's common welfare, and consider themselves life partners. This type of requirement is fairly typical, as is the additional requirement that the employee's relationship must have lasted some specified minimum period of time, such as 6 or 12 months. The employee must usually give the employer an affidavit that these requirements have been satisfied.

By the late-1990s, an estimated 10 percent of employers provided medical expense benefits to domestic partners. (A smaller percentage of employers offer other types of group benefits.) Most plans provide benefits to domestic partners engaged in either heterosexual or homosexual relationships. Some plans provide benefits only to persons of the opposite sex of the employee, and a small number of plans limit benefits only to persons of the same sex. The rationale for the latter is that persons of opposite sexes can obtain benefits by marrying, whereas this option is not available to persons of the same sex.

The number of employees obtaining coverage for domestic partners has been relatively small, with many employers experiencing enrollment of less than 1 percent when only partners of the same sex are covered. Some employers have experienced enrollment of up to 4 percent if partners of either sex are covered. (Enrollments of partners of the opposite sex are more than double the enrollments of partners of the same sex.) This low enrollment is due primarily to two factors. First, the domestic partner is probably also working and has medical expense coverage from his or her employer. Second, some employees are unwilling to make their living arrangement or sexual preference known in the workplace.

Despite predictions that domestic partners would have adverse claims experience (primarily due to AIDS), the claims experience has been good. This is probably due in part to the fact that domestic partners, on the average, tend to be younger and therefore probably healthier than employees in general. Also, same-sex partners have few maternity claims. Most, if not all, insurers that levied surcharges on premiums for domestic partners when the coverage was new have now dropped the surcharges.

COORDINATION OF BENEFITS

In recent years, the percentage of individuals having duplicate group medical expense coverage has increased substantially and is estimated to be about 10 percent. Probably the most common situation is the one in which a husband and wife both work and have coverage under their respective employers' noncontributory plans. If the employer of either spouse also provides dependent coverage on a noncontributory basis, the other spouse (and other dependents if both employers provide such coverage) is covered under both plans. If dependent coverage is contributory, it is necessary for a couple with children to elect such coverage under one of their plans. However, because a spouse is considered a dependent, he or she also has duplicate coverage when the election is made. Note that this duplicate coverage can be avoided if dependent coverage can be elected for children only. This option exists under many but not all plans. Duplicate coverage may also arise under the following circumstances:

- An employee has two jobs.
- Children are covered under both a parent's and a stepparent's plans.
- An employee elects coverage under a contributory plan, even though he or she is covered as a dependent under another plan. This could result from ignorance or from an attempt to collect double the amount if a claim should occur. In many cases, this coverage is elected because it is broader, even though it still results in an element of duplicate coverage.

Duplicate coverage can also occur if an individual has coverage under a group plan that is not provided by an employer. A common example involves children whose parents have purchased accident coverage for them through their schools.

In the absence of any provisions to the contrary, group medical expense plans are obligated to provide benefits in cases of duplicate coverage as if no other coverage exists. However, to prevent individuals from receiving benefits that exceed their actual expenses, group medical expense plans contain a *coordination-of-benefits (COB) provision,* under which priorities are established for the payment of benefits by each plan covering an individual.

Most states do not require medical expense products of insurance companies, the Blues, HMOs, or PPOs to have a COB provision. If one is used, however, it must comply with the appropriate state rules. Most COB provisions are based on the Group Coordination of Benefits Model Regulation promulgated by the NAIC. This regulation, which applies to traditional insurance products and other products subject to insurance regulation, is periodically revised, and all or portions of one of the versions have now been adopted by almost all states. As with all NAIC model legislation and regulations, some states have adopted the COB provisions with variations. Most states also have adopted a virtually identical COB provision for use by HMOs.

Although some flexibility is allowed, virtually all COB provisions apply when other coverage exists through the group insurance plans or other group benefit arrangements (such as the Blues, HMOs, or self-funded plans) of another employer. They may also apply to no-fault automobile insurance benefits and to student coverage that is either sponsored or provided by educational institutions. However, these provisions virtually never apply (and cannot in most states) to any other coverages provided under contracts purchased on an individual basis outside the employment relationship.

Determination of Primary Coverage

The usual COB provision stipulates that any other plan without the COB provision is primary and that any plan with it is secondary. If more than one plan has a COB provision, the following priorities are established:

- Coverage as an employee is usually primary to coverage as a dependent. The exception to this rule occurs if a retired person is covered (1) by Medicare, (2) under a retiree plan of a former employer, and (3) as a dependent of a spouse who is an active employee. In this case, coverage as a dependent is primary, Medicare is secondary, and the retiree plan pays last.
- Coverage as an active employee (or as that person's dependent) is primary to coverage as a retired or laid-off employee (or as that person's dependent). This rule is ignored unless both plans contain the rule.
- Coverage as an active employee (or that person's dependent) is primary to a plan that provides COBRA continuation benefits. This rule is also ignored unless both plans contain the rule.
- If the specific rules of a court decree state that one parent must assume responsibility for his or her child's health care expenses and the plan of that parent has actual knowledge of the terms of the court decree, then that plan is primary.
- If the parents of dependent children are married or are not separated (regardless of whether they have ever been married) or if a court awards joint custody without specifying that one parent has the responsibility to provide health care coverage, the plan of the parent whose birthday falls earlier in the calendar year is primary and the plan of the parent with the later birthday is secondary.
- If the parents of dependent children are not married, are separated (regardless of whether they have ever been married), or are divorced and if there is no court decree allocating responsibility for the child's health care expenses, the following priorities apply:
  - The plan of the parent with custody is primary.
  - The plan of the stepparent who is the spouse of the parent with custody is secondary.
  - The plan of the parent without custody is tertiary.
  - The plan of the stepparent who is the spouse of the parent without custody pays last.
- If none of the previous rules establishes a priority, the plan covering the person for the longest period of time is primary. If this rule also fails to determine the primary plan, then allowable expenses are shared equally among the plans.

Determination of Benefits Payable: A Simple Example

The actual mechanics of the previously described COB provision are demonstrated in the following example, which assumes that a person has coverage under the plans of two employers:

■ EXAMPLE

Plan A has PPO coverage that pays allowable expenses in full as long as network preferred providers are used. If nonnetwork providers are used, there is (1) a $500 annual deductible, (2) 80 percent coinsurance subject to a $3,000 out-of-pocket limit and (3) a $1 million lifetime maximum.

Plan B has traditional comprehensive major medical expense coverage with (1) a $200 calendar-year deductible, (2) 80 percent coinsurance subject to a $1,000 out-of-pocket limit and (3) a $2 million lifetime maximum.

Assume also that this person incurs the following expenses for a surgical procedure:

Semiprivate room for 5 days at $800 per day	$4,000
Other hospital charges	3,500
Surgeon's fees	3,000
Total expenses	$10,500

Assume that (1) neither plan contains a COB provision, (2) plan A is primary, and (3) network providers were used. In this case, plan A would pay the full $10,500, and plan B would pay $9,300 after deductions for the $200 deductible and the $1,000 out-of-pocket limit that applies to the coinsurance provision. Consequently, the insured would collect a total of $19,800, or $9,300 in excess of his or actual expenses.

If the example is changed so that plan B is primary and nonnetwork providers are used for plan A, plan B will still pay $9,300. However, plan A only will pay $8,000, which is 80 percent of the expenses above the nonnetwork deductible. In this case, the insured would collect $17,300, still significantly more than his or her actual expenses.

Before the COB provision is used, it must first be determined whether the provision applies to a given claim. It applies only if the sum of the benefits under the plans involved (assuming there is no provision) exceeds an individual's allowable expenses. *Allowable expenses* are defined as any necessary, reasonable, and customary items of expense, all or a portion of which are covered under at least one of the plans that provides benefits to the person for whom the claim is made. However, under a primary plan, the amount of any benefit reductions resulting from a covered person's failure to comply with the plan's provisions (such as second opinions or precertification) is not considered an allowable expense. In addition, the difference between the cost of a private hospital room and the cost of a semiprivate hospital room is not considered an allowable expense unless the patient's stay in a private room is medically necessary. When the allowable expenses are determined, any deductibles, percentage participation from coinsurance, and plan maximum are ignored.

In the previous example, the entire $10,500 is considered allowable expenses. Because the sum of the benefits otherwise payable under the two plans (either $19,800 or $17,300, depending on which plan is primary) exceeds this amount, the COB provision applies. If the sum of the benefits did not exceed the allowable expenses, the COB provision would not apply and each plan would pay its benefits as if it were the only existing plan.

When the COB provision applies, a person receives benefits equal to 100 percent of his or her allowable expenses and no more. The primary plan pays its benefits as if no other coverage exists, and the secondary plan (or plans) pays the remaining benefits. If plan A in this example is primary, it will pay $10,500, and plan B will pay nothing because 100 percent of the insured expenses have been paid. If plan B is primary, it will pay $9,300 and plan A will pay the remaining $2,200 of the insured's expenses.

Determination of Benefits: Some Complexities

In actual practice, the determination of benefits payable may be much more complex than the previous simple example. While many of these complexities are beyond the scope of this book, a few issues are addressed. These include the following:

- Determination of benefits payable by each plan
- Benefit banks
- Coordination of benefits with self-funded plans

Before proceeding farther, however, one important point needs to be made: Coordination of benefits is between two (or more) specific plans, each of which has its own rules. While generalizations can be made, the ultimate benefits paid depend on the specific rules of each plan.

Determination of Benefits Payable by Each Plan

The earlier example lumped expenses together into three broad categories and assumed that they were fully covered by each plan, except for any deductibles and percentage participation by the insured. An actual benefit calculation looks at every charge billed by the hospital and surgeon and determines to what extent that charge is covered. It is possible that some charges will not be paid in full because they exceed reasonable and customary charges or because of exclusions. In addition, some managed care plans limit benefits for nonnetwork services to what is paid to network providers. It is common for this to be significantly below billed charges.

Benefit Banks

Some medical expense plans have *benefit banks* (also called *benefit reserves*) in which COB savings from being a secondary payer accumulate for future claims when the plan is also the secondary payer. Assume, for example, that a plan is secondary and pays $1,000 of a claim for which the plan would have paid $15,000 if it had been primary. The $14,000 savings is credited to an account for the insured and can be withdrawn for reimbursement of future allowable medical expenses to the extent they that are not 100 percent reimbursed. Assume further that $4,000 of allowable expenses result from a future claim, and for some reason the primary and secondary payers pay only a total of $3,500. This $500 shortfall will be withdrawn from the $14,000 balance in the benefit bank so that the insured has a 100 percent reimbursement. Balances in the benefit bank usually revert to zero at the end of a specified period, most commonly a calendar year.

Coordination of Benefits with Self-Funded Plans

Self-funded plans are not bound by the state COB rules that apply to insurance contracts and HMO plans, but as a rule they use provisions that are identical or very similar. However, they are free to use any type of COB provision.

Some self-funded plans use a provision so that their payment as a secondary payer is limited to the amount that would reach the limits of their own plan. For example, assume that two self-funded plans would each cover only 80 percent of an insured's medical expenses after a $250 deductible. The secondary payer would pay nothing because the limits of its own plan had already been reached by the primary plan. If the secondary plan had a lower deductible, such as $200, the secondary plan would pay $50. This type of provision, which in effect preserves deductible and coinsurance in the COB process, is not allowed under the NAIC model regulation previously discussed.

A few self-funded plans coordinate benefits with plans under which an individual is eligible for coverage, even if the individual is not covered under that plan. For example, the self-funded plan might provide coverage for an employee's dependents. If a dependent spouse works outside the home and is eligible for his or her own employer-provided coverage, the self-funded plan would pay on a secondary basis, whether or not the spouse signed up for his or her employer's plan.

Finally, self-funded plans have been designed so that they are excess or "always secondary" to any other medical expense plan. The most extreme situation occurs if a person is covered under two self-funded plans, each of which takes an always-secondary approach. Each plan pays as if it were secondary. In the earlier example where the insured has $10,500 of covered expenses, this means that plan A pays $2,200 and plan B pays nothing. This total of $2,200 is less than either plan would pay if it were primary. This issue has been the subject of several court cases, and some (but not all) courts have stated that the always-secondary position cannot prevail. While these courts have ordered an equitable payment of benefits to the covered person, that person has been forced to take the matter to court.

A similar situation exists if a person is covered under a self-funded plan that is always secondary (but would be primary if the state's rules applied) and an insured plan that is legitimately secondary because of the state's COB rules. However, the results are usually somewhat different. In most states, the insured plan must pay the covered person two amounts—the first, what the insured plan is obligated to pay as the secondary plan, and the second, the difference between what the self-funded plan pays on a secondary basis and what it would have paid if it had settled the claim as the primary payer of benefits. This second amount is considered an advance to the covered person, and the insured plan receives a right of subrogation. In other words, the insured plan has the right to take legal action to recover the amount of the advance from the self-funded plan. If the amount is recovered, the advance is, in effect, repaid. If there is no recovery, the covered person has no obligation to repay the insured plan.

RELATIONSHIP WITH MEDICARE

Because most employees and their dependents are eligible for Medicare on reaching age 65 (and possibly under other circumstances), a provision that eliminates any possible duplication of coverage is necessary. The simplest solution is to exclude any person eligible for Medicare from eligibility under the group contract. However, in most cases this approach conflicts with the Age Discrimination in Employment Act, which prohibits discrimination in welfare benefit plans for active employees.

Medicare Secondary Rules

As mentioned in Chapter 9, Medicare is often the secondary payer to employer-provided medical expense coverage. Employers with 20 or more employees must make coverage available under their medical expense plans to active employees aged 65 or older and to active employees' spouses who are eligible for Medicare. Unless an employee elects otherwise, the employer's plan is primary and Medicare is secondary. Except in plans that require large employee contributions, it is doubtful that employees will elect Medicare to be primary because employers are prohibited from offering active employees or their spouses a Medicare carve-out, a Medicare supplement, or some other incentive not to enroll in the employer's plan.

Medicare is the secondary payer of benefits in two other situations. The first situation involves persons who are eligible for Medicare benefits to treat end-stage renal disease with dialysis or kidney transplants. Medicare provides these benefits to any insured workers (either active or retired) and to their spouses and dependent children, but the employer's plan is primary during the first 30 months of treatment only; after that time, Medicare is primary and the employer's plan is secondary. It should be noted that the employer's plan could totally exclude dialysis and/or kidney transplants, in which case Medicare would pay. However, the employer is prevented by law from excluding these benefits for the first 30 months if they are covered thereafter. This rule for renal disease applies to medical expense plans of all employers, not just those with 20 or more employees.

Medicare is also the secondary payer of benefits to disabled employees (or the disabled dependents of employees) under age 65 who are eligible for Medicare and who are covered under the medical expense plan of large employers (defined as plans with 100 or more employees). Medicare, however, does not pay anything until a person has been eligible for Social Security disability income benefits for two years. The rule applies only if an employer continues medical expense coverage for disabled persons; there is no requirement for such a continuation.

When an employer's plan is primary, Medicare payments are made for any expenses that are covered by Medicare but not by the employer's plan. For purposes of these payments, Medicare deductibles, copayments, and percentage participation generally do not apply, although Medicare benefits are limited to what would have been paid in the absence of the employer's plan.

Medicare Carve-Outs and Supplements

An employer's plan may cover certain persons aged 65 or older who are not covered by the provisions of the Age Discrimination in Employment Act—specifically, retirees and active employees of firms with fewer than 20 employees. Although there is nothing to prevent an employer from terminating coverage for these persons, many employers provide them with either a Medicare carve-out or Medicare supplement.

With a *Medicare carve-out,* plan benefits are reduced to the extent that benefits are payable under Medicare for the same expenses. (Medicare may also pay for some expenses not covered by the group plan.) For example, if a person who incurs $1,000 of covered expenses is not eligible for Medicare, $720 in benefits is paid under a medical expense plan that has a $100 deductible and an 80 percent coinsurance provision. However, if the same person is eligible for Medicare and if Medicare pays $650 for the same expenses, the employer's plan pays only $70, for a total benefit of $720.

Some medical expense plans use a more liberal carve-out approach and reduce covered expenses (rather than benefits payable) by any amounts received under Medicare. In the previous example, the $650 paid by Medicare would be subtracted from the $1,000 of covered expenses, which would leave $350. After the deductible and coinsurance are applied to this amount, the employer's plan would pay $200, so the covered person would receive a total of $850 in benefits, or $130 more than a person not eligible for Medicare.

As an alternative to using a carve-out approach, some employers use a *Medicare supplement* that provides benefits for certain specific expenses not covered under Medicare. These include (1) the portion of expenses that is not paid by Medicare because of deductibles, coinsurance, or copayments and (2) certain expenses excluded by Medicare, such as prescription drugs. Such a supplement may or may not provide benefits similar to those available under a carve-out plan.

TERMINATION OF COVERAGE

In the absence of any provisions for continuation or conversion, group medical expense coverage of an employee generally ceases on the earliest of the following:

- The date on which employment terminates (In some plans, coverage ceases on the last day of the month in which employment terminates.)
- The date on which the employee ceases to be eligible
- The date on which the master contract terminates
- The date on which the overall maximum benefit of major medical coverage is received
- The end of the last period for which the employee has made any required contribution

Coverage on any dependent usually ceases on the earliest of the following:

- The date on which he or she ceases to meet the definition of dependent
- The date on which the coverage of the employee ceases for any reason except the employee's receipt of the overall maximum benefit
- The date on which the dependent receives the overall maximum benefit of major medical coverage
- The end of the last period for which the employee has made any required contribution for dependent coverage

However, coverage often continues past these dates because of federal legislation or employer practices.

Continuation of Coverage under COBRA

The Consolidated Omnibus Budget Reconciliation Act of 1985, or COBRA, requires that group health plans allow employees and certain beneficiaries to elect to have their current health insurance coverage extended at group rates for up to 36 months following a "qualifying event" that results in the loss of coverage for a "qualified beneficiary." The term *group health plan* as used in the act is broad enough to include medical expense plans, dental plans, vision care plans, and prescription drug plans, regardless of whether benefits are self-insured or provided through other entities, such as insurance companies, HMOs, or PPOs. COBRA applies even if the cost of a plan is paid solely by employees, as long as the plan would not be available at the same cost to an employee if he or she were not employed. There is one exception to this rule: Voluntary benefit plans under which the employer's only involvement is to process payroll deductions are not subject to COBRA.

Church and government plans are exempt from COBRA, but the act applies to all other employers who had the equivalent of 20 or more full-time employees on a typical business day during the preceding calendar year. For example, an employer who had 10 full-time and 16 half-time employees had the equivalent of 18 full-time employees and is not subject to COBRA. Failure to comply with the act results in an excise tax of up to $100 per day for each person denied coverage. The tax can be levied on the employer as well as on the entity (such as an insurer or HMO) that provides or administers the benefits.

Since the passage of COBRA, a *qualified beneficiary* has been defined as any employee, or the spouse or dependent child of the employee, who on the day before a qualifying event was covered under the employee's group health plan. HIPAA expanded the definition to include any child who is born to or placed for adoption with the employee during the period of COBRA coverage. This change gives automatic eligibility for COBRA coverage to the child as well as the right to have his or her own election rights if a second qualifying event occurs.

Under the act, each of the following is a qualifying event if it results in the loss of coverage by a qualified beneficiary or an increase in the amount the qualified beneficiary must pay for the coverage:

- The death of the covered employee
- The termination of the employee for any reason except gross misconduct (This includes quitting, retiring, or being fired for anything other than gross misconduct)
- A reduction of the employee's hours so that the employee or dependent is ineligible for coverage
- The divorce or legal separation of the covered employee and his or her spouse
- For spouses and children, the employee's eligibility for Medicare
- A child's ceasing to be an eligible dependent under the plan

The act specifies that a qualified beneficiary is entitled to elect continued coverage without providing evidence of insurability. The beneficiary must be allowed to continue coverage identical to that available to employees and dependents to whom a qualifying event has not occurred.

Coverage for persons electing continuation can be changed when changes are made to the plan covering active employees and their dependents. The continued coverage must extend from the date of the qualifying event to the earliest of the following:

- 18 months for employees and dependents when the employee's employment has terminated or coverage has been terminated because of a reduction in hours. This period is extended to 29 months for a qualified beneficiary if the Social Security Administration determines that the beneficiary was or became totally disabled at any time during the first 60 days of COBRA coverage.
- 36 months for other qualifying events.
- The date the plan terminates for all employees.
- The date the coverage ceases because of a qualified beneficiary's failure to make a timely payment of premium.
- The date a qualified beneficiary subsequently becomes entitled to Medicare or becomes covered (as either an employee or dependent) under another group health plan, provided the group health plan does not contain an exclusion or limitation with respect to any preexisting condition. If the new plan does not cover a preexisting condition, the COBRA coverage can be continued until the earlier of (1) the remainder of the 18- or 36-month period or (2) the time when the preexisting-conditions provision no longer applies. Note that COBRA coverage is not affected by entitlement to benefits under Medicare or coverage under another group plan if this entitlement or coverage existed at the time of the qualifying event.

If a second qualifying event (such as the death or divorce of a terminated employee) occurs during the period of continued coverage, the maximum period of continuation is 36 months. For example, if an employee terminates employment, the employee and family are eligible for 18 months of COBRA coverage. If the employee dies after 15 months, a second qualifying event has occurred for the employee's spouse and dependent children. The normal period of COBRA continuation resulting from the death of an employee is 36 months. However, because the spouse and children have already had COBRA coverage for 15 months, the second qualifying event extends coverage for an additional 21 months.

At the termination of continued coverage, a qualified beneficiary must be offered the right to convert to an individual insurance policy if a conversion privilege is generally available to employees under the employer's plan.

Notification of the right to continue coverage must be made at two times by a plan's administrator. First, when a plan becomes subject to COBRA or when a person becomes covered under a plan subject to COBRA, notification must be given to an employee as well as to his or her spouse. Second, when a qualifying event occurs, the employer must notify the plan administrator, who then must notify all qualified beneficiaries within 14 days. In general, the employer has 30 days to notify the plan administrator. However, an employer may not know of a qualifying event if it involves divorce, legal separation, or a child's ceasing to be eligible for coverage. In these circumstances, the employee or family member must notify the employer within 60 days of the event, or the right to elect COBRA coverage is lost. The time period for the employer to notify the plan administrator begins when the employer is informed of the qualifying event, as long as this occurs within the 60-day period.

The continuation of coverage is not automatic; it must be elected by a qualified beneficiary. The election period starts on the date of the qualifying event and may end not earlier than 60 days after actual notice of the event to the qualified beneficiary by the plan administrator. Once coverage is elected, the beneficiary has 45 days to pay the premium for the period of coverage prior to the election.

Under COBRA, the cost of the continued coverage may be passed on to the qualified beneficiary, but the cost cannot exceed 102 percent of the cost to the plan for the period of coverage for a similarly situated active employee to whom a qualifying event has not occurred. The extra 2 percent is supposed to cover the employer's extra administrative costs. The one exception to this rule occurs for months 19 through 29 if an employee is disabled, in which case the premium can then be as high as 150 percent. Qualified beneficiaries must have the option of paying the premium in monthly installments. In addition, there must be a grace period of at least 30 days for each installment.

COBRA has resulted in significant extra costs for employers. Surveys indicate that coverage is elected by approximately 20 percent of those persons who are entitled to a COBRA continuation. The length of coverage averages almost one year for persons eligible for an 18-month extension and almost two years for persons eligible for a 36-month extension. While significant variations exist among employers, claim costs of persons with COBRA coverage generally run between 150 percent and 200 percent of claim costs for active employees and dependents. Moreover, administrative costs are estimated to be about $20 per month for each person with COBRA coverage.

Continuation of Coverage in Addition to COBRA

Even before the passage of COBRA, it was becoming increasingly common for employers (particularly large employers) to continue group insurance coverage for certain employees—and sometimes their dependents—beyond the usual termination dates. Obviously, when coverage is continued now, an employer must at least comply with COBRA. However, an employer can be more liberal than COBRA by paying all or a portion of the cost, providing continued coverage for additional categories of persons, or continuing coverage for a longer period of time. Some states have continuation laws for insured medical expense plans that might require coverage to be made available in situations not covered by COBRA. One example is coverage for employees of firms with fewer than 20 employees; another is coverage for periods longer than those required by COBRA.

Retired Employees

Even though not required to do so by the Age Discrimination in Employment Act, many employers continue coverage on retired employees. Although coverage can also be continued for retirees' dependents, it is often limited only to spouses. Retired employees under age 65 usually have the same coverage as the active employees have. However, coverage for employees aged 65 or older (if included under the same plan) may be provided under a Medicare carve-out or a Medicare supplement. The lifetime maximum for persons eligible for Medicare is often much lower (such as $5,000 or $10,000) than for active employees.

The subject of retiree benefits has become a major concern to employers since the Financial Accounting Standards Board (FASB) phased in new rules between 1993 and 1997 for the accounting of postretirement benefits other than pensions. These rules require that employers do the following:

- Recognize the present value of future retiree medical expense benefits on the firm's balance sheet with other liabilities.
- Record the cost for postretirement medical benefits in the period when an employee performs services. This is comparable to the accounting for pension costs.
- Amortize the present value of the future cost of benefits accrued prior to the new rules.

These rules are in contrast to the long-used previous practice of paying retiree medical benefits or premiums out of current revenue and recognizing these costs as expenses when paid. Although the rules are logical from a financial accounting standpoint, the effect on employers has been significant. Employers who have elected to immediately recognize the liability have had to show reduced earnings and net worth. Firms that have elected to amortize the liability (often because immediate recognition would wipe out net worth) will be affected for years to come.

The FASB rules have resulted in two major changes by employers. First, many employers have lowered or eliminated retiree benefits or are considering such a change. However, there are legal uncertainties as to whether benefits that have been promised to retirees can be eliminated or reduced. Many employers also feel that there is a moral obligation to continue these benefits. As a result, most employers are not altering plans for current retirees or active employees who are eligible to retire. Instead, the changes apply to future retirees only. These changes, which seem to be running the gamut, include the following:

- The elimination of benefits for future retirees.
- The shifting of more of the cost burden to future retirees by reducing benefits. Such a reduction may be accomplished by providing lower benefit maximums, covering fewer types of expenses, or increasing copayments.
- Adding or increasing retiree sharing of premium costs after retirement.

- Shifting to a defined-contribution approach to funding retiree benefits. For example, an employer might agree to pay $5 per month toward the cost of coverage after retirement for each year of service by an employee. Thus, an employer would make a monthly contribution of $150 for an employee who retired with 30 years of service, but the employer would make a contribution of only $75 for an employee with 15 years of service. Many plans of this nature have been designed so that the employer's contribution increases with changes in the consumer price index, subject to maximum increases (such as 5 percent per year).
- Encouraging retirees to elect benefits from managed care plans. With this approach, retirees are required to pay a significant portion of the cost if coverage is continued through a traditional indemnity plan.

A second change is that employers have increasingly explored methods to prefund the benefits. However, there are no alternatives for prefunding that are as favorable as the alternatives for funding pension benefits. One alternative is the use of a 501(c)(9) trust (or VEBA). As discussed in Chapter 14, there are limitations on the deductibility of contributions to a 501(c)(9) trust. Furthermore, a 501(c)(9) trust can be used to fund retiree benefits only if it is currently being used to fund benefits for active employees.

Another alternative is to prefund medical benefits within a pension plan. Contributions are tax deductible, and earnings accumulate tax free. The IRS rules for qualified retirement plans permit the payment of benefits for medical expenses from a pension plan if certain requirements are satisfied:

- The medical benefits must be subordinate to the retirement benefits. This rule is met if the cost of the medical benefits provided does not exceed 25 percent of the employer's aggregate contribution to the pension plan. For many employers, this figure is too low to allow the entire future liability to be prefunded.
- A separate account must be established and maintained for the monies allocated to medical benefits. This account can be an aggregate account for nonkey employees, but individual separate accounts must be maintained for key employees, and medical benefits attributable to a key employee (and his or her family members) can be made only from the key employee's account.
- The employer's contributions for medical benefits must be ascertainable and reasonable.

Although the rules for funding retiree medical benefits in a pension plan are restricted and administratively complex, they offer an employer the opportunity to deduct at least a portion of the cost of prefunded benefits.

Surviving Dependents

Coverage can be continued for the survivors of deceased active employees and/or deceased retired employees. However, coverage for the survivors of active employees is not commonly continued beyond the period required by COBRA, and coverage for the survivors of retired employees may be limited to surviving spouses. In both instances, the continued coverage is usually identical to what was provided prior to the employee's death. It is also common for the employer to continue the same premium contribution level.

Laid-off Employees

Medical expense coverage can be continued for laid-off workers, and large employers frequently provide such coverage for a limited period. Few employers provide coverage beyond the period required by COBRA, but some employers continue to make the same premium contribution, at least for a limited period of time.

Disabled Employees

Medical expense coverage can be continued for an employee (and dependents) when he or she has a temporary interruption of employment, including one arising from illness or injury. Many employers also cover employees who have long-term disabilities or who have retired because of a disability. In most cases, this continuation of coverage is contingent on satisfaction of some definition of total (and possibly permanent) disability. When continuing coverage for disabled employees, an employer must determine the extent of employer contributions. For example, the employer may continue the same premium contribution as for active employees, although there is nothing to prevent a different contribution rate—either lower or higher.

Extension of Benefits

When coverage is terminated rather than continued, most medical expense providers extend benefits for any covered employee or dependent who is totally disabled at the time of termination. However, the disability must have resulted from an illness or injury that occurred while the person was covered under the provider's contract. Generally, the same level of benefits is available as before termination. Although some contracts cover only expenses associated with the same cause of disability, other contracts cover any expenses that would have been paid under the terminated coverage, regardless of cause.

As a general rule, the extension of benefits generally ceases after 12 months, or when the individual is no longer totally or continuously disabled, whichever comes first.

Conversion

Except when termination results from the failure to pay any required premiums, medical expense contracts usually contain (and are often required to contain) a conversion provision, whereby most covered persons whose group coverage terminates are allowed to purchase individual medical expense coverage without evidence of insurability and without any limitation of benefits for preexisting conditions. Covered persons commonly have 31 days from the date of termination of the group coverage to exercise this conversion privilege, and coverage is then effective retroactively to the date of termination.

This conversion privilege is typically given to any employee who has been insured under the group contract (or under any group contract it replaced) for at least three months, and it permits the employee to convert his or her own coverage as well as any dependent coverage. In addition, a spouse or child whose dependent coverage ceases for any other reason may also be eligible for conversion (for example, a spouse who divorces or separates, and children who reach age 19).

A person who is eligible for both the conversion privilege and the right to continue the group insurance coverage under COBRA has two choices when eligibility for coverage terminates. He or she can either elect to convert under the provisions of the policy or elect to continue the group coverage. If the latter choice is made, the COBRA rules specify that the person must again be eligible to convert to an individual policy within the usual conversion period (31 days) after the maximum continuation-of-coverage period ceases. Policy provisions may also make the conversion privilege available to persons whose coverage terminates prior to the end of the maximum continuation period.

The provider of the medical expense coverage has the right to refuse the issue of a "conversion" policy to anyone (1) who is covered by Medicare or (2) whose benefits under the converted policy, together with similar benefits from other sources, would result in overinsurance according to the insurance company's standards. These similar benefits may be found in other coverages that the individual has (either group or individual coverage) or for which the individual is eligible under any group arrangement.

The use of the word *conversion* is often a misnomer. In actuality, a person whose coverage terminates is given only the right to purchase a contract on an individual basis at individual rates. Most Blue Cross–Blue Shield plans and some HMO plans offer a conversion policy that is similar or identical to the terminated group coverage. However, most insurance companies offer a conversion policy (or a choice of policies) that contains a lower level of benefits than existed under the group coverage. Traditionally, the conversion policy contained only basic hospital and surgical coverages, even if major medical coverage was provided under the group contract. Now many insurance companies provide (and are required to provide in many states) a conversion policy that includes major medical benefits, which do not necessarily have to be as broad as those under the former group coverage.

Some plans offer a conversion policy that is written by another entity. For example, an HMO might enter into a contractual arrangement with an insurance company. In some cases, the HMO and insurance company are commonly owned or have a parent-subsidiary relationship.

Self-funded plans, which are exempt from state laws that mandate a conversion policy, may still provide such a benefit. Rather than providing coverage directly to the terminated employee, an agreement is usually made with an insurance company to make a policy available. This agreement is typically part of a broader contract with the insurer to also provide administrative services and/or stop-loss protection. Because the availability of a conversion policy results in a charge (such as $.65 per employee per month), most self-funded plans do not provide any continuation of coverage beyond what is required by COBRA.

Group-to-Individual Portability

HIPAA makes it easier for individuals who lose group medical expense coverage to find alternative coverage in the individual marketplace. The purpose of the federal legislation seems to be to encourage states to adopt their own mechanisms to achieve this goal. The federal rules apply in a state only if the state fails to have its own plan in effect.

Most states have adopted their own plans so that the federal rules have not become effective. The state alternative must do all the following:

- Provide a choice of health insurance coverage to all eligible individuals
- Not impose any preexisting-conditions restrictions
- Include at least one policy form of coverage that is either comparable to comprehensive health coverage offered in the individual marketplace or comparable to or a standard option of coverage available under the group or individual laws of the state

In addition, the state must implement one of the following:

- One of the NAIC model laws on individual market reform
- A qualified high-risk pool
- Certain other mechanisms specified in the act

If a state fails to adopt an alternative to federal regulation, then insurance companies, HMOs, and other health plan providers in the individual marketplace are required to make coverage available on a guaranteed-issue basis to individuals with 18 or more months of creditable coverage and whose most recent coverage was under a group health plan. Coverage does *not* have to be provided to an individual who has other health insurance or who is eligible for COBRA coverage, Medicare, or Medicaid. No preexisting-conditions exclusions can be imposed. Health insurers have three options for providing coverage to eligible individuals:

1. They may offer every health insurance policy they offer in the state.
2. They may offer their two most popular policies in the state, based on premium volume.
3. They may offer a low-level and a high-level coverage as long as they contain benefits that are similar to other coverage offered by the insurer in the state.

Rules similar to those described in Chapter 9 for group health insurance coverage require the renewal of individual coverage.

CLAIMS

Medical expense contracts that provide benefits on a service basis (such as HMOs and the Blues) generally do not require that covered persons file claim forms. Rather, the providers of services perform any necessary paperwork and are then reimbursed directly.

Medical expense contracts that provide benefits on an indemnity basis typically require that the insurance company (or other provider) be given a written proof of loss (that is, a claim form) concerning the occurrence, character, and extent of the loss for which a claim is made. This form usually contains portions that must be completed and signed by the employee, a representative of the employer, and the provider of medical services.

The period during which an employee must file a claim depends on the provider of coverage and any applicable state requirements. An employee generally has at least 90 days (or as soon as is reasonably possible) after medical expenses are incurred to file. Some insurance companies require that they be notified within a shorter time (such as 20 days) about any illness or injury on which a claim may be based, even though they give a longer time period for the actual filing of the form itself.

Individuals have the right under medical expense plans to assign their benefits to the providers of medical services. Such an assignment, which authorizes the insurance company to make the benefit payment directly to the provider, may generally be made by completing the appropriate portion of the claim form. In addition, the insurance company has the right (as it does in disability income insurance) to examine any person for whom a claim is filed at its own expense and with the physician of its own choice.

Most self-funded plans contain subrogation provisions. If state law allows, they are also commonly contained in the group medical expense contracts of HMOs, PPOs, the Blues, and insurance companies. A subrogation provision gives the plan (or the organization that provides plan benefits) the right to recover from a third party who is responsible through negligence or other wrongdoing for a covered person's injuries that result in claims being paid. If a covered person receives a settlement from the third party (or their liability insurance company) for medical expenses that the plan has already paid, the covered person must reimburse the plan. The plan also has the right to seek a recovery for benefits paid if legal action is not taken by the person who receives benefits.

FEDERAL TAXATION

In many respects, the federal tax treatment of group medical (including group dental) expense premiums and benefits parallels that of other group coverage if they are provided through an insurance company, a Blue Cross–Blue Shield plan, an HMO, or a PPO. Contributions by the employer for an employee's coverage or the coverage of the employee's dependents are tax deductible to the employer, as long as the employee's overall compensation is reasonable. Employer contributions do not create any income tax liability for an employee. Moreover, benefits are not taxable to an employee except when they exceed any medical expenses incurred. The value of any employer-provided coverage for an employee's domestic partner, minus any employee contributions, represents taxable income to the employee unless the partner qualifies under IRS rules as the employee's dependent.

One major difference between group medical expense coverage and other forms of group insurance is that a portion of an employee's contribution for coverage may be tax deductible as a medical expense if that individual itemizes his or her income tax deductions. Under the Internal Revenue Code, individuals are allowed to deduct certain medical care expenses (including dental expenses) for which no reimbursement was received. This deduction is limited to expenses (including amounts paid for insurance) that exceed 7.5 percent of the person's adjusted gross income.

If a sole proprietorship or partnership pays the cost of medical expense coverage for a proprietor or partner (including dependent coverage), this amount constitutes taxable income to the proprietor or partner. However, the proprietor or partner may be entitled to an income tax deduction for a percentage of this amount. As a result of recent legislation, this deduction is 60 percent through 2001, 70 percent in 2002, and 100 percent thereafter. The deduction cannot exceed the individual's earned income from the proprietorship or partnership that provides the medical expense plan, and the deduction is available only if the proprietor or partner is not eligible to participate in any subsidized medical expense plan of another employer of the proprietor, the partner, or the proprietor's or partner's spouse. It is important to recognize that this is not an itemized deduction; rather, it is a deduction in arriving at adjusted gross income. The remainder of the cost of the medical expense coverage can be deducted as an itemized expense to the extent that it and other medical expenses exceed the 7.5 percent threshold previously described.

As of 1999, there is one circumstance under which a self-employed person, other than a more-than-2 percent owner-employee of an S corporation, can receive a 100 percent deduction for his or her medical expense coverage. This occurs only if the spouse is a bona fide employee of the self-employed person. The medical coverage is then provided to the spouse, who elects dependent coverage for the self-employed person. The self-employed person then pays the entire premium and takes a business deduction for the medical expense coverage provided to an employee. However, the IRS has indicated that such an arrangement will be challenged if the spouse's involvement in the business consists of nominal or insignificant services that have no economic substance or independent significance. Note that if there is a significant investment of the spouse's separate assets in the business, the spouse is employed in the business as a joint owner and treated as self-employed person rather than an employee for purposes of the medical expense insurance.

The tax situation may be different if an employer provides medical expense benefits through a self-funded plan (referred to in the Internal Revenue Code as a *self-insured medical reimbursement plan*), under which employers either (1) pay the providers of medical care directly or (2) reimburse employees for their medical expenses. If a self-funded plan meets certain nondiscrimination requirements for highly compensated employees, the employer can deduct benefit payments as they are made, and the employee has no taxable income. If a plan is discriminatory, the employer still receives an income tax deduction. However, all or a portion of the benefits received by "highly compensated individuals," but not by other employees, are treated as taxable income. A *highly compensated individual* is defined as (1) one of the five highest-paid officers of the firm, (2) a shareholder who owns more than 10 percent of the firm's stock, or (3) one of the highest-paid 25 percent of all the firm's employees. There are no nondiscrimination rules if a plan is not self-funded and provides benefits through an insurance contract, a Blue Cross–Blue Shield plan, an HMO, or a PPO.

To be considered nondiscriminatory, a self-funded plan must meet certain requirements regarding eligibility and benefits. The plan must provide benefits (1) for 70 percent or more of "all employees" or (2) for 80 percent or more of all eligible employees if 70 percent or more of all employees are eligible. The following can be excluded from the all-employees category without affecting the plan's nondiscriminatory status:

- Employees who have not completed three years of service.
- Employees who have not attained age 25.
- Part-time employees. Anyone who works fewer than 25 hours per week is automatically considered a part-time employee. Persons who work 25 or more but fewer than 35 hours per week, may also be counted as part-time, as long as other employees in similar work for the employer have substantially more hours.
- Seasonal employees. Anyone who works fewer than seven months of the year is automatically considered a seasonal employee. Persons who work between seven and nine months of the year may also be considered

seasonal, as long as other employees have substantially more months of employment.

■ Employees who are covered by a collective-bargaining agreement if accident-and-health benefits were a subject of collective bargaining.

Even if a plan fails to meet the percentage requirements regarding eligibility, it can still qualify as nondiscriminatory, as long as the IRS is satisfied that the plan benefits a classification of employees in a manner that does not discriminate in favor of highly compensated employees. This determination is made on a case-by-case basis.

To satisfy the nondiscrimination requirements for benefits, the same type and amount of benefits must be provided for all employees covered under the plan, regardless of their compensation. In addition, the dependents of other employees cannot be treated less favorably than the dependents of highly compensated employees. However, because diagnostic procedures are not considered part of a self-funded plan for purposes of the nondiscrimination rule, a higher level of this type of benefit is permissible for highly compensated employees.

If a plan is discriminatory in either benefits or eligibility, highly compensated employees must include the amount of any "excess reimbursement" in their gross income for income tax purposes. If highly compensated employees receive any benefits that are not available to all employees covered under the plan, these benefits are considered an excess reimbursement. For example, if a plan pays 80 percent of covered expenses for employees in general but 100 percent for highly compensated employees, the extra 20 percent of benefits constitutes taxable income.

If a self-funded plan discriminates in the way it determines eligibility, highly compensated employees have excess reimbursements for any amounts they receive. The amount of this excess reimbursement is determined by a percentage that is calculated by dividing the total amount of benefits highly compensated employees receive (exclusive of any other excess reimbursements) by the total amount of benefits paid to all employees (exclusive of any other excess reimbursements). Using the previous example, assume a highly compensated employee receives $2,000 in benefits during a certain year. If other employees receive only 80 percent of this amount (or $1,600), the highly compensated employee has received an excess reimbursement of $400. If the plan also discriminates in the area of eligibility, the highly compensated employee incurs additional excess reimbursement. For example, if 60 percent of the benefits (ignoring any benefits already considered excess reimbursement) are given to highly compensated employees, 60 percent of the remaining $1,600 ($2,000 – $400), or $960, is added to the $400, for a total excess reimbursement of $1,360.

If a plan provides benefits only for highly compensated employees, all benefits received are considered an excess reimbursement, because the percentage is 100 percent.

STUDY QUESTIONS

1. Explain the effect of the NAIC Model Regulation on Group Coverage Discontinuance and Replacement when group insurance coverage is transferred.

2. What dependents are typically eligible for coverage under a medical expense plan?

3. a. What is a medical child support order?
   b. What makes such an order qualified?
   c. What are the obligations of a plan administrator who receives a medical child support order?

4. How does the Health Insurance Portability and Accountability Act limit the use of preexisting-conditions provisions in medical expense plans?

5. What is the relationship between creditable coverage and the length of a person's preexisting-conditions period?

6. Holly incurred $5,000 of medical expenses that, except for deductibles and coinsurance, are fully covered under the medical expense plan provided by her employer. She is also covered as a dependent under her husband's plan. Holly's plan has a $100 deductible and an 80 percent coinsurance provision; her husband's plan has a $200 deductible and 90 percent coinsurance. How much will Holly collect from each plan if the traditional COB approach is used?

7. Under what circumstances is Medicare the secondary payer of medical expense benefits?

8. a. What employers are subject to the health insurance continuation provisions of COBRA?
   b. What are the penalties for noncompliance?

9. With respect to the health insurance continuation provisions of COBRA, answer each of the following:
   a. What is a qualifying event?
   b. Who are eligible qualifying beneficiaries?
   c. For what length of time must coverage be continued?

10. a. Briefly describe how medical expense coverage provided to retired employees may differ from that provided to active employees.
    b. What are the ways in which employers have modified medical expense plans as a result of the new FASB rules?

11. a. Under what circumstances is an employee or dependent eligible to convert medical expense coverage that has terminated?
    b. What type of coverage can be obtained under the conversion provision?

12. Describe the group-to-individual portability rules of the Health Insurance Portability and Accountability Act.

13. How does the claims process differ with respect to medical expense plans providing benefits on a service basis and medical expense plans providing benefits on a an indemnity basis?

14. Under what circumstances do benefits under insured group medical expense plans result in taxable income to an employee?

15. To what extent and under what circumstances are contributions for group medical expense coverage deductible for federal income tax purposes if paid by
    a. the employer?
    b. the employees?

CHAPTER 13

Group Dental Insurance and Other Group Insurance Benefits

- Identify the sources of group dental insurance benefits and explain the provisions contained in dental insurance contracts.

- Explain the reasons why long-term care insurance is needed and describe the provisions found in group long-term care products.

- Describe the approaches used to provide group legal expense benefits.

- Describe the characteristics of voluntary benefit plans and explain their similarities to and differences from group insurance.

- Briefly describe the status of property and liability insurance as an employee benefit.

$\mathbf{P}$reviou s chapters have considered the three traditional types of group insurance: life insurance, disability income insurance, and medical expense insurance. This chapter focuses on three of the newer and/or less common types of group insurance coverage: group dental insurance, group long-term care insurance, and group legal expense insurance. It also covers voluntary benefit plans, which may be either group or individual insurance. Finally, there is a brief discussion of property and liability insurance as a group benefit.

GROUP DENTAL INSURANCE

Since the early 1970s, group dental insurance has been one of the fastest-growing employee benefits. It has been estimated that in the past 25 years, the percentage of employees who have dental coverage has grown from about 5 percent to more than 60 percent. More than 90 percent of firms with 500 or more employees make coverage available. Many employee benefit consultants feel that by the early part of the next century most employees, except for those who work for very small employers, will have dental coverage.

To a great extent, group dental insurance contracts have been patterned after group medical expense contracts, and they contain many similar, if not identical, provisions. Like group medical expense insurance, however, group dental insurance has many variations. Dental plans may be limited to specific types of expenses or they may be broad enough to cover virtually all dental expenses. In addition, coverage can be obtained from various types of providers, and benefits can be in the form of either services or cash payments.

The concept of managed care has had a significant role in the evolution of group dental insurance plans. However, this role has been somewhat different from that in medical expense plans. Group dental plans are more likely than medical expense plans to provide benefits on a traditional fee-for-service basis, but they are also more likely to take a managed care approach to providing those benefits. The most common example of the latter is the emphasis on providing a higher level of benefits for preventive care. As group dental plans have become more prevalent, the percentage of persons receiving preventive care has continued to increase; as a result, the percentage of persons needing care for more serious dental problems has continued to decrease.

One other difference between group medical expense plans and group dental plans is that providers of managed dental care arrangements have been more likely to offer coverage to very small groups.

The federal taxation of dental premiums and benefits is the same as that described in Chapter 12 for medical expense premiums and benefits.

Providers of Dental Coverage

Group dental benefits may be offered by insurance companies, dental service plans, the Blues, and managed care plans. Like medical expense coverage, a significant portion of dental coverage is also self-funded. An employer may either self-administer the plan or use the services of a third-party administrator. In either case, the plan may use a preferred-provider network to provide dental services.

Insurance Companies

Insurance companies are a major provider of dental coverage, often on an indemnity basis. Coverage is usually offered independently of other group insurance coverages, but it may be incorporated into a major medical contract. If it is part of a major medical contract, the coverage is often referred to as an *integrated dental plan,* and the benefits are frequently subject to the same provisions and limitations as benefits that are available under a separate dental plan.

Dental Service Plans

Most states have dental service plans, often called *Delta Plans* or *Delta Dental Plans* that along with the Blues write approximately one-quarter of dental coverage. However, the extent of their use varies widely by state, and western states generally have larger and more successful plans than states in other parts of the country. The majority of these plans are nonprofit organizations that are sponsored by state dental associations. In addition, they are patterned after Blue Shield plans, and dentists provide service benefits on a contractual basis. Also like Blue Shield, state Delta Plans are coordinated by a national board, Delta Dental Plans, Inc.

Blue Cross and Blue Shield

Many Blue Cross and Blue Shield plans also provide dental coverage. In some cases, the Blues have contractual arrangements that are similar to those that dental service plans have with dentists; in other cases, benefits are paid on an indemnity basis just as if an insurance company were involved. Finally, a few of the Blues market dental coverage through Delta Plans in conjunction with their own medical expense plans.

Managed Care Plans

A significant and growing amount of dental coverage is provided through managed care plans, often sponsored by insurance companies or the Blues. However, the majority of dental benefits are provided through traditional fee-for-service plans. Because dental expenses are more predictable than medical expenses, the emphasis on preventive care by managed care plans provides a real potential to hold down future costs.

Coverage can be obtained from dental health maintenance organizations (DHMOs), which operate like health maintenance organizations but provide dental care only. Like HMOs, DHMOs can take the form of closed-panel plans or individual practice associations. Estimates are that about one-quarter of employers offer a DHMO option to employees but usually as an alternative to a fee-for-service plan.

Coverage can also be obtained from PPOs, which have enjoyed rapid growth in recent years. Point-of-service plans have also become increasingly common for providing dental coverage.

Self-Funded Plans

For several years, it has been common for large employers to self-fund dental benefits, and recently the concept has spread to smaller employers. Under the technique, often called *direct reimbursement,* the employee visits the dentist, pays the bill, and then submits the bill to the employer or a third-party administrator for reimbursement. This process often generates significant savings for the employer, largely because of a significant savings in administrative costs. The claims process is relatively simple because most reimbursements are small in size, and large claims do not exist because of caps on benefit amounts. The number of claims is also fairly stable from year to year. One problem that often occurs in self-funding of benefits is the lack of control over utilization. However, this has been a minimal problem in dental treatment because employees seem to be reluctant to visit the dentist unless it is absolutely necessary.

Contractual Provisions

Although group dental insurance contracts have been patterned after group medical expense contracts, some of their provisions are different, and others are unique to dental coverage. These provisions pertain to eligibility, benefits, exclusions, benefit limitations, predetermination of benefits, and termination.

Eligibility

In contributory plans, most employers use the same eligibility requirements for dental coverage as they use for medical expense coverage. However, some employers have different probationary periods for the two coverages. Probationary periods are used because members of a group who previously had no dental insurance usually have a large number of untreated dental problems. In addition, because many dental care expenditures are postponable, an employee who anticipates coverage under a dental plan in the future is inclined to postpone treatment that is not crucial. Depending on the group's characteristics, the number of first-year claims for a new plan or for new employees and their dependents under an existing dental plan can be expected to run between 20 percent and 50 percent more than long-run annual claims. Therefore, to counter this higher-than-average number of claims, some employers use a longer probationary period for dental benefits than for medical expense benefits. Other employers may have the same probationary period for both types of coverage but will impose waiting periods before certain types of dental expenses will be covered (such as 12 months for orthodontics).

Longer-than-usual probationary periods or waiting periods initially minimize claims, but unless an organization has a high turnover rate, the result may be false economy. Many persons who do not have coverage merely postpone treatment until they do have coverage. This postponement may actually lead to increased claims, because existing dental conditions only become more severe and then require more expensive treatment. For this reason, some benefit consultants feel that dental plans should at most contain relatively short probationary and waiting periods.

Another method of countering high first-year claims is to require evidence of insurability. For example, an insurance company might require any person who desires coverage from the dental plan to undergo a dental examination. If major dental problems are disclosed, the person must have them corrected before insurance coverage becomes effective.

Because dental expenditures are postponable and somewhat predictable, the problem of adverse selection under contributory plans is more severe for dental insurance than for many other types of group insurance. To counter this adverse selection, insurance companies impose more stringent underwriting (including eligibility) requirements on contributory dental plans than they do on other types of group insurance. In addition, most insurance companies insist on a high percentage of participation (such as 80 percent or 85 percent), and a few will not write contributory coverage. Many insurance companies also insist on having other business besides dental coverage from the employer.

The problem of adverse selection is particularly severe when persons desire coverage after the date on which they were initially eligible to participate. These persons most likely want coverage because they or someone in their family needs dental treatment. Dental insurance contracts contain several provisions that try to minimize this problem, including one or a combination of the following:

- Reducing benefits (usually by 50 percent) for a period of time (such as one year) following the late enrollment.
- Reducing the maximum benefit to a low amount (such as $100 or $200) for the year following the late enrollment.
- Excluding some benefits for a certain period (such as one or two years) following the late enrollment period. This exclusion may apply to all dental expenses except those that result from an accident, or it may apply only to a limited array of benefits (such as orthodontics and prosthetics).

Benefits

Most dental insurance plans pay for almost all types of dental expenses, but a particular plan may provide more limited coverage. One characteristic of dental insurance that is seldom found in medical expense plans is the inclusion of benefits for both routine diagnostic procedures (including oral examinations and X-rays) and preventive dental treatment (including teeth cleaning and fluoride treatment). In fact, a few dental plans actually require periodic oral examinations as a condition for continuing eligibility. There is clear evidence that the cost of providing these benefits is more than offset by the avoidance of expensive dental procedures that are required when a condition is not discovered early or when preventive treatment has not been given.

In addition to benefits for diagnostic and preventive treatment, benefits for dental expenses may be provided for the following categories of dental treatment:

- Restoration (including fillings, crowns, and other procedures used to restore the functional use of natural teeth)
- Oral surgery (including the extraction of teeth as well as other surgical treatment of diseases, injuries, and defects of the jaw)
- Endodontics (treatment for diseases of the dental pulp within teeth, such as root canals)
- Periodontics (treatment of diseases of the surrounding and supporting tissues of the teeth)
- Prosthodontics (the replacement of missing teeth and structures by artificial devices such as bridgework and dentures)
- Orthodontics (the prevention and correction of dental and oral anomalies through the use of corrective devices such as braces and retainers)

Most dental plans will usually cover any expenses that arise from the first five categories listed above, and they may include benefits for orthodontics. Whatever benefits are provided may be on a scheduled basis, on a nonscheduled basis, or on some combination of the two.

Scheduled Plans. A scheduled dental plan is similar to a surgical expense plan in which benefits are paid up to the amount specified in the fee schedule. Table 13-1 is an excerpt from one such dental schedule.

Most scheduled dental plans provide benefits on a first-dollar basis and contain no deductibles or specified coinsurance percentage. However, benefit maximums are often lower than are reasonable and customary charges, thereby forcing employees to bear a portion of the costs of their dental services. For example, if a schedule is designed to provide maximum benefits that are equal to approximately 80 percent of reasonable and customary charges, employees are in effect subject to an 80 percent coinsurance provision. To encourage diagnostic and preventive services, some dental schedules are designed so that the fees for these services are almost completely covered, while benefits for other dental services are paid at a lower level.

Unlike a surgical schedule, which lists only the more common surgical procedures, a dental schedule is essentially an all-inclusive list of the covered

TABLE 13-1
Fee Schedule

Dental Services	Maximum Benefit
Diagnostic:	
Initial oral examination	$ 15
Periodic oral examination	10
Preventive:	
Prophylaxis (14 years of age or older)	30
Prophylaxis (under 14 years of age)	20
Prosthodontics:	
Complete upper denture	400

dental services. If a service is not on the list, most contracts will cover it, but only if the schedule contains what could be considered a suitable substitute. In addition, any benefits paid will be limited to the amount specified for the substitute service.

Although once common, scheduled dental plans are now used less frequently than either nonscheduled plans or combination plans.

Nonscheduled Plans. Nonscheduled dental plans, often called *comprehensive dental plans,* are the most common type of dental coverage. They resemble major medical expense contracts because dental expenses are paid on a reasonable and customary basis, subject to any exclusions, limitations, or copayments in the contract. The use of the term *nonscheduled* is something of a misnomer because many nonscheduled plans actually do contain a schedule of the covered dental services, but they do not list specific benefit amounts for individual services.

Nonscheduled dental plans usually have both deductibles and coinsurance provisions. Although a single deductible and a single coinsurance percentage may apply to all dental services, the more common practice is to treat different classes of dental services in different ways. The typical nonscheduled dental plan breaks dental services into three broad categories: diagnostic and preventive services, basic services (such as fillings, oral surgery, periodontics, and endodontics), and major services (such as inlays, crowns, dentures, and orthodontics).

Diagnostic and preventive services are typically covered in full and are not subject to a deductible or percentage participation. (They are, however, subject to any other contract limitations.) The other two categories are generally subject to an annual deductible (usually between $25 and $100 per person). In addition to the deductible, the cost of basic services may be subject to a high coinsurance percentage (most often 80 percent), while major services are subject to a lower percentage (most often 50 percent).

While significant variations exist among DHMOs, these plans are likely to have no deductibles or lower deductibles than fee-for-service plans. They are also much more likely to cover basic services in full and provide a higher level of reimbursement for major services other than orthodontics.

Combination Plans. Combination plans contain features of both scheduled and nonscheduled plans. The typical combination plan covers diagnostic and preventive services on a reasonable and customary basis but uses a fee schedule for other dental services.

Exclusions

Exclusions are found in all dental plans, but their number and type vary. Some of the more common exclusions are charges for the following:

- Services that are purely cosmetic, unless necessitated by an accidental bodily injury while a person is covered under the plan (Orthodontics, although often used for cosmetic reasons, can usually also be justified as necessary to correct abnormal dental conditions.)
- Replacement of lost, missing, or stolen dentures or other prosthetic devices
- Duplicate dentures or other prosthetic devices
- Oral hygiene instruction or other training in preventive dental care
- Services that do not have uniform professional endorsement
- Occupational injuries to the extent that benefits are provided by workers' compensation laws or similar legislation
- Services furnished by or on behalf of government agencies, unless there is a requirement to pay
- Certain services that began prior to the date that coverage for an individual became effective (e.g., a crown for which a tooth was prepared prior to coverage)

Limitations

Dental insurance plans also contain numerous limitations that are designed to control claim costs and to eliminate unnecessary dental care. In addition to deductibles and coinsurance, virtually all dental plans have overall benefit maximums. Except for DHMOs, which usually do not have a calendar-year limit, most plans contain a calendar-year maximum (varying from $500 to $2,000) but no lifetime maximum. However, some plans have only a lifetime maximum (such as $1,000 or $5,000), and a few plans contain both a calendar-year maximum and a large lifetime maximum. These maximums may apply to all dental expenses, or they may be limited to all expenses except those that arise from orthodontics (and occasionally periodontics). In the latter case, benefits for orthodontics are subject to a separate, lower lifetime maximum, typically between $500 and $2,000.

Most dental plans limit the frequency with which some benefits are paid. Routine oral examinations and teeth cleaning are usually limited to once every six months, and full-mouth X-rays to once every 24 or 36 months. The replacement of dentures may also be limited to one time in some specified period (such as five years).

The typical dental plan also limits benefits to the least expensive type of accepted dental treatment for a given dental condition. For example, if either a gold or silver filling can be used, benefit payments will be limited to the cost of a silver filling, even if a gold filling is inserted.

Predetermination of Benefits

About half of dental contracts provide for a pretreatment review of certain dental services by the insurance company. Although this procedure is usually not mandatory, it does allow both the dentist and the patient to know just how much will be paid under the plan before the treatment is performed. In addition, it enables the insurance company (or other provider of benefits) to have some control over the performance of procedures that are unnecessary or more costly than necessary, by giving patients an opportunity to seek less costly care (possibly from another dentist) if benefits will be limited.

In general, the predetermination-of-benefits provision (which goes by several names, such as *precertification* or *prior authorization*) applies only in nonemergency situations and when a dentist's charge for a course of treatment exceeds a specified amount (varying from $200 to $300). The dentist files a claim form (and X-rays, if applicable) with the insurance company just as if the treatment had already been performed. The insurance company reviews the form and returns it to the dentist. The form specifies the services that will be covered and the amount of reimbursement. If and when the services are actually performed, payment is made to the dentist by the insurance company after the claim form has been returned with the appropriate signatures and the date of completion.

When the predetermination-of-benefits provision has not been followed, benefits are still paid. However, neither the dentist nor the covered person knows in advance what services will be covered by the insurance company or how much the insurance company will pay for these services.

Termination

Coverage under dental insurance plans typically terminates for the same reasons it terminates under medical expense coverage (described in Chapter 12). Rarely is there any type of conversion privilege for dental benefits, even when the coverage is written as part of a major medical contract. However, dental coverage is subject to the continuation rules of COBRA.

Benefits for a dental service received after termination may still be covered as long as (1) the charge for the service was incurred prior to the termination date and (2) treatment is completed within 60 or 90 days after termination. For example, the charge for a crown or bridgework is incurred once the preparation of the tooth (or teeth) has begun, even though the actual installation of the crown or bridgework (and the billing) does not take place until after the coverage terminates. Similarly, charges for dentures are incurred on the date the impressions for the dentures are taken, and charges for root canal therapy are incurred on the date the root canal is opened.

GROUP LONG-TERM CARE INSURANCE

In the 1980s, insurance companies started to market long-term care insurance policies to individuals. Many of the earlier policies had limited benefits and expensive premiums. As the products have evolved, benefits have improved while premiums have remained stable or decreased. As is often the case, success in the individual marketplace led to interest in group long-term care insurance as an employee benefit. The first group long-term plan was written in 1987, and a small but growing number of employers, mostly large ones, now make coverage available. The number of insurance companies writing coverage has also grown, but the number still remains relatively small and is primarily limited to the largest group insurance carriers.

At best the growth of group long-term care insurance can be described as slow and cautious for several reasons. First, the individual long-term care insurance market is still in an evolving state, due partially to the lack of adequate actuarial data to design and price coverage. The situation is not unlike the early days of disability income insurance. Second, the tax status of group long-term care coverage has been uncertain, with most tax experts feeling that employer-provided benefits, unlike medical expense benefits, would result in taxation to employees. To the extent that employers want to spend additional benefit dollars, they want to spend them on benefits for which employees receive favorable tax benefits. As a result, almost all group long-term care plans have been financed solely by employee contributions. However, the Health Insurance Portability and Accountability Act (HIPPA) now provides favorable tax treatment for long-term care insurance. The effect of this act is discussed later in this chapter. Third, there has been uncertainty about whether long-term care can be included in a cafeteria plan on a tax-favored basis. This issue has also been addressed by HIPPA (which states that long-term care can't be included). Finally, participation in group plans has been modest because older employees who feel they have a need for the coverage often find it too expensive. A surprise, however, with many of the early plans has been the higher-than-expected participation by employees in the 40-to-50 age bracket.

Before a description of the existing plans is undertaken, it is important to discuss the need for long-term care protection and the sources already available to meet this need.

The Need for Long-Term Care

The need for long-term care arises from the following factors:

- An aging population
- Increasing costs
- The inability of families to provide full care
- The inadequacy of insurance protection

An Aging Population

Long-term care has traditionally been thought of as a problem primarily for the older population. The population aged 65 or over is the fastest-growing age group; today, it represents about 11 percent of the population, a figure that is expected to increase to between 20 percent and 25 percent over the next 50 years. The segment of the population aged 85 and over is growing at an even faster rate. While less than 10 percent of the "over 65" group is over age 85 today, this percentage is expected to double over the next two generations.

An aging society presents changing problems. Those who needed long-term care in the past were most likely to have suffered from strokes or other acute diseases. With longer life spans, a larger portion of the elderly will be incapacitated by chronic conditions such as Alzheimer's disease, arthritis, osteoporosis, and lung and heart disease—conditions that often require continuing assistance with day-to-day needs. The likelihood that a nursing home will be needed increases dramatically with age. One percent of persons between the ages of 65 and 74 reside in nursing homes, and the percentage increases to 6 percent between the ages of 75 and 84. At age 85 and over, the figure rises to approximately 25 percent.

It should be noted that the elderly are not the only group of persons who need long-term care. Many younger persons are unable to care for themselves because of handicaps resulting from birth defects, mental conditions, illnesses, or accidents.

Increasing Costs

More than $50 billion is spent each year on nursing home care. This cost is increasing faster than inflation because of the growing demand for nursing home beds and the shortage of skilled medical personnel. The cost of complete long-term care for an individual can also be astronomical, with annual nursing home costs of $30,000 to $50,000 and more not unusual.

The Inability of Families To Provide Full Care

Traditionally, long-term care has been provided by family members, often at considerable personal sacrifice and great personal stress. However, it is becoming more difficult for families to provide long-term care for the following reasons:

- The geographic dispersion of family members
- Increased participation in the paid work force by women and children
- Fewer children in the family
- More childless families
- Higher divorce rates
- The inability of family members to provide care because they themselves are growing old

The Inadequacy of Insurance Protection

Private medical expense insurance policies (both group and individual) almost always have an exclusion for convalescent, custodial, or rest care. Some policies, particularly group policies, do provide coverage for extended-care facilities and for home health care. In both cases, the purpose is to provide care in a manner that is cheaper than care in a hospital. However, coverage is provided only if a person also needs medical care; benefits are not provided if a person is merely "old" and needs someone to care for him or her.

Medicare is also inadequate because it does not cover custodial care unless this care is needed along with the medical or rehabilitative treatment provided in skilled nursing facilities or under home health care benefits.

Sources of Long-Term Care

There are several sources other than insurance that are available for providing long-term care. However, there are drawbacks associated with each source.

One source is to rely on personal savings. Unless a person has substantial resources, however, this approach may force an individual and his or her dependents into poverty. It may also mean that the financial objective of leaving assets to heirs will not be met.

A second source is to rely on welfare. The Medicaid program in most states will provide benefits, which usually include nursing home care, to the "medically needy." However, a person is not eligible unless he or she is either poor or has exhausted most other assets (including those of a spouse). There is also often a social stigma associated with the acceptance of welfare.

Life-care facilities are growing in popularity as a source of meeting long-term care needs. With a life-care facility, residents pay an "entrance fee" that allows them to occupy a dwelling unit but usually does not give them actual ownership rights. The entrance fee may or may not be refundable if the resident leaves the facility voluntarily or dies. As a general rule, the greater the refund is, the higher the entrance fee will be. Residents pay a monthly fee that includes meals, some housecleaning services, and varying degrees of health care. If a person needs long-term care, he or she must give up the independent living unit and move to the assisted-living or nursing home portion of the facility, but the monthly fee normally remains the same. The disadvantages of this option are that the cost of a life-care facility is beyond the reach of many persons, and a resident must be in reasonably good health and able to live independently at the time the facility is entered. Therefore the decision to use a life-care facility must be made in advance of the need for long-term care. Once such care is needed or is imminent, this approach is no longer viable.

A few insurers now include long-term care benefits in some cash-value life insurance policies. Essentially, an insured can begin to use this accelerated benefit while still living. For example, if the insured is in a nursing home, he or she might receive a benefit equal to 25 percent or 50 percent of the policy face. However, any benefit reduces the future death benefit payable to heirs.

Group Long-Term Care Policies

Most of the early group long-term care policies were designed for specific large employers, and much variation existed. For the last few years, most insurance companies have had a standard group long-term care product, which in virtually all cases is consistent with the provisions in the Long-Term Care Insurance Model Act of the National Association of Insurance Commissioners. The result is that group policies tended to be comparable to the broadest policies sold in the individual marketplace.

Effect of Health Insurance Portability and Accountability Act

The tax treatment of long-term care insurance was made more favorable by HIPAA. Because favorable tax treatment is given only if long-term care insurance policies meet prescribed standards, the nature of most long-term coverage has changed. In most cases, the imposition of federal standards results in broader coverage for consumers. However, Congress seems to have been concerned with the revenue loss associated with this tax legislation. As a result, policies that are modified to comply with the federal standards may in some cases actually provide more limited coverage than has been previously required in several states, particularly with respect to qualifying for benefits.

It should be emphasized that the long-term care changes in the act are primarily changes in the income tax code. States still have the authority to regulate long-term care insurance contracts. They have no obligations to bring state rules and regulations into conformity with these tax changes. However, all states allow "qualified" contracts so that consumers can obtain the new tax benefits.

In the individual marketplace, there are both "qualified" contracts and contracts that do not meet the new HIPAA rules—called *nonqualified contracts*—and there is some debate over which type of contract is better. However, in the group marketplace, most, if not all, of the contracts are qualified.

Eligibility for Favorable Tax Treatment. The act provides favorable tax treatment to a qualified *long-term care insurance contract*. This is defined as any insurance contract that meets all the following requirements:

- The only insurance protection provided under the contract is for *qualified long-term care services*.
- The contract cannot pay for expenses that are reimbursable under Medicare.
- The contract must be guaranteed renewable.
- The contract does not provide for a cash surrender value or other money that can be borrowed or paid, assigned, or pledged as collateral for a loan.
- All refunds of premiums and policyholder dividends must be applied as future reductions in premiums or to increase future benefits.
- The policy must comply with various consumer protection provisions. For the most part, these are the same provisions contained in the NAIC model act and already adopted by most states. However, the new federal act requires the issuer of any level-premium contract to offer a nonforfeiture benefit that can take the form of one of the following: paid-up insurance, extended term insurance, a shortened benefit period, or any similar benefit allowed by regulations that might be issued.

The act defines *qualified long-term care services* as necessary diagnostic, preventive, therapeutic, curing, treating, and rehabilitative services, as well as maintenance or personal care services that are required by a chronically ill individual and are provided by a plan of care prescribed by a licensed health care practitioner.

A *chronically ill person* is one who has been certified as meeting one of the following requirements:

- The person is expected to be unable to perform, without substantial assistance from another person, at least two activities of daily living (ADLs) for a period of at least 90 days due to a loss of functional capacity. The act allows six ADLs, and a qualified long-term care policy must contain at least five of the six. These ADLs are eating, bathing, dressing, transferring from bed to chair, using the toilet, and maintaining continence. (The secretary of health and human services is permitted to prescribe regulations so that a person having a level of disability similar to the level of disability of a person who cannot perform two activities of daily living would also be considered chronically ill.)

■ Substantial services are required to protect the individual from threats to health and safety due to substantial cognitive impairment, even if the person can perform all other ADLs.

Federal Income Tax Provisions. A qualified long-term care insurance contract is treated as accident and health insurance. Therefore any employer contributions are deductible to the employer and do not result in any taxable income to an employee. Benefits received under a group plan are received tax free by an employee with one possible exception. Under contracts written on a per diem basis, proceeds are excludable from income up to $190 per day in 2000. (This figure is indexed annually.) Amounts in excess of $190 are also excludable to the extent that they represent actual costs for long-term care services.

Coverage cannot be offered through a cafeteria plan on a tax-favored basis. In addition, if an employee has a flexible spending account for unreimbursed medical expenses, any reimbursements for long-term care services must be included in the employee's income.

With some exceptions, expenses for long-term care services, including insurance premiums, are treated like other medical expenses. That is, self-employed persons may deduct a portion of premiums paid, and persons who itemize deductions can include the cost of long-term care services, including insurance premiums, for purposes of deducting medical expenses in excess of 7.5 percent of adjusted gross income. However, there is a cap on the amount of personally paid long-term care insurance premiums that can be claimed as medical expenses. These limits for 2000, based on a covered individual's age and subject to cost-of-living adjustments, are shown in Table 13-2.

TABLE 13-2

Age	Annual Deductible Limit per Covered Individual
40 or younger	$ 220
41–50	410
51–60	820
61–70	2,200
Older than 70	2,750

Deductions cannot be taken for payments made to a spouse or relative who is not a licensed professional with respect to such services.

Policy Characteristics

Eligibility for Coverage. The typical eligibility rules (that is, full-time employee, actively at work, and so on) apply to group long-term care policies. At a minimum, coverage can be purchased for an active employee and/or spouse. Many policies also provide coverage to retirees and to other family members such as children, parents, parents-in-law, and, possibly, adult children. There is a maximum age for eligibility, but it is frequently as high as age 85 and may be higher.

Cost. As previously mentioned, the cost of group long-term care coverage is almost always borne by the employee. Initial premiums are usually based on five-year age brackets and increase significantly with age. For example, one plan has an annual premium of $300 for persons aged 40 to 44 and $975 for persons aged 60 to 65. Once coverage is elected, premiums remain level and do not increase when a person enters another age bracket. Coverage is guaranteed renewable, so premiums can be increased by class.

Under some plans, premiums are payable for life. Under other plans, premiums are higher but cease at retirement age. Such a plan is analogous to a life insurance policy that is paid up at age 65. Virtually all plans contain a waiver-of-premium provision that becomes effective when a covered person starts to receive benefits.

Levels of Care. There are several types of care that group long-term care policies can provide. All group policies cover the first three items on the following list, and most policies can provide coverage for all the listed items. However, to receive coverage for some benefits, such as home health care, a covered person might have to elect the benefit and pay an increased premium.

- *Skilled-nursing care,* which consists of daily nursing and rehabilitative care that can be performed only by or under the supervision of skilled medical personnel and must be based on a doctor's orders.
- *Intermediate care,* which involves occasional nursing and rehabilitative care that must be based on a doctor's orders and can be performed only by or under the supervision of skilled medical personnel.
- *Custodial care,* which is primarily to handle such personal needs as walking, bathing, dressing, eating, or taking medicine and can usually be provided by someone without professional medical skills or training.
- *Home health care,* which is received at home, and includes part-time skilled nursing care, speech therapy, physical or occupational therapy, part-time services from home health aides, and help from homemakers or chore workers.
- *Adult day care,* which is received at centers specifically designed for the elderly who live at home but whose spouses or families are not available to stay home during the day. The level of care received is similar to that provided for home health care. Most adult day care centers also provide transportation to and from the center.
- *Care coordination,* which includes the services of a licensed health care practitioner who can access a person's condition, evaluate care options, and develop an individualized plan of care that provides the most appropriate services.
- A *bed reservation benefit,* which continues payments to a long-term care facility for a limited time (such as 20 days) if a patient must temporarily leave because of hospitalization. Without a continuation of payments, the bed may be rented to someone else and unavailable on the patient's release from the hospital.

■ *Respite care,* which allows occasional full-time care at home for a person who is receiving home health care. Respite-care benefits enable family members (or other persons) who are providing much of the home care to take a needed break.

Some policies provide other types of benefits. These include, for example, the purchase or rental of needed medical equipment, emergency alert systems, and assisted-living benefits for facilities that provide care for the frail elderly who are no longer able to care for themselves but do not need the level of care provided in a nursing home.

Benefits. Benefits are usually limited to a specific dollar amount per day, with $50 to $150 being common. A few plans allow participants to select varying benefit levels (for example, $50, $75, $100, $150, or $200 per day) when coverage is initially elected. Benefits may vary by level of care, with the highest benefits being provided for skilled nursing care and the lowest level for home health care and/or adult day care if they are covered. For example, home health care benefits are often paid at one-half the level of custodial care benefits. Annual respite care benefits are usually limited to some multiple, such as 20, of the maximum daily benefit. Most states require that insurance companies offer protection against inflation, usually in the form of benefits increasing periodically based on some index such as the consumer price index. However, inflation increases are often capped at some annual maximum, such as 3 percent.

While a few group long-term care plans provide benefits for an unlimited duration, most limit benefits to a period of time, ranging from three to seven years, or to some equivalent dollar maximum. It should be noted that most persons who enter nursing homes either are discharged or die within two years. However, it is not unusual for stays to last seven years or longer. As in the case of disability income insurance, benefits are often subject to a waiting period, which may vary from 10 to 150 days with 90 days being most common.

Some policies provide for a full restoration of benefits if a covered person has recovered and not been receiving long-term care benefits for a certain period of time, often 180 days. In the absence of such a provision, maximum benefits for a subsequent claim are reduced by the amount of any benefits previously paid.

Eligibility for Benefits. Eligibility for benefits under group long-term care policies is based on meeting the requirements of a chronically ill person as previously described. With respect to ADLs, most policies specify that the covered person be unable to perform at least two out of six ADLs (without substantial assistance from another person) for at least 90 days. However, some policies use a criterion of two out of five ADLs.

There is a second criterion for eligibility, which if satisfied results in the payment of benefits even if the ADLs can be performed. This criterion is based on cognitive impairment, which can be caused by Alzheimer's disease, strokes, or other brain damage. Cognitive impairment is generally measured through tests performed by trained medical personnel.

Because eligibility for benefits often depends on subjective evaluations, most insurance companies use some form of case management. Case management may be mandatory, with the case manager determining eligibility, working with the physician and family to decide on an appropriate type of care, and periodically reassessing the case. Case management may also be voluntary, with the case manager making recommendations about the type of care needed and providing information about the sources for care.

Underwriting. If a group is large enough, coverage is provided on a guaranteed-issue basis for employees who are actively at work. Other categories of eligible persons and employees of small groups are usually subject to individual underwriting, in a manner similar to that in the marketplace for individual long-term care insurance.

Unlike medical expense insurance, a long-term care policy usually does not contain a preexisting-conditions provision. There is little need for such a provision because insurers are required in most states to underwrite at the time coverage is written and are not allowed to use post claims underwriting. If properly underwritten at that time, claims within usual preexisting-conditions periods are very unlikely to occur. In addition, waiting periods for benefits often serve a similar purpose.

Exclusions. Several exclusions are found in group long-term care policies:

- War
- Institutional care received outside the United States
- Treatment for drug or alcohol abuse
- Intentionally self-inflicted injury
- Attempted suicide
- Confinement or care for which benefits are payable under workers' compensation or similar laws
- Confinement or care for which the covered person or the covered person's estate is not required to pay

In contrast to many older individual policies, group contracts have not been written to exclude organic-based mental diseases such as Alzheimer's disease.

Renewability and Portability. Group long-term care plans are guaranteed renewable. If a participant leaves employment, the group coverage can usually be continued on a direct-payment basis, under either the group contract or an individual contract.

GROUP LEGAL EXPENSE INSURANCE

Plans that cover the legal expenses of employees have been a common benefit in several European countries for many years. However, until the mid-1970s, the concept was not widely used in the United States. The plans that did exist were almost always established by unions and were financed from general union funds. Usually, the legal services were provided by attorneys who were employed by the unions, and the only legal services covered were those limited to job-related difficulties, such as suspensions or workers' compensation disputes.

The limited extent of legal expense plans was due to the existence of several obstacles, all of which have been substantially reduced or eliminated in recent years as a result of changes to state and federal laws. In 1973, the Taft-Hartley Act was amended to make legal expense benefits a new subject of collective bargaining, and the Tax Reform Act of 1976 gave favorable tax treatment to certain legal expense plans by providing that neither the premiums paid by employers nor the benefits received under the plans constitute taxable income to employees. As a result of these changes, the number of legal expense plans grew considerably, particularly for union employees as a result of collective bargaining. These plans are typically negotiated trusteeships that provide benefits on an uninsured basis. Some employers have established voluntary plans—possibly as part of a cafeteria plan—under which an employee can elect to participate if he or she desires. In most cases, the employee pays the full cost of the coverage on an after-tax basis. It is also becoming increasingly common for employers to offer some legal expense benefits under employee-assistance plans.

Current Tax Treatment

Under provisions of the 1976 tax act, Section 120 of the Internal Revenue Code was established. This Code section allowed an employer to pay annual premiums to a "prepaid legal services plan" of up to $70 for each employee without the employee's incurring any taxable income. To qualify as a prepaid legal services plan, a group legal expense plan had to meet specific requirements regarding funding and nondiscrimination. Section 120 was always subject to a sunset provision, but the date of expiration was extended several times. However, the section was allowed to expire at the end of 1992. Unless Section 120 is revived at some future date (and periodically there continue to be bills in Congress to do this), any premiums paid by the employer for group legal expenses coverage are treated as taxable income for employees. Benefits are taxable if a plan is self-funded. If Section 120 is revived, favorable tax treatment could also be provided to group legal expense benefits available (within limits) under a cafeteria plan.

The cost of legal expense plans is deductible for the employer. Employees, however, have taxable income to the extent of employer payments. If the plan is prefunded, the employee is taxed on his or her share of the premium paid and benefits are received tax free. If a plan is self-funded by the employer, the employee's taxable income is the value of the benefits paid by the plan.

Types of Plans

The types of group legal expense plans vary significantly in the ways they provide legal services. When an employer or negotiated trusteeship establishes a group legal expense plan, benefits can be self-funded or purchased from another organization. These other organizations include state bar associations, groups of attorneys, or other organizations (either profit or nonprofit) formed for this purpose. However, most group legal expense coverage is purchased from a relatively small number of organizations, several of which have recently affiliated with insurance companies.

Existing plans fall into one of three types of arrangements:

1. Referral and discount plans
2. Access plans
3. Comprehensive plans

Referral and Discount Plans

The most basic form of legal expense plan is one that involves referrals and discounts. Plan members are referred to an attorney who provides services based on a fee schedule or at a discount from his or her usual fees, but the attorney's charges are paid by the plan member. In some cases, plan members may be eligible to be referred to attorneys who provide free services, such as a clinic for low-income persons or an attorney hotline of a local bar association.

Access Plans

This form of legal expense plan, sometimes also called a *telephone access plan,* provides plan members with unlimited legal consultation over the telephone for most legal matters. The plan may also provide simple legal services, such as the preparation of wills or powers of attorney or the review of legal documents.

Plan members are referred to an attorney for more complex legal matters. The attorney will often provide an initial free consultation (usually either one-half or one hour), after which the attorney will bill at some discount (often 25 percent) from normal fees. A plan member is responsible for paying this discounted fee.

Access plans can often be provided at a cost of $5 to $10 per month per member.

Comprehensive Plans

Most legal expense plans can be categorized as comprehensive plans, and premiums usually fall in the range of $10 to $20 per month per member, depending on the level of services provided.

In addition to telephone consultation, comprehensive plans cover in-office and trial work of attorneys. The term *comprehensive* may be a slight misnomer because most plans are not designed to cover 100 percent of a member's potential legal services; 80 to 90 percent is probably a better figure.

Comprehensive plans usually contain a list of covered services. While there are significant variations among plans, most cover at least the following:

- Unlimited legal advice by telephone
- Document review and preparation
- Name changes
- Adoptions
- Purchase or sale of primary residences
- Eviction defense
- Civil actions
- Driver's license suspension
- Juvenile court proceedings
- Consumer protection
- Bankruptcy
- IRS audits
- Debt collection
- Child custody and support
- Divorce, but possibly only for the covered employee and not dependents

If a particular legal service that is required is not on the list of covered services, there may be some limited coverage as long as the service is not otherwise excluded. This limited service, for example, may be in the form of telephone consultation or a limited amount of work by the attorney, such as two to four hours per family per year.

Legal expense plans have exclusions, and common exclusions include the following:

- Business activities or transactions
- Preparation of tax returns
- Class-action suits
- Actions involving the legal expense plan
- Actions involving the employer
- Actions involving the union that bargained for the coverage
- Cases that have contingent fees

Comprehensive plans take three approaches to the method by which a plan member may select an attorney. Many plans use a closed-panel approach, under which a panel of attorneys has agreed to provide covered services at a predetermined fee or hourly rate for which they bill the plan. The plan member selects the attorney, and benefits are generally available at little or no additional cost. However, plans may limit some benefits to a scheduled maximum (such as $500) and usage limitation (such as four hours). A few plans also have deductibles and copayments.

Other plans are open-panel. A plan member can choose any licensed attorney; however, plan benefits are usually subject to scheduled dollar maximums.

Many plans are modified-panel plans. Under such plans, a plan member may choose either a panel attorney, as in a closed-panel plan, or select his or her own attorney. The election of a panel attorney often results in benefits being paid in full, while the election of a nonpanel attorney results in the use of benefit maximums.

VOLUNTARY BENEFITS

A major area of growth for insurance companies in recent years has been through the marketing of voluntary benefits for employees, some of which have already been discussed in this book. These products—which can be either group insurance or individual insurance—vary considerably among insurance companies. Even the names used to describe these products are not uniform, with terminology like *payroll deduction plans* and *worksite marketing* often being used. For purposes of this book, *voluntary benefits* will be defined as products provided by the employer that the employee purchases and for which he or she pays 100 percent of the premium.

It is difficult to measure the precise extent of voluntary benefits because statistics are often included with other group or individual products sold by a company. However, surveys indicate that more than half of the employers with 20 to 100 employees make voluntary benefit products available. This figure increases to 90 percent for employers with 1,000 or more employees. It is also estimated that more than half of the employers that provide voluntary benefit plans make at least three products available.

Reasons for Increase in Popularity

Voluntary benefits have increased in popularity in recent years, primarily because of employers' attempts to contain the rising costs of employee benefits. For example, an employer may determine that it cannot afford to institute a new group insurance program and pay any portion of the cost of coverage. Even though employees would naturally like to have the employer share in the cost, the ease of payroll deduction and more liberal underwriting still make a payroll deduction plan attractive to them. In addition, the portability of the coverage is often appealing.

Voluntary benefits have also grown in popularity as a method of providing individual insurance coverage to supplement the benefits provided under a group plan financed by the employer. For example, an employer may pay for a group long-term disability income plan that provides benefits equal to 50 percent of salary. Voluntary benefits then allow employees to purchase additional protection. Or the employer may pay for short-term disability income protection only and make long-term protection available under a voluntary benefit plan.

Changes in demographics make it increasingly difficult for employers to offer an overall benefit plan that meets the needs of all employees. One alternative is to offer a cafeteria plan. Another option is to provide a basic core of benefits that all employees want. Additional benefits, such as long-term care insurance, can be offered on a voluntary basis.

Another reason for the increase in the popularity of voluntary benefits is the increased availability of products. More insurance companies have entered the market to obtain additional revenue at a time when revenue from other sources has been decreasing. As is often the case, this has sometimes resulted in lower costs and more liberal underwriting. However, before entering the voluntary benefits market, agents should be sure they are dealing with a stable company whose market line will stay current with the changing demands of the marketplace.

Market Characteristics

The voluntary market is very diverse. The remainder of this section briefly describes some of the variations.

Insurance Company Involvement

It is estimated that between 150 and 200 insurance companies offer voluntary benefits, with the number of companies offering individual products being about double the number of companies offering group products and with some companies offering both individual and group products. For a few companies, 50 to 100 percent of their premium income is from voluntary products. For the majority of companies, the figure is under 10 percent.

As a general rule, individual carriers tend to target employers with fewer employees than do group carriers. However, many insurance companies will provide coverage for the employees of almost any size employer. Most companies target employees in the middle income range.

Types of Products Available

The major goal of most insurance companies in the voluntary market is to sell life insurance to employees and their dependents. Individual carriers are heavily concentrated in this market. Life insurance is also the most popular product of group carriers, but they are more likely to also offer health insurance products.

Life insurance products run the gamut from basic term insurance to variable universal life insurance and include accidental death and dismemberment insurance. The most prevalent health insurance products are short-term and long-term disability income. Major medical coverage is seldom offered, but some insurance companies sell specified-disease policies and hospital-indemnity coverage. Dental insurance, prescription drug coverage, and vision coverage are also found, usually in the group insurance market. An increasingly common product is long-term care insurance. A few companies also write property and liability insurance.

Depending on the size of the employer, group products can be tailored to the employer's needs. In the individual marketplace, some providers of voluntary products sell the standard products that are listed in their rate books. Other carriers have specialized products for this market. This is common for universal life insurance and among companies that specialize in voluntary benefits.

Underwriting

Surveys of both employers and employees indicate that the success of a voluntary benefit plan is affected by insurance company underwriting. Although some voluntary benefits are individually underwritten, most plans are responsive to market demands and use either simplified underwriting or guaranteed issues, with group coverage being more likely than individual coverage to have the latter. As a general rule, employers want guaranteed-issue coverage unless simplified underwriting will result in significant cost savings to employees. Several factors affect the underwriting policy of an insurance company, including size, participation level, and issue limits. For example, an insurance company might use simplified underwriting for its universal life product if there is a minimum 8 percent participation rate among employers with 500 employees and the issue limit is $100,000. For a group of 50 employees, the percentage might be 15 and the issue limit, $85,000. For guaranteed issue, the figures might be 35 percent and $80,000 for employers with 500 employees and 55 percent and $50,000 for employers with 50 employees.

Cost

It is estimated that voluntary benefits are about 10 percent less expensive than coverage purchased in the individual marketplace outside the employment relationship. However, significant variations exist. Even when there is no cost differential, the ease of payroll deduction is appealing to employees.

Because both employers and employees have considerable interest in voluntary products being offered on a tax-favored basis, benefits may be provided under a cafeteria plan. However, the use of a cafeteria plan may pose problems, and some benefit consultants feel that voluntary benefits should be kept separate from a firm's cafeteria plan. The issue arises over regulation by ERISA. Most voluntary plans, being employee pay all, are exempt from ERISA rules, which is a definite plus from the employer's perspective. Any benefits purchased under a cafeteria plan are technically purchased with employer funds, even if made with voluntary salary reductions. It is argued that this would bring a voluntary benefit plan under ERISA rules. In 1996 the Pension and Welfare Benefits Administration issued an advisory opinion that ERISA did not apply to premium-conversion plans (also called *premium-only plans*) used to allow before-tax salary reductions for medical expense benefits. However, the government has not addressed the issue of other voluntary benefits.

Methods of Premium Payment

The vast majority of voluntary benefits use payroll deduction (also referred to as *salary allotment* or *salary reduction*) as the method for premium payments, with the employer remitting the premiums to the insurance company. Some insurance companies will bill employees directly if an employer is unwilling to participate in a payroll deduction arrangement. Payroll deduction is very popular with employees, however, and direct billing will probably have an adverse effect on plan participation, although it may also reduce the rate at which coverage lapses when employment terminates.

Premiums are usually determined by the benefits purchased and the frequency of payroll deductions. However, life insurance is often sold on a money-purchase basis. The term *money purchase* comes from the fact that amounts of coverage are sold on the basis of what can be purchased with a given premium, such as $1, $2, or $5 per week (or other period). Because the amount of coverage is a function of the employee's attained age, larger amounts of coverage are available to younger employees than to older employees.

Some insurance companies sell universal life insurance on a money-purchase basis, but other companies take a different approach. Rather than selecting the desired premium, employees choose the amount of pure death protection. Several options—such as $10,000, $25,000, and $50,000—may be offered, and the available options may vary by salary level or position. A minimum periodic premium will then be specified for each option and a given employee's age. The premium will be sufficient to generate a cash value at retirement age if the insurer's current interest assumptions are met. Employees, however, can elect to pay higher premiums so that a larger cash value will develop. Some insurers set the initial premium at a multiple of the pure insurance cost (such as twice the cost); others make it an amount that will generate a cash value equal to a percentage (such as 50 percent) of the original amount of insurance. After the policy has been in force for a specified time period, employees typically have flexibility in premium levels similar to what is available to persons purchasing universal life insurance outside the employment relationship.

Portability

Individual products are automatically portable when an employee terminates employment. However, there are several possibilities with group coverage. In a few cases, coverage ceases; in some cases, the employee must convert to an individual policy. In most cases, the employee can continue the group coverage on a direct-bill basis.

Premiums often remain the same after termination of employment, but they may have to be paid less frequently. For example, instead of paying a monthly periodic deduction, an individual may be billed quarterly. Under some plans, an extra administrative charge is made for the cost of direct billing.

Enrollment

Enrollment in voluntary plans can take many forms, and most insurance companies use more than one method. For individual policies, the agent or broker is usually involved in the enrollment process. Group plans also frequently use group sales representatives. Some insurance companies use professional enrollers, and some occasionally undertake direct-mail enrollment.

Numerous methods are employed to encourage plan enrollment. Printed materials often are provided to employees in the workplace and may even be sent to the employees' homes. Meetings frequently are held with employees, usually on a group basis. Other methods of communicating the plan include the use of videotapes and toll-free telephone numbers.

PROPERTY AND LIABILITY INSURANCE

The current status of property and liability insurance as an employee benefit is that, for several years, it has been offered by a few large employers. Detailed statistics from the insurance industry are difficult to obtain, but most estimates indicate that only a small percentage of personal property and liability insurance is provided as the result of an employer-arranged plan. This slow growth can be traced to several factors, namely, lack of favorable tax treatment, a low potential for cost savings, a lack of employer enthusiasm, and regulatory restrictions.

Most employer-provided property and liability insurance plans are not true group insurance but are payroll deduction plans of individual insurance. The cost of these plans is usually borne entirely by the participating employees. Besides handling the payroll deductions, the employer has little, if any, responsibility for plan administration. Employees are solicited by representatives of the insurance company, usually by mail or phone. Some insurance companies may actually have agents on or near the employer's premises, but most insurance companies give group members toll-free numbers to contact their representatives.

Payroll deduction property and liability insurance plans are usually not experience rated but are offered at a slight discount because of the administrative savings associated with mass marketing. Premiums for employees vary because they are based on the same factors as individual property and liability insurance (such as age, driving record, or value of the home), which also means that some employees may be ineligible for coverage. Most plans offer automobile insurance, and a few also offer other coverages such as homeowners' insurance and umbrella liability insurance. Employees usually have the same choices regarding the amount and type of coverage that they would have in the individual marketplace, and the contracts offered are usually identical. However, modifications that attempt to decrease the cost of the payroll deduction coverage are sometimes made. These include larger deductibles and provisions in the automobile insurance policy that eliminate coverage for medical expenses to the extent that they are paid under the employer's medical expense plan.

A few companies offer property and liability insurance on a true group basis and use both a master contract and experience rating for the group. All employees are usually eligible. The coverages offered to the employees are usually the same as those offered under payroll deduction plans, but the rating structure tends to be less refined, particularly for automobile insurance. Instead of having several dozen classifications that are based on factors such as age, sex, and driving record, there may only be three or four classifications based solely on driving record. In virtually all cases when true group property and liability plans are made available, the insurance company will insist on employer contributions of between 25 percent and 50 percent of the cost of the coverage and on participation by a large percentage of employees, possibly as high as 75 percent.

STUDY QUESTIONS

1. What types of limitations are often imposed upon benefits for a person enrolling in a dental insurance plan after his or her initial eligibility period has ended?

2. Why are dental insurance plans more likely than medical expense plans to include benefits for routine examinations and preventive medicine?

3. Describe the limitations often contained in dental expense plans to control claims costs and to eliminate unnecessary dental treatment.

4. a. What factors result in the need for long-term care insurance?
   b. What are the reasons for the cautious growth of group long-term care insurance?

5. What sources other than long-term care insurance coverage are available to meet the need for long-term care?

6. a. How did the Health Insurance Portability and Accountability Act affect long-term care insurance?
   b. What are the tax advantages associated with a qualified long-term care insurance contract?

7. Describe the typical provisions found in group long-term care insurance policies for each of the following:
   a. Persons eligible for coverage.
   b. Current and future premiums
   c. Levels of care covered
   d. Level and duration of benefits
   e. Eligibility for benefits
   f. Treatment of preexisting conditions.
   g. Exclusions
   h. Renewability and portability

8. Compare referral and discount legal expense plans with access plans.

9. a. What types of legal services are covered under most comprehensive legal expense plans?
   b. What are the common exclusions?
   c. What are the approaches by which a plan member may be able to select an attorney?

10. Describe the voluntary benefit market with respect to each of the following:
    a. Insurance company involvement
    b. Types of products available
    c. Underwriting
    d. Cost
    e. Methods of premium payment

11. a. To what extent are voluntary benefits portable?
    b. How are premium payments affected if coverage is continued after termination of employment?

12. Describe the types of plans that may be used to provide group property and liability insurance.

Alternative Funding Methods

In recent years, employers have increasingly considered—and often adopted—benefit funding methods that are alternatives to the traditional, fully insured group insurance contract. Under the traditional group insurance contract, the employer pays premiums in advance to the insurance company, which then has the financial responsibility both for paying claims (if and when they occur) and for assuming the administrative expenses associated with the contract. In addition, the insurance company bears the risk that claims will be larger than anticipated.

REASONS FOR ALTERNATIVE FUNDING

The increasing interest in alternatives to the traditional, fully insured group arrangement has focused on two factors: cost savings and improved cash flow. To a large extent, this interest has grown in response to the rising cost of medical care, which has resulted in an increase in the cost of providing medical expense benefits. Even though alternative funding methods are most commonly used for providing medical expense benefits, many of the methods described here are also appropriate for other types of benefits.

Cost Savings

Savings can result to the extent that either claims or the insurance company's retention can be reduced. Retention—the portion of the insurance company's premium over and above the incurred claims and dividends—includes such items as commissions, premium taxes, risk charges, and profit. Traditionally, alternative funding methods have not focused on reducing claims, because the same benefits have been normally provided (and therefore the same claims have been paid) regardless of the funding method used. However, this focus has changed as state laws and regulations increasingly mandate the types and levels of benefits that must be contained in medical expense contracts. To the extent that these laws and regulations apply only to benefits that are included in insurance contracts, employers can avoid providing these mandated benefits by using alternative funding methods that do not involve insurance contracts. It should be noted that federal mandates apply to benefit plans, not just insurance contracts, and cannot be avoided by self-funding.

Modifications of fully insured contracts are usually designed either to lower or eliminate premium taxes or to reduce the insurance company's risk and, consequently, the risk charge. Alternative funding methods that involve a degree of self-funding may be designed to also reduce other aspects of retention and to reduce claims by excluding mandated benefits.

Improved Cash Flow

Under a fully insured contract, an employer has the ability to improve cash flow because premiums are collected before the funds are actually needed to pay claims. The employer generally is credited with interest while these funds are held in reserves. Alternative funding arrangements that are intended to improve cash flow are designed either to postpone the payment of premiums to the insurance company or to keep the funds that would otherwise be held in reserves in the employer's hands until the insurance company needs them. Such an arrangement is particularly advantageous to the employer when these funds can be invested at a higher rate of interest than that credited by the insurance company to reserves. It must be remembered, however, that earnings on funds invested by the employer generally are subject to income taxation, while interest credited to reserves by the insurance company is tax free.

METHODS OF ALTERNATIVE FUNDING

Totally self-funded (or self-insured) employee benefit plans are the opposite of traditional, fully insured group insurance plans. Under totally self-funded plans, the employer is responsible for paying claims, administering the plan and bearing the risk that actual claims will exceed those expected. However, very few employee benefit plans that use alternative methods of funding have actually turned to total self-funding. Rather, the methods used typically fall somewhere between the two extremes.

The methods of alternative funding can be divided into two general categories: those that primarily modify traditional, fully insured group insurance contracts and those that have some self-funding (either partial or total). The first category includes these methods:

■ Premium-delay arrangements
■ Reserve-reduction arrangements
■ Minimum-premium plans
■ Cost-plus arrangements
■ Retrospective-rating arrangements

These alternative funding methods are regarded as modifications of traditional, fully insured plans because the insurance company has the ultimate responsibility for paying all benefits promised under the contract. Most insurance companies allow only medium-sized and large employers to use these modifications, and although practices differ among insurance companies, generally a group insurance plan must generate between $150,000 and $250,000 in claims or have a minimum number of covered persons, such as 50 or 100, before these funding methods become available to the employer.

The second category of alternative funding methods consists of the following:

■ Total self-funding from current revenue and self-administration
■ Self-funding with stop-loss coverage and/or ASO arrangements
■ Funding through a 501(c)(9) trust

In contrast to the first category of alternative funding methods, some of these alternatives can be used by small employers.

Premium-Delay Arrangements

Premium-delay arrangements allow the employer to defer payment of monthly premiums for some time beyond the usual 30-day grace period. In fact, these arrangements lengthen the grace period, most commonly by 60 or 90 days. The practical effect of premium-delay arrangements is that they enable the employer to have continuous use of the portion of the annual premium that is approximately equal to the claim reserve. For example, a 90-day premium delay allows the employer to use three months' worth (or 25 percent) of the annual premium for other purposes. This amount roughly corresponds to what is usually in the claim reserve for medical expense coverage. Generally, the larger this reserve is on a percentage basis, the longer the premium payment can be delayed. Because the insurance company still has a statutory obligation to maintain the claim reserve, it must use other assets besides the employer's premiums for this purpose. In most cases, these assets come from the insurance company's surplus.

A premium-delay arrangement has a financial advantage to the extent that an employer can earn a higher return by investing the delayed premiums than by accruing interest on the claim reserve. In actual practice, interest is still credited to the reserve, but this credit is offset by either an interest charge on the delayed premiums or an increase in the insurance company's retention.

On termination of an insurance contract with a premium-delay arrangement, the employer is responsible for paying any deferred premiums. However, the insurance company is legally responsible for paying all claims incurred prior to termination, even if the employer fails to pay the deferred premiums. Consequently, most insurance companies are concerned about the employer's financial position and credit rating. For many insurance companies, the final decision of whether to enter into a premium-delay arrangement, or any other alternative funding arrangement that leaves funds in the hands of the employer, is made by the insurer's financial experts after a thorough analysis of the employer. In some cases, this may mean that the employer will be required to submit a letter of credit or some other form of security.

Reserve-Reduction Arrangements

A reserve-reduction arrangement is similar to a premium-delay arrangement. Under the usual reserve-reduction arrangement, the employer is allowed (at any given time) to retain an amount of the annual premium that is equal to the claim reserve. Generally, such an arrangement is allowed only after the contract's first year, when the pattern of claims and the appropriate amount of the reserve can be more accurately estimated. In succeeding years, if the contract is renewed, the amount retained is adjusted according to changes in the size of the reserve. As with a premium-delay arrangement, the monies retained by the employer must be paid to the insurance company on termination of the contract. Again, the advantage of this approach lies in the employer's ability to earn more on these funds than it would earn under the traditional insurance arrangement.

A few insurance companies offer another type of reserve-reduction arrangement for long-term disability income coverage. Under a so-called limited-liability arrangement, the employer purchases from the insurance company a one-year contract in which the insurer agrees to pay claims only for that year, even though the employer's "plan" provides benefits to employees for longer periods. Consequently, enough reserves are maintained by the insurance company to pay benefits only for the duration of the one-year contract. At renewal, the insurance company agrees to continue paying the existing claims as well as any new claims. In effect, the employer pays the insurance company each year for existing claims as the benefits are paid to employees, rather than when disabilities occur. A problem for employees under this type of arrangement is the lack of security for future benefits. For example, if the employer goes bankrupt and the insurance contract is not renewed, the insurance company has no responsibility to continue benefit payments. For this reason, several states do not allow this type of arrangement.

The limited-liability arrangement contrasts with the usual group contract in which the insurance company is responsible for paying disability income claims to an employee for the length of the benefit period (as long as the employee remains disabled). On average, each disability claim results in the establishment of a reserve equal to approximately five times the employee's annual benefit.

Minimum-Premium Plans

Minimum-premium plans were designed primarily to reduce state premium taxes. However, many minimum-premium plans also improve the employer's cash flow.

Under the typical minimum-premium plan (sometimes called limited self-funding), the employer assumes the financial responsibility for paying claims up to a specified level, usually from 80 percent to 95 percent of estimated claims (with 90 percent most common). The specified level may be determined on either a monthly or an annual basis. The funds necessary to pay these claims are deposited into a bank account that belongs to the employer. However, the actual payment of claims is made from this account by the insurance company, which acts as an agent of the employer. When claims exceed the specified level, the balance is paid from the insurance company's own funds. No premium tax is levied by the states on the amounts the employer deposits into such an account, as would have occurred if these deposits had been paid directly to the insurance company. In effect, for premium-tax purposes the insurance company is considered to be only the administrator of these funds and not a provider of insurance. Unfortunately, the Internal Revenue Service considers these funds to belong to the employer, and death benefits represent taxable income to beneficiaries. Consequently, minimum-premium plans are used to insure disability income and medical expense benefits rather than life insurance benefits.

Under a minimum-premium plan, the employer pays a substantially reduced premium, subject to premium taxation, to the insurance company for administering the entire plan and for bearing the cost of claims above the specified level. Because such a plan may be slightly more burdensome for an insurance company to administer than would a traditional group arrangement, the retention charge may also be slightly higher. Under a minimum-premium arrangement, the insurance company is ultimately responsible for seeing that all claims are paid, and it must maintain the same reserves that would have been required if the plan had been funded under a traditional group insurance arrangement. Consequently, the premium includes a charge for the establishment of these reserves, unless some type of reserve-reduction arrangement has also been negotiated.

Some insurance regulatory officials view the minimum-premium plan primarily as a loophole used by employers to avoid paying premium taxes. In several states, there have been attempts to seek court rulings or legislation that would require premium taxes to be paid either on the funds deposited in the bank account or on claims paid from these funds. Most of these attempts have been unsuccessful, but court rulings in California require the employer to pay premium taxes on the funds deposited in the bank account. If similar attempts are successful in the future, the main advantage of minimum-premium plans will be lost.

Cost-Plus Arrangements

Cost-plus arrangements (often referred to by other names such as *flexible funding*) may be used to fund other types of employee benefits, but they generally are used by large employers to provide life insurance benefits. Under such an arrangement, the employer's monthly premium is based on the claims paid by the insurance company during the preceding month, plus a specified retention charge that is uniform throughout the policy period. To the extent that an employer's claim experience is better than that assumed in a traditional premium arrangement, the employer's cash flow is improved. However, an employer with worse-than-expected experience, either during the early part of the policy period or during the entire policy period, could also have a more unfavorable cash flow than if a traditional insurance arrangement were used. To prevent this from occurring, many insurance companies place a maximum limit on the employer's monthly premium so that the aggregate monthly premiums paid at any time during the policy period do not exceed the aggregate monthly premiums that would have been paid if the cost-plus arrangement had not been used.

Retrospective-Rating Arrangements

Under retrospective-rating arrangements, the insurance company charges the employer an initial premium that is less than what would be justified by the expected claims for the year. In general, this reduction is between 5 percent and 10 percent of the premium for a traditional group insurance arrangement. However, if claims plus the insurance company's retention exceed the initial premium, the employer is called upon to pay an additional amount at the end of the policy year. Because an employer usually has to pay this additional premium, one advantage of a retrospective-rating arrangement is the employer's ability to use these funds during the year.

This potential additional premium is subject to a maximum amount based on some percentage of expected claims. For example, assume that a retrospective-rating arrangement bases the initial premium on the fact that claims will be 93 percent of those actually expected for the year. If claims in fact are below this level, the employer receives an experience refund. If they exceed 93 percent, the retrospective-rating arrangement is triggered, and the employer has to reimburse the insurance company for any additional claims paid, up to some percentage of those expected, such as 112 percent. The insurance company bears claims in excess of 112 percent. In this manner, some of the risk associated with claim fluctuations is passed on to the employer, reducing both the insurance company's risk charge and any reserve for claim fluctuations. The amount of the reductions depends on the actual percentage specified in the contract, above which the insurance company is responsible for claims. This percentage and the one that triggers the retrospective-rating arrangement are subject to negotiations between the insurance company and the employer. In general, the lower the percentage that triggers the retrospective-rating arrangement, the higher the percentage above which the insurance company is fully responsible for claims. In addition, the better the cash-flow advantage to an employer, the greater the risk of claim fluctuations.

In all other respects, a retrospective-rating arrangement is identical to the traditional group insurance contract.

Total Self-Funding from Current Revenue and Self-Administration

The purest form of a self-funded benefit plan is one in which the employer pays benefits from current revenue (rather than from a trust), administers all aspects of the plan, and bears the risk that benefit payments will exceed those expected. In addition to eliminating state premium taxes, avoiding state-mandated benefits, and improving cash flow, the employer has the potential to reduce its operating expenses to the extent that the plan can be administered at a lower cost than the insurance company's retention (other than premium taxes). A decision to use this kind of self-funding plan is generally considered most desirable when all the following characteristics are present:

■ Predictable claims. Budgeting is an integral part of the operation of any organization, and it is necessary to budget for benefit payments that will have to be paid in the future. This can best be done when a specific type of benefit plan has a claim pattern that is either stable or shows a steady trend. Such a pattern is most likely to occur in those types of benefit plans that have a relatively high frequency of low-severity claims. Although a self-funded plan may still be appropriate when the level of future benefit payments is difficult to predict, the plan will generally be designed to include stop-loss coverage (discussed later in this chapter).

■ A noncontributory plan. Several difficulties arise if a self-funded benefit plan is contributory. Some employees may resent paying their money to the employer for benefits that are contingent on the firm's future financial ability to pay claims. If claims are denied, employees under a contributory plan are more likely to be bitter toward the employer than they would be if the benefit plan were noncontributory. Finally, ERISA requires that a trust be established to hold employees' contributions until the plan uses the funds; both the establishment and maintenance of the trust result in increased administrative costs to the employer.

■ A nonunion situation. Self-funding of benefits for union employees may not be feasible if a firm is subject to collective bargaining. Self-funding (at least by the employer) clearly cannot be used if benefits are provided through a negotiated trusteeship. Even when collective bargaining results in benefits being provided through an individual employer plan, unions often insist that benefits be insured to guarantee that union members will actually receive them. An employer's decision about whether to use self-funding is most likely motivated by the potential to save money. When unions approve self-funding, they also frequently insist that some of the savings be passed on to union members through additional or increased benefits.

■ The ability to effectively and efficiently handle claims. One reason that many employers do not use totally self-funded and self-administered benefit plans is the difficulty in handling claims as efficiently and effectively as an insurance company or other benefit-plan administrator would handle them. Unless an employer is extremely large, only one person or a few persons will be needed to handle claims. Who in the organization can properly train and supervise these people? Can they be replaced if they should leave? Will anyone have the expertise to properly handle the unusual or complex claims that might occur? Many employers want some insulation from their employees in the handling of claims. If employees are unhappy with claim payments under a self-administered plan, dissatisfaction (and possibly legal actions) will be directed toward the employer rather than toward the insurance company. The employer's inability to handle claims, or its lack of interest in wanting to handle them, does not completely rule out the use of self-funding. As will be discussed later, employers can have claims handled by another party through an administrative-services-only (ASO) contract.

■ The ability to provide other administrative services. In addition to claims, the employer must determine whether the other administrative services normally included in an insured arrangement can be provided in a cost-effective manner. These services are associated with plan design, actuarial calculations, statistical reports, communication with employees, compliance with government regulations, and the preparation of government reports. Many of these costs are relatively fixed, regardless of the size of the employer, and unless the employer can spread these costs out over a large number of employees, self-administration will not be economically feasible. As with claims administration, an employer can purchase needed services from other sources.

■ The ability to obtain discounts from medical care providers if medical expense benefits are self-funded. In order to obtain much of the cost savings associated with managed care plans, the employer must be able to secure discounts from the providers of medical care. Large employers whose employees live in a relatively concentrated geographic region may be able to enter into contracts with local providers. Other employers may use the services of third-party administrators who have either established or entered into contracts with preferred-provider networks.

The extent of total self-funding and self-administration differs significantly among the different types of group benefit plans. Plans that provide life insurance or accidental death and dismemberment benefits do not usually lend themselves to self-funding because of infrequent and large claims that are difficult to predict. Only very large employers can expect stable and predictable claims on an annual basis. In addition, federal income tax laws impede the use of self-funding for death benefits, because any payments to beneficiaries are considered taxable income for beneficiaries. Such a limitation does not exist if the plan is insured.

The most widespread use of self-funding and self-administration occurs in short-term disability income plans, particularly those in which the maximum duration of benefits is limited to six months or less. For employers of most any size, the number and average length of short-term absences from work are relatively predictable. In addition, the payment of claims is relatively simple, because benefits can be (and usually are) made through the usual payroll system of the employer.

Long-term disability income benefits are occasionally self-funded by large employers. Like death claims, long-term disability income claims are difficult to predict for small employers because of their infrequent occurrence and potentially large size. In addition, because small employers receive only a few claims of this type, self-administration of such claims is economically unjustifiable.

The larger the employer, the more likely that its medical expense plan is self-funded. The major problem with a self-funded medical expense plan is not the prediction of claims frequency but rather the prediction of the average severity of claims. Although infrequent, claims of $500,000 to $1,000,000 or more do occasionally occur. Most small and medium-sized employers are unwilling to take a chance that they might have to pay such a large claim. Only employers with several thousand employees are large enough to assume the risk that such claims will regularly occur and have the resources that will be necessary to pay any unexpectedly large claims. This does not mean that smaller employers cannot self-fund medical benefits. To avoid the uncertainty of catastrophic claims, these employers often self-fund basic medical expense benefits and insure major medical expense benefits or self-fund their entire coverage but purchase stop-loss protection.

It is not unusual to use self-funding and self-administration in other types of benefit plans, such as those providing coverage for dental care, vision care, prescription drugs, or legal expenses. Initially, it may be difficult to predict the extent to which these plans will be utilized. However, once the plans have "matured," the number and dollar amount of claims tends to be fairly stable. Furthermore, these plans are commonly subject to maximums so that the employer has little or no risk of catastrophic claims. Although larger employers may be able to economically administer the plans themselves, smaller employers commonly purchase administrative services.

Self-Funding with Stop-Loss Coverage and/or ASO Arrangements

Two of the problems associated with self-funding and self-administration are the risk of catastrophic claims and the employer's inability to provide administrative services in a cost-effective manner. For each of these problems, however, solutions have evolved—namely, stop-loss coverage and ASO contracts—that still allow an employer to use elements of self-funding. Although an ASO contract and stop-loss coverage can be provided separately, they are commonly written together. In fact, most insurance companies require an employer with stop-loss coverage to have a self-funded plan administered under an ASO arrangement, either by the insurance company or by a third-party administrator.

Until recently, stop-loss coverage and ASO contracts were generally provided by insurance companies and were available only to employers with at least several hundred employees. However, these arrangements are increasingly becoming available to small employers, and in many cases the administrative services are now being purchased from third-party administrators who operate independently from insurance companies.

Stop-Loss Coverage

Aggregate stop-loss coverage is one form of protection for employers against an unexpectedly high level of claims. If total claims exceed some specified dollar limit, the insurance company assumes the financial responsibility for those claims that are over the limit, subject to the maximum reimbursement specified in the contract. The limit is usually applied on an annual basis and is expressed as some percentage of expected claims (typically between 115 percent and 135 percent). This arrangement can be thought of as a form of reinsurance and is treated as such by some regulatory officials. It is interesting to note that the employer is responsible for payment of all claims to employees, including any payments that are received from the insurance company under the stop-loss coverage. In fact, because the insurance company has no responsibility to the employees, no reserve for claims must be established.

Aggregate stop-loss coverage results in (1) an improved cash flow for the employer and (2) a minimization of premium taxes, because they must be paid only on the stop-loss coverage. However, these advantages are partially (and perhaps totally) offset by the cost of the coverage. In addition, many insurance companies insist that the employer purchase other insurance coverages or administrative services to obtain aggregate stop-loss coverage.

Stop-loss plans may also be written on a specific basis, similar to the way an insured plan with a deductible is written. In fact, this arrangement (most commonly used with medical expense plans) is often referred to as a *big-deductible plan* or as *shared funding*. The deductible amount may vary from $1,000 to $250,000 but is most commonly in the range of $10,000 to $20,000. It is usually applied on an annual basis and pertains to each person insured under the contract. Although stop-loss coverage was once written primarily for large employers, more recently it also has been written for employers with as few as 25 employees. These plans have particular appeal for small employers who have had better-than-average claims experience but who are too small to qualify for experience rating and the accompanying premium savings.

The deductible specified in the stop-loss coverage is the amount the employer must assume before the stop-loss carrier is responsible for claims and is different from the deductible that an employee must satisfy under the medical expense plan. For example, employees may be given a medical expense plan that has a $200 annual deductible and an 80 percent coinsurance provision. If stop-loss coverage with a $5,000 limit has been purchased, an employee will have to assume the first $200 in annual medical expenses, and the plan will then pay 80 percent of any additional expenses until it has paid a total of $5,000. At that time, the stop-loss carrier will reimburse the plan for any additional amounts that the plan must pay to the employee. The stop-loss carrier has no responsibility to pay the employer's share of claims under any circumstances, and most insurance companies require that employees be made aware of this fact.

Misunderstandings often arise over two variations in specific stop-loss contracts. Most contracts settle claims on a *paid* basis, which means that only those claims paid during the stop-loss period under a benefit plan are taken into consideration in determining the liability of the stop-loss carrier. Some stop-loss contracts, however, settle claims on an *incurred* basis. In these cases, the stop-loss carrier's liability is determined on the basis of the date a loss took place rather than when the benefit plan actually made payment. For example, assume an employee was hospitalized last December, but the claim was not paid until this year. This is an incurred claim for last year but a paid claim for this year.

A second variation has an impact on an employer's cash flow. Assume an employer has a medical expense plan with a $20,000 stop-loss limit and that an employee has a claim of $38,000. If the stop-loss contract is written on a *reimbursement basis,* the employer's plan must pay the $38,000 claim before the plan's administrator can submit an $18,000 claim to the stop-loss carrier. If the stop-loss contract is written on an *advance-funding basis,* the employer's plan does not actually have to pay the employee before seeking reimbursement.

Most insurance companies that provide stop-loss coverage for medical expense plans also agree to provide a conversion contract to employees whose coverage terminates. However, the employer must pay an additional monthly charge to have this benefit for employees.

ASO Contracts

Under an ASO contract, the employer purchases specific administrative services from an insurance company or from an independent third-party administrator. These services usually include the administration of claims, but they may also include a broad array of other services. In effect, the employer has the option to purchase services for those administrative functions that can be handled more cost-effectively by another party. Under ASO contracts, the administration of claims is performed in much the same way as it is under a minimum-premium plan; that is, the administrator has the authority to pay claims from a bank account that belongs to the employer or from segregated funds in the administrator's hands. However, the administrator is not responsible for paying claims from its own assets if the employer's account is insufficient.

In addition to listing the services that will be provided, an ASO contract also stipulates the administrator's authority and responsibility, the length of the contract, the provisions for terminating and amending the contract, and the manner in which disputes between the employer and the administrator will be settled. The charges for the services provided under the contract may be stated in one or some combination of the following ways:

- A percentage of the amount of claims paid
- A flat amount per processed claim
- A flat charge per employee
- A flat charge for the employer

Payments for ASO contracts are regarded as fees for services performed, and they are therefore not subject to state premium taxes. However, one similarity to a traditional insurance arrangement may be present: The administrator may agree to continue paying any unsettled claims after the contract's termination but only with funds provided by the employer.

Funding Through a 501(c)(9) Trust

Section 501(c)(9) of the Internal Revenue Code provides for the establishment of voluntary employees' beneficiary associations, commonly called either *501(c)(9) trusts* or *VEBAs,* which are funding vehicles for the employee benefits that are offered to members. The trusts have been allowed for many years, but until the passage of the Tax Reform Act of 1969, they were primarily used by negotiated trusteeships and association groups. The liberalized tax treatment of the funds accumulated by these trusts resulted in their increased use by employers as a method of self-funding employee benefit plans. However, the Tax Reform Act of 1984 imposed more restrictive provisions on 501(c)(9) trusts, and their use has diminished somewhat, particularly by smaller employers who previously had overfunded their trusts primarily as a method to shelter income from taxation.

Advantages

The use of a 501(c)(9) trust offers the employer some advantages over a benefit plan that is self-funded from current revenue. Contributions can be made to the trust and can be deducted for federal income tax purposes at that time, just as if the trust were an insurance company. Appreciation in the value of the trust assets or investment income earned on the trust assets is also free of taxation. The trust is best suited for an employer who wishes to establish either a fund for claims that have been incurred but not paid or a fund for possible claim fluctuations. If the employer does not use a 501(c)(9) trust in establishing these funds, contributions cannot be deducted until they are paid in the form of benefits to employees. In addition, earnings on these funds are subject to taxation.

Although the Internal Revenue Code requires that certain fiduciary standards be maintained regarding the investment of the trust assets, the employer does have some latitude and does have the potential for earning a return on the trust assets that is higher than what is earned on the reserves held by insurance companies. A 501(c)(9) trust also lends itself to use by a contributory self-funded plan, because ERISA requires that, under a self-funded benefit plan, a trust must be established to hold the contributions of employees until they are used to pay benefits.

There is also flexibility regarding contributions to the trust. Although the IRS will not permit a tax deduction for overfunding a trust, there is no requirement that the trust must maintain enough assets to pay claims that have been incurred but not yet paid. Consequently, an employer can underfund the trust in bad times and make up for this underfunding in good times with larger-than-normal contributions. However, any underfunding must be shown as a contingent liability on the employer's balance sheet.

Disadvantages

The use of a 501(c)(9) trust is not without its drawbacks. The cost of establishing and maintaining the trust may be prohibitive, especially for small employers. In addition, the employer must be concerned about the administrative aspects of the plan and the fact that claims might deplete the trust's assets. However, as long as the trust is properly funded, ASO contracts and stop-loss coverage can be purchased.

Requirements for Establishment

To qualify under Section 501(c)(9), a trust must meet certain requirements, some of which may hinder its establishment. These requirements include the following:

- Membership in the trust must be objectively restricted to those persons who share a common employment-related bond. IRS regulations interpret this broadly to include active employees and their dependents, surviving dependents, and employees who are retired, laid off, or disabled. Except for plans maintained pursuant to collective-bargaining agreements, benefits must be provided under a classification of employees that the IRS does not find to be discriminatory in favor of highly compensated individuals. It is permissible for life insurance, disability, severance pay, and supplemental unemployment compensation benefits to be based on a uniform percentage of compensation. In addition, the following persons may be excluded in determining whether the discrimination rule has been satisfied: (1) employees who have not completed three years of service, (2) employees under age 21, (3) seasonal or less-than-half-time employees, and (4) employees covered by a collective-bargaining agreement if the class of benefits was subject to good-faith bargaining.
- With two exceptions, membership in the trust must be voluntary on the part of employees. Members can be required to participate (1) as a result of collective bargaining or (2) when participation is not detrimental to them. In general, participation is not regarded as detrimental if the employee is not required to make any contributions.
- The trust must provide only eligible benefits. The list of eligible coverages is broad enough that a trust can provide benefits because of death, medical expenses, disability, and unemployment. Retirement benefits, deferred compensation, and group property and liability insurance cannot be provided.

- The sole purpose of the trust must be to provide benefits to its members or their beneficiaries. Trust assets can be used to pay the administrative expenses of the trust, but they cannot revert to the employer. If the trust is terminated, any assets that remain after all existing liabilities have been satisfied must either be used to provide other benefits or be distributed to members of the trust.
- The trust must be controlled by (1) its membership, (2) independent trustees (such as a bank), or (3) trustees or other fiduciaries, at least some of whom are designated by or on behalf of the members. Most 501(c)(9) trusts are controlled by independent trustees selected by the employer.

Limitation on Contributions

The contributions to a 501(c)(9) trust (except collectively bargained plans for which Treasury regulations prescribe separate rules) are limited to the sum of (1) the qualified direct cost of the benefits provided for the taxable year and (2) any permissible additions to a reserve (called a *qualified asset account*). The qualified direct cost of benefits is the amount that would have been deductible for the year if the employer had paid benefits from current revenue.

The permissible additions may be made only for disability, medical, supplemental unemployment, severance pay, and life insurance benefits. In general, the amount of the permissible additions includes (1) any sums that are reasonably and actuarially necessary to pay claims that have been incurred but remain unpaid at the close of the tax year and (2) any administration costs with respect to these claims. If medical or life insurance benefits are provided to retirees, deductions are also allowed for funding these benefits on a level basis over the working lives of the covered employees. However, for retirees' medical benefits, current medical costs must be used rather than costs based on projected inflation. In addition, a separate account must be established for postretirement benefits provided to key employees. Contributions to these accounts are treated as annual additions for purposes of applying the limitations that exist for contributions and benefits under qualified retirement plans.

The amount of certain benefits for which deductions are allowed is limited. Life insurance benefits for retired employees cannot exceed amounts that are tax free under Section 79. Annual disability benefits cannot exceed the lesser of (1) 75 percent of a disabled person's average compensation for the highest three years or (2) $135,000. (This amount is subject to periodic indexing.) Supplemental unemployment compensation benefits and severance benefits cannot exceed 75 percent of average benefits paid plus administrative costs during any two of the immediately preceding seven years. In determining this limit, annual benefits in excess of $45,000 cannot be taken into account.

In general, it is required that the amount of any permissible additions be actuarially certified, although deductible contributions can be made to reserves without such certification as long as certain safe-harbor limits on the size of the reserve are not exceeded. The safe-harbor limits for supplemental unemployment compensation benefits and severance benefits are the same as the amounts previously mentioned. For short-term disability benefits, the limit is equal to 17.5 percent of benefit costs (other than insurance premiums for the current year), plus administrative costs for the prior year. For medical benefits, the percentage is 35 percent. The Internal Revenue Code provides that the limits for life insurance benefits and long-term disability income benefits will be those prescribed by regulations. However, no regulations have been issued.

Employer deductions cannot exceed the limits as previously described. However, any excess contributions may be deducted in future years to the extent that contributions for those years are below the permissible limits.

There are several potential adverse tax consequences if a 501(c)(9) trust does not meet prescribed standards. If reserves are above permitted levels, additional contributions to the reserves are not deductible and earnings on the excess reserves are subject to tax as unrelated business income. [This effectively negates any possible advantage of using a 501(c)(9) trust to prefund postretirement medical benefits.] In addition, an excise tax is imposed on employers maintaining a trust that provides disqualified benefits. The tax is equal to 100 percent of the disqualified benefits, which include (1) medical and life insurance benefits provided to key employees outside the separate accounts that must be established, (2) discriminatory medical or life insurance benefits for retirees, and (3) any portion of the trust's assets that revert to the employer.

STUDY QUESTIONS

1. What are the reasons for increased employer interest in using alternative methods to fund employee benefit plans?

2. Why is an insurance company concerned with the financial position and credit rating of an employer to whom it issues a group insurance contract that contains a premium-delay arrangement?

3. a. Why are reserve-reduction arrangements usually not used during the first year of a group insurance contract?
   b. What is the responsibility of the employer under a reserve-reduction arrangement if an insurance contract is terminated?

4. a. Explain how minimum-premium plans minimize premium taxes.
   b. What is the responsibility of the insurance company under a minimum-premium plan for paying claims and maintaining reserves?

5. Explain the mechanics of retrospective rating.

6. Explain the conditions that are generally considered desirable before an employer should use total self-funding.

7. Why are life insurance benefits usually not self-funded?

8. What is the difference between aggregate stop-loss coverage and specific stop-loss coverage?

9. a. What are the tax advantages of a 501(c)(9) trust that are not present in benefit plans self-funded from current revenue?
   b. What conditions must be satisfied for a 501(c)(9) trust to meet IRS requirements?
   c. What are the limitations in amounts that may be contributed to a 501(c)(9) trust?

CHAPTER 15

Group Insurance Rate Making

OBJECTIVES

■ Describe the process by which manual premium rates are calculated.

■ Explain how manual premium rates are used to determine group term life insurance premiums, both for large groups and for small groups.

■ Identify the ways in which the manual rating process for other types of group insurance differs from the process for group term life insurance.

■ Explain the rationale for experience rating.

■ Describe the process of using experience rating to calculate dividends.

■ Explain how experience rating for determining prospective premiums differs from experience rating for calculating dividends.

 One of the least understood aspects of group insurance is the pricing process. In the simplest sense, group insurance pricing is no different from pricing in other industries. The insurance company must generate enough revenue to cover its costs (claims and expenses) and to contribute to the net worth of the company. However, this similarity is often overlooked because of the unique terminology that is associated with insurance pricing and because the price of a group insurance product is initially determined on the basis of expected, but uncertain, future events rather than on current tangible cost estimates. In addition, a group insurance plan may be subject to experience rating, so that the final price to the consumer can be determined only after the coverage period has ended.

The purpose of this chapter is not to make readers experts in the actuarial intricacies of group insurance pricing, commonly referred to as *rate making,* but rather to provide an understanding of basic principles and concepts. Rate making consists of two distinct steps: (1) the determination of a unit price, referred to as a *rate* or *premium rate,* for each unit of benefit (such as each $1,000 of life insurance) and (2) the determination of the total price, or premium, that the policyholder will pay for the entire amount of coverage purchased. The mechanics of rate making differ, depending upon whether a particular group is subject to manual rating or experience rating. When manual rating is used, the premium rate is determined independently of a particular group's claims; when experience rating is used, the past claims experience of a group is considered in determining future premiums for the group and/or in adjusting past premiums after a policy period has ended.

The major objective of rate making for all types of group insurance is to develop premium rates that are both adequate and equitable. Adequate rates must be sufficient to cover both incurred claims and expenses and to generate the desired profit or contribution to the insurance company's surplus. Obviously, the success and solvency of any group insurance operation is contingent on the long-run adequacy of premium rates. Therefore, several states, concerned about the solvency of insurance companies, have laws and regulations regarding the adequacy of rates. The most significant of these is the New York law that prohibits any insurance company doing business in that state from issuing in any state a group health insurance contract (either medical expense or disability income) that does not appear to be self-supporting on the basis of reasonable assumptions concerning expected claims and expenses.

Equitable rates require that each group pay a premium that reflects the cost of providing coverage to that group. Again, practical considerations and state regulations act to encourage equity. The overpricing of group coverage for some segments of the market will result in lost business; the underpricing for other segments will attract unprofitable business. Most states also have laws and regulations that try to encourage equity by prohibiting unfair discrimination in insurance rates. The objective of equity has resulted in group insurance rates that differ because of such factors as the age, sex, and income distribution of a group's members and the size of a group, its geographic location, its occupational hazards, and its claims experience. As is discussed later, the factors that are considered vary with the type of group insurance coverage.

MANUAL RATING

In the manual rating process, premium rates are established only for broad classes of group insurance business, and the insurance company does not consider the past claims experience of a particular group when determining that group's rates. However, claims experience is not entirely ignored because the aggregate claims experience for a class of business is used to determine the premium rates for that class.

Manual rating is used with small groups for which no credible individual claims experience is available. This lack of credibility exists because the group's size makes it impossible to determine whether other-than-average claims experience is due to random chance or is truly reflective of the group. Manual rating is also frequently used to determine the initial premiums for groups that are subject to experience rating, particularly when a group's past experience is unobtainable or when a group is being written for the first time. Experience rating typically uses a weighting of manual rates and the actual experience of a group to determine the premium. (Rates for very large groups may be based solely on a group's own experience.)

Rating Basis

Prior to the actual calculation of manual premium rates, it is necessary to develop a basis on which the rates will be determined. This involves a decision regarding (1) what benefit unit to use, (2) the extent to which rates will be refined by factors affecting claims, and (3) the frequency with which premiums will be paid.

Benefit Unit

Subject to certain adjustments, the premium for a group is calculated by multiplying the premium rate by the number of benefit units provided. While variations do occasionally exist, the benefit units predominantly used for the most common types of group insurance are shown in Table 15-1.

Factors Affecting Claims

As previously mentioned, equity requires that rates reflect those factors that result in different claims experience for different groups. Although there are variations among insurance companies, the following factors are used by most insurance companies to determine rates for life, disability income, medical expense, and dental insurance: the sex, age, geographic location, occupa-

TABLE 15-1
Common Benefit Units Used in Group Insurance

Type of Group Insurance	Benefit Unit
Term life (including accidental death and dismemberment)	Each $1,000 of death benefit
Short-term disability income	Each $10 of weekly income
Long-term disability income	Each $100 of monthly income
Medical expense (including dental)	Each employee and each category of dependents

tion, and income of group members; the size of the group; and the length of time that rates will be used.

Sex. The sex of insured persons is taken into account for determining rates for life, disability income, medical expense, and dental insurance.

Age. Age is also used as a rating factor for life, disability income, and medical expense insurance. Dental insurance rates usually do not take age into consideration.

Geographic Location. At one time, geographic location was a rating factor for medical expense and dental insurance only. However, an increasing number of insurance companies are using geographic variations for determining life and disability income insurance rates. For these latter types of insurance, rates may not be determined separately for a wide variety of locations. Rather, the insurance company may have only two or three rate schedules, with each schedule applying to several different geographic locations on the basis of past claims experience.

Occupation. Occupation is virtually always reflected in both group term life and accidental death and dismemberment insurance rates. It may also be reflected in disability income, medical expense, and dental insurance rates, but the number of groups for which it is of concern is relatively small. Consequently, some companies ignore it as a rating factor but may not write such coverages when certain occupations are involved.

Income. At one time, the income level of group members was commonly used as a factor in establishing disability income, medical expense, and dental insurance rates. Currently, income level is still a factor in determining dental insurance premiums, but it is more likely to be an underwriting consideration in disability income and medical expense insurance.

Size. The size of a group also affects rates because the proportion of the premium needed for expenses decreases as the size of a group increases. All manual premium rates are based on an assumption that the size of a group falls within a certain range. If the size of a group varies from this range, an appropriate rate adjustment is made to reflect this differential. In addition, many insurers reserve the right to rerate a group during the period of the contract if the group changes in size by a certain percentage. This is particularly important in an era of downsizing and mergers.

Time. A final factor considered in the calculation of rates is the length of time for which the rates will be used. This is a concern primarily for coverages that involve medical and dental claims, which over time will be expected to increase in severity because of inflation. In inflationary times, monthly rates that are guaranteed for three months can be lower than those guaranteed for one year.

Frequency of Premium Payment Period

Because group insurance premiums are usually paid monthly, this is the period for which rates are generally determined. When premiums can be paid less frequently (such as annually), they are usually slightly lower than the sum of the monthly premiums for the same period of coverage.

Calculation of Manual Rates

Manual rating involves the calculation of the manual premium rates (also called *tabular rates*) that are quoted in an insurance company's rate book. These manual rates are applied to a specific group insurance case to determine a final premium rate (sometimes called an *average premium rate*) that then will be multiplied by the number of benefit units to obtain a premium for the group.

There are three different manual rating methods. However, if identical assumptions are used, each method should result in approximately the same premium for any given group. The first method determines separate manual premium rates for groups with certain characteristics that an insurance company feels will affect claims experience. A second approach establishes a single standard manual rate that is adjusted in the premium-calculation process to compensate for any characteristics that deviate from those of the standard group. A third method merely combines the first two approaches and considers some factors in determining the manual premium rate and other factors in determining the final premium rate.

The first step in the calculation of manual premium rates is the determination of the net premium rate, which is the amount necessary to support the cost of expected claims. For any given classification, the net premium rate is calculated by multiplying the probability (frequency) of a claim's occurring by the expected amount (severity) of the claim. For example, if the probability that an employee aged 50 will die in the next month is .0005, then the monthly net premium for each $1,000 of coverage is .0005 × $1,000, or $.50. Because premiums are collected before claims are paid, the insurance company adjusts this figure downward for anticipated interest earnings on these funds.

In general, insurance companies that write a large volume of any given type of group insurance rely on their own experience in determining the frequency and severity of future claims. Insurance companies that do not have enough past data for reliable future projections can turn to many sources for useful statistics. Probably the major source is the Society of Actuaries, which regularly collects and publishes aggregate data on the group insurance business that is written by a number of large group insurance companies. Other sources of information are industry trade organizations and various agencies of the federal government.

The second and final step in the calculation of manual premium rates is the adjustment of the net premium rates for expenses, a risk charge, and a contribution to surplus. Expenses include commissions, premium taxes, claims settlement costs, and other costs associated with the acquisition and servicing of group insurance business. The risk charge represents a contribution to the insurance company's contingency reserve as a cushion against unanticipated and catastrophic amounts of claims. The contribution to surplus or net worth represents the profit margin of the insurance company. While mutual companies are legally nonprofit, they, like stock insurance companies, require a contribution to net worth that is a source of financing for future growth.

From the standpoint of equity, the adjustment of the net premium rate is complex. Some factors, such as premium taxes and commissions, vary with the premium charge; however, the premium tax rate is not affected by the size of a group, whereas the commission rate decreases as the size of a group increases. To a large degree, the expenses of settling claims vary with the number, and not the size, of claims. It costs just as much administratively to pay a $10,000 claim under a group life insurance plan as it does to pay a $100,000 claim. Certain other costs tend to be fixed regardless of the size of a group. For simplicity, some insurance companies adjust, or load, their net premium rates by a constant percentage. However, other insurance companies consider the different patterns of expenses by using a percentage plus a constant charge. For example, if the net premium rate is $.60, this might be increased by 20 percent plus $.10 to arrive at a manual premium rate of $.82 (that is, $.60 × 1.2 + $.10). Because neither approach adequately accounts for the difference in expenses as a result of a group's size, another adjustment based on the size of the group will be made in the calculation of the final premium rate.

Calculation of Premiums

Probably the best way to explain the actual calculation of group insurance premiums is to discuss some examples. The following analysis begins with a group term life insurance, with a later discussion on how the structure of manual premium rates and the premium calculation process differ for certain other types of group insurance.

Group Term Life Insurance

The mechanics of calculating a final premium rate and the premium for a particular group vary among insurance companies because of the differences in methods of preparing manual premium rates and the process by which adjustments are made to these rates.

The following example begins with Table 15-2, which is an abbreviated version of a set of rates on a monthly basis per $1,000 of coverage at selected ages. As with most rate tables, the ages are those at a person's attained age (nearest birthday).

These rates are loaded for expenses and assume that the coverage contains a waiver-of-premium provision on disabled lives, accidental death and dismemberment coverage, and a conversion privilege. Consequently, the rates are higher than if none of these additional benefits were included. When an employee converts coverage to an individual policy, a charge is assessed against the group insurance business of an insurance company to reflect the increased mortality that results from the adverse selection on conversions. The amount of this assessment (commonly $50 to $75 per $1,000 of converted insurance) is transferred to the individual insurance department of the company to compensate it for having to write the converted business at too low a rate.

The premium-calculation process starts with the determination of an "unadjusted cost," based on a census of the covered employees and the manual rates. For example, assume a firm has 230 employees. For the sake of simplicity, also assume that each of these employees has $25,000 of life insurance and that the group has the age distribution shown in Table 15-3. The unadjusted cost is then calculated as shown in Table 15-4.

TABLE 15-2

Age at Nearest Birthday	Male Rate	Female Rate
20	$ 0.16	$ 0.10
25	0.18	0.11
30	0.21	0.12
35	0.24	0.15
40	0.37	0.21
45	0.48	0.30
50	0.81	0.48
55	1.24	0.75
60	1.87	1.12
65	2.83	1.70
70	4.35	2.52

TABLE 15-3

Age	Males	Females
25	20	30
30	0	30
35	10	30
40	30	10
45	30	10
50	20	10

TABLE 15-4

Age	Sex	Number of Employees		Amount of Coverage (in Thousands)		Unadjusted Rate (per Thousand)		Unadjusted Cost
25	M	20	×	25	×	$0.18	=	$ 90.00
35	M	10	×	25	×	0.24	=	60.00
40	M	30	×	25	×	0.37	=	277.50
45	M	30	×	25	×	0.48	=	360.00
50	M	20	×	25	×	0.81	=	405.00
25	F	30	×	25	×	0.11	=	82.50
30	F	30	×	25	×	0.12	=	90.00
35	F	30	×	25	×	0.15	=	112.50
40	F	10	×	25	×	0.21	=	52.50
45	F	10	×	25	×	0.30	=	75.00
50	F	10	×	25	×	0.48	=	120.00
					Total unadjusted cost	=	$1,725.00	

The second step is to reduce the sum of the unadjusted cost by a percentage based on the volume of a group insurance case as determined by its monthly premium. The reductions used in this example are shown in Table 15-5 (for selected premiums).

Thus, the initial monthly premium for the group in this example is

Unadjusted cost	$1,725.00
Minus expense reduction (7 percent)	− 120.75
Adjusted monthly premium	$1,604.25

TABLE 15-5

Monthly Premium Before Reduction	Percentage Expense Reduction
Under $200	0%
200–249	1
250–299	2
.	.
.	.
.	.
1,000–1,499	6
1,500–1,999	7
2,000–3,999	8
.	.
.	.
.	.
60,000–79,999	19
80,000 and over	20

The initial monthly premium is also used to calculate the final monthly premium rate per $1,000 of protection for the group:

$$\text{Monthly premium rate per thousand} = \frac{\text{Adjusted monthly premium}}{\text{Total volume (in thousands)}}$$

$$= \frac{\$1,604.25}{(230 \times \$25,000) \div \$1,000}$$

$$= \frac{\$1,604.25}{5,750}$$

$$= \$0.28$$

This final monthly premium rate (usually rounded to either the nearest cent or one-tenth of a cent) is used throughout the first policy year and is multiplied each month by the amount of insurance in force to calculate the monthly premium due. Adjustments to the final monthly premium rate as a result of changes in the makeup of employees by age or sex are not made until the beginning of the next policy year as part of the renewal process. The initial rate is guaranteed for at least one year, assuming no change in the benefit structure of the plan. However, two- and three-year rate guarantees are not unusual.

Manual rates are designed so that policies for most industries can be written at those rates. However, employers in industries that are considered hazardous may be charged higher rates. These increased rates are usually in the form of a surcharge per $1,000 of coverage that is added to the unadjusted cost before the expense reduction percentage is applied. For example, an industry that would be expected to have about one death claim per year per 1,000 employees in excess of those assumed in the manual rates might be charged for this excess mortality with a surcharge of $.06 per $1,000 of coverage per month. Therefore, the adjusted monthly premium would be calculated as follows:

Unadjusted cost	$1,604.25
Plus industry surcharge	+ 345.00
Total cost before expense reduction	$1,949.25
Minus expense reduction (7 percent)	− 136.45
Adjusted monthly premium	$1,812.80

Similarly, the expectation of two extra death claims per year would result in an added premium of $.12 per $1,000 per month, or $690.

Variations for Large Groups. Insurance companies use the premium-calculation process discussed above for most groups over a certain size, usually from 10 or more to 50 or more lives, but variations do exist. For example, some insurance companies do not incorporate a charge for a waiver of premium or accidental death and dismemberment coverage into their manual rates. Rather, an extra charge, which usually differs by industry, is added for this coverage. Also, some companies use (and are required to use in a few states) manual rates that vary by age but not sex. These unisex rate tables are based on assumptions about the ratio of males to females in the group. However, an adjustment is usually made in the premium-calculation process if the actual group ratio differs from this assumption.

Some companies incorporate a level of expenses into their manual rate so that there is no expense reduction for a certain-size group. In the final premium-calculation process, an adjustment is made; larger groups receive an expense reduction while smaller groups receive an expense surcharge. Table 15-6 is one such table of adjustments.

TABLE 15-6

Monthly Premium Before Adjustment	Percentage Adjustment
Under $200	+25%
200–249	+22
.	.
.	.
700–799	+1
800–999	0
1,000–1,099	−1
.	.
.	.
50,000–74,999	−14
75,000 and over	−15

Variations for Small Groups. The manual-rating process for small groups, including those written by multiple-employer trusts, differs from that of large groups in several ways. In general, the manual rates are banded by age, typically in five-year intervals. Table 15-7 is an example of one such monthly rate table for each $1,000 of coverage.

An unadjusted cost is developed based on a census of the employees by age and by sex unless unisex rates are used. Because the manual rates are loaded for most expenses, and because the groups written tend to be reasonably close in size, typically no adjustment for size is made. However, to compensate for the expenses of periodic billings, most insurance companies apply a flat fee to all groups, commonly between $10 and $20 per billing. Some companies do not levy this charge if the premium is paid annually. To reflect the administrative costs associated with record keeping, some insurance companies also levy a modest one-time expense charge when coverage is added for a new employee.

TABLE 15-7		
Age at Nearest Birthday	**Male Rate**	**Female Rate**
Under 30	$0.24	$0.10
30–34	0.24	0.13
35–39	0.25	0.15
40–44	0.36	0.20
45–49	0.58	0.36
50–54	0.91	0.54
55–59	1.55	0.79
60–64	1.93	1.02
65–69	3.30	1.81
70 and over	6.80	3.23

In contrast to large groups—for which the initial monthly premium is used to determine a monthly premium rate that applies for a specified period of time—the monthly premium rate for small groups is recalculated each month based not only on the volume of insurance but also on changes in the makeup of employees by age and sex (unless unisex rates are used), just as if the group were being newly written. However, most insurance companies do guarantee that the manual rates used when the group was initially written (and any future manual rates applicable to the group) remain applicable for some period of time, with 12 months being common.

Accidental Death and Dismemberment Insurance

Accidental death and dismemberment insurance is usually not written as a separate coverage, but rather it is added by an endorsement to a group term life insurance contract. A single manual rate typically applies to all employees regardless of age or sex, but it will vary depending on whether coverage is written (1) for nonoccupational accidents or (2) on a 24-hour basis for both nonoccupational and occupational accidents. The rate for nonoccupational coverage generally does not vary by industry and ranges from $.02 to $.05 per $1,000 of principal sum per month. However, the rate for coverage on a 24-hour basis does vary by industry, and, although it falls within this same range for low-risk industries, it may be several times higher for hazardous industries. Some companies calculate a separate cost for the accidental death and dismemberment coverage and add it to the charge for the group term life insurance. However, because most employers purchase accidental death and dismemberment coverage, other insurance companies incorporate the cost into the manual rates for group term life insurance. When this is done, the principal sum is equal to the amount of life insurance protection that is purchased, and an additional charge is levied only if a higher level of accidental death and dismemberment coverage is desired.

Dependent Life Insurance

Dependent life insurance may be added as additional coverage to a group life insurance contract that provides life insurance protection for employees. Because dependent life insurance coverage is usually a modest fixed amount (such as $2,000 on the spouse and $1,000 on each child) that generates a relatively small additional premium, a very simplified rate structure tends to be used. However, several variations do exist. Some insurance companies have a single flat rate, independent of the type or number of dependents, for each employee who has dependent coverage. Other companies have two separate flat rates: one for the spouse's coverage and the other for the children's coverage. The rate for the children's coverage is a family rate regardless of the number of children, and it is based upon an average-sized family.

Flat rates are based on the assumption that the group has an average age mix of employees. If the group of employees is older than average, the flat rate for dependent coverage may be adjusted (particularly when it applies to spouses) to reflect the likelihood that the dependents are also above average in age when compared with the dependents of most other groups. A flat rate is commonly used when the cost of dependent coverage is paid entirely by the employees. The uniform charge is easy to communicate to employees, and it simplifies the payroll-deduction process for the employer.

Some insurance companies also use a rate for dependent coverage that varies with the employee's age, thereby assuming that older employees have older dependents. Basing the rate on the employee's age may seem illogical, but it is administratively simpler and less expensive than having to determine the ages of dependents. A single variable rate may apply to the total family coverage for the spouse and all children, or it may apply only to the spouse. In this latter case, a flat rate is generally used if coverage for the children is also provided.

It is becoming less common to see dependent life insurance added to the basic group life coverage for an employee. Instead, this coverage is more frequently being written as an employee-pay-all voluntary benefit, with higher amounts of coverage available.

Short-Term Disability Income Insurance

In addition to varying by age, sex, and possibly geographic location, manual rates for short-term disability income insurance also differ by (1) the maximum benefit period, (2) the length of the waiting period, and (3) the writing of coverage either on a 24-hour basis or only for nonoccupational disabilities.

Some insurance companies (particularly for small groups) have only a single standard short-term disability income plan that they sell, and therefore they only need a single manual rate table. Other companies allow the employer some flexibility in designing the plan to be purchased, and rather than make adjustments to a single rate table, these companies usually have several rate tables that vary by such factors as maximum benefit period (such as 13 or 26 weeks) and waiting period (such as seven days for all disabilities or seven days for illnesses and no waiting period for injuries). If any other variations are allowed, appropriate adjustments are made.

An adjustment may be made for the nature of the industry the group represents. Ignoring the occupational injuries and diseases that are covered under workers' compensation insurance, a few occupations are still characterized by higher-than-average disability income claims. As an alternative to a rate adjustment, some insurance companies have underwriting standards that prohibit the writing of coverage for these groups.

TABLE 15-8		
Monthly Manual Rates per $10 Weekly Benefit		
Age	**Male**	**Female**
Under 30	$0.48	$1.25
30–34	0.52	1.25
35–39	0.56	1.25
40–44	0.72	1.21
45–49	0.81	1.21
50–54	1.01	1.31
55–59	1.21	1.53
60–64	1.61	1.61
65–69	2.01	2.01
70 and over	2.16	2.16

Until the passage of amendments to the Pregnancy Discrimination Act and various state laws, it was common for insurance companies to have one manual rate for plans that did not provide benefits for pregnancy-related disabilities and another for plans that did provide such benefits. Because most employers can no longer exclude pregnancy as a cause of disability, rates for coverage without this benefit are usually not published, except for the employers of small groups that still have an option regarding this benefit.

In contrast to group life insurance for which the rates for females are lower than the rates for males, disability income rates are higher for females. Ignoring pregnancy-related disabilities, the claims of females at younger ages still somewhat exceed those of males. However, because male and female claims are comparable at older ages, the rates for later years seldom vary. Table 15-8, which illustrates one insurance company's monthly manual rates per $10 of weekly benefit for 26 weeks following a seven-day waiting period, shows how this rate differential is even more pronounced at younger ages if maternity coverage is included.

In the past, it was common for short-term disability income rates to be expressed on the basis of each $10 of weekly benefit. This is probably still the norm, but some insurance companies are now expressing their rates in terms of a higher weekly benefit, such as $50 or $100.

Long-Term Disability Income Insurance

Like short-term disability income rates, the manual rates for long-term coverage vary by age, sex, the length of the benefit period, the length of the waiting period and possibly geographic location. In addition, the manual rates reflect the fact that benefits will be integrated with Social Security and certain other disability income benefits for which an employee might be eligible. To the extent that variations are allowed in the integration provision that was assumed in developing the manual rates, an adjustment will be made during premium calculation. As is also the case with short-term rates, an adjustment might be made for certain occupations.

Unlike short-term disability income rates that are commonly expressed on the basis of a weekly benefit, long-term rates are typically expressed on the basis of a monthly benefit, usually per $100. In contrast to the coverages previously discussed, long-term disability claims fluctuate with general economic conditions. Consequently, insurance companies review and possibly revise their manual rates (and/or their underwriting standards) as economic conditions change. The period of time for which rates are guaranteed from one to three years, depending on the industry in which the employees work.

Medical Expense Insurance

In many ways, the manual rates for medical expense insurance (and also dental insurance) are similar to those for disability income insurance because variations exist by age, sex, and the provisions of the plan, including the size of the deductible, the coinsurance percentage, and the level of benefits. Most insurance companies have manual rates for the few standard plans that will be sold, and only large employers are given the flexibility to deviate from these plans. Any such deviation will then be reflected in adjustments to the manual rates. Adjustments may also be made to the manual rates if the employer is in an industry that is characterized by higher-than-average claims.

One other factor, geographic location, is always a variable in the manual rates because of the significant differences in medical costs across the country. Depending on group size, an adjustment for location may be made in one of two ways. For large groups, the rating process usually starts with a manual rate that does not consider the location of employees. Each county (or other geographic subdivision) where coverage will be written is then assigned a factor that is based on the cost of health care in that location compared with the average cost that is assumed in the manual rates. For example, if costs in Seattle were 20 percent higher than average, the city would have a factor of 1.2 assigned to it. If all a firm's employees were there, the manual rates for that group would be multiplied by a location factor of 1.2 in the process of determining the group's premium. If employees were in several locations, a composite factor would be calculated as shown in Table 15-9.

TABLE 15-9				
	Number of Employees	Location Factor		Product
Seattle	100	×	1.2 =	120
Kansas City	70	×	1.0 =	70
Birmingham	30	×	.7 =	21
	200			211

$$\text{Location Factor} = \frac{\text{Total product}}{\text{Total number of employees}} = \frac{211}{200} = 1.055$$

Consequently the manual rate for this group would be increased by 5.5 percent because of the location of the employees.

A slightly different approach is used for small groups. Because employees are usually in one location, many companies have manual rate tables for between 10 and 20 rating territories, and each geographic area in which employees are located is assigned a specific territorial rating. The territorial classifications to the right are from the rating manual of one insurance company for some areas in three of the states where it writes business. The areas are identified by the first three digits of the ZIP code.

Table 15-10, an excerpt from the manual rate tables of the same company, shows how the monthly cost for coverage under a plan written through one of its multiple-employer trusts varies by geographic area.

This example lists manual rates for dependent coverage that are applied regardless of the number of children or the ages of the dependents. For any size group, this is one of several possible methods for pricing dependent coverage. Another method uses rates that vary by the number of children. Some rating structures also take the ages of dependents into consideration.

Because medical expense claims are continually increasing as a result of inflation, a trend factor must be applied to past claims experience when manual rates are developed. This is a complex and often perplexing task for most providers of medical expense coverage. Not only has the overall cost of medical care increased faster than the general cost of living (as measured by the consumer price index), but the increases have been erratic from year to year and virtually impossible to predict with any degree of accuracy. In addition, because these increases vary significantly for each category of medical expenses, different trend factors must be applied to different categories of claims.

California	
900–901	19
902–905	18
941	15
950–951	10
920–923	9
932–933	7
Georgia	
303	6
300, 302, 311, 314	5
309	4
Nebraska	
680, 685	3
683–684, 686–693	2
New Mexico	
Entire State	2

TABLE 15-10

Employee's Age	Class of Coverage	Area 3	Area 6	Area 10	Area 19
30–34	Male	$ 94	$123	$142	$ 205
30–34	Female	119	179	269	257
30–34	Employee and spouse	213	306	411	462
30–34	Employee, spouse, and children	348	452	510	756
30–34	Female employee and children	254	329	368	551
45–49	Male	166	214	250	360
45–49	Female	179	242	282	423
45–49	Employee and spouse	345	456	532	783
45–49	Employee, spouse, and children	489	632	740	1060
45–49	Female employee and children	323	418	490	700

At one time, group insurance premium rates were guaranteed for at least 12 months and possibly for as long as two or three years. However, to protect themselves against unexpected increases in claims due to increases in the cost of medical care, some insurance companies now guarantee medical expense rates for no more than six months. In fact, a number of multiple-employer trusts have only three-month guarantees or they contain provisions whereby rates can be increased at any time, provided notice of the rate increase is given 30 or 60 days in advance. Some companies allow an employer to select the length of the rate guarantee, such as six months or one year. However, the longer the rate guarantee, the higher the rate.

Dental Insurance

Although the rating of dental insurance is similar in many ways to the rating of medical expense insurance, there are some significant differences. Most insurance companies do not vary their manual rates by the ages of group members. Rather, an adjustment is usually made for the income levels of employees, because higher-paid persons are much more likely to obtain dental care. This adjustment is usually in the form of a percentage based on the extent to which the portion of employees with incomes higher than some figure (such as $30,000) exceeds the proportion of such employees that is assumed in the manual rates. An adjustment is also made for certain occupations (such as salespeople or teachers) that use dental services more frequently than average. Finally, the manual rates are usually increased when a plan is new (or expands benefits) if the employees have been informed beforehand. Under these circumstances, there is a tendency to postpone needed dental care until the plan is installed.

EXPERIENCE RATING

With experience rating, an insurance company considers a group's claims experience, either at the issue date or at the end of a policy period, when determining the premium rate for that group. When applied prospectively (that is, to future periods), experience rating is used to determine (1) adjustments in renewal premiums (either upward or downward) for those groups whose claims experience has deviated from what was expected and (2) initial premiums for large groups that change insurance carriers.

In addition to determining the premium rate for the next policy period (usually 12 months), experience rating is also used to compute the refund for those groups that had better claims experience than anticipated. This refund is commonly referred to as a *dividend* by mutual insurance companies and a *retrospective rate credit* or *premium refund* by stock insurance companies. (Because the majority of group insurance business is written by mutual companies, the term *dividend* will be used here.) Under some experience-rating arrangements, the premium at the end of a policy period may also be retroactively adjusted upward if a group's claims experience has been worse than anticipated, and an additional premium will be charged. These arrangements are not very common and were discussed in Chapter 14.

Rationale for Experience Rating

One argument in favor of experience rating is that it achieves the ultimate degree of premium equity among policyholders. Even though manual rating also results in equity because it considers the obvious factors that affect claims, it is impossible to measure and make adjustments in the manual rates for such factors as lifestyle, working conditions, and morale, all of which contribute to the level of claims experience. Experience rating is also the most cost-effective way to reflect the general health of a group in the premium that is charged.

Probably the major reason for using experience rating is the competition that exists in the group insurance marketplace. If an insurance company were to use identical rates for all groups regardless of their experience, the employers with good experience would soon seek out insurance companies that offered lower rates, or they would turn to self-funding as a way to reduce costs. The insurance company that did not consider claims experience would therefore be left with only the poor risks. This is exactly the situation that led most of the Blues to abandon community rating for group insurance cases above a certain size. Experience rating allows an insurance company to acquire and retain the "better" cases (from a claims experience standpoint) and to determine an appropriate premium for the groups that have worse-than-average claims experience.

Dividend Calculation

It is perhaps putting the cart before the horse to explain experience rating for dividend purposes (which occurs at the end of a policy period) before discussing its use to determine premiums (which occurs at the beginning of that period). However, calculating dividends tends to be more complicated and is easier to discuss first. An explanation follows of how the experience-rating process is different for determining premiums on a prospective basis.

At first glance, the process of using experience rating to determine dividends appears complex. However, the actual mechanics are relatively simple, and much of the confusion stems from the fact that the process is lengthy. In addition, both the format and the terminology vary somewhat among insurance companies. This discussion focuses on the illustration in Table 15-11 and explains the steps used to calculate the dividend for a group medical expense insurance case of about 450 lives. Although this illustration can be considered a typical example of a dividend calculation, variations could have been (and often are) used.

TABLE 15-11
Illustrative Dividend Calculation

1. Premiums paid		$1,950,000
2. Stop-loss limit (per claim)		$ 250,000
3. Incurred claims [a + (c − b)]		$1,620,000
a. Paid claims (below stop-loss limit)	$1,590,000	
b. Beginning reserve for claims	$ 400,000	
c. Ending reserve for claims	$ 430,000	
4. Expected claims		$1,700,000
5. Credibility factor		.8
6. Claims charge [(0.8 × 3) + (0.2 × 4)]		$1,636,000
7. Retention charge (d + e + f + g + h − i)		$ 225,000
d. Charge for stop-loss coverage	$ 40,000	
e. Commissions	$ 80,000	
f. Premium taxes	$ 40,000	
g Administration	$ 30,000	
h. Contingency reserve (risk charge) and	$ 60,000	
surplus contribution		
i. Interest on reserves	$ 25,000	
8. Dividend earned [1 − (6 + 7)]		$ 89,000
9. Deficit carried forward from prior periods		$ 42,000
10. Deficit to be carried forward to future periods		
(8 − 9) if less than 0		–
OR		
Dividend payable (8 − 9) if greater than 0		$ 47,000

Premiums Paid

Step 1 shows the total amount of premiums that the policyowner actually paid during the experience-rating period (usually one year) before any adjustment was made to reflect the actual experience of the group. In most instances, this is the sum of 12 monthly premiums. The premiums paid may have been based on manual rates or on the group's past experience.

Stop-Loss Limit

Step 2 specifies the stop-loss limit—the maximum amount of any claim that is charged to the group in the experience-rating calculation. Its purpose is to minimize the effect of any chance fluctuations that might occur from year to year because of catastrophic losses within the group. These chance fluctuations tend to become relatively smaller as the size of a group increases, and a stop-loss limit may not be used for very large groups.

The stop-loss limit in medical expense insurance is usually expressed as a dollar amount per claim, and the actual figure is subject to negotiation between the policyowner and the insurance company. In this illustration, $250,000 is used. Therefore, if a claim of $400,000 is incurred because of a premature birth, only the first $250,000 of the claim will be used in the experience-rating calculation.

Obviously, a charge must be made somewhere for incorporating a stop-loss provision into an experience-rating contract, since the insurance company is obligated to pay any excess amount over the stop-loss limit. The charge in this illustration is shown in step 7. In effect, this charge for stop-loss coverage can be viewed as a manual-rate charge for losses in excess of some limit, with only those losses below the limit subject to experience rating.

Incurred Claims

Step 3 involves the determination of incurred claims, which are those claims attributable to the recently ended period of coverage that was subject to experience rating (that is, the *experience period*). It may seem as if the incurred claims are those claims that were paid during the experience period. Unfortunately, it is not that simple. Some of the claims that were paid during the experience period may actually be attributable to previous periods and must be subtracted from the incurred claims. In addition, other claims that are attributable to the experience period may not have been reported or may be in the course of settlement. However, their value must be estimated. Therefore, an appropriate determination of incurred claims is as follows:

Incurred claim	=	claims paid during the experience period
	−	claims paid during the experience period but incurred during previous periods
	+	estimate of claims incurred during the experience period but to be paid in future periods

In actual practice, incurred claims are usually expressed as follows:

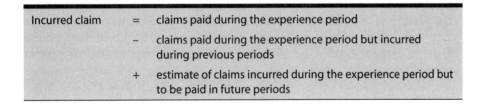

Incurred claims	=	paid claims
	+	ending claim reserve
	−	beginning claim reserve
		or
Incurred claims	=	paid claims
	+	change in claim reserve

This *claim reserve,* which is often referred to as the *open-and-unreported claim reserve,* represents an estimate by the insurance company for (1) claims that have been approved but not yet paid, (2) claims that are in the course of settlement, and (3) claims that have been incurred but not yet reported (often referred to as *IBNR*). In addition, when disability income coverage or medical expense coverage is experience rated, an additional amount must be added to this estimate for any claims that have been incurred, reported, and approved but are not yet payable. Essentially, these claims arise from disabilities or current medical claims that will continue beyond the experience period.

Based on past experience, most insurance companies can closely estimate the percentage of claims that are paid after the close of the experience period for a given type of coverage. While this estimate reflects companywide experience and may not reflect the experience of a particular policyowner, it is usually applied to each group insurance case rather than determining the claim reserve on a case-by-case basis. In general, the claim reserve is based either on a percentage of the annual premium (before experience rating) or on a percentage of claims paid. The first approach is most common for small groups, and the latter approach tends to be used for large groups. This percentage varies considerably by type of coverage, with the claim reserve for group term life insurance usually ranging between 10 and 15 percent of the annual premium (and up to 25 percent if a waiver of premium for disability is included), and the claim reserve for medical expense coverage often ranging from 20 to 65 percent, depending on what benefits are involved.

Expected Claims

The amount of expected claims in step 4 represents the portion of the premiums paid that the insurance company has anticipated would be necessary to pay claims during the experience period. This amount may have been derived either from average experience, as in manual rating, or from the past experience of the particular group.

Credibility

The credibility factor (step 5), which can vary from zero to one, is a statistical measure of the reliability of the group's past experience. In other words, it is a measure of the probability that the group's actual experience is a true reflection of the group and is not the result of chance occurrences. The credibility factor varies by the size of the group and the type of coverage. In general, the larger the group, the greater the reliability of estimates (because of the law of large numbers). In addition, actual experience tends to deviate less from the estimates of expected claims (on a relative basis) as the frequency of claims rises. Therefore, a greater degree of credibility can be attributed to a group's medical expense claims than to its life insurance claims.

In actual practice, credibility factors are usually based on the size of a group. as determined by the number of persons (lives) who are insured. However, some insurance companies base their credibility factors on the annual premium of a group. The factors vary somewhat among insurance companies, but the excerpt in Table 15-12 from the rate manual of one insurance company, and which is used for this illustration, is a typical example of the first approach.

Adjustments in these factors may be made to reflect any characteristics of either the group or the insurance contract that are not the norm. For example, an older group of employees might be assigned a higher credibility factor than a younger group whose claims are more likely to be due to random fluctuations. In addition, the level of any stop-loss limit may have an effect. As the stop-loss charge is increased (meaning the stop-loss limit is lowered), the credibility that can be assigned to the remaining claims below the stop-loss limit also increases.

TABLE 15-12		
Size of Group (Lives)	Long-Term Disability Income Insurance and Life Insurance	Medical Expense Insurance and Short-Term Disability Income Insurance
100	0.0	0.2
200	0.2	0.5
400	0.4	0.8
600	0.7	1.0
800	0.9	1.0
1,000 or more	1.0	1.0

Similarly, the size of the credibility factor may be influenced by the amount of the risk charge levied on the group for establishing a contingency reserve. If an insurance company has an adequate contingency reserve for a group insurance case, it is more likely to allow the use of a higher credibility factor than can be statistically justified. This practice results in reduced claims charges for years when the employer has good experience and increased claims charges for years when it has bad experience. Although it is desired by employers with a history of better-than-average claims experience, a higher-than-justified credibility factor leads to a larger-than-usual deficit for a group with bad experience. It also increases the probability that the employer will terminate the contract before the deficit is eliminated. A larger contingency reserve can balance the financial consequences of this possibility.

Claims Charge

Once the credibility factor is determined, the process of calculating what claims will be charged against the group in the experience period is relatively simple and can be expressed by the following formula:

Claims charge	=	(z) (incurred claims subject to experience rating)
	+	$(1 - z)$ (expected claims)
where z is the credibility factor.		

In effect, the claims charge is a weighted average of (1) the incurred claims that are subject to experience rating and (2) the expected claims, with the incurred claims being assigned a weight equal to the credibility factor and the expected claims being assigned a weight equal to one minus the credibility factor. In step 6 of Table 15-11, the claims charge is calculated as follows:

Claims charge	=	.8 ($1,620,000) + (1 − .8) ($1,700,000)
	=	.8 ($1,620,000) + .2 ($1,700,000)
	=	$1,296,000 + $340,000
	=	$1,636,000

If a credibility factor of 1.0 is used, the claims charge is equal to the incurred claims that are subject to experience rating, and the expected claims are not taken into consideration.

Retention

The retention (step 7) in a group insurance contract is usually defined as the excess of premiums paid over claims payments and dividends. It consists of charges for (1) the stop-loss coverage, (2) expenses (commissions, premium taxes, and administrative expenses), (3) a risk charge, and (4) a contribution to the insurance company's surplus. In this particular illustration, the sum of these charges is reduced by the interest that is credited to certain reserves—the claim reserve and any contingency reserves—that the insurance company holds to pay future claims attributable to this contract. However, some insurance companies do not subtract this interest when determining retention; rather, they treat it as an additional premium paid.

For large groups, each item in the retention is calculated separately, based on the group's actual experience. For small groups, a formula is usually applied that is based on insurance company averages. This formula varies by the size of a group and the type of coverage involved, and most often it is either a percentage of the claims charge or a flat charge plus a percentage of the claims charge.

Dividend Earned

The dividend earned (step 8) is computed by adding the retention to the claims charge and then subtracting this sum from the premiums paid. This is the dividend amount attributable to the group insurance case for the current experience period.

Previous Deficits

Under most experience-rated group insurance plans, any deficits from past periods must be made up before any future dividends are paid. Whenever the sum of the claims charge and the retention charge for any experience period exceeds the premiums paid and results in a negative dividend earned, there is a deficit. In step 9 of Table 15-11, a $42,000 deficit from previous periods exists. Interestingly, the insurance company has no opportunity to recover this deficit if the insurance contract is not renewed. However, the fact that there is always a chance of nonrenewal is one of the reasons why a risk charge is levied.

As additional protection against the nonrenewal of insurance contracts that have a deficit, some insurance companies require that part of any dividend earned be placed in a *claims fluctuation reserve* when experience is favorable. Monies are drawn from the reserve to indemnify the insurance company for the years in which there is a deficit. Because this reserve lessens the possibility that the insurance company will lose money on a group insurance case, it is usually accompanied by a lower risk charge.

Dividend Payable

The final step in the dividend-calculation process (step 10) is to establish whether a dividend is payable. This is determined by subtracting any deficit that has been carried forward (or placed in a claims fluctuation reserve) from the dividend earned for the experience period. If this figure is positive, it is the amount of the dividend; if the figure is negative, it is the amount of the cumulative deficit that is to be carried forward.

In this illustration, only one type of coverage is experience rated. However, when an employer has more than one type of coverage that is experience rated with the same insurance company, a single dividend is usually determined for the combined package. This typically involves the determination of a separate claims charge for each coverage and a single retention charge for the entire package. Because "losses" for one type of coverage are often offset by "gains" for other types of coverage, the relative fluctuation in the overall experience tends to be less than the fluctuations in the experience of some or all of the individual coverages. Therefore, the overall premium can often be reduced (or the dividend increased) because the insurance company will levy a lower risk charge and/or require a lower contingency reserve.

Variations for Other Types of Coverage

In some types of group insurance, particularly group term life insurance, there is considerable disparity in the amounts of coverage, and top executives often have much greater coverage than the lowest-paid employees. Claims that arise from the deaths of employees who have large amounts of coverage can have a significant effect on a group's experience for the years in which they occur. Consequently, several methods have been used to exclude these claims (or at least a portion of them) from the process of determining the claims charge in experience rating. One of these methods is the stop-loss limit that was previously mentioned. However, its primary purpose is to limit the claims charge because of a higher-than-anticipated frequency of claims, rather than because of a few high-severity claims. Some of the other methods used to handle these large claims are the following:

■ Excess-amounts pooling. This approach limits the amount of insurance that is subject to experience rating on any one person. Amounts over the limit are not experience rated but are subject to manual rates based on the ages of the individuals involved. This results in a "pooling" or an "insurance" charge that is added to either the claims charge or the retention charge, depending on the insurance company's practice. These excess amounts may also be subject to evidence of insurability.

■ A lower credibility factor. Under this method, the credibility factor normally used for a certain-size group is reduced if there is a significant difference between the smallest and largest amounts of coverage. This results in more weight being placed on the group's expected claims than on their incurred claims.

■ An extra contingency reserve. Under this approach, the excess of claims above a certain limit is ignored in the experience-rating process for dividend purposes but is charged against a contingency reserve that has been established (with an appropriate annual charge) for this reason.

Two other factors enter into the incurred claims amount for group term life insurance: disability claims and conversion charges. In addition to death claims, there may be disability claims if a group insurance contract contains a waiver-of-premium provision or another type of disability provision. Once a waiver-of-premium claim has been approved, a charge is made for future death claims, because no future premiums will be received for the disabled employee. This charge is based on the probability that the disabled employee will die prior to recovery or termination of coverage (for example, at age 65). On the average the charge will be about $750 for each $1,000 of coverage. If the insurance contract continues, an additional $250 per $1,000 of coverage will be charged if a death claim is paid. If the employee recovers or coverage terminates prior to death, the $750 charge will be credited back to the policyowner.

As mentioned earlier in this chapter, a conversion charge is levied against the group insurance department of an insurance company to reflect the increased mortality on converted coverage. In the experience-rating procedure, this charge is transferred to the group policyowner as a charge per $1,000 of coverage converted (commonly $50 to $75).

Renewal Rating

Experience rating is also often used to develop future premiums for group insurance cases based on the past experience of the group. For the most part, the procedure is similar to that for determining dividends, and in fact the two procedures are usually done at the same time. However, there are some differences. In most cases, the experience-rating period is three to five years instead of a single year, and thus cumulative premiums and charges for this period are used. In addition, a more conservative (that is, lower) credibility factor is normally applied. For example, an insurance company that uses a credibility factor of .8 for dividend purposes for a particular case might use a factor of .6 for renewal rating. Furthermore, because a premium is being developed for the future, it is also necessary to adjust past claims and the retention, not only to reflect current cost levels but also to include expected trends for the next year. Adjustments must also be made to account for any changes in the coverage. Once a renewal premium expected to be sufficient to cover claims and retention is calculated, an additional amount is added for future dividends. This amount in effect becomes a safety margin for the insurance company should both claims and retention be higher than anticipated; otherwise, it is returned as an experience dividend to the policyholder.

Experience rating may also be used to develop the initial premiums for any transferred business, requiring that the insurance company obtain past data from the policyholder regarding its experience with the previous carrier. A policyholder may be reluctant to provide this information because poor experience (and the resulting rate increase) is often the reason for changing insurance companies. However, the existence of the poor claims experience is exactly the information the insurance company needs. In fact, some insurance companies actually refuse to write transferred coverage, particularly for large groups, unless verifiable prior claims experience is provided.

If possible, the past data are used to determine what the premiums and charges would have been if the new contract had been written by the new carrier in previous years. If this can be accomplished, the procedure is a simplified application of the principles previously described. If it cannot be accomplished, manual rating may be used for small groups, but judgment may play a large role in determining the premiums for large groups.

STUDY QUESTIONS

1. The major objective of rate making is to develop rates that are adequate and equitable. What is meant by adequate and equitable?

2. In addition to determining the benefit unit, what decisions must be made in developing a basis on which manual premium rates can be established?

3. Describe the steps in the calculation of manual premium rates.

4. What characteristics of a group are usually considered in determining disability income rates that are not likely to be considered in determining term life insurance rates?

5. How do insurance companies protect themselves against increases in medical expense claims costs due to inflation?

6. a. What is the rationale for the use of experience rating?
   b. Identify the situations in which experience rating may be used.

7. What is the purpose of a stop-loss limit?

8. Explain why paid claims differ from incurred claims.

9. Given the following information for a group insurance contract, calculate its claims charge:

Premiums paid	$250,000
Claims paid	$190,000
Beginning claim reserve	$ 25,000
Ending claim reserve	$ 35,000
Stop-loss limit	120% of premiums paid
Expected claims	$160,000
Credibility factor	.7

10. How does the credibility factor for a group vary by the size of the group and the type of insurance coverage?

11. Why might the full amount of a dividend earned not be paid to a group insurance policyholder?

12. How does experience rating for determining renewal rates differ from experience rating for calculating dividends?

Other Nonretirement Benefits and Cafeteria Plans

CHAPTER 16

Other Nonretirement Benefits: Meeting Personal and Family Needs

- Explain why employers often provide fringe benefits.

- Identify the types of payments that employers may make to employees for time not worked and explain the tax consequences of each benefit.

- Describe the types of extra cash payments that employers may provide to employees and explain the tax consequences of each.

- Describe the types of services employers often provide to employees and explain the tax consequences of each.

In the first chapter, employee benefits were divided into five categories:

1. Legally required social insurance payments
2. Payments for private insurance and retirement plans
3. Payments for time not worked
4. Extra payments to employees
5. Services to employees

Variations exist among employers, but typically about one-quarter of the sum spent on employee benefits is devoted to payments for legally required social insurance programs. More than one-third is spent on employee benefits devoted to payments for retirement plans and group insurance. Often overlooked is the significance of all the remaining types of benefits that may be provided to employees, which as a group account for between one-quarter and one-third of the employee benefit dollars employers spend. Many of these benefits are designed to meet specific personal needs of employees and their families. Because the list is extensive, not every possible benefit is described. Rather, the discussion is devoted to the following list of more commonly provided "other" benefits:

- Vacations
- Holidays
- Personal time off with pay
- Personal time off without pay (family leave)
- Supplemental unemployment benefit plans
- Educational assistance
- Moving-expense reimbursement
- Suggestion awards
- Service awards
- Productivity and safety achievement awards
- Holiday bonuses and gifts
- No-additional-cost services
- Employee discounts
- Dependent-care assistance
- Adoption assistance
- Wellness programs
- Employee-assistance programs
- Financial planning programs for executives
- Preretirement counseling programs
- Transportation/free parking
- Company cars
- Subsidized eating facilities

Some of these benefits, such as holidays and vacations, are provided by most employers; other benefits, such as financial planning, are provided by relatively few employers. There are many reasons that an employer may provide a certain array of benefits: to satisfy specific needs of its employees, for competitive reasons, or because of traditions within its locality or industry. Collective bargaining, the personal whims of the employer, and state laws may also play a role.

With rare exceptions, the cost of providing these benefits is tax deductible to the employer. However, the tax treatment of employees receiving benefits varies, and the treatment of each benefit is described separately.

MEANING OF HIGHLY COMPENSATED EMPLOYEE

Several of the benefits discussed in this chapter are subject to nondiscrimination rules. Specifically, these benefits are educational assistance, service awards, safety achievement and productivity awards, no-additional-cost services, employee discounts, dependent-care assistance, adoption assistance, and employee-assistance programs. In each case, there are rules designed to prevent or discourage the benefit plan from discriminating in favor of highly compensated employees.

The consequences of a plan's being discriminatory vary. In some cases, no employees can receive benefits on a tax-favored basis; in other cases, this penalty applies to highly compensated employees only.

As used in this chapter, a highly compensated employee is one who meets the definition in Sec. 414(q) of the Internal Revenue Code. This definition is also used for the nondiscrimination rules that apply to qualified retirement plans. A *highly compensated employee* is an employee who meets one of the following criteria:

- Is a 5 percent owner of the firm during the current year or was a 5 percent owner during the previous year.
- Had compensation from the employer in excess of $85,000 during the previous year. However, the employer can elect to define this category of employees as only those whose compensation puts them in the top 20 percent of the organization's employees. The $85,000 figure is subject to periodic indexing.

It is interesting to note that this definition of highly compensated employee is not the same as the one used with the nondiscrimination rules for self-insured medical reimbursement plans or the one used for cafeteria plans.

PAYMENTS FOR TIME NOT WORKED

Vacations

In terms of employer cost, the most significant benefit mentioned in this chapter is paid vacations. In 1999, the U.S. Chamber of Commerce estimated that the cost to employers of providing vacations to employees was equal to almost 5 percent of base pay.[1] The number of vacation days given to employees increased steadily from World War II until the adverse economic times of the late 1970s. During the last few years, this trend has leveled off, and few companies have increased the number of vacation days provided.

While the specifics of vacation plans vary widely, most plans are based on length of service, and the number of vacation days given to any particular employee normally increases over time. There is usually a short waiting period (three to six months) during which employees are ineligible for vacations, but for competitive reasons there is often no waiting period for management employees. Table 16-1 is one employer's benefit schedule for its vacation plan.

Some firms have different schedules for different classes of employees, with higher-paid employees tending to have more vacation time, particularly in the earlier years of service. In contrast to many types of benefits, vacation benefits are often given to part-time employees.

TABLE 16-1
Vacation Plan Benefit Schedule

Length of Service	Vacation Days
First 6 months	0
After 6 months	1 for each month in the remaining calendar year (maximum of 10)
1–5 years	10
6–15 years	15
16 years or more	20

In recent years, many employers have adopted cafeteria plans, in which employees have some choice in designing their own benefit plans. Although most companies with cafeteria plans have a basic vacation schedule that is separate from the cafeteria plan, employees may have the option of using their benefit dollars to purchase extra vacation days, often subject to approval of their supervisor and usually subject to a maximum additional number of days.

Several major issues must be addressed in properly designing a vacation plan. One is the treatment of unused vacation days. Some employers require that any unused vacation days be forfeited; others allow them to be carried over to the next year, subject to certain limitations. A few businesses compensate employees for unused vacation days. Another issue is the question of when employees can take their vacations. In general, supervisory approval is necessary, and vacations may not be allowed during busy work times. Junior employees may also have to schedule their vacations around those of senior employees so that the number of people away from work at the same time is minimized. Other issues that must be addressed are those of how unused vacation days will be treated upon termination of employment and whether sicknesses and holidays occurring during vacation periods will be treated as vacation days.

The compensation employees receive during periods of vacation is treated the same as compensation for time worked and is taxed accordingly.

---

[1] U.S. Chamber of Commerce, *1999 Employee Benefits Study.*

Holidays

Employers normally pay employees for certain holidays. At a minimum, employees usually receive pay for the following:

- New Year's Day
- Memorial Day
- The Fourth of July
- Labor Day
- Thanksgiving
- Christmas

Most employees receive at least six and sometimes as many as 11 or 12 additional holidays, which may include the following:

- Martin Luther King's Birthday
- Washington's Birthday
- Lincoln's Birthday
- Presidents' Day
- Good Friday
- Columbus Day
- The Friday after Thanksgiving
- Veterans Day
- Christmas Eve
- New Year's Eve
- The employee's birthday
- Various state holidays

For some institutions, such as banks, holidays are prescribed by law. However, for most companies, management decides which holidays to provide, subject to collective bargaining if applicable.

When a scheduled holiday falls on a Saturday, employees who normally do not work on that day are given the preceding Friday off. When a holiday falls on Sunday, it is normally observed on Monday. Restaurants and retail establishments are increasingly open for business on holidays. When this occurs, employees who work are usually paid at least time and a half and sometimes as much as triple time.

Some companies, realizing that not all employees want to take the same holidays, try to satisfy these needs by adopting holiday plans that include a minimum number of scheduled holidays coupled with a specific number of "floating holidays" to be taken at an employee's discretion. Usually, there is no requirement that the days taken actually be holidays, so in effect they become additional vacation days in lieu of holidays.

Like vacation pay, holiday pay is taxed as regular income.

Personal Time Off with Pay

Because personal situations that require an employee to be away from work occasionally arise, many employers allow employees to take time off with pay for certain reasons, the more common of which are the following:

- Reserve/National Guard duty. Laws sometimes require that employees be given time off for reserve or National Guard duty, but there is no stipulation that pay continue during this period. However, the majority of employers compensate their employees for the difference between their regular pay and any compensation received for the reserve or National Guard duty.

- Jury duty. Most employers grant (and may be required to grant) time off for jury duty. Because employees are usually compensated for jury duty, some employers pay only the difference between this amount and an employee's regular pay. However, the amount paid for jury duty is small and often just barely covers an employee's extra expenses. Therefore, many employers continue regular compensation with no deduction.

- A death in the family. Employers often allow up to five days off with pay for the death of family members. At a minimum, this usually includes the death of a parent, child, spouse, or other relative residing in the household. Some employers allow a shorter period of time, such as a day or half a day, to attend funerals of other relatives and sometimes even persons other than relatives.

- Sabbatical leaves. Sabbatical leaves are well established as employee benefits at educational institutions. Typically, faculty members are permitted an extended leave of a semester or a year after a specified period of service, such as seven years. During the sabbatical leave, the faculty member receives full or partial pay while performing no services for the employer. Meanwhile, the faculty member is often required to complete a research project or some similar activity as a condition of the sabbatical. Noneducational employers, particularly those having employees with professional degrees, sometimes provide similar benefits to professional employees to give them an opportunity to engage in research or study that is not directly job related.

Some less common reasons for which employers may allow time off with pay include the employee's getting married and serving as a witness in a court proceeding. Because still other personal reasons for needing time off may arise, employers may grant two or three days of personal leave that can be taken at an employee's discretion.

Personal Time Off Without Pay (Family Leave)

For many years, most industrialized countries have had legislation that enables employees to be away from work for extended periods without jeopardizing their jobs. The reasons for such leave vary among countries, as does the extent to which the employer must continue to provide pay and benefits to an employee on leave.

Over the last two decades, an increasing number of American employers have voluntarily begun to allow employees to take time off without pay. Reasons for such leave may include active military duty, extended vacations, honeymoons, education, the birth or adoption of a child, and the illness of a family member. Usually, such time off has been subject to the approval of the employer. Family leave is becoming more and more common as many states and the federal government adopt family-leave legislation.

State Laws

In recent years, the legislatures of almost every state have considered family-leave legislation, and more than half the states have enacted such legislation. As a general rule, these laws allow an employee to take an unpaid leave of absence for reasons such as the birth or adoption of a child and the illness of a family member. The length of leave allowed varies considerably among states, but it usually ranges from three to six months. When the family leave is completed, the employer is required to allow the employee to return to the same or a comparable job.

Almost all family-leave laws apply to public employers, and about half of the laws apply to private employers with more than a minimum number of employees, usually in the range of 25 to 100. In all states, employers are allowed to limit family leave to employees who have met certain eligibility requirements. While these requirements vary, the most common requirement is at least one year of full-time employment. At a minimum, most family-leave laws allow an employee to continue medical expense coverage at his or her own cost. Some laws require all employee benefits to be made available.

Federal Law

In 1993, the first federal family-leave legislation—the Family and Medical Leave Act—became effective. Unlike some federal legislation, it applies not only to private employers but also to nonprofit organizations and government entities, including Congress. The provisions of this legislation cover only a small percentage of the nation's employers but approximately two-thirds of all employees.

Despite concerns by employers that the act would increase costs and lower productivity, the actual effect seems to have been minimal, partly because many large employers already had leave policies similar to the act's provisions. A report issued in May 1996 by the Bipartisan Commission on Family and Medical Leave reported the following:

- Approximately 90 percent of employers reported that there was no noticeable effect on productivity, profitability, and growth as a result of the act.
- Only about 16 percent of the persons eligible for leave actually took it. The vast majority of persons who did not take leave for which they were eligible said they could not afford the resulting wage loss.
- The median length of leave time is 10 days.
- The group most likely to take leave is employees between the ages of 25 and 34.

The act applies only to employers with more than 50 employees within a 75-mile radius. To comply with the 50-employee requirement, an employer needs only to have that many employees during each workday for a period of 20 or more calendar weeks during the current or preceding calendar year. Part-time employees and employees on unpaid leaves of absence are included in the calculation. The 50-employee requirement is based on "joint employment," which means that two or more related companies can be treated as a single employer on the basis of factors such as common management, interrelations between operations, centralized control of labor relations, and the degree of common ownership or management. The 75-mile radius is based on the shortest route on public roads or public transportation.

With some exceptions, a worker must be allowed to take up to 12 weeks of unpaid leave in any 12-month period for the birth or adoption of a child; to care for a child, spouse, or parent with a serious health condition; or for the worker's own serious health condition that makes it impossible to perform a job. An employer may use any one of the following four methods to determine the 12-month period to which the family leave applies:

- The calendar year
- Any fixed 12-month period
- The 12-month period beginning with any employee's first day of leave
- A rolling 12-month period measured backward from the date leave is used

With one exception, the method chosen must apply uniformly to all employees. The exception occurs if a multistate employer operates in one or more states that have family-leave legislation that mandates a method different from the one chosen. In that case, the employer is permitted to comply with the state's requirement for employees located in that state but must use the chosen method for employees in other states.

A serious health condition is defined as one that requires continuing treatment from a health care provider. The regulations implementing the act generally define this as meaning that the condition will require absence from work, school, or regular daily activities for more than three calendar days.

However, the regulations also include treatment for pregnancy and certain chronic conditions, such as diabetes and asthma, as being serious health conditions even though treatment at any time may last less than three days. In addition, the definition includes health problems that are not ordinarily incapacitating on a day-to-day basis, but for which a person must undergo a series of multiple treatments. Examples in the regulations include chemotherapy or radiation for cancer, kidney dialysis, and physical therapy for severe arthritis. The regulations specifically exclude the following from the definition of a serious health condition: common colds, flu, upset stomach, and routine dental problems. Stress is also excluded, but mental illness arising from stress can qualify.

The act applies to both full-time and part-time employees. The latter must be allowed to take leave on a basis that is proportional to that given to full-time employees. However, leave can be denied to anyone who has not worked for the employer for at least one year and worked at least 1,250 hours during that period.

In most cases, the rules allow employees to take leave intermittently or by working a reduced week, but only with the employer's approval. The exception is that leave because of a person's or family member's serious health condition may be taken whenever medically necessary.

An employer is allowed to substitute an employee's accrued paid leave for any part of the 12-week period of family leave. In addition, an employer can deny leave to a salaried employee within the highest-paid 10 percent of its work force if the leave would create a substantial and grievous injury to the organization's operations.

An employee is required to provide 30 days' notice for foreseeable leaves for birth, adoption, or planned medical treatment. The employer can require that an employee provide a doctor's certification of a serious illness. An employer can also require a second opinion but must pay for the cost.

During the period of leave, an employer has no obligation to continue an employee's pay or most benefits, and the employee is ineligible for unemployment compensation. However, an employer must continue to provide medical and dental benefits during the leave as if the worker were still employed. The employee must continue to pay any required plan contributions and must be given a 30-day grace period for such payments. The employer is also required to send the employee a notice no later than 15 days before the grace period expires, stating that coverage will be terminated if the premium is not paid. The employer is allowed to recover the cost of premiums paid by the employer during the leave if the employee does not return to work for reasons other than (1) the continuance, recurrence, or onset of a health condition (as previously defined) affecting the employee or the employee's spouse, parent, or child, or (2) other cirucumstances beyond the employee's control.

Upon return from leave, an employee must be given his or her old job or an equivalent job. The employee must also be allowed to regain any benefits that were enjoyed prior to the leave without meeting any requalification requirements. With respect to retirement plans, any period of leave must be treated as continued service for purposes of vesting and eligibility to participate.

Employers must comply with the new federal law as well as with any applicable state laws. Because most existing state laws have at least one provision that is broader than the federal legislation, an employer must have a complete understanding of both laws.

An employer should have a clear, written family-leave policy that is consistently enforced. In establishing this policy, the employer should address such issues as

- Eligibility requirements
- Employee certification of need for leave
- Employee rights upon returning from leave
- Employer rights if employee terminates at end of leave

The federal law requires that an employer post a notice explaining the Family and Medical Leave Act, a sample of which is contained in material from the Labor Department, which administers the law. In addition, if an employer does not provide employees with guidance about their rights and obligations under the act in employee manuals or handouts, this information must be provided to an employee at the time he or she requests it.

Supplemental Unemployment Benefit Plans

Collective-bargaining agreements may require that employers contribute to a supplemental unemployment benefit (SUB) plan that is designed to supplement state unemployment insurance benefits for workers who are unemployed. These plans rarely exist for nonunion employees. Benefits are often payable for at least a year and with regular unemployment benefits may be as high as 95 percent of what the worker was earning while employed.

SUB plans typically require that employers contribute to a SUB fund on the basis of the compensation of currently active employees, and employee contributions may also be required. The fund is usually maintained by trustees selected by the collective-bargaining agent, and it is frequently a common fund maintained for several employers. Employer contributions to the fund are income tax deductible, and if the fund is properly designed, earnings on fund assets may also be exempt from income taxation. Benefit payments to employees are fully taxable.

EXTRA PAYMENTS TO EMPLOYEES

Educational Assistance

For several years the Internal Revenue Code has provided favorable tax treatment to employees who receive benefits from their employers for educational assistance. Section 127 of the Code, which allows employees to receive annually the first $5,250 of these benefits on a tax-free basis, is scheduled to expire for courses beginning after December 31, 2001. (However, the date has been extended several times before and will probably be extended again, or the Code section may be made permanent.) For benefits to be tax free, the employer's plan cannot discriminate with respect to eligibility in favor of officers, shareholders, highly compensated employees, or their dependents. In addition, no more than 5 percent of the benefits may be paid out to shareholders or owners (or their dependents) who are more-than-5-percent owners of the firm.

Eligible benefits include tuition, fees, and books. The costs of supplies and equipment are also included as long as they are not retained after completion of the course. Meals, lodging, and transportation associated with educational expenses cannot be received tax free, nor can tax-free educational assistance be provided for graduate-level courses. For purposes of Sec. 127, a graduate-level course is defined as any course taken by an employee who has a bachelor's degree or is receiving credit toward a more advanced degree, if the particular course can be taken for credit by any individual in a program leading to a law, business, medical, or other advanced academic or professional degree. Courses involving sports, games, or hobbies are also ineligible for favorable tax treatment. Although an employer's plan can pay for any of these types of courses, an employee will be taxed on the value of the employer's contribution to their cost.

Many employers provide reimbursement for certain educational expenses that do not qualify for favorable tax treatment under Section 127. While such reimbursements result in taxable compensation for an employee, the employee may be eligible for a federal income tax deduction (subject to the 2-percent-of-adjusted-gross-income floor on miscellaneous itemized deductions) if he or she itemizes deductions. The deduction is allowed for educational expenses that are incurred (1) to maintain or improve a skill required in employment or (2) to meet the express requirements of the employer as a condition for retaining employment. Other types of educational expenses, such as costs incurred to qualify the employee for a new trade or business, are not deductible.

Moving-Expense Reimbursement

To attract new employees and to encourage current employees to move to suit the employer's needs, many businesses provide reimbursement for moving expenses. Such reimbursement is includable in an employee's income, but the employee is allowed certain offsetting income tax deductions if specified rules are satisfied. To receive the deductions, the employee must have moved because of a change in job location. In addition, the employee must satisfy both a distance test and a time test. The distance test requires that the employee's new workplace be at least 50 miles farther from the employee's old residence than the employee's old workplace (or at least 50 miles from the employee's old residence if the employee was previously unemployed). The time test requires that the employee work full-time in the general location of the new residence for at least 39 weeks during the 12 months following the move. An employee may take the applicable deductions in anticipation of satisfying the time test, but additional taxes will be payable if the time test is not ultimately met.

If all the preceding rules are satisfied, an employee may deduct the following expenses:

- Transportation expenses in moving household goods and personal effects
- Travel and lodging (but not meal) expenses in moving to the new residence

An employer may pay for other expenses, such as expenses to sell an old residence, premove travel to look for a new residence, or temporary living costs at the new location. Because these reimbursements will be taxable income without a corresponding deduction, the employer may give the employee a bonus to offset the increased tax.

Suggestion Awards

Some employers, particularly those in manufacturing industries, give awards to employees who make suggestions that will improve the operating efficiency of the firm if implemented. The awards are often a percentage of the firm's estimated savings over some specified future period of time but may be subject to a maximum dollar amount. If a suggestion plan is properly administered, the benefits of the plan may far exceed its costs while at the same time increasing the motivation and involvement of employees.

Suggestion awards are included in an employee's gross income for tax purposes.

Service Awards

Many employers provide awards to employees for length of service. These awards are often nominal for short periods of service (five or ten years) and may consist of such items as key chains, flowers, or pens. Awards typically increase in value for longer periods of service, and employees may actually be given some choice in the award received.

If the value of a service award is *de minimis,* it is not included in an employee's income. To be *de minimis* the value of the benefit must be so minimal that accounting for the cost of the benefit would be unreasonable or administratively impractical. Service awards of higher value may also be excludable from an employee's income if they are considered qualified plan awards. However, the total amount excludable from an employee's income for qualified plan awards (which also include awards for safety) cannot exceed $1,600 per year. Qualified plan awards must be provided under a permanent written program that does not discriminate in favor of officers, shareholders, or highly compensated employees. In addition, the average annual cost of all awards under the plan cannot exceed $400.

Productivity and Safety Achievement Awards

Some employers provide awards for productivity and safety achievement. Productivity awards are fully treated as compensation. However, while awards for safety achievement given to professional, administrative, managerial, or clerical employees are fully taxable, such awards are treated as qualified plan awards for other employees and are included in the $1,600 excludable figure mentioned previously under service awards.

Holiday Bonuses and Gifts

Many employers give gifts or bonuses to employees, particularly at Christmastime. Because the value of such gifts is typically small, some employees tend to resent gifts of money. Therefore, gifts such as liquor or a ham are often given.

As with service awards, a holiday gift does not result in taxation for an employee as long as the market value of the gift is small.

SERVICES TO EMPLOYEES

No-Additional-Cost Services

Employers in many service industries provide their employees with free or discounted services. Examples include telephone service to employees of phone companies and airline tickets to employees of airlines. As long as the following rules are satisfied, the cost of these services is not includable in an employee's gross income for tax purposes:

- The services cannot be provided on a basis that discriminates in favor of highly compensated employees.
- The employer must not incur any significant additional cost or lost revenue in providing the services. For example, giving a standby ticket to an airline employee if there were unsold seats on a flight would satisfy this requirement, but giving an airline ticket to an employee when potential paying customers were denied seats would not.
- The services must be those that are provided in the employer's line of business in which the employee actually works. Therefore, if a business owns both an airline and a chain of hotels, an employee of the hotels can be given a room as a tax-free benefit but not an airline ticket. However, unrelated employers in the same line of business, such as airlines, may enter into reciprocal arrangements under which employees of any party to the arrangement may obtain services from the other parties.

Employee Discounts

Just as no-additional-cost services are an important employee benefit in certain service industries, discounts on the merchandise sold by manufacturers and retailers are an important benefit to employees in these industries. Discounts may also be provided on services sold by other types of businesses; for example, there may be a reduction in the commission charged by a brokerage house or insurance company.

Rules similar to those discussed for no-additional-cost services apply to discounts. Employees have no taxable income as long as the discounts are made available on a nondiscriminatory basis and are provided on goods or services ordinarily sold to nonemployees in the employer's line of business in which the employee works. However, there are some additional rules. Discounts received on real estate or on personal property normally held as an investment (for example, gold coins or securities) are not received tax free. Furthermore, there is a limit on the size of a discount that can be received tax free. For merchandise, the discount cannot exceed the gross profit percentage of the price at which the merchandise is offered for sale to customers. For example, if an employer had a gross profit margin of 40 percent on a particular product and an employee purchased the merchandise at a 50 percent discount, the extra 10 percent would be taxable income to the employee. In the case of services, including insurance policies, the tax-free discount cannot exceed 20 percent of the price at which the service is offered to nonemployee customers in the normal course of the employer's business. The type of service that cannot be received tax free involves loans that financial institutions give to employees at a discounted rate of interest.

Dependent-Care Assistance

Changes in society and in the work force often create changing needs for both employers and employees. When the work force was largely male and most families had two parents, caring for children and older parents frequently was the female spouse's responsibility. As the number of families headed by two wage earners or by single parents has increased, so has the need for dependent care. This change in demographics has also created problems for employers. Caring for family members can lead to increased absenteeism, tardiness, turnover, and time taken as family leave. Workplace morale can also suffer if the employer is viewed as insensitive to employee responsibilities.

The nature of employee benefit plans has changed as employers have increasingly responded to the need for dependent care. Child-care benefits are increasingly common, and a small but growing number of firms also make eldercare benefits available. Firms that have dependent-care assistance plans generally feel that such plans alleviate the problems cited in the previous paragraph. Furthermore, the availability of such benefits at a firm often makes it easier for the firm to attract new employees.

In addition to a formal dependent-care assistance plan, there are other ways in which employers can respond to employee needs to care for family members. These include flexible work schedules, part-time employment, job sharing, salary reduction options under cafeteria plans, and family-leave policies that are more liberal than those required by federal and state laws.

Child-Care Plans

Several alternative types of benefits can be provided under child-care plans. A few employers maintain on-site day care centers, and the number is growing. On the other hand, some employers have closed down on-site centers and provide alternative forms of assistance because of the following problems encountered with on-site centers:

- Difficulty in obtaining qualified child-care providers.
- Difficulty in obtaining liability insurance.
- Difficulty, time, and expense associated with obtaining necessary zoning variances and child-care licenses.
- Distractions caused by parents and children being in close proximity to each other.
- Underutilization. While this type of facility would be expected to be popular, many employees prefer other alternatives. A site close to home is often more appealing than a location that may involve a long commute for parent and child. An on-site location may be less convenient if both parents share in child-care activities. Employees may also prefer a different type of child-care arrangement.

Some employers provide benefits by supporting a limited number of off-site child-care centers. The employer may make arrangements to reserve spaces for employees' children at these centers and/or arrange for corporate discounts for employees.

Probably the most common approach is to provide reimbursements to employees who make their own arrangements for child care, either at child-care centers or in their own home or the home of a care provider. Reimbursement is sometimes tied to pay levels, with lower-paid workers receiving higher reimbursements.

When employees are required to make their own arrangements under a child-care plan, employers may provide information and referral services—often through a contract with community or private referral services. In addition to providing assistance in locating a quality child-care center, these services can provide help in finding drop-in facilities when the usual child-care arrangement has fallen through or when school is closed for a day. They may also maintain a list of persons who will care for temporarily ill children at home or for children after school hours. Such services may also be a source of information about facilities that can be used during summer and other school vacations.

Eldercare Benefits

While benefits to care for elderly dependents are much less prevalent than benefits for child care, the need for these benefits continues to grow as parents live longer. In addition, because many couples have delayed having children until later in life, they have become part of what is often referred to as the "sandwich generation"; they must care for elderly parents at the same time that they are raising their own children.

Although eldercare benefits may take a variety of forms, frequently they are much like those provided under child-care plans. Within limits, the employer may pay for costs associated with home care for elderly dependents or care at day care facilities for the elderly. One interesting development in this area is the establishment of centers that care for both children and the elderly, with the elderly assisting in such activities as the feeding and teaching of the children. Studies have shown that the two groups are very compatible. Children, particularly those without grandparents nearby, benefit from the attention and knowledge they receive from the elderly, while the elderly achieve a feeling of usefulness.

Other employer activities with respect to eldercare may include the following:

- Providing seminars on issues affecting the elderly
- Providing information on available eldercare services and how to use these services
- Sponsoring support groups where employees can share experiences and learn from others
- Expanding employee-assistance plans to include eldercare
- Making long-term care insurance available to employees and including parents as an eligible group for coverage

Taxation of Benefits

Under the Internal Revenue Code, dependent care is a tax-free benefit to employees up to statutory limits as long as certain requirements are met. The amount of benefits that can be received tax free is limited to $5,000 for single parents and married persons who file jointly and to $2,500 for married persons who file separately. The benefits must be for care to a qualifying individual—a child under age 13 for whom the employee is allowed a dependency deduction on his or her income tax return or a taxpayer's spouse or other dependent who is mentally or physically incapable of caring for himself or herself. Although benefits must generally be for dependent care only, educational expenses at the kindergarten or preschool level can also be paid.

Dependent-care benefits are subject to a series of rules. If the rules are not met, highly compensated employees are taxed on the amount of benefits received. However, the benefits for other employees still retain their tax-free status. The following are the rules that must be met:

- Eligibility, contributions, and benefits under the plan cannot discriminate in favor of highly compensated employees or their dependents.
- No more than 25 percent of the benefits may be provided to the class composed of persons who own more than a 5 percent interest in the firm.
- Reasonable notification of the availability of benefits and the terms of the plan must be provided to eligible employees.
- By January 31 of the following year, each employee must receive an annual statement that indicates the amounts paid or expenses incurred by the employer to provide benefits.
- The average benefit provided to non–highly compensated employees must be at least 55 percent of the average benefit provided to highly compensated employees.

In meeting the 55-percent-of-benefit test, an employer can exclude employees earning under $25,000 if benefits are provided through a salary reduction agreement. For both the 55-percent-of-benefit test and the nondiscrimination rule for eligibility, an employer can exclude employees who (1) are under age 21, (2) have not completed one year of service, or (3) are covered under a collective-bargaining unit that has bargained for dependent-care benefits.

Even if an employer does not provide assistance for dependent care, other tax-saving options may be available to employees. Under the Code, a tax credit (subject to limits) is available for child-care expenses. In addition, the employer may have the opportunity to make before-tax contributions to a cafeteria plan that includes dependent care as an option.

Adoption Assistance

While many types of benefits have long been available to natural parents because of the birth of a child, comparable benefits historically have not been available to adoptive parents. Over the last few years, this disparity has begun to change. Even before the passage of family-leave legislation, many employers had established comparable leave policies for natural parents and adoptive parents; for example, if an employer allowed maternity leave (either paid or unpaid) for a new mother, no distinction was made between natural mothers and adoptive mothers. Leave may also be available for time involved in qualifying for the adoption and taking possession of the child.

A smaller number of employers provide reimbursement for some or all of the following expenses associated with adoption:

- Legal fees
- Adoption agencies' fees
- The birth mother's medical expenses

- The adoptive parents' medical expenses for physical examinations required by the adoption source
- The child's uninsured medical expenses
- Foster care charges for the child prior to placement with the adoptive family
- Transportation expenses associated with taking custody of the child.
- Extra expenses associated with foreign adoptions.

Reimbursements are generally available only to employees who have satisfied some minimum service requirement, most commonly one year. Amounts typically range from $1,000 to $3,000 per adoption, but higher amounts may be paid for adoptions involving handicapped children or children from a foreign country. There may also be a lifetime cap, such as $6,000.

Prior to 1997, adoption assistance for costs other than medical expenses generally represented taxable income to an employee. Beginning in 1997, employer payments of up to $5,000 per child for qualified adoption expenses can be excluded from an employee's gross income if an employer has an adoption-assistance program that satisfies IRS requirements. The amount is increased to $6,000 for certain children with special needs.

The adoption-assistance program must be a separate written plan, and employees must have reasonable notification of the availability of the program and its benefits. The program cannot discriminate in favor of highly compensated employees or their dependents, and no more than 5 percent of the benefits under the plan can be paid to shareholders or owners (or their dependents) who are more-than-5-percent owners of the firm.

Qualified adoption expenses include reasonable and necessary adoption fees, court costs, attorney's fees, travel expenses, and other expenses directly related to the legal adoption of an eligible child, defined as a child who is under age 18 or who is incapable of caring for himself or herself. Expenses incurred in adopting a spouse's child or carrying out a surrogate parenting arrangement are not qualified adoption expenses, nor are expenses that are reimbursed from other sources. In addition, expenses to adopt a foreign child are not qualified adoption expenses unless the adoption becomes final.

The $5,000 (or $6,000) exclusion from gross income is available to employees with an adjusted gross income of $75,000 or less, and married couples must file joint returns to obtain the exclusion. For employees with higher adjusted gross incomes, the exclusion is gradually phased out until it is eliminated when adjusted gross income reaches $115,000.

There is also a similar tax credit available to all taxpayers for adoption expenses, but the credit is not available for expenses that were paid by employer-provided adoption assistance, regardless of whether the employer paid the expenses through an adoption-assistance program. However, the credit can be used for expenses not reimbursed by an employer's plan.

Wellness Programs

Traditional benefit programs have been designed to provide benefits (1) to employees for their medical expenses and disabilities or (2) to their dependents if the employee should die prematurely. In the last few years, there has been an increasing trend among employers, particularly large corporations, to initiate programs that are designed to promote the well-being of employees (and possibly their dependents). Some of these programs have been aimed at the discovery and treatment of medical conditions before they become severe and result in large medical expenses, disabilities, or death. Other programs have focused on changing employees' lifestyles to eliminate the possible causes of future medical problems. A few programs, such as those that make flu shots available to employees, actually provide medical treatment. Recent studies have shown that the costs of establishing and maintaining many of these programs are more than offset by the lower amounts paid for medical expense, disability, and death benefits. In addition, if long-term disabilities and premature deaths can be eliminated, the expenses associated with training new employees can be minimized. Many firms also feel that these programs increase productivity by improving the employees' sense of well-being, their work attitudes and their family relationships.

Medical Screening Programs

The use of a medical screening program to discover existing medical conditions is not new, but it has often covered the costs (frequently up to some dollar limit) of routine physical examinations for only selected groups of management employees. Although this benefit may be highly valued by these employees and its use as an executive benefit has been increasing somewhat, there are doubts—even among the medical profession—as to its cost-effectiveness, particularly when it is provided on an annual basis. Certain medical conditions will undoubtedly be discovered during a complete physical, but most of them could also be diagnosed by less frequent and less costly forms of medical examinations.

In recent years, there has been a significant increase in the number of employers that sponsor periodic medical screening programs that detect specific medical problems, such as hypertension (high blood pressure), high cholesterol levels, breast cancer, prostate cancer, and colorectal cancer. Generally, such screenings are conducted at the employment site during regular working hours. Sometimes, a screening is conducted by a physician, but it is usually performed by lower-paid medical professionals. In addition, screenings can sometimes be obtained at little or no cost through such organizations as the American Red Cross, the American Heart Association, or the American Cancer Association.

Lifestyle Management Programs

Lifestyle management programs are primarily designed to encourage employees and often their dependents to modify their behavior so that they will lead healthier lives. Most of these programs strive to discover and eliminate conditions that increase the likelihood of cardiovascular problems (the source of a significant percentage of medical expenses and premature deaths). Some of these conditions (such as obesity and smoking) are obvious, but medical screening can also detect less obvious conditions like hypertension, high cholesterol levels, and the degree of an employee's physical fitness. The types of programs often instituted to promote cardiovascular health include the following:

- Smoking-cessation programs.
- Fitness programs. These may consist of formal exercise programs or only exercise facilities (such as swimming pools, exercise rooms, or jogging tracks). Some employee benefit consultants question whether facilities for competitive sports (such as racquetball courts) can be cost justified because their availability is limited and they are often a source of injuries.
- Weight-reduction programs.
- Nutrition programs. These are often established in conjunction with weight-reduction programs, but they can also teach methods of cholesterol reduction even if there is no weight problem.
- Stress-management programs.

These programs may be available to any employees who express an interest in them, or they may be limited to those employees who have been evaluated and found to be in a high-risk category for cardiovascular disease. This evaluation may consist of questionnaires regarding health history, blood pressure reading, blood chemistry analyses, and fitness tests. Generally, these evaluations and meetings to describe the programs and their value are conducted during regular working hours. However, the programs themselves are usually conducted during non-working hours, possibly at lunchtime or just after work.

Many wellness programs are designed to include employees, their spouses, and, sometimes, other family members. In many instances, it will not be possible to change an employee's lifestyle unless the lifestyle of his or her entire family also changes. For example, it is not very probable that an employee will stop smoking if his or her spouse also smokes and is making no attempt to stop. Similarly, a weight-reduction or nutrition program will probably be more effective if all family members alter their eating habits.

Programs designed to eliminate alcohol or drug abuse are another example of lifestyle management. Participation may be voluntary, or it can be mandatory for employees who are known to have alcohol or drug problems and who want to keep their jobs. When these programs have been successful, many employers have found a decrease in employee absenteeism.

Some employers have also instituted programs that seek to minimize back problems—the reason for a large percentage of employee absenteeism and disability claims. These programs are generally intended for employees who have a history of back trouble, and they consist of exercises as well as education in how to modify or avoid activities that can aggravate existing back conditions.

More recently, many employers have become concerned with the spread of AIDS and its effect on the cost of benefit plans. As a result, they have instituted educational programs aimed at encouraging employees to avoid activities that may result in the transmission of AIDS.

The employer may either conduct these wellness activities on the premises or use the resources of other organizations. For example, overweight employees might be sent to Weight Watchers, employees with alcohol problems might be encouraged to attend Alcoholics Anonymous, and employees with back problems might be enrolled in programs at a local YMCA.

Employers in increasing numbers are subscribing to wellness newsletters and are distributing them to employees. To encourage wellness for the entire family, these newsletters are often mailed to employees' homes.

Taxation of Benefits

Because medical screening programs are treated as medical benefits for tax purposes, employees have no taxable income as a result of participating in these programs. Unless the cost of providing lifestyle management programs is *de minimis,* participation will probably result in taxation to employees. The costs of programs that promote general health, such as programs for smoking cessation or weight control, are not considered medical expenses. While the cost of providing these programs to employees is deductible by the employer, an employee will incur taxable income unless the purpose of the program is to alleviate a specific medical problem. There is one exception to this general rule: Employees incur no taxable income as a result of being provided with or using athletic facilities that are located on the employer's premises.

Employee-Assistance Programs

As the trend toward fostering wellness in the workplace continues, an increasing number of employers are establishing employee-assistance programs. These programs are designed to help employees with certain personal problems through a plan that provides the following:

- Treatment for alcohol or drug abuse
- Counseling for mental problems and stress
- Counseling for family and marital problems
- Financial, legal, and tax advice
- Referrals for child care or eldercare
- Crisis intervention

Numerous studies have shown that proper treatment of these problems is very cost-effective and leads to a reduction in hospital costs, disability claims, the number of sick days, and absenteeism. It is also argued that employee morale and productivity are increased as a result of the concern shown for employees' personal problems.

Traditionally, employee-assistance programs have used job performance as the basis for employer concern. Essentially, an employee was told that his or her work was substandard and asked if a problem existed that he or she would like to discuss with someone. If the employee said yes, referral was made to an appropriate counselor or agency. No attempt was made by the employee's supervisor to diagnose the specific problem. Newer employee-assistance programs go beyond this approach by allowing employees who have problems to go directly to the program and seek help. Dependents can usually use the employee-assistance program and can often seek help without the employee's knowledge.

Another recent trend in employee-assistance programs is to coordinate them more closely with the employer's medical expense plan. For example, several employee-assistance programs act as the gatekeeper for mental health and substance abuse services. An employee must go through the employee-assistance program before benefits can be received under his or her medical expense coverage. The objective of this approach is to establish a course of treatment that will have maximum effectiveness for the costs incurred.

Access to an employee-assistance program is through a counselor; this counselor may be a company employee, but most often he or she is employed by a professional organization that specializes in providing such programs. Information disclosed to the counselor by the employee is kept confidential. Many problems can be solved by discussion between the counselor and the employee, and most plans have 24-hour counseling available, through either a telephone hotline or on-duty personnel. If the counselor cannot solve an employee's problem, it is the counselor's responsibility to make a preliminary determination about the type of professional help that the employee should receive. In many cases, this treatment can be provided under existing medical expense or legal expense plans or through community agencies. The costs of other types of treatment are usually paid totally or in part by the employer.

As long as the treatment is for the purpose of alleviating medical conditions, including mental illness, an employee has no taxable income. If the treatment is for a nonmedical condition, the employee will have taxable income as the result of employer payments.

Financial Planning Programs for Executives

Employers are increasingly providing financial planning as a benefit to employees. Although, traditionally, this benefit was limited to a small number of top executives, many firms are now expanding their programs to include middle management employees in the $50,000 to $100,000 annual salary range.

In addition, financial planning education and advice are now offered to many employees as part of a broader preretirement-counseling program. Any program in overall financial planning must take into consideration the benefits that are provided or that are potentially available under group insurance plans, under social insurance programs, and through the individual efforts of employees.

The concept of providing financial planning for top executives has been widely practiced for many years, particularly in large corporations. Businesses have deemed this financial planning benefit as necessary for such executives (who have limited time for their own financial affairs), so that they can be free to devote their full talents to important business decisions. A company may also find it easier to attract and retain executives who look on the financial planning program as a way to make existing compensation more valuable (for example, by providing a larger spendable income through tax planning or a greater accumulation of wealth through investment planning).

Although group meetings are sometimes used (for example, to explain certain types of investments or changes in the tax laws), most financial planning programs provide for individual counseling of employees to suit their own particular circumstances and needs.

Types of Planning

Financial planning is composed of many separate but interrelated activities:

- Compensation planning, including the explanation of employee benefits and an analysis of any available compensation options
- Preparation of tax returns
- Estate planning, including the preparation of wills and planning to both minimize estate taxes and maintain proper estate liquidity
- Investment planning, including both investment advice and investment management
- Insurance planning, including information on how to meet life insurance, medical expense, disability, property, and liability needs

A financial planning program may be designed to provide either selected services from the list above or a comprehensive array of services. Comprehensive financial planning can be thought of as a series of interrelated and continuing activities that begin with the collection and analysis of personal and financial information, including the risk attitudes of an employee. This information is used (1) to establish the priorities and time horizons for attaining personal objectives and (2) to develop the financial plan that will meet these objectives. Once the plan is formulated, the next critical step is the actual implementation of the plan. A proper financial planning program should also include a process for measuring the performance of any plan so that, if unacceptable, either the plan can be changed or the employee's objectives revised.

Sources of Financial Planning

A few firms provide financial planning services using the organization's own employees. Most firms purchase the services either from outside specialists (such as lawyers, accountants, insurance agents, or stockbrokers) or from companies or individuals that do comprehensive financial planning.

Significant differences exist among financial planning firms. Some operate solely on a fee basis and give only advice and counseling, in which case it is the employee's responsibility to have his or her own attorney, insurance agent, or other financial professional implement any decisions. These financial planning firms often work closely with the other professionals in handling the employee's affairs. The cost of using a fee-only financial planning firm varies, depending upon what services it provides, but initial fees of $5,000 per employee and annual charges of $1,000 to $2,000 are not uncommon.

Other financial planning firms operate on a product-oriented basis and sell products (usually insurance or investments) in addition to other financial planning services. The fact that these firms receive commissions from the products they sell may eliminate or reduce any fees paid by the employer. Unfortunately, the insurance or investment advice of these firms may be slanted in favor of the products they sell. Therefore, employers must make sure that the advice of outside specialists will be unbiased and will be presented in a professional manner.

Taxation

Fees paid for financial planning are tax deductible by the employer as long as the total compensation paid to an employee is reasonable. The amount of any fees paid to a financial planning firm or other professional on behalf of an individual employee becomes taxable income to the employee. However, an employee may be able to take miscellaneous itemized deductions for certain services relating to tax matters and investment advice. Services that the employer provides to executives on an individual basis also result in taxable income.

Preretirement Counseling Programs

Businesses, aware of the pitfalls that await unprepared retired employees, have increasingly begun to offer preretirement counseling. It has been estimated that this benefit is offered by approximately 75 percent of companies with 20,000 or more employees. For companies with fewer than 1,000 employees, the figure is closer to 15 percent or 20 percent. Most of these companies have made this benefit available to all employees over a specific age (such as 50 or 55), but an increasing number of organizations allow employees of any age to participate. Retired employees may also be invited to take advantage of any program benefits that are of interest to them.

Preretirement counseling programs differ from financial planning programs for executives in that there is very little individual counseling. Rather, employees meet in groups to listen to media presentations and speakers, and they are given the opportunity to ask questions and discuss their concerns. This counseling may take place during non-working hours, but there is an increasing tendency to have it provided during working hours, often in a concentrated, one-day or two-day period. Most companies encourage spouses to participate. Often, one program is developed for all employees, although some organizations vary their programs for different classifications of employees (such as management employees and blue-collar workers).

When these programs are successful, the fears that many employees have about retirement are alleviated. They learn that, with proper planning, retirement can be not only financially comfortable but also a meaningful period in their lives.

Financial Planning

Some preretirement counseling programs devote at least half their time to the financial aspects of retirement. Because proper financial planning for retirement must begin many years prior to actual retirement, the amount of time devoted to this subject will be greatest in programs that encourage employees to begin participation at younger ages.

Some financial planning meetings help employees identify and determine what their financial needs will be after retirement and what resources will be available to meet those needs from the company's benefit plans and from Social Security. If retirement needs will not be met by these sources, employees are informed about how their individual efforts can supplement retirement income through savings or investments. They are also told about the specific advantages and risks associated with each method of saving or investment. In addition, issues such as the need for wills and estate planning may be discussed. Such preretirement financial planning is unlikely to provide investment advice on an individual basis or through an investment management service, as described in the previous section on financial planning programs for executives. However, some employers do give employees financial planning reports that are prepared through a computerized financial planning system. These reports, which may vary in length from 20 to 60 pages, are generated from the data on a questionnaire completed by the employee. They may provide advice on such topics as the additional amount of money that should be saved for retirement or compare the cost of working with the cost of retiring.

Many employers now make available computer software that employees can use to derive varying scenarios related to retirement, education funding, and the like by entering basic personal and financial data. The major advantage of these computer programs is that an employee can quickly evaluate alternative assumptions about factors such as retirement dates and savings rates. One potential drawback to the use of computer programs is the lack of employee understanding about the assumptions and reasoning that lie behind the input into the program and the output that results. Therefore, it is important that the introduction of such computer programs be accompanied by proper training in their purpose, use, and interpretation.

Other Aspects of Preretirement Counseling

Preretirement counseling also focuses on other aspects of retirement besides financial needs. The following are some of the questions that must be faced by most retired workers and that are often addressed in preretirement counseling programs:

- Living arrangements. What are the pros and cons of selling a house and moving into an apartment or condominium? Is relocation to the Sunbelt, away from family members and friends, advisable?
- Health. Can changes in lifestyle lead to healthier retirement years?
- Free time. How can the time that was previously devoted to work be used? What opportunities are available for volunteer work, part-time employment, or continuing education? What leisure activities or community activities can be adopted that will continue into retirement? (Studies have shown that alcoholism, divorce, and suicide tend to increase among the retired. Much of this increase has been attributed to the lack of activities to fill free time and to the problems encountered by husbands and wives, who are constantly together for the first time in their lives.)

Sources of Preretirement Counseling

An employer may establish and maintain its own program of preretirement counseling. However, many organizations (such as benefit-counseling firms and the American Association of Retired Persons) have developed packaged programs that are sold to other organizations. These programs typically consist of media presentations and information regarding the types of speakers that should be used in counseling sessions. Generally, these packaged programs are flexible enough to be used with almost any type of employee group. Most firms actually conduct preretirement counseling programs with a combination of their own employees and outside speakers or organizations. It is becoming common to see the use of an employer's own retirees in the counseling process.

Taxation

As long as no specific services are provided to employees on an individual basis, they do not have taxable income to report as a result of participating in preretirement counseling programs.

Transportation/Free Parking

Some employers have long provided transportation benefits to employees as a fringe benefit. These benefits have been in the form of various types of reimbursement for commuting expenses, the use of company-owned vehicles for vanpooling, and free parking. However, except for free parking, employees have usually had taxable income as a result of these benefits. To increase the use of public transportation and decrease the reliance on the use of private passenger automobiles, the Comprehensive National Energy Policy Act of 1992 changed the tax rules governing transportation benefits. As a result of the act, the Internal Revenue Code provides favorable taxation for transportation benefits that meet the definition of a qualified transportation fringe, which includes the following:

- Transportation in a commuter highway vehicle if such transportation is in connection with travel between the employee's residence and place of employment. The commuter vehicle must have a capacity of at least six adults other than the driver. In addition, at least 80 percent of the mileage use of the vehicle must reasonably be expected to be for transporting employees to and from work and must occur when at least one-half of the seating capacity of the vehicle is filled. Traditional vanpools, in which one employee usually has possession of an employer-provided vehicle to drive other employees to work, come under this definition as long as these criteria are satisfied.
- Transit passes. These include any pass, token, fare card, voucher, or similar item entitling a person to transportation as long as such transportation is on a mass-transit facility or in a commuter highway vehicle as previously described.
- Qualified parking. This includes parking provided on or near the business premises of the employer or near a location from which the employee commutes to work by using a mass-transit facility or a commuter highway vehicle. Qualified parking does not include any parking on or near a premises used by the employee for residential purposes.

The value of the benefit under a qualified transportation fringe is excluded from gross compensation up to the following amounts, which are subject to cost-of-living adjustments:

- $100 per month in the aggregate for any transit passes and transportation in a commuter highway vehicle.
- $175 per month for qualified parking.

Amounts in excess of the above and the value of employer transportation benefits that do not meet the definition of a qualified transportation fringe are fully taxable to employees.

Three additional points should be made about qualified transportation benefits. First, they can be provided on a discriminatory basis. Second, the employer can either provide the benefits directly or give a cash reimbursement to the employee, with one exception: Cash reimbursement for a transit pass is not acceptable if such a pass is available for direct distribution by the employer to the employee. Third, when an employer does not wish to assume the cost of the benefits, they can still be provided under an arrangement that allows an employee to enter into a compensation-reduction agreement up to the applicable limits. However, such a compensation-reduction agreement is irrevocable during its specified term even if the employee is no longer eligible for the transportation benefits.

Company Cars

Employers often provide employees with company cars (or other types of vehicles). In addition to using a vehicle for business purposes, an employee may also be allowed to use the car for commuting to and from work and for other personal purposes. However, an employee who drives a company car for personal use must include the value of this use in his or her taxable income.

The method for valuing the use of a car is determined by the employer, and several choices are available. The most common method for valuing the car is for the employer to report an annual cost that is a percentage of the car's annual lease value. This value is determined by a table prepared by the Internal Revenue Service and is based on a car's fair market value, unless an employer can clearly justify a lower value. Under this table, a car with a fair market value of $20,000 to $20,999 has an annual lease value of $5,600. This figure is then multiplied by the ratio of personal-use miles to total miles. For example, if 20 percent of the miles driven are personal miles, the employer must report $1,120 of income for the employee. Additional income must also be reported if the employer pays for gas.

A second alternative is for the employer to annually report the entire lease value of the car as taxable income. If the employer uses this alternative, the employee can claim an income tax deduction for any business use of the vehicle if the employee itemizes his or her deduction. However, the deduction is subject to the 2 percent floor requirement for miscellaneous deductions. This alternative is less favorable to the employee but administratively less burdensome to the employer.

A third alternative is to report a value that is based solely on the employee's use of the vehicle. Under IRS regulations, a flat mileage rate may be used for each personal mile driven. The mileage rate ($.325 in 2000) is adjusted annually. This alternative is available only if a car's fair market value does not exceed a specified value ($15,400 in 2000) and one of the following criteria is satisfied: (1) more than 50 percent of the car's use is for business, (2) the car is used each day in an employer-sponsored commuting pool, or (3) the car is driven at least 10,000 miles per year and is used primarily by employees.

The final alternative is available if the employer has a written policy that the employee must commute in the vehicle and cannot use the vehicle for other than minimal personal use. In this case, the value of the car's use is $1.50 times the number of one-way commutes or $3.00 times the number of round-trip commutes.

Subsidized Eating Facilities

Employers often provide fully or partially subsidized eating facilities for employees. While lunch is the most commonly served meal, breakfast and dinner may also be served. Such facilities offer a place for employees to discuss common issues and may minimize the chance that employees will take prolonged lunch periods at off-site restaurants. The popularity of these facilities tends to vary with the price of meals, the convenience of alternative places to eat, and the quality of the food served.

The subsidized value of meals served to employees is excluded from taxable income as long as the meals are (1) provided on the business premises and (2) furnished for the convenience of the employer. In general, meals are considered to be furnished for the employer's convenience if there are inadequate facilities in the area for employees to obtain meals within a reasonable period of time. If the requirements regarding the business premises and/or the convenience of the employer are not satisfied, the subsidized value of any meals consumed by employees is included in taxable income.

Employees are not allowed to deduct any portion of the cost they pay for individual meals. However, if an employee is required to have a fixed periodic charge for meals deducted from wages or salary (such as $15 per week), this amount is excluded from taxable income.

STUDY QUESTIONS

1. What design features are usually found in paid vacation plans?

2. What factors other than employee benefit decisions determine the holidays on which a business is closed?

3. Under what circumstances might an employer allow employees to have time off with pay?

4. Describe the family-leave legislation that exists at both the state and federal levels.

5. With respect to an educational assistance plan that meets the requirements of Code Section 127, explain
   a. the amount of benefits that may be received tax free.
   b. the types of benefits that may be received.
   c. the nondiscrimination rules that apply.

6. Under what circumstances may each of the following employer-provided services be received tax free by employees?
   a. No-additional-cost services
   b. Employee discounts
   c. Adoption assistance
   d. Employee-assistance programs
   e. Financial planning programs
   f. Transportation
   g. Free parking
   h. Subsidized eating facilities

7. What types of benefits may be available under each of the following types of programs?
   a. Child-care
   b. Eldercare
   c. Adoption assistance

8. What are the advantages that may offset the cost of wellness programs?

9. Why are many wellness programs designed to include family members of employees?

10. a. What is the purpose of employee-assistance plans?
    b. How do employee-assistance plans operate?

11. Explain how financial planning programs for executives differ from the financial planning that is available under preretirement counseling programs.

12. In addition to financial planning, what are the other aspects of preretirement counseling programs?

Cafeteria Plans

OBJECTIVES

- Explain the rationale for the use of cafeteria plans.

- Describe the general nature of cafeteria plans and identify the various types of cafeteria plans.

- Explain the barriers that must be overcome before a cafeteria plan can be implemented.

- Explain the issues that must be resolved to properly design a cafeteria plan.

In the past, with the possible exception of an HMO option, employees have had little or no opportunity to decide how employer dollars are to be spent on employee benefits. Some organizations have had benefit plans that give a limited number of key executives some choice in the selection of types and levels of employee benefits that will be provided to them with employer contributions. Although many organizations have benefit programs in which optional or supplemental benefits may be elected by all (or many) employees, the cost of these benefits must normally be borne by the employees on an after-tax, payroll-deduction basis.

More recently, however, many organizations have established benefit programs in which all (or almost all) employees can design their own benefit packages by purchasing benefits with a prespecified amount of employer dollars from a number of available options. Generally, these cafeteria plans (often referred to as *flexible benefit plans* or *cafeteria compensation plans*) also allow additional benefits to be purchased on a payroll-deduction basis. Today, it is estimated that more than 25 percent of employers with more than 500 employees have a full-fledged cafeteria plan. Most of these employers and many smaller employers offer premium-conversion plans and/or flexible spending accounts.

THE RATIONALE FOR CAFETERIA PLANS

The growth in employee benefits has caused two problems. First, some employers feel that many employees do not recognize and appreciate the magnitude of their employee benefits; indeed, as benefits increase, employee appreciation often seems to decrease. Advocates of cafeteria plans argue that by giving employees a stated dollar amount with which they must select their own benefits (from a list of options), employees become more aware of the actual cost of these benefits and are more likely to appreciate the benefits they choose.

A second problem is that the inflexible benefit structure of conventional employee benefit plans does not adequately meet the various benefit needs of all employees, often leading to employee dissatisfaction. For example, single employees often resent the medical coverage that married employees receive for their families because the single employees receive no benefit of corresponding value. Similarly, employees who have no dependents often see little value in life insurance and would prefer other benefits. Those who favor the concept of cafeteria plans feel that such dissatisfaction can be minimized if employees have the option to select their own benefits. Advocates of cafeteria plans argue that this increased employee satisfaction will result in a better employee-retention record and in greater ability to attract new employees.

Some employers see the cafeteria approach to benefit planning as an opportunity to control the escalating benefit costs associated with inflation and with the new requirements of recently enacted federal and state legislation. Because a cafeteria plan is essentially a defined-contribution plan rather than a defined-benefit plan, it provides a number of opportunities for controlling increases in costs. For example, it may encourage employees to choose medical expense options that have larger deductibles or a greater degree of managed care so that they can more efficiently use the fixed number of dollars allotted to them under the plan. A cafeteria plan may also enable the employer to pass on to the employees any increased benefit costs that result from having to comply with legislation that mandates additional benefits. In addition, because increases in employer contributions are not directly related to increases in benefit costs, the employer can grant percentage increases in the amounts available for benefits that are less than the actual overall increase in employee benefit costs.

It should be noted that early cafeteria plans were designed primarily to meet the varying needs of employees. In contrast, newer plans are much more likely to be instituted as a cost-saving technique.

THE NATURE OF CAFETERIA PLANS

In its purest sense, a cafeteria plan can be defined as any employee benefit plan that allows an employee to have some choice in designing his or her own benefit package by selecting different types or levels of benefits that are funded with employer dollars. At this extreme, a benefit plan that allows an employee to select an HMO as an option to an insured medical expense plan can be classified as a cafeteria plan. However, the more common use of the term *cafeteria plan* denotes something much broader—a plan in which choices can be made among several different types of benefits and, possibly, cash.

Prior to the addition of Section 125 to the Internal Revenue Code in 1978, the use of cafeteria plans had potentially adverse tax consequences for an employee. If an employee had a choice among benefits that were normally nontaxable (such as medical expense insurance or disability income insurance) and benefits that were normally taxable (such as life insurance in excess of $50,000 or cash), then the doctrine of constructive receipt resulted in an employee's being taxed as if he or she had elected the maximum dollar amount of taxable benefits that could have been obtained under the plan. For example, if an employee could have elected cash in lieu of being covered under the employer's medical expense plan but chose to remain in the medical expense plan, that employee was considered to have taxable income merely because cash could have been elected. Obviously, this tax environment was not conducive to the use of cafeteria plans unless the only benefits offered were normally of a nontaxable nature.

Permissible Benefits

Section 125 of the Code defines a cafeteria plan as a written plan under which all participants are employees and under which all participants may choose between two or more benefits consisting of (1) *qualified benefits* and (2) cash. Qualified benefits essentially include any welfare benefits excluded from taxation under the Internal Revenue Code except scholarships and fellowships, transportation benefits, educational assistance, no-additional-cost services, employee discounts, and *de minimis* fringe benefits. The latter include dependent life insurance coverage in amounts of $2,000 or less. The Health Insurance Portability and Accountability Act (HIPPA) expanded this list of exceptions to include any product that is advertised, marketed, or offered as long-term care insurance. Thus medical expense benefits (other than long-term care insurance), disability benefits, accidental death and dismemberment benefits, vacations, and dependent-care assistance (such as day care centers) can be included in a cafeteria plan. The Code also allows group term life insurance to be included, even in amounts exceeding $50,000. In general, a cafeteria plan cannot include benefits that defer compensation except for a qualified Section 401(k) or similar plan.

The prohibition of benefits that defer compensation has an important impact on vacation benefits. If an employee elects vacation benefits for the plan year of a cafeteria plan, the vacation days cannot be carried over into the following plan year because this would be a deferral of compensation. (Note: Regular vacation days are considered to have been taken before the additional days elected under the cafeteria plan.) However, an employee can elect to exchange these days for cash as long as the election is made and the cash is actually received prior to the end of the plan year. If this is not done, the days are forfeited and their value is lost.

The term *cash* is actually broader than it would otherwise appear. In addition to the actual receipt of dollars, a benefit is treated as cash as long as (1) it is not a benefit specifically prohibited by Section 125 as cash and (2) it is provided on a taxable basis. This latter provision means that either (1) the cost of the benefit is paid by the employee with after-tax dollars on a payroll-deduction basis or (2) employer dollars are used to obtain the benefit, but the employer reports the cost of the benefit as taxable income for the employee. This rule would allow the inclusion of group automobile insurance or long-term care insurance in a cafeteria plan but not on a tax-favored basis. It also allows long-term disability coverage to be provided on an after-tax basis, so that disability income benefits can be received tax free.

The list of benefits that Section 125 specifically prohibits from being treated as cash includes any benefits provided under Section 117 (scholarships and tuition expenses) and Section 132 (various fringe benefits such as discounts and transportation benefits) of the Internal Revenue Code.

As long as a benefit plan offering choice meets the definition of a cafeteria plan, the issue of constructive receipt does not apply. Employees will have taxable income only to the extent that normally taxable benefits—group term life insurance in excess of $50,000 and cash—are elected. An employer can have a benefit plan that offers choice but does not meet the statutory definition of a cafeteria plan. In such a case the issue of constructive receipt will come into play if the plan contains any benefits that normally result in taxable income.

Choice of Medical Expense Plans

Employers often allow employees a choice of medical expense plans for themselves or their employees. However, there is often confusion over whether this choice constitutes a cafeteria plan. If it does, the employer will need to comply with the rules of Section 125 and ERISA or be subject to the statutory penalties for noncompliance.

Assume an employer has a noncontributory medical expense plan that allows employees to elect among two or more managed care plans. If this is the only choice offered to employees, it is not a cafeteria plan because there is no cash option. It is only a choice among qualified benefits.

Now assume that an employer gives employees the option of electing either a noncontributory managed care plan or an indemnity plan for which the employee must make a monetary contribution on an after-tax basis. Again, by itself this is not a cafeteria plan because there is no option of electing cash. However, if employees are allowed to pay their share of the premiums for the indemnity plan on a before-tax basis through a premium-conversion plan (discussed later in this chapter), a cafeteria plan has been created under Section 125. Because salary reductions technically become employer dollars, the employees who elect salary reductions are considered to be choosing between cash and a qualified benefit.

Some employers allow an employee to elect out of medical expense coverage and receive cash. For example, some employees may feel that they do not need coverage under the employer's plan because they are adequately covered under their spouse's plans. If the cost to provide coverage to employees is $2,000 per year, the employer might feel financially justified in offering these employees $1,000 to waive coverage. Since these employees have a choice between the medical expense coverage and cash, a cafeteria plan has been created.

Benefit Election

Section 125 requires that benefit elections under a cafeteria plan be made prior to the beginning of a plan year. These elections cannot be changed during the plan year except under certain specified circumstances if the plan allows such changes. While there is no requirement that these changes be included in a plan, some or all of them are included in most plans.

The Internal Revenue Service (IRS) regulations regarding election changes had remained unchanged through most of the 1990s. In 1997, however, regulations with proposed changes were issued, and employers were allowed to use either the old or the new regulations. In early 2000, the proposed regulations were made final with some modifications; they must be used for plan years beginning on or after January 1, 2001. At the same time, the IRS issued another set of proposed regulations to address issues not covered by the new regulations. Employers also are allowed to use these regulations for plan years beginning on or after January 1, 2001.

The regulations allow new cafeteria plan elections for specified *changes in status*. In addition, the regulations specify that any new cafeteria plan elections are allowed only if an employee, spouse, or dependent gains or loses eligibility for coverage, and the cafeteria plan election change corresponds with that gain or loss in coverage. The acceptable changes in status include the following:

- Legal marital status (including marriage, death of a spouse, divorce, legal separation, or annulment)
- Number of dependents (resulting from birth, adoption, commencement or termination of an adoption proceeding, or death)
- Employment status (the termination or commencement of employment by the employee, spouse, or dependent)
- Work schedule (a reduction or increase in hours of employment by the employee, spouse, or dependent, including a switch between part-time and full-time employment, a strike or a lockout, and commencement of or return from an unpaid leave of absence)
- Dependent status under a health plan for unmarried dependents
- Residence or worksite of the employee, spouse, or dependent

Regulations address several specific issues. For example, increases in group term insurance coverage and disability income coverages are allowed in the case of marriage, birth, adoption, or placement for adoption. Decreases in coverage are allowed for divorce, legal separation, annulment, or death of a spouse or dependent. The regulations also allow employees to make election changes if, during the plan year, (1) a new benefit package is offered or a benefit package is eliminated or (2) a change is made in the coverage of an employee's spouse or dependent. In addition, an employee can make a change as a result of an open-enrollment change by a spouse or dependent whose employer's plan has a different period of coverage. Finally, an employee can make a change as a result of a spouse's or dependent's change under his or her own cafeteria plan, as long as that change conforms to the regulations.

Even if none of the above rules are met, election changes are permitted in cafeteria plans as a result of changes in coverage or premiums because of HIPAA, COBRA, eligibility for Medicare, or a legal judgment, decree, or order resulting from divorce, legal separation, annulment, or change in legal custody.

Payroll Deductions and Salary Reductions

Under some cafeteria plans, employees are allowed to allocate only a predetermined employer contribution to benefits. Other cafeteria plans are designed so that employees can obtain additional benefits with optional payroll deductions or salary reductions.

Many cafeteria plans that provide a wide array of benefits allow an employee to elect an after-tax payroll deduction to obtain additional benefits. For example, under a cafeteria plan an employee might be given $200 per month with which to select varying types and levels of benefits. If the benefits the employee chooses cost $240, the employee has two options—either to decrease the benefits selected or to authorize a $40 payroll deduction. Even though the payroll deduction is on an after-tax basis, the employee gains to the extent that the additional benefits can be selected through a group arrangement at a lower cost than in the individual marketplace.

Section 125 also allows employees to purchase certain benefits on a before-tax basis through the use of a premium-conversion plan or a flexible spending account (FSA). Premium-conversion plans or FSAs, both of which are technically cafeteria plans, can be used by themselves or incorporated into a more comprehensive cafeteria plan. They are most commonly used alone by small employers who are unwilling to establish a broader plan, primarily for cost reasons. The cafeteria plans of most large employers contain one or both of these arrangements as an integral part of the plan.

Before-tax salary reductions reduce taxable income for federal income tax purposes. In most (but not all) states, they also reduce the income subject to state tax.

Premium-Conversion Plans

A premium-conversion plan (also called a *premium-only plan*, or *POP*) allows an employee to elect a before-tax salary reduction to pay his or her premium contribution to any employer-sponsored health or other welfare benefit plan. For example, an employer might provide medical expense coverage to employees at no cost but make a monthly charge for dependent coverage. Under a premium-conversion plan, the employee can pay for the dependent coverage with a before-tax salary reduction.

As a rule, premium-conversion plans are established for medical and dental expenses only. If such plans are used for group term life insurance, the cost of coverage in excess of $50,000 must be reported as income, which defeats the purpose of the salary reduction. If these plans are used for disability income coverage, benefits will be taxable as noncontributory employer-provided coverage because the amount of any salary reduction is considered to be the employer's money.

Flexible Spending Accounts (FSAs)

An FSA allows an employee to fund certain benefits on a before-tax basis by electing to take a salary reduction, which can then be used to fund the cost of any qualified benefits included in the plan. However, FSAs are used almost exclusively for medical and dental expenses not covered by the employer's plan and for dependent-care expenses.

The amount of any salary reduction is, in effect, credited to an employee's reimbursement account, and benefits are paid from this account when an employee properly files for such reimbursement. Reimbursements are typically made on a monthly or quarterly basis. The amount of the salary reduction must be determined prior to the beginning of the plan year. Once the amount is set, changes are allowed only under the specified circumstances previously mentioned for benefit elections. A separate election must be made for each benefit, and the funds are accounted for separately. Monies from a salary reduction for one type of expense cannot be used as reimbursement for another type of expense.

If the monies in the FSA are not used during the plan year, they are forfeited. Because forfeited funds are considered plan assets, they can be used only for the payment of benefits and reasonable administrative expenses. Under ERISA rules, forfeitures may be used to do the following:

- Defray the administrative costs of the plan.
- Protect the underwriting integrity of the plan. This includes the use of these funds to reimburse the plan for benefits paid that exceed a terminated employee's contributions. For example, an employee who contributed $100 per month might be eligible to collect a full annual reimbursement of $1,200 in the first month of participation. If the employee terminated employment at that time, the plan would have paid out $1,100 more than it had taken in.
- Reallocate contribution to the following plan year. Such reallocations must be on a per capita basis for all participants and cannot be based on amounts each employee originally contributed.

The ERISA rules specifically prohibit the donating of forfeitures to charity or the reversion of such amounts to the employer for general business expenses.

An election to participate in an FSA program not only reduces a salary for federal income tax purposes but also lowers the wages on which Social Security and Medicare taxes are levied. As a result, those employees who end up below the Social Security wage-base limit after the reduction pay less in Social Security taxes, and their future income benefits under Social Security may be reduced. However, the reduction in future benefits is small in most cases, unless the salary reduction is large. It should be noted that the employer's share of Social Security and Medicare tax payments also decreases. In some cases, the employer's savings may actually be large enough to fully offset the cost of administering the FSA program.

One issue faced by employers over the years has been whether to limit benefit payments to the amount of an account balance or to allow an employee at any time during the year to receive benefits equal to his or her annual salary reduction. For example, say an employee contributes $100 per month to an FSA to provide benefits for the cost of unreimbursed medical expenses. During the first month of the plan, the employee earns only $100 of the $1,200 annual contribution. If the employee incurs $300 of unreimbursed medical expenses during the month, should he or she be allowed to withdraw $100 or the full $300? The objection to allowing a $300 withdrawal is that the employer will lose $200 if the employee terminates employment before making any further contribution. IRS regulations do not give the employer any choice with respect to health benefits (that is, medical and dental expenses); FSAs must allow an amount equal to the full annual contribution to be taken as benefits any time during the year. Therefore, the employee is entitled to a benefit of $300 after the first month. However, IRS regulations do allow a choice in reimbursement policies for other types of benefits, such as dependent-care expenses. For these benefits, most plans limit aggregate benefits to the total contributions made up until the time when benefits are received.

TYPES OF PLANS

Core-Plus Plans

Probably the most common type of full-fledged cafeteria plan is one that offers a basic core of benefits to all employees, plus a second layer of optional benefits that permits an employee to choose which benefits he or she will add to the basic benefits. These optional benefits can be "purchased" with dollars, or credits, that are given to the employee as part of the benefit package. If these credits are inadequate to purchase the desired benefits, an employee can make additional purchases with after-tax contributions or with before-tax salary reductions under a premium-conversion plan and/or an FSA.

Perhaps the best way to demonstrate how cafeteria plans operate is to include a brief description of some existing plans.

■ EXAMPLE 1

An educational organization with 3,000 employees offers a core-plus plan. While this type of plan is common, it should be noted that the list of optional benefits in this example is more extensive than what is found in most cafeteria plans.

All employees receive a minimum level of benefits, called basic benefits, as follows:

- Term life insurance equal to one-half of salary
- Travel accident insurance (when on the employer's business)
- Disability income insurance
- Two to four weeks' vacation

continued

■ **EXAMPLE 1** *(continued)*

Employees are also given flexible credits, equal to between 3 percent and 6 percent of salary (depending on length of service, with the maximum reached after ten years), which can be used to purchase additional, or "optional," benefits. There is a new election of benefits each year, and no carryover of any unused credits is allowed. The optional benefits are the following:

- An array of medical expense options. Although there is no charge for HMO coverage, a charge is made for coverage under an indemnity plan, and additional flexible credits are given if a person elects no medical expense coverage.
- Additional life insurance up to $4\frac{1}{2}$ times salary.
- Accidental death insurance when the basic travel accident insurance does not apply.
- Dental insurance for the employee and dependents.
- Up to two weeks' additional vacation time.
- Cash.

If an employee does not have enough flexible credits to purchase the desired optional benefits, additional amounts may be contributed on a payroll-deduction basis for all but additional vacation time. Also, a salary reduction may be elected for contributions to an FSA that provides dependent-care benefits.

A variation of the core-plus approach is having the core plan be an "average" plan for which the employee makes no contribution. If certain benefits are reduced, the employee may then receive credits that can be used either to increase other benefits or, if the plan allows, to increase cash compensation. Additional benefits can typically be obtained through employee payroll deductions.

■ **EXAMPLE 2**

This plan covers 15,000 nonunion employees in one division of a major industrial conglomerate.

Employees may elect to reduce certain benefits and receive credits that can be either used to purchase additional benefits, taken in cash, or contributed to the company's 401(k) plan. Additional benefits may be purchased through payroll deduction.

The plan applies to four types of benefits:

1. Medical expense insurance
2. Employee life insurance

continued

■ **EXAMPLE 2** *(continued)*

3. Accidental death and dismemberment insurance
4. Dependent life insurance

Several medical expense insurance options are available. The standard coverage, for which there is neither a charge nor a credit, is a point-of-service plan. Employees may elect a traditional indemnity plan, but this option results in a charge. Several HMO options are also available, all of which result in credits.

There are several employee life insurance options that range from one-half to five times salary. The standard coverage for which there is no credit or charge is 1½ times salary.

Although several supplemental accidental death and dismemberment options and a single dependent life insurance option are available, they result in a charge to the employee. So, in effect, there is no basic benefit for these areas.

Modular Plans

Another type of cafeteria plan is one in which an employee has a choice among several predesigned benefit packages. Typically, at least one of the packages can be selected without any employee cost. If an employee selects a more expensive package, he or she will be required to contribute to the cost of the package. Some employers may also include a bare-bones benefit package, which results in cash being paid to an employee who selects it.

Under some cafeteria plans using this approach (often referred to as a *modular approach*), the predesigned packages may have significant differences. A comparison of two packages may show one to be better than others in certain cases but inferior in other cases. Other plans using this approach have virtually identical packages, the major difference being the option selected for medical expense coverage. For example, the plan of one large bank offers coverage by three traditional insured plans, two HMOs and a preferred-provider organization.

Modular plans are popular among employees for two reasons. First, adverse selection can be more easily controlled under modular plans than under core-plus plans. Second, modular plans are easier to administer and communicate. For both these reasons, small employers who have full-fledged cafeteria plans are most likely to take a modular approach.

■ **EXAMPLE 3**

A large financial institution's cafeteria plan covers almost 20,000 employees. There are seven predesigned benefit packages that can be chosen, with each package designed for a specific segment of the employee population. Each package has one of three medical expense plans and varying amounts of group term life insurance. The packages contain differing combinations of dental insurance, vision coverage and dependent-care benefits. All offer the same level of disability income coverage.

A "cost" is associated with each package. Some packages cost an employee nothing, other packages require an employee contribution, and at least one option has a negative cost, meaning that an employee who selects it receives additional cash compensation. The cost of each package can vary for two reasons. First, an employee elects whether to have medical expense coverage for dependents. Second, HMO and PPO choices are available in many of the employee locations.

Salary-Reduction-Only Plans

The final example is a cafeteria plan that consists solely of the two types of salary reduction that can be used in a cafeteria plan—a premium-conversion plan and an FSA.

■ **EXAMPLE 4**

Employees of a small nonprofit organization are allowed to elect salary reductions for each of the following:

■ The employee's share of the cost of medical and dental insurance premiums for dependents. (Under this plan, the employer pays the full cost of the employee's coverage.)

■ Qualifying medical care expenses. These are any medical (including dental) expenses normally deductible on Schedule A of an employee's federal income tax return (without regard to any gross income limitations). Note that these deductible expenses must not have been reimbursed by insurance.

■ Eligible dependent-care expenses. These are expenses for the types of benefits that could be provided in a qualified program for dependent-care assistance. The maximum annual salary reduction for this category of benefits is limited to $5,000 to prevent the plan from being discriminatory; otherwise, too large a portion of the benefits would be provided to highly compensated employees.

continued

■ **EXAMPLE 4** *(continued)*

Employees can request reimbursements for medical care and dependent-care expenses at the end of each month and must file an appropriate form accompanied by documentation (bills and receipts) to support their request. For administrative purposes, reimbursement requests must be for amounts of at least $50, except in the last quarter of the year.

The maximum reimbursement at any time for dependent-care expenses is the accumulated amount in an employee's account.

OBSTACLES TO CAFETERIA PLANS

Certain obstacles must be overcome before a cafeteria plan can be successfully implemented. Recent changes in federal tax laws and proper plan design would seem sufficient to overcome many of these obstacles. However, it must be realized that any organization that adopts a cafeteria plan other than a simple FSA program or premium-conversion plan will face a complex, costly, and time-consuming project.

The Legislative Environment

Undoubtedly, the largest obstacle to cafeteria plans for several years was the unsettled federal income tax picture. This picture was finally clarified in 1984 by the passage of the Tax Reform Act and the IRS issuance of regulations governing cafeteria plans. Since then, the number of cafeteria plans has grown significantly, particularly among large firms. However, almost every year, either a federal tax bill alters Section 125 in some way, new IRS regulations are issued, or proposals for change are made by elected officials. The benefits that can be included in a cafeteria plan are changed, the nondiscrimination rules are altered, or the rules for FSAs are "clarified." This continuing uncertainty has caused many employers to take a wait-and-see attitude toward cafeteria plans.

Meeting Nondiscrimination Rules

Section 125 imposes complex nondiscrimination tests on cafeteria plans, causing many employees to view cafeteria plans unfavorably. If these tests are not met, adverse tax consequences for key employees and/or highly compensated employees may actually result in higher taxable income for these employees than if no cafeteria plan existed. From a practical standpoint, the test is usually met if an employer has a full-fledged cafeteria plan that applies to all employees. However, care must be exercised in designing a plan that either covers only a segment of the employees or has only a small percentage of employees participating. The latter situation often occurs with FSAs.

As is often the case, the nondiscrimination tests are not applicable if a plan is maintained under provisions of a collective-bargaining agreement.

The Concentration Test

Under the concentration test, no more than 25 percent of the tax-favored benefits provided under the plan can go to key employees (as defined for the Section 79 nondiscrimination rules). This test is a particular problem if an employer has a large percentage of key employees and if key employees, as higher-paid individuals, contribute large amounts to an FSA.

If a plan fails the concentration test, key employees must include in gross income the maximum taxable benefits that could have been elected under the plan. In effect, these employees are subject to the doctrine of constructive receipt.

The Eligibility Test

Cafeteria plans are subject to a two-part eligibility test, both parts of which must be satisfied. The first part of the test stipulates that no employee be required to complete more than three years of employment as a condition for participation and that the employment requirement for each employee be the same. In addition, any employee who satisfies the employment requirement and is otherwise entitled to participate must do so no later than the first day of the plan year following completion of the employment requirement unless the employee has separated from service in the interim.

The second part of the test requires that eligibility for participation must not be discriminatory in favor of highly compensated employees, who are defined as any of the following:

- Officers
- Shareholders who own more than 5 percent of the voting power or value of all classes of the firm's stock
- Employees who are highly compensated based on all facts and circumstances
- Spouses or dependents of any of the above

The eligibility test uses Table 17-1, which is found in IRS regulations and can best be explained with the following example.

An employer has 1,000 employees—800 non–highly compensated and 200 highly compensated. The percentage of non–highly compensated employees is 80 percent (800/1,000), for which the table shows a safe harbor percentage of 35. This means that if the percentage of non–highly compensated employees eligible for the plan is equal to at least 35 percent of the percentage of highly compensated employees eligible, the plan satisfies the eligibility test. Assume that 160 people, or 80 percent of the highly compensated employees, are eligible. Then at least 28 percent, or 224, of the non–highly compensated employees must be eligible for the plan (calculations: $.80 \times .35 = .28$ and $.28 \times 800 = 224$).

The table also shows an unsafe harbor percentage of 25 percent. Using this figure instead of 35 percent yields 160 employees. If fewer than this number of non–highly compensated employees are eligible, the eligibility test is failed.

If the number of eligible non–highly compensated employees falls between the numbers determined by the two percentages (from 160 to 223 employees in this example), IRS regulations impose a facts-and-circumstances test to determine whether the eligibility test is passed or failed. According to the regulations, the following factors will be considered: (1) the underlying business reason for the eligibility classification, (2) the percentage of employees eligible, (3) the percentage of eligible employees in each salary range, and (4) the extent to which the eligibility classification is close to satisfying the safe harbor rule. However, the regulations also state that none of these factors alone is determinative, and other facts and circumstances may be relevant.

If a plan fails the eligibility test, highly compensated employees must include in gross income the maximum taxable benefits that could have been elected under the plan.

Nondiscriminatory Contributions and Benefits

Cafeteria plans cannot discriminate in favor of highly compensated participants with respect to contributions or benefits. Section 125 states that a cafeteria plan is not discriminatory if the plan's nontaxable benefits and total benefits (or the employer contributions allocable to each) do not discriminate in favor of highly compensated employees. In addition, a cafeteria plan providing health benefits is not discriminatory if contributions under the plan for each participant include an amount equal to one of the following:

TABLE 17-1

Non–Highly Compensated Employee Concentration Percentage	Safe Harbor Percentage	Unsafe Harbor Percentage
0–60	50.00	40.00
61	49.25	39.25
62	48.50	38.50
63	47.75	37.75
64	47.00	37.00
65	46.25	36.25
66	45.50	35.50
67	44.75	34.75
68	44.00	34.00
69	43.25	33.25
70	42.50	32.50
71	41.75	31.75
72	41.00	31.00
73	40.25	30.25
74	39.50	29.50
75	38.75	28.75
76	38.00	28.00
77	37.25	27.25
78	36.50	26.50
79	35.75	25.75
80	35.00	25.00
81	34.25	24.25
82	33.50	23.50
83	32.75	22.75
84	32.00	22.00
85	31.25	21.25
86	30.50	20.50
87	29.75	20.00
88	29.00	20.00
89	28.25	20.00
90	27.50	20.00
91	26.75	20.00
92	26.00	20.00
93	25.25	20.00
94	24.50	20.00
95	23.75	20.00
96	23.00	20.00
97	22.25	20.00
98	21.50	20.00
99	20.75	20.00

- 100 percent of the health benefit cost for the majority of similarly situated (that is, having family or single coverage) highly compensated employees
- At least 75 percent of the health benefit cost for the similarly situated participant with the best health benefit coverage

Contributions exceeding either of these amounts are nondiscriminatory if they bear a uniform relationship to an employee's compensation.

The Employer's Obligation

Under the most liberal cafeteria plan, each employee has an unrestricted choice of the benefits that his or her employer provides. Some critics of this concept argue that both the motivational and the security aspects of a cafeteria plan may be damaged by unwise employee selection, because many employees may not have the expertise to select the proper benefits. In addition, there is concern about the organization's moral and, perhaps, legal obligation to prevent employees from financial injury through faulty decisions. These concerns have been incorporated into the design of most plans presently in existence: employees are given both certain basic benefits that provide a minimum level of security and a series of optional benefits on top of the basic ones.

Negative Attitudes

Some negative attitudes toward cafeteria plans have been expressed by employees, insurers, and unions. No cafeteria plan can be truly successful without the support of the employees involved. To win the employees' initial support and to overcome any potential negative attitudes, companies that contemplate the development of such programs must spend a considerable amount of time and resources in making sure that employees are adequately informed about (1) the reasons for the proposed program, (2) its advantages and disadvantages, and (3) its future implications. For best results, the opinions of employees should be solicited and weighed, and employees should be involved in various aspects of the decision-making process.

Some insurers have been reluctant to participate in cafeteria plans. A few seem unwilling to try anything new; others are concerned about the problem of adverse selection as a result of employee choice. However, as explained below, the problem of adverse selection can be minimized.

Unions have also had a negative attitude. Union management often feels that bargaining for a cafeteria plan is contrary to the practice of bargaining for the best benefit program for all employees. There is also concern that a cafeteria plan will be used primarily as a cost-containment technique to pass on the cost of future benefit increases to union members. Consequently, the existing programs often apply only to nonunion employees.

Adverse Selection

When employees are allowed a choice in selecting benefits, the problem of adverse selection arises. This means that employees who are likely to have claims tend to pick the benefits that will minimize their out-of-pocket costs. For example, an employee who previously selected a medical expense option with a high deductible might switch to a plan with a lower deductible if medical expenses are ongoing. An employee who previously rejected dental insurance is likely to elect this benefit if dental care is anticipated in the near future.

It should be noted that adverse selection is a problem whether a plan is insured or self-funded. The problem even exists outside of cafeteria plans if choice is allowed. However, the degree of choice within a cafeteria plan tends to make the potential costs more severe unless actions are taken to combat the problem.

Several techniques are used to control adverse selection in cafeteria plans. Benefit limitations and restrictions on coverage can be included if a person wishes to add or change coverage at a date later than initial eligibility. This technique has been common in contributory benefit plans for many years. Another technique is to price the options accordingly. If an option is likely to encourage adverse selection, the cost to the employee for that option should be higher than what would have been charged if the option had been the only one available. Such pricing has been difficult in the past, but it is becoming easier and more accurate as more experience with cafeteria plans develops. The need to control adverse selection is also one reason for the use of predesigned, packaged plans. If, for example, the medical expense plan in one option is likely to encourage adverse selection, the option may not include other benefits for which adverse selection is also a concern (such as dental benefits). To further offset increased costs from the medical expense plan, the option may also offer minimal coverage for other types of benefits.

Cost

It is an accepted fact that an organization that adopts a cafeteria plan will incur initial development and administrative costs that are over and above those of a more traditional benefit program. Some of this extra cost is the value of the employee hours that must be spent in preparing the program for implementation. Another sizable portion must be paid for the reprogramming of the organization's computer system to include necessary information and to accept the employees' benefit elections. ERISA also requires the annual filing of Form 5500.

Until recently, the cost of a cafeteria plan was beyond the means of all but large employers. However, packaged plans developed by many insurers now make this approach financially available to employers with only a few hundred employees.

Continuing costs will depend on such factors as the benefits included in the plan, the number of options available with each benefit, the frequency with which employees may change benefit elections, and the number of employees covered by the plan. Firms with cafeteria plans have incurred added costs because of the need for additional employees to administer the program and additional computer time to process employee choices. However, these costs have been regarded as small in relation to the total cost of providing employee benefits. In addition, as cafeteria plans have grown in popularity, many vendors have developed software packages that can be used to provide administrative functions more cost-effectively.

ISSUES IN PLAN DESIGN

Before committing itself to the establishment of a cafeteria program, an employer must be sure a valid reason exists for converting the company's traditional benefit program to a cafeteria approach. For example, if there is strong employee dissatisfaction with the current benefit program, the solution may lie in clearly identifying the sources of dissatisfaction and making appropriate adjustments in the existing benefit program, rather than in shifting to a cafeteria plan. However, if employee dissatisfaction arises from widely differing benefit needs, conversion to a cafeteria plan may be quite appropriate. Beyond having a clearly defined purpose for converting from a traditional benefit program to a cafeteria program and being willing to bear the additional administrative costs associated with a cafeteria approach, the employer must face a number of considerations in designing the plan.

The Type and Amount of Benefits To Include

Probably the most fundamental decision that must be made in designing a cafeteria plan involves determining what benefits should be included. An employer who wants the plan to be viewed as meeting the differing needs of employees must receive employee input concerning the types of benefits perceived as most desirable. An open dialogue with employees will undoubtedly lead to suggestions that every possible employee benefit be made available. The enthusiasm of many employees for a cafeteria plan will then be dampened when the employer rejects some—and possibly many—of these suggestions for cost, administrative, or psychological reasons. Consequently, it is important that certain ground rules be established regarding the benefits that are acceptable to the employer.

The employer must decide whether the plan should be limited to the types of benefits provided through traditional group insurance arrangements or be expanded to include other benefits. At a minimum, it is important to ensure that an overall employee benefit program provide employees with protection against all major areas of personal risk. This suggests a benefit program with at least *some* provision for life insurance, disability income protection, medical expense protection, and retirement benefits, but it is not necessary that *all* these benefits be included in a cafeteria plan. For example, most employers have a retirement plan that is separate from their cafeteria plan because of Section 125 requirements. Other employers make a 401(k) plan one of the available cafeteria options.

In some respects, a cafeteria plan may be an ideal vehicle for providing less traditional types of benefits. Two examples are extra vacation time and child care. Some plans allow an employee to use flexible credits to purchase additional days of vacation. When available, this option has proven a popular benefit, particularly among single employees. A problem may arise, however, if the work of vacationing employees must be assumed by nonvacationing employees, in addition to their own regularly assigned work. Those not electing extra vacation time may resent doing the work of someone else who is away longer than the normal vacation period.

In recent years, employers have been under increasing pressure to provide care for employees' children, which represents an additional cost if added to a traditional benefit program. Employees who include child-care benefits in a cafeteria plan can pay for the cost of such benefits, possibly with dollars from an FSA. However, lower-paid employees may be better off financially by paying for child care with out-of-pocket dollars and electing the income tax credit available for dependent-care expenses.

One question that sometimes arises is whether dependent life insurance should be included in a cafeteria plan. As mentioned previously, amounts of $2,000 or less do not fit the definition of a qualified benefit and cannot be included. If the amount of coverage available exceeds $2,000, the benefit can be provided as long as it is treated as a cash benefit. An employee who elects coverage with employer-provided dollars will have taxable income as determined by Uniform Premium Table I. Because this amount will exceed the actual cost of the coverage in some cases, dependent life insurance is often made available outside a cafeteria plan. When it is included in a cafeteria plan, there is frequently a requirement that it be purchased with after-tax salary reductions.

Cost is an important consideration in a cafeteria plan. The greater the number of benefits, particularly optional benefits, the greater the administrative costs. A wide array of options may also be confusing to many employees and require extra personnel to counsel employees or to answer their questions.

Level of Employer Contributions

An employer has considerable latitude in determining the amount of dollars that will be available to employees to purchase benefits under a cafeteria plan. These dollars may be a function of one or more of the following factors: salary, age, family status, and length of service.

A major difficulty arises in situations in which the installation of a cafeteria plan is not accompanied by an overall increase in the amount of the employer's contributions to the employee benefit plan. It is generally felt that each employee should be provided with enough dollars so that he or she can purchase optional benefits that, together with basic benefits, are at least equivalent to the benefits provided by the old plan.

Including a Premium-Conversion or FSA Option

A premium-conversion or FSA option under a cafeteria plan enables employees to lower their taxes and, therefore, increase their spendable income. Ignoring any administrative costs, there is probably no reason not to offer this option to employees for benefits such as dependent care or for health insurance premiums. However, salary reductions for unreimbursed medical expenses pose a dilemma. While such deductions save taxes for an employee, they may also result in his or her obtaining nearly 100 percent reimbursement for medical expenses, which may negate many of the cost-containment features in the employer's medical expense plan.

Change of Benefits

Because employees' needs change over time, a provision regarding their ability to change their benefit options must be incorporated in a cafeteria plan. As a rule, changes are allowed prior to the beginning of the plan year. Additional changes may be allowed as long as they are permissible under Section 125 regulations.

Two situations often affect the frequency with which benefits may be changed. First, charges to employees for optional benefits must be adjusted periodically to reflect experience under the plan. If charges for benefits rise between dates on which employees may change benefit selections, the employer must either absorb these charges or pass them on to the employees, probably through increased payroll deductions. Consequently, most cafeteria plans allow benefit changes on annual dates that are the same as the dates when charges for benefits are recalculated as well as the dates on which any insurance contracts providing benefits under the plan are renewed.

The second situation arises when the amount of the employer's contribution is based on compensation. If an employee receives a pay increase between selection periods, should he or she be granted more dollars to purchase additional benefits at that time? Under most cafeteria plans, the dollars available to all employees are calculated only once a year, usually before the date by which any annual benefit changes must be made. Any changes in the employee's status during the year will have no effect on the employer's contribution until the date on which a recalculation is made in the following year.

STUDY QUESTIONS

1. Explain the advantages claimed for cafeteria plans.

2. a. What types of welfare benefits can be provided under a cafeteria plan?
   b. What types of retirement benefits can be provided?
   c. What is meant by a cash benefit?

3. A benefit plan may offer employees choices among benefits but not satisfy the statutory definition of a cafeteria plan. What are the implications of such a situation?

4. a. When must benefit elections be made under a cafeteria plan?
   b. To what extent can a cafeteria plan permit changes in benefit elections?

5. a. What is the advantage of funding employee benefits through a premium-conversion plan or an FSA?
   b. What types of benefits are usually funded through premium-conversion plans and FSAs?
   c. What happens to balances in an FSA if they are not used for expenses incurred during the election period?

6. What is the difference between a core-plus cafeteria plan and a modular plan?

7. Other than meeting nondiscrimination rules and adverse selection, what are the obstacles to establishing cafeteria plans?

8. What types of nondiscrimination rules apply to cafeteria plans?

9. What techniques can be used to control adverse selection in a cafeteria plan?

10. Briefly discuss the issues that must be addressed in designing a cafeteria plan.

PART FIVE

Retirement Plans

Introduction to Qualified Plans

- Describe the fundamental management objectives in designing and implementing pension plans.

- Identify major policy issues motivating government regulation of qualified retirement plans.

- Explain the general requirements that must be met by qualified pension plans with respect to each of the following:
    1. Eligibility and plan coverage
    2. Nondiscrimination in benefits and contributions
    3. Funding requirements
    4. Vesting
    5. Limitations on benefits and contributions
    6. Payout restrictions
    7. Top-heavy rules

- Identify the tax advantages of qualified pension plans.

- List the broad types of qualified plans and their primary characteristics.

- Briefly explain the government's regulatory structure for qualified plans.

Retirement plans are among the most common employee benefits offered by employers. Nearly half of all benefit spending by employers goes to retirement benefits,[1] and employees rate retirement benefits as the second most important employee benefit, after health insurance.[2] Moreover, retirement plans are probably the most complicated benefit—in terms of design, administration, and taxation—commonly provided by employers. The purpose of this chapter is to explain the reasons for this importance and complexity and to provide an introduction to pension plan design and government regulation of pension plans.

MANAGEMENT OBJECTIVES IN PENSION PLAN DESIGN

Generally, a primary management objective in designing and maintaining a pension program is to maximize those factors by which the plan improves employee productivity. In other words, to maximize the extent to which the costs of the plan represent investment rather than pure expense. A pension plan improves productivity by attracting and keeping a better work force and providing incentives for good work performance. Although the quantitative evidence for the productivity relationship for specific pension plan features is relatively scanty at this time, there has been much qualitative experience in this area.

Benefit managers and pension planners must begin with an overall idea of what employer objectives can be promoted by a pension plan. While not every potential objective can be met with a single plan—in fact, some are conflicting—it's useful to begin this chapter by noting broadly what pension plans can do. Here are the basic objectives:

- *Help employees with retirement saving.* This is the most fundamental reason for pension plans and it shouldn't be overlooked. Most employees, even highly compensated employees, find personal savings difficult. It is difficult not merely for psychological reasons but also because our tax system and economy are oriented toward consumption rather than savings.

  For example, the federal income tax system imposes tax on income from savings (even if it is not used for consumption) with only three major exceptions: (1) deferral of tax on capital gains until realized, (2) benefits for investment in a personal residence, and (3) deferral of tax and other benefits for qualified retirement plans and IRAs. In other words, a qualified retirement plan is one of only three ways our government encourages savings through the tax system—but it is available only if an employer adopts the plan. (IRA benefits are very limited.)

- *Tax deferral for owners and highly compensated employees.* While many employees in all compensation categories can benefit from pension plans, owners and other key employees have more money available for saving,

[1]Employee Benefit Research Institute, Facts from EBRI, www.ebri.org/facts/, Feb. 1999.

[2]Employee Benefit Research Institute, EBRI Notes, Washington, D.C. (8/94).

have higher compensation, have longer service with the employer, and often are older than regular employees; thus they can benefit more from pension plans. When designing a plan for a business owner, a typical objective is to maximize the benefits for the owner (or, in some cases, to minimize the discrimination *against* the highly compensated employee that is built into some of the qualified pension plan rules.)

■ *Help recruit, retain and retire employees.* These "three Rs" of compensation policy are important in designing pension plans. The plan can help recruit employees by matching or bettering pension benefit packages offered by competing employers; it can help retain employees by tying maximum pension benefits to long service; and it can help retire employees by allowing them to retire with dignity—without a drastic drop in living standard—when their productivity has begun to decline and the organization needs new members.

■ *Encourage productivity directly.* Certain types of plan design can act as employee incentives; this is particularly true of plans whose contributions are profit-based or those providing employee accounts invested in stock of the employee.

■ *Discourage collective bargaining.* An attractive pension package—as good as or better than labor union-sponsored plans in the area—can help to keep employees from organizing into a collective bargaining unit. Collective bargaining often poses major business problems for some employers.

THE GOVERNMENT'S ROLE—PENSION POLICY ISSUES

Management objectives are one major factor in pension design; the other is the government regulatory structure. This section discusses the development of the government's role in this area.

A relatively complete discussion of plan types and terminology will appear later in this chapter, but one very important concept must be understood at the outset. Most employees covered under an employer-sponsored retirement plan are covered under what is known as a *qualified* retirement plan. A qualified plan is one that receives certain valuable federal tax benefits, but its design, funding, and administration must meet an extraordinarily complex set of federal statutory and regulatory requirements. Most federal regulation in this area specifically preempts state and local regulation. The tax benefits from such plans to both employer and employee are generally (though not always) adequate to justify the inconvenience of this severe regulatory regime. A *nonqualified* plan is any other retirement or deferred compensation plan. Nonqualified plans are subject to much simpler federal regulation, along with less favorable tax treatment. Nonqualified plans are used primarily for executive compensation arrangements that replace or supplement qualified plan coverage for a selected group of highly compensated executives. These are discussed in Chapter 28.

The government's role in the retirement income area has been dictated primarily by historical factors. Beginning in the late 19th century, the economy of the United States changed fairly rapidly from predominantly agricultural to predominantly industrial and service oriented. Coinciding with this change—and probably in response to it—the large, supportive extended family of the agricultural economy was largely replaced by smaller, more fragmented family units. The shift away from agriculture reduced the amount of economically useful work available to older people, and family structural changes reduced the amount of family support for the aged.

Because of these economic and social trends, people generally must make specific plans for their retirement. This is a difficult matter for most individual employees to do alone and, consequently, employer-sponsored pension plans have become increasingly important.

In the 20th century, federal government involvement in retirement plans for the aged also greatly expanded. The federal government's involvement is twofold. For most people, the most obvious federal government program in this area is the Social Security system adopted in the 1930s to provide direct benefit payments to the aged. But even before the Social Security system was adopted, the federal government became involved in a more traditional way by measures designed to encourage the private pension system.

Governments tend to be reluctant to adopt direct payment arrangements for dependent individuals, particularly in the United States—a reflection of the generally conservative social values of the American public. Historically, governments have tended to look first at private organizations to act in this area. This is one reason why charitable institutions, such as orphanages and hospitals, have for centuries been granted various forms of tax exemption.

In the tradition of encouraging private initiatives, in the 1920s the federal government began encouraging private, employer-sponsored retirement plans by providing two kinds of tax benefits. First, pension funds were made tax exempt under the Revenue Acts of 1921 and 1926. Then, in the Revenue Act of 1928, employer contributions to plan funds were made currently deductible by the employer, even though benefits were not paid to employees until later years. These basic provisions still apply and form the basis for today's vast federal regulatory scheme for qualified plans.

The embryonic private pension system of the 1920s declined significantly during the depression of the 1930s. This was one reason for the adoption of the Social Security system. However, since the 1940s, private pension plans have revived to an enormous degree. Assets in private pension plans now amount to more than three trillion dollars,[3] which constitutes a very substantial portion of the nation's entire capital.

Because of the large sums involved, any tax benefits provided to qualified plans cost the government a great deal in lost tax revenues; the government

---

[3.]Employee Benefit Research Institute, *EBRI Databook on Employee Benefits,* 4th ed. (1997), Washington, D.C. (figures as of end of 1995).

estimate is well over $75 billion annually.[4] This large "tax expenditure" is often given as a primary justification for the exhaustive scheme of government regulation that now applies to qualified pension plans. Fundamentally, the argument is that the large tax expenditure is designed to help prevent individuals from becoming dependent on the government in retirement. Consequently, the government attempts to make sure that plan benefits go where they are most needed so that this tax expenditure is cost effective. Much pension regulation is aimed at discouraging plans that primarily benefit highly-compensated employees who have other sources of retirement income. Other rules are intended to assure that the large sums set aside for plan benefits are managed in the exclusive interest of plan participants and beneficiaries.

In practice, the government frequently adopts new or modified statutes and regulations relating to pensions without clear or articulated long-range policy objectives. The absence of a coherent federal retirement policy is currently a critical federal policy issue. Current issues in pension regulation include those covered in the following sections.

Tax Revenue Loss

At times, revenue-raising needs outweigh retirement policy issues in Congress. The tax benefits for qualified plans cause a substantial apparent decrease in tax revenues. The criticism is also frequently made that too much of the tax benefit goes to high-income individuals who don't need government help. Whatever the merits of this argument, it is indisputable that "fine tuning" the rules to reduce tax benefits for certain plan participants can increase tax revenues in the short run, without the political pain of visibly "raising taxes." The need to raise revenue has motivated many recent changes in the qualified plan law, and it probably will be a factor in future legislation. Changes of this type are often enormously complex as a result of the need to carefully target the group whose benefits are to be reduced, typically the owner-employees of closely held businesses. Revenue-motivated changes are often criticized as resulting in bad retirement policy.

Discrimination in Favor of Highly Compensated Employees

Although a major thrust of virtually all qualified plan legislation since the 1940s has been to discourage employers from discriminating in their plans in favor of highly compensated employees, a considerable amount of such discrimination is still possible, as discussed throughout this text. Because of this, much qualified plan legislation has been designed to reduce the "tax shelter" aspects of qualified plans, particularly those for smaller businesses whose owner-employees receive substantial benefits. Many of the most complex and

---

[4.]Office of Management and Budget, *Budget of the United States Government, Fiscal Year 1999.* The estimated total annual tax loss for all employee benefit provisions was $200 billion.

awkward provisions of the law, such as the top-heavy rules discussed in Chapter 25, were designed in this vein.

Seemingly, it would be easy to eliminate the discrimination problem by simple, appropriate benefit or contribution limits. However there is a countervailing policy consideration. Small businesses, collectively, employ a large and increasing segment of the work force. Owners of these businesses may not be interested in maintaining a qualified plan for their employees unless the plan provides substantial, and possibly disproportionate, benefits for the owners themselves. This policy issue, therefore, involves tension between tax-benefit equity and efficiency on the one hand, and the need to encourage small business retirement plans on the other. No simple resolution of this is likely in the near future, and complex legislative compromises on this issue will probably continue to emerge from Congress.

Encouraging Private Saving

Surprisingly, in view of the trillions invested in pension plans, relatively little policy emphasis has been given to the role of the qualified plan rules in encouraging private savings. One problem is that policy makers agree neither on the appropriate level for private savings nor on whether government policy should encourage savings rather than allowing the free market to set the level. Another factor is that economists are divided about the efficacy of the qualified plan provisions in encouraging savings. Some economists argue that these plans merely displace private saving that would take place in any event. Nevertheless, the savings issue is an ongoing factor in the policy debate.

Interest-Group Pressures

As the foregoing discussion indicates, retirement policy poses difficult problems even if viewed from a neutral intellectual viewpoint. The actual political climate, of course, is not neutral. The qualified plan business is large and involves many firms and individuals. Most of these organizations eagerly and frequently convey their views to Congress in great technical detail. This complicates the resolution of issues and makes change more difficult.

Mandatory Retirement Plan Coverage

A presidential commission formed in the late 1970s to study pension policy recommended the establishment of a Minimum Universal Pension System (MUPS) for all workers, to be funded by employers at an initial rate of at least 3 percent of payroll.[5] The MUPS benefit would be completely portable from job

---

[5]*Coming of Age: Toward a National Retirement Income Policy,* President's Commission on Pension Policy, 1981.

to job. In general, the MUPS approach is not popular with employers and benefit plan designers, who prefer the flexibility of current rules; at the present time, Congress is not considering it seriously.

Age and Sex Discrimination

Age and sex discrimination have not been addressed by Congress specifically as retirement plan issues. However, recent federal legislative and regulatory activity related to employment discrimination in general has affected retirement plans, as discussed later in this text.

QUALIFIED PLAN CHARACTERISTICS

The term *qualified plan* is not amenable to a simple definition; in a sense, it requires all of Part Five of this text to provide an adequate definition. Nevertheless, it is helpful to take a brief overall look at the most significant requirements before getting into the details. These requirements are discussed in appropriate detail in subsequent chapters.

Eligibility and Plan Coverage

The plan can have almost any kind of initial eligibility provision, except for specific restrictions based on age or service. Generally, no minimum age over 21 can be required, nor can more than one year of service be required for eligibility. In addition, the plan *in operation* must generally cover at least 70 percent of all non–highly compensated employees. These rules have many complex exceptions and limitations, as discussed in Chapter 19.

Nondiscrimination in Benefits and Contributions

Generally speaking, a qualified plan may not discriminate, either in plan benefits or employer contributions to the plan, in favor of highly compensated employees. The law includes a detailed definition of *highly compensated* for this purpose. However, the plan contribution or benefit can be based on the employee's compensation or years of service, which often will provide a higher benefit for certain highly compensated employees. In addition, the qualified plan can be integrated with Social Security so that a greater contribution or benefit is available for higher-paid employees whose compensation is greater than an amount based on the Social Security taxable wage base. Because of the possibilities for abuse in these areas, the rules for Social Security integration, discussed in Chapter 20, are complex.

Funding Requirements

Generally, a qualified plan must be funded in advance of the employee's retirement. This can be done either through contributions to an irrevocable trust fund for the employee's benefit or under an insurance contract. There are strict limits on the extent to which the employer can exercise control over the plan fund. The fund must be under the control of a *fiduciary*—the legal designation for a person who holds funds of another—and must be managed solely for the benefit of plan participants and beneficiaries.

Vesting Requirements

Under the vesting rules, an employee must be given a nonforfeitable or *vested* benefit at the normal retirement date specified in the plan and, in case of termination of employment prior to retirement, after a specified period of service. For example, one common vesting provision grants a fully vested benefit after the employee has attained five years of service, with no vesting until then. If the plan has this vesting provision, an employee who leaves after, say, four years of service with the employer will receive no plan benefit even though the employer has put money into the plan on his behalf over the four-year period. However, an employee who leaves after five or more years of service will receive the entire plan benefit earned up until that time.

The vesting rules are discussed more fully in Chapter 19. These rules are designed to make it more difficult for employers to deny benefits to employees by selectively discharging or turning over employees.

Limitations on Benefits and Contributions

To limit the use of a qualified plan as a tax shelter for highly compensated employees, Section 415 of the Internal Revenue Code contains a limitation on the plan benefit or employer contributions, depending on the type of plan. Under these limitations, a plan cannot generally provide an annual pension of more than $90,000 (as indexed for inflation) or annual employer and employee contributions of more than $30,000. The limitations are discussed further in Chapter 25. Practically speaking, these limits are high enough so that only highly compensated participants are likely to encounter them.

Benefits for highly compensated employees are further limited by a requirement that only the first $150,000 (as indexed) of a participant's compensation can be taken into account in a plan's contribution or benefit formula.

Payout Restrictions

To ensure that qualified plan benefits are used for their intended purposes, there are various restrictions on benefit payouts. Certain plans (pension plans in particular) do not allow withdrawals of funds before termination of employment. In addition, there is a 10 percent penalty on withdrawal of funds from any qualified plan before early retirement, age 59½, death, or disability, with certain exceptions. Funds cannot be kept in the plan indefinitely; generally, the payout must begin by April 1 of the year after the participant's attainment of age 70½, in specified minimum annual amounts. Loans from the plan to participants are restricted.

Top-Heavy Rules

To reduce the possibility of excessive discrimination in favor of business owners covered under a qualified plan, special rules are provided for *top-heavy plans*. Basically, a top-heavy plan is one that provides more than 60 percent of its aggregate accumulated benefits or account balances to key employees. A plan that is top-heavy must meet a special rapid vesting requirement and provide minimum benefits for nonkey employees.

TAX BENEFITS OF QUALIFIED PLANS

The most important tax advantage of a qualified plan is best understood by comparison with the rules applicable to a nonqualified deferred compensation plan. In a nonqualified plan, the timing of the employer's income tax deduction for compensation of employees depends on when the compensation is included in the employee's income. If the employer puts no money aside in advance to fund the plan, there is no deduction to the employer until the retirement income is paid to the employee, at which time the employee also reports the compensation as taxable income. If the employer puts money aside into an irrevocable trust fund, insurance contract, or similar fund for the benefit of the employee, the employer can get an immediate tax deduction, but then the employee is taxed immediately; there is no tax deferral for the employee.

These rules do *not* apply to a qualified plan. In a qualified plan, the employer obtains a tax deduction for contributions to the plan fund (within specified limits) for the year the contribution is made. Employees pay taxes on benefits when they are received. The combination of an immediate employer tax deduction plus tax deferral for the employee can be obtained only with a qualified plan.

Besides this basic advantage, there are other tax benefits for qualified plans. Four advantages are usually identified:

1. The employer gets an immediate deduction, within certain limits, for amounts paid into the plan fund to finance future retirement benefits for employees.
2. The employee is not taxed at the time the employer makes contributions for that employee to the plan fund.

3. The employee is taxed only when plan benefits are received. If the full benefit is received in a single year, it may be eligible for special favorable "lump sum" income taxation.
4. Earnings on money put aside by the employer to fund the plan are not subject to federal income tax while in the plan fund; thus the earnings accumulate tax free.

CLASSIFICATION OF QUALIFIED PLANS

There are two broad classifications of qualified plans. The first classification differentiates between pension plans and profit-sharing plans and the second between defined-benefit and defined-contribution plans. These broad classifications are useful in identifying plans that meet broad overall goals of the employee. Once detailed employer objectives have been determined, a specific qualified plan program can be developed for the employer using one or more of the types of plans from a menu of specific plan types. The specific plan types contain a lot of flexibility in design to meet employer needs, and one or more different plans or plan types can be designed covering the same or overlapping groups of employees to provide the exact type of benefits that the employer desires.

Pension and Profit-Sharing Plans

One way of broadly classifying qualified plans is to distinguish between pension plans and profit-sharing plans. A *pension plan* is a plan designed primarily to provide income at retirement. Thus, benefits are generally not available from a pension plan until the employee reaches a specified age, referred to as the *normal retirement age*. Some plans also provide an optional benefit at an earlier age (the *early retirement age*). The design of a pension plan benefit formula must be such that an employee's retirement benefit is reasonably predictable in advance. Because the object of a pension plan is to provide retirement security, the employer must keep the fund at an adequate level. Pension plans are subject to the *minimum funding* rules of the Code, and these generally require that the employer make regular deposits to avoid a penalty.

By contrast, a *profit-sharing plan* is designed to allow a relatively short-term deferral of income; it is a somewhat more speculative benefit to the employee because the employer's contribution can be based on profits. Furthermore, a profit-sharing plan can provide for a totally discretionary employer contribution so that even if the employer has profits in a given year, the employer need not make a contribution for that year. The minimum funding rules do not apply. However, there must be substantial and recurring contributions or the plan will be deemed to be terminated.

In a profit-sharing plan, it is difficult to determine the employee's benefit in advance, and the plan is considered more an incentive to employees than a predictable source of retirement income. Because it is not exclusively designed for retirement income, employees may be permitted to withdraw funds from the plan before retirement. The plan may allow amounts to be withdrawn as early as two years after the employer has contributed them to the plan. However, as with any qualified plan, preretirement withdrawals may be subject to a 10 percent penalty. Finally, the deductible annual employer contribution is limited to 15 percent of payroll, an amount less than would usually be deductible under a pension plan.

Defined-Benefit and Defined-Contribution Plans

Qualified plans are also divided into defined-benefit and defined-contribution plans. A *defined-contribution plan* has an *individual account* for each employee; defined-contribution plans are, therefore, sometimes referred to as individual-account plans. The plan document describes the amount the employer will contribute to the plan, but it does not promise any particular benefit. When the plan participant retires or otherwise becomes eligible for benefits under the plan, the benefit will be the total amount in the participant's account, including past investment earnings on the amounts put into the account. The participant can look only to his or her own account to recover benefits; he or she is not entitled to amounts in any other account. Thus, the participant bears the risk of bad plan investments.

In a *defined-benefit plan* the plan document specifies the amount of benefit promised to the employee at normal retirement age. The plan itself does not specify the amount the employer must contribute annually to the plan. The plan's actuary will determine the annual contribution required so that the plan fund will be sufficient to pay the promised benefit as each participant retires. If the fund is inadequate, the employer is responsible for making additional contributions. There are no individual participant accounts, and each participant has a claim on the entire fund for the defined benefit. Because of the actuarial aspects, defined-benefit plans tend to be more complicated and expensive to administer than defined-contribution plans.

Specific Types of Qualified Plans

As Figure 18-1 indicates, within the broad categories (pension, profit-sharing, defined-benefit, defined-contribution), there are specific types of plans available to meet various retirement-planning objectives.

Defined-Benefit Pension Plan

All defined-benefit plans are pension plans; they are designed primarily to provide income at retirement. A defined-benefit plan specifies the benefit in terms of a formula, of which there are many different types. Such formulas may state the benefit in terms of a percentage of earnings measured over a

FIGURE 18-1
Types of Qualified Plans

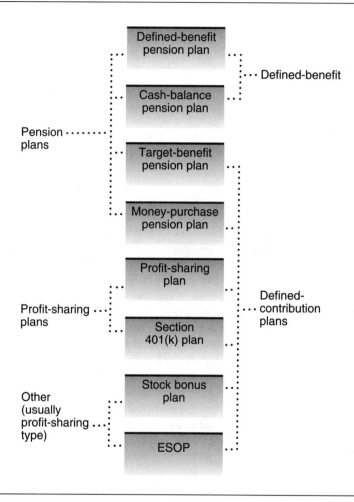

specific period of time, and might also be based on years of service. For example, a defined-benefit plan might promise a monthly retirement benefit equal to 50 percent of the employee's average monthly earnings over the five years prior to retirement. Or instead of a flat 50 percent, the plan might provide something like 1.5 percent for each of the employee's years of service, with the resulting percentage applied to the employee's earnings averaged over a stated period. Employer contributions to the plan are determined actuarially. Thus, for a given benefit, a defined-benefit plan will tend to result in a larger employer contribution on behalf of employees who enter the plan at older ages, because there is less time to fund the benefit for them.

Cash-Balance Pension Plan

In a cash-balance plan (also called a *guaranteed account plan* and various other titles), each participant has an "account" that increases annually as a result of two types of credits: a compensation credit, based on the participant's compensation, and an interest credit equal to a guaranteed rate of interest. As a result of the guarantee, the participant does not bear the investment risk. Unlike defined-benefit formulas, the plan deposits are not based on age, and younger employees receive the same benefit accrual as those hired at older ages. The plan is funded by the employer on an actuarial basis; the plan fund's actual rate of investment return may be more or less than the guaranteed rate, and employer deposits are adjusted accordingly. Technically, because of the guaranteed minimum benefit, the plan is treated as a defined-benefit plan. From the participant's viewpoint, however, the plan appears very similar to a money-purchase plan, described below.

Target-Benefit Pension Plan

A target plan uses a benefit formula (the "target") like that of a defined-benefit plan. However, a target plan is a defined-contribution plan and, therefore, the benefit consists solely of the amount in each employee's individual account at retirement. Initial contributions to a target plan are determined actuarially, but the employer does not guarantee that the benefit will meet the target level, so the initial contribution level is not adjusted to reflect actuarial experience. Like a defined-benefit plan, a target-benefit plan provides a relatively higher contribution on behalf of employees entering the plan at older ages.

Money-Purchase Pension Plan

A money-purchase pension plan is a defined-contribution plan that is in some ways the simplest form of qualified plan. The plan simply specifies a level of contribution to each participant's individual account. For example, the plan might specify that the employer will contribute each year to each participant's account an amount equal to 10 percent of that participant's compensation for the year. The participant's retirement benefit is equal to the amount in the account at retirement. Thus, the account reflects not only the initial contribution level but also any subsequent favorable or unfavorable investment results obtained by the plan fund. The term *money purchase* arose because in many such plans, the amount in the participant's account at retirement is not distributed in a lump sum but rather is used to purchase a single or joint life annuity for the participant.

Profit-Sharing Plan

As described earlier, the significant features of a profit-sharing plan are that employer contributions are, within limits, discretionary on the part of the employer and that employee withdrawals before retirement may be permitted. Profit-sharing plans that are designed to allow employee contributions are sometimes referred to as *savings* or *thrift plans*.

Section 401(k) Plan

A Section 401(k) plan, also called a *cash* or *deferred plan,* is a plan allowing employees to choose (within limits) to receive compensation either as current cash or as a contribution to a qualified profit-sharing plan. The amount contributed to the plan is not currently taxable to the employee. Such plans have become popular because of their flexibility and tax advantages. However, such plans must include restrictions that may be burdensome to the employer or the employees. The most significant restrictions are a requirement of immediate vesting for amounts contributed under the employee election and restrictions on distribution of these amounts to employees prior to age 59½.

Stock Bonus Plan

The stock bonus plan resembles a profit-sharing plan except that employer contributions are in the form of employer stock rather than cash and the plan fund consists primarily of employer stock.

The fiduciary requirements of the pension law forbid an employer to invest more than 10 percent of a pension plan fund in stock of the employer company. This prevents the employer from utilizing pension plan funds primarily for financing the business rather than providing retirement security for employees. However, the 10 percent restriction does not apply to profit-sharing or stock bonus plans.

Stock bonus plans are intended specifically to give employees an ownership interest in the company at relatively low cost to the company. Stock bonus plans are also used by closely held companies to help create a market for stock of the employer.

ESOP

Employee stock ownership plans (ESOPs) are similar to stock bonus plans in that most or all of the plan fund consists of employer stock: employee accounts are stated in shares of employer stock. However, ESOPs are designed to offer a further benefit: the employer can use an ESOP as a mechanism for financing the business through borrowing or "leveraging." Various tax incentives exist to encourage this.

PLANS FOR SPECIAL TYPES OF ORGANIZATIONS

Plans Covering Partners and Proprietors

Under federal tax law, partners and proprietors (sole owners) are not considered employees of their unincorporated business, even if they perform substantial services for the business. By comparison, shareholders of a corporate business who are employed by the business are considered employees for retirement planning and other employee benefit purposes. For many years, there were restrictions on the benefits available from a qualified plan to partners or proprietors. Special plans called *Keogh* or *HR#10* plans were used if partners or proprietors were covered. Since 1983, most of these restrictions no longer apply, and qualified plans can cover partners and proprietors on virtually the same terms as regular employees of the business.

S Corporations

An S corporation is a corporation that has made an election to be treated substantially like a partnership for federal income tax purposes. Certain shareholder employees of S corporations were once subject to qualified plan restrictions similar to those for partners and proprietors; however, after 1983, most of these restrictions do not apply. Thus, as with partners and proprietors, S corporation shareholder-employees are now treated basically like regular employees for qualified plan purposes. However, an S corporation employee who owns more than 2 percent of the corporation's stock is treated as a partner for *other* employee benefit purposes, such as group life and health plans.

Multiple Employer, Collectively Bargained, and Multiemployer Plans

In this text, if not stated otherwise, it is assumed that any qualified plans referred to are maintained by a single employer or by a group of related employers. It is possible, however, for more than one employer or related group to participate in a single qualified plan. If such a plan is established under a collective bargaining agreement (as is usually the case), it is referred to as a *collectively bargained plan*. With a collectively bargained plan, the plan is usually designed and maintained by a labor union, and employers who recognize the union as a bargaining agent for their employees agree to contribute to the plan on a basis specified in the collective bargaining agreement. If the plan is not the result of a collective bargaining agreement, it is referred to as a *multiple employer plan*. Such plans might, for example, be maintained by trade associations of employers in a certain line of business. There are special rules for applying the participation and other requirements to these plans.

There are also provisions for a special type of collectively bargained plan known as a *multiemployer plan* (Code Section 414(f)). A multiemployer plan is a plan to which more than one employer is required to contribute and that is maintained under a collective bargaining agreement covering more than one employer; the Department of Labor can also impose other requirements by regulation. Presumably, most large collectively bargained plans will qualify as multiemployer plans. Because of the nature of the multiemployer plan, the funding requirements are somewhat more favorable than for other plans. However, the employer may incur a special liability on withdrawing from the plan.

GOVERNMENT REGULATION OF QUALIFIED PLANS

It was noted earlier in this chapter that a qualified retirement plan receives special federal tax benefits in return for being designed in accordance with rules imposed by the federal government. This section of the chapter will discuss how the federal government imposes these rules. The federal rules are the most important because federal law generally preempts state and local laws in the qualified plan area.

Benefit planners need a basic understanding of the federal regulatory scheme. Planners must often interpret the significance of various official rules and interact with government organizations. These government rules and organizations must be understood in order to be effective in plan design and management.

Government regulation is expressed through the following, in the order of their importance: (1) statutory law, (2) the law as expressed in court cases, (3) regulations of government agencies, and (4) rulings and other information issued by government agencies.

Statutory Law

Theoretically, the highest level of regulatory law is the U.S. Constitution because all regulation must meet constitutional requirements, such as due process of law and equal protection for persons under the law. However, relatively few issues of federal regulation are actually resolved under constitutional law. For practical purposes, the "law" as expressed by statutes passed by the U.S. Congress is the highest level of authority and is the basis of all regulation; court cases, rulings, and regulations are simply interpretations of statutes passed by Congress. If the statute was detailed enough to cover every possible case, there theoretically wouldn't be any need for anything else. But despite the best efforts of Congressional drafting staffs, the statutes can't cover every situation.

Benefit planners should become as familiar as possible with statutory law because it is the basis for all other rules, regulations, and court cases. One of the main causes for confusion among nonexperts is a lack of understanding of the relative status of sources of information. That is, while a rule found in the Internal Revenue Code is fundamental, a statement in an IRS ruling or instructions to IRS forms may be merely a matter of interpretation that is relatively easy to "plan around."

In the benefits area, the sources of statutory law are:

■ *Internal Revenue Code (the Code).* The tax laws governing the deductibility and taxation of pension and employee benefit programs are fundamental. These are found primarily in Sections 401-425, with important provisions also in Sections 72, 83, and other sections.

■ *ERISA (Employee Retirement Income Security Act of 1974), as amended, and other labor law provisions.* Labor law provisions such as ERISA govern the nontax aspects of federal regulation. These involve plan participation requirements, notice to participants, reporting to the federal government, and a variety of rules designed to safeguard any funds that are set aside to pay benefits in the future. There is some overlap between ERISA and the Code in the area of plan participation, vesting, and prohibited transactions.

■ *Pension Benefit Guaranty Corporation (PBGC).* The PBGC is a government corporation set up under ERISA in 1974 to provide termination insurance for participants in qualified defined-benefit plans up to certain limits. In carrying out this responsibility, the PBGC regulates plan terminations and imposes certain reporting requirements on covered plans that are in financial difficulty or in a state of contraction.

■ *Securities laws.* The federal securities laws are designed to protect investors. Benefit plans may involve an element of investing the employees' money. While qualified plans are generally exempt from the full impact of the securities laws, if the plan holds employer stock, a federal registration statement may be required and certain securities regulations may apply.

■ *Civil rights laws.* Benefit plans are part of an employer's compensation policies; these plans are subject to the Civil Rights Act of 1964, which prohibits employment discrimination on the basis of race, religion, sex, or national origin.

■ *Age discrimination.* The Age Discrimination Act of 1978, as amended, has specific provisions aimed at benefit plans, as discussed throughout this book.

■ *State legislation.* ERISA contains a broad "preemption" provision under which any state law in conflict with ERISA is preempted—has no effect. If ERISA does not deal with a particular issue, however, there may be room for state legislation. For example, there is considerable state legislation and regulation governing the types of group term life insurance contracts that can be offered as part of an employer plan. There are also certain areas where states continue to assert authority even though ERISA also has an impact, as in the area of creditors' rights to pension fund assets.

Court Cases

The courts enter the picture when a taxpayer decides to appeal a tax assessment made by the IRS. The courts don't act on their own to resolve tax or other legal issues. Consequently, the law as expressed in court cases is a crazy-quilt affair that offers some answers but often raises more questions than it answers. However, after statutes, court cases are the most authoritative source of law. Courts can and do overturn regulations and rulings of the IRS and other regulatory agencies.

A taxpayer wishing to contest a tax assessment has three choices: (1) the Federal District Court in the taxpayer's district, (2) the United States Tax Court, or (3) the United States Claims Court. Tax law can be found in the decisions of any of these three courts.

All three courts are equally authoritative. Most tax cases, however, are resolved by the U.S. Tax Court, because it offers a powerful advantage: The taxpayer can bring the case before the Tax Court without paying the disputed tax. All the other courts require payment of the tax followed by a suit for refund.

Decisions of these three courts can be appealed to the Federal Court of Appeals for the applicable federal "judicial circuit"—the U.S. is divided into 11 judicial circuits. The circuit courts sometimes differ on certain points of tax law; as a result, tax and benefit planning may depend on what judicial circuit the taxpayer is located in. Where these differences exist, one or more taxpayers will eventually appeal a decision by the Court of Appeals to the United States Supreme Court to resolve differences of interpretation among various judicial circuits, but this process takes many years and the Supreme Court may ultimately choose not to hear the case. Congress also sometimes amends the Code or other statute to resolve these interpretive differences.

Regulations

Regulations are interpretations of statutory law that are published by a government agency; in the benefits area, the most significant regulations are published by the Treasury Department (the parent of the IRS), the Labor Department, and the PBGC.

Regulations are structured as abstract rules, like the statutory law itself. They are not related to a particular factual situation, although they often contain useful examples that illustrate the application of the rules. Currently, Treasury regulations are often issued in question-and-answer form.

The numbering system for regulations is supposed to make them more accessible by including an internal reference to the underlying statutory provision. For example, Treasury Regulation Section 1.401(k)-2 is a regulation relating to Section 401(k) of the Internal Revenue Code. Labor Regulation Section 2550.408b-3 relates to Section 408b of ERISA.

Issuance of regulations follows a prescribed procedure involving an initial issuance of *proposed regulations* followed by hearings and public comment, then *final regulations*. The process often takes years. Where taxpayers have an urgent need to know answers, the agency may issue *temporary regulations* instead of proposed regulations. Technically, temporary regulations are binding, while proposed regulations are not. However, if a taxpayer takes a position contrary to a proposed regulation, the taxpayer is taking the risk that the regulation will ultimately be finalized and be enforced against him.

Rulings and Other Information

IRS Rulings

IRS rulings are responses by the IRS to requests by taxpayers to interpret the law in light of their particular fact situations. A *General Counsel Memorandum (GCM)* is similar to a ruling, except that the request for clarification and guidance is initiated from an IRS agent in the field during a taxpayer audit, rather than directly from the taxpayer.

There are two types of IRS rulings—*Revenue Rulings,* which are published by the IRS as general guidance to all taxpayers, and *Private Letter Rulings (PLRs),* which are addressed only to the specific taxpayers who requested the rulings. The IRS publishes its Revenue Rulings in IRS Bulletins (collected in Cumulative Bulletins [CB] each year). Revenue rulings are binding on IRS personnel on the issues covered in them, but often IRS agents will try to make a distinction between a taxpayer's factual situation and a similar one covered in a ruling if the ruling appears to favor the taxpayer.

PLRs are not published by the IRS, but are available to the public with taxpayer identification deleted. These "anonymous" PLRs are published for tax professionals by various private publishers. They are not binding interpretations of tax law except for the taxpayer who requested the ruling, and even then they apply only to the exact situation described in the ruling request and do not apply to even a slightly different fact pattern involving the same taxpayer. Nevertheless. PLRs are very important in research because they are often the only source of information about the IRS position on various issues.

Other Rulings

The Department of Labor and the PBGC issue some rulings in areas of employee benefit regulation under their jurisdiction. DOL rulings include the *Prohibited Transaction Exemption (PTEs)* which rule on types of transactions that can avoid the prohibited transaction penalties—for example, sale of life insurance contracts to qualified plans.

Other Information

Because of frequent changes in the tax law, the IRS has been unable to promulgate regulations and rulings on a timely basis, and has increasingly used less formal approaches to inform taxpayers of its position. These include various types of published *Notices* and even speeches by IRS personnel. Finally, many important IRS positions are found only in *IRS Publications* (pamphlets available free to taxpayers) and *instructions* for filling out IRS forms. The IRS also maintains telephone question-answering services, but the value of these for information on complicated issues is minimal.

STUDY QUESTIONS

1. List four major management objectives for a pension plan and explain how the plan helps achieve these objectives.

2. What are the underlying social and historical reasons for the federal government's involvement in regulating private pension plans?

3. List some of the general features required for qualified retirement plans.

4. Identify the tax benefits available to the employer and the employees from a qualified plan.

5. Explain the difference between a pension plan and a profit-sharing plan.

6. Compare defined-benefit plans with defined-contribution plans with respect to
   a. administrative costs.
   b. individual account balances for participants.
   c. risk of bad plan investments.
   d. need for an actuary.

7. Identify the types of defined-contribution plans and their primary features.

8. Discuss the coverage available to partners and sole proprietors under qualified plans.

9. How are shareholder-employees treated under an S corporation for purposes of qualified plans?

10. Distinguish between multiple-employer plans, collectively bargained plans, and multiemployer plans.

11. Explain the role of the courts in interpreting the tax laws pertaining to qualified plans.

12. What are the respective regulatory roles of Treasury Regulations, IRS Revenue Rulings, and IRS Private Letter Rulings?

CHAPTER 19

Plan Qualification Requirements

OBJECTIVES

- Explain the eligibility and participation requirements that must be met by qualified retirement plans with respect to
    1. age and service requirements.
    2. maximum age limits.
    3. years of service.
    4. breaks in service.
    5. overall coverage tests.

- Explain the coverage rules when an employer has
    1. a group of employees in a collective bargaining unit.
    2. separate lines of business.
    3. affiliated or commonly controlled related employers.

- Explain the vesting requirements for qualified plans.

- Explain why most pension plans are noncontributory.

- Discuss the importance of normal, early, and late retirement ages in a qualified plan.

- Describe the federal nontax antidiscrimination provisions that apply to qualified plans.

A basic problem in discussing qualified plans is the great variety of possible plan types. Many of the qualified plan rules apply to all types of qualified plans. In any complete discussion, there is a possibility that the same rules will be repeated again and again in different contexts. To minimize this problem, this chapter and the next two chapters will contain a relatively complete discussion of pension plans and the rules that apply to them. This is appropriate because pension plans are the most complex and significant of qualified plans, involving the majority of employees covered under qualified plans and well over half of the funds held by qualified plans. Because the qualified plan rules will be discussed thoroughly in these three chapters, only a brief review of these rules is necessary in Chapters 22 and 23, which discuss profit-sharing and other qualified plans.

Qualified plan design is particularly complicated because there is constant interaction between the employer's objectives and the limits imposed by the qualified plan rules of the Internal Revenue Code and other provisions of the law. In this text, the approach will be to discuss both aspects of plan design together—plan design topics will be discussed from the standpoint of employer objectives and how these objectives can be accomplished within the limitations imposed by the qualified plan rules.

STRUCTURE AND DESIGN OF A QUALIFIED PLAN

A qualified plan is a labyrinth of concepts and terminology. One way to thread the labyrinth is to follow an employee covered under a typical defined-benefit pension plan. This may help to introduce the process of qualified plan design discussed in these chapters.

■ **EXAMPLE**

Suppose Clutch Company has a qualified defined-benefit plan. When employee Tom Bill is hired, he does not automatically become a participant because he must first meet the plan's eligibility requirements, basically consisting of a definition of the covered group and a waiting period. When Tom enters the plan and becomes a plan *participant,* Clutch Company must begin to put money into a fund designed to accept, invest, accumulate, and pay out money belonging to the plan. Also, when Tom enters, he begins to *accrue benefits* under the plan. In the Clutch Plan, as in many plans, the amount of benefit accrued each year is determined by estimating the benefit Tom will receive at retirement and allocating that amount in a specified manner over each of Tom's anticipated years of employment prior to his expected retirement date.

Because the Clutch Plan does not allow loans to participants or provide incidental insurance coverage (although it could do these things), Tom will receive no benefit from the plan until he terminates employment with Clutch. If he terminates before retirement and before he has served Clutch long enough to be vested,

continued

> ■ **EXAMPLE** (*continued*)
>
> he will receive nothing even though he has accrued a benefit under the plan. If he terminates after vesting, he will receive all or a portion of his benefit accrued to that date. This benefit will begin immediately if he has reached either the plan's specified early retirement age or normal retirement age. These ages are 62 and 65 in the Clutch Plan, a typical choice of ages that is within the limits of the qualified plan law. If Tom has not reached either of these ages, the Clutch Plan will not pay benefits until he reaches age 65. If the benefit is very small, Tom will be paid his benefit immediately in a cash lump sum. Except for this, the plan gives Tom a choice of various forms of benefit at retirement; all of these are of equal value to the plan—a life annuity, an annuity for the joint lives of Tom and his wife, or several others.

This little scenario illustrates the major planning decisions. These are, as discussed in this and the next several chapters:

■ What group of employees should be covered under the plan? (Chapter 19)
■ Should there he a waiting period for plan entry by new employees? (Chapter 19)
■ Should the plan be funded solely by the employer or should employees contribute? (Chapter 19)
■ What is the plan's normal retirement age and how are earlier and later retirement treated? (Chapter 19)
■ What is the plan benefit at retirement? (Chapter 20)
■ How fast do benefits accrue to employees? (Chapter 20)
■ What do employees receive on termination of employment before retirement (what is the vesting schedule)? (Chapter 20)
■ What provisions should the plan have for employees who terminate employment because of death or disability? (Chapter 20)
■ Who should hold the plan funds and on what terms? (Chapter 21)
■ What will the plan cost the employer each year? (Chapter 21)
■ In what form are benefits paid? (Chapter 24)

ELIGIBILITY AND PARTICIPATION

The employer must decide what group is to be covered by the qualified plan. In a closely held business, the employer will often want to provide a large portion of the plan's benefits to controlling and key employees and minimize benefits for rank and file employees. In larger plans, employers will often want to provide a different qualified plan (or no plan) for different groups of employees for various reasons; for example, the existence of collective bargaining units with separate plans, a desire for different benefit structures for hourly and salaried employees or differences in benefit policy for employees at different geographic locations.

In reviewing the many limitations imposed on the plan designer by the qualified plan rules, note that the overriding purpose for most of these rules is to prevent discrimination by the employer in favor of highly compensated employees. A secondary purpose, related to the first, is to provide and maintain some security of benefits for participants, particularly participants who are not highly compensated. Most of the qualified plan rules can be explained by these rationales; most questions about the meaning of particular rules and how they apply in a particular situation can be resolved by referring to these basic purposes of the law.

The Code imposes two types of limitations on the employer's freedom to designate the group of employees to be covered under the plan. The first limitation applies to the plan as it exists on paper—the eligibility provisions written into the plan. The second type of limitation applies to the plan in operation and provides minimum coverage requirements in the form of three alternative coverage tests. Both limitations are contained in Code Section 410 and its accompanying regulations and rulings.

First of all, as to plan coverage in the document itself, the designer has a good deal of freedom. The plan may cover only employees at a certain geographic location, employees in a certain work unit, salaried employees only, hourly employees only, or almost any other variation. However, when eligibility is restricted on the basis of age or service with the employer, there are specific limits.

AGE AND SERVICE REQUIREMENTS

Although not all plans have age or service conditions for entry, many employers prefer such conditions because they help to avoid the cost of carrying an employee on the records as a plan participant when the employee quits after a short period of service. Generally, a plan cannot require more than one year of service before eligibility, and an employee who has attained the age of 21 must be permitted to participate in the plan if the employee has met the other participation requirements of the plan. Both age and service requirements can be imposed. For example, for an employee hired at age 19, the plan can require that employee to wait until age 21 to participate in the plan. However, an employee hired at age 27 cannot be required to wait more than one year before participating in the plan.

As an alternative to the one-year waiting period, a plan may provide for a waiting period of up to two years if the plan provides immediate 100 percent vesting upon entry. (In most other cases, graduated vesting is allowed—see the discussion in Chapter 20.) The two-year provision is often used by employers with very few employees and a high turnover rate—for example, a self-employed physician with one or two clerical or technical employees who have high mobility in their labor market. With a two-year provision, few of the employees may ever be covered.

One problem with these age and service requirements is that it is often desirable for a plan to have *entry dates*—that is, specific dates during the year in which plan participation is deemed to begin—to simplify recordkeeping. The regulations provide that no employee may be required to wait for participation more than six months after the plan's age and service requirements are met.[1] Thus, a plan having entry dates must adjust its eligibility provisions accordingly.

■ EXAMPLE

The Blarp, Inc., pension plan wishes to have a one-year, age 21 entry requirement and to use an entry date or dates. Any of the following options will meet the requirement in the regulations:

- Two entry dates in the year, six months apart, with participants entering on the next entry date after they satisfy the one-year, age 21 condition
- One entry date, but a minimum entry age of no more than 20½ and a maximum waiting period of six months
- One entry date, with participants entering the plan on the date nearest (before or after) the date on which the one-year, age 21 requirement is satisfied

---

All qualified plans are subject to the age 21 requirement, except for a plan maintained exclusively by a tax-exempt educational institution as defined in Code Section 170(b)(1)(a)(ii). To avoid coverage of temporary employees such as graduate teaching assistants, such a plan may provide a minimum age of 26, but the plan must have 100 percent vesting after one year of service.

Maximum Age Limits and Coverage of Older Employees

Coverage of employees who enter a defined-benefit or target plan when they are close to the plan's retirement age can present a funding problem because there are relatively few years available to fund the benefit. If the participant enters the plan within a few years of retirement, the employer contribution may be burdensome. For example, using a given set of actuarial assumptions, the annual cost to fund the same benefit of $1,000 per month at age 65 varies with age at entry as shown in the table.

Age at Plan Entry	Annual Cost
30	$ 537
50	3,410
55	6,391
60	15,783
62	28,521
64	92,592

The age discrimination law prohibits exclusion of employees who enter at later ages. However, as discussed later under "Retirement Age," a plan can

---

[1.]Regulations Section 1.410(a)–4(b)(1).

define normal retirement age as the fifth anniversary of plan entry for a participant entering within five years of normal retirement age. This provides at least five years for funding. Alternatively, the time for funding the benefit can be extended simply by having the plan delay the beginning of benefit payments beyond retirement age, but payments cannot be delayed beyond the tenth anniversary of plan participation, and benefit payments must begin no later than April 1 of the year after attainment of age 70½ or at retirement, if later; see Chapter 24.

Definition of Year of Service

The term *year of service* is used in different ways in the qualified plan rules. It is used to define the age and service rules for eligibility that were just discussed, and is also used in connection with the vesting and benefit accrual rules discussed in Chapter 20. Because it plays such an important part in these rules, it has a specific definition under the law.

Generally, a year of service is a 12-month period during which the employee has at least 1,000 hours of service.[2] For purposes of determining eligibility, the *initial* 12-month period must be measured beginning with the date the employee begins work for the employer. For other purposes, the 12-month accounting period used by the plan (the *plan year*) can generally be used. For example, suppose the plan uses the calendar year as the plan year. If an employee began work on June 1, 2001, the initial 12-month period for determining whether the 1,000-hour requirement had been met would be June 1, 2001, through May 31, 2002. If the employee did not perform 1,000 hours of service during that period, the plan could begin the next measuring period on January 1, 2002, with subsequent years being determined similarly on the basis of the plan year.

The employer may determine hours of service using payroll records or any other type of records that accurately reflect the hours worked. Alternatively, the regulations allow a plan to use "equivalency" methods for computing hours of service. These equivalencies allow employees to be credited with hours worked based on completion of some other unit of service such as a shift, week, or month of service, without actual counting of hours worked.

Breaks in Service

A larger employer may reduce the cost of a plan somewhat by including a *break-in-service provision* in the plan's eligibility requirements. Under such a provision, an employee whose continuous service for the same employer is interrupted loses credit (upon returning to work) for service prior to the break and must again meet the plan's waiting period for eligibility. For a smaller employer, breaks in service followed by reemployment are relatively rare and

---

[2] See Code Sections 410(a)(3) (eligibility) and 411(a)(5) (vesting), and regulations thereunder.

such a provision may have no substantial cost impact other than possibly to complicate plan administration.

The rules under which a plan may interrupt service credits for breaks in service are somewhat complicated. The rules are set out in Code Section 410(a)(5) and regulations thereunder, as well as Labor Regulations Section 2530.200b. A one-year break in service for this purpose is defined as a 12-month period during which the participant has 500 or fewer hours of service. Service prior to a break cannot be disregarded until there is a one-year break in service. If the employee then returns to work, prebreak service may be disregarded (and the participant regarded as a new employee for participation purposes) within the following three limitations:

1. Service prior to the one-year break in service does not have to be counted unless the returned employee completes a year of service. Participation is then effective as of the first day of the plan year in which eligibility was reestablished.

2. If the plan has a two-year, 100 percent vesting eligibility provision, prebreak service need not be counted if the employee did not complete two years of service before the break.

3. If the participant had no vested benefits at the time of the break, prebreak service need not be counted if the number of consecutive one-year breaks in service equals or exceeds the greater of five or the participant's years of service before the break. For example, suppose that participant Arlen works for Maple Corporation for eight months, quits, and then returns seven years later. For purposes of determining eligibility in the Maple Corporation Plan, Arlen's eight months of prebreak service do not have to be counted.

Other Eligibility Criteria Related to Age and Service

Because the age and service limitations must be met by the plan document as drafted, the IRS will scrutinize the plan to ascertain whether there are eligibility criteria that indirectly base eligibility on age and service. For example, the employer may wish to exclude part-time employees. The IRS views an exclusion of part-timers as a service-based eligibility provision. If the plan has a one-year service requirement for entry, it will exclude all employees who never work 1,000 hours or more in any year. However, the plan cannot exclude part-timers who work 1,000 hours or more in a year, but less than a full year, because such a requirement would be seen as a service requirement that violated the one-year, 1,000-hour rule. However, even if some part-timers must be included, the plan is allowed to have a benefit formula that provides smaller benefits for them because of their lesser compensation, or because part-time service is given less credit for benefit purposes than full-time service.

The IRS will also look at how a plan is actually operated to make sure that the age and service limitations are not violated. For example. suppose an employer has a plan for Division B of the business, and employment in Division B requires five years of service in Division A. Division B has a qualified plan and Division A does not. This service requirement, although outside the plan itself, could be seen as an attempt to circumvent the service limitation for the plan maintained by Division B.

OVERALL COVERAGE TESTS

In addition to the specific rules relating to age and service eligibility provisions, the second major limitation on the employer's freedom to exclude employees from a qualified plan is a set of two alternative statutory tests (Code Section 410) to be applied to the plan in actual operation to determine if coverage is discriminatory. A qualified plan must satisfy one of two coverage tests:

1. The *ratio percentage test:* The plan must cover a percentage of nonhighly compensated employee that is at least 70 percent of the percentage of highly compensated employees covered.
2. The *average benefit test:* The plan must benefit a nondiscriminatory classification of employees, and the average benefit, as a percentage of compensation, for all non–highly compensated employees of the employer, must be at least 70 percent of that for highly compensated employees.

In addition, no defined-benefit plan can be qualified unless it covers, on each day of the plan year, the lesser of (1) 50 employees of the employer or (2) 40 percent or more of all employees of the employer [Code Section 401(a)(26)].

Employees Excluded

In applying these tests, certain employees are not taken into account:

- Employees who have not satisfied the plan's minimum age and service requirements, if any
- Employees included in a collective bargaining unit, if there is evidence that retirement benefits were the subject of good-faith bargaining under a collective bargaining agreement
- Employees excluded under a collective bargaining agreement between air pilots and employers under Title II of the Railway Labor Act
- Employees who are nonresident aliens and who receive no earned income from sources within the United States

The coverage tests apply not only at the plan's inception but on an ongoing basis. Generally, all of the nondiscrimination requirements must be met by a plan on at least one day of each quarter of the plan's taxable year [Code Section 401(a)(6)]. Although the IRS does not perpetually monitor a plan's compliance with the percentage coverage requirements, these requirements give the IRS an ongoing weapon to challenge a plan that may have become discriminatory.

Highly Compensated

For purposes of the coverage tests just described (and for many other employee benefit purposes as well), Code Section 414(q) provides a specific definition of a *highly compensated employee*. A highly compensated employee is any employee who during the preceding year met either of the following tests:

■ Was at any time an owner of a more than 5 percent interest in the employer or
■ Received compensation from the employer in excess of $80,000 (this nominal $80,000 amount is indexed annually for inflation; the 2000 amount is $85,000).

Features of the Average Benefit Test

In some respects, the average benefit test is the least stringent of the two coverage tests, and many types of plan design will be able to qualify only under this test. For example, a common plan design provides separate plans for salaried and hourly employees. In many cases, neither plan individually—the salaried plan in particular—can meet the ratio percentage test and thus meets the average benefit test.

The average benefit test is two-pronged. First, the plan must cover a *nondiscriminatory classification* of employees. Because of this aspect of the test, the IRS has a degree of discretion in the determination of whether a classification is nondiscriminatory. However, the IRS has issued detailed regulations as guidance in interpreting whether there is a nondiscriminatory classification.

The second requirement of the average benefit test is that the *average benefit,* as a percentage of compensation for non–highly compensated employees, must be at least 70 percent of that for highly compensated employees. In making this determination, all employees, whether covered or not under the plan in question, are counted and benefits from all qualified plans are taken into account.

Examples of Plan Coverage Meeting Various Tests

■ Acme Trucking Company has ten employees, three of whom are highly compensated. A qualified plan covers the three highly compensated employees and five of the seven nonhighly compensated employees. This plan meets the ratio percentage test because it covers at least 70 percent of nonhighly compensated employees.

- Barpt Products, Inc., has 20 employees, 5 of whom are highly compensated. If a qualified plan covers four of the highly compensated employees (80 percent), then the plan meets the ratio percentage test if it covers at least 56 percent of non–highly compensated employees—70 percent of 80 percent—or, in this case, nine nonhighly compensated employees.
- Flim Company, Inc. has 500 employees, 100 of whom are salaried. Flim has a plan for salaried employees that covers 50 employees. Flim has received a determination from the IRS that the 50 salaried employees covered do not form a discriminatory classification, presumably because some low-paid salaried employees are covered as well as highly paid employees. The Flim Company Plan will qualify, so long as benefits are provided for non–highly compensated employees as a group that are at least 70 percent of those for highly compensated employees as a group. Thus, some kind of retirement plan coverage for the hourly employees would be necessary.

Plans for Separate Lines of Business

If an employer has separate lines of business, the participation tests can be applied separately to employees in each line of business [Code Section 414(r)]. A separate line of business must be operated for bona fide business reasons and must have at least 50 employees. If highly compensated employees constitute more than a specified percentage of the employees in the separate line of business, special guidelines apply or IRS approval may be required to use the separate line of business provision.

The separate line of business provision may allow a larger employer, or a controlled group of employers, to design separate plans—with separate coverage provisions—for its various operations. This increases the flexibility available in plan design to some extent.

SERVICE FOR PREDECESSORS AND OTHER EMPLOYERS

A plan of one employer generally does not need to give an employee credit for service with another employer. There are some situations, however, in which this is required. Under collectively bargained, multiemployer, or multiple employer plans, service with more than one employer may have to be taken into consideration. Also, if the employer has chosen to take over or maintain the plan of a predecessor employer, service for the predecessor must be given credit. The IRS has not yet made clear what is meant by "predecessor employer," leaving some doubt as to the rules in this area. A common situation is the incorporation of a partnership and the continuation of the qualified plan of that partnership by the new corporation. The IRS once took the position that corporate employees who were partners in the prior partnership may not be given credit for prior service as partners. However, the IRS currently will probably permit this so long as regular employees receive full credit for service under the partnership.

Finally, service credit must be given for service with all employers under common control. The definition of *common control,* an important concept in the qualified plan area, is discussed in general terms below.

COMMONLY CONTROLLED EMPLOYERS

Often an employer organization (incorporated or unincorporated) is owned or controlled in common with other such organizations. The qualified plan designer often must coordinate plan coverage for the first employer with plan coverage for employees of other members of the commonly controlled group of employers.

The Code has several provisions relating to this issue; their basic objective is to prevent a business owner from getting around the coverage and nondiscrimination requirements for qualified plans by artificially segregating employees to be benefited from the plan into one organization with the remainder being employed by subsidiaries or organizations with lesser plan benefits or no plan at all. While this is still technically possible, the controlled group rules restrict this practice considerably.

Controlled Group Rules in General

Because the forms of business ownership can be tangled and complex, the common control rules for qualified plans are appropriately complicated. There are three sets of these rules.

1. Under Code Section 414(b), all employees of all corporations in a *controlled group* of corporations are treated as employed by a single employer for purposes of Sections 401, 408(k), 410, 411, 415, and 416. The major impact of this comes from the participation rules of Section 410, which require that the participation and coverage tests be applied to the entire controlled group rather than to any single corporation in the group. Code Section 414(c) provides similar rules for commonly controlled partnerships and proprietorships.
2. Code Section 414(m) provides that employees of an *affiliated service group* are treated as employed by a single employer. This requirement similarly has its major impact in determining participation in a qualified plan; however, it applies to other employee benefit requirements as well.
3. A *leased employee* is treated as an employee of the lessor corporation under certain circumstances, under Code Section 414(n).

Some examples will give a general idea of the impact of these provisions on plan design; a detailed discussion is beyond the scope of this book. Note that the common thread of these examples is that the related organization's employees must be *taken into account* in applying the participation rules. This does not mean that these employees must necessarily be covered.

- Alpha Corporation owns 80 percent of the stock of Beta Corporation. Alpha and Beta are members of a parent subsidiary controlled group of corporations. In applying the participation and coverage rules of Code Section 410, Alpha and Beta must be considered as a single employer.
- Bert and Harry own stock as shown in the chart at the left:

Owner	Corporation A	Corporation B
Bert	60%	60%
Harry	30	30
	90%	90%

Corporations A and B are a brother-sister controlled group. Thus, A and B must be considered as a single employer for purposes of Code Section 410 and most other qualified plan rules.

- Medical Services, Inc., provides administrative and laboratory services for Dr. Sam and Dr. Joe, each of whom is an incorporated sole practitioner. Dr. Sam and Dr. Joe each own 50 percent of Medical Services, Inc. If either Dr. Sam or Dr. Joe adopts a qualified plan, employees of Medical Services, Inc., will have to be taken into account in determining if plan coverage is nondiscriminatory.
- Calculators Incorporated, an actuarial firm, contracts with Temporary Services, Inc., an employee-leasing firm, to lease employees on a substantially full-time basis. The leased employees will have to be taken into account in determining nondiscrimination in any qualified plan of Calculators, unless Temporary maintains a minimum (10 percent nonintegrated) money-purchase pension plan for the leased employees.

VESTING

A qualified plan must provide a minimum nonforfeitable, or vested, benefit for participants who attain certain service requirements. Once vested, the participant cannot forfeit this minimum vested benefit. For example, the plan cannot require that an employee forfeit part or all of the vested benefit required by the Code even if the employee commits an act of misconduct, such as embezzlement or going to work for a competitor. The strictness of the vesting rules was designed to provide additional benefit security and to protect employees against arbitrary acts of the employer.

Vesting at Normal Retirement Age and Termination of Employment

The plan must provide a fully vested benefit at the normal retirement age. The plan must also provide that benefits are vested under a specified "vesting schedule" during the participant's employment, so that if the participant terminates employment prior to retirement age, he or she is entitled to a vested benefit with some stated minimum amount of service. The vested benefit can be payable immediately on termination or deferred to the plan's normal retirement age.

If the plan provides for employee contributions, the participant's accrued benefit is divided between the part attributable to employee contributions and the part attributable to employer contributions. The part attributable to employee contributions must at all times be 100 percent vested. The part attributable to employer contributions must be vested in accordance with a vesting schedule set out in the plan.

There is some flexibility in designing a vesting schedule in order to meet various employer objectives. However, the vesting schedule must be at least as favorable as one of two alternative minimum standards, five-year vesting or three- to seven-year vesting.

Five-Year Vesting

The vesting schedule satisfies this minimum requirement if an employee with at least five years of service is 100 percent vested in the employer-provided portion of the accrued benefit. This rule is satisfied even if there is no vesting at all before five years of service. This rule is sometimes referred to as *cliff vesting*.

Three- to Seven-Year Vesting

Years of Service	Vested Percentage
3	20
4	40
5	60
6	80
7 or more	100

A vesting schedule satisfies this minimum standard if the vesting is at least as fast as in the following table on the right:

In applying the vesting rules, all of a participant's years of service for the employer must be taken into account, even years prior to plan participation, except that years of service prior to age 18 may be excluded. The plan's vesting schedule may also ignore service prior to a break in continuous service with the employer; however, there are elaborate restrictions on how this may be done [Code Section 411(a)(6)].

Probably the most common vesting provision in defined-benefit plans is the five-year provision, because of its simplicity and because it is generally the most favorable to the employee. Defined-contribution plans are often designed with a more generous (to the employee) vesting schedule using the three- to seven-year schedule or one that is even faster.

Top-Heavy Vesting

To complete this discussion, it should be mentioned that plans that are top-heavy, as defined in the Code, are required to provide faster vesting than under

Years of Service	Vested Percentage
2	20
3	40
4	60
5	80
6 or more	100

most of the schedules previously mentioned. The top-heavy minimum vesting schedule is shown in the table at the left:

A 100 percent vesting provision with two years' eligibility also meets the top-heavy minimum vesting requirement. Top-heavy plans are discussed in detail in Chapter 25. As discussed below, the top-heavy requirements have a significant impact in designing a vesting schedule for plans of smaller employers.

Choosing a Vesting Schedule

Choosing an appropriate vesting schedule is an important plan design decision. When a pension plan participant terminates employment, invested funds contributed to the plan for that participant in excess of any benefits paid to the participant on termination (forfeitures) are generally used to reduce future employer costs for the pension plan. Strict vesting, therefore, can reduce a pension plan's cost to the employer. In a defined-contribution plan, forfeitures also can be reallocated to remaining participants' accounts. Thus, there should be a reason for adopting more than a strict minimum vesting schedule. Some reasons for using liberal vesting include the need to provide employee incentive and involvement in situations where a five-year vesting schedule might appear too remote and therefore of no value to employees. Also, a simplified liberal vesting schedule may reduce administrative costs.

Vesting on Plan Termination

The final vesting rule relates to a plan that has terminated. The IRS will regard a plan as having terminated either if it is formally terminated or if the employer permanently ceases to make contributions to the plan (see Chapter 26). When a plan is terminated, all benefits must be fully vested to the extent funded. Therefore, when a defined-contribution plan terminates, all participants are immediately 100 percent vested in their account balances. When a defined-benefit plan terminates, participants are 100 percent vested in their accrued benefits; however, if the plan funds are insufficient, they are vested only to the extent that the plan is funded. Many terminated qualified defined-benefit plans are insured by the Pension Benefit Guaranty Corporation (PBGC). The provisions that come into operation on plan termination under the PBGC rules will be discussed in Chapter 26.

WHO WILL PAY FOR THE PLAN?

Most qualified pension plans are funded entirely by the employer. Pension plans requiring contributions by employees, referred to as *contributory plans,* were once popular but are currently of diminishing importance. There are two reasons for this. First, employee contributions to a qualified plan other than "salary reductions" (see below) are *after-tax* contributions—the employee receives no tax deduction or exclusion for the contribution. Also, employee contributions involve administrative complications such as Code Section 401(m), discussed in Chapter 22.

Many employers believe that retirement plan benefits are appreciated more by employees if the employees themselves contribute (or feel that they are contributing) toward their cost. In most cases, of course, most of an employee's income comes in the form of compensation from the employer, so there is some degree of illusion in this approach. Some employers may also believe that a contributory approach lowers plan costs, but this is not actually true. To the extent that a contributory approach results in the loss of tax benefits (in effect, losing a contribution to the plan by the U.S. Treasury), a contributory plan actually costs the employer more for the same level of benefits. A better justification for contributory plans is that they give the employee some degree of choice in allocating his or her compensation between cash and deferred benefits.

Currently, the most favorable contributory plan design is to use *salary reductions* in a plan that is permitted to use salary reductions—a Section 401(k) plan, a Section 403(b) plan, a Section 457 plan, or a SIMPLE plan (discussed in later chapters). Qualified pension plans cannot use salary reductions, except for some older plans that were "grandfathered" (permitted to use older law) when current law was enacted. Salary reductions are subject to FICA and FUTA (Social Security and federal unemployment) taxes but not to federal income tax. Thus, the tax benefits of qualified plans are not completely lost to the employee if the salary reduction approach is used.

RETIREMENT AGE

A plan's *normal retirement age* is the age at which a participant can retire and receive the full specified retirement benefit. A defined-benefit plan must specify a normal retirement age in order to fully define the benefit. Defined-contribution plans do not need a normal retirement age for this purpose, but they may have a normal retirement age in order to specify an age at which participants can retire and begin to receive benefits or, as discussed below, an age beyond which no further employer contributions will be made.

Under Code Section 411(a)(8), a plan's normal retirement age can be no greater than the latest of:

- age 65 or
- the fifth anniversary of plan entry if a participant entered within five years of normal retirement age.

Thus, for example, a plan having a normal retirement age of 65 could provide normal retirement at age 67 for a participant entering at age 62.

Although most plans use 65 as the normal retirement age, the plan may specify an earlier normal retirement age. The use of an earlier normal retirement age in a defined-benefit plan requires that funding be accelerated—larger amounts must be contributed to the plan each year to fund each employee's benefit because the benefit will become payable at an earlier date. For plans in which tax sheltering is a primary consideration, such as plans oriented toward key employees in a closely held business, the use of the earliest possible normal retirement age can provide significant additional tax benefits by increasing the deductible plan contributions each year. However, if the normal retirement age is less than the Social Security retirement age, the Section 415 limitations are reduced, as discussed in Chapter 25. This tends to provide some limit on the use of unrealistically low normal retirement ages.

The IRS considers a plan's retirement age to be an actuarial assumption. Therefore, the requirement of "reasonableness" for actuarial assumptions, as discussed in Chapter 21, also puts some limit on the use of unrealistically low normal retirement ages.

Early Retirement

A qualified plan may designate an *early retirement age* at which an employee may retire and receive an immediate benefit. The early retirement benefit is usually reduced below that payable at normal retirement. The plan may have some service requirement for early retirement, such as ten years of service, or it may permit early retirement simply upon attainment of the early retirement age.

Under most defined-benefit plans, the monthly early retirement benefit is reduced below the monthly normal retirement benefit payable at age 65 because of two factors. First, the early retirement benefit will usually be limited to the participant's accrued benefit, and the participant will often have not accrued the full benefit at early retirement. Second, most plans require an actuarial reduction. The actuarial reduction is a mathematical adjustment based on (1) longer life expectancy at early retirement, (2) loss of investment earnings to the plan fund due to payments beginning earlier, and (3) loss of the possibility that the participant might die before payments begin—mortality.

Most plans do not require employer consent for early retirement. If employer consent is required, the IRS limits the early retirement benefit to the vested accrued benefit that would be payable if the employee terminated employment unilaterally, in order to avoid the possibility that the employer will favor highly compensated employees in granting early retirement benefits.

For defined-contribution plans, early retirement is usually treated the same as a termination of employment, and the benefit payable at early retirement is simply the amount of the participant's account balance as of that date. Thus, many defined-contribution plans do not specify an early retirement age.

Some employers offer a "subsidized" early retirement benefit—one that is reduced by less than the full amount dictated by the three factors discussed above—as an incentive for retirement. The subsidized benefit is often offered during a limited "window" period, during which the employee must either choose the benefit or lose the opportunity to receive it forever (or at least until the employer decides to offer another window benefit). There are specific legal protections under the Age Discrimination Act for employees in this situation.

Late Retirement

A qualified plan design should also cover the possibility of late retirement— retirement after the normal retirement age. Under the age discrimination rules discussed below, the plan must continue benefit accruals for employees who continue working after the normal retirement age unless the plan's benefit formula stops benefit accruals after a specified number of years and the employee has enough years of service to cease accruals for that reason. Benefit formulas must be designed carefully to ensure appropriate treatment of older employees. In smaller businesses, older participants are often owners or key employees who will want the plan to provide substantial benefits. On the other hand, many larger employers want to encourage earlier retirement and will want to provide only the minimum late retirement benefit required under the law.

NONTAX FEDERAL REGULATION AFFECTING QUALIFIED PLANS

As discussed in this chapter, the tax-law requirements for qualified plans include numerous provisions to prevent discrimination in favor of highly compensated employees. Other federal statutes also have some impact on qualified plan benefit and contribution formulas:

- The Civil Rights Act of 1964 prohibits employers from discriminating on the basis of race, color, religion, sex, or national origin. Sex discrimination, as discussed below, is the only issue under this law that has a significant practical impact on pension benefit design.
- The Age Discrimination in Employment Act (Title 29 USC) prohibits discrimination by employers on the basis of age; the major implications of this provisions are also discussed below.
- The Americans with Disabilities Act (Title 42 USC) prohibits discrimination against disabled employees. This would prohibit special pension provisions applicable only to disabled employees and might also require general pension provisions to be changed to accommodate disabled employees. The law is broadly written and its full implications, including its effect on retirement plans, are not yet entirely apparent.
- The Family and Medical Leave Act of 1993 (Title 29 USC Sees. 2601 et seq.) generally requires employers with 50 or more employees to provide

12 weeks per year of unpaid leave for childbirth, adoption, health condition or care for a sick family member. When the employee returns, all accrued pension and other employee benefits must be restored, but the employer is not required to provide accrual of benefits during the period of the leave.

Sex Discrimination

Of the issues arising under these nontax federal statutes, sex discrimination is the one issue that has the most direct relevance to pension plan design.

Sex discrimination as it relates to qualified plans, annuities, and life insurance is a subject that is not yet completely resolved, but some clear rules for qualified plan design have emerged. The issue arises from the statistical fact that women, as a group, live longer than men. This means that if actuaries make separate calculations for men and women, the same periodic annuity costs more for women than for men of the same age. Or, for a given annuity premium, the periodic annuity amount is lower for women than for men.

The Civil Rights Act of 1964, like its predecessor, the Equal Pay Act of 1963, provides that it is an unlawful employment practice for an employer

> to discriminate against any individual with respect to his compensation, terms, conditions or privileges of employment, because of such individual's race, color, religion, sex or national origin [Section 2000e-2(a), Civil Rights Act of 1964].

It is clear that qualified plan benefits are part of an employee's compensation; it was not originally clear, however, what constituted sex discrimination in a qualified plan.

- Must the plan provide the same periodic benefit for both men and women employees?
- Must the plan provide only the same employer contribution to the plan?

Early federal administrative guidelines under the Equal Pay Act of 1963 indicated that an employer satisfied the nondiscrimination requirement if it provided either equal periodic benefits or equal contributions. However, in 1972, the Equal Employment Opportunities Commission (EEOC) issued a revised sex discrimination guideline under the Civil Rights Act of 1964: To avoid sex discrimination in retirement plans, the employer must provide equal periodic benefits to men and women employees in all circumstances. Employers originally resisted this guideline, but recent court cases clearly point in this direction. The first significant case went to the United States Supreme Court, *Los Angeles Department of Water and Power v. Manhart*, 435 US 702 (1978). That case involved a contributory pension plan of a municipality. The Supreme Court held that the plan could not require women to pay higher contributions than men to receive equal periodic benefits upon retirement. Subsequently, the Supreme Court held in *Arizona Governing Committee v. Norris*, 103 S.Ct. 3492 (1983), that a municipal retirement plan could not provide sex-based annuity choices at retirement. No employer contributions were involved—only employee contributions.

Although technically the Manhart and Norris cases did not completely establish that the Civil Rights Act requires equal periodic benefits for men and women in an employer-provided retirement plan under all circumstances, the trend of the cases favors an equal-benefit approach and virtually all planners assume this to be the law.

Most qualified plans already avoid obvious sex discrimination problems. Most defined-benefit plans provide the same normal retirement benefit for men and women employees; most defined-contribution plans provide the same employer contribution for men and women employees. Discrimination problems arise when a qualified plan (either defined-benefit or defined-contribution) offers participants a choice of benefits including a retirement annuity. Most plan designers advise using only unisex annuities (those providing the same annuity rate for both men and women) for this purpose. Similarly, if a qualified plan offers life insurance as an incidental benefit (see Chapter 20), the life insurance cost to the employee must be determined on a unisex basis. However, in determining the annual deposit to a defined benefit plan, the sex of covered employees may be taken into account, because it affects only the employer's costs and not the ultimate benefit that the employee will receive.

The sex discrimination issue is complicated by the fact that the Civil Rights Act does not govern the pricing of insurance products; private insurance companies, therefore, currently are allowed to use sex as a factor in determining life insurance and annuity rates. The argument has been made that when a qualified plan uses a group pension contract for funding, sex-based annuity options should be allowed under the group contract. However, it is the employer, not the insurance company, that provides the pension as part of an employee's compensation. In view of this and the trend of the court cases, insurance companies no longer offer sex-based annuities as part of a group pension contract.

Even if employers remove any conceivable sex discrimination from qualified plan documents, if the plan is designed so that participants can withdraw their benefits at retirement, effective sex discrimination will still be possible so long as sex-based annuities are available from insurance companies. In that situation, men can withdraw their benefits and purchase an annuity from an insurance company providing greater periodic payments than women would be able to purchase for the same amount (or payments greater than those available under the plan if the plan provides a unisex annuity). Because of this and other related problems, the law may at some point reconsider the question whether insurance companies should be allowed to determine annuity and life insurance premiums on the basis of sex.

There is no doubt that sex is a relevant actuarial classification, as is any ascertainable factor affecting life expectancy, which could conceivably include such things as race, religion, or national origin. Insurance companies do not commonly use race or other potentially offensive actuarial factors, regardless of their relevance as predictors of life expectancy. However, they are strongly attached to the use of sex classifications and have vigorously opposed restrictions proposed in Congress.

Both sides of the controversy view the issue as one of fairness. Advocates of sex classification argue that unisex annuity rates are unfair to men, who should be allowed to purchase annuities reflecting their group's life expectancy. Opponents argue that it is unfair to attribute to an individual the characteristics of a group to which that individual belongs, regardless of whether the individual actually possesses those characteristics. Ultimately, Congress may have to determine the appropriate social policy in connection with insurance company practices.

Age Discrimination

The federal Age Discrimination in Employment Act,[3] as amended in 1978, 1986, and 1989, has an impact on qualified plans. The Age Discrimination Act applies to workers and managers of any business that engages in interstate transactions (a very broad category) and employs at least 20 persons during the year. Certain hazardous occupations are excluded as well as executive employees who would be entitled, upon retirement, to an annual pension of $44,000 or more over and above Social Security benefits.

The main provision of the Age Discrimination Act that affects qualified plans is that which prohibits involuntary retirement at any age. A qualified plan must not in any way require mandatory retirement.

In addition, Code Sections 411(b)(1)(H) and 411(b)(2) deal specifically with benefits for older workers. In general, older workers must be treated the same as younger workers with regard to plan contributions (for a defined-contribution plan) and benefit accruals (for a defined-benefit plan). However, for a defined-benefit plan, the benefit formula can provide that benefits are fully accrued not at a specified age but after a specified number of years of service, such as 25. This will cut off further benefit accrual for many older employees, but it is permitted. If a plan provides for normal retirement at 65 with actuarial increases for later retirement, the actuarial increases are credited toward any requirement of benefit accrual that applies. For example, if a plan provides a benefit of $1,000 per month beginning at age 65 or an actuarially adjusted $1,100 per month beginning at age 66, the extra $100 is counted as an additional benefit accrual.

[3.]29 USC.

STUDY QUESTIONS

1. Describe the coverage of employees who enter into a defined-benefit or a target plan when they are close to the plan's normal retirement age.

2. For purposes of a qualified plan, explain what requirements an employee must satisfy to earn credit for a year of service.

3. Jane Chaney worked two years for BIGGO and acquired two years of service under BIGGO's defined-benefit plan. The BIGGO Company has a vesting schedule that grants a fully vested benefit after the employee has attained five years of service with no vesting until then. Jane left after two years, but returned to work after a four-year absence. Will Jane's break in service cause her to lose her prebreak service? Explain.

4. Which of the following employees of the Kelvin Company are considered highly compensated employees for nondiscrimination purposes?

	Salary
Kathy Kelvin (100 percent stock owner/president)	$400,000
Lou Jane (vice president/treasurer)	180,000
Manny Martin	47,000
Nancy Norris	40,000
Oprah Oliver	22,000
Peter Peaquin	20,000

5 a. The Alpha Company has 20 employees, six of whom are highly compensated. The Alpha Plan covers the six highly compensated employees and 11 of the 14 employees who are not highly compensated. Does the Alpha Plan pass the ratio percentage test?
   b. The Beta Company has ten employees, two of who are highly compensated. The Beta Plan covers the two highly compensated employees and covers seven of the eight employees who are not highly compensated. Does the Beta Plan pass the ratio percentage test?

6. For qualified plan purposes, what is the significance of treating more than one business as a controlled group of corporations?

7. Explain whether the following vesting schedules comply with the vesting rules.

a.

Years of Service	Percentage Vested
0–9	0%
10	100

b.

Years of Service	Percentage Vested
1	50%
2	60
3	70
4	80
5	90
6	100

c.

Years of Service	Percentage Vested
0–4	0%
5	50
6	100

8. Explain whether the following vesting schedule meets the vesting schedule rules for top-heavy plans.

Years of Service	Percentage Vested
0–1	0%
2	20
3	40
4	60
5	80
6 or more	100

9 a. Under what conditions would you recommend that an employer choose a restrictive vesting schedule for the plan?
   b. Under what conditions would you recommend that an employer choose a liberal vesting schedule for the plan?

10. The president of The New England Cannery (250 employees) is undecided about whether her company's qualified pension plan should provide for employee contributions.
   a. Explain the advantages and disadvantages of including mandatory employee contributions in the plan.
   b. What type of plan eliminates the problem of lost tax benefits arising from employee contributions?

11. a. Why do defined-benefit plans use a normal retirement age requirement?
   b. What is the latest normal retirement age that a qualified plan may use?
   c. What are the advantages and disadvantages of using a pre-65 normal retirement age in a closely held business?

12. Why are early retirement benefits typically reduced below the monthly normal retirement benefit payable at age 65?

13. Explain how sex discrimination in retirement benefits is still possible even if there is no explicit discrimination in the pension plan documents.

CHAPTER 20

Pension Benefit Formulas

OBJECTIVES

- Describe the types of retirement benefit formulas that can be included in defined-contribution pension plans and in defined-benefit plans.

- Explain the planning reasons for integrating a qualified plan formula with Social Security benefits.

- Describe offset and integration level formulas and explain the integration rules applying to such formulas.

- Explain how pension plans can provide inflation protection.

- Describe the purpose for the accrued-benefit rules.

- Explain how benefits are paid on nonretirement terminations of employment.

- Describe the preretirement and postretirement survivorship benefits that must be provided by qualified plans.

- Explain the extent to which incidental death benefits and disability benefits may be included in qualified plans.

T he central issue in qualified plan design is the plan's benefit formula. A variety of approaches are possible to meet the needs of the employer and employee, within the restrictions to be discussed here.

The discussion of benefit formulas in this chapter is organized as follows:

- Defined-contribution formulas
- Defined-benefit formulas including cash-balance formulas
- Integration of plan formulas with Social Security
- Inflation protection
- The accrued benefit
- Benefits at termination of employment
- Death and disability benefits

DEFINED-CONTRIBUTION FORMULAS

A defined-contribution plan is much simpler than a defined-benefit plan. In a defined-contribution plan, the plan specifies the amount that the employer will contribute to the plan. There are two basic types of contribution formulas for defined-contribution pension plans—the *money-purchase* formula and the *target-benefit* formula. For a money-purchase formula, the annual employer contribution is usually a stated percentage of each employee's compensation—for example, 6 percent of compensation. The target-benefit formula uses an actuarial approach, providing larger contribution percentages for older plan entrants.

The following advantages have been identified for defined-contribution plans (including both pension and profit-sharing types) over defined-benefit plans:

- Defined-contribution plans with their individual, periodically reported, and valued employee accounts are easier for the employee to understand and appreciate as a valuable benefit.
- Administration and government regulations are generally simpler for defined-contribution plans. For example, Pension Benefit Guaranty Corporation (PBGA) coverage and reporting requirements do not apply to defined-contribution plans (see Chapter 26) and ongoing actuarial services are not required for defined-contribution plans.
- Defined-contribution plans fit the nature of today's work force, which experiences frequent job-changing, thereby putting a premium on a portable benefit that increases steadily from the first day of employment. Few employees enjoy the luxury of a 40-year career with the same employer, which typically provides the best result for defined-benefit plan participants.

In terms of the number of plans, defined-contribution plans—including profit-sharing and pension plans—constitute about 70 percent of all qualified plans. However, if a comparison is made on the basis of employees covered under qualified plans, the result is the opposite—about 60 percent of such employees are in defined-benefit plans. This indicates, not surprisingly, that defined-benefit plans tend to cover larger groups, although defined-benefit plans are often used for smaller groups as well.

Money-Purchase Formulas

In a money-purchase plan, as in all defined-contribution plans, there is an individual account for each employee. The amount of the benefit at retirement is equal to the employee's account balance at the retirement date or at a valuation date near the time of the retirement date. The plan may provide for payment of the benefit in a lump sum; a variety of payment options, including annuity benefits, may also be made available. The accounts of all employees are usually commingled for investment purposes; each account is kept separate administratively, so that the account increases and decreases in accordance with the investment performance of the fund. Thus, the benefit available at retirement cannot be predicted exactly. Investment risk lies with the employee. If the employee's account is less than anticipated, the employer is not required to make additional contributions.

As Table 20–1 shows, money-purchase plans tend to provide a better benefit for employees who enter the plan at younger ages because a longer period of time is available to accumulate plan contributions and compound these contributions with investment earnings. If the employer has employees with a wide range of ages at the inception of the plan, this feature of a money-purchase plan makes it impossible to provide older employees with retirement income that is comparable—as a percentage of their preretirement income, the replacement ratio—to that of the younger employees. As discussed later, comparable replacement ratios for older and younger employees can be better achieved with a target plan or defined-benefit plan.

TABLE 20-1
Defined-Contribution Plan Accumulations

Age at Plan Entry	Account Balance at Retirement
25	$213,609
30	147,913
40	67,676
50	26,888
55	14,783
60	6,153

Assumptions: Annual employer contributions: $1,000 per employee; retirement age: 65; average investment return: 7%.

Target Plans

From a planning point of view, the target plan is a hybrid of the defined-contribution and defined-benefit approaches. Under a target plan, the employer chooses a target level of retirement benefit using a benefit-formula approach similar to that used in designing a defined-benefit plan.

For example, the target level might be some percentage of each participant's final-average compensation. At the plan's inception, an actuarial calculation is made of the level annual contribution amount (for each participant) that would be required to fully fund this benefit at the participant's normal retirement date. These level amounts are then actually contributed by the employer to the plan each year. Unlike a defined-benefit plan, however, there is no change in the level contribution amount if actual investment return or mortality varies from the assumptions used in determining the initial contribution level, unless the plan is actually amended. Therefore, at retirement, the amount actually available may be more or less than anticipated. The plan has individual accounts for each participant, and unlike a defined-benefit plan, each employee's benefit is limited to the amount actually in his or her individual account.

Because a target plan is a defined-contribution plan, it is subject to the Section 415 limits applicable to defined-contribution plans. As discussed further in Chapter 25, under this limit the annual addition to each participant's account cannot exceed the lesser of 25 percent of compensation or $30,000 (dollar figure subject to indexing for inflation; $30,000 in 2000). For some older employees, this limit might prevent making a large enough contribution to fund the target benefit. For example, if an employee enters the plan at age 60 and earns $50,000, the target formula might require a contribution of $15,000 annually, but the actual contribution would be limited to $12,500 (25 percent of $50,000). This disadvantage of a target plan does not apply to a defined-benefit plan, for which the applicable Section 415 limit is not based on the annual contribution (see Chapter 25).

Target plans are an example of a more general type of benefit/contribution formula design based on what is known as *cross-testing*. A cross-tested defined-contribution formula is tested for discrimination in favor of the highly compensated by looking at employees' projected benefits at retirement (assuming they continue in employment until retirement age) rather than testing the contribution formula directly. Cross-testing is discussed in more detail in Chapter 22 in connection with profit-sharing plans, specifically age-weighted profit-sharing formulas. Currently, employers considering this approach in benefit design are likely to be more interested in age-weighted profit-sharing plans than in target pension plans, because profit-sharing plans have more flexibility in annual contribution levels. Target plans, like all pension plans, require that the employer commit to a fixed annual contribution obligation.

DEFINED-BENEFIT FORMULAS

In a defined-benefit plan, the plan formula specifies the benefit that will be paid to the employee rather than the amount of the contribution. There are no individual accounts for employees and, consequently, the employee does not bear the risk of bad investment results. Payment of the promised benefit is an obligation of the employer and the employer is required to fund the plan in advance so that sufficient funds will be available. Within certain limits, benefits in a defined-benefit plan are insured by the federal government through the PBGC.

Defined-benefit plans are the most complex of all qualified plans. The benefit formulas themselves tend to be complex because of the variety of employer objectives sought. The actuarial funding approach requires additional administrative costs for the plan. Hence, the law dealing with defined-benefit plans is appropriately complex.

General Characteristics of Defined-Benefit Formulas

Defined-benefit formulas have two basic characteristics that determine their use in pension plan design. First, the amount of an employee's benefit is not necessarily directly related to total compensation from the employer during the period the employee is covered under the plan. This means that the employer can design the plan with reference to a desired retirement income level for an employee, even if the employee had relatively low compensation in certain years or participated in the plan for a relatively short time.

The second basic characteristic is that defined-benefit formulas can favor those employees who enter the plan at later ages. This is because the benefit for such employees is a stated amount—often the same amount payable to employees who entered the plan at earlier ages—even though the employer's annual cost for funding the benefit is greater for employees entering the plan at later ages. As an example, consider three employees having the same compensation of $50,000 annually and a plan providing a benefit of 50 percent of this compensation at age 65. If these employees entered the plan at ages 30, 40, and 50, the employer's level annual cost to provide the same retirement benefit for each is illustrated in Table 20–2.

These basic characteristics relate to the two principal types of employer objectives that can be met with a defined-benefit plan. One objective is to provide a reasonable income replacement ratio for all covered employees. The flexibility of defined-benefit formulas permits this. The other type of objective is philosophically quite different—the objective of providing the maximum tax shelter under the plan for key employees. In a closely held business where this objective is often dominant, key employees are typically older at the plan's inception. Thus, the second basic defined-benefit plan characteristic illustrated in Table 20–2 is significant, as is the flexibility of defined-benefit formula design.

TABLE 20-2
Entry Age and Defined-Benefit Contribution

Age at Entry	Employer Contribution Each Year to Retirement
30	$ 1,971
40	4,309
50	10,847

Replacement Ratio Approach

In adopting an income replacement ratio approach to benefit formula design, the starting point is to examine the census of the employees to be covered and determine an appropriate level of retirement income. For all but the lowest-paid employees, a retiree's standard of living can usually be maintained with less than 100 percent of preretirement income. Some reasons for this are that there are no work-related expenses after retirement, that the need to save after retirement is reduced, and that living expenses of older persons tend to be less than those of working persons. Certain expenses of older persons that tend to go up, such as medical care, are often covered under Medicare or other health insurance. Replacement ratios for lower income employees should be higher because an individual closer to the subsistence level tends to spend most of his or her income for basic items such as food and shelter, and these expenses at a basic level are not likely to decline after retirement. Qualified plans that use this approach typically aim at providing about 50 to 75 percent of preretirement gross (before-tax) income from the plan plus Social Security retirement benefits.

An appropriate benefit formula is designed to provide the desired replacement ratio, using the design rules discussed in the rest of this chapter. The annual cost of the plan is then determined. If this exceeds the employer's cost objectives, the plan must be redesigned until the cost comes within the appropriate range. It is also possible to vary the annual cost by varying the actuarial methods and assumptions used, as discussed in Chapter 21.

Types of Formulas

Many different benefit formulas have been developed to meet various plan design objectives. A large degree of variation is possible, within the limits of the benefit accrual rules and rules for integration with Social Security, discussed later, and the general nondiscrimination requirements for qualified plans covered in Chapter 19. The possible benefit formulas can be divided into specific types. The IRS distinguishes two types of benefit formulas, the flat-benefit formula and the unit-benefit formula.

Flat-Benefit Formula

This type of formula does not take an employee's service into account. Such a benefit formula might be either a *flat-amount* formula, such as a formula providing a benefit of $100 per month at retirement for each employee, or a *flat-percentage* formula—for example, a benefit of 40 percent of compensation at retirement.

The flat-amount approach is usually suitable only for a group of employees having almost the same compensation levels because most pension planners would want to take differing compensation levels into account in determining the retirement income level. However, the flat-amount formula has the advantage of simplicity. The flat-percentage approach takes differing compensation into account and is frequently used. The plan's definition of compensation, as discussed below, is an important element of this formula.

All flat-benefit formulas raise the problem of fairness among employees with differing amounts of service with the employer. Many employers would prefer not to give the same benefit to short- and long-service employees, even though they have the same compensation levels. This objection often can be resolved by having a minimum period of service required in order to receive the full stated dollar amount or percentage, with reductions for lesser amounts of service. A more definite solution is to use a unit-benefit formula, discussed next.

Unit-Benefit Formula

A unit-benefit formula is based on the employee's service. Some unit-benefit formulas take only service, not compensation, into account—for example, a benefit of $10 per month for each year of service. As with the flat benefit formula, such a formula is usually only suitable for a group having a fairly narrow range of compensation. Such formulas are sometimes used in collectively bargained plans. A unit-benefit formula may also take compensation into account—for example, a formula providing a benefit of 1 percent of compensation for each year of service (or to state it another way, 1 percent of compensation times the employee's years of service). Under this formula, an employee who retired with 15 years of service would receive a retirement benefit equal to 15 percent of compensation.

Past Service. When a unit-benefit plan is installed for an existing, rather than new, employee group, the employer must decide whether to give service credit only for prospective or future service or to give some credit for existing employees' prior service for the employer. In small, closely held businesses, the owners and key employees often have considerable past service compared with other employees; it is particularly common to have past-service provisions in such plans. Past-service credit can be provided in many ways, so long as there is no discrimination in favor of highly compensated employees. Past service can be treated the same as future service, or the formula can provide lesser credit for past service.

The ability to utilize past service is one of the major advantages of a defined-benefit plan over a defined-contribution plan. For example, suppose a plan is adopted by an employer with two employees, one age 30 with 5 years of prior service and the other age 50 with 25 years of prior service. If a defined-contribution plan is adopted, the younger employee will have at age 65 a plan account representing 35 years of employer contributions, while the older employee will have only 15 years of contributions at retirement. However, a unit-benefit plan providing an annual benefit of 1 percent of compensation for each year of past and future service would allow each employee to retire at age 65 with an annual benefit of 40 percent of compensation.

The Cash-Balance Formula

The cash-balance formula—sometimes referred to as a *guaranteed-account formula,* as well as by other names—is a type of hybrid between defined-benefit and defined-contribution approaches that is in a sense the opposite of the other hybrid, the target formula. In the target formula, employer contributions are based on age at entry, but ultimate benefits are not guaranteed. With a cash-balance formula, employer contributions are based on compensation, not on age at entry; the ultimate benefit (account balance) is subject to a guaranteed rate of return.

In a cash-balance plan, accounts are set up for each participant. Unlike the accounts in a defined-contribution plan, there is no investment risk—the accounts are merely a computational formality. The accounts are credited at least annually with two types of credits, a pay credit and an interest credit.

The pay credit is generally a percentage of compensation. The pay credit formula may be integrated with Social Security; for example, the plan might provide a pay credit each year of 2 percent of each participant's total earnings plus 3 percent of the participant's earnings above an integration level related to the Social Security taxable wage base. A cash-balance formula must meet the rules for integrating a defined-benefit plan (see discussion beginning on page 519). The actuary typically will do this by showing that the "worst case"—the most discriminated-against participant—will receive at least as much as under the defined-benefit integration rules.

The interest credit is an amount representing earnings on the participant's account balance. To meet the definitely determinable rule applicable to pension formulas, the interest credit must be an amount that is defined in the plan and not subject to the employer's discretion. For example, the interest credit each year might be defined as the lesser of the change in the Consumer Price Index (CPI) for the preceding year or the one-year rate for Treasury securities. However, the employer can have the option of crediting actual plan earnings, if these are higher.

Because there are no true individual accounts—participants have a guaranteed minimum benefit that can be legally satisfied out of the entire plan fund—the plan does not meet the definition of a defined-contribution plan and is thus technically a defined-benefit plan. Consequently, the plan is subject to a more complex legal environment; it is subject to PBGC reporting and termination requirements and the requirement of actuarial certification.

The employer's cost for the plan is determined actuarially because of the guarantee features. Costs can be controlled to some extent by choosing appropriate factors for the interest credits. However, if interest credits do not keep pace with actual plan earnings, participants are likely to be dissatisfied with the plan.

Despite the plan's technical status as a defined-benefit plan, a cash-balance plan looks to participants very much like a money-purchase plan and serves some of the same objectives. Typically, the cash-balance plan will be attractive to younger employees because benefits (and employer costs) build up faster in

FIGURE 20-1

Comparison of Cash-Balance and Traditional Defined-Benefits (DB) Plans

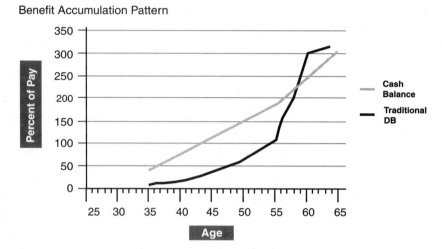

Traditional Defined-Benefits versus
Cash-Balance Plan Employee Hired at Age 30

Source: *Employee Benefits Journal*, June 1999.

the employee's earlier years than in a traditional defined-benefit plan (see Figure 20.1). Thus, it is attractive to employers wishing to retain younger employees or allocate pension costs in a way that does not discriminate against younger employees. At the same time, the guarantee features help to meet some of the retirement security objectives of the traditional defined-benefit plan.

Cash-balance plans have attracted current interest because some large companies have announced that they are converting their regular defined-benefit plans to the cash-balance variety. Some employers that have a traditional defined-benefit plan have become dissatisfied with the plan because of the rising costs for employees nearing retirement and the belief that younger employees do not find traditional defined-benefit plans attractive. Termination of the defined-benefit plan and substitution of a defined-contribution plan, if any, is costly to the employer because most or all of existing plan assets have to be immediately credited to participants. A less costly alternative is to revise the existing plan's formula into a cash-balance formula. Generally, the new formula provides a benefit equal to the greater of the cash-balance formula applied over all years of service or the amount earned under the old defined-benefit formula up to the date of the conversion. Existing benefits earned by employees are not lost, but some older employees may not receive much additional benefit under the cash-balance formula. Some plans provide a phase-in period to ease this adjustment.

The IRS has identified certain potential tax issues in these conversions, including the question whether there is any age discrimination resulting from the conversion, an issue not currently resolved. The IRS is currently requiring "technical advice" on any cash-balance conversion submitted for a determination letter. This means, in effect, that each case must be sumitted to the National Office of the IRS. Meanwhile, Congress has been considering legislation on the issue. However, a basic principle of pension and employment law is that an employer is not generally obligated to continue any pension or other employment benefit indefinitely without charge or reduction, unless it has contractually agreed to do so. Consequently, new law in this area probably will be limited to a requirement of improved disclosure of a proposed conversion to employees, so they can plan their retirements accordingly.

Definition of Compensation

For formulas that are based on compensation, the definition of compensation provides some flexibility in planning. Definitions of compensation can be classified into two categories: *career average* and *final average*. With a career-average formula, the employee's compensation over the entire working period is averaged. Another way of putting this is that the benefit earned in a given year of service is based on the compensation for that year. Any defined-contribution formula is effectively a career-average formula, but defined-benefit plans can also use the career-average approach. In a final-average formula, the compensation used is averaged over a specified period of years, usually chosen to produce a relatively high benefit. For example, the compensation used in the benefit formula could be defined as compensation over the employee's five final years of service. To guard against the possibility of a salary decrease in the final years of service due to partial disability or other cause, many plans define compensation as the compensation over a specified consecutive period during which the average compensation is the highest.

In defining compensation for plan purposes, a decision must be made whether to use total compensation (salary or wages plus bonuses, overtime, and so forth) or some lesser amount, such as base salary only. Flexibility is permitted here, but if anything other than total compensation is used, the method chosen must not produce discrimination. For example, excluding overtime pay in the benefit formula might be discriminatory if lower-paid workers typically receive substantial overtime pay while prohibited group employees do not.

INTEGRATION OF QUALIFIED PLANS WITH SOCIAL SECURITY

Qualified plan formulas can be designed to reflect, or integrate with, the participants' Social Security benefits. Integration of a plan with Social Security avoids duplication of plan benefits by those of Social Security and also tends to lower the employer's cost for the plan, for a given level of total benefits. More than half of all private qualified plans are integrated with Social Security, and the percentage is even higher among defined-benefit plans considered separately. The reason for this is the obvious overlap between private retirement benefits and the Social Security benefit. Although this is a complication, it provides advantages in private plan design.

Purpose and Effect of Social Security Integration

The existence of Social Security benefits is relevant to a number of objectives in designing a qualified plan.

- The objective of providing an appropriate income replacement ratio must take into account the fact that the employee will receive Social Security benefits as well as benefits from the plan. If plan benefits alone are considered for this purpose, the actual replacement ratio will often be very different from what was intended.
- The objective of plan efficiency can be met only if retirement benefits from Social Security are considered in designing the plan. Otherwise, private plan benefits for some employees may duplicate benefits they already receive from Social Security.
- For a small business owner who is interested in maximizing the tax sheltering-benefits from the qualified plan, an integrated plan provides a method by which the plan benefit or contribution formula can, to a considerable extent, discriminate in favor of higher paid employees. In fact, in the tax law, the Social Security integration rules are referred to as the "permitted disparity" rules, referring to the maximum extent to which the plan's benefit or contribution formula can deviate from a uniform percentage of compensation. Therefore, the objective of maximizing the tax-sheltering benefits of the qualified plan will generally lead to a consideration of integrating the plan with Social Security.
- Finally, with regard to the employer's cost objectives, an integrated plan may provide a satisfactory level of retirement benefits to all employees at the lowest possible employer cost.

The integration rules are based on the way the OASDI Social Security benefit is calculated. For simplicity, this benefit will be referred to in this chapter as OASDI.

OASDI uses a unit-benefit type of formula based on the employee's past years of work experience and the employee's compensation income in each of those years. More credit is given for the "first dollars" of compensation than for larger amounts; for compensation in a given year that exceeds the taxable wage base for that year, there is no benefit credit. The OASDI calculation was covered in detail in Chapter 3.

FIGURE 20-2
Integrated Plan—Portion of Replacement Income
(50% of Final Average Compensation [FAC]) Provided by OASDI and Private Plan

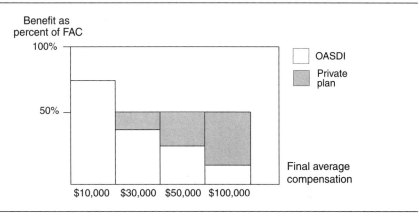

The integration rules are designed to allow a private qualified plan to provide a benefit that is a mirror image of OASDI so that the two sources of retirement income together form a retirement program that is non-discriminatory. Because of the nature of the OASDI calculation, Social Security alone provides a higher percentage of income replacement for lower-paid employees than for higher-paid employees. Thus, the private plan may correspondingly provide a proportionately greater benefit for the higher paid. Figures 20–2 and 20–3 illustrate this qualitatively. In all cases, note how OASDI integration allows the private plan, considered alone, to discriminate substantially in favor of the highly compensated, both in terms of benefit amounts and percentages of compensation.

FIGURE 20-3
Integrated Plan—Sources of Total Retirement Benefit
(Qualitative Diagram for Illustration, Not for Calculation)

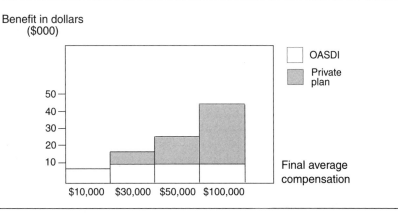

An employer has much less freedom in integrating a qualified plan with OASDI than in integrating other types of benefit plans such as disability income plans. Because of the potential for discrimination, Code Section 401(a)(5) and 401(1) and associated regulations and IRS rulings impose detailed limitations on integrating qualified plans.

Under the principles of Code Section 401(1), there are two basic approaches by which a qualified plan can be integrated with OASDI—the *offset approach* and the *integration-level approach* (sometimes called the *excess approach*). Under the offset approach, a specified fraction of the benefit is subtracted from the benefit otherwise payable under the plan. The offset approach can be used only with a defined-benefit plan. Under the integration-level approach, the plan specifies a level of compensation called the *integration level*. Benefits or contributions below this integration level are provided at a lower rate than benefits or contributions for compensation above the integration level. An integration-level approach can be used with both defined-benefit and defined-contribution plans. The rules will be discussed in detail next, beginning with the integration of defined-benefit plans.

Integration of Defined-Benefit Plans

Offset Approach

As indicated above, a defined-benefit plan can be integrated with OASDI using either the offset approach or the integration-level approach. Because the offset approach is simpler, it will be discussed first.

With the offset method, the private plan benefit is initially structured to provide the replacement ratio desired, without taking OASDI into account. Then the benefit formula is modified to subtract a specified amount to reflect the employee's OASDI benefit. For example, an offset formula might read as follows:

> Upon retirement, the participant shall be entitled to a monthly retirement benefit equal to 60 percent of the participant's final average monthly compensation, less ½ percent of the participant's monthly final average compensation for each year of service. If the participant retired with 20 years of service and monthly final average compensation of $10,000, the benefit would be $6,000 less $1,000 [10% of $10,000] or $5,000.

An offset approach cannot result in a complete elimination of the private plan benefit. The plan benefit may not be reduced by more than the *maximum offset allowance,* which is

- for any year of service, 4 percent of the participant's final average compensation;
- for total benefits, ¾ percent of the participant's final average compensation multiplied by the participant's years of service with the employer, not in excess of 35.

Furthermore, in no event can the maximum offset allowance be more than 50 percent of the plan benefit that would have accrued without the offset.

The ¾ percent fraction is reduced if the participant's final average compensation exceeds an amount referred to as *covered compensation*. (See Table 20–4 on page 527 and the explanation that follows.) The IRS is scheduled to publish annually a table with the appropriate offset factors for brackets of final average compensation that exceed covered compensation.

An offset plan must base benefits on average annual compensation for at least a three-year period, or the total number of the participant's years of service, if less. The ¾ percent factor in the maximum excess allowance is actuarially reduced for early retirement benefits. For this purpose, an early retirement benefit is any unreduced benefit other than disability benefits beginning before the Social Security retirement age. The ¾ percent factor is to be reduced by ¹⁄₁₅ for each of the first five years that the benefit's commencement date precedes Social Security retirement age, and by an additional ¹⁄₃₀ for each of the next five years that the benefit commencement date precedes the Social Security retirement age, with actuarial reductions for additional years (more than ten) of commencement prior to the Social Security retirement date.

OASDI is currently subject to indexing to reflect increases in the cost of living. However, the benefit paid by a private integrated plan cannot be reduced to reflect postretirement increases in OASDI, even if an offset formula is used. In other words, the amount of benefit payable to a participant from the plan itself generally will be fixed when the participant retires, regardless of changes in OASDI paid thereafter to the participant.

As will be evident after reviewing the rules for Social Security integration using the integration-level approach, the principal advantage of an offset formula is its simplicity, both in designing the plan and in communicating the plan effectively to employees.

Integration-Level Approach

Under the integration-level approach in a defined-benefit plan, a specified level of compensation, called the *integration level*, is defined by the plan. The plan then provides the participant a higher rate of benefits for compensation above the integration level than for compensation below the integration level. This clearly is a mirror image to the OASDI benefit structure, which provides a lower (zero) rate of benefits above a specified compensation level (the taxable wage base) than it does for compensation below the taxable wage base.

An example of a formula using an integration-level approach is

Upon retirement, a participant will be entitled to an annual retirement benefit equal to 30 percent of the participant's final average annual compensation up to $7,000, plus 56 percent of the participant's final average annual compensation in excess of $7,000.

Another way of drafting the same formula is:

Upon retirement, a participant will be entitled to an annual retirement benefit equal to 30 percent of the participant's full final average annual compensation, plus 26 percent of the participant's final average compensation in excess of $7,000.

The integration level in both plans is $7,000.

Under the Code, two percentages are defined. The excess-benefit percentage is the benefit as a percentage of compensation above the integration level. The base-benefit percentage is the percentage provided for compensation up to and including the integration level. The difference between these two percentages cannot exceed the maximum excess allowance. The maximum excess allowance is ¾ percent for any year of service, or in total, ¾ percent multiplied by the participant's years of service up to 35.

For example, if the plan provides a benefit of 1 percent of compensation below the integration level for each year of service, then it can provide no more than 1.75 percent of compensation above the integration level for each year of service. Or, for a participant with 35 years of service, if the plan provides a benefit of 30 percent of final average compensation below the integration level, it cannot provide more than 56.25 percent of compensation above the integration level. (The spread of 26.25 percent is ¾ of 1 percentage point multiplied by 35 years of service.)

Furthermore, the maximum excess allowance can be no greater than the base percentage. Thus, if a plan provides 10 percent of final average compensation below the integration level, it can provide no more than 20 percent of compensation above the integration level.

The maximum permitted integration level is the appropriate amount from the IRS table of covered compensation (see Table 20–3). This table essentially gives the average of the taxable wage base over the 35-year period prior to an employee's retirement, as explained further below. Covered compensation can be taken from either the exact or the rounded figures in Table 20-3. Because this amount varies with each participant's age, some planners may prefer to use a uniform dollar amount as the integration level for all participants to make the plan simpler and easier to communicate to participants. It should be permissible to use any uniform dollar amount that does not exceed the covered compensation from Table 20–3 for the oldest possible prospective employee of the employer.

The Covered Compensation Table

In specifying the maximum integration levels and the maximum percentages that may be used in integration-level plans, IRS actuaries have made a computation based on the value of OASDI benefits. Because the integrated private plan is designed to be a mirror image of the OASDI benefit, the maxi-

TABLE 20-3
2000 Covered Compensation Table

Calendar Year of Birth	Calendar Year of Social Security Retirement	2000 Covered Compensation	Calendar Year of Birth	Calendar Year of Social Security Retirement	2000 Covered Compensation
1907	1972	$ 4,488	1938	2004	$42,984
1908	1973	4,704	1939	2005	44,940
1909	1974	5,004	1940	2006	46,896
1910	1975	5,316	1941	2007	48,816
1911	1976	5,664	1942	2008	50,688
1912	1977	6,060	1943	2009	52,488
1913	1978	6,480	1944	2010	54,252
1914	1979	7,044	1945	2011	55,992
1915	1980	7,692	1946	2012	57,708
1916	1981	8,460	1947	2013	59,376
1917	1982	9,300	1948	2014	60,900
1918	1983	10,236	1949	2015	62,340
1919	1984	11,232	1950	2016	63,660
1920	1985	12,276	1951	2017	64,920
1921	1986	13,368	1952	2018	66,072
1922	1987	14,520	1953	2019	67,164
1923	1988	15,708	1954	2020	68,220
1924	1989	16,968	1955	2022	70,116
1925	1990	18,312	1956	2023	71,004
1926	1991	19,728	1957	2024	71,820
1927	1992	21,192	1958	2025	72,528
1928	1993	22,716	1959	2026	73,176
1929	1994	24,312	1960	2027	73,764
1930	1995	25,920	1961	2028	74,304
1931	1996	27,576	1962	2029	74,748
1932	1997	29,304	1963	2030	75,180
1933	1998	31,128	1964	2031	75,564
1934	1999	33,060	1965	2032	75,864
1935	2000	35,100	1966	2033	76,092
1936	2001	37,092	1967 or later	2034	76,200
1937	2002	39,072			

(continued)

TABLE 20-3 *(continued)*
2000 Covered Compensation Table

2000 Rounded Table	
Year of Birth	Covered Compensation
1934	$33,000
1935–1936	36,000
1937	39,000
1938	42,000
1939	45,000
1940–1941	48,000
1942–1943	51,000
1944	54,000
1945–1946	57,000
1947–1948	60,000
1949–1950	63,000
1951–1953	66,000
1954-1955	69,000
1956-1959	72,000
1960-1964	75,000
1965 or later	76,200

mum integration level in private plans should correspond generally to the maximum compensation taken into account in determining the OASDI benefit. For this purpose, the IRS has promulgated the *covered compensation* table. Covered compensation represents an averaging of the taxable wage base that has been in effect over each employee's working career. As shown in Table 20–3, the covered compensation figure will, therefore, vary, depending on the year in which the employee reaches age 65 and becomes eligible for full OASDI retirement benefits. The relevance of the table of covered compensation is that, as described above, it specifies the maximum integration level permitted for most types of defined benefit plans.

Integration of Defined-Contribution Plans

Because the benefits in a defined-contribution plan are based on the participant's account balance, the integration rules for defined-contribution plans apply to the amounts allocated to participants' accounts rather than to the benefits. Only an integration-level approach, not an offset, can be used.

The integration level for a defined-contribution plan is generally the taxable wage base for the year. While other integration levels may be used, under IRS regulations, this generally reduces the excess contribution percentage allowable. Table 20–4 gives the taxable wage base for recent years. The integration rules for defined-contribution plans are further stated in terms of two defined quantities: the *base contribution percentage* is the plan's contribution level for compensation below the integration level, while the *excess contribution percentage* is the contribution level for compensation above the integration level. The difference between the excess contribution percentage and the base contribution percentage cannot be more than:

- the base contribution percentage or
- the greater of (a) 5.7 percent or (b) the old-age Social Security tax rate.

Under this rule, a plan having a zero base-contribution percentage would also have to have a zero excess-contribution percentage. Therefore, it is not possible to have a plan that provides no contribution at all for participants at compensation levels below the integration level.

Some examples of the application of the rules are as follows:

- A plan providing a 4 percent base-contribution percentage could provide no more than 8 percent excess-contribution percentage.
- A plan providing a 6 percent base-contribution percentage could provide no more than an 11.7 percent excess-contribution percentage, assuming the old-age Social Security tax rate is less than 5.7 percent.

Multiple Plans

If the employer has more than one plan covering the same employee, both plans cannot be fully integrated. The degree of integration must be cut back in one or both. The most common approach is to fully integrate one plan (typically a defined-benefit plan) and not to integrate the other (typically a defined-contribution plan).

TABLE 20-4
Social Security Taxable Wage Base

Year	Taxable Wage Base (Annual)
1972	$ 9,600
1973	10,800
1974	13,200
1975	14,100
1976	15,300
1977	16,500
1978	17,700
1979	22,900
1980	25,900
1981	29,700
1982	32,400
1983	35,700
1984	37,800
1985	39,600
1986	42,000
1987	43,800
1988	45,000
1989	48,000
1990	51,300
1991	53,400
1992	55,500
1993	57,600
1994	60,600
1995	61,200
1996	62,700
1997	65,400
1998	68,400
1999	72,600
2000	76,200

Summary of Integration Rules

Qualified plan benefit or contribution formulas can be integrated with OASDI to reflect the value of the employer's OASDI contribution for the employee. This reduces plan costs by avoiding duplication of benefits provided by OASDI. It also tends to provide relatively higher plan benefits for highly compensated employees.

continued

Summary of Integration Rules *(continued)*

Defined-Benefit Plans

A defined-benefit plan can be integrated using either the offset or the integration level method:

- The maximum offset allowance is ¾ percent of final average compensation for any year of service, or a total of ¾ percent multiplied by years of service up to 35; total offset can't exceed 50 percent of benefit otherwise payable.
- The maximum integration level is covered compensation. Maximum excess allowance is ¾ percent for any year of service, or, in total, ¾ percent multiplied by years of service up to 35.

Defined-Contribution Plans

A defined-contribution plan may use only the integration level approach. The maximum integration level is the taxable wage base for the year. The difference between the base contribution percentage and the excess-contribution percentage can't exceed the lesser of the base-contribution percentage or the non-Medicare OASDI tax rate.

INFLATION PROTECTION

Inflation has been a persistent feature of the U.S. economy, at least since World War II. Although the rate of inflation has gone up and down during that period, many economists believe that some degree of inflation is a permanent structural feature of our economy. A qualified plan, particularly a defined-benefit pension plan, is a theoretically long-range program; benefit levels are often determined for a 25-year-old employee's benefits that will not be paid until 40 years later. Thus, inflation is a serious problem in the design of pension plans.

Although no really satisfactory solution to the problem of inflation in private pension plans has yet been devised, there are some planning approaches that can help with this problem. A distinction can be made between approaches that are applied in the preretirement period while the employee is still at work and in the postretirement period, when the employee is least able to protect against inflation.

Preretirement Inflation

Some types of benefit design are inherently better able to cope with preretirement inflation than others. If the plan benefit depends on employee compensation, the final-average definition of compensation usually does a better job protecting the employee against inflation than the career-average definition because the final-average definition bases benefits on the employee's highest compensation level. Much of the increase in an employee's compensation level over a working career merely reflects inflation. Other reasons for compensation increases are increases in general employee productivity and increases in the individual employee's merit, and both are also appropriately reflected in the retirement benefit. If the plan does not use a final-average formula, the employer should consider periodically reviewing the plan's benefit level in light of inflation and amending the plan to increase benefits as appropriate. It is also possible to include an automatic mechanism in the plan under which future benefit levels for current employees are increased in accordance with some kind of formula based on the inflation rate; however, this is rarely done.

Defined-contribution plans provide some inflation protection not available under defined-benefit plans because the benefit in the defined-contribution plan depends on the value of the investments in each participant's account. In the long run, a reasonably diversified investment portfolio tends to increase in value to keep pace with inflation. This is not necessarily true for short periods; in the 1970s, for example, common stocks often declined even as inflation reached new heights. However, most economists believe that the long-range linkage between asset values and inflation will continue, so defined-contribution plans can be useful in dealing with inflation. Naturally, for this to occur the investment portfolio has to be chosen to emphasize the types of assets— common stocks, for example—that typically show inflation-related growth.

A defined-contribution plan, however, has a disadvantage similar to that of a career-average benefit formula: contributions to the participant's account in the early years are based on then-current compensation, which typically is at a low level compared with later years. This disadvantage tends to reduce the advantage of possible investment-related growth.

Postretirement Inflation

In the postretirement period, one approach to inflation protection in defined benefit plans is indexing of retirement benefits. With an indexed formula, the plan provides that the benefit is to be increased after retirement in accordance with some formula contained in the plan. The design problem here is the choice of a formula that is affordable by the employer and that accurately reflects the impact of inflation on retirees.

One approach is to use the consumer price index (CPI), a price index provided by the government. The CPI is a measure of the relative rise from month to month of a "market basket" of consumer products purchased by a hypothetical average consumer. There is some debate as to whether the CPI accurately reflects the impact of inflation, particularly on retirees, because it may emphasize rising prices of items not normally purchased by retirees or, conversely, may understate the impact of rising prices for items particularly important to retirees. At one time, for example, the CPI had a large component reflecting the cost of new housing, which typically is not a significant item in retirees' budgets.

The government also provides various types of wage indexes indicating the increase in wages in specific portions of the work force. Theoretically, it is possible to index retirement benefits in accordance with a wage index. Based on past experience, this would produce a larger increase in retirement benefits than a price index because wage indexes reflect increases in productivity that have historically outdistanced inflationary price increases. However, in short-term periods, wage indexes can fall behind cost indexes such as the CPI. A theoretical advantage of wage indexing is that retirees will obtain the same protection against inflation as people currently in the work force (but no better). Whatever the merits of this argument, however, wage indexes are rarely used.

A third approach to indexing is to use a formula for increasing benefits that is included in the plan itself and is not dependent on external price or wage indexes. Such a formula makes it easier for the employer to anticipate the cost of the benefit increases. The risk of possibly running ahead of the CPI can be minimized by providing that the formula increase will not exceed an amount determined by reference to the CPI or other chosen economic indexes.

Indexed pension benefits are obviously attractive to participants, but currently they are not extensively used in the private pension system. This is because even a small annual or periodic percentage increase in pension benefits can result in a very large increase in the ultimate cost of the benefit. Private employers, therefore, often avoid indexing because of the possibility of incurring an uncontrollable future liability. However, indexing is quite common in pension programs of federal, state, and local government units. Elected officials often grant indexed pensions to government employees with the implicit expectation that taxpayers in the future (after current officials' terms have expired) will accept tax increases to fund the increased pension costs.

In the private sector, probably the most common mechanism for dealing with postretirement inflation is to increase pension benefits through ad hoc "supplemental payments" to retirees. At one time, there was some concern that a program of supplemental payments might be deemed a separate pension plan involving various federal regulatory complexities. However, to encourage employers to make such supplemental payments, the Labor Department has issued relatively permissive regulations concerning these payments. Under these regulations [Labor Regulations Section 2510.32(g)], a supplemental payment plan will not be treated as a separate pension plan but rather as a welfare plan, which is subject to much simpler regulatory requirements if the amount paid is limited by a formula that effectively restricts it to the cost-of-living increases that have occurred since the retirees' pension payments commenced. The supplemental payments can be made out of the employer's general assets or from a separate trust fund established for them. In addition, there are special provisions [Code Section 415(k)(2)] allowing employees to contribute additional amounts to a defined-benefit plan to provide cost-of-living adjustments to benefits.

THE ACCRUED BENEFIT

Under the vesting rules for qualified plans, many employees will be entitled to a benefit from their qualified plan if they terminate employment before retirement. Also, if an employer terminates a plan before all employees have retired, plan participants generally receive the benefits they have earned at that point. Therefore, the plan must provide a means of determining the amount of benefit payable to employees with a given termination date. To do this, the qualified plan benefit is treated as having been earned over the employee's entire period of employment. The amount of benefit earned as of a given date is referred to as the *accrued benefit* at that date.

The concept of the accrued benefit is also important in certain actuarial methods for determining annual plan costs, as discussed in Chapter 21.

Every qualified plan must include a means for determining the participant's accrued benefit. Furthermore, to prevent discrimination, Code Section 411(b) and extensive IRS regulations under Code Section 401(a)(4) require that benefits accrue at minimum specified rates. The purpose of the Section 411(b) benefit accrual rules is to prevent the plan from having an excessive amount of what is known as *backloading*. An extreme example of a backloaded plan would be one that had a normal retirement age of 65 with a provision that no employee who terminated employment prior to age 63 would receive any benefit under this plan. In effect, all of the benefits under this plan would accrue during the two years between ages 63 and 65. This much backloading is not permitted under current rules. Obviously, the purpose of the accrual rules is to prevent employers from favoring highly compensated employees who are the ones most likely to continue employment to later ages. Incidentally, the benefit accrual rules do not prohibit frontloading—rapid benefit accrual during a participant's earlier years of employment. However, few employers would have any reason for designing a frontloaded plan.

Benefit Accrual Rules

In a defined-contribution plan, a participant's accrued benefit is simply equal to the balance in that participant's account under the plan. The account balance includes employer and employee contributions, forfeitures from accounts of other employees, and investment earnings on the account, less any distributions from the account. If a defined-contribution plan has a nondiscriminatory contribution formula, there normally is no problem of backloading. Consequently, there are no specific rates of accrual required for defined-contribution plans.

For defined-benefit plans, however, benefits must accrue at a rate specified in Code Section 411(b). The plan's accrual rate must be at least as fast as one of three alternative minimum rules:

1. *Three Percent Rule.* Under this rule, the benefit accrued by a participant during each year of participation must be at least 3 percent of the maximum benefit that a hypothetical participant can accrue by entering at the plan's earliest entry age and participating until normal retirement.
2. *133⅓ Percent Rule.* Under this rule, the rate of benefits accrued in any given plan year cannot be more than 133⅓ percent of the rate of benefit accrual during any prior year.

3. *Fractional Rule.* Under this rule, the benefit the employee has accrued at the date of termination must be proportionate to the normal retirement benefit. The following requirement must be satisfied:

$$\frac{\text{Benefit on}}{\text{termination}} = \frac{\text{Normal retirement benefit if participant continued to normal retirement age}} \times \frac{\text{Years of actual participation}}{\text{Years of participation if terminated at normal retirement}}$$

■ **EXAMPLE**

Suppose that an employee has participated in the plan for 20 years and terminates at age 55. The plan's normal retirement age is 65. If the employee had continued working to age 65, the plan would have provided an annuity of $12,000 per year beginning at age 65. The fractional rule would require a termination benefit of at least two-thirds of this, or $8,000 annually beginning at age 65. If the plan does not provide at least this amount, it must meet one of the other two benefit accrual rules or it will be disqualified.

The tendency is for most plans to provide a termination benefit based on the fractional rule, because it is simpler to design and explain to participants.

Fully insured plans—plans that are funded exclusively by the purchase of insurance contracts providing level annual premium payments to retirement and providing benefits guaranteed by an insurance company—are not specifically subject to the preceding three accrual rules if the accrued benefit meets the following tests:

■ The accrued benefit is not less than the cash surrender value of the participant's insurance contracts at any time.
■ The insurance premiums are paid up, the insurance contracts are not subject to a security interest and there are no policy loans outstanding.

The assumption is that if all these conditions are satisfied, plans funded with insurance contracts will automatically meet or exceed the benefit accrual test. Note that this exception applies only to fully insured plans, not to all plans that use an insurance contract or contracts for funding. The use of insurance contracts in plan funding is discussed in Chapter 21.

BENEFITS AT TERMINATION OF EMPLOYMENT

The vesting provisions of a plan determine the amount of benefit that a participant is entitled to receive upon terminating employment prior to retirement.

In a defined-contribution plan, the termination benefit is the vested portion of the participant's account balance. In defined-contribution plans, particularly profit-sharing plans, the account balance usually is distributed to the participant in full at termination of employment. It is technically possible to defer the distribution to the participant's normal retirement date, but this is rarely done in defined-contribution plans because it causes additional expense to the plan with little or no corresponding benefit to the employer or the plan. However, the plan may give the participant the option to leave the funds on deposit in the plan for withdrawal at a later date, to allow the participant to take advantage of the tax-deferred investment medium afforded by the plan, with a possible loss of favorable income tax treatment on the later plan distribution (see Chapter 24).

For a defined-benefit plan, the benefit on termination of employment is more complicated. The benefit will be the vested accrued benefit as of the date of termination, determined under the vesting and the accrual rules already described. Use the same example as in the discussion of the fractional accrued-benefit rule, again supposing that an employee terminates employment at age 55 after 20 years of service and the plan's normal retirement age is 65. If the participant is fully vested and the accrued benefit is $8,000 as discussed in the earlier example, an annuity of $8,000 per year will be payable beginning at age 65.

To make sure that terminated participants actually receive deferred vested benefits at retirement, which may be many years after termination, the employer must report all deferred vested benefits of terminated participants to the Social Security Administration, which then can inform retirees of their rights to benefits from plans of former employers. This reporting is done on the Form 5500 series (Chapter 26).

In some cases, the deferred vested benefit may be such a small amount that keeping track of it until the participant's retirement is merely a nuisance for both employer and employee. The employer can cash-out a distribution—that is, pay cash to the employee in lieu of the deferred vested benefit—without the employee's consent, so long as the entire benefit is distributed and the employer portion of the benefit so distributed does not exceed $5,000. The involuntary cashout must be within one year of termination of participation in the plan; the plan must have a provision permitting the employee to repay the cashout to the plan if the employee was not fully vested at the time of termination, in case the employee should resume participation in the plan. A cashout of a benefit that exceeds the $5,000 limit can be made, but only with the consent of the employee.

DEATH AND DISABILITY BENEFITS

Qualified plans are intended primarily to provide retirement benefits or, in the case of profit-sharing and similar plans, deferred-compensation benefits. However, the regulations indicate that a plan may provide for the payment of incidental death benefits through insurance or otherwise, and also that the plan may provide for the payment of a pension due to disability. Moreover, a qualified plan must in certain circumstances provide a survivorship pension to the participant's spouse.

Currently under Code Section 401(a)(11), two types of survivorship benefits are required: the *qualified joint and survivor annuity* and the *qualified preretirement survivor annuity*. All pension plans must provide these, but profit-sharing plans need not provide them if the participant's vested account balance is payable as a death benefit to the spouse. ESOPs and stock bonus plans generally do not have to provide spousal survivorship benefits.

Qualified Joint and Survivor Annuity

The qualified joint and survivor annuity is a postretirement death benefit for the spouse. Plans subject to this requirement must provide, as an automatic form of benefit, an annuity for the life of the participant with a survivor annuity for the life of the participant's spouse. The survivor annuity must be not less than 50 percent of nor greater than the annuity payable during the joint lives of participant and spouse. The spouse annuity must be continued even if the spouse remarries. The joint and survivor annuity must be at least the actuarial equivalent of the plan's normal form of benefit or any optional form of benefit offered under the plan. Optional benefit forms are discussed further in Chapter 24.

The qualified joint and survivor form must be offered automatically to a married participant at retirement. The participant may elect to receive another form of benefit if the plan so provides; however, the spouse must consent in writing to the election and the consent form must be notarized or witnessed by a plan representative. An election to waive the joint and survivor form must be made during a 90-day period ending on the annuity starting date. A waiver of the joint and survivor annuity can be revoked—the participant can change the election during the 90-day period. The plan administrator must provide the participant with a notice of the election period and an explanation of the consequences of the election within a reasonable period before the annuity starting date.

Preretirement Survivor Annuity

Code Section 401(a)(11) mandates a preretirement death benefit for the spouse of a vested plan participant. The survivor annuity payable if the participant dies before retirement is the amount that would have been paid under a qualified joint and survivor annuity, computed as if the participant had either (1) retired on the day before his or her death or (2) separated from service on the date of death and survived to the plan's earliest retirement age, then retired with an immediate joint and survivor annuity. For a defined-contribution plan, a qualified preretirement survivor annuity is an annuity for the life of the surviving spouse actuarially equivalent to at least 50 percent of the participant's vested account balance as of the date of death.

As with the qualified joint and survivor annuity, a participant can elect to receive an alternative form of preretirement survivorship benefit, including a benefit that does not provide for the spouse. However, written consent by the spouse is required for such an election. The right to make such an election must be communicated to all participants with a vested benefit who have attained age 32, and the participant can elect to waive the preretirement survivor annuity at any time after age 35.

Subsidizing Survivor Annuities

A plan can provide that a participant who receives either the qualified joint and survivor annuity or the preretirement survivor annuity will receive an annuity payment lower than the amount that would be paid under a straight-life annuity; the reduction reflects the extra cost to the plan of the survivorship feature. For example, the normal form of benefit might be a straight-life annuity of $1,000 per month, but the joint and survivor annuity might pay only $800 per month while both spouses survived, then $400 per month to the survivor. However, a plan is permitted to subsidize all or part of the cost of the survivorship feature. If the survivorship feature is fully subsidized, the plan does not have to allow the participant to elect an alternative form of benefit.

Incidental Death Benefits

A qualified plan may provide a death benefit over and above the survivorship benefits required by law. In a defined-contribution plan, probably the most common form of death benefit is a provision that the participant's vested account balance will be paid to the participant's designated beneficiary in the event of the participant's death before retirement or termination of service. Defined-benefit plans, unless they use insurance as discussed later, usually do not provide an additional death benefit; in such cases, the survivors receive no death benefit except for whatever survivor annuity the plan provides.

To provide any substantial preretirement death benefit, it is usually necessary for the plan to purchase life insurance. This provides the plan with significant funds at a participant's death; it is particularly important in the early years of a participant's employment, when the participant's accrued benefit is still relatively small. An insured preretirement death benefit can be provided in either a defined-benefit or defined-contribution plan. Contributions to the plan by the employer may be used to pay life insurance premiums, as long as the amount qualifies under the tests for incidental benefits.

In general, the IRS considers that nonretirement benefits such as life, medical, or disability insurance in a qualified plan will be incidental and therefore permissible, as long as the cost of providing these benefits is less than 25 percent of the cost of providing all the benefits under the plan. In applying this approach to life insurance benefits, the 25 percent rule is applied to the portion of any life insurance premium that is used to provide current life insurance protection. Any portion of the premium used to increase the cash value of the policy is considered a contribution to the plan fund available to pay retirement benefits and is not considered in the 25 percent limitation.

The IRS has ruled, using its general 25 percent test, that if a qualified plan provides death benefits using ordinary life insurance (life insurance with a cash value), the death benefit will be considered incidental if either (1) less than 50 percent of the total cumulative employer contribution credited to each participant's account has been used to purchase ordinary life insurance or (2) the face amount of the policies does not exceed 100 times the anticipated monthly normal retirement benefit or the accumulated reserve under the life insurance policy, whichever is greater. In practice, defined-benefit plans using ordinary life insurance are usually designed to take advantage of the 100-times rule, while defined-contribution plans, including profit-sharing plans, that use ordinary life contracts generally make use of the 50 percent test.

If term insurance contracts are used to provide the death benefit, the 25 percent test will be applied to the entire premium, and the aggregate premiums paid for insurance on each participant should be less than 25 percent of aggregate additions to the employee's account. Term insurance is sometimes used to fund death benefits in defined-contribution plans but rarely in defined-benefit plans.

The discussion so far is somewhat simplified because insurance can be used in qualified plans in many ways, and the IRS has issued many rulings, both revenue rulings and letter rulings, applying the basic 25 percent test to a variety of different fact situations. Thus, there is considerable room for creative design of life insurance-funded death benefits within qualified plans.

If life insurance is provided for a participant through a qualified plan (i.e., by using employer contributions to the plan to pay premiums for the insurance), part or all of the cost of the insurance is currently taxable to the participant. Life insurance provided by the plan is not considered part of a Section 79 group term plan, and consequently the $50,000 exclusion under Section 79 does not apply.

If cash value life insurance is used and if all of the death proceeds are payable to the participant's estate or beneficiary, the term cost, or cost of the "pure amount at risk," is taxable income to the employee. The term cost is the difference between the face amount of insurance and the cash surrender value of the policy at the end of the policy year. In other words, the cost of the policy's cash value is not currently taxable to the employee because the cash value is considered part of the plan fund to be used to provide the retirement benefit. The term cost is calculated using either a table of rates (Table 20–5) provided by the IRS, known as the PS 58 table, or the insurance company's rates for individual one-year term policies, if these are lower and if the insurance company actually offers such policies.

TABLE 20-5
PS 58 Rates, One-Year Term Premiums for $1,000 of Life Insurance Protection*

Age	Premium	Age	Premium	Age	Premium
15	$1.27	37	$ 3.63	59	$ 19.08
16	1.38	38	3.87	60	20.73
17	1.48	39	4.14	61	22.53
18	1.52	40	4.42	62	24.50
19	1.56	41	4.73	63	26.63
20	1.61	42	5.07	64	28.98
21	1.67	43	5.44	65	31.51
22	1.73	44	5.85	66	34.28
23	1.79	45	6.30	67	37.31
24	1.86	46	6.78	68	40.59
25	1.93	47	7.32	69	44.17
26	2.02	48	7.89	70	48.06
27	2.11	49	8.53	71	52.29
28	2.20	50	9.22	72	56.89
29	2.31	51	9.97	73	61.89
30	2.43	52	10.79	74	67.33
31	2.57	53	11.69	75	73.23
32	2.70	54	12.67	76	79.63
33	2.86	55	13.74	77	86.57
34	3.02	56	14.91	78	94.09
35	3.21	57	16.18	79	102.23
36	3.41	58	17.56	80	111.04
				81	120.57

*These rates are used in computing the cost of pure life insurance protection that is taxable to the employee under qualified pension and profit-sharing plans.
The rate at insured's attained age is applied to the excess of the amount payable at death over the cash value of the policy at the end of the year.

If the plan uses term insurance rather than cash-value insurance to provide an insured death benefit, the cost of the entire face amount of insurance is taxable to the employee. Similarly, if the plan provides medical or disability insurance for participants, the entire cost of the insurance is taxable to the employee, unless the insurance can be excluded under Code Section 106 as part of the employer's medical or disability plan.

Planning Considerations

It is relatively uncommon for a qualified plan to provide medical, disability or term life insurance to participants because the tax treatment provides no advantage to the employee in so doing. It is more common, however, to use cash-value life insurance as funding for the plan because the cost to the employee using the PS 58 table or the insurance company's term rates may prove to be a relatively favorable way to provide life insurance. The use of life insurance for funding qualified plans will be discussed further in Chapter 21.

The decision whether to include life insurance in a qualified plan relates to the employee benefit design objective of efficiency. The employer must first decide whether and to what extent it will provide death benefits to employees. Death benefits can be provided for employees under group term plans and other plans as well as providing them as an incidental benefit in qualified plans. The death benefit should be designed to produce the lowest employer and employee cost for the benefit level desired. A death benefit should be included in the qualified plan only to the extent it is consistent with this objective.

Disability Benefits from Qualified Plans

A qualified plan may provide as an incidental benefit a pension payable upon disability. The plan must provide a specific definition of disability. Usually some minimum service or age requirements are imposed to appropriately restrict the class of participants entitled to the disability pension. The disability benefit may be the participant's accrued benefit actuarially reduced because of a commencement date earlier than normal retirement, or the plan may provide some subsidy of the disability benefit to be sure that it is adequate for the participant's needs.

It is becoming increasingly common for companies to cover disability through separate benefit programs, often insured. These were discussed in Chapter 8. Such programs tend to be fairer and more efficient than providing disability coverage as an incidental benefit under a qualified plan. In all events, the planner should be sure that there is no duplication of disability coverage between the qualified plan and a separate short-term- or long-term-disability plan of the employer.

Qualified plans that do not provide immediate disability coverage prior to normal retirement age should, however, include some provision for the treatment of the employee's retirement benefit if the employee becomes disabled. Separate long-term-disability programs usually cease paying benefits when the participant reaches age 65 or other normal retirement age. After this age, the company's retirement plan must provide whatever income the participant will receive from the employer. Therefore, from an employee's standpoint, the plan should be designed so that the retirement benefit will be adequate when long-term-disability benefits cease. For example, the plan might provide that a participant who is disabled as defined in the plan will continue to receive service credit for purposes of vesting or benefit accrual, or both. The definition of disability in the plan should be coordinated with the definition in the employer's long-term-disability plan. The plan also should indicate what definition of compensation will be used to determine retirement benefits if the participant becomes disabled before retirement.

STUDY QUESTIONS

1. a. How are employer contributions usually determined under a money-purchase plan?
   b. What determines the amount of an employee's retirement benefit under a money-purchase plan?

2. Explain why a target plan is considered a hybrid of the defined-contribution and defined-benefit approaches.

3. Why are defined-benefit plans the most complex of all qualified plans?

4. Explain how you can design a defined-benefit formula to favor employees who enter a plan at a later age.

5. Describe the replacement ratio approach to benefit formula design.

6. a. What is a flat-benefit formula?
   b. Explain how a flat-benefit formula may create a problem of fairness among employees.
   c. How can this problem be resolved?

7. A firm has two long-time, devoted employees. A retirement plan is about to be adopted and the employer desires to provide these two older employees with an adequate retirement benefit at retirement.
   a. What type of plan should the employer adopt?
   b. What special provision should be included in the plan to achieve the employer's objective?

8. Distinguish between a career-average formula and a final-average formula in a defined-benefit plan.

9. What is the purpose of the rules for integrating qualified plans with Social Security?

10. Briefly describe the integration rules for
    a. offset plans.
    b. integration-level plans.
    c. defined-contribution plans.

11. What kinds of qualified plans are inherently better able to cope with preretirement inflation?

12. For defined-benefit plans, benefits must accrue at an accrual rate that must be at least as rapid as one of the three alternative minimum rules. What are these rules?

13. What is the effect on the accrual rules on a plan that is funded exclusively by insurance contracts?

14. a. What is a qualified joint and survivor annuity?
    b. What rules affect the amount of the joint and survivor annuity?
    c. What requirements apply to a joint and survivor annuity that must be offered to married participants as part of a qualified plan?

15. a. What is a preretirement survivor annuity?
    b. How is the amount of a preretirement survivor annuity determined?

16. Explain the rules that determine whether a death benefit that is funded with life insurance is considered incidental in a qualified plan.

17. Explain how the taxable income to an employee is determined when employer-provided life insurance is included in a qualified plan.

18. Why might you recommend that an employer include life insurance in a qualified plan?

CHAPTER 21

Pension Plan Funding

OBJECTIVES

■ Describe the general features of each of the following pension funding instruments and explain when each might best be used:
  1. Trusts
  2. Individual life insurance and annuity contracts
  3. Group permanent contracts
  4. Group deposit administration contracts
  5. Immediate-participation guarantee contracts

■ Explain how separate accounts and the new money technique can overcome the disadvantages associated with the commingling of pension funds.

■ Identify the circumstances under which a plan sponsor should use a guaranteed investment contract and an investment-guarantee contract.

■ Distinguish between accrued-benefit actuarial cost methods and projected-benefit methods for determining pension costs.

■ Explain the concept of a supplemental liability and how the use of a supplemental liability increases flexibility in pension funding.

■ Describe the actuarial cost methods that are specifically permitted by ERISA.

■ Explain the minimum funding standards of the Internal Revenue Code and the operation of the funding standard account.

■ Explain the rules for deductibility of employer contributions to qualified pension plans.

The assets of a qualified plan must be held either by a trustee or by an insurance company. It is also possible to hold plan funds in a bank custodial account that is not technically a trust, but under Code Section 401(f), such an account is treated the same as a trust for all practical purposes. The trustee or insurance company is referred to as the plan's *funding agency*.

Plan assets are held by a funding agency under a legal document called a *funding instrument*—either a *trust agreement* or an *insurance contract,* depending on the funding agency. There are many legal requirements applicable to a funding instrument; these are discussed in this chapter and in Chapter 26. Within these requirements, however, there is opportunity for flexibility in plan design, funding procedures, and investment policy. The employer's choices in these areas are an important part of qualified plan design.

TRUSTS

The trust is the leading funding agency for qualified plans, in terms of both the number of employees covered and aggregate plan assets. A trust used for qualified plan funding is based on the same general principles of trust law as trusts used for other purposes, such as estate planning and administering the affairs of minors or incompetent persons. A trust is an arrangement involving three parties—the grantor of the trust, the trustee, and the beneficiaries. In qualified plan funding, the grantor is the employer and the beneficiaries are the employees. The trustee is a party holding funds contributed by the employer for the benefit of employees.

Legally speaking, a trustee is a fiduciary. A fiduciary is a person or organization that holds money on behalf of someone else (here the plan participants and beneficiaries) and that must administer that money solely in the interest of those other persons. The trustee's compensation is a fee for services rendered; the trustee is prohibited from personally profiting as a result of investing the trust funds.

The duties of a qualified plan trustee, like those of any other trustee, are set out in a formal trust agreement. Usually, the duties of a plan trustee are to accept employer contributions, invest those contributions, accumulate the earnings, and pay benefits to plan participants and beneficiaries out of the plan fund. The trustee performs these acts only at the direction of the plan administrator and not at the trustee's own discretion. However, in some cases, a trustee is given direct responsibility for choosing plan investments or choosing an investment adviser. The trustee must account periodically to the plan administrator or the employer for all investments, receipts, and disbursements. The trustee does not guarantee the payment of benefits or the adequacy of the trust fund to pay benefits. That remains the obligation of the employer.

A trustee may be an individual or group of individuals or a corporation such as a bank or trust company. Often employers name individual trustees, such as the company president or a major shareholder, to obtain an extra measure of control over plan assets. This is permissible under the law; however, when acting as trustee, such an individual is legally obligated to act solely in the interests of the plan participants and beneficiaries and not in the interests of the employer or shareholders.

Although a qualified plan trust is created and exists under the laws of the state in which it is established, the most significant provisions of trust law affecting qualified plan trusts have been codified in federal statutes that supersede state law whenever they apply. The area of trust investments and related issues is treated in more detail in Chapter 26.

INSURANCE CONTRACTS

Allocated and Unallocated Funding in Insurance Contracts

Insurance companies offer a variety of contracts either designed specifically for qualified plan funding or adaptable to it. In theory, an employer could negotiate a contract with the insurance company with provisions specifically tailored to the employer's needs. In practice, however, insurance contracts tend to fall into specific types, with some but not complete flexibility in their terms. This is partly a result of the fact that an insurance contract—particularly a life insurance contract—cannot be the subject of unfettered negotiation between insurer and contractholder. Often, the terms of the contract require state regulatory approval and, consequently, the insurer is not interested in varying them for each individual contractholder. Also, historical practices and needs in the insurance industry have determined the form of many of the contracts.

Insurance contracts used in funding qualified plans can be divided into *allocated* and *unallocated* types. When funding is allocated under an insurance contract, this means that the insurer has assumed the employer's obligation to pay specific benefits to specific participants. The employer is still primarily responsible, but under the terms of the insurance contract, participants and the employer can look to the insurance company for payment of specific amounts. With unallocated funding, the insurance company acts as a holder of the funds, much like a bank trustee. With unallocated funding, the insurance company is, of course, obligated to deal prudently with the funds, but it makes no guarantee that the funds will be adequate to pay any specific benefits under the plan. An insurance contract used in a qualified plan can be either purely allocated or purely unallocated, or can offer a mixture of both.

Insurance contracts can be classified—and will be discussed—in this order:

Allocated Contracts

- Individual life insurance or annuity contracts
  1. Fully insured plans
  2. Combination plans
- Group permanent contracts
- Group deferred annuity contracts

Unallocated Contracts

- Deposit administration contracts
- Immediate participation guarantee contracts

INSURANCE CONTRACTS USING ALLOCATED FUNDING

Individual Life Insurance and Annuity Contracts

For qualified plans of employers with few employees, particularly defined-benefit plans, one of the most common funding methods traditionally has been the use of individual life insurance or annuity contracts. These contracts are typically level premium contracts. Once a benefit level for a given employee has been determined, the benefit is funded using a single insurance or annuity contract with equal annual premiums paid by the employer until the employee's retirement. It is relatively simple to see how annuity contracts can be used in this manner; however, the use of life insurance contracts requires some explanation.

The somewhat complex spectrum of life insurance products can be divided into two types of contracts—those providing only term insurance and those with a cash value. Term insurance contracts are not suitable as funding instruments for qualified plans, although they can be used by the plan to provide incidental insurance. Cash value contracts, on the other hand, can be used in a qualified plan to provide both retirement benefits and death benefits. This is because these contracts are designed to accumulate a reserve that, if the insured lives long enough, grows to a size sufficient to pay the entire face amount of the contract's death benefit. The purpose for the accumulation of this reserve is to allow the policy to be offered to the insured with the assurance of a level premium for a long period of time—the excess cost in early years is used to provide insurance in later years. Term insurance, by comparison, increases in cost each year as the insured grows older; there is no reserve for any period longer than one year. The reserve feature of cash value contracts means that such a contract is an investment medium that can be used in funding a qualified plan.

The most familiar cash value insurance contract, usually referred to as the *whole life contract,* provides increasing cash values up to a quite advanced age, such as 90 or more. Prior to that time, the scheduled cash value is usually less than the face amount of the death benefit, although many policies provide dividends that accelerate the cash value increase considerably. A whole life policy cannot be used to provide the sole funding for the retirement benefit in a qualified plan with a normal retirement age of 65, because the cash value at age 65 is usually insufficient. Under the incidental test for death benefits described in the preceding chapter, the death benefit in a qualified plan cannot be more than 100 times the expected monthly pension. For example, if the plan provides a monthly pension of $100 per month, no more than $10,000 of

FIGURE 21-1
Fully Insured Versus Combination Plan

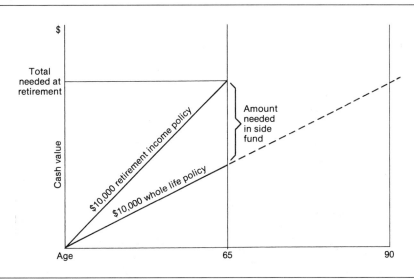

whole life insurance can be provided, and the cash value of a $10,000 policy at age 65 is usually insufficient to provide a pension of $100 per month. If whole life policies are used to fund a qualified plan, the plan fund must be supplemented with a side fund or conversion fund, as discussed under "Combination Plans" below. To fund a qualified plan benefit with life insurance alone, policies with rapidly increasing cash values must be used; one such policy commonly used is referred to as a *retirement income policy*. The difference in cash value buildup between a retirement income policy and a whole life policy is represented in Figure 21-1.

Use of Retirement Income Policies

The individual retirement income policies used in qualified plans are usually similar to such policies offered to the general public for use outside qualified plans. The plan design options for a plan funded with such policies are somewhat limited because of the characteristics of the policies themselves. The plans are usually defined-benefit plans providing a life income at retirement in a specified amount, usually expressed in units of $10 per month. When the plan is initially installed, benefit levels are projected for each employee, and a policy is purchased for each employee sufficient to provide these projected benefits. If an employee's projected benefit increases—for example, if the benefit formula is based on compensation and the employee's compensation increases—then a second, additional policy must be purchased for the employee to provide the benefits in excess of the original amount. Thus, the employee's eventual benefit at retirement may be provided under more than one policy.

Because retirement income contracts are basically life insurance policies, the plan provides a preretirement death benefit usually determined under the 100-to-1 formula. Death benefits may be made subject to medical examinations or insurance may be made available on a guaranteed issue basis (i.e., without medical examinations), usually subject to a minimum number of participants, such as five. If medical examinations are required and a participant is uninsurable, the retirement benefit is unaffected, but the death benefit may be reduced or eliminated.

The plan's vesting provisions must, of course, meet the vesting rules described in the preceding chapter. To accomplish this, at termination of employment the policies may be distributed to the participant in return for a payment by the participant to the plan of the amount of any nonvested cash values in the policy. Alternatively, the plan may retain the policy and use it to provide a deferred vested benefit at the participant's retirement age.

Use of Retirement Annuity Contracts

Retirement annuity contracts are individual contracts used in funding qualified plans in a manner similar to retirement income contracts. However, as the name implies, these are not life insurance contracts; therefore, the plan usually provides no death benefit other than a return of the annuity premiums or the annuity's cash value, whichever is greater. Thus, the death benefit under a retirement annuity contract is relatively small in a participant's earlier years in the plan.

The employer is the contractholder under both types of fully insured individual contract plans, although sometimes a trustee is designated as contractholder for administrative convenience. The employer's sole responsibility for funding the plan is to make the premium payments when due. All benefits are guaranteed by the insurance company and if the employer has paid all premiums, it has no further responsibility as long as the insurance company remains solvent.

Under these contracts, the insurance company provides certain credits to the employer to offset premium costs. Because the plan must meet the "exclusive benefit" rule applicable to all qualified plans, these credits cannot be paid to the employer in cash. Credits include policy dividends, credits for withdrawal of a participant who is not fully vested, and credits for participants who continue working beyond the normal retirement date.

Combination Plans

A combination plan is a plan that funds a participant's benefit with a whole life policy or policies (i.e., policies whose cash value buildup is relatively slow), plus an additional unallocated trust fund called a *side fund* or *conversion fund* to provide the additional amount needed at retirement to fund the retirement benefit. This type of funding is frequently used for defined-benefit plans of small employers, because it combines the advantages of an insured death benefit with some of the flexibility of an unallocated trust fund.

The whole life policies used in combination plans are generally the same as those offered by insurance companies to individuals for purposes other than retirement plans. Almost any type of cash value policy can be used, including some of the newer forms, such as universal life policies, that provide substantial investment return compared with older types of cash value policies. As with fully insured plans, the employer is the policyholder although, again, a trustee can be used to hold the policies; this trustee can be the same as the trustee of the side fund.

As with fully insured plans, the plan design is to some extent based on the features of the policy used. However, additional flexibility is provided because of the side fund. A whole life policy is purchased for each participant when initial projected benefit levels are established; additional policies are provided for each participant if that participant's projected benefit increases because of increases in compensation or changes in the plan. The employer is responsible for paying premiums on policies, with the insurance company guaranteeing the death benefit and the cash value of the policies. However, the employer is responsible for insuring the adequacy of the side fund. The employer may use its own consulting actuary for purposes of determining funding levels for the side fund, although the insurance company can provide these services if the employer wishes. The employer also determines how the side fund will be invested, although, again, the insurance company can hold these funds under a deposit administration type of contract to be discussed later.

Table 21–1 illustrates the typical features of a combination plan. Note that the amount of life insurance (face amount of each policy) is determined using the 100-to-1 test. The total cost to the employer is the sum of the annual premiums plus the deposit to the side fund. At each participant's retirement, the policy cash value and the balance in the side fund will be combined to provide the retirement benefit. Typically, the plan will provide that an annuity will be purchased from the insurance company at this time at guaranteed rates. If the amount in the side fund is more than is necessary to provide the benefit specified in the plan, the excess remains in the plan, thus allowing the employer to reduce future contributions to the side fund. On the other hand, if the side fund is insufficient at retirement to provide the plan benefit, the employer must make up the difference.

TABLE 21-1
Illustration of Defined-Benefit Combination Plan

	Employee	
	A	B
Age at entry	48	30
Projected monthly retirement benefit	$ 2,250	$ 1,250
Face amount of insurance	225,000	125,000
Gross annual premium	6,399	1,647
Annual side fund deposit	10,174	1,405
Policy cash value at retirement	81,225	65,250
Side fund at retirement (5 percent assumed return)	276,075	133,250

In the event of death before retirement, the combination plan typically provides a death benefit to the participant's beneficiary equal to the policy's full face amount. This is particularly beneficial in the case of a participant who dies early, before the cash value or the side fund have built up to significant amounts. If the participant terminates employment with a vested benefit, the plan provides a deferred vested benefit using a portion of the cash value of insurance contracts on the participant's life plus a portion of the side fund.

Combination funding can also be used for defined-contribution plans, such as money-purchase pension plans or profit-sharing plans. Because the 100-to-1 test for incidental insurance benefits is difficult to apply in such situations, the amount of insurance is usually designed to meet the other "incidental" test—aggregate insurance premiums less than 50 percent of total contributions. In a defined-contribution plan, individual accounts in the side fund must be maintained for each participant. The retirement benefit is usually a lump sum equal to the cash value of the policy or policies plus the amount in the participant's individual side fund account. Alternatively, this amount could be distributed as an equivalent annuity. If the participant dies before retirement, the death benefit in such a plan usually is the face amount of the life insurance plus the participant's individual side fund account, although the plan may limit the death benefit to the insurance amount alone.

Group Permanent Contract

To facilitate the use of cash-value life insurance contracts in qualified plans of larger employers, insurance companies can write these contracts on a group basis. Such contracts are referred to as *group permanent contracts*. The group permanent contract is used to provide a funding structure similar to that of corresponding individual contracts, with similar plan design considerations and costs. The major difference is group underwriting. Sometimes a minimum number of employees is required, usually 10 to 25. With group underwriting, life insurance is written without evidence of insurability up to a limit specified in the plan.

A group permanent (whole life) contract can be designed to provide relatively slow buildup of cash values and, therefore, a lower cost to the employer, so that it can be used together with a side fund in much the same manner as a combination plan utilizing individual policies.

Group Deferred Annuity Contract

The group deferred annuity contract is, historically, an important form of allocated funding for pension plans. Under this contract, there is no life insurance. Employer contributions are used to purchase single premium deferred annuities for employees based on the amount of annuity accrued by the participant each year.

As an illustration, suppose that in a given year, an employee earns (accrues) a pension increment of $10 per month beginning at age 65. The premium for this amount of deferred annuity is determined, and similar determinations are made for other covered employees. The total annuity premium charged to the employer this year is the sum of all such premiums for all employee credits earned during the year. Next year, the premium is the cost of all deferred annuities earned by employees during that year. Thus, unlike the types of contracts discussed so far, the group deferred annuity contract does not generate a level premium but, other things being equal, tends to produce an increasing premium because the cost of a given amount of deferred annuity increases with increasing age. For an entire employee group, however, the annual premium will not necessarily show an increasing trend because of retirements, deaths, and terminations of employment.

Because the entire premium under a group deferred annuity contract is determined by the insurance company, the employer has little control over the amount and timing of pension costs. There are typically withdrawal credits, deferred retirement credits, and dividends or premium rate adjustments, but these also are largely beyond the control of the employer. Because of the lack of employer flexibility in funding, as well as the availability of better investment results using other contracts, group deferred annuity contracts are rarely used today.

INSURANCE CONTRACTS USING UNALLOCATED FUNDING

The basic characteristic of unallocated funding instruments in a qualified plan is that employer contributions to the plan are not initially allocated to provide specific benefits. In an insurance contract with unallocated funding, the insurance company thus does not assume the risk of paying specific benefits. Instead, the contributions are held in an undivided fund, similar to a trust fund, until annuities are purchased at an employee's retirement or until benefits are actually paid to employees. Where long-term investment results are more favorable than the investment assumptions used by insurance companies for allocated contracts, the unallocated type of contract provides an advantage to the employer because the employer contribution level can be made lower initially and the employer can retain use of the money saved. Thus, unallocated contracts have been developed by insurance companies primarily to compete with other funding agencies, such as bank trust departments.

Group Deposit Administration Contract

In the conventional type of group deposit administration (DA) contract, employer contributions to fund benefits for employees who have not yet retired are held in an unallocated account, referred to as the *active life fund, annuity purchase fund, deposit administration fund, purchase payment fund*, or something similar. As each participant reaches retirement age, an amount is taken from the active life fund sufficient to purchase an annuity for that participant in the amount provided by the plan. The annuity purchase rate is determined by the insurance company under the terms of the DA contract. Typically, a DA contract provides a limited guarantee of annuity purchase rates. For example, the contract may guarantee annuity purchase rates for contributions paid during the first five years of the contract, with a year-to-year guarantee thereafter. More liberal guarantees are sometimes made available by insurers to remain competitive.

Under a DA contract, the rate of contributions to the fund is determined by the employer, using a reasonable actuarial method of the employer's choosing, subject to the minimum funding standards and other rules discussed later in this chapter. The employer is entirely responsible for the adequacy of the active life fund and must make contributions accordingly. The insurance company does not determine the premium or funding level. Also, the lack of allocated funding allows the same flexibility in designing the plan's benefit structure as is available under a trust fund plan. Benefit and funding flexibility are the main reasons for the attractiveness of unallocated funding instruments to employers.

In addition to design flexibility, insurance companies can provide investment features under DA contracts that make these contracts attractive. Most DA contracts provide a minimum investment rate guarantee. As with annuity purchase rate guarantees, the investment rate guarantee will typically apply to contributions paid during the first five years of the contract, with a year-to-year guarantee thereafter; more liberal guarantees may be made available from time to time to increase the attractiveness of these contracts.

Immediate Participation Guarantee Contract

The conventional DA contract just described retains one difference from a fully unallocated fund—the purchase of annuities as participants reach retirement. In determining annuity purchase rates, the insurer includes a factor for expenses, and also a factor for a "contingency reserve" to cover the possibility of adverse actuarial experience. This amount must be conservatively determined by the insurance company, because if the annuity purchase rate turns out to be excessive, the company can return part of the excess through dividends on the contract; if the purchase rate is insufficient, the insurance company cannot require the contractholder to make additional payments.

Many employers, particularly those with many employees, would prefer to assume all of the risks of making postretirement benefit payments to avoid the withdrawal of funds to purchase annuities, thereby maintaining control of the funds for a longer period of time. The immediate participation guarantee (IPG) contract was developed to provide for this market.

In most respects, the IPG contract is similar to the conventional DA contract. The principal difference is in the method of providing annuities to participants reaching retirement. Under an IPG contract, there is a single fund into which all plan contributions by the employer are deposited. Under some IPG contracts, the fund is charged directly with benefit payments as they are made. Under other contracts, the IPG fund is charged as each employee reaches retirement with a single annuity premium; however, this is done in such a way as to provide the effect of a trust fund; for example, through annual cancellation and reissuance of annuities.

Although some insurers offer no guarantees under IPG contracts, principal and minimum investment return guarantees are sometimes made available. As with conventional DA contracts, separate accounts funding can be made available under an IPG contract.

SEPARATE ACCOUNTS FUNDING AND NEW MONEY

The investment of qualified plan funds under an insurance contract can involve certain disadvantages relating to the commingling of the employer's pension funds with those of other employers or with other funds of the insurance company. Separate accounts funding and the new money technique are methods by which two of these disadvantages can be mitigated.

Separate Accounts

Separate accounts funding was developed to avoid commingling pension assets with all of the general assets of the insurance company because an insurance company's general assets have traditionally been invested in long-term, low-return investment vehicles, sometimes subject to legal restrictions on investments. With separate accounts funding, the insurance company makes available one or more special accounts, separate from its general asset accounts, solely for investment of pension money. Such separate accounts may have a specified investment philosophy; for example, one type of account might be invested in common stocks, another in bonds, another in real estate mortgages, another in money market instruments, and so forth. The qualified plan sponsor is then given the option to invest various portions of the plan fund in one or more of the separate accounts. The funds so designated are commingled with similar funds of other qualified plans, as in a common or collective trust fund. If an individual plan fund is large enough, an insurer may also offer the employer an individual separate account only for that employer with whatever mix of assets the employer designates.

New Money

Because many of the insurance contracts available for qualified plan funding involve the mingling of an employer's pension contributions with money invested in previous years, the investment return credited on a given year's contributions is not necessarily equal to the return that could have been earned if the amounts contributed had been newly invested that year. This can present a problem under contracts giving employers discretion as to how much to contribute to the fund during a given year, as is generally true under DA and IPG contracts. Where the composite return provided under the insurance contract is greater than that available for new investments, the employer will tend to maximize contributions, while contributions will be minimized when new outside investments can obtain a higher rate of return than under the contract. To alleviate such problems, insurers have developed methods to credit each block of qualified plan contributions with the rate of return at which the funds were actually invested. There are a number of ways of accomplishing this; such techniques are referred to as *new money, investment year,* or *investment generation* methods.

New money methods must not only credit plan contributions for a given year with the current investment rate for that year, but must also take account of the fact that contributions from past years are constantly being reinvested at current rates. Thus, a plan contribution made in Year 1 is credited with the new money rate for Year 1. For Year 2, the Year 1 contribution is credited not with the Year 2 rate, but with a composite of the Year 1 rate and the Year 2 rate, to reflect the fact that a portion (but only a portion) of the Year 1 money will be reinvested in Year 2.

Two broad methods of accounting for these changes are the *declining-index* method and the *fixed-index* method. Under the declining-index method, the amount of money associated with a particular year gradually declines as the amount originally invested in that year is reinvested in later years. Thus, under the declining-index method, the amount invested in Year 1 in the previous example would decline in Year 2 to reflect the fact that part of it was reinvested in Year 2. Under the fixed-index method, the amount associated with the initial investment year remains the same, and the rate of return credited to that amount is adjusted to reflect reinvestments without changing the original principal amount. The two methods generally produce the same results.

ACTUARIAL METHODS AND ASSUMPTIONS

The final or ultimate cost of a qualified plan cannot be determined until the last benefit dollar has been paid to the last surviving plan participant. However, the ultimate cost is not of immediate concern to the employer. Rather, the employer wants to know what the annual cost burden of the plan will be, particularly over the first several years of the plan. For a defined-contribution plan, this is not difficult to determine; the plan document itself specifies the amount of annual contribution that is required, usually in terms of some parameter of business operations, such as payroll or profits. Thus, it is not difficult to get an idea of the kind of burden the business will be assuming if it adopts this kind of plan. For a defined-benefit plan, however, actuarial methods and assumptions determine the annual cost, because the plan itself specifies only the benefits that will be paid.

In the past, employers had a great deal of flexibility in funding defined-benefit plans. In fact, prior to ERISA, it was not necessary even to fund such plans in advance; benefit payments could be made as they came due. Another method sometimes used was terminal funding—funding the benefit in full at the participant's retirement, usually through purchase of an annuity from an insurance company. Under current law, however, all qualified defined-benefit plans subject to the funding provisions of ERISA must provide advance funding over the working lives of the participants, using an actuarial cost method and assumptions. The ERISA funding requirements apply basically to all qualified defined-benefit plans of private employers. Certain government and church plans are exempted from coverage, as well as certain types of plans having no employer contributions. Also, fully insured plans are treated under special rules described later in this chapter in the discussion of minimum funding standards.

An *actuarial cost method* is a method of determining an annual employer contribution for a given set of plan benefits and group of employees. The method produces a schedule of annual contributions aimed at providing a plan fund sufficient to make all benefit payments when they come due without any further contributions by the employer. *Actuarial assumptions* refer to assumptions about future investment return and the character of the employee group that are made in order to determine the annual contribution.

Great variety and complexity are possible in actuarial methods and assumptions. Because of this, many people who are otherwise experts in the benefits area tend to regard actuarial methods as a technical subject that should be left solely to actuaries. However, the choice of actuarial methods and assumptions is such an important factor in determining the timing of plan costs—and, therefore, the tax benefits from the plan—that anyone involved in the benefits area should have a basic knowledge of actuarial concepts.

Because of the complexity of the subject and the specialized terminology involved, it is difficult to treat actuarial methods in a brief and concise way. As with so many considerations in the design of qualified plans, there are two interrelated aspects to the issue. First are the basic concepts used by pension actuaries; then there are the limits imposed by the Internal Revenue Code and ERISA on the types of methods and assumptions permitted for a qualified plan.

Accrued-Benefit and Projected-Benefit Approaches for Determining the Plan's Normal Cost

We will begin with a discussion of the basic concepts and terminology. The actuary's starting point is a determination of the amount that will be required at retirement to fully fund each active employee's benefit. For example, suppose that Clutch Company is planning to adopt a defined-benefit plan. The annual retirement benefit will be 50 percent of each employee's salary at retirement,

Employee	Age	Current Salary	Projected Annual Retirement Benefit
A	60	$100,000	$50,000
B	50	60,000	30,000
C	45	40,000	20,000
D	30	25,000	12,500

with the benefits payable as a straight-life annuity. Clutch's employee census and projected benefits look like those in the table shown on the left.

For simplicity, it is assumed in this example that salary at retirement is equal to current salary, even though it is permissible for funding purposes to make certain assumptions about salary changes, as discussed later. At any rate, the actuary's task is to determine an annual deposit to the plan fund that will ensure that as each employee retires there is enough money in the fund to fully fund the retirement benefit.

Initially, this discussion will focus on methods for determining annual deposits over each employee's working career prior to retirement, designed to fully fund that employee's benefit. The total of such amounts for all employees is the plan's annual *normal cost*. In some actuarial methods, the total cost is divided into two elements. Under this approach, only part of the cost is funded by deposits calculated over employees' working careers (the normal cost). The remainder of the plan's cost, or the *supplemental liability,* which is usually an amount attributable to past service, is funded through deposits over a fixed period of years without reference to participants' retirement dates. This type of funding can provide flexibility in the annual contribution level, as will be discussed.

The Internal Revenue Code does not specifically prescribe what actuarial methods must be used, only that a method must be "reasonable" [Section 412(c)(3)]. However, the regulations state that to be reasonable, the actuarial method must determine the normal cost in one of two ways:

1. The normal cost must be an "amount equal to the present value of benefits accruing under the method for a particular plan year."
2. The normal cost must be expressed as "a level dollar amount or a level percentage of pay."

Actuarial cost methods used for qualified plans determine the normal cost using one of these two approaches: the first is referred to as the *accrued-benefit approach* and the second is the *projected-benefit approach.*

Accrued-Benefit Approach

Under this method of determining the normal cost, the normal cost for a particular year is the amount needed to currently fund all the benefits earned for service with the employer that year. The first step in the method, therefore, is to determine the amount of retirement benefit accrued by each employee during the current year. This depends on the plan formula; some formulas may specify the amount accrued for each year of service, while for others, the total amount will have to be determined and then spread over the years of service remaining to retirement, usually on a pro rata basis, although the plan can specify otherwise within the limits of the benefit accrual rules. Pro rata accrual will be used for the plan of the Clutch Company described above. Thus, if normal retirement age is 65, the annual benefit accrual under the Clutch Plan would be as shown on the right.

The next step is to compute the amount that must be contributed this year to fund each of these benefits currently—that is, the present value of the annual accrual. For simplicity, we will assume that all employees survive and continue in service with the employer until age 65. (Mortality and turnover assumptions are permitted, however, as discussed later.) The only factor in the present-value calculation then is an assumption as to the rate of investment return. The actuary must determine the rate of investment return to be assumed. The Code does not put specific limits on the range of permissible rates, but the rate must be reasonable, as with other actuarial assumptions. For reference, Table 21–2 is a present-value factor table for a 6 percent investment return assumption. Either a table or a formula may be used.

The final factor needed is the annuity purchase rate. This is the lump sum needed at retirement to provide a straight-life annuity of $1 per year. The annuity purchase rate is based on the plan's retirement age, the life expectancy of the retiree and the assumed investment return in the postretirement period. For illustration, an annuity purchase rate of $9.50 will be used for the Clutch Plan. As an example, an accrued benefit of $10,000 per year at that rate would require an accumulation of $95,000 at age 65. Our calculation under the accrued-benefit method then is as follows:

Employee	Projected Annual Retirement Benefit	+ Years to Retirement =	Annual Benefit Accrual
A	$50,000	5	$10,000
B	30,000	15	2,000
C	20,000	20	1,000
D	12,500	35	357

TABLE 21-2
Present-Value Factors

Years to Retirement	Present Value at 6 Percent
5	.7473
15	.4173
20	.3118
25	.2330
35	.1301
40	.0972

Employee	Annual Accrual	×	Annuity Rate	×	Present Value Factor	=	Present Value
A	$10,000		$9.50		.7473		$70,993
B	2,000		9.50		.4173		7,929
C	1,000		9.50		.3318		2,962
D	357		9.50		.1301		441
Total							$83,325

This calculation shows, for example, that $70,993 must be deposited now to provide a benefit of $10,000 per year for Employee A at age 65 (five years from now), $70,993 being the present value of the $95,000 required to purchase the

$10,000 annuity at age 65. The normal cost for the current year is the sum of the present values of the annual accruals for all employees, or $83,325.

It should be noted from the present-value table that the present-value factor increases as the participant gets closer to retirement. The accrued-benefit method, therefore, produces a steadily increasing normal cost for a given group of active employees. However, as employees leave the group by retiring or terminating employment, their benefit no longer enters the calculation. Correspondingly, new employees entering the plan will add to the normal cost. Thus, when the accrued-benefit method is used in actual situations, the employer's annual normal cost may increase, decrease, or level off.

Projected-Benefit Methods

The projected-benefit methods determine the normal cost by developing a level annual cost for each employee's benefit instead of the steadily rising costs resulting under the accrued-benefit method. A simple illustration of this can be provided using the data and assumptions for the Clutch Plan discussed previously.

(1) Employee	(2) Projected Annual Benefit	×	(3) Annuity Rate	=	(4) Accumulation Required at Age 65	(5) Years to Retirement	(6) Level Annual Deposit (6%) Required To Attain (4)
A	$50,000	×	$9.50	=	$475,000	5	$79,494
B	30,000		9.50		285,000	15	11,551
C	20,000		9.50		190,000	20	4,872
D	12,500		9.50		118,750	35	1,005
Total							$96,922

The calculation of the normal cost under the projected-benefit approach begins with the entire projected benefit at retirement, then a calculation (column 6) of the level deposits necessary each year to provide an ultimate accumulation at retirement age sufficient to provide the projected benefit at an assumed annuity rate. (Column 6 can be calculated from the information in columns 4 and 5, plus an interest assumption—6 percent was used here—using a pocket calculator having an installment savings program, a computer with the same program, or actuarial tables.) The normal cost for the Clutch Plan is the total of the amounts in column 6, or $96,922. The addition of mortality, turnover, or other actuarial assumptions would complicate the calculation, but the principles are the same. Note that the normal cost provided initially under this method is higher than the normal cost using the accrued-benefit method. This is what one would expect because of the level funding approach in the projected-benefit approach.

Several actuarial cost methods use the projected-benefit approach. These can be divided into *individual* and *aggregate* methods. With individual methods, the plan's normal cost is determined as the sum of separate annual costs determined for each employee. This is the approach used in the example just completed. With aggregate methods, the normal cost is determined by reference to the total benefits and salaries of all employees covered under the plan rather than on an individual basis. Basically, this is done by determining the normal cost as a percentage of payroll of all employees covered by the plan. The normal cost percentage is defined as

$$\frac{\text{Present value of projected benefits} - \text{Plan assets}}{\text{Present value of future salaries}}$$

For a new plan, of course, the value of plan assets will initially be zero.

An advantage of an aggregate method is that, as the above formula indicates, the value of plan assets is taken into account in determining each year's normal cost percentage; thus, the method automatically makes adjustments for investment results or other fund experience, such as mortality or turnover, that deviate from the actuarial assumptions. With individual methods, such adjustments are made after an actuarial valuation and are amortized separately over a period of years, as will be discussed.

Amortization of Past Service Cost (Supplemental Liability)

Flexibility in funding is gained by splitting the funding into two elements — the normal cost and a *supplemental liability*. As previously discussed, the supplemental liability is usually related to an initial liability for funding past service benefits. While the normal cost of a plan is designed to be funded over the period prior to each employee's retirement, the entire supplemental liability may be funded or *amortized* over a fixed period of years, even if this period extends beyond the retirement dates of some plan participants. Under ERISA, the amortization period for new single-employer plans cannot exceed 30 years. A full tax deduction for the supplemental liability amortization, however, can be obtained for an amortization over as little as ten years, as discussed under "Deductibility of Pension Plan Contributions" later in this chapter.

An actuarial cost method that includes a supplemental liability provides some flexibility in the amount the employer must contribute each year. Once a plan's actuarial methods and assumptions have been determined, the amount of the normal cost has been correspondingly determined. It may be difficult for an employer to change actuarial methods and assumptions to adjust the normal cost to a more financially comfortable level in the future. However, the portion of the plan funding attributable to amortizing the supplemental liability can be varied by the employer from year to year so long as the amount is at least enough to meet the 30-year amortization requirement.

Actuarial Assumptions

The importance of actuarial assumptions has been mentioned previously. The following are some commonly used actuarial assumptions with some indication of when and how they are used.

Interest or Investment Return

This is the actuarial assumption that is most basic and must always be used. It reflects the time value of money—the fact that $1 deposited currently will grow over the years to some amount greater than $1. Actuaries typically use conservative rates of return for defined-benefit plans because of the plan's long-range nature and the necessity for security. The lower the rate used, the greater the annual deposit required.

Mortality

A mortality assumption reflects the possibility that some participants in the employee census may die before reaching retirement age and the amounts contributed to the plan on their behalf will be available to fund benefits of other participants, assuming the plan does not pay these amounts out fully as a death benefit. A mortality assumption accordingly reduces the current contribution to the plan. A mortality assumption may not be appropriate for a small group—say, less than ten employees. It is hard to predict mortality in such a small group: often all the members of the group will live to retirement, thus producing underfunding if a mortality assumption has been used.

Turnover

A turnover assumption reflects the possibility that some employees will terminate employment without a fully vested retirement benefit. Again, a turnover assumption tends to reduce current costs for the plan. But, as with mortality, a turnover assumption may not be appropriate for a small group of employees where turnover is difficult to predict.

Salary Scale

If plan benefits depend on future salaries, it is unrealistic to make a benefit projection based on current salaries. Therefore the plan may include an assumption that salaries will increase at a specified rate over time. It is impractical to assume an increase based on a high inflation rate, because this would produce enormous projected benefits for younger employees. Therefore, a salary scale typically uses a relatively conservative long-term rate based on annual increases of a few percentage points.

Choosing Actuarial Assumptions

The regulations under Code Section 412 permit assumptions of the four types indicated above, so long as they use "reasonable" factors. Each assumption must be reasonable under IRS guidelines.

Certain types of assumptions that might be considered actuarially appropriate are specifically prohibited by the regulations. The regulations do not allow a funding method to anticipate changes in plan benefits that become effective in a future plan year, except for collectively bargained plans. Also, a funding method may not anticipate the future entry of new employees into the plan, except for current employees who have not yet satisfied the plan's participation requirements.

Penalty for Overstatement of Pension Liabilities

If the IRS assesses additional taxes because an employer's pension plan used unreasonable actuarial assumptions, under Code Section 6662, it can also impose a penalty on the additional tax liability ranging from 10 to 30 percent, based on the extent of the actuarial overstatement.

Some Specific Permissible Actuarial Cost Methods

The choice of actuarial cost method is limited only by the code requirement that the method be reasonable and a few corresponding requirements in the regulations. Thus, a wide variety of actuarial cost methods is available through variations on the concepts discussed earlier.

- Accrued-benefit or projected-benefit approach for determining normal cost
- Individual or aggregate methods, if the projected-benefit approach is used
- Whether to use a supplemental liability

Six specific methods are briefly discussed here because they are specifically mentioned in ERISA Section 3(31) as acceptable methods. Because of this legislative endorsement, many plans use one of these methods.

Accrued-Benefit Method

The accrued-benefit method, sometimes called the *unit-credit method,* is a method under which future service costs are funded using a normal cost determined by an accrued-benefit method; past service liability is treated separately. This is essentially the method discussed earlier in some detail in the first example for the Clutch Plan.

Individual Level-Premiums Method

This is a method without separate funding for past service benefits, so that the entire cost of the plan is funded through the normal cost. In this method, the normal cost is determined on a projected benefit or level cost basis for each participant separately, with the total normal cost for the plan being the sum of the level cost computed for each participant. The second example for the Clutch Plan illustrates this method.

Entry-Age Normal Method

This is another method under which past service liability is funded separately from the normal cost. The normal cost of the plan each year is the sum of the level costs for each participant. However, the level cost for each participant is determined as if the participant had entered the plan at the age when that participant's benefits began to accrue—the entry age. If entry ages occur before the plan is instituted—that is, if the plan provides past service benefits—then the normal cost will not by itself fully fund the plan. The amount of the past service liability is the present value of the total normal costs, which were never actually paid, occurring between each employee's entry age and the establishment of the plan. This past service liability is then amortized under the applicable rules.

Aggregate Method

This method and the next two methods are aggregate cost methods because they determine normal cost with reference to total benefits and salaries of all plan participants, rather than making determinations on an individual basis. The "plain" aggregate method does not separately fund past service cost, so there is no initial past service liability. The normal cost percentage is determined from the following formula:

$$\frac{\text{Present value of projected benefits} - \text{Plan assets}}{\text{Present value of future salaries}}$$

Attained-Age Normal Method

This is a variation of the plain aggregate method designed to create an initial past service liability to increase funding flexibility. Under the attained-age normal method, the amount of the initial past service liability is determined using the accrued-benefit method. The normal cost percentage is then determined under the following formula:

$$\frac{\text{Present value of projected benefits} - \left(\begin{array}{c} \text{Plan} \\ \text{assets} \end{array} + \begin{array}{c} \text{Unfunded initial} \\ \text{past service liability} \\ \text{under the accrued-} \\ \text{benefit method} \end{array} \right)}{\text{Present value of future salaries}}$$

Frozen Initial Liability Method

This is a further variation on the aggregate method, and it also determines an initial past service liability to increase funding flexibility. The frozen initial liability method uses a projected-benefit method, such as the entry-age normal method, to determine the initial past service liability. As with the attained-age normal method, the remaining benefits are funded through future normal cost determined under the aggregate method. Accordingly, the normal cost percentage formula is

$$\frac{\text{Present value of projected benefits} - \left(\begin{array}{c} \text{Plan} \\ \text{assets} \end{array} + \begin{array}{c} \text{Unfunded initial} \\ \text{past service liability} \\ \text{under the entry-age} \\ \text{normal method} \end{array} \right)}{\text{Present value of future salaries}}$$

The best way to understand how these actuarial cost methods operate is to work through examples of the various types for a given plan and employee group. A good example is found in "How to Select Acceptable Actuarial Methods for Defined-Benefit Pension Plans." by Kirk F. Maldonado in *The Journal of Taxation,* July 1982.

A comparison of the annual cost for a given plan under the six methods shows how important the choice of method is and how much flexibility is available. In the Maldonado article, the cost for a given plan for each of the six ERISA methods was determined. The plan provides an annual retirement benefit of 40 percent of the employee's salary for his or her final year, and the benefits are to be paid monthly in the form of a straight-life annuity. For simplicity, possible deferred vested benefits for terminating employees were not taken into account. The employee census data are shown on the right.

Age	Age When Hired (Entry Age)	Years of Past Service	Current Salary
60	40	20	$10,000
50	45	5	50,000
30	30	0	25,000
25	25	0	10,000

Comparison of First-Year Funding Cost		
Funding Method	**Minimum Contribution**	**Maximum Deduction**
Individual methods:		
Accrued-benefit	$34,742	$50,162
Individual level-premiums	81,938	81,938
Entry-age normal	34,546	51,831
Aggregate methods:		
Aggregate	52,318	52,318
Attained-age normal	36,594	52,014
Frozen initial liability	34,668	51,953

For the first year, the cost comparison from the article is shown above.

The column headed "Minimum Contribution" indicates the normal cost plus a 30-year amortization of the supplemental liability, if any, for each method. The column headed "Maximum Deduction" indicates the normal cost plus a ten-year amortization of the supplemental liability. The employer's actual first-year contribution for a given funding method, could be either amount or any amount in between, as the employer determines.

Choosing an Actuarial Cost Method

The initial choice of an actuarial cost method may be affected by the employer's concerns as to how plan costs will be spread over future years. The accrued-benefit method will often produce a lower initial cost than other methods and might be chosen if the employer wishes to minimize costs at the plan's inception with the expectation of increased funding in later years. Sometimes this deferral of funding can be a problem. For example, in the 1950s, plans of large manufacturing companies often used the accrued-benefit method because they expected continuing expansion of their work force and thus increasing contributions. However, with the decline in manufacturing in the 1970s, many such plans became underfunded.

Some employers might prefer to *maximize* initial contributions. This is often the case when a plan benefits mostly key employees and the employer wishes to maximize tax sheltering effects. in that case, a level cost method such as the individual level-premiums method may produce the highest annual cost. A very high initial annual cost can sometimes be provided using the individual level-premiums method with past service liability amortized over a ten-year period. However, if highly paid participants are within ten years of retirement, the individual level-premiums method *without* a supplemental liability will generally provide a higher annual tax deductible contribution.

Sometimes, employers wish to match pension costs as closely as possible to payroll costs. In that situation, the aggregate method is typically used because it expresses normal cost as a percentage of participants' compensation and thus rises automatically with payroll costs. The aggregate method is typically used with larger employee groups for this reason, although it produces the same results with a smaller group of employees as well.

Methods that spread costs over too many years can produce problems of underfunding. For example, using a supplemental liability for past-service benefits and spreading these benefits over a 30-year period can result in underfunding if participants with large projected benefits are close to retirement.

If a plan's initial funding method proves unacceptable in practice, the plan administrator can change the method. Code Section 412(c)(5) requires IRS approval for a change in funding method; however, under Revenue Procedure 85-29, such changes will be automatically approved in most routine situations. Changes in actuarial assumptions generally do not require IRS approval.

Ongoing Actuarial Valuations

The discussion so far has focused on actuarial methods for determining plan costs for the initial year. In subsequent years, the plan experience is likely to deviate somewhat from the assumptions made in determining first-year cost. If the deviations are significant enough, one response may be to change the actuarial methods or assumptions. There are, however, other ways to deal with variations from the initial assumptions.

The assets of all qualified plans are valued periodically by the actuary. Under ERISA, the valuation must be made at least once every three years. If the plan assets are found to be insufficient, there is an actuarial deficiency (or *experience loss*), which is made up with increased contributions that are usually deposited *(amortized)* over a period of years. Similarly, if there is an actuarial surplus (or *experience gain*), contributions are decreased over future years. The minimum funding standards, discussed below, determine how rapidly these experience gains and losses must be amortized.

The valuation of the plan's assets may be made on the basis of any reasonable valuation method, as long as the method takes into account the fair market value of the assets—rather than using cost or some other purely formal method of valuation. The regulations under Section 412 specify rules that must be used in variation. For example, debt instruments may be valued by amortizing the difference between initial cost and maturity value over the life of the bond, because it may not be possible to determine current fair market value by market quotations. Also, because valuations are relatively infrequent, the plan can use any reasonable and consistent procedure for averaging actual market value over a period of years or smoothing out the fluctuations in the market value of assets.

MINIMUM FUNDING STANDARDS

The minimum funding standards of Code Section 412 and corresponding ERISA provisions provide the legal structure for enforcing the advance funding requirement that applies to qualified pension plans. A plan to which the minimum funding standard applies must maintain a *funding standard account*. The funding standard account is annually charged with the plan's normal cost and certain other costs and credited with certain items that benefit the plan. At the end of the year, if the charges exceed the credits, there may be an *accumulated funding deficiency*. In that case, there is a penalty tax and other enforcement provisions. The penalty tax consists of an initial tax of 5 percent of the deficiency, with an additional 100 percent tax if the deficiency is not corrected after notification by the IRS.

Obviously, the employer's objective is to *balance* the funding standard account for each year. If the employer is unable to make sufficient contributions to do this, the employer can request a waiver from the IRS of the minimum funding standard for the plan year or request an extended amortization period for certain plan liabilities.

The employer is not required to contribute annually any more to the plan than an amount referred to as the *full funding limitation,* even if the funding standard account would then be left with a deficit for the plan year. This important limitation is generally defined as the difference between the accrued actuarial liability of the plan computed under the plan's funding method (or if this is not possible, under the entry-age normal method) and the value of the plan assets. Finally, certain plans are allowed to establish an *alternative minimum funding standard account* and can then avoid a funding deficiency by avoiding a deficit in either the funding standard account or the alternative minimum funding standard account, whichever is lesser. The alternative minimum funding standard account is somewhat simpler than the funding standard account and it is usually possible to avoid a deficit with a lower employer contribution.

Exemptions from the Minimum Funding Standard

The minimum funding standard rules basically apply to all qualified pension plans. However, government plans, church plans that have not elected to be treated as qualified plans, and various types of plans having no employer contributions are exempted in Code Section 412.

More significantly, the minimum funding standards do not apply to profit-sharing or stock bonus plans. Technically, the standards apply to defined-contribution pension plans as well as defined-benefit pension plans. However, for defined-contribution pension plans (money-purchase and target plans), the minimum funding standard will be met so long as the employer contributes the amount required under the plan's contribution formula each year.

Fully insured plans—those funded exclusively by the purchase of individual insurance or annuity contracts—are specifically exempted from the minimum funding standards, as long as the following requirements are met:

- The contracts provide for the payment of premiums in equal annual amounts over a period no longer than the preretirement period of employment.
- The plan benefits are equal to those guaranteed by the insurance carrier under the contracts.
- The premiums on the contracts have been paid when due or, if there has been a lapse, the policy has been reinstated.
- No rights under the insurance contract have been subject to a security interest at any time during the plan year.
- No policy loans are outstanding at any time during the plan year.

Plans that are fully insured under group contracts are also exempt from the minimum funding standard, as long as the contracts meet conditions similar to those previously listed. These would ordinarily have to be group contracts providing fully allocated funding.

DEDUCTIBILITY OF PENSION PLAN CONTRIBUTIONS

Excessive contributions to a pension plan fund, if they are allowed to be deducted, will accelerate the employer's tax deduction and thereby increase the tax benefit of the qualified plan beyond what is considered appropriate. To prevent this, there are specific limits on the amount of pension plan contributions that an employer can deduct in a given plan year.

Unlike the deduction limit for profit-sharing plans, which is 15 percent of payroll (see Chapter 22), the deduction limit for pension plans is based on actuarial considerations. For a given plan year, an employer can deduct contributions to a pension plan up to a limit determined by the largest of three amounts [Code Section 404(a)(1)].

1. The amount necessary to satisfy the minimum funding standard for the year.
2. The amount necessary to fund benefits based on past and current service on a level funding basis over the years remaining to retirement for each employee. However, if the remaining unfunded cost for any three individuals is more than 50 percent of the total of the unfunded costs, fundings for those three individuals must be distributed over a period of at least five taxable years.
3. An amount equal to the normal cost of the plan plus, if there is a supplemental liability, an amount necessary to amortize the supplemental liability in equal annual payments over a ten-year period.

In determining the applicable limitation, the funding methods and the actuarial assumptions used must be the same as those used for purposes of the minimum funding standards. Furthermore. the tax deduction for a given plan year cannot exceed the full funding limitation that was discussed earlier. Thus, there is little incentive for the employer to contribute beyond the full funding limitation.

Although these limits are expressed in actuarial language, the implications are relatively easy to understand. First of all, if the plan is funded on the basis of individual insurance contracts, the second limit will generally be the one applicable to the plan because most such contracts have premiums determined on the basis of level funding for the years remaining until retirement for each employee. On the other hand, plans funded with group contracts and trust funds using a variety of actuarial methods and assumptions will generally be governed by the third alternative limit.

Note that this limit specifies the *maximum* deductible amount. The amount required to be contributed under the minimum funding standard as applied to the plan may be somewhat less than this limit. Therefore, in a given plan year, the employer's actual contribution and deduction may be less than the maximum limit that applies. This is one of the reasons why a defined-benefit plan with a group pension contract or trust fund can be relatively flexible for the employer. Between the minimum limit required by the minimum funding standards and the maximum deductible limit discussed earlier, there may be a relatively comfortable range of contributions that can be adjusted according to the employer's specific financial situation.

Technically, the rules previously stated apply to both defined-benefit and defined-contribution pension plans. However, for defined-contribution plans, the minimum funding standards are satisfied whenever the employer makes the annual contributions specified by the plan document. In other words, the limit on the amount deductible under a defined-contribution pension plan is simply the amount specified in the plan document. For example, the plan document in a money-purchase plan might require that each year the employer must contribute an amount equal to 6 percent of each employee's compensation to that employee's account. The total of such contributions would then be both the amount required by the minimum funding standard and the maximum amount deductible.

If an employer has a combination of defined-benefit and defined-contribution plans covering the same employee or employees, a percentage deduction limit applies. The deduction for a given year cannot exceed the greater of 25 percent of the common payroll (compensation of employees covered under both plans) or the amount required to meet the minimum funding standard for the defined-benefit plan alone. As discussed in Chapter 25, this provision has its greatest impact on highly compensated employees.

Penalty for Nondeductible Contributions

Generally, there is no advantage in contributing more to a plan than is deductible, because not only is the deduction for the excess unavailable but under Code Section 4972, a 10 percent penalty is imposed on the nondeductible portion of the contribution, with some exceptions. However, if nondeductible contributions are made, they can be carried over and deducted in future years. The deduction limit for future years, however, applies to the combination of carried-over and current contributions.

Timing of Deductions

The rules for timing of contributions and deductions for qualified plans are relatively favorable. Contributions will be deemed to be made by the employer for a given taxable year of the employer, and will be deductible for that year, if they are made by the time prescribed for filing the employer's tax return for that year, including extensions. For example, a corporation using a calendar year could contribute to the plan for 2001 as late as September 15, 2002 (the basic tax filing date of March 15, plus the maximum six-month extension). The rules for timing of contributions and deductions are the same for both cash and accrual-method taxpayers; there is no advantage for this purpose in using the accrual method.

STUDY QUESTIONS

1. a. What is a trust?
   b. What is the role of a trustee?

2. Explain why a retirement income policy can be the sole funding vehicle for a qualified pension plan, but an ordinary life insurance policy cannot normally be so used.

3. a. Describe a combination plan.
   b. What are the typical features of a combination plan?

4. How does a group permanent contract differ from individual policies used to fund qualified plans?

5. a. What are the basic characteristics of unallocated funding instruments in a qualified plan?
   b. What is the advantage in using them?

6. What makes an IPG contract different from the conventional DA contract?

7. Why is it important for anyone involved with employee benefits to understand actuarial cost methods and actuarial assumptions?

8. a. Explain how an accrued-benefit approach is used to determine the normal cost for a qualified plan.
   b. How does the projected-benefit approach for determining the normal cost of a qualified plan differ from the accrued-benefit approach?

9. a. Under what circumstances is supplemental liability incurred?
   b. Over what period of time may supplemental liability be amortized?

10. Which actuarial cost method should be chosen in each of the following situations?
    a. The Metro Company, a growing corporation, wishes to minimize costs at the plan's inception with the expectation of increased funding in later years.
    b. Infant Care, Inc., a small, closely held pediatric care group with highly paid participants who are within ten years of retirement, wishes to maximize initial contributions in order to maximize tax shelter.
    c. Middleco, a mid-sized manufacturing firm, wishes to match pension costs as closely as possible to payroll costs.

Profit-Sharing and Similar Plans

CURRENT QUALIFIED PLAN TRENDS

Although only the traditional types of pension plans discussed in earlier chapters involve an employer commitment to adequate retirement income for employees, trends in management, the economy, and the workforce have produced a gradual erosion in qualified pension plan coverage and a movement toward "nonretirement" plans—that is, defined-contribution plans that provide a form of savings and incentive benefits for employees without a specific funding commitment by the employer. (See Figure 22–1.) The reasons for this trend include the following:

- Competition and cost pressures to minimize wage and benefit costs
- Increasing acquisition, dissolution, and reorganization of business enterprises discourage employer long-term commitment to employees
- Decline in collective bargaining; labor unions have traditionally favored the defined-benefit plan
- Increased mobility in the workforce; the 40-year career with one employer has become a rarity
- Employers are using more part-time employees, leased employees, and independent contractors who would generally receive little benefit from a traditional pension plan
- Increase in families with two wage earners; traditional pension plans tend to duplicate benefits in such cases

This chapter will discuss the following:

- Qualified profit-sharing plans
- Savings or thrift plans
- Employer stock plans (stock bonus plans and ESOPs)

Increasingly, the trend in qualified planning is toward salary savings plans such as 401(k) plans, which are primarily funded through employee salary reductions that are contributed to the plan. These plans are typically combined with the traditional employer-funded profit-sharing plans, or with those in which employer contributions match the employee salary reductions. Salary savings plans are discussed in the next chapter. First, to fully understand how salary savings plans work, the basic profit-sharing plan and its variants will be discussed in this chapter.

QUALIFIED PROFIT-SHARING PLANS

The basic profit-sharing plan is a defined-contribution plan in which employer contributions are typically based in some manner on the employer's profits, although there is no actual requirement for the employer to have prof-

FIGURE 22-1
Pension Coverage

Pension Coverage
For wage and salary workers in private industry

Defined-Benefit Plans - % Covered

Defined-Contribution Plans - % Covered

	WORKERS COVERED	EMPLOYER CONTRIBUTION
	In millions	*In billions*
1975	26.8	$24.2
1991	25.7	$30.1

	WORKERS COVERED	EMPLOYER CONTRIBUTION
	In millions	*In billions*
1975	3.9	$12.8
1991	17.1	$81.0

SOURCE: *U. S. Department of Labor, Pension and Welfare Administration.*

its in order to contribute to the plan. Even a nonprofit organization may have a "profit-sharing" plan. The general characteristics are as follows:

- The employer contribution may be specified as a percentage of annual profits each year or, for even more flexibility, the plan may provide that the employer determines the amount to be contributed on an annual basis, with the option of contributing nothing even in years in which there are profits or, conversely, making contributions in unprofitable years.
- The plan must have a nondiscriminatory formula for allocating the employer contribution to the accounts of employees.
- Because the plan is a defined-contribution plan, the benefit from it consists of the amount in each employee's account, usually distributed as a lump sum at retirement or termination of employment.

- The plan may permit employee withdrawals or loans during employment.
- Eligibility and vesting are usually liberal because of the incentive nature of the plan.
- Forfeitures from employees who terminate employment are usually reallocated to the accounts of remaining participants, thus making the plan particularly attractive to long-service employees.
- The main price for the advantages of the design is that the employer's annual deduction for contributions to the plan is limited to 15 percent of the payroll of employees covered under the plan.

Eligibility and Vesting

Profit-sharing plans are typically designed with relatively liberal eligibility and vesting provisions, compared with pension plans. This is because the employer generally wishes the incentive objective of the plans to operate for short-term as well as long-term employees, and also because the simplicity of administering a profit-sharing plan makes it less necessary to exclude short-term employees to reduce plan administrative costs. Thus, many profit-sharing plans permit employees to enter the plan immediately upon becoming employed, or after a short waiting period—for example, until the next date on which the plan assets are valued. A great variety of vesting provisions are used, and they are typically tailored to the employer's specific needs.

As a qualified plan, a profit-sharing plan is subject to the restrictions on eligibility and vesting provisions discussed in detail in earlier chapters. In summary, a minimum age requirement greater than 21 is not permitted, nor can a waiting period for entry be longer than one year, or up to $1\frac{1}{2}$ years if entry is based on plan entry dates. Under the age discrimination law, no maximum age for entry can be prescribed (and contributions must continue for as long as the employee continues to work). The coverage tests discussed in Chapter 19 apply to a profit-sharing plan as they do to all qualified plans.

The vesting requirements discussed in Chapter 19 are also applicable to profit-sharing plans. A profit-sharing plan is more likely to discriminate in favor of highly compensated employees as a result of high employee turnover and the use of forfeitures, as discussed below. Therefore, the IRS may require the more stringent three- to seven-year vesting schedule in new profit-sharing plans. Most profit-sharing plans use a vesting schedule that is at least as generous as this schedule. Even more stringent vesting is required if the plan is top-heavy (Chapter 25).

Employer Contribution Provision

There is great flexibility in designing an employer contribution provision for a profit-sharing plan. The contribution provision can be either *discretionary* or of the *formula* type.

With the discretionary provision, the company's board of directors determines each year what amount will be contributed. It is not necessary for the company actually to have current or accumulated profits. Many employers will wish to contribute the maximum deductible amount each year, but a lesser amount can be contributed.

Although employers are permitted to omit contributions under a discretionary provision, the IRS requires that contributions be "substantial and recurring." If too many years go by without contributions, the IRS is likely to find that the plan has been terminated, with the consequences discussed in Chapter 26 (basically 100 percent vesting for all plan participants and distribution under a specified payment schedule). No specific guidelines are given by the IRS as to how many years of omitted contributions are permitted, so the decision to skip a profit-sharing contribution must always be made with some caution.

With a formula contribution provision. a specified amount must be contributed to the plan whenever there are profits. Typically, the amount is expressed as a percentage of profits determined under generally accepted accounting principles. There are no specific IRS restrictions on the type of formula, so flexibility is possible. For example, the plan might provide for a contribution of 7 percent of all current profits in excess of $50,000, possibly with a limitation on the amount deductible for the year. There is also considerable freedom in defining the term *profit* in the plan. For example, profit before taxes or after taxes can be used, with before-tax profits being the most common. Profit as defined in the plan can also include capital gains and losses or accumulated profits from prior years. Even an employer that is organized under state law as a "nonprofit" corporation can have a profit-sharing plan funded from a suitably defined surplus account.

The advantage of the formula approach is that it is more attractive to employees than the discretionary approach and more definitely serves the incentive purpose of the plan. However, if a formula approach is adopted, the employer must remember that the formula amount must always be contributed to the plan; the formula constitutes a continuing legal and financial obligation for the business as long as the plan remains in effect. It is possible to draft formulas that take into account possible adverse financial contingencies. Without such provisions, the formula may have to be amended in the future in the event of financial difficulty.

Allocations to Employee Accounts

The plan's contribution provision determines the total amount contributed to the plan for all employees. The plan must also have a formula under which appropriate portions of this total contribution are allocated to the individual accounts of employees. Here there is less flexibility because the allocation provision must meet nondiscrimination requirements. The law provides that contributions must be allocated under a definite formula that does not discriminate in favor of highly compensated employees. Any formula that meets these requirements can be acceptable, but most formulas allocate to participants on the basis of their compensation, compared with the compensation of all participants. That is, after the total employer contribution is determined, the amount allocatable to a given participant is

$$\text{Total employer contribution} \times \frac{\text{Participant's compensation}}{\text{Compensation of all participants}}$$

If compensation is used in the allocation formula, the plan must define compensation in a way that does not discriminate. Compensation might include only base pay or might be total compensation including bonuses or overtime. Only the first $150,000 (as indexed for inflation) of each employee's compensation can be taken into account in the plan formula.

Service is another factor often used in the formula for allocating employer contributions. However, since highly compensated employees are likely to have long service, the IRS will probably require a showing that any service-based formula will not produce discrimination.

Age-Based Allocation Formula and Cross-Testing

Under IRS regulations, it is possible for a profit-sharing plan's allocation formula to take the participant's *age at plan entry* into account. That is, the plan can provide a greater allocation percentage of compensation to a participant who entered the plan at, say, age 55 than to a participant who entered at age 25. The purpose of this allocation method is to provide the late entrant with a more adequate benefit at retirement, given the fact that the late entrant has fewer years to accumulate plan contributions. The advantages of this approach are similar to those for the target pension plan discussed in Chapter 20. Compared with a target plan, the age-based profit-sharing plan has the additional advantage that the employer is not "locked-in" to an annual contribution obligation, which may make this approach attractive to smaller or less stable businesses.

Age-based profit-sharing allocation formulas and target plans are examples of a method of discrimination testing known as *cross-testing*. A cross-tested defined-contribution plan is tested for discrimination in favor of the highly compensated as if it were a defined-benefit plan. That is, projected benefits at retirement age are determined for all participants in the defined-contribution plan (by assuming that the current level of contributions to each participant's account continues each year until that participant's retirement age). These projected benefits, as a percentage of each participant's compensation, are then tested for discrimination. If lower-paid employees are generally younger than highly compensated employees, cross-testing may allow relatively low contribution levels (percentages of compensation) for the lower-paid employees because the contributions for the younger employees are projected over a longer period of time than those for the older employees. Cross-tested plans are often used by smaller businesses to provide substantial contributions for highly compensated employees, with relatively low costs for coverage of other employees.

Forfeitures

A forfeiture is an unvested amount remaining in a participant's account when the participant terminates employment without being fully vested under the plan's vesting schedule. Thus, forfeitures can occur in any defined-contribution plan that does not have 100 percent immediate vesting. Forfeitures can be reallocated to accounts of other participants or used to reduce future employer contributions. In a profit-sharing plan, forfeitures are usually reallocated to participants to provide an additional incentive for continuing service.

Forfeitures must be allocated in a nondiscriminatory manner. In most plans, forfeiture allocations are made in the same manner as allocations of employer contributions—on the basis of compensation or a combination of compensation and service. The IRS usually will not accept a forfeiture allocation provision based on account balances of remaining participants because such a provision may provide substantial discrimination.

Analysis of profit-sharing plans of smaller employers that have existed for a number of years generally shows that by far the largest account balances are those for highly compensated participants. This is because the combination of higher compensation, longer service (and therefore more years in the plan), and low turnover among the highly compensated group eventually produces a great disparity in account balances. This phenomenon is, in fact, one of the reasons why closely held businesses adopt profit-sharing plans. As such, they are not deemed to be discriminatory. However, if a plan contains any features designed to multiply this inherent discrimination (such as forfeiture allocation based on account balance), the IRS generally will not approve it.

Integration with Social Security

The allocation formula of a profit-sharing plan may be integrated with Social Security to avoid duplication of benefits and reduce plan costs to the employer. Under those rules, as discussed earlier, the integration level is generally equal to the taxable wage base for the year, although other levels are used in some cases. The difference between the plan's excess contribution percentage (contribution percentage for compensation above the integration level) and its base contribution percentage (contribution percentage for compensation up to the integration level) cannot be more than the lesser of

- the base contribution percentage or
- the greater of (a) 5.7 percent or (b) the old-age Social Security tax rate.

The integrated plan gives credit to the employer for contributions made to Social Security as if they had been made to the plan, thus overall providing a nondiscriminatory allocation formula.

As an example of integrated formulas, if the plan uses an integration level of $76,200, it could provide a base allocation percentage of 10 percent of compensation below $76,200, plus an allocation of 5.7 percent of compensation above $76,200, assuming the old-age Social Security tax rate is less than 5.7 percent. Or if the plan provided 4 percent of compensation below the integration level, it could provide no more than 4 percent of compensation above the integration level.

Plan allocations counted toward the 5.7 percent limitation must include not only employer contributions for the year but also any forfeitures allocated to the participant's account. For example, suppose that for the year 2000 a plan has two participants with compensation as shown below. For 2000, the employer contributes $5,000 to the plan and a forfeiture of $8,000 is available for allocation to participants' accounts. The plan's integration level is $76,200. Under the plan's allocation formula, each participant's account is to receive the maximum permitted percent of plan contributions plus forfeitures for compensation above $76,200 (up to 5.7 percent). The remaining amount of the plan contributions plus forfeitures are allocated in proportion to total compensation. Plan allocations, shown below, show that the amount in the sixth column is arrived at by subtracting the excess allocation (total of column five) from the $13,000 of contributions plus forfeitures; this remaining amount of $12,430 is multiplied by a fraction, the numerator which is the participant's total compensation and the denominator of which is the total payroll. This allocation meets the integration rules because the amount allocated to compensation below $76,200 is more than 5.7 percent.

Employee		2000 Compensation	Compensation above $76,200	5.7% of Excess	Allocation of Remainder	Total Allocation
A		$86,200	$10,000	$570	$10,857	$11,157
B		15,000	0	0	1,843	1,843
	Payroll	$101,200				$13,000

Deduction of Employer Contributions

Under Code Section 404(a)(3), the maximum amount that an employer can deduct for contributions to a profit-sharing plan is 15 percent of the compensation paid or accrued during the taxable year to all employees who participate in the profit-sharing plan. This is an employer deduction limit based on compensation of all covered employees; it is not a rule stating that allocations to individual participants' accounts are limited to 15 percent of their compensation. The limitation on annual additions to individual accounts, the Section 415 limit, is discussed below.

An employer can contribute to a profit-sharing or a stock bonus plan in excess of the 15 percent limit, but the excess is not deductible and is subject to a 10 percent penalty under Section 4972. The excess amount can be carried over to a future year and deducted then, but deductions in the future year for current contributions plus carryovers are still subject to the 15 percent of payroll limit.

Combined Profit-Sharing and other Plans

If an employer has both a defined-benefit plan and a profit-sharing or other defined-contribution plan covering a common group of employees, the total contribution for both plans cannot exceed 25 percent of compensation of the common group of employees. However, if a greater contribution is necessary to satisfy the minimum funding standard for the defined-benefit plan, the employer will always be able to make and deduct this contribution.

Section 415 Limits

The Section 415 limits (discussed in more detail in Chapter 25) that apply to profit-sharing plans are those applicable to all defined-contribution plans. The annual addition to any participant's account cannot exceed the lesser of 25 percent of the participant's compensation or $30,000 (as indexed for inflation). For a profit-sharing plan, the annual addition includes the participant's share of any forfeitures as well as employer and employee contributions. This means that when forfeitures are allocated to a participant's account, the amount of employer contributions that can be allocated may be reduced. The Section 415 limits usually affect only highly compensated employees covered under the plan.

Investment Earnings and Account Balances

As a defined-contribution plan, a profit-sharing plan must provide separate accounts for each participant. However, unless the plan contains a provision permitting participants to direct investments (discussed below), the plan trustee or other funding agents will generally pool all participants' accounts for investment purposes. The plan must then provide a mechanism for allocating investment gains or losses to each participant. Most methods for doing this effectively allocate such gains and losses in proportion to the participant's account balance.

IRS revenue rulings require accounts of all participants to be valued in a uniform and consistent manner at least once each year, unless all plan assets are immediately invested in individual annuity or retirement contracts meeting certain requirements. The plan usually will specify a *valuation date* or dates on which valuation occurs. Investment earnings, gains, and losses are allocated to participants' accounts as of this date.

Participant-Directed Investments

Under ERISA Section 404c, any "individual account" plan (such as a profit-sharing, stock bonus, or money-purchase pension plan) can include a provision allowing the participant to direct the trustee or other funding agent as to the investment of the participant's account.

If the plan administrator provides a broad range of investment choices—so that the participant's choice has real meaning—then the trustee and other plan fiduciaries are not subject to fiduciary responsibility for the investment decision.[1] A plan can technically allow unlimited choice of investments, but this increases the plan's administrative burdens. Often, a family of mutual funds is offered as an investment option to increase the administrative feasibility of participant direction. At least three investment alternatives must be included.

Investment direction gives the participant a considerable degree of control over the funds in his or her account. It is frequently used in profit-sharing plans, particularly those for closely held businesses where the controlling employees have by far the largest accounts. On the other hand, to the extent that participant direction of investments removes the security provided by the fiduciary rules, such a provision is at odds with a plan objective of providing retirement security, and it would not be appropriate if this were a major objective of the plan for a particular employee group.

To prevent certain abuses associated with participant-directed investments, the Code provides that an investment by a participant-directed qualified plan account in a *collectible* will be treated as if the amount invested were distributed to the participant as taxable income to the participant. A collectible is defined in Code Section 408(m) as a work of art, rug or antique, metal or gem, stamp or coin (excluding certain federal and state-issued coins), alcoholic beverage, or any other tangible personal property designated as a collectible by the IRS.

Withdrawals during Employment and Loan Provisions

The incentive (rather than retirement security) focus of profit-sharing plans tends to dictate that participants be given the opportunity to control or benefit from their accounts even before retirement or termination of employment. There are various ways to do this. One such provision is a participant-directed account, as discussed above. Another is a special feature permitted in profit-sharing plans but not in pension plans—a provision for account withdrawals from the plan during employment.

---

[1] Labor Regulation Section 2550.404c-1.

The regulations require that employer contributions under a profit-sharing plan must be accumulated for at least two years before they can be withdrawn by participants.[2] However, in some revenue rulings, the IRS has permitted a plan provision allowing employees with at least 60 months of participation to withdraw employer contributions, including those made within the previous two years. Also, revenue rulings have permitted a plan provision for withdrawal in the case of "hardship," including contributions made within the previous two years. *Hardship* must be sufficiently defined in the plan and the definitions must be consistently applied.[3] All these limitations apply only to amounts attributable to employer contributions to the plan. If the plan permits employee contributions, the employee contributions can be withdrawn at any time without restriction.

In considering the design of withdrawal provisions, it is important to keep in mind that the taxation and early-withdrawal penalty rules act as disincentives for participants to withdraw plan funds. These rules (discussed in Chapter 24) indirectly reduce the advantages of using a qualified plan as a medium for preretirement savings.

Many plan designers prefer to have a prohibition or at least restrictions on withdrawals from the employer-contributed portion of the account. This is because favorable investment results sometimes depend on having a pool of investment money that is relatively large and not subject to the additional liquidity requirements imposed by the possibility of participant withdrawals. Some typical restrictions found in profit-sharing plans include a requirement that the participant demonstrate a need for the money coming within a list of authorized needs either set out in the plan or promulgated by the plan administrator and applied consistently. Such needs might include educational expenses for children, home purchase or remodeling, sickness or disability, and so forth. Another method of restricting plan withdrawals is to provide a penalty on a participant who withdraws amounts from the plan (in addition to the 10 percent federal penalty tax, which also applies). A plan penalty might include suspension of participation for a period of time, such as six months after the withdrawal. The plan penalty cannot, however, deprive a participant of any previously vested benefit.

Loan provisions are appropriate for profit-sharing plans. Again, however, a generous loan provision in a plan may have the effect of reducing the amount of funds available for other plan investments.

Incidental Benefits

The regulations permit profit-sharing plans to provide as an incidental benefit life, accident, or health insurance for the participant and the participant's

---

[2.]Revenue Ruling 73-55, 1973-2 CB 130; Rev. Rul. 71-295, 1971-1 CB 184; Rev. Rul. 80-155, 1980-1 CB 84.

[3.]Rev. Rul. 68–24, 1968–1 CB 150.

family. Incidental life insurance is the only one that is commonly provided. If employer contributions are used to provide insurance, the incidental benefit limitations described in Chapter 21 must be met.

If the plan provides incidental whole life insurance, the usual test is that aggregate premiums for each participant must be less than 50 percent of the aggregate of employer contributions allocated to the participant's account. If the plan purchases term insurance or accident and health insurance, the aggregate premiums must be less than 25 percent of the employer contributions allocated to the participant's account. The current IRS position is that universal life premiums also must meet the 25 percent limit. Note that these tests apply to the *aggregate*—that is, the total contributions made for all years at any given time. If either of these limits is exceeded, the plan could be disqualified. However, insurance premiums paid with employer-contributed funds that have accumulated for at least two years are not subject to these limitations.

If the employee dies before normal retirement age, the plan can provide that the face amount of the policies plus the balance credited to the participant's account in the profit-sharing plan can be distributed to the survivors without the life insurance violating the incidental benefit requirement. This can be done even though the amount of life insurance might be more than 100 times the account balance expressed as an expected monthly pension.

If life insurance is provided by the plan, the term insurance cost is currently taxable to the employee under the PS 58 table (see Chapter 21) or the insurer's term insurance rates, as discussed in Chapter 6. Accident and health insurance provided by an employer under the plan might not be taxable because of the exclusion provided for employer-provided health insurance. However, there usually is no particular benefit in providing accident and health insurance under a profit-sharing plan. It is usually provided in a separate plan not connected with the profit-sharing plan.

SAVINGS PLANS

Almost any qualified plan can have a provision for employee contributions to supplement the plan fund or benefit. A plan that is designed particularly to exploit the possibility of employee contributions is often referred to as a *savings plan* or *thrift plan*. The term *savings plan* will be used here to describe a plan featuring employee *after-tax* contributions. Salary-reduction [401(k)] plans are discussed in Chapter 23.

Design of Savings Plans

A savings plan is a defined-contribution plan so that employees can have separate accounts. Usually, qualified savings plans are designed as profit-sharing plans (rather than money-purchase pension plans) because only a profit-sharing plan permits account withdrawals during employment, and this is an important feature of the plan if the plan is to be described to employees as a savings medium. Thus, a savings plan can generally be described as a *contributory profit-sharing plan.*

The typical savings plan features employee contributions matched by the employer. Plan participation is voluntary; employees elect to contribute a chosen percentage of their compensation up to a maximum percentage specified in the plan. The employer then makes a matching contribution to the plan. The matching may be dollar for dollar, or the employer may put in some multiple or submultiple of the employee contribution rate. For example, typically a plan might permit an employee to contribute annually any whole percentage of compensation from 1 to 6 percent. The plan might then provide that the employer contributes at the rate of half the chosen employee percentage; thus, if the employee elects to contribute 4 percent of compensation, the employer would contribute an additional 2 percent.

If the plan's maximum contribution level is too high, there is a possibility of discrimination because only higher-paid employees could be in a position to contribute to the plan, and only they would receive full employer matching contributions. To prevent this type of discrimination, there is a specific numerical test applicable to after-tax employee contributions. Under this test [Code Section 401(m)], a plan is not deemed discriminatory for a plan year if, for highly compensated employees, the total of employee contributions (both matched and voluntary) plus employer matching contributions does not exceed certain numerical limits similar to those applicable to Section 401(k) plans, discussed in the next chapter. Administration of the Section 401(m) limits can be complex and costly.

Apart from the features relating to employee contributions, savings plans generally follow the rules for profit-sharing plans described earlier. In designing a savings plan, emphasis is usually put on features relating to the objective of providing a savings medium for employees. Thus, a savings plan usually has generous provisions for vesting, employee withdrawal of funds, plan loans, and investment flexibility.

Advantages and Disadvantages of Savings Plans

Savings plans have been very popular in the past and continue to be so, despite the advent of other types of plans, such as Section 401(k) plans, that provide greater tax leverage. Some older savings plans have been converted to add a 401(k) feature while retaining the provision for additional after-tax contributions by employees. Like all qualified plans, a savings plan provides a tax-deferred savings medium because earnings in the plan fund are not taxable until the employee's account is distributed.

A savings plan usually does not maximize the potential tax deduction available for plan contributions, because it involves after-tax contributions by the employee—contributions that are not deducted or excluded for federal income or Social Security tax purposes. A greater degree of tax deductibility can be provided with other types of plans, such as regular profit-sharing plans or Section 401(k) plans. However, some of these plans may require a greater employer outlay for the plan itself (although not necessarily for the overall compensation package). These other plans may also entail greater restrictions on the funds, which may make them a less attractive savings medium from the employee's standpoint.

USING EMPLOYER STOCK IN QUALIFIED PLANS

For a number of years, the Internal Revenue Code has included special provisions for qualified plans that invest primarily in employer securities. Congress wants to encourage these plans on the premise that it is desirable to give employees some ownership interest in the company for which they work. The most important special benefit is the leveraging technique for ESOPs, described below, that allows the employer to use the ESOP as a means of financing corporate growth. There are also provisions that encourage the use of a stock plan to help create a market for employer stock.

There are two types of qualified plans that invest primarily in employer securities, the traditional *stock bonus plan* and the *employee stock ownership plan* (ESOP). In addition, a regular profit-sharing plan may invest in employer stock without limit, and profit-sharing plans are sometimes used, formally or informally, for this purpose. Qualified pension plans may not invest more than 10 percent of their assets in employer stock, so pension plans are not very useful as employer stock plans.

Advantages of Investing in Employer Stock

There are certain employer and employee advantages to any plan that invests in employer stock, including a regular profit-sharing plan, a stock bonus plan, or an ESOP.

- A market can be created for employer stock. This has many planning implications and is discussed in detail below.
- The employer can obtain a deduction for noncash (that is, employer stock) contributions to the plan.
- Employees receive an ownership interest in the company, which may act as a performance incentive.
- As described below, unrealized appreciation of stock is not taxed to the employee at the time of distribution.

Stock Bonus Plan

The stock bonus plan is the older of the two types of qualified plans that invest primarily in employer securities. Under the regulations, a stock bonus plan is a qualified defined-contribution plan similar to a profit-sharing plan, except that the employer's contributions are not necessarily dependent on profits; benefits are distributable in the stock of the employer company.

Typically, the plan contribution formula is based on employee compensation. Employer contributions to the plan may be made in cash or directly in the form of employer securities, newly issued or otherwise. Shares of stock are allocated to participants' accounts under a formula that must meet the same nondiscrimination requirements as the allocation formula in a profit-sharing plan. Some stock bonus plans also provide for after-tax employee contributions or salary reductions. (A salary reduction stock plan is sometimes referred to as a *KSOP*.)

The value of each participant's account in a stock bonus plan is stated in terms of a certain number of shares of employer stock. The value of the account varies with the value of the underlying employer stock. Dividends on the shares can be used to increase participants' accounts, or cash dividends can be paid through the plan directly to participants as currently taxable income, in which case the employer gets a tax deduction.

Plan Distributions

Distributions from both stock bonus plans and ESOPs are generally subject to the same restrictions applicable to distributions from any qualified plan. Thus, distributions prior to age $59\frac{1}{2}$, death, disability, or retirement are subject to a 10 percent penalty, with some exceptions. However, for a stock bonus plan or ESOP, there is no requirement of providing a joint and survivor annuity or other spousal death benefit.

Because an employee retains the investment risk in the employer company until the stock is distributed, a deferred distribution to a terminated employee would not be appropriate, so payouts from stock bonus plans or ESOPs have a special earlier beginning date than that for other qualified plans. Distributions from a stock bonus plan or ESOP must occur no later than one year after the end of the fifth plan year after the employee's separation from service or no later than one year after retirement, disability, or death.

In general, the plan must distribute benefits in the form of employer stock. However, the participant can be given the option of receiving cash of equal value, subject to a right to receive employer stock. If the participant receives stock that is not traded on an established market, the participant has a right to require that the employer repurchase the securities under a fair valuation formula. This is referred to as the *"put" requirement*. If an employee exercises the put option on distribution—that is, sells the securities back to the plan—the participant must be paid over no more than five years, and during that time the plan must provide adequate security for the payment.

Voting Rights

If the employer company is closely held, plan participants must be given the right to vote with respect to stock held for them in the plan on corporate issues requiring more than a majority of the outstanding common shares. If the employer stock is publicly traded, participants must be permitted to vote on all issues.

Taxation of Employees

In addition to the usual tax advantages for qualified plans, an additional employee tax benefit provided by the Code for a plan holding employer stock is the deferral of taxation of unrealized appreciation. When the plan makes a lump-sum distribution including employer stock, the unrealized appreciation of the stock—that is, the difference between the value of the stock when contributed to or purchased by the trust and its value when distributed to the employee—is not taxable to the employee at the time of the distribution to the extent that it (1) represents nondeductible employee contributions or (2) represents employer contributions, and the participant's entire account is distributed within one taxable year as a result of death, the attainment of age 59½, or the employee's separation from the service of the employer.

This means that the taxable amount of a lump-sum distribution from a stock bonus plan does not include unrealized appreciation of employer securities if the recipient is entitled to the special tax treatment for lump-sum distributions in general. The unrealized appreciation is taxable only when the employee or other recipient sells the securities at a later date. The unrealized appreciation amount is taxable as a capital gain when the stock is sold.

Deductibility of Contributions

As indicated above, the employer can deduct a contribution to a stock bonus plan in the form of employer securities as well as cash. Deductions for contributions can be taken even if there are no current or accumulated profits. The deduction limit is the same as that for a profit-sharing plan—15 percent of covered payroll.

Employee Stock Ownership Plan (ESOP)

The ESOP is a stock bonus plan with an important additional feature: If certain requirements are met, the plan can be used by the employer company as a means of raising funds on a tax-favored basis. The funds can be used for any corporate purposes, which can include acquiring the assets or stock of another company.

In effect, an ESOP allows an employer to indirectly borrow money from a bank and repay the loan with fully deductible repayment amounts. The repayment amounts are deductible in full because they are structured as contributions to an ESOP; normally, only the interest portion of a loan repayment would be tax deductible.

FIGURE 22-2

How an ESOP is Used by an Employer
To Obtain Financing with Tax-Deductible
Loan Repayments

This bit of tax magic (see Figure 22-2) is accomplished by first having the plan trustee borrow money from a bank or other lender. The borrowed money is then used to purchase a block of employer stock from the employer. Shares of this stock also will subsequently be allocated to participants' accounts in the ESOP as plan contributions are made. The employer makes periodic plan contributions to the ESOP and obtains a tax deduction for them. These plan contributions are designed to be enough to enable the plan trustee to gradually repay the loan to the bank. The net result is that the employer immediately receives the full proceeds of the bank loan and in effect pays off the loan through tax-deductible contributions to the plan on behalf of plan participants.

Because the ESOP normally has no financial status independent of the employer, the employer usually must guarantee the loan to the bank. If the plan gives collateral for the loan, the collateral may consist only of qualifying employer securities.

Contribution Formulas and Accounts

An ESOP's contribution allocation formula may not be integrated with Social Security because plan allocations must be based on total compensation. In other respects, contribution formulas and participants' accounts are handled in the same manner as for the stock bonus plan described earlier.

Deductibility of Contributions

The rules for contribution deductibility for an ESOP are somewhat different from those for a stock bonus plan or profit-sharing plan. If employer contributions to the ESOP are applied to the repayment of a loan, amounts applied by the plan to repay the loan principal are deductible by the employer up to a limit of 25 percent of compensation of employees covered under the plan. Amounts used to repay interest are deductible without any percentage limit.

Plan Distributions

The distribution rules, voting rights, and taxation considerations regarding ESOP distributions are the same as those discussed earlier in connection with stock bonus plans.

Diversification Requirement

To reduce investment risks, participants in ESOPs who have reached age 55 with ten years of service are entitled to an annual election requiring the employer to diversify investment in the participant's account. The plan must offer at least three investment options, other than employer stock, to the participant for diversification purposes.

Creating a Market for Closely Held Stock

In small companies, it is often important for shareholders to find a market for their stock for financial and estate planning purposes. Many types of plans have been designed to enable the use of company funds for purchasing stock, such as stock redemption and corporate-owned life insurance plans. An ESOP or stock bonus plan can also be helpful for this purpose. The shareholder can sell stock to the plan during lifetime or at death, generally with favorable tax results. These techniques involve various complexities and must be designed with some care.

STUDY QUESTIONS

1. a. What is a profit-sharing plan?
   b. Explain how the eligibility and vesting requirements of profit-sharing plans differ from the eligibility and vesting requirements of pension plans.

2. a. Describe the two types of contribution formulas that can be used for a profit-sharing plan.
   b. Why is a formula approach more attractive to employees?

3. a. Explain the importance of the allocation formula in a profit-sharing plan.
   b. What is the usual allocation formula?

4. Explain how the allocation formula of a profit-sharing plan may be integrated with Social Security.

5. a. What is the maximum amount that an employer can deduct for contributions to a profit-sharing plan?
   b. What is the maximum annual addition to any participant's account in a profit-sharing plan?

6. Explain the ramifications of participant-directed investments.

7. a. To what extent are preretirement withdrawals allowed from profit-sharing plans?
   b. Describe the restrictions on withdrawals of employer contributions from profit-sharing plans.

8. a. What incidental benefits are allowed in profit-sharing plans?
   b. What limitations are placed on incidental life insurance benefits?

9. a. What are the typical features of savings (thrift) plans?
   b. What are the advantages and disadvantages of savings plans?

10. a. Describe the characteristics of a stock bonus plan.
    b. How do ESOPs differ from stock bonus plans?

401(k) and Other Salary Savings Plans

SALARY SAVINGS PLANS IN GENERAL

A *salary savings plan,* as it is called here (there is no single accepted term for these plans), is a plan under which employees are given a choice, or election, to receive a part of their compensation in cash or to contribute it to a qualified plan or similar arrangement under which the amount contributed to the plan is not subject to income taxation in the year in which it is contributed. Instead, income tax on the contributions and investment earnings on those contributions is deferred until actual withdrawals are made by the employee. Amounts contributed by the employee under such an arrangement are sometimes referred to as *elective deferrals.*

In the last decade, such plans have become extremely popular with employers and employees as a result of the trends discussed at the beginning of the preceding chapter, as well as specific advantages of the salary savings approach such as the following:

- No annual funding commitment for the employer except to the extent that the plan requires a matching or formula contribution
- Initial cost to the employer is minimized because elective deferral amounts come out of existing cash payroll
- No long-term liability for employer
- Benefits have high portability to employee—fast vesting, annual or more frequent account valuation, easy for employee to understand how much has accumulated
- Employee has option to save at desired level (or not to save at all)
- Apparent administrative simplicity (although complex plans with directed investment may be as costly to administer as a defined benefit plan)

Many salary savings plans make use of directed investment provisions (where the employee chooses the investments for his or her account, usually among a family of mutual funds), so that the employee's choices regarding savings programs are further enhanced.

The trend toward this type of qualified benefit is not without its disadvantages. Overall, the movement from the traditional pension plan to profit-sharing and salary savings approaches, however inevitable, probably results in a reduction in potential retirement income for employees, although employees who change jobs frequently (an increasing category of employees) may do better with the newer types of arrangement, as long as they do not dissipate their account accumulations before retirement. Many mobile workers, however, tend to spend distributions from profit-sharing or salary savings plans when they change jobs, particularly if the distribution is relatively small. Another emerging problem, in the case of plans using directed investment provisions, is that employees tend not to make good investment allocations in their plan accounts and, overall, may earn less on their money than if the employer chose the investments. Employees who do well with salary savings plans tend to be people who would save wisely and well for retirement even without the plan, thus raising questions as to the social utility of these plans. These problems, along with already well-known demographic problems with Social Security, threaten to haunt American society in the early 21st century as the baby boomers retire. Some time soon, we will have to better address, both individually and as a society, the issue of retirement income adequacy.

Among the general public, the best-known salary savings plan is the 401(k) plan, which is basically a qualified profit-sharing plan with an elective deferral feature. In addition, there are several other plan types (SIMPLEs, 403(b) tax-deferred annuity plans, and Section 457 plans) that, although not qualified plans, provide elective deferrals and have much the same income tax and other consequences for the participants. These plans are discussed together in this chapter because of their practical similarity, but the student must be careful to note that they all have different rules and all are different from qualified plans.

SECTION 401(K) PLANS (CASH OR DEFERRED PLANS)

A qualified cash or deferred profit-sharing plan, usually referred to as a *401(k) plan* because the special rules for these plans are found in Code Section 401(k), is a qualified profit-sharing or stock bonus plan that incorporates an option for participants to put money into the plan or receive it as taxable cash compensation. In other words, a 401(k) plan differs from a regular profit-sharing plan in that employees can participate in deciding how much of their compensation is deferred. Amounts contributed to the plan are not federal income taxable to participants until they are withdrawn; this is a significant advantage over contributions to a savings plan, which are taxable to the employee before contribution to the plan. However, 401(k) amounts for which the employee can elect to receive either cash or a plan contribution—elective deferrals—are subject to an annual limit of $9,500, indexed for inflation (2000 figure is $10,500).

A 401(k) plan can be an independent plan or the 401(k) feature can be included with a regular profit-sharing, savings, or stock bonus plan of the employer. The plan can be designed in a number of ways to combine both employer and employee contributions, or the entire plan can be funded through salary reductions by employees.

Eligible Employers

Section 401(k) plans can be adopted only by private employers, including tax-exempt organizations. They are not available to government employers. As discussed later in this chapter, government employers may be eligible to adopt Section 403(b) or Section 457 plans to provide results somewhat similar to 401(k) plans.

Advantages and Disadvantages

Section 401(k) plans are currently very attractive to employees. First, they have the basic attraction of all qualified plans—they provide a tax-deferred savings medium. But 401(k) plans have an additional advantage by giving employees an opportunity to choose the amount of deferral according to their individual need for savings. From the employee's viewpoint, a 401(k) plan appears much like an individual IRA, but with additional advantages: The 401(k) plan has higher contribution limits than an IRA, in certain cases it provides special averaging on qualifying lump-sum withdrawals, and the withdrawal provisions during employment are slightly less restrictive.

From the employer's viewpoint, 401(k) plans are favorable because the entire plan can be funded through salary reductions by employees. Thus, the plan provides no direct additional compensation costs to the employer. Because of the popularity of the plan with employees, partly due to good publicity for these plans in the media, the employer can obtain employee goodwill with this type of plan at a relatively low cost. There are also some actual dollar savings in using the 401(k) type of design, because salary reductions by employees may reduce employer expense for workers' compensation and unemployment compensation insurance by reducing the payroll subject to those taxes.

The 401(k) type of design has some disadvantages, but in reviewing these it is important always to ask disadvantages to whom and disadvantages compared with what? First of all, the $9,500 (indexed) annual limit on elective deferrals is lower than that for other types of qualified plan contributions. However, as a practical matter, this limit primarily affects highly compensated employees. Another disadvantage is that a 401(k) plan is a qualified plan and as such is much more complicated than simply leaving savings up to individual employees, either through individual IRAs or otherwise. Also, the 401(k) plan is a qualified profit-sharing plan, not a pension plan, so the employer's deduction is limited to 15 percent of the covered payroll. That is, the total of the employer contribution and nontaxable employee salary reductions cannot exceed 15 percent of covered payroll. Generally speaking, integration of a 401(k) formula with Social Security is not possible, but the 401(k) nondiscrimination rules nevertheless permit significant discrimination in favor of higher-paid employees. Section 401(k) plans are more difficult to administer than regular qualified plans because of the additional rules (discussed later) that must be satisfied. Deferral amounts must be 100 percent vested; thus, there is no opportunity for the employer to save on plan costs by making use of employee forfeitures on Section 401(k) deferral amounts. Finally, distributions to employees prior to termination of employment are more restrictive than for a regular qualified plan. However, these restrictions are more liberal than those for an IRA.

Salary-Reduction 401(k) Plan

The regulations permit a 401(k) plan to be funded entirely through employee elections to reduce salary by a specified amount and contribute the reduced amount to the plan. Most plans are structured this way. The major appeal of this approach is that the plan can be funded based on existing salary scales without any specific additional costs to the employer. Also, the plan can be described to employees as being somewhat like an IRA.

For purposes of the 15 percent deduction limit and the annual-additions limit of Section 415(c), salary reductions are treated as employer contributions to the plan. However, the annual-additions 25 percent limit is applied to the gross salary before salary reductions.

■ **EXAMPLE**

Suppose an employer has two employees whose gross salaries and salary-reduction contributions to a 401(k) plan for a given year are as follows:

	Gross Salary	Salary Reduction Elected	Salary after Reduction
Pat	$21,000	$1,000	$20,000
Mike	31,000	1,000	30,000

Neither participant exceeds the $9,500 (as indexed; 2000: $10,500) limit on elective deferrals. The deduction limit for plan contributions in this case is 15 percent of the payroll of reduced salaries—here, 15 percent of $50,000, or $7,500, which is well in excess of the $2,000 actually contributed to the plan. The annual-additions limit for each participant is 25 percent of their gross salary, or $30,000 if less. For example, for Pat, the annual-additions limit is 25 percent of $21,000. or $5,250. Note that for both Pat and Mike the annual-additions limit is lower than the indexed $9,500 elective deferral limit, indicating how little impact this limit has on lower-income employees. (See Chapter 25 for further discussion of the annual additions limit.)

Salary reductions must be elected by employees before compensation is earned; that is, before they render the services for which compensation is paid. If elections are made after compensation has been earned, the doctrine of constructive receipt prevents the employee from excluding the salary reduction from taxable income. The regulations indicate that salary reductions must be made before the beginning of the calendar year for which the reduction is effective.

Employer Matching Contributions

Under this approach, participating employees can elect salary reductions, with the employer making a matching contribution to the plan. The employer share can be dollar-for-dollar, or some specified fraction of the employee's contribution. Matching can be limited to a specified percentage of each employee's compensation. For example, a plan might provide that an employee can elect salary reductions up to 6 percent of compensation, with the employer contributing an additional 1 percent of compensation for each 2 percent of employee salary reduction.

A significant advantage to this approach is that employer matching encourages plan participation by lower-paid employees. This helps to meet the qualification tests for 401(k) plans—the actual deferral percentage tests discussed later.

Employer Profit-Sharing Contributions

The plan also may provide for additional employer contributions not related to salary reductions by employees. These contributions can be completely discretionary or subject to a formula, as in the case of a regular profit-sharing plan. These contributions can be allocated in any manner permitted in a profit-sharing plan, including a simple uniform percentage of the participant's compensation as well as integration with Social Security or an age-weighted or cross-tested approach.

Employee After-Tax Contributions

The plan may permit employees to make additional after-tax contributions to the plan—that is, contributions not subject to the elective deferral rules and subject to income tax. These contributions are treated like employee contributions to a thrift or savings plan, discussed earlier.

Coverage Requirements

Because a 401(k) plan is a qualified profit-sharing plan, it must meet all the eligibility and coverage requirements discussed earlier for qualified plans in general. However, substantial additional participation by lower-paid employees may indirectly be required to meet the actual deferral percentage requirements applicable under Section 401(k) as discussed below.

Vesting of Employee Accounts

Vesting requirements in a 401(k) plan may depend on the source or identity of the plan contributions.

- Nontaxable employee salary reductions or elective deferrals made under a Section 401(k) cash or deferral option must be immediately 100 percent vested.
- Any after-tax employee contributions must be 100 percent immediately vested, as in qualified savings or thrift plans, discussed earlier.

■ Employer contributions to the plan must meet the usual vesting rules for qualified plans, discussed in Chapter 19. That is, the plan must have a vesting schedule for employer contributions that at least meets one of the ERISA minimum vesting standards (five-year vesting or three- to seven-year vesting).

$9,500 Limit on Elective Deferrals

Code Section 402(g) imposes a $9,500 annual limit on elective deferrals for each plan participant. The limit is imposed on the total of elective deferrals under all 401(k) plans, Section 403(b) tax-deferred annuity plans, and SIMPLEs covering the participant. The plan may not permit elective deferral contributions in excess of this limit. The $9,500 limit is adjusted for cost-of-living changes (2000: $10,500).

Actual Deferral Percentage (ADP) Tests

It has long been recognized that because higher-paid employees have more discretionary income and, in particular, more income to save, any qualified plan that allows employees to choose deferral or cash will be used disproportionately by higher-paid employees. The concept of cash or deferral plans has existed for a long time, but until Congress enacted Section 401(k) in 1978, these plans were not permitted by statute because of this potential discrimination problem. The most important provision of Section 401(k) is a series of tests designed to prevent disproportionate use of these plans by higher-paid employees. These are the actual deferral percentage (ADP) tests.

These tests are in the nature of an additional nondiscrimination rule that must be met by 401(k) plans in addition to the usual rules for qualified plans. A qualified 401(k) plan must meet one of the following two tests in actual operation:

1. The ADP for eligible highly compensated employees must not be more than the ADP of all other eligible employees multiplied by 1.25 (i.e., it must not exceed this percentage by more than 25 percent).
2. The ADP for eligible highly compensated employees must not exceed the lesser of (a) 200 percent of the ADP of all eligible nonhighly compensated employees or (b) the ADP for all eligible nonhighly compensated employees plus 2 percentage points.

The ADP for a given year is

$$\frac{\text{Employer contribution to plan for employee (or salary reduction)}}{\text{Employee's compensation}}$$

This amount is computed for each employee and averaged for each of the two groups (highly compensated, non–highly compensated).

A few examples will illustrate the operation of the ADP tests better than any extended explanation.

■ **EXAMPLE 1:**

10 percent of compensation bonus which the employee can take as cash or as a contribution (deferral) to the 401(k) plan; only employee A is highly compensated.

Employee	Compensation	Cash	Deferral	ADP
A	$30,000	$1,350	$1,650	5.5%
B	15,000	750	750	5
C	10,000	600	400	4

Test 1 is satisfied; ADP for highly compensated (A only) is 5.5%; ADP for non–highly compensated is 4.5% (average of 4% and 5%); 1.25 times 4.5% is 5.625%.

■ **EXAMPLE 2:**

6 percent of compensation bonus; D, E, and F are highly compensated.

Employee	Compensation	Cash	Deferral	ADP
D	$100,000	$ 0	$6,000	6%
E	80,000	0	4,800	6
F	60,000	0	3,600	6
G	40,000	800	1,600	4
H	30,000	600	1,200	4
I	20,000	400	800	4

Plan fails test 1 (1.25 × 4% is less than 6%) but passes test 2 (ADP for highly compensated is no more than two percentage points greater and less than two times 4%).

These examples are simplified for illustrative purposes. In actual practice, the ADP for non–highly compensated employees is generally determined for the preceding year to simplify administration. There are also "safe harbor" approaches to plan design that can provide simplified administration and compliance with nondiscrimination tests.

Designing a Plan To Meet the ADP Tests

Obviously, it is critical to design the 401(k) plan so that the ADP tests are met; otherwise the plan will fail to qualify and all tax benefits will be lost. Fortunately, it is not as difficult as plan designers once believed and disqualifications are rare. Some of the methods used to ensure compliance are as follows:

- *Mandatory deferral.* For example, an employer contributes 5 percent of compensation for all employees that must be deferred and allows an additional 2 percent under a cash or deferral option. This plan will always meet the second ADP test.
- *Limiting deferral by the higher paid.* This approach involves administrative problems. The highly compensated group must be identified and deferral must be monitored, with a mechanism to stop deferrals at an appropriate point during the year if necessary. Alternatively, excess deferrals for highly compensated employees can be computed at the end of the year and corrective distributions, including interest earnings, made to affected employees. Such corrective distributions are income-taxable to the recipients and must be made within 2½ months after the end of the plan year to avoid an additional penalty tax. Instead of cash distributions if the plan permits after-tax contributions, these excess amounts can be retained in the plan and recharacterized as after-tax contributions within 2½ months after the plan year. Related matching contributions can be forfeited and generally cannot be distributed.
- *Counting on the popularity of the 401(k) approach.* In actual practice, many companies find that participation by lower-paid employees is substantial. It is not unusual for 75 percent of all employees of an organization to participate in the plan. This may eliminate the problem without any special mechanisms coming into effect.

Because of the ADP tests, not every employer is suitable for a 401(k) plan. Because substantial participation by lower-paid employees is necessary, pay levels must be reasonably high in the organization, at least high enough so that some amount of retirement saving is possible by most of the employees.

Distribution Restrictions

Account balances attributable to amounts subject to the cash or deferral election—the 401(k) amounts—are subject to special distribution restrictions. These amounts may not be distributed earlier than on retirement, death, disability, separation from service, hardship, age 59½, or termination of the plan. Also, as with any qualified plan distribution, the 10 percent early withdrawal penalty applies. Amounts attributable to matching and profit-sharing contributions can generally be withdrawn according to the rules for profit-sharing plans discussed earlier.

The income taxation of distributions from 401(k) plans, including both 401(k) and non-40l(k) amounts in the plan, follows the usual rules for qualified plan distributions. The qualified plan rules relating to loans and plan distributions are discussed in detail in Chapter 24.

Social Security and Employment Taxes

Section 401(k) plans are an exception to the general rule that contributions by an employer to a qualified plan are free of federal employment taxes (Social Security [FICA] and unemployment tax (FUTA)). The popularity of 401(k) plans when first introduced caused such a noticeable reduction in federal employment tax revenues that Congress made special rules for 401(k) plans. Under current law, 401(k) amounts subject to an employee election to defer instead of receiving cash (elective deferrals) are subject to FICA and FUTA, whether these are contributed through salary reduction or employer bonuses. FICA and FUTA do not apply to non-40l(k) amounts—matching or profit-sharing contributions made by the employer to the plan that are not subject to elective deferrals.

In general, state unemployment compensation and workers' compensation payments are not required for either employer contributions or salary reductions in a 401(k) plan.

SIMPLEs

In an attempt to increase coverage of employer-sponsored plans, Congress has provided certain simplified arrangements that are not qualified plans but provide employers and employees some of the same benefits as qualified plans. One such arrangement, structured as a salary savings plan somewhat similar to a 401(k) plan, is the SIMPLEs (savings incentive match plans for employees). SIMPLEs are employer-sponsored plans under which plan contributions are made to the participating employees' IRA's. SIMPLEs also can be part of a 401(k) plan, but this arrangement is somewhat more complicated than a SIMPLE/IRA. Tax-deferred contribution levels are generally significantly higher than the $2,000/$4,000 deductible limit for individual IRAs (Chapter 27). SIMPLEs feature employee salary reduction contributions (elective deferrals) coupled with employer matching contributions.

SIMPLEs are easy to adopt and generally simple to administer, while providing employees with the tax-deferred retirement savings benefits of a qualified plan. However, qualified plans potentially can provide higher contribution levels. An employee's salary reductions under a SIMPLE can be no greater than $6,000 annually.

Eligible Employers

Any employer may adopt a SIMPLE if it meets the following requirements:

- The employer has 100 or fewer employees.
- The employer does not maintain a qualified plan, 403(b) plan, or SEP except for a collectively bargained plan.

Advantages and Disadvantages

SIMPLEs can be adopted by completing a simple IRS form (Form 5304-SIMPLE or 5305-SIMPLE) rather than by the complex procedure required for qualified plans. Benefits of a SIMPLE/IRA are totally portable by employees because funding consists entirely of IRAs for each employee and employees are always 100 percent vested in their benefits. Employees own and control their accounts, even after they terminate employment with the original employer. Individual IRA accounts allow participants to benefit from good investment results, as well as run the risk of bad results. As with a 401(k) plan, a SIMPLE can be funded in part through salary reductions by employees.

However, SIMPLEs have some disadvantages. As with profit-sharing or salary savings plans in general, employees cannot rely on a SIMPLE to provide an adequate retirement benefit. First, benefits are not significant unless the employee makes significant regular salary reduction contributions. Such regular contributions are not a requirement of the plan. Furthermore, employees who enter the plan at older ages have only a limited number of years remaining prior to retirement to build up their SIMPLE accounts. Also, annual contributions generally are restricted to lesser amounts than would be available in a qualified plan. SIMPLE contributions are limited by the maximum $6,000 (as indexed; 2000: $6,000) salary reduction permitted for each participant (plus the employer's matching contribution). This contrasts with the $9,500 (as indexed; 2000: $10,500) annual salary reduction permitted for 401(k) or 403(b) plans. Distributions from SIMPLEs/IRAs are not eligible for the 5-year (or 10-year) averaging provisions available for certain qualified plan distributions. (Five-year averaging is repealed for years after 1999, but 10-year averaging is available even after 1999.)

Design Features of SIMPLEs

The following are the most significant Internal Revenue Code requirements for SIMPLEs (Section 408(p):

- The employer must have 100 or fewer employees (only employees with at least $5,000 in compensation for the prior year are counted) on any day in the year.
- The employer may not sponsor another qualified plan, 403(b) plan, or SEP under which service is accrued or contributions made for the same year the SIMPLE is in effect, except for a plan covering exclusively collective bargaining employees.
- Contributions may be made to each employee's IRA or to the employee's 401(k) account. In effect, there are thus two types of SIMPLEs—those that include the 401(k) requirements and those funded through IRAs. SIM-

PLEs meeting the 401(k) requirements are rarely adopted and will not be discussed further here.

- Employees who earned at least $5,000 from the employer in the preceding two years and are reasonably expected to earn at least $5,000 in the current year can contribute (through salary reductions) up to $6,000 (as indexed; 2000: $6,000) annually.
- The employer is required to make a contribution equal to either

  a. a dollar-for-dollar matching contribution up to 3 percent of the employee's contribution (the employer can elect a lower percentage, not less than 1 percent, in not more than two out of the past five years) or
  b. 2 percent of compensation for all eligible employees earning at least $5,000 (whether or not they elect salary reductions).

In a SIMPLE/IRA plan, each participating employee maintains an IRA. Employer contributions are made directly to the employee's IRA, as are any employee salary reduction contributions. Employer contributions and employee salary reductions, with the limits discussed above, are not included in the employee's taxable income.

Direct employer contributions to a SIMPLE are not subject to Social Security (FICA) or federal unemployment (FUTA) taxes. However, as with 401(k) plans, employee salary reduction contributions are subject to FICA and FUTA. The impact of state payroll taxes depends on the particular state's laws. Both salary reductions and employer contributions may be exempt from state payroll taxes in some states.

Distributions to employees from a SIMPLE/IRA plan are treated as distributions from an IRA. All the restrictions on IRA distributions apply and the distributions are taxed the same. The taxation of IRA distributions is discussed in Chapter 27.

Installation of a SIMPLE

Installation of a SIMPLE can be very easy. The employer merely completes IRS Form 5304-SIMPLE or Form 5305-SIMPLE. Form 5305-SIMPLE provides for a "designated financial institution" for participant investments, while Form 5304-SIMPLE does not have this provision, which some plan sponsors and participants may find restrictive. Under a SIMPLE, salary reduction elections must be made by employees during a 60-day period prior to January 1 of the year for which the elections are made. The form does not have to be sent to the IRS or other government agency.

The reporting and disclosure requirements for SIMPLEs are simplified if the employer uses Form 5304-SIMPLE or 5305-SIMPLE. The annual report form (5500 series) need not be filed if these forms are used. In other cases, reporting and disclosure requirements are similar to those for a qualified profit-sharing plan.

SECTION 403(B) TAX-DEFERRED ANNUITY PLANS

The 403(b) plan is another specialized plan that is available to some employers as an alternative or supplement to a qualified plan. The 403(b) plan was provided as a result of Congress's concern that employees of tax-exempt organizations might not have adequate qualified plan coverage. Tax-exempt employers may have relatively little money available for employee benefits, and the tax deductibility of a qualified plan does not act as an incentive because the tax-exempt employer pays no federal income taxes. As a result, Congress enacted Code Section 403(b), which, within limits, allows employees of certain tax-exempt organizations to have money set aside for them by salary reductions or direct employer contributions in a tax-deferred plan somewhat similar to a qualified plan.

Section 403(b) plans are an important consideration in designing the benefit program for any tax-exempt employer. However, today many tax-exempt employers have regular qualified plans for their employees, with the Section 403(b) plan being made available as a supplemental retirement or savings program. Tax-exempt, but not government, employers can adopt 401(k) plans as well as 403(b) plans, so such employers may be in a position to choose between the two approaches for salary savings. For most tax-exempts, the 403(b) plan is somewhat more advantageous than a 401(k) plan.

Section 403(b) plans are sometimes referred to as *tax-deferred annuity (TDA) plans* or *tax-sheltered annuities,* but because these terms also can refer to annuities not covered under Section 403(b), the term *Section 403(b) plans* will be used here to avoid confusion.

Eligible Employers

Employees of the following two types of organizations are eligible to adopt Section 403(b) plans:

1. A tax-exempt employer described in Code Section 501(c)(3)—an employer "organized and operated exclusively for religious, charitable, scientific, testing for public safety, literary or educational purposes, or to foster national or international amateur sport competition . . . or for the prevention of cruelty to children or animals." Section 501(c)(3) also requires that the organization benefit the public rather than a private shareholder or individual and that the organization refrain from political campaigning or propaganda to influence legislation.
2. An educational organization with a regular faculty and curriculum and a resident student body that is operated by a state or municipal agency—in other words, a public school or college. This is the only type of government employer that can adopt a 403(b) plan.

Thus, Section 403(b) plans are available to a wide range of familiar non-profit institutions such as churches, private and public schools and colleges, hospitals, and charitable organizations.

To participate in a Section 403(b) plan of an eligible employer, the participant must be a full- or part-time employee. This is significant because tax-exempt organizations often have ties with persons who are independent contractors rather than employees. For example, many physicians on a hospital staff technically are not employees but rather independent contractors. A person is an employee when the employer exercises control or has the right to control the person's activities as to what is done and when, where, and how it is done. The question of employee status also affects federal income tax withholding, employment taxes (Social Security and federal unemployment), and participation in other fringe benefit plans of the employer. If the employer wishes to cover a person under a Section 403(b) plan, it must at least treat that person consistently as an employee for all these purposes.

To be eligible for a Section 403(b) plan, a public school employee must perform services related directly to the educational mission. The employee can be a clerical or custodial employee, as well as a teacher or principal; a political officeholder is eligible only if the person has educational training or experience.

Coverage and Participation Tests

Section 403(b) plans to which the employer makes contributions are subject to relatively complicated nondiscrimination requirements. Employer matching contributions are also subject to the tests described in the discussion of savings and thrift plans. However, if the plan is funded entirely through employee salary reductions, as many plans are, these requirements do not apply. There is a simpler nondiscrimination requirement for salary reductions, however: if the plan permits salary reductions for any employee, then it must permit salary reductions of more than $200 for any other employee, except for those covered under a Section 457 plan or Section 401(k) plan or under another 403(b) plan. Certain part-time and student employees can be excluded.

A Section 403(b) plan (except for a church-related, public school, or public college plan) is covered under the age and service provisions of ERISA Section 202, which are the same as the analogous age and service code provisions for qualified plans. Thus, if a Section 403(b) plan uses age or service eligibility, these can be no greater than age 21 and one year of service. However, age and service requirements are rarely used in Section 403(b) plans.

The Limits on the Employee's Annual Contributions

Determining the maximum amount that can be contributed for an employee under a 403(b) plan is quite complicated. There are at least three steps in the computation, and if the plan is based on employee salary reductions, as most plans are, there are five basic steps summarized following.

1. The 403(b) annual exclusion allowance. The starting point in the computation is a provision unique to 403(b) plans, the annual exclusion allowance. The formula for the annual exclusion allowance for an employee is

- 20 percent of the participant's includable compensation from the employer multiplied by
- the employee's total years of service for the employer, minus
- amounts contributed to the plan in prior years that were excluded from the employee's income.

Includable compensation in general is gross compensation including salary reductions. For example, if a participant has a salary of $30,000 and elects a salary reduction of $5,000 to the 403(b) plan, his includable compensation for purposes of this formula is $30,000, even though his taxable compensation is only $25,000.

The third item—the amount subtracted from the 20 percent times years of service amount—must include contributions by the employer to regular qualified plans on behalf of the employee. If the qualified plan is a defined-benefit plan, the amount deemed to be contributed for the employee is to be determined under recognized actuarial principles or under a formula provided in the regulations.

2. The Section 415 annual additions limit. The determination of the maximum 403(b) contribution for higher-income employees is complicated by the fact that although a Section 403(b) plan is not a qualified plan, the Section 415 limitation for defined-contribution plans applies. Thus, the annual addition to any participant's account cannot exceed the lesser of 25 percent of compensation or $30,000, even if the exclusion allowance would produce a higher figure.

■ **EXAMPLE**

Doctor Staph is an employee of the Tibia Hospital and has annual compensation of $200,000 this year. She has four prior years of service for Tibia Hospital, during which the hospital has contributed $5,000 to her account in a Section 403(b) plan. No amounts have been contributed to any qualified plan on her behalf. Her exclusion allowance for the Section 403(b) plan this year is 20 percent of her includable compensation of $200,000 times her five years of service, or a total of $200,000, less contributions for prior years of $5,000, or $195,000. However, since this exceeds the applicable Section 415 limit of $30,000, $30,000 is the most that can be contributed to the Section 403(b) plan for Doctor Staph this year.

If the participant has more than one employer, all Section 403(b) plans of all employers must be combined for purposes of the Section 415 limit. However, if the employee participates in a regular qualified plan or plans as well as the Section 403(b) plan, it usually is not necessary to combine the qualified plans and the 403(b) plan for purposes of the Section 415 limit [Section 415(g) and Regulations Section 1.415-8].

3. Section 415 catch-up alternatives. The third step relates to a special feature in applying the Section 415 limit to a 403(b) plan. The Section 415 limit (25 percent/$30,000) may not be exceeded in any year, while the regular exclusion allowance is increased by prior service. This works a hardship on long-service employees who have had relatively low Section 403(b) contributions in prior years. Under the regular exclusion allowance, their prior service would otherwise permit large contributions to catch up for past years. For employees of educational institutions, hospitals, and home-health service agencies—but not other employers—the Code contains catch-up alternatives to the regular Section 415 limitation that are aimed at long-service employees. Under the catch-up alternatives, the 25 percent of compensation limit under Section 415 is not always applied, thus permitting Section 403(b) contributions in excess of 25 percent of the current year's compensation. However, in no event can the $30,000 limitation be exceeded, even under the catch-up alternatives.

4. Salary reduction limitation. The fourth step in determining the maximum 403(b) contribution applies to salary reduction plans. For such plans, there is a limit of $9,500 on annual salary reductions for each participant. This limit applies to the total (for each employee) of Section 403(b) salary reductions, SIMPLEs, and 401(k) salary reductions under plans of all the employee's employers. The $9,500 is indexed for cost-of-living increases (2000: $10,500). The $9,500 limit does not apply to direct employer contributions to the participant's account; thus, the total can be more than $9,500, as long as the exclusion allowance and the Section 415 limit are not exceeded.

The amount contributed to the plan by a salary reduction will not be subject to income taxes if the salary-reduction election is made properly. For these amounts to avoid taxation, the salary reductions must be made under the same rules discussed in connection with 401(k) plans concerning the timing of the election. As with 401(k) salary reductions, although the amounts are not currently subject to income tax to the participant, they are subject to Social Security and federal unemployment (FICA and FUTA) taxes.

5. Salary reduction catch-up. As a final step in the process of determining the maximum 403(b) annual contribution, there is a further catch-up provision to raise the $9,500 salary reduction limit for employees having at least 15 years of service with the employer. The catch-up limit [Code Section 402(g)] allows additional salary reductions above the $9,500 limit (as indexed) equal to the least of

- $3,000;
- $15,000 less prior catch-up contributions; or
- $5,000 times the employee's years of service with the employer, less all prior salary reductions with that employer.

Types of Investments for 403(b) Plans

Section 403(b) plan funds must be invested in either

- annuity contracts purchased by the employer from an insurance company or
- mutual fund shares held in custodial accounts [referred to as *403(b)(7) accounts*].

Many different types of annuities may be used for Section 403(b) plans. Thus, the annuities can be individual or group contracts, level or flexible premium annuities, and fixed dollar or variable annuities. Face-amount certificates providing a fixed maturity value and a schedule of redemptions are also permitted. In addition, the annuity contract may provide incidental amounts of life insurance for the employee; however, the value of such insurance is taxable to the employee each year under the PS 58 table. The annuity contracts can provide the employee a choice of broad types of investment strategy—for example, a choice between investment in a fixed-income fund and an equity-type fund. However, if the contract gives the employee specific powers to direct the investments of the fund, the IRS will regard the employee as in control of the account for tax purposes and the employee will be currently taxed on the fund's investment income.

Annuity contracts used in Section 403(b) plans must be nontransferable. This means that they cannot be sold or assigned as collateral to any person other than the insurance company issuing the contract. However, the employee is permitted to designate a beneficiary for death benefits or survivorship annuities. Because similar restrictions apply to annuities transferred to participants from qualified plans, most insurance companies use the same standard provisions for both types of annuity contracts.

Mutual fund accounts [403(b)(7) accounts] are used in 403(b) plans much as they are in 401(k) plans, and can give participants the opportunity to allocate their accounts according to their own investment strategies by providing a family of funds with different investment approaches.

Distributions and Loans from Section 403(b) Plans

Distributions from Section 403(b) plans are subject to rules similar to those applicable to qualified 401(k) plans; however, there are differences in detail. Withdrawal restrictions are quite complicated. In general, withdrawals are not permitted from 403(b)(7) custodial accounts (mutual funds) or from any salary-reduction 403(b) account except for withdrawals after age 59½, or upon death, disability, separation from service, or financial hardship. These withdrawal restrictions technically do not apply to annuity-type 403(b) accounts funded by direct employer contributions rather than salary reductions. However, this "loophole" is of limited usefulness because all early withdrawals are subject to the 10 percent early distribution penalty of Code Section 72(t). As discussed in Chapter 24, this penalty applies to most distributions prior to age 59½ from qualified plans, IRAs, and Section 403(b) plans. The penalty applies even to distributions that are permitted; for example, many hardship distributions from Section 403(b) plans will be subject to the penalty.

Other qualified plan distribution rules also apply to Section 403(b) plans. Distributions must begin by April 1 of the calendar year following the attainment of age 70½ or actual retirement, if later. The minimum annual distribution thereafter is a level amount spread over the participant's life expectancy or over the joint life expectancies of the participant and beneficiary, as discussed in Chapter 24.

Loans

Section 403(b) plans with either annuity or mutual-fund accounts may permit loans on the same basis as regular qualified plans. Plan loans are discussed in Chapter 24. Because of the restrictions on Section 403(b) distributions, plan loan provisions are particularly important to employees and should be considered in any Section 403(b) plan.

Taxation of Section 403(b) Plans

A Section 403(b) plan provides the same general tax advantages as a qualified plan. Thus, plan contributions within the limits of the exclusion allowance are not currently taxable to the employee. Investment earnings on plan funds are also not currently taxable.

However, the taxation of distributions from Section 403(b) plans is somewhat less favorable than for qualified plans. The full amount of any distribution from a Section 403(b) plan, whether during employment or at termination of service, is fully taxable as ordinary income to the participant, except for any cost basis the participant has in the distribution. A cost basis could result if the employee paid tax previously on any amount contributed to the plan or reported PS 58 costs if the plan provides incidental life insurance. There are no averaging or capital-gain provisions for the taxable amount of a distribution from a Section 403(b) plan. The bad tax effect of having all of the income taxable in a single year can be alleviated only by having a periodic form of payout from the plan. A periodic distribution from a Section 403(b) plan is taxed under the annuity rules the same as an annuity from a qualified plan.

Death benefits are also subject to somewhat less favorable income tax treatment than death benefits from qualified plans. The averaging and capital gain provisions are not available to the beneficiary. Section 403(b) death benefits are included in the gross estate of the deceased participant for federal estate tax purposes. However, if they are paid to a spouse, they escape estate taxation under the unlimited marital deduction. In other cases, there may be no estate tax because the tax applies only to relatively large estates (those over about $600,000, subject to increase to $1,000,000 by 2007).

Regulatory and Administrative Aspects

A Section 403(b) plan is considered a pension plan, rather than a welfare benefit plan, for purposes of the reporting and disclosure provisions. The reporting and disclosure requirements applicable are similar to those applicable to qualified plans, as discussed in Chapter 26. However, as with qualified plans, Section 403(b) plans of government units and churches that have not elected to come under ERISA are exempt from these requirements, unless mutual funds rather than annuity contracts are used for funding. If a Section 403(b) plan is purely of the salary reduction type and does not include any direct employer contributions, the reporting and disclosure and other regulatory requirements are greatly reduced.

SECTION 457 PLANS

These plans are primarily used by government employers. Government employers may have qualified plans for employees, except that they are not eligible to adopt 401(k) plans. And, only a very limited category of government employers (public schools) can adopt 403(b) plans. Thus, the opportunity to offer employees a plan of the salary savings type is very limited. Section 457 provides the only alternative in designing a salary savings arrangement for most government employers. Plans designed under this Code provision are not qualified plans; moreover the rules are in many cases very different from those discussed previously in this chapter. The rules were enacted by Congress primarily to forestall perceived abuses in retirement plans of government employers rather than to benefit government employees, so they are somewhat lacking in flexibility or generosity.

Eligible Employers

Section 457 applies to government employers and to employers that are exempt from federal income tax. However, these plans are not much used by private tax-exempt organizations because better alternatives such as 401(k) plans are available.

Limit on Amount

The amount deferred annually by an employee under these plans cannot exceed the lesser of $7,500 or one-third of the employee's taxable compensation, reduced by any salary reductions under a Section 403(b) plan or SIMPLE. The $7,500 limit is indexed for inflation (2000: $8,000). This ceiling can be increased in each of the last three years before normal retirement age, to the lesser of $15,000 or the regular ceiling plus the total amount of potential deferral that was not used in prior years. If an individual has more than one employer, the total deferred for all employers must not exceed these limits.

Other Rules

- Elections to defer compensation under Section 457 are made monthly, under an agreement entered into before the beginning of the month.
- For government employers, employee salary deferrals must be placed in a trust fund or custodial account. However, for private tax-exempt employers, the plan cannot be funded—all deferred compensation and income therefrom remains the property of the employer.
- Plan distributions cannot be made before separation from service or "unforeseeable emergency."
- Plan distributions must meet the minimum distribution rules of Section 401(a)(9) regarding beginning date (April 1 after age 70½ or retirement—see Chapter 24).
- A special incidental death benefit provision applies—the participant must expect to receive at least two-thirds of the total payout where there is a survivor annuity.
- Plan distributions are taxable in full when received. They are not eligible for five- or ten-year averaging and cannot be rolled over into an IRA.
- There are no specific coverage requirements—the plan can be offered to all employees, or any group of employees, even a single employee. However, for a tax-exempt organization (but not for a government organization) the participation, fiduciary, and other ERISA rules may apply.

If the state or local government employer or tax-exempt employer has a nonqualified deferred-compensation plan that does not comply with Section 457—for example, one that exceeds the limits—then it is treated for tax purposes as a funded plan, whether or not it is actually funded. This means that the deferred amount is includable in the participant's income when there is no substantial risk of forfeiture. This does, however, provide some opportunity for governments and tax-exempts to design plans for top executives above the $7,500 limit by including forfeiture provisions.

STUDY QUESTIONS

1. Describe a qualified Section 401(k) plan. Include the following points in your description.
   a. What are the advantages and disadvantages of a 401(k) plan?
   b. What are the vesting requirements in a 401(k) plan?
   c. What is the limit on elective deferrals under a 401(k) plan?

2. Fixemup, P.C., is a professional corporation for a group of four doctors, two nurses, and one receptionist. The census data for the current year is as follows:

	Salary/Percentage of Stock Ownership	401(k) Contributions
Dr. Able	$90,000/50%	8%
Dr. Baker	85,000/30	8
Dr. Resident	44,000/20	8
Dr. Intern	35,000/0	8
Nurse Marmer	25,000/0	5
Nurse Devries	25,000/0	5
Receptionist Smith	15,000/0	0

   Does the Fixemup, P.C., 401(k) plan meet the ADP test? Explain.

3. What are the major similarities and differences between a SIMPLE/IRA and a qualified 401(k) plan?

4. Explain the rules for SIMPLE matching contributions.

5. What types of organizations may adopt a 403(b) plan for employees?

6. Ed Greave's salary in his first year of employment with a nonprofit charitable organization is $50,000. He elects a salary reduction under a Section 403(b) plan. What is the maximum salary reduction possible for Ed Greave?

7. Describe the major differences between a salary-reduction type Section 403(b) plan and a qualified Section 401(k) plan.

8. What types of organizations are subject to Code Section 457?

9. Compare a 457 plan for a government employer with a qualified Section 401(k) plan.

Qualified Plan Distributions and Loans

MANAGEMENT ISSUES IN DESIGN OF DISTRIBUTION PROVISIONS

Employee interests are best served by maximum flexibility in plan distribution provisions. However, plan designers may find it necessary to reduce this flexibility somewhat to meet the employer's management objectives.

First of all, flexibility increases administrative complexity and costs. In addition, flexibility can potentially cause cash-flow and liquidity problems to the plan fund. Finally, flexibility can create extremely complex federal income tax problems, due to the inordinately complex rules in this area. The rules are merely summarized in this chapter, but the reader will undoubtedly note that even this summary is startlingly complicated. The complexity is probably due more to congressional inattention to this issue rather than to any clear policy rationale. Simplification is on the congressional agenda.

The complex distribution rules are management's problem as well as the participant's because employees often ask employers about the tax treatment of a plan distribution. An employer's wrong answer likely will subject the employer to liability to reimburse the employee for any excess tax payments that result. And management cannot simply "stonewall" on this issue by refusing to advise employees on tax treatment of distributions because employee resentment as well as legal liability may result that can negate the value of the plan as an employee incentive.

The planner's objective in designing plan distribution provisions is to provide employees with the maximum amount of distribution flexibility that is consistent with management's needs as outlined above. In a small business with limited personnel management resources, this may dictate only very limited distribution flexibility. For example, some smaller plans provide for distributions only in the form of a lump sum at retirement or termination of employment.

Normal Form of Benefit

A qualified plan must specify not only the amount of the benefit but the form of the benefit. In a defined-benefit plan, the *normal form of benefit* is the basic "defined benefit," the form that quantifies the benefit due and provides a standard for calculating equivalent alternative benefits. At one time, the normal form was the form a participant received if he or she did not choose an alternative form, but this is not necessarily true because of joint and survivor provisions.

The normal form in a defined-benefit plan is usually either a straight-life annuity or a life annuity with period certain. A straight-life annuity simply provides periodic (usually monthly) payments for the participant's life. A life annuity with period certain provides periodic payments for the participant's life, but additionally provides that if the participant dies before the end of a specified period of years, payments will be continued until the end of that period to the participant's designated beneficiary. Specified periods of 10, 15, and 20 years are commonly used.

In comparing defined-benefit plans, it must be remembered that straight-life and life annuities with periods certain are not equivalent; a plan providing an annuity of $100 per month for life with period certain as the normal form of benefit provides a significantly larger benefit than a plan providing $100 per month as a straight-life annuity. Period-certain annuities as the normal form of benefit are most commonly found in plans using insurance contracts for funding.

As discussed in Chapter 20, a pension plan must provide a qualified joint and survivor annuity for the participant and spouse automatically to a married participant (unless the participant elects otherwise). To avoid discrimination against single participants, most plans provide that the qualified joint and survivor annuity is "actuarially equivalent" to the normal form. For example, if the normal retirement benefit would be $1,000 per month as a straight-life annuity, the qualified joint and survivor annuity might be something like $800 per month to the participant for life, then $400 per month to the spouse for life. However, the plan can partially or fully subsidize the joint and survivor annuity; for example, it might provide a straight-life annuity of $1,000 per month or a $1,000/$500 joint and survivor annuity. This might be desirable to the employer even though it would discriminate against unmarried participants.

Defined-contribution pension plans can provide an annuity as the normal benefit form. This is particularly common if an insurance contract is used for funding. The amount of the annuity depends on the participant's account balance at retirement, with annuity purchase rates specified in the insurance contract, if any. Optional forms of benefit, particularly a lump sum, are usually provided in defined-contribution plans.

Optional Alternative Forms of Benefit

Participants generally benefit from having a choice of benefit forms as an alternative to the normal form. Participants can then choose a benefit that is structured in accordance with their individual financial needs, family situations, and retirement activities. In defined-benefit plans, the most common alternative forms (assuming a straight-life annuity as the normal form) are, in addition to the qualified joint and survivor annuity that must be offered, (1) joint and survivor annuities for the participant and spouse or other beneficiary, with varying survivorship annuity percentages such as 50 percent, 75 percent, and 100 percent, and (2) annuities for the participant and beneficiary, with varying periods certain, such as 5, 10, 15, or 20 years. The plan also can allow payouts over a fixed period of years without a life contingency. All these options are subject to the limitations described below.

To avoid undesirable or prohibited discrimination among employees in different situations, the plan should provide that any optional benefit is actuarially equivalent to the normal form of benefit. Under Code Section 401(a)(25), the actuarial assumptions used for this purpose must be specified in the plan, either by stating the actuarial interest and other factors or by specifying an equivalency table for the various benefits, to avoid employer discretion in favor of highly compensated employees.

Lump-Sum Option

A lump-sum distribution can provide planning flexibility for participants. Lump-sum distribution provisions are most common in defined-contribution plans; in fact, in a profit-sharing plan, the lump sum is often the only distribution option. However, even a defined-benefit plan can offer a lump-sum option. The Code provides in Section 417(e) that the lump sum must be at least that determined on the basis of interest and mortality factors specified in the Code.

Higher-income participants often would like a lump sum because they have other sources for retirement income and wish to invest their plan funds in riskier, high-return investment vehicles. A defined-contribution plan can be designed to accommodate this need to some extent within the plan, however, by providing participant investment direction. Also, investment results within the plan are enhanced by the tax deferral on plan income and may provide an effective rate of return that the participant cannot match outside of the plan. However, funds cannot be left in the plan indefinitely; distributions must generally begin at age 70½ or retirement, if later.

In some defined-benefit plans, particularly insured plans, the assumptions used for funding are too conservative. For example, a plan may have accumulated $140,000 to fund a benefit of $12,000 per year to a retiree. In many cases, however, it might be possible for a retiree to individually invest $140,000 and receive a better return than $12,000 per year for life. Thus, the retiree might rather have a $140,000 lump sum from the plan fund than the plan's annuity benefit. In some cases, this situation results from bad plan design, while in others it is done deliberately to increase the benefit for key employees. The Code limits the extent to which this can be done by prescribing minimum interest and mortality assumptions.

Distribution Restrictions

Plan distributions can be designed to provide considerable flexibility, but they must be designed within a rather complex network of rules that have been accumulating in the law over many years. These rules are aimed at protecting the financial interests of participants and, more significantly, they are designed to limit the use of qualified plans merely as a tax-sheltered investment medium for key employees. The significant rules are as follows:

- Distinctions between the types of distributions permitted in pension plans as opposed to profit-sharing plans

- Rules preventing employers from unjustly delaying benefit payments
- Minimum distribution requirements
- Early distribution penalties
- Incidental benefit requirements
- Nonalienation rules

Pension versus Profit-Sharing Plans

The IRS generally will not allow a pension plan to pay benefits prior to retirement, early retirement, death, or disability, although some limited cash-out provisions may be allowed in the event of termination of employment prior to these events, as previously discussed. With a profit-sharing plan, there is much more flexibility, and the plan may allow in-service distributions, as discussed in Chapter 22. However, the 10 percent penalty described below may deter employees from making certain withdrawals.

Delaying Benefit Payments

Under Code Section 401(a)(14), all qualified plans must provide for payment not later than the 60th day after the latest of the following three dates:

1. The earlier of age 65 or the plan's normal retirement date
2. The tenth anniversary of the participant's entry into the plan
3. The participant's termination of service with the employer

The plan may allow the participant to elect a payout that begins at a date later than this maximum limit. However, the extent to which a participant can stretch out payments is limited by the rules discussed in the next section.

Minimum Distribution Rules

Congress does not like qualified plans to be used as tax shelters for funds that are not actually needed by participants for retirement income. Therefore, Code Section 401(a)(9) requires that plan distributions begin no later than April 1 of the calendar year following the later of the year in which the employee attains age 70½ or the year of actual retirement. If the employee owns more than 5 percent of the employer, deferral to the actual retirement date is not permitted.

Furthermore, the distribution must be either in a lump sum or a periodic distribution over a specified period. Basically, the distribution must be paid in substantially equal annual amounts over the life of the employee or the joint lives of the employee and a designated beneficiary. Alternatively, the distribution may be made over a stated period that does not exceed the life expectancy of the employee or the life expectancy of the employee and a designated beneficiary. This permits period-certain annuity payouts, as long as the period certain does not exceed the life expectancy limits. A periodic distribution based on an ongoing recalculation of life expectancy is permitted, which tends to stretch out payments somewhat because life expectancy is extended by continuing survival. However, life expectancy can be recalculated no more often than annually. Cost-of-living increases in pension payments to retirees are permitted as long as they are not designed to circumvent the minimum distribution rules.

The minimum distribution rules also have provisions applicable to distributions made to a beneficiary if the employee dies before the entire plan interest is distributed. If distributions to the employee have already begun, the remaining portion of the employee's interest must be distributed at least as rapidly as under the method in effect prior to death. For example, if the employee elected a 20-year period certain annuity and the employee died after ten years, the remaining interest could be distributed in equal annual installments over a term not exceeding ten years. The beneficiary could, however, elect to accelerate these payments.

If the employee dies before distributions have begun, the plan's death benefit must be distributed within five years after the employee's death, with an exception. The five-year restriction is not applicable if (1) any portion of the plan benefit is payable to a designated beneficiary, (2) the beneficiary's interest will be distributed over the life of the beneficiary or over a period not extending beyond the life expectancy of the beneficiary and (3) distributions begin no later than one year after the employee's death. If the designated beneficiary is the surviving spouse, the beginning of the distribution can be delayed to the date on which the employee would have attained age 70½.

Early Distribution Penalty

Code Section 72(t) provides a tax penalty for early distributions from qualified plans. This penalty provision was added by Congress to encourage plan participants to use qualified plans primarily for retirement and not merely for deferral of compensation. The 10 percent penalty tax applies to distributions from a broad range of tax-advantaged retirement plans. As applied to regular qualified plans and 403(b) plans, the penalty applies to all distributions *except* distributions

- made on or after attainment of age 59½;
- made to a beneficiary or employee's estate on or after the employee's death;
- attributable to disability;
- that are part of a series of substantially equal periodic payments made at least annually over the life or life expectancy of the employee, or the joint lives or life expectancies of the employee and beneficiary (separation from service is required);
- made after a separation from service after age 55;

- related to certain tax credit ESOP dividend payments;
- to the extent of medical expenses deductible for the year under Code Section 213, whether or not actually deducted.

The penalty also applies to IRAs and IRA-funded plans (SEPs and SIMPLE/IRAs), with a somewhat different list of exceptions—see Chapter 27. Under this penalty provision, a plan may be permitted to make a distribution to an employee without disqualifying the plan, but the distribution may nevertheless be subject to penalty. For example, many hardship distributions from 401(k) plans or 403(b) tax-deferred annuity plans will be subject to the penalty tax.

Despite the penalty, withdrawals from qualified plans may still be important to participants in many situations—to obtain emergency funds, for example. Therefore, plan designers may wish to provide withdrawals in plans, where permitted, despite the existence of the 10 percent penalty.

Incidental Benefit Requirements

Some types of optional benefit forms provide substantial payments to persons other than the participant after the participant's death—for example, a 20-year-certain annuity with payments continued to a beneficiary. Because these are death benefits, they must be incidental.

Code Section 401(a)(9)(G) and corresponding regulations provide rules for determining whether survivorship benefits are incidental. For example, if a participant has a 10-year life expectancy at retirement, he or she could not elect a 25-year certain annuity because this would result in too much of the expected benefit to be paid as a death benefit. This incidental rule does not apply to a survivor annuity for spouses; thus, for example, a plan could provide a joint and 50 percent survivor annuity for a 65-year-old retiree and his 25-year-old spouse, even though actuarially, the participant's present interest in the benefit would be less than half of the total.

Nonalienation Rules

A qualified plan must provide that plan benefits may not be assigned or alienated [Code Section 401(a)(13)]. This means, for example, that a plan participant can't pledge future anticipated qualified plan payments as security for a bank loan. For divorce, child support, and similar domestic disputes, there are special provisions discussed later in this chapter.

Examples

The distribution restrictions described in the preceding pages appear so complex as to defy summary. Probably the best way to see how these restrictions work is to look at some examples. Consider the following proposed plan distribution options, offered to a married male participant in a qualified defined-benefit plan retiring at age 65. Assume that the participant and his spouse have waived any required joint and survivor annuity. The following options will be analyzed to see if they are permissible under the distribution restrictions:

- A joint and 100 percent survivor annuity for the lives of the participant and his daughter, age 35
- A 25-year period-certain annuity for the lives of the participant and his spouse
- Equal periodic distributions over five years beginning when the participant reaches age 75
- Equal monthly payments over a fixed period equal to the participant's life expectancy, but if the participant survives, the payout period is extended (the monthly payments are actuarially reduced) annually to reflect the increased life expectancy

The first potential distribution would meet the first restrictions of Section 401(a)(9), because it extends over the lives of a participant and named beneficiary, but it does not meet the incidental benefit tests under the regulations. According to tables in the regulations, no more than a 60 percent survivor annuity could be payable to the daughter.

The second distribution—the 25-year period-certain annuity for the lives of the participant and spouse would meet Section 401(a)(9) as long as the joint life expectancy of the participant and spouse is at least 25 years. As for the incidental test, the regulations provide that a survivor annuity for a spouse will generally qualify regardless of the difference in ages.

The third option, a distribution beginning at age 75, is not permitted because distributions must begin not later than April 1 following the calendar year in which the employee reaches age 70½.

Finally, a fixed-period payout over the participant's life expectancy, with annual recalculations of life expectancy, is permitted. This can be an advantageous way of receiving the benefit because payments can continue to a relatively advanced age, reducing the danger that retirement income will stop while the participant is still living.

FEDERAL TAXATION OF DISTRIBUTIONS

Plan distributions generally are taxed in accordance with the rules for taxing annuity payments found in Code Section 72. A lump sum distribution from a plan is generally taxed in full on receipt unless it is rolled over to an IRA, as discussed below. This section deals with *federal* income and estate taxation. Some states apply similar tax treatment, but there is considerable variation. Federal taxes are usually the dominant factor in the overall tax burden on plan distributions.

The initial step in determining the taxation of a qualified plan distribution is determining the *taxable amount* of the distribution. For a distribution upon retirement, disability, or termination of employment, the taxable amount consists of the total amount of the distribution less the following amounts, sometimes referred to as the employee's *cost basis* in the plan:

- The total nondeductible contributions made by the employee (in the case of a contributory plan)
- The total cost of life insurance reported as taxable income by the participant, assuming that the plan distribution is received under the same contract that provided the life insurance protection
- Any employer contributions previously taxed to the employee (for example, where a nonqualified plan later became qualified)
- Certain employer contributions attributable to foreign services performed before 1963
- Amounts paid by the employee in repayment of loans that were treated as distributions
- In the case of a stock bonus plan or other stock plan, the net unrealized appreciation, as discussed in Chapter 23

The first two items in the list are the ones most frequently encountered. If the employee is self-employed or was self-employed in the past, the items excludable from the taxable amount are slightly different from the above list. The most important difference is that for a self-employed person who is an owner/employee (a more-than-10-percent owner of an unincorporated business), the insurance costs (the second item above) are not part of the cost basis.

The simplest way to describe the taxation of qualified plan distributions is to distinguish between those benefits that are paid out fully in a single taxable year of the participant and those that are spread out over more than one taxable year. The latter are discussed first.

Payment over More than One Taxable Year

If the plan distribution is made over more than one taxable year of the employee, the usual annuity rules apply to taxation of the distribution. The distribution will be taxable to the participant or beneficiary in the year received, except to the extent that there is a cost basis to be recovered.

In general, basis is recovered using a table specified in Section 72 of the Code. The total basis is to be divided by a number from the table, and the resultant amount is the amount of each monthly payment that is nontaxable. The table for a payout based on a single life is as follows:

Age on annuity starting date	Number of anticipated payments
Not more than 55	360
More than 55–60	310
More than 60–65	260
More than 65–70	210
More than 70	160

There is an additional table for annuities paid over the life of more than one individual:

Combined age of annuitants	Number of payments
Not more than 110	410
More than 110 but not more than 120	360
More than 120 but not more than 130	310
More than 130 but not more than 140	260
More than 140	210

■ **EXAMPLE**

Employee Green retires at age 65 and is entitled to a pension of $1,000 per month, based on his single life expectancy. Green's cost basis in the plan is $26,000. Green pays taxes on $900 per month; the remaining $100 of his monthly pension is excluded from tax ($26,000 divided by the factor from the table, 260)

If the recipient receives payments long enough for the entire basis to be recovered, subsequent payments are taxable in full. Correspondingly, if the recipient dies before the entire basis is recovered, there is an income deduction allowable to the beneficiary for the unrecovered basis.

Payment in One Taxable Year

If the qualified plan distribution is paid to the participant in a single taxable year, the taxable amount (the amount in excess of the participant's cost basis as described above) potentially is all taxable to the participant as ordinary income in the year received. Because this can increase the participant's effective tax rate by pushing up the marginal tax bracket in that year, a special one-time relief provision applies if the distribution qualifies as a *lump-sum distribution* and is received after age 59½. A lump-sum distribution must meet all of the following requirements:

- It is made in one taxable year of the recipient.
- It represents the entire amount of the employee's benefit in the plan.
- It is payable on account of the participant's death, attainment of age 59½ separation from service (non–self-employed person only), or disability (self-employed person only).
- It is from a qualified plan.
- Except for death benefits, the employee must have participated in the plan for at least five years prior to the distribution.

In determining whether the entire amount of the employee's benefit has been distributed, all pension plans maintained by the employer are treated as a single plan, all profit-sharing plans are treated as one plan, and all stock bonus plans are treated as one plan.

If the distribution qualifies as a lump-sum distribution, the taxable amount of the distribution (the amount remaining after the cost basis is subtracted) is eligible for special tax treatment in certain cases, owing to expiring tax provisions that are retained ("grandfathered") for long-term plan participants. For participants who attained age 50 before 1986, there is a "ten-year averaging" computation. For amounts accumulated before 1974, a special capital-gain treatment is available. All other distributions are treated as ordinary income, to the extent of the taxable amount.

Taxation of Death Benefits from Qualified Plans

The income tax treatment described above also applies in general to plan death benefits paid to beneficiaries of participants. That is, if the death benefit is paid as periodic payments, the annuity rules described above generally apply; if the death benefit qualifies as a lump-sum distribution, the special favorable tax treatment is available to the beneficiary. However, if the death benefit is payable under a life insurance contract held by the plan, the pure insurance amount paid—the difference between the policy's face amount and its cash value is excluded from tax.

■ **EXAMPLE**

Employee Haines dies before retirement and his beneficiary receives a lump-sum death benefit from the plan consisting of $100,000 of the proceeds of a cash-value life insurance contract, the cash value of which was $50,000. The plan was noncontributory, and Haines reported a total of $8,000 of insurance costs on his income tax return during his lifetime as a result of the plan's insurance coverage. The taxable amount of this distribution to the beneficiary is the total distribution of $100,000 less the following:

- The pure insurance amount ($100,000 minus the cash value of $50,000) and
- Haines's cost basis—in this case, only the $8,000 of insurance cost reported during his lifetime.

The taxable amount is therefore $42,000. This amount is taxable income to the beneficiary, subject to the special averaging provisions described above, if applicable.

Federal Estate Tax

The federal estate tax on qualified plan death benefits affects only highly compensated participants (those with a gross estate of at least $675,000) (2000 figure) and is discussed further in Chapter 25.

QUALIFIED DOMESTIC RELATIONS ORDERS

The prohibition against nonalienation of benefits does not apply to an assignment of a benefit under a *qualified domestic relations order (QDRO)*. Under Code Section 414(p), a QDRO is a decree, order, or property settlement under state law relating to child support, alimony, or marital property rights that assigns a participant's plan benefits to a spouse, former spouse, child, or other dependent of the participant. Currently, therefore, a participant's plan benefits generally become the subject of negotiation in domestic disputes. The pension law itself does not indicate how such benefits are to be divided; this is still a matter of state domestic relations law. The QDRO provision simply provides a means by which state court orders in domestic relations issues can be enforced against plan trustees.

To protect plan administrators and trustees from conflicting claims, a QDRO cannot assign a benefit that the plan does not provide. Also, a QDRO cannot assign a benefit that is already assigned under a previous order. If, under the plan, a participant has no right to an immediate cash payment from the plan, a QDRO cannot require that the trustees make such a cash payment. If a cash settlement is desired, the parties will generally agree to allow one participant to keep the entire plan benefit and pay compensating cash to the other.

LOANS FROM QUALIFIED PLANS

The law permits loans, within limits, to participants in regular qualified plans and Section 403(b) tax-deferred annuity plans. However, a participant cannot borrow from a plan unless the plan document specifically permits loans, and as discussed below, loan provisions may not be appropriate for all plans. Loans from IRAs and SEPs are effectively prohibited; they are treated as taxable distributions and may be subject to penalties for premature distribution. Also, loans from a qualified plan to an owner/employee (a proprietor or more than 10 percent partner in an unincorporated business) or to an employee of an S corporation who is a more-than-5-percent shareholder in the corporation are prohibited transactions subject to the prohibited transaction penalties.

Limits on Loan Amount

Under Code Section 72(p), loans will be recognized as loans (rather than taxable current distributions) only to the extent that the loan, together with all other outstanding loans, does not exceed the lesser of

- $50,000 reduced by the highest outstanding loan balance during the preceding one-year period or
- one-half of the present value of the vested accrued benefit of the employee under the plan.

A loan up to $10,000 may be made even if this is more than one-half of the present value of the employee's vested accrued benefit. Some examples are shown to the right:

Vested Accrued Benefit	Maximum Aggregate Loans
$120,000	$50,000
40,000	20,000
15,000	10,000

Terms of Loans

To obtain loan treatment, the loan must be repayable by its terms within five years. The rule noted above for reducing the $50,000 limit by the loan balance in the preceding year was designed to prevent avoidance of the five-year limit by simply repaying and then immediately reborrowing the same amount every five years. The five-year requirement does not apply to any loan used to acquire a principal residence of the participant.

Transactions with an effect similar to that of loans (for example, the pledging of an interest in a qualified plan or a loan made against an insurance contract purchased by a qualified plan) are also covered by the loan limitations and rules.

If the plan permits loans, they must be made available on a nondiscriminatory basis. Also, the loans must be adequately secured and bear a reasonable rate of interest. Usually, the security for a plan loan is simply the participant's vested accrued plan benefit. Interest on the loan is generally consumer interest that is not deductible as an itemized deduction unless secured by a home mortgage. However, if the loan is to a key employee as defined in the top-heavy rules or is secured by 401(k) or 403(b) elective deferrals, interest is not deductible in any event.

Any loan that does not meet these requirements will be treated as a current distribution and may be currently taxable to the employee when received.

Should the Plan Permit Loans?

Whether the plan should permit loans depends on the employer's objectives for the plan. Plan loan provisions are often desired by the controlling employees of closely held businesses because a plan loan provides the advantage of tax sheltering the plan funds without losing control of the cash. However, the same considerations may make plan loans desirable for regular employees as well. A disadvantage of plan loans is that if they are too extensively utilized, they deplete the plan funds available for investment. More fundamentally, however, plan loan provisions are inconsistent with a primary plan objective of providing retirement security. Thus, they are less common in pension plans than in profit-sharing plans. Plan loan provisions are particularly uncommon in defined-benefit plans because such plans have no individual participant accounts; it is complicated to convert a participant's vested accrued benefit to a cash equivalent at a given time to determine the amount of loan that can be allowed. Plan loans also add significant administrative costs to the plan.

STUDY QUESTIONS

1. a. What is meant by the "normal form of benefit" in a defined-benefit plan?
   b. What optional forms of benefit are commonly made available to participants?

2. What is the distinction between types of preretirement distributions allowable in a pension plan and types allowable in a profit-sharing plan?

3. a. What is the latest date on which a qualified plan may allow retirement benefits to commence?
   b. What is the latest age at which a participant of a qualified plan must begin to receive benefits?

4. Explain the minimum distribution rules applicable to a beneficiary if
   a. the employee dies before the entire plan interest is distributed.
   b. the employee dies before distributions have begun.

5. Which of the following plan distributions is not subject to the 10 percent Section 72(t) penalty?
   a. A lump-sum distribution to a participant age 55
   b. A death benefit payable to a beneficiary upon the death of an employee age 52
   c. A lump-sum benefit payable to a disabled employee age 57
   d. A life annuity payable beginning immediately upon separation from service to an employee age 45
   e. A distribution of $30,000 to employee Slick who plans to use the money to build a swimming pool prescribed by his doctor for arthritis treatments
   f. A distribution from a 401(k) plan to an employee age 52 who qualifies under the plan's "extreme hardship" distribution provision

6. Joe Smith retired at age 65 with a pension of $400 per month. His life expectancy is 20 years. To what extent is his pension benefit taxable if Smith's cost basis is $16,400?

7. a. What requirements must a lump-sum distribution meet to qualify for special tax treatment?
   b. What is the special tax treatment that is available?

8. Explain how death benefits from a qualified plan are taxed.

9. The ABC Company (an S corporation) has a qualified money-purchase plan that allows employees to take loans up to the maximum legal limit. What is the maximum loan that can be taken by the following employees?

Employee	Vested Account Balance	Percentage of Corporate Ownership
a. Don Taich	$ 17,000	0%
b. Peter Demunney	$160,000	0
c. Dana N. Runn	$200,000	50

10. What are the advantages and disadvantages of designing a plan that includes a loan provision?

CHAPTER 25

Plan Restrictions Aimed at Highly Compensated Employees

Congress and the IRS have long been convinced that the tax advantages of qualified plans can be abused by plans that confer most of their benefits on highly paid key employees, typically employees who are stockholders or partners in a closely held business. Such plans are arguably inconsistent with the social policy behind the qualified plan provisions. Therefore, the law contains a variety of provisions particularly aimed at this type of abuse. The provisions discussed in this chapter will have little actual effect on plans typically designed for larger employers. However, these rules technically apply to *all* plans, and thus they must be considered at least in drafting every plan.

There is a large community of pension planners who specialize in designing plans to avoid the provisions discussed in this chapter, so from time to time Congress and the IRS add new rules to close various "loopholes" that plan designers have found. Thus, the provisions discussed here have become the most complex in the entire pension law.

CEILING ON COMPENSATION

The most fundamental limit of this type is the rule [Code Section 401(a)(17)] that only the first $150,000 of each employee's compensation (as indexed for inflation; 2000: $170,000) can be taken into account in a qualified plan's contribution or benefit formula. For example, if an employee earns $300,000 in 2000 and is covered under a money-purchase pension plan with a 10 percent of compensation contribution formula, the contribution for that employee in 1997 is limited to $17,000 (10 percent of $170,000, rather than 10 percent of $300,000).

LIMITATIONS ON INDIVIDUAL BENEFITS OR ANNUAL ADDITIONS (SECTION 415 LIMITS)

Section 415 of the Internal Revenue Code contains limitations on the amount of benefit or annual account additions that any participant can receive under a qualified plan. These limitations are intended to prevent the qualified plan from being used as an individual tax-sheltering device beyond any reasonable need for retirement savings. They have their greatest impact on small businesses where one or more of the business owners are plan participants. However, the limitations also can have an impact on larger plans that cover high-salaried executives. There are two types of Section 415 limits—one for defined-benefit plans and one for defined-contribution plans.

Defined-Benefit Plans

For defined-benefit plans, the applicable limitation restricts the amount of *benefit* that any individual can receive. Basically, the plan cannot permit a benefit at age 65 (or the Social Security retirement age, if later) that exceeds the lesser of 100 percent of the participant's compensation averaged over the three years of highest compensation, or $90,000 (as indexed) annually. A pension of up to $10,000 annually can be paid even if it exceeds the 100 percent limit, but this $10,000 floor applies only if the participant has never been covered by a defined-*contribution* plan.

The benefit limit of Section 415 applies to employer-provided benefits only. If the plan provides for employee contributions (which is relatively rare in defined-benefit plans), these employee contributions can be used to increase benefits above the Section 415 limit.

The limits as stated above apply to a benefit in the form of either a straight-life annuity or a qualified joint-and-survivor annuity. However, the limits must be actuarially adjusted if the normal retirement benefit is something else—for example, a ten-year period-certain annuity. No adjustment is made for preretirement death or disability benefits. Also, there is an increase in the limit in the event of late retirement.

The $90,000 limit is now adjusted for inflation in $5,000 increments under a formula based on Social Security benefit amounts in effect. In 2000, for example, the limit reached $135,000.

The $90,000 limit is actuarially adjusted for retirement ages earlier or later than the Social Security retirement age. This prevents acceleration of funding (and tax deductions) simply by choosing a normal retirement age earlier than 65. The limit is also actuarially increased for retirement later than the Social Security retirement age. Table 25-1 illustrates the adjustments to the basic $90,000 limit for a participant born before 1938 whose Social Security retirement age is 65.

As indicated, the Section 415 benefit limitation must be part of every qualified plan document. The plan language must, therefore, prohibit the accrual of any benefit in excess of the limit. For any given employee, however, except an employee who is contemplating retirement in the current plan year, it is impossible to know what the applicable dollar limitation under Section 415 will be in the year of retirement. Nevertheless, the IRS does not allow benefits to be accrued in excess of the Section 415 limits based on current compensation and the current dollar limit, even for a participant far from retirement.

TABLE 25–1
Retirement Age and Maximum Benefit

Retirement Age	Maximum Dollar Benefit
55	$ 42,400
60	61,419
62	72,000
65	90,000
70	155,843

Assumptions: 1971 Group Annuity (Male) Table with interest at 5 percent, life annuity. Revenue Ruling 80-253 indicates what assumptions will be considered reasonable for this purpose. For the actuarial increase after age 65, under Code Section 415(b)(2)(E)(iii), the interest rate assumption cannot be greater than the lesser of 5 percent or the plan's actuarial interest rate assumption.

Defined-Contribution Plans

For a defined-contribution plan, the Section 415 limitation is a restriction not on the benefit, but on the *annual addition* to each participant's account.

The annual addition cannot exceed the lesser of 25 percent of the participant's annual compensation or $30,000. Like the dollar limit for defined-benefit plans, the $30,000 limit is adjusted for inflation in $5,000 increments. The 2000 figure is $30,000.

The annual addition to each participant's account includes three elements:

1. Employer contributions including employee salary reductions
2. Reallocated forfeitures from other participants' accounts
3. Nondeductible (after tax) employee contributions

The following example shows how the annual-additions limit will affect a participant's account in a hypothetical plan. In the example, a forfeiture amount is available that is allocated to the employee's account in proportion to compensation.

Employee Compensation	Maximum Annual Addition	Forfeiture Allocated	Maximum Employer Contribution
$ 20,000	$ 5,000	$ 2,000	$ 3,000
50,000	12,500	5,000	7,500
100,000	25,000	10,000	15,000
200,000	30,000	20,000	10,000

It is important to note that both of the Section 415 limitations apply to individual participants, not to the plan as a whole. Also, it should be noted that the annual-additions limit is not a limit on the amount that the employer can deduct for income tax purposes. The deduction limits are a separate set of rules from the Section 415 limits, and the two items should not be confused. However, no deduction can ever be taken for an employer contribution that causes an employee's benefit or account to exceed the Section 415 limit.

Combined Deduction Limit

A combined deduction limit [Code Section 404(a)(7)] has the effect of restricting the benefits of many combination plans. If an employer maintains a defined-contribution and a defined benefit-plan covering the same employer or employees, the employer's annual tax deduction for the plans cannot exceed 25 percent of the compensation of the employees covered under both plans. The 25 percent deduction limit can be exceeded only to meet the minimum funding requirements for the defined-benefit plan. For older plan entrants, the defined-benefit funding level will often exceed 25 percent of compensation, thus (depending on the overall nature of the employee group) potentially eliminating the possibility of adding a defined-contribution plan. For example, if there is only one participant, or only one highly paid participant and a few others (such as the typical plan for a doctor or dentist), this will be the case.

■ EXAMPLE

Dr. X, age 55, adopts a plan providing a pension of $75,000 a year (50 percent of compensation) at retirement age 65. Annual cost is $44,428 (8 percent interest assumption) which is 30 percent of Dr. X's compensation. Thus, if Dr. X is the only employee, under the limits of Section 404(a)(7) there is no room for additional deductible contributions to a defined-contribution plan.

TOP-HEAVY PLANS

The *top-heavy* rules are another addition to the arsenal of weapons Congress has provided against the use of qualified plans by small businesses primarily as tax shelters for owners and highly compensated employees. The rules (Code Section 416) provide additional requirements that must be met by all qualified plans that meet the definition of top-heavy. To summarize, the top-heavy requirements do the following:

- Put a ceiling on the amount of a participant's compensation that may be taken into account in a plan contribution or benefit formula
- Provide faster vesting of benefits for plan participants who are not key employees
- Provide minimum unintegrated benefit or contribution levels for plan participants who are not key employees
- Reduce the aggregate Section 415 limit on contributions and benefits for key employees in certain situations
- Restrict distributions to key employees

The top-heavy restrictions must be written into the plan document itself, even a plan for a large employer that is unlikely ever to be top-heavy. The plan document must provide that if the plan meets the definition of top-heavy on a given determination date, all of the top-heavy restrictions automatically become part of the plan. So long as the plan is not top-heavy, the top-heavy restrictions need not necessarily apply, although, of course, the planner is free to add these restrictions to the plan even if it is not top-heavy.

Definition of Top-Heavy

A defined-benefit plan is a top-heavy plan for a given plan year if (as of the determination date—see below) the present value of the accumulated accrued benefits for participants who are key employees is more than 60 percent of the present value of all accumulated accrued benefits in the plan. A defined-contribution plan is considered top-heavy if, as of the determination date, the sum of the account balances of participants who are key employees exceeds 60 percent of the aggregate value of the accounts of all employees. Benefits and account balances attributable to both employer and employee contributions are to be taken into account, except for accumulated voluntary deductible employee contributions or rollovers from other plans. The present value of a participant's accrued benefit or the value of the participant's account balance is to be increased by any aggregate distributions made with respect to the participant during the five-year period ending on the determination date. Plans of related groups can be lumped together, and if the contributions or benefits of the overall group are top-heavy, each plan in the group will be considered top-heavy.

Determination Date

The determination date for any given plan year is the last day of the preceding plan year. For the first year of the new plan, the determination date is the last day of the first plan year. The IRS also has the authority to apply the top-heavy provisions on the basis of years other than plan years.

Definition of Key Employee

A key employee is any participant in the plan, including a self-employed person, who at any time in the four preceding years was an officer earning more than 50 percent of the Section 415 defined-benefit dollar limit, an employee owning one of the ten largest interests in the employer (under attribution-of-ownership rules), a more-than-5-percent owner, or a more-than-1-percent owner earning more than $150,000. Because the term *officer* is not clearly defined, there is a limit on the number of employees that can be treated as officers. No more than 50 employees can be treated as officers in general, while for small employers the limit on the number of officers is the greater of three individuals or 10 percent of the employees (presumably the highest paid). For example, suppose a small company has 25 employees. In determining who are key employees, the IRS cannot designate more than three of these employees (the greater of three individuals or 10 percent of the employees) as officers.

Note that *key employee* is defined differently from *highly compensated employee* used in all other nondiscrimination provisions of the law.

In determining ownership in the business for purposes of identifying key employees, the top-heavy provisions have rules for attributing stock ownership from related persons, and there are special rules for aggregating commonly controlled groups of employers and affiliated service groups.

An illustration of what constitutes a top-heavy plan might be helpful in defining the concept of top-heavy.

> ■ **EXAMPLE**
>
> Suppose that a corporation with ten employees has a defined-contribution money-purchase pension plan. The employees include Wolfe (president and sole shareholder), Hare (vice-president), and Flynn (foreman). All of the other employees are clerical or production workers paid by the hour. The IRS would most likely identify the three named employees as the plan's key employees. As of the end of the 2000 plan year, aggregate account balances of all participants in the plan total $200,000. The account balances for Wolfe, Hare, and Flynn total $100,000. On these facts, the plan is not top-heavy for the plan year 2001 because the aggregate account balances for the three key employees total less than 60 percent of the total account balances as of the determination date, the end of 2000. However, suppose that in 1999 Wolfe received a distribution of $100,000 from the plan. In this case, the account balances as of the end of 2000 would have to be increased by the amount of this distribution, so they would total $300,000. The account balances for the key employees would then be $200,000, because the $100,000 distribution to Wolfe would have to be included for this purpose. Now the plan would be deemed to be top-heavy for the plan year 2001 because the account balances for key employees would be more than 60 percent of the total.

Although the example above involved a plan of a small employer that fell on the line between being top-heavy and avoiding that status, planners find that virtually all plans of employers with fewer than ten employees will be top-heavy at all times. Key employees in such businesses usually have not only higher salaries but also much longer service than regular employees, so their account balances or accrued benefits are much higher as a percentage of the total. Therefore, the top-heavy rules become an additional set of qualification requirements that must be met by all small plans.

Additional Vesting Requirements for Top-Heavy Plans

Years of Service	Vesting Percentage
2	20
3	40
4	60
5	80
6 or more	100

If a plan meets the definition of top-heavy, the plan provisions must meet one of two special vesting schedules applicable during years in which the plan is top-heavy. One alternative is 100 percent after two years of service. The other alternative is six-year graded vesting, as shown on the left.

Minimum Benefit Requirements

A qualified plan must provide minimum benefits or contributions for top-heavy years. For defined-benefit plans, the benefit for each nonkey employee must be at least a minimum percentage of average compensation. The applicable minimum percentage of compensation for a given employee is two multiplied by the number of the employee's years of service, with a maximum percentage of 20 percent (i.e., ten years of service or more). The average compensation used for this test will generally be based on the highest five years of compensation.

For a defined-contribution plan, employer contributions during a year of topheaviness must be not less than 3 percent of each nonkey employee's compensation.

A top-heavy plan can consider only nonintegrated benefits in meeting the vesting and minimum benefit requirements. That is, these requirements must be met based on benefits from the plan itself. Benefits received by the participant from Social Security cannot be taken into account.

QUALIFIED PLANS FOR OWNERS OF UNINCORPORATED BUSINESSES

The owner of an unincorporated business often works full time or performs substantial services for the business as its proprietor or one of its partners. However, under the law such a person is not technically an employee of the business, but is referred to instead as a *self-employed person*. For many years, partners and proprietors were not eligible to be covered under qualified plans adopted by their unincorporated businesses. Beginning in 1962, qualified plan coverage was allowed, but only under very restricted conditions. In particular, there was a relatively low limit on the amount that could be contributed to the plan (or on the benefit provided by the plan) for partners and proprietors. The special plans designed under these restrictions were known as *Keogh* or *HR-10* plans. These restrictions were enough to induce many unincorporated businesses to incorporate, simply so that the partner or proprietor could become a legally recognized *employee* of the business and be eligible for full qualified plan coverage. However, for plan years beginning after 1983, most of these previous restrictions were eliminated and partners and proprietors were able to participate fully in qualified plans adopted by their unincorporated businesses. There are, however, a few differences in the treatment of unincorporated businesses, most of them related to basic differences in the form of business.

Earned Income

An unincorporated business is not treated for federal income tax purposes as a taxable entity but rather as a conduit for passing the business's taxable income or loss through to the partners or proprietor. By comparison, a corporation is a tax-paying entity, and income can be passed through to owners only in the form of salaries representing reasonable compensation for services rendered or as dividends. Because of this difference, plan benefits or contributions for partners and proprietors are based on a defined amount referred to as *earned income,* which is intended to be comparable to the *compensation* that employees receive.

Earned income is the partner's or proprietor's share of the net earnings of the business after taking all appropriate business deductions, and without including nontaxable income. However, earned income includes only earnings with respect to the trade or business in which the personal services of the partner or proprietor are a material income-producing factor. For example, the net profits of an investment type business could not be treated like compensation in order to provide a benefit under a qualified plan for a partner who provided no personal services to the business.

The fact that earned income is determined after all business deductions creates a computational complication. Business deductions include the plan contribution itself, as well as one-half the Social Security self-employment tax that is based on net income [Code Section 164(f)]. An illustration will show this without getting into the details of the algebra.

■ **EXAMPLE**

Dot Matrix is a self-employed computer consultant with no regular employees. She earned $100,000 of net income in 2000, not counting her Keogh plan contribution and the deduction for self-employment tax. Her deduction for self-employment tax is $6,063.48. The Keogh plan is a money-purchase plan calling for an annual contribution of 25 percent of earned income. How much can Dot contribute? The answer is $18,787.31. This amount is 25 percent of Dot's earned income. Her earned income is equal to

Initial net income		$100,000.00
Less Self-employment tax deduction	$ 6,063.48	
Keogh contribution	18,787.31	
Earned income		$ 75,149.21

Insurance

Another group of special rules applies to a qualified plan providing insurance for a partner or proprietor. No deduction can be taken by the business for plan contributions that are allocatable to the purchase of incidental life, health, or accident insurance for the partner or proprietor. If cash-value life insurance is used, the deduction is denied for the portion of the premium allocatable to pure insurance protection, but the remainder of the premium is deductible as a plan contribution. The amounts not deducted are taxable income to the business owners, because all taxable income of a partnership or proprietorship flows through to the individual owners. Therefore, there are no PS 58 costs to include in the owner's income if insurance has been purchased because the full cost of the insurance has already been included in the owner's income. However, unlike regular employees, the owners do not obtain a cost basis for the cost of the insurance to apply to any distribution from the qualified plan.

EARLY TERMINATION RULE FOR 25 HIGHEST-PAID EMPLOYEES

Potentially, a qualified defined-benefit plan can be used as a one-time tax shelter for key employees if it is designed with the expectation that most of the key employees will retire within a few years, taking most of the plan assets out for their retirement, thus terminating the plan. For many years, the Regulations [Section 1.401–4(c)] have contained a provision designed to limit this abuse by requiring defined-benefit plans to limit benefits for the 25 highest-paid employees if they are paid out within ten years of the plan's establishment or the plan terminates within ten years.

In such cases, benefits to the 25 highest-paid employees are limited by limiting the total employer contributions used to fund such benefits. The employer contributions for each such employee cannot exceed the greater of $20,000 or 20 percent of the first $50,000 of employee compensation multiplied by the number of years the plan was in effect prior to the benefit payment or plan termination. Often, this will produce a lower limit on benefits than the Section 415 benefit limit.

FEDERAL ESTATE TAX TREATMENT OF QUALIFIED PLAN BENEFITS

The federal estate tax is a tax separate from the income tax that is imposed on the value of a decedent's property at the time of death. The estate tax is payable out of the decedent's estate and, therefore, reduces the amount available to the beneficiaries. Only a small percentage of decedents—less than 5 percent—have enough wealth to be concerned about the estate tax because of a high initial minimum tax credit applicable to the estate tax. No estate tax return need be filed for a decedent whose gross estate is less than $675,000 (in 2000). This amount is scheduled to rise incrementally to $1,000,000 in 2006. Also, there is an unlimited marital deduction for federal estate tax purposes—that is, there is no federal estate tax imposed on property transferred at death to a spouse, regardless of the amount.

As a general rule, a lump-sum death benefit, or the present value of an annuity payable to a beneficiary from a qualified plan, is includable in the estate of a deceased participant for federal estate tax purposes. For some high-income participants, avoiding federal estate taxes on the plan benefit will be important. Their estates may be large enough to attract imposition of some federal estate tax. The marital deduction may not be significant, because they may not wish to pay the plan benefit to a spouse—they may be widowed or divorced or may wish to provide for another beneficiary. Also, even if the benefit is payable to a spouse, a spouse is often about the same age as the decedent, and thus within relatively few years most of the property transferred to the spouse is potentially subject to federal estate tax again at the spouse's death. As a result, it is often useful to design a qualified plan death benefit that can be excluded from the participant's estate.

The general rule of the federal estate tax is that all items of property are includable unless a specific code provision excludes them. Thus, qualified plan death benefits are generally includable because there is no specific exclusion. However, the estate tax law does have a specific provision dealing with life insurance, Section 2042. Under Section 2042, life insurance proceeds are includable in a decedent's estate if the decedent has "incidents of ownership" in the insurance policies. Incidents of ownership are various rights under the policy, particularly the right to designate the beneficiary. If a qualified plan death benefit is provided through a life insurance policy, in most places this provision would require inclusion because the participant retains the right to name the beneficiary. Noninsured death benefits presumably would not be excludable in any event.

STUDY QUESTIONS

1. a. Why are so many provisions of the qualified plan law aimed primarily at the closely held business?
   b. How do Congress and the IRS often react to aggressive design by pension planners?

2. What is the purpose of the Section 415 limitations on qualified plan benefits and contributions?

3. a. What is the basic Section 415 limitation on benefits from a defined-benefit plan?
   b. Under what circumstances might this basic limit be adjusted?

4. a. What is the basic Section 415 limitation on annual additions to a defined-contribution plan?
   b. What elements are included in annual additions?

5. a. Describe the reasons for the combined limit under Section 415 when an employee is a participant in a defined-benefit and a defined-contribution plan with the same employer.
   b. Briefly describe the rule that applies to benefits and contributions when such dual participation exists.

6. Assume a corporation has 15 employees and that three employees, Tom, Ed, and Jim, individually earn more than $60,000 annually. They are the only officers of the corporation. The remaining employees are hourly paid and clerical workers. Assume that the aggregate account balances of all participants in the firm's defined-contribution plan are equal to $200,000, and for Tom, Ed and Jim the total is $100,000.
   a. Who are the plan's key employees? Explain.
   b. Is the plan top-heavy? Explain.

7. Explain how each of the following is affected if a qualified plan is top-heavy:
   a. Vesting.
   b. Minimum benefits.
   c. Section 415 limits

8. Explain how the rules applying to qualified plans of unincorporated businesses differ from those applying to the qualified plans of corporations.

9. Explain the early termination rule for the 25 highest-paid employees of a qualified plan.

10. What is the federal estate tax treatment of qualified plan benefits?

CHAPTER 26

Plan Installation and Administration; Investments; Plan Termination

OBJECTIVES

■ Describe the basic steps that must be taken to install a qualified plan and explain the significance of an advance-determination letter.

■ Explain the reporting and disclosure requirements that apply to qualified plans.

■ Describe the impact of the ERISA fiduciary requirements and other investment restrictions on qualified plans.

■ Explain the procedures for terminating a qualified plan and describe the general coverage of plan termination insurance provided by the Pension Benefit Guaranty Corporation (PBGC).

TABLE 26–1

Checklist for Installation of Quicklime Construction Company, Inc. (calendar-year taxpayer), Employees' Profit-Sharing Plan *(effective January 1, 2000)*

BEFORE DECEMBER 31, 2000
1. Board must pass resolution adopting the plan. It is sufficient for the board to adopt either a preliminary draft of the plan or a simple resolution listing the major provisions of the plan.
2. Trust instrument must be executed. (Under state law, a nominal contribution to the trust corpus may also be necessary in order to establish the existence of the trust.) If there is a separate group pension contract, the contract need not be in final form before December 31, 2000, but application must have been accepted by insurer and partial payment made.
3. Plan should be communicated to employees. (There is no specific statutory deadline for this, but communication before the end of the year is recommended.) Communication can be oral (e.g., at employee meetings) or written. Alternatively, the Summary Plan Description (SPD) can be used for this purpose.

BEFORE EMPLOYER'S TAX-FILING DATE (March 15, 2001; extension to September 15, 2000, is possible)
1. Execute plan in final form. (Plan may be adopted subject to right to rescind if determination letter is not obtained.)
2. Make 2000 contribution to trust. (Plan may allow contribution to be returned if plan does not qualify.)

WITHIN 120 DAYS AFTER PLAN IS ADOPTED BY BOARD OF DIRECTORS (e.g., if resolution adopted December 31, 2000, by April 30, 2001)
    Furnish SPD to participants. (See "Reporting and Disclosure" in this chapter.)

BEFORE FILING APPLICATION FOR DETERMINATION WITH IRS
Time
    No statutory deadline. However, should be filed before employer's tax-filing date (March 15, 2000, plus extensions). Filing of letter will extend the retroactive amendment date to give time to amend plan to meet IRS objections, if any.
What to file
    Form (5300 series)
    Other schedules as required under Form 5300 instructions and IRS procedures
    Plan—executed
    Trust Agreement—executed (or Insurance Contract)
    Other items (e.g., Power of Attorney)—depending on circumstances

ON OR BEFORE JULY 31, 2001 (AND EACH JULY 31 THEREAFTER)
File Annual Report (Form 5500 Series) with IRS (see "Reporting and Disclosure")

PLAN INSTALLATION

Installing a qualified plan can be fairly complex, particularly if the plan is complicated and the employer wishes to maximize the tax benefits by having the plan effective at the earliest possible date. The best way to discuss the installation process is to use as a framework for reference the checklist for the installation of a hypothetical qualified plan provided in Table 26-1. This checklist should be used for general discussion only; IRS guidelines for plan installation are frequently revised, and procedures may even vary from one Internal Revenue district to another.

Adoption of the Plan

To be effective during a particular year, the plan must be adopted by the employer during that year. For a corporation, the corporate board should pass a resolution adopting the plan before the end of its year for the plan to become effective during that year. It is not proper to back date documents for this purpose—the board must actually act legally before the end of the year. It may not be necessary to draft the final form of the plan at this time; however, the board usually can adopt a resolution merely outlining the basic provisions of the plan. If the plan uses a trust, the trust must be established before the end of the year in which the plan is to be effective. This means that a trust agreement must be executed between the employer and the trustee, and at least a nominal principal contribution may be necessary to establish the existence of the trust. If the plan uses an insurance contract as a funding instrument, the insurer must have accepted the terms of the agreement before the end of the year, although the contract may not be put into final form until sometime later. The plan and insurance contract should be finalized prior to the time the employer makes its first plan contribution other than a nominal contribution required to establish the trust or insurance contract; this usually means the employer's tax filing date, because as discussed in Chapter 21, the plan contribution for a given year can be deferred to the tax filing date for that year.

Plan Year

It is possible to establish a plan with a plan year that is different from the employer's taxable year. In that case, one plan year will end and another will begin in the same taxable year of the employer. The employer can then take a deduction that taxable year for a contribution on behalf of either plan year or for partial contributions for both taxable years; however, the employer must follow a consistent procedure so there is no undue tax benefit. For simplicity, unless otherwise indicated in this chapter, it will be assumed that the plan year is the same as the employer's taxable year.

Advance Determination Letters

A central feature of the plan installation process is usually an application to the IRS District Director for a determination letter stating that the plan as designed is a qualified plan eligible for the accompanying tax benefits. It is not necessary for the plan to have such a letter to be qualified; any plan that complies with the applicable Code provisions is a qualified plan. However, if there is no advance determination by the IRS, the IRS will not examine the plan until the time comes for an audit of the employer's tax returns. If the IRS finds at that time that the plan is not qualified, the possible tax consequences can be disastrous: the loss of the employer's tax deductions for plan contributions, the taxation of all plan contributions to participants, and the loss of the trust's tax-exempt status. To avoid this, most employers consider it desirable to have the IRS review the plan in advance and issue a determination letter. There are some other advantages to the determination letter procedure. The process of IRS review will often reveal drafting problems that might otherwise have gone unnoticed. During the review procedure, the IRS usually suggests any changes in the plan that are necessary to make it qualify.

There is a retroactive amendment procedure that allows the employer to make amendments to the plan effective for a prior year if the amendments are necessary to make the plan qualify. In general, retroactive plan amendments may be made up to the employer's tax filing date for the year in question, plus extensions. For example, if a corporate employer uses a calendar year, the tax filing date for the year 2000 is March 15, 2001, with possible extensions to September 15, 2001. Thus, an employer could install a qualified plan effective January 1, 2000, and could amend the plan retroactively to January 1, 2000, as late as September 15, 2001. The filing of a determination letter prior to this deadline extends the retroactive amendment procedure while the determination letter request is pending—this is another advantage of requesting an IRS determination letter.

Generally, the employer wishes to make the plan effective as early as possible to obtain the maximum tax deduction at the outset. This can present a problem if, on filing the application for determination, the IRS finds the plan not qualified and retroactive amendments are unavailable or the employer does not wish to make the amendments the IRS suggests. The employer's prior contributions to the plan then might not be retrievable because the trust generally must be an irrevocable trust. To avoid this problem, the plan can be drafted making the plan's existence and the employer's contribution contingent on obtaining a determination letter.

The IRS provides various forms for purposes of making an application for determination. Some of these are described in the checklist (Table 26-1). IRS publishes an annually revised Revenue Procedure that prescribes the requirements for an Application for Determination.

One final point should be made concerning IRS determination letters. Determination letters indicate that the IRS has approved the plan on the basis of the plan documents and the facts submitted to it. They are no guarantee that the plan qualifies and will continue to qualify if these facts are not accurate or if the facts change at a subsequent date. Therefore, the continuing qualification of the plan must always be a concern of the employer and its employee benefit advisers.

Master, Prototype, and Pattern Plans

A qualified plan must be evidenced by a formal written document. Because of the many complex provisions that must be included, it is not unusual for such documents to run to 50 pages or more. If all of the plan language is custom designed, the drafting expense alone can be considerable.

Various methods have been devised to simplify plan drafting for smaller employers. One of the most common is the use of master and prototype plans offered by financial institutions and other types of plan advisers. A *prototype plan* is a standardized plan form, such as a prototype profit-sharing plan or a prototype money-purchase pension plan, usually offering some choice of provisions in the important features. For example, the plan might allow the employer to specify the contribution rate or choose the vesting schedule. A master plan is similar to a prototype plan, but the term *master plan* usually refers to a plan form designed by a financial organization and adopted only by employers that wish to use that financial organization for plan funding. The IRS also allows law firms to use *pattern plans;* these are plans using language that has been examined and approved by the IRS, thus allowing speedier IRS approval of plans to the extent they use the pattern language. Also, most qualified plan consultants use standardized plan language of one kind or another to a considerable extent to reduce drafting costs, even if they do not provide formal master, prototype, or pattern plans.

PLAN ADMINISTRATION

Plan administration encompasses a host of clerical and managerial functions related to a plan, including record keeping, receipt and disbursement of funds, claim administration, and investments. The discussion of plan administration in this chapter will focus on specific obligations imposed by ERISA and the Internal Revenue Code affecting plan administration.

Many of the administrative requirements of the law involve penalties for noncompliance, so it is important to impose these duties on specific individuals or groups of individuals to limit the scope of this liability to a known group. Otherwise, persons involved with the plan might find themselves held responsible for actions over which they may think they have no control. This problem is greatest in the area of investment decisions; therefore, it is important to be as specific as possible in the plan and trust agreement as to who has responsibility for making investment decisions and how these persons are chosen.

Employee Benefit Plans Other than Qualified Plans

As discussed in Chapter 5, many of the requirements of ERISA apply to a broad range of employee benefit plans as well as to qualified plans. In general, all of the rules discussed in the sections of this chapter beginning with "Plan Administration" through the section on "Unrelated Business Income" apply to all employee benefit plans, with the exceptions noted in the next paragraph. The rules are discussed in detail here because they typically have a much greater impact on qualified plans than on other plans, particularly the fiduciary rules.

The following employee benefit plans (retirement and other) are exempt from the fiduciary and reporting and disclosure requirements of ERISA:

- Government plans
- Church plans (unless they elect to be covered)
- Plans maintained solely to comply with workers' compensation, unemployment compensation, or disability insurance laws

In addition, through regulations issued by the secretary of labor, certain types of plans have been declared not to be employee welfare benefit plans and are thus exempt from the regulations of ERISA. Among these are the following:

- Compensation for work performed under other than normal circumstances, including overtime pay and shift, holiday, or weekend premiums
- Compensation for absences from work due to sickness, vacation, holidays, military duty, jury duty, or sabbatical leave and training programs to the extent such compensation is paid out of the general assets of the employer
- Group insurance programs under which (1) no contributions are made by the employer; (2) participation is completely voluntary for employees; (3) the sole function served by the employer, without endorsing the program, is to collect premiums through payroll deduction and remit the amount collected to the insurer; and (4) no consideration is paid to the employer in excess of reasonable compensation for administrative services actually performed. (Most of the mass-marketed plans described in Chapter 13 fall into this category.)

Plan Administrator

Any employee benefit plan subject to ERISA is required to name a plan administrator in the plan document. If none is named, the employer is assumed to be the plan administrator. Some employers prefer to designate a plan committee to be the plan administrator. This committee is usually made up of a group of management and sometimes rank-and-file employees responsible for administering the plan. If this is done, the plan should spell out how committee members are to be named, so that there can be no doubt who has the responsibility of plan administrator. Many employers prefer to simply designate the employer as plan administrator, with administration duties delegated to specific employees, usually in the personnel department, in the same manner as other management functions are carried out. Where the plan is funded through an insurance contract, some administrative duties may be carried out by the insurance company for a fee; this is particularly likely for smaller employers where the amount of administrative work involved does not justify the employment of a qualified plan specialist. Often, plan administrators also rely on outside benefit consultants for assistance with various administrative duties.

Claims Procedure

One of the plan administrator's duties is to evaluate employee claims for benefits and to direct the trustee or other fund holder to make payments as appropriate. If the plan is properly drafted, there should be little ambiguity about whether a particular participant or beneficiary is entitled to a plan benefit. However, due to the complexity of many plan provisions, disputes sometimes arise.

Every plan must include a written procedure under which a claimant can appeal the denial of a plan benefit to the plan administrator. There are specific time limits, 60 to 120 days generally, within which the plan administrator must make a decision on the appeal. The purpose for the claims procedure requirement is to require plans to develop internal procedures for evaluating claims so that participants will not always be compelled to bring a lawsuit against the plan if a claim is denied. If a claim dispute cannot be satisfactorily resolved internally, however, claimants have the right to sue and many will do so.

Tax Withholding

Distributions from a qualified retirement plan are subject to federal income tax withholding in a manner similar to payments of wages or other compensation. However, a recipient can elect not to have tax withholding on the qualified plan distribution, without providing any reason. (This, of course, will not relieve the recipient of any obligation to pay whatever income taxes are due.) The payer of the plan distribution must notify the recipient of the right not to have taxes withheld.

The withholding requirement applies to both lump-sum distributions and periodic payments. The liability for withholding is imposed on the payer of the distribution, but the plan administrator will be held liable unless the plan administrator directs the payer to withhold the tax and provides the payer with the information necessary to make the withholding. If the payer is a different person from the plan administrator, a trustee for example, it is important that there is a clear understanding between the parties about the responsibilities for withholding.

Reporting and Disclosure

The reporting and disclosure provisions, enacted as part of ERISA in 1974, impose a variety of duties on employee benefit plans to report or disclose various plan information to the government and plan participants. The purpose of the reporting and disclosure provisions is to indirectly discourage various plan abuses on the theory that wrongdoers will be deterred by knowing that their wrongdoing may be exposed to public view. This approach to federal regulation is based on the success of the securities laws of the 1930s and is common in other areas of federal regulation. The statutory format in ERISA for reporting and disclosure is extremely complex and confusing, and many modifications of the original statutory procedure have since been made by regulation, although the underlying statutes remain the same.

The reporting and disclosure requirements currently consist of this series of reports, some annual and some not, that must be provided to the participant or filed with the government or both:

- *Summary Plan Description (SPD).* The SPD is a document intended to describe the plan to its participants in plain language. Whether they ask for it or not, it must be furnished to participants within 120 days after the plan is established or 90 days after a new participant enters the plan. There is no government form for the SPD; it can be designed according to the employer's specifications. However, the contents of the SPD are specified in minute detail by Department of Labor regulations. These regulations require, among other things, clear identification of the plan sponsor and funding entities, the plan's eligibility requirements, any possibilities of losses or forfeiture of benefits, procedures for making claims for benefits under the plan, and a prescribed statement of the participant's rights under the law.

    There is also a plain language requirement, and this can be extremely important in practice. If a participant or beneficiary claims a benefit and is disappointed to find that the benefit was not provided under the plan, it is quite likely that the disappointed claimant will find a lawyer who will look closely at the SPD for any ambiguities that might provide grounds for a lawsuit. Such lawsuits sometimes prove successful.

- *Annual Report (Form 5500).* This form is the centerpiece of the reporting requirements. The form is filed only with the IRS, but is made available to both the IRS and the Department of Labor. The form includes detailed financial information about the plan, including a signed report by an independent, qualified public accountant, along with any separate financial statements forming the basis of the independent accountant's report. If a qualified plan is subject to the minimum funding requirements, a signed report by the plan's enrolled actuary must be included, along with a certified actuarial valuation.

    Plans covering fewer than 100 participants are subject to simpler reporting requirements designed to reduce the cost of compliance for these plans. To get a better idea of the scope of the reporting requirements, it is useful to obtain from the IRS copies of Form 5500 and accompanying instructions and review them. These are available on the IRS web site.

    Form 5500 also includes schedule SSA, a schedule identifying participants who have separated from service during the year with deferred vested benefits under the plan. It is provided by the IRS to the Social Security

Administration so that at retirement any former participant may be notified of a deferred vested benefit from the plan.

■ *Report on Termination, Merger, or Other Changes (Forms 5310 and 5310A).* The plan administrator of a plan covered under the PBGC plan termination insurance discussed later in this chapter must notify the PBGC in advance of the termination. The Code and ERISA also contain a number of other reporting requirements in the event of a plan termination, merger, split up, transfer of assets and various other similar events. These are generally reported on Form 5310 or 5310A.

■ *Individual Benefit Statement.* On written request, the plan administrator must furnish an individual participant or beneficiary with a prescribed statement of his or her vested and unvested current plan benefits. This need not be furnished more than once a year. Some plan administrators provide these individual statements annually, even without a request from participants or beneficiaries.

The Health Insurance Portability and Accountability Act (HIPAA) imposes some additional requirements for information that must be included in summary plan descriptions for group health plans. (See the definition in Chapter 9.) These include the following:

■ Whether a plan is self-funded or whether an insurer (including a health maintenance organization) is responsible for the administration or financing of a plan

■ The name and address of any insurer responsible for administration or financing of a plan, the extent to which benefits under the plan are guaranteed by a contract or policy issued by the insurer, and the nature of any administrative services provided by the insurer

■ The office of the Department of Labor from which a participant may obtain information about HIPAA

ERISA does not require that a summary plan description be provided on a specific form, only that certain information be provided. Some employers use a single document; other employers incorporate much of the required information into the employee benefits handbook provided to their employees. Electronic transmissions of summary plan descriptions and other required information for participants are acceptable as long as certain conditions are met:

■ Electronic documents may be used only for participants who can access the documents at work and convert them to paper form.

■ The plan administrator must take appropriate measures to ensure that documents are actually received, such as the use of return receipt electronic mail features.

- The electronic documents must be prepared in accordance with style, format, and content requirements of Department of Labor regulations.
- Each participant must be notified, electronically or in writing, which documents will be furnished electronically, the significance of such documents, and the fact that paper copies of the documents can be received free of charge.
- The plan administrator must furnish a paper copy of any electronically submitted documents free of charge on request of a participant.

The reporting requirements are enforced by various types of penalties, including criminal penalties for willful violations or false statements.

In addition to the specific forms that must be filed or distributed, the reporting and disclosure requirements include a variety of sunshine provisions that give government agencies and participants rights to inspect and copy various documents and records relevant to the plan and its operation. Also, to obtain an advance determination letter or other IRS ruling, the plan documents usually must be submitted to the IRS.

INVESTMENT ISSUES

Investment issues are among the most complex and significant issues relating to employee benefit plans, involving the fiduciary relationship of plan sponsors to participants and beneficiaries, as well as larger issues of public policy. In this section, some basic rules and some of the more frequently occurring investment issues are discussed.

Fiduciary Requirements of ERISA and the Internal Revenue Code

A relationship in which one person holds and administers money or property belonging to another is legally described as a *fiduciary* relationship. A funded employee benefit plan, therefore, involves fiduciary relationships—plan assets are held by a trustee or insurance company, under the direction of the employer, on behalf of plan participants and beneficiaries. The rules governing fiduciary relationships are generally a subject of state law; however, in the case of qualified plans and other employee benefit plans, federal law (primarily ERISA) has superimposed specific federal fiduciary requirements that supersede state law where applicable. The federal requirements are usually stricter than the superseded state law requirements. While these rules are applicable to most employee benefit plans, they have their greatest impact on qualified pension and profit-sharing plans because welfare-benefit plans are typically insured or unfunded, although the use of funded welfare-benefit plans is increasing.

The fiduciary requirements were not intended as a helpful guide for employers and trustees in administering qualified plans. They do not spell out the specific responsibilities of each person involved in designing and maintaining the plan. Rather, the rules are intended to spread a net of liability over various persons involved with the plan, aimed at maximizing the protection of participants and beneficiaries. Thus, there are not always simple rules explaining how employers, trustees, and other persons should act with regard to qualified plans; rather, they must be aware of their fiduciary responsibilities and do their best to comply with them or avoid them.

The definition of *fiduciary* is broad enough to include the employer, the plan administrator, and the trustee. It also includes a wide variety of other possible targets. However, the government has stated that an attorney, accountant, actuary, or consultant who renders legal, accounting, actuarial, or consulting services to the plan will not be considered a fiduciary solely as a result of performing those services. Also, labor regulations exclude broker/dealers, banks, and reporting dealers from being treated as fiduciaries simply as a result of receiving and executing buy-sell instructions from the plan. Furthermore, a person giving investment advice will be considered a fiduciary only with respect to the assets covered by that investment advice.

Every plan must specify a *named fiduciary* in the plan document. The purpose of this requirement is not to limit liability to named persons, but rather to provide participants and the government with an easy target in case they decide to take legal action against the plan. Of course, other unnamed fiduciaries can also be included in the legal action.

The duties of fiduciaries specified in the law are primarily of an investment nature. According to ERISA Section 404, a fiduciary must do the following:

- Discharge duties with respect to a plan solely in the interest of the participants and the beneficiaries
- Act for the exclusive purpose of providing benefits to participants and their beneficiaries and defraying the reasonable expenses of administering the plan.
- Act with the care, skill, prudence, and diligence under the prevailing circumstances that a prudent man acting in a like capacity and familiar with such matters would use in the conduct of an enterprise of a like character and with like aims
- Diversify the investments of the plan to minimize the risk of large losses, unless under the circumstances it is clearly prudent not to do so.
- Follow the provisions of the documents and instruments governing the plan, unless inconsistent with ERISA provisions

In interpreting the prudent-man requirement, labor regulations indicate that the fiduciary must, in making an investment, determine that the particular investment is reasonably designed as part of the plan's portfolio to further the purposes of the plan. The fiduciary must consider (1) the composition of the portfolio with regard to diversification, (2) the liquidity and current return of the portfolio relative to the anticipated cash flow requirements of the plan, and (3) the projected return of the portfolio relative to the funding objectives of the plan.

A major exception to the diversification requirement applies to holdings of employer securities and employer real property. An eligible individual account plan (a profit-sharing, stock bonus, or employee stock ownership plan that specifically permits the holding of employer real property or qualifying employer securities) may hold such property in any amount, and may even hold such property as the exclusive assets of the plan. Other plans can hold such property only up to the extent of 10 percent of the fair market value of the plan assets. The purpose of this exception is, of course, to encourage the adoption of employer stock plans of the type discussed in Chapter 22. A qualifying employer security means employer stock or marketable debt obligations meeting the various requirements of ERISA Section 407. Employer real property is real property owned by the plan and leased to the employer, again under limitations set out in ERISA Section 407.

Fiduciaries can delegate fiduciary responsibilities and, therefore, avoid direct responsibility for performing the duty delegated. For example, the employer can delegate duties relating to the handling and investment of plan assets to a trustee, and investment management duties can be delegated to an appointed investment manager. The plan must provide a definite procedure for delegating these duties. The delegation of a fiduciary duty does not remove all fiduciary responsibility. A fiduciary will be liable for a breach of fiduciary responsibility of any other fiduciary under certain circumstances.

The broad scope of the fiduciary liabilities indicates that, in addition to careful delegation of fiduciary duties to well-chosen trustees and advisers, the employer should take care that its liability insurance coverage adequately covers any liabilities that might arise out of the fiduciary responsibility provisions. ERISA specifically prohibits a plan from excusing or exculpating any person from fiduciary liability, but individuals and employers are permitted to have appropriate insurance and employers can indemnify plan fiduciaries.

Prohibited Transactions

In addition to the general fiduciary requirements already described, both Code Section 4975 and ERISA Section 406 include a specific list of "don'ts" for employee benefit plans, including qualified plans. Under these rules, a *party-in-interest* is forbidden to do any of the following, with a number of exceptions described later:

- Sale or exchange, or leasing, of any property between the plan and a party-in-interest
- Lending of money or other extension of credit between the plan and a party-in-interest

- Furnishing of goods, services, or facilities between the plan and a party-in-interest
- Transfer to, or use by or for the benefit of, a party-in-interest of any assets of the plan
- Acquisition, on behalf of the plan, of any employer security or employer real property in excess of the limits described previously in this chapter

A *party-in-interest*—the Code uses instead the term *disqualified person*—is defined very broadly, again to bring the largest possible number of persons into the net to provide the maximum protection for plan participants. A party-in-interest includes the following:

- Any fiduciary, counsel, or employee of the plan
- A person providing services to the plan
- An employer, if any of its employees are covered by the plan
- An employee organization, any of whose members are covered by the plan
- An owner, direct or indirect, of a 50 percent or more interest in an employer or employee organization
- Various individuals and organizations related to those on this list, under specific rules given in Code Section 4975 and ERISA Section 406

Because of the breadth of the prohibited transaction rules, certain specific exclusions are provided in the law, and the IRS and Department of Labor are also given the authority to waive the prohibited transaction rules in certain circumstances.

First, the specific statutory exemptions: Loans to participants or beneficiaries are permitted under the rules discussed in Chapter 24. A loan to an ESOP by a party-in-interest is also permitted under certain circumstances to permit the ESOP to function as described in Chapter 22. Similar provisions permit such a plan to acquire employer securities or real property without violating the prohibited transaction rules. Also, the plan is allowed to pay a reasonable fee for legal, accounting, or other services performed by a party-in-interest. There are provisions permitting various financial services to the plan by a bank or insurance company that is a party-in-interest. Other provisions exempt normal benefit distributions from any possible conflict with the prohibited transaction rules.

In addition to the specific statutory exemptions, the Department of Labor has broad authority to grant an exemption to the prohibited transaction rules for a transaction or a class of transactions, after finding that the exemption is administratively feasible, in the interest of the plan and its participants and beneficiaries, and protective of their rights. There are specific administrative procedures for obtaining such exemptions. Pursuant to this authority, the Department of Labor has granted, among others, a class exemption permitting the sale of life insurance policies by participants to the plan or by the plan to participants. Another exemption, PTE84–14, permits a wide variety of transactions by qualified plan asset managers (QPAMs) such as banks and insurance companies. Individual exemptions have been granted for a variety of transactions, usually involving a sale to the plan by a party-in-interest of property that represents a particularly favorable investment opportunity for the plan.

Penalties

A violation of the prohibited transaction rules can result in a two-step penalty under the Internal Revenue Code, with the initial penalty equal to 15 percent of the amount involved, and an additional 100 percent penalty if the transaction is not corrected within a certain period of time. A violation of the prohibited transaction rules can also result in penalties for breach of fiduciary liability.

Unrelated Business Income

The trust fund under a qualified plan and trust funds used in some other self-insured employee benefit plans, such as Section 501(c)(9) trusts, are given a broad exemption from federal income tax similar to that granted to a variety of other institutions and organizations, such as churches, schools, and charities. However, such tax-exempt organizations are subject to federal income tax on *unrelated business taxable income* according to Code Sections 511–514. Unrelated business taxable income is income of a tax-exempt organization from a trade or business that is not related to the function that is the basis for the tax exemption. For example, if a charitable organization operates a full-time shoe store in a shopping center, the shoe store income would be taxable to the charity. However, the charity's tax exemption for its other income probably would not be jeopardized unless the effect of operating the shoe store was to shift the focus of the organization totally away from its exempt function.

The basic function of an employee benefit plan trust is to receive, invest, and distribute plan funds to participants and beneficiaries. Thus, passive investment income of the plan trust is usually not unrelated business income unless the investment is debt-financed, as described in the next paragraph. Problems sometimes arise in distinguishing passive investments from activities that might be considered a trade or business. The law specifically exempts dividends, interest, annuities, and royalties, as well as rents from real property and from personal property leased with real property. However, the wide variety of possible leasing arrangements indicates that each rental arrangement must be looked at on the basis of its own facts and circumstances. For example, a number of revenue rulings have held that investments in manufacturing or railroad equipment for leasing constituted an unrelated trade or business, even though these leasing arrangements are usually looked on by investors as strictly investment activities. Another revenue ruling, however, allows a qualified plan trust to hold shares in a real estate investment trust without incurring unrelated business taxable income. In short, the possible impact of unrelated business taxable income is an additional factor that must be taken into account by the investment advisers of a benefit plan trust.

Code Section 514 specifies that income from *debt-financed property* is to be treated by a tax-exempt organization as unrelated business taxable income. However, there is an exception in Section 514(c)(9) for qualified plans holding certain real estate investments that typically are highly leveraged or debt-financed. Therefore, such investments may still be advantageous to a qualified plan, particularly if they provide long-term growth or other benefits.

Investment Policy

The policy baseline for the investment of qualified plan funds is set by the rules previously discussed—the exclusive-benefit rule, the prudent-expert rule, the diversification requirement, liquidity requirements, the plan document itself, and the additional limitations imposed by the prohibited transaction and unrelated business income provisions. Within these constraints, however, a broad range of investment strategies is possible.

Growth-Oriented Strategies

Trustees governed by fiduciary rules aimed primarily at the preservation of principal generally do not follow aggressive, growth-oriented investment strategies, and pension trustees are no exception. However, qualified plan design offers a number of opportunities for incorporating growth-oriented investment strategies without running into fiduciary problems.

Defined-contribution plans can provide that part or all of each participant's account be put in a participant-directed account, with the participant then choosing the investment strategy. This relieves the trustee of liability for that choice if the plan meets requirements of Department of Labor regulations under ERISA Section 404c. Also, defined-contribution plan funds can be invested in pooled accounts of a bank or insurance company that offer participants choices of investment strategies—an equity fund, a fixed-income fund, and so on.

For defined-benefit plans, there is no provision for participant direction of investment; however, as discussed in Chapter 21, defined-benefit plan funds can be invested in insurance company funds utilizing separate account funding, with a choice by the employer of investment strategies such as equity or fixed income. It is also possible to structure the trust agreement to allow the employer to recommend investments, and the employer can pursue a growth-oriented strategy. In such a case, of course, the employer is still responsible for the adequacy of the pension fund and is subject to full fiduciary liability for its investment recommendations. Finally, there is the possibility of designing a plan to invest primarily in employer securities, which can be viewed as a type of growth-oriented investment strategy.

Risk

Most of the ERISA investment rules can be seen as prescriptions for avoiding risk, particularly the risk of large losses; for example, the requirement for diversification of investments. Within the ERISA limits, however, the qualified plan investment manager, like any investor, must balance risk and return.

Social Effects

According to the Employee Benefit Research Institute,[1] at the end of 1992, private pension funds (trusted and insured) in the United States totaled about $2.8 trillion, with government-employee funds comprising an additional $1.3 trillion. This is a sizable portion of the nation's capital. If there is any pattern to the investment strategies of qualified plan investment managers, such a pattern is likely to have an effect on the economy and on society. Because so much pension money is held and invested by large institutions such as banks and insurance companies, current pension investment policies largely reflect the views of these organizations. In general, such organizations will tend to invest in conventional ways that support the status quo. The question is often raised whether there is a role in pension investing for active attempts to support a particular social result not dictated merely by market conditions.

Existing legislation and other laws relating to qualified plan investments focus primarily on fiduciary aspects of the relationship between plan managers and participants; they do not address issues of social policy. That is, they encourage investment managers to invest so as to prevent direct losses to participants and beneficiaries, but they do not deal with possible indirect losses that may accrue to participants and beneficiaries as a result of trends in overall pension investment policy that may be contrary to the social and economic interests of plan participants.

Social Investing

In recent years, objections to prevailing pension investment policies have been raised, particularly on behalf of unionized employees in large manufacturing industries. Although these objections are not always clearly stated, four types of arguments can be distinguished. First, it is stated that the usual pension investment policies contribute to the disinvestment in basic manufacturing industries that has been occurring, particularly in certain geographic areas such as the Midwest. This results in the loss of jobs for persons covered under the pension plans, with the attendant economic and social costs, and also in disinvestment in housing and other facilities in communities where plan participants live. Second, it is stated that pension investors can undercut the union movement by investing in nonunionized corporations. Third, pension investment policies allegedly can affect the welfare of workers adversely by investing in corporations that violate health, safety, or nondiscrimination

---

[1] *EBRI Databook on Employee Benefits,* 3rd ed. (1995).

principles. Finally, some object to investing in certain corporations on moral or political grounds (not directly related to the interests of plan participants), such as environmental pollution or weapons production. Although advocates of social investment for union pension funds sometimes make common cause with religious and academic groups who advocate social investment policies for church or university endowment funds, it is clear that on this issue the interests of unionized employees are quite distinct.

A decision by a pension investment manager to pursue a social investment strategy that attempts to avoid one or more of these objections raises a number of issues. The first relates to fiduciary responsibility. Does a social investment strategy result in a lower return on the fund? There are some studies indicating that an investment portfolio of "good guy" investments has a lower return. However, such studies usually choose the "good" investments using a broad range of criteria, so they do not indicate the effects of narrower targeting such as simply excluding nonunion employers. The "efficient markets" theory proposed by some economists would suggest that in the long run an investment strategy based on social investing should have no effect on investment return, so long as investments are sufficiently diversified and the market includes other investors who do not use the same social criteria.

Some social investment advocates suggest that even if the return is lower, the indirect social and economic benefits to plan participants are a compensating factor. However, under current fiduciary law, both state and federal, this argument probably could not protect an investment manager in the event of a lawsuit by a plan participant injured directly by a low return on the fund. Suggestions have been made in Congress to amend federal legislation to permit social investment of various types, but no such provision has yet been enacted. The Department of Labor is reportedly studying the issue, but no regulations or rulings in this area have been issued.

A second problem is, assuming a social investment strategy has been chosen, how does the investment manager evaluate possible investments to determine their compliance with the chosen social criteria? It is currently difficult to identify corporations that meet even such simple criteria as compliance with health and safety legislation. There are various social investment indices available, but these are generally inadequate as guidance in any specific program of social investing. Because of these difficulties, social investing usually involves additional administrative costs.

The pension investment community has generally reacted with some hostility to social investing, with most pension advisers taking the view that any considerations other than the traditional ones of risk and return have no part in pension investment decisions, and that it would be a violation of fiduciary responsibility to use other criteria.

PLAN TERMINATION

To be qualified, the regulations require that a plan be "permanent." By this it is meant only that the employer must not have an *initial* intention of operating the plan for a few years to obtain tax benefits and then terminating it. Thus, despite the permanence requirement, qualified plans can be terminated and often are.

A plan can be terminated unilaterally by the employer, unless a collective bargaining agreement or other employment contract prohibits it. If an employer does not formally terminate a plan, but merely discontinues contributions to it, the IRS may find that the plan has been terminated, with the same consequences as if a formal termination had been made by the employer. It is also possible to have a *partial termination* of a plan, which usually means that the plan is terminated for an identifiable group of employees, such as employees at a given geographic location, while it is continued for other employees.

When Should a Plan Be Terminated?

If a qualified plan ceases to be an effective method of compensating employees, or becomes too expensive for the employer, it should be terminated. However, under the rules discussed in this chapter, a proposed termination may have such undesirable consequences that the employer will decide to continue the plan, possibly in amended form. As discussed below, the substitution of a different plan or plans may avoid some of the undesirable consequences of simply terminating the old plan.

Asset-Reversion Terminations

Defined-benefit plans are sometimes terminated not because they are too costly or ineffective but because the employer wants to take out some of the plan's assets. If the plan is fully funded, excess plan assets will revert to the employer, if the plan so provides. The assets that revert are taxable income to the employer.

For some time, commentators have expressed concern that the applicable law in this area favors stripping of assets from qualified plans, with a possible detriment to the retirement security of employees. Congress initially responded to this concern by imposing a 10 percent tax on asset reversions, in addition to the income tax payable on the reversion amount. This tax was criticized as merely penalizing employers slightly without any direct benefit to employees. Consequently, the law was changed; the penalty is now set at 50 percent of the reversion amount unless (1) the employer adopts a replacement plan, (2) the employer provides pro rata increases in the benefits of participants in the terminated plan totaling at least 20 percent of the reversion, or (3) the employer is in bankruptcy. If any of these three conditions is met, the excise tax is 20 percent rather than 50 percent (Code Section 4980).

Consequences of Termination

If an employer terminates a plan within a few years after its inception, the employer must usually show that the termination resulted from *business necessity* or the IRS will infer that the permanence requirement for qualification never existed. The plan will thus be treated as a nonqualified deferred compensation arrangement, resulting in a loss of tax benefits for both employer and employees. If the plan is terminated after many years of operation, the IRS will not raise a presumption of impermanence so long as the plan is properly funded and termination does not result in prohibited discrimination.

Plan termination results in immediate 100 percent vesting for some or all employees. With a defined-benefit plan, 100 percent vesting means that the accrued benefits of affected participants become 100 percent vested at the time of termination, to the extent the plan is funded. Most defined-benefit plans are insured by the PBGC, and the further complications involved are discussed below. At termination, with a defined-contribution plan, participants become 100 percent vested in their account balances derived from employer contributions, regardless of where they stand otherwise on the vesting schedule. This precludes the possibility of any future forfeitures (and therefore, in a profit-sharing plan, any future reallocation of forfeitures). Obviously, the purpose of the vesting remedy is to limit the possibility of any discrimination resulting from termination of the plan.

THE PENSION BENEFIT GUARANTY CORPORATION AND ITS PLAN INSURANCE

If an employer encounters financial difficulty and is forced to terminate or curtail a qualified defined-benefit plan, the ultimate payment of plan benefits is often jeopardized. If the plan uses an insurance company contract as the funding medium, the employee's benefit is usually to some extent guaranteed by the insurance company. However, the use of trust funds predominates in defined-benefit plans, and these funds usually involve no insurance company guarantees. Actuarial funding methods assume that plans will be in existence indefinitely. As a result, the plan fund in many cases is, at a given moment, inadequate to fund all of the benefits accrued under the plan if the plan terminates at that moment.

Recognizing this problem, Congress established a scheme of mandatory plan insurance for certain defined-benefit plans as part of ERISA (Title 4) in 1974. The insurance is administered by a quasi-governmental corporation called the Pension Benefit Guaranty Corporation (PBGC). Defined-contribution plans do not involve the same benefit security problems as defined-benefit plans because the participant's accrued benefit is always equal to the participant's account balance. Therefore, the PBGC plan insurance scheme does not apply to defined-contribution ("individual account") plans.

Plans Covered

PBGC coverage can be summarized by stating that, in general, all qualified defined-benefit plans are covered, while individual account (defined-contribution) plans are not covered. With respect to defined-benefit plans, the usual exclusions applicable to ERISA provisions apply: there is no PBGC coverage for federal, state, and local government plans; church plans (unless the plan elects coverage); plans with no employer contributions; plans for highly compensated individuals or substantial owners; plans frozen prior to ERISA; and various other exclusions.

Benefits Insured

The PBGC does not insure or guarantee all benefits provided under a qualified defined-benefit plan covered by PBGC insurance. A distinction is made between *basic* and *nonbasic* benefits. The PBGC is required under the terms of its federal charter to insure basic benefits. PBGC is allowed to extend coverage to nonbasic benefits, but it has not yet done so.

There are numerous conditions and limitations on what qualifies as a guaranteed basic benefit, set out in Part 2613 of the PBGC regulations. The most significant limitations are as follows:

- The benefit must be nonforfeitable or vested. This refers to vesting that existed under the terms of the plan immediately prior to plan termination, not to benefits that became vested solely on account of plan termination.
- The benefit must be a "pension benefit"—a benefit payable as an annuity to a retiring or terminating participant or surviving beneficiary, providing a substantially level retirement income to the recipient. Consequently, the PBGC generally does not insure a lump-sum benefit.
- There is a dollar limitation on the amount of monthly payment the PBGC will guarantee. Regardless of the plan provisions, the insured monthly benefit is limited to one-twelfth of the participant's average annual gross income from the employer during the highest paid five consecutive calendar years or lesser number of years of active participation. Furthermore, in no event will the insured benefit exceed a dollar limit, originally $750 monthly in 1974, which is subject to an indexation procedure. For plans terminated in 2000, the limit was $3,221.59 monthly. The dollar limitation applies to a benefit in the form of a straight-life annuity beginning at age 65 and payable monthly. The limit is adjusted actuarially for other forms of benefits.
- The participant must be "entitled" to the benefit as of the date of plan termination. Generally, this means that the recipient must have satisfied the conditions of the plan necessary to establish the right to receive the benefit (other than mere application for it or satisfying a waiting period) prior to the plan termination date. Also, the benefit must be payable to or for the benefit of a natural person (not, for example, a corporation).

PBGC Funding and Premiums

The PBGC has established several funds to provide benefit guarantees. It has the power to borrow up to $100 million from the U.S. Treasury if necessary. However, the PBGC is expected to be self-supporting and is therefore required to charge insurance premiums for its guarantees. For single employer plans, the basic annual premium for 2000 is $19 per participant. For certain underfunded plans, an additional annual premium may be required, depending on the amount of the plan's unfunded vested benefits. Congress has the authority through a joint resolution procedure to review and change PBGC rates from time to time, based on various factors set out in the law. Payment of the premiums is mandatory, and is enforced by various penalties.

Plan Termination Procedures

Reportable Events

The PBGC becomes involved with a plan that is terminating or encountering various difficulties in somewhat complex ways. First of all, the plan administrator is obligated to report to the PBGC certain events that could potentially cause financial difficulty. There is a long list of these *reportable events;* some significant ones are these:

- An IRS or Department of Labor disqualification of the plan
- A plan amendment decreasing retirement benefits
- A decrease in the number of active participants to less than 80 percent of the number at the beginning of the plan year or 75 percent of the number at the beginning of the previous plan year
- A determination by the IRS that there has been a termination or partial termination of the plan
- A failure to meet the minimum funding standards
- An inability by the plan to pay benefits when due
- Certain large distributions to a substantial owner
- A plan merger, consolidation, or transfer of its assets
- The occurrence of another event indicative of a need to terminate the plan—the regulations refer to such items as insolvency of the employer or a related employer and certain breakups of commonly controlled groups of employers

If the consequences of these reportable events are significant enough, the plan can be *involuntarily terminated* by the PBGC. Also, of course, a *voluntary termination* can be carried out by the plan administrator under one of the two procedures described below. In any event, the actual termination of a plan covered by PBGC guarantees is carried out under detailed procedures set out in the law.

Allocation of Plan Assets on Termination

The PBGC termination procedures revolve around the rules for allocation of the assets of a terminated defined-benefit plan under ERISA Section 4044. On termination, such plan assets must be allocated in descending order to the following categories:

- Benefits attributable to voluntary employee contributions.
- Benefits attributable to mandatory employee contributions.
- Annuity benefits attributable to employer contributions that were, or could have been, in "pay status" as of three years prior to termination. A benefit in "pay status" means a benefit being paid to a retired (nonactive) employee. The high priority reflects the fact that such employees are least able to protect themselves against a failure of the plan fund.
- All other PBGC guaranteed benefits.
- All other vested benefits.
- All other plan benefits.

Any amount remaining after these categories may revert to the employer, if the plan so provides.

Voluntary Plan Termination

ERISA Section 4041(a) provides for two types of voluntary termination procedures, the *standard termination* and the *distress termination*. A plan is eligible for the standard termination only if assets at the termination date are sufficient to provide for all *benefit commitments* as of the termination date. A benefit commitment to a participant or beneficiary means all benefits guaranteed by the PBGC as described earlier, but determined without certain limitations, such as the maximum dollar limit or the restriction on benefits in effect for less than 60 months before plan termination. Certain early retirement supplements and plant closing benefits also come within the definition of benefit commitments. If benefit commitments are not met, a voluntary termination must follow the distress termination procedures.

With a standard termination, the plan administrator must provide 60 days advance notice of intent to terminate to participants, beneficiaries, and other affected parties.

The plan administrator must begin distributing plan assets at the end of the 60-day determination period if the PBGC has not issued a notice of noncompliance and if the plan assets are sufficient to meet benefit commitments. The assets are distributed in accordance with the priorities of ERISA Section 4044 described above. Assets must be distributed either through the purchase of annuities from an insurance company to provide plan benefits or in some other manner providing adequate benefit security.

A distress termination is available only if one of three distress criteria is met:

1. Each contributing sponsor of the plan or substantial member of a controlled group sponsoring the plan must be in a liquidation proceeding under federal bankruptcy law or similar state law; or
2. The sponsor must be involved in a reorganization in bankruptcy or an insolvency proceeding; or
3. The plan administrator demonstrates to the PBGC that unless the termination occurs, the sponsor will not be able to pay its debts and will be unable to continue in business, or the cost of providing benefits under the pension plan has become unreasonably burdensome (for example, because of a declining work force).

On a distress termination, the plan administrator must submit to the PBGC information similar to that required under a standard termination, plus information related to the distress criteria. If the PBGC determines that there are sufficient plan assets to fulfill benefit commitments, the plan administrator may begin to distribute the assets in accordance with ERISA Section 4044.

Contingent Liability of Employer

In the event of a plan termination covered by PBGC insurance, the employer must reimburse the PBGC for the PBGC's liability for guaranteed benefits in excess of the plan's assets. However, under ERISA Section 4062, any amount of the employer's liability that exceeds 30 percent of the employer's net worth, can be deferred under "commercially reasonable" terms. This PBGC remedy may be of limited value for large bankrupt employers with no net worth or financial resources.

Multiemployer Plans

The previous discussion of termination procedures applies primarily to single employer plans or plans of controlled groups of employers. The termination problems are somewhat different where contributions to the plan are made by a number of unrelated employers—that is, a multiemployer plan such as a plan adopted under industrywide collective bargaining agreements. For such plans, there are different asset allocation provisions and somewhat different provisions for involuntary termination by the PBGC.

The most significant difference from single employer plans involves the *withdrawal liability* of an employer that completely or partially withdraws from a multiemployer plan. A sale of the employer's assets in an arm's-length transaction will not be treated as a withdrawal as long as the purchaser of the business continues the plan, the purchaser provides an acceptable surety bond or escrow deposit for five years after the sale, and the seller of the business remains secondarily liable for five years. If an employer withdraws from the plan, the employer's withdrawal liability is an amount based on the withdrawing employer's share of unfunded vested benefits under the plan. The withdrawing employer must pay all or a substantial portion of the withdrawal liability to the plan on a periodic basis over a number of years. The law provides for the PBGC to establish a supplemental fund to reimburse multiemployer plans for any uncollectible employer withdrawal liabilities.

STUDY QUESTIONS

1. What are the steps necessary for an employer to adopt a qualified plan for a given year?

2. a. Why is it desirable to obtain an advance determination letter for a qualified plan?
   b. What recourse might be available to an employer if the IRS finds a plan is not qualified?

3. What types of employee benefit plans are exempt from the fiduciary, reporting, and disclosure requirements of ERISA?

4. a. What is the purpose of the reporting and disclosure provisions of ERISA?
   b. Briefly describe the reports ERISA requires qualified plans to provide to participants or to the federal government.

5. What objectives were the fiduciary requirements of ERISA enacted to accomplish?

6. What are the investment responsibilities of a fiduciary under ERISA?

7. Explain why each of the following is or is not a prohibited transaction.
   a. The sale of real estate owned by the ABC Plan to the wife of the treasurer of the ABC Company.
   b. Loaning money from the plan to an officer of the corporation. The plan contains a loan provision that permits loans on a nondiscriminatory basis.
   c. The acquisition of 25 percent of employer stock by a defined-benefit plan.
   d. The acquisition of real estate from the plan for less than its market value by the plan's trustee.

8. What is unrelated business taxable income and what is the effect of having it?

9. The Faulty Corporation installed a pension plan five years ago and because of declining profits, the firm is considering terminating the plan to help prevent insolvency.
   a. What will be the IRS's likely reaction to this termination? Explain.
   b. What alternatives are available to the corporation other than terminating the plan?

10. What qualified plan benefits are insured by the Pension Benefit Guaranty Corporation?

Individual Retirement Plans and Simplified Employee Pensions

Certain tax-favored arrangements that are not technically qualified plans can offer employees the same tax deferral advantages as the qualified plans discussed in previous chapters. These nonqualified but tax-favored arrangements are individual retirement accounts and simplified employee pensions. Where these plans are available, they can be a useful supplement or alternative to a qualified plan adopted by an employer.

INDIVIDUAL RETIREMENT PLANS

Complete retirement planning, at least from the employee's viewpoint, requires consideration of individual retirement accounts or annuities (IRAs), which allow individuals to adopt a plan that provides tax deferral benefits somewhat similar to those available from an employer plan. The role of IRAs is a limited one, however. Individuals who are participants in qualified plans and whose income exceeds specified limits are limited or excluded altogether from eligibility for IRA deductions. And no employee can contribute more than $2,000 annually to an IRA (or $4,000 including a spousal IRA).

IRAs can be used by employers as part of their employee plan design, either through simply sponsoring an IRA plan or adopting an arrangement known as a *simplified employee pension (SEP),* under which employer contributions are made systematically to employees' IRAs. SEPs permit a contribution level similar to that for a qualified plan and are viewed as an alternative to a qualified plan.

Eligibility for IRAs

To be eligible for an IRA, an employee or self-employed person must have compensation or earned income.[1] Compensation or earned income means income received from services actually performed by the individual. This includes compensation from self-employment as well as from an employer. The definition has been extended to also include taxable alimony received by a divorced spouse. It does not include investment income, any amount received as a pension or annuity, or any amount received as deferred compensation.

Deduction Limit

The annual IRA deduction limit for an individual is the lesser of $2,000 or the individual's earned income.

Deductible IRA contributions are restricted to the following:

[1.]Most of the IRA rules are found in Code Sections 219 and 408 and related regulations; these references will not be repeated in this chapter.

- Individuals who are not active participants in an employer-maintained retirement plan for any part of the retirement plan year ending with or within the individual's taxable year
- Any other individual, as long as the individual (or married couple if a joint return is filed) has adjusted gross income below a specified limit. If the adjusted gross income exceeds this limit, the $2,000 IRA limit is reduced under a formula that eventually permits no deduction

The *active participant* restriction applies if the individual is an active participant in any of the following:

- A regular qualified plan
- A Section 403(b) tax-deferred annuity plan
- A simplified employee pension (SEP)
- A federal, state, or local government plan, not including a Section 457 nonqualified deferred-compensation plan

If an otherwise eligible person actively participates in an employer plan, the available IRA deduction is reduced below $2,000 if the AGI of the taxpayer is within the phaseout ranges indicated in the chart shown to the right, with the deduction eliminated entirely if the AGI is above the upper limit of the phaseout range.

		Married Filing	Married Filing
IRA Active Participant AGI Phaseout Ranges			
Year	**Single**	**Jointly**	**Separately**
1998	$30,000 – $40,000	$50,000 – $ 60,000	$0 – $10,000
1999	31,000 – 41,000	51,000 – 61,000	0 – 10,000
2000	32,000 – 42,000	52,000 – 62,000	0 – 10,000
2001	33,000 – 43,000	53,000 – 63,000	0 – 10,000
2002	34,000 – 44,000	54,000 – 64,000	0 – 10,000
2003	40,000 – 50,000	60,000 – 70,000	0 – 10,000
2004	45,000 – 55,000	65,000 – 75,000	0 – 10,000
2005	50,000 – 60,000	70,000 – 80,000	0 – 10,000
2006	50,000 – 60,000	75,000 – 85,000	0 – 10,000
2007 and later	50,000 – 60,000	80,000 – 100,000	0 – 10,000

The reduction in the IRA deduction for those affected is computed by multiplying the IRA limit ($2,000 or 100 percent of compensation) by a fraction equal to

$$\frac{\text{Taxpayer's adjusted gross income} - \text{full deduction limit}}{\$10,000}$$

There is a $200 floor under this formula—if the result comes out to less than $200, the taxpayer can contribute and deduct $200.

■ **EXAMPLE 1:**

A married couple, both of whom are active participants in a regular qualified plan, files a joint return and has an AGI of $55,000 in 2000.

$$\frac{\$\ 3,000}{\$10,000} \times \$2,000 = \$600$$

$$\$\ 2,000\ -\ \$600 = \$1,400 \text{ IRA deduction limit}$$

■ **EXAMPLE 2:**

A single person, an active participant in a qualified plan, has an AGI of $41,500 in 2000.

$$\frac{\$\ 9,500}{\$10,000} \times \$2,000 = \$1,900$$

$$\$\ 2,000\ -\ \$1,900 = \$100$$

However, the individual may contribute $200, the floor amount

---

Spousal IRAs

The spousal IRA provision permits married couples who file a joint return to make a higher level of deductible IRA contributions (up to a total of $4,000 annually) in some cases by permitting an additional deduction for the non-working spouse. If one spouse is nonworking or earns less than the other spouse, the maximum amount deductible for the lower-earning spouse is the lesser of (1) $2,000 or (2) 100 percent of the lower-earner's compensation, plus 100 percent of the higher-earner's compensation minus the amount taken as an IRA deduction by the higher earner.

■ **EXAMPLE**

Individual Pat earns $30,000 and Pat's spouse, Chris, is not working. The couple may contribute and deduct up to $2,000 annually to an IRA for Chris. If Pat is eligible for an IRA, the couple may also contribute and deduct up to $2,000 for Pat's IRA.

If an individual is an "active participant" as described in the preceding section, his or her spouse will not be deemed to be an active participant. Therefore, an IRA will be available even if the other spouse is an active participant. However, this deductible contribution is phased out for AGI between $150,000 and $160,000 (so the deduction is unavailable for AGI of $160,000 or more).

Nondeductible IRAs

Individuals not permitted to make deductible IRA contributions may, nevertheless, make such contributions on a nondeductible basis, up to the usual $2,000/100 percent limit. The total of any individual's annual IRA contributions both deductible and nondeductible, together with Roth IRA contributions (see below) cannot exceed $2,000. Nondeductible contributions (but not income on those contributions) are tax free when ultimately distributed to the individual. If nondeductible contributions to an IRA are made, any amounts withdrawn are treated as partly tax free and partly taxable under rules similar to the exclusion ratio calculation for annuities under Code Section 72.

Roth IRAs

A Roth IRA is a specialized form of nondeductible IRA. Contributions to a Roth IRA are nondeductible, but distributions (including earnings on accumulated contributions) are tax free as long as certain requirements are satisfied. Roth IRAs are not limited or prohibited if the individual is an active participant in a qualified plan, as with deductible IRAs. Many individuals will have a choice between using the traditional IRA or contributing to the new Roth IRA. As indicated above, total contributions for the year (to either type of IRA) can not exceed $2,000.

The maximum contribution to a Roth IRA is phased out for individuals with AGIs between $95,000 and $110,000 (pro rata reduction over $15,000 income spread). For joint filers the phaseout occurs for AGIs between $150,000 and $160,000 (pro rata reduction over $10,000 income spread). Unlike traditional IRAs, contributions can even be made after attainment of age 70½. For distributions to be tax free they generally have to be made after the participant attains age 59½, although exceptions are made if payments are made on account of death or disability or used for qualifying first-time homebuyer expenses. An otherwise eligible distribution won't be qualified if made within the five-tax-year period beginning with the first tax year for which a contribution was made to an individual's Roth IRA. If a nonqualifying distribution is made, amounts representing earnings are subject to both income tax and the 10 percent penalty tax that currently applies to early distributions from regular IRAs and other qualified retirement plans (see below). However, Roth IRA contributions can be withdrawn first, before earnings are taxed.

Other Restrictions on IRAs

Because the IRA is designed primarily for retirement savings, no IRA deduction is allowed to an individual for the taxable year in which the individual attains age 70½ or any later year.

Contributions to an IRA must be made in cash; contributions of property such as an insurance policy are not permitted.

Excess Contributions

A contribution in excess of the deductible limits described above is an *excess contribution* subject to an annual nondeductible 6 percent excise tax (Code Section 4973). The excise tax continues to be applied each year until the contribution is withdrawn from the IRA. Many complex rules apply to excess contributions; their complexity seems out of proportion to the actual issue involved.

Timing of Contributions

An IRA for any given year may be established up to the time for filing the tax return for the given year, not including extensions. Deductible contributions for a given year may be made within the same time limit. This "last minute" feature of IRAs helps to explain a lot of their popularity. For example, suppose Frank Filer works out a draft of his 2000 tax return on April 1, 2001, and discovers that he owes the government $600. His local savings bank is running an advertising campaign touting its IRAs and offering to lend money to contribute to an IRA. Frank does some quick figuring and discovers that if he borrows $2,000 from the bank and contributes it to an IRA, it will wipe out his tax liability and he will be entitled to a $160 tax refund, enough to make the first monthly payment on the loan. This may be a more attractive deal to Frank than borrowing $600 to pay taxes.

Limitations on IRA Distributions

To limit any benefits for nonretirement distributions from IRAs, there is a penalty under Code Section 72(t) for certain early IRA distributions similar to the early distribution penalty applicable to qualified plans. The IRA early distribution penalty is 10 percent of the taxable amount of any distribution except for the following:

- Distributions made on or after attainment of age 59½
- Distributions made to a beneficiary or employee's estate on or after the employee's death
- Distributions attributable to disability
- Distributions that are part of a series of substantially equal periodic payments made at least annually over the life or life expectancy of the participant, or the joint lives or life expectancies of the participant and beneficiary
- Certain distributions to unemployed individuals for health insurance premiums
- Distributions to the extent they are eligible for an itemized medical expense

- Distributions to pay for certain higher education expenses for the taxpayer, spouse, child, or grandchild
- Distributions up to $10,000 for first-home purchases

Loans from IRAs are treated as distributions and, therefore, are not available for practical purposes. This is another aspect of IRAs that makes them less flexible than regular qualified plans, which allow loans.

There is an *upper limit* on the length of time amounts may be maintained in an IRA. Distributions from an IRA must begin no later than April 1 of the year following the year in which the individual attains age 70½. The distribution may be in the form of a lump sum or periodic payments. The minimum annual distribution is a periodic payment determined on the basis of a period not extending beyond the life expectancy of the individual or the joint life expectancy of the individual and a designated beneficiary. If an individual or beneficiary dies before the entire interest is distributed, the remaining amount must, within five years after the death, be distributed or applied to the purchase of an immediate life annuity for the beneficiary for a term not exceeding the life expectancy of the beneficiary. In general, these rules are the same as the rules under Section 401(a)(9) for distributions from qualified plans, discussed in Chapter 24.

If the assets of the IRA are not distributed at least as rapidly as described above, there is an excise tax of 50 percent of the *excess accumulation* (Code Section 4974). The excess accumulation is the amount by which the minimum amount required to be distributed during a given year (under the above rules) exceeds the amount actually distributed during the year. The IRS is allowed to waive the 50 percent penalty to avoid penalizing reasonable errors.

Taxation of Distributions

The amount distributed from an IRA is taxable as ordinary income in the year of receipt. Lump-sum distributions are taxable when received and do not qualify for the special capital-gain or averaging provisions applicable to lump-sum distributions from qualified plans. An IRA annuity is taxed under the Section 72 annuity rules—payments based on deductible contributions and all investment earnings are ordinary income and are taxable in full as received. Nondeductible IRA contributions, if any, are recovered tax free through an exclusion ratio applied to each payment.

The value of an annuity or lump sum received by any beneficiary of a participant in an IRA is included in the deceased participant's gross estate for federal estate tax purposes. However, if the beneficiary is a spouse, there is no estate tax because of the unlimited marital deduction under the estate tax. Even for a nonspouse beneficiary, there may be no estate tax if the estate is relatively small—less than $675,000 (scheduled to rise to $1 million in 2007).

Funding of IRAs

The code provides two funding vehicles for IRAs: individual retirement accounts and individual retirement annuities.

Individual Retirement Accounts

An individual retirement account must be a plan established under a written trust created or organized in the United States for the exclusive benefit of the individual creating the IRA. A written custodial agreement can also be used. The written instrument must include the following provisions:

- The contributions must be in cash and not exceed $2,000 on behalf of any individual.
- The trustee must be a bank or "other person" approved by the IRS.
- No part of the trust fund will be invested in life insurance contracts. Annuities, however, can be purchased.
- An individual's account is nonforfeitable.
- The assets of the trust will not be commingled with other property except in a common trust fund or common investment fund.
- The individual's account must be distributed in accordance with certain distribution requirements, such as the age 70½ provision and the minimum distribution requirement.

Many banks and other savings institutions are actively marketing trusteed IRAs. Brokerage houses and mutual funds also market trusteed IRAs. These technically use a bank as trustee but the bank's role is purely formal and the investor views the broker or fund as the sponsor of the IRA.

A bank or institution acting as trustee or custodian may prepare its own prototype trust agreement and submit the agreement to the IRS for approval on Form 5306. Alternatively, the IRS has issued prototype trust and custodial agreements (Forms 5305 and 5305A), which, if used, are automatically qualified. An individual who deposits funds in an IRA that uses an approved form of trust agreement does not have to submit the IRA to the IRS for approval.

Individual Retirement Annuities

An individual may fund an IRA by purchasing an *individual retirement annuity*. An individual retirement annuity is a contract that is issued by an insurance company and that meets requirements parallel to those listed above for individual retirement accounts. The premium for the annuity may not be fixed, so the only insurance product that can be used is a flexible premium annuity. Both fixed-dollar and variable annuities can be used.

Insurance companies that wish to market individual retirement annuities may apply for IRS approval of their own prototype contracts. As with trusteed plans, an individual who purchases an approved prototype individual retirement annuity contract does not apply separately for IRS approval of the individual IRA plan.

Rollovers

To increase the amount of investment flexibility available to participants in IRAs and qualified plans, the Code contains a number of provisions relating to the use of IRAs as vehicles for investment *rollovers*. Three types of tax-favored rollovers are possible.

Rollover from One IRA to Another

There is no current taxation if an individual withdraws an amount out of an IRA trust fund, IRA annuity or retirement bond plan and invests part or all of it in another IRA plan. To receive this treatment, the amount to be rolled over must be paid into another IRA plan not later than the sixtieth day after the withdrawal. If such a rollover is made, no additional tax-free rollover of this type is permitted for period of one year thereafter.

A direct transfer of an account from one IRA trustee to another (with the participant never receiving the money) is not treated as a rollover for purposes of these rules. Thus, a direct transfer can be used as a way of avoiding the one-year rule.

Rollover of Distribution from Qualified Plan or Annuity

An IRA may be used as a vehicle for receiving the proceeds of a distribution from a qualified plan or a Section 403(b) plan, thereby avoiding immediate taxation on the distribution. If the rollover amount is transferred to the participant, however, tax must be withheld. To avoid this, the rollover should be a direct transfer from the plan trustee to the IRA trustee. All or any portion of the amount received can be rolled over. The 100 percent/$2,000 limit does not apply to a rollover contribution. If the rollover is made by the participant (rather than as a direct transfer), the rollover contribution must be made on or before the sixtieth day after receipt of the distribution. An existing IRA can be used, or a new one may be set up.

The part of the distribution that is rolled over into the IRA will not be currently taxable to the recipient. The usual rules for taxation of IRA distributions will apply when this amount is subsequently withdrawn. Any part of the distribution from the qualified plan or Section 403(b) plan that is not rolled over into the IRA will be taxable at the time of receipt under the usual rules for taxation of distributions, except that the averaging provisions may not be used.

In deciding whether or not to roll over all or part of the proceeds of a distribution from a qualified plan to an IRA, the alternatives must be considered. A lump-sum distribution from a qualified plan may qualify for the special averaging provisions of the Code. Thus, even though a distribution that is not rolled over is taxable immediately, it is taxable under advantageous provisions if it qualifies as a lump-sum distribution. A distribution that is rolled over will not be taxed immediately; taxation will be deferred to the time when it is withdrawn from the IRA. However, this subsequent distribution, like any IRA distribution, is not eligible for the averaging provisions; rather, the taxable amount is taxed as ordinary income.

Despite the possible loss of averaging, however, the mere deferral of taxes resulting from a rollover may be advantageous. Furthermore, taxes on investment earnings of the IRA are also deferred until the rollover amount is distributed. Although it is somewhat complex, the tax consequences of the two alternatives can be calculated (under appropriate assumptions) and compared; some financial planners provide such advice to their clients. Computer software for this purpose is now widely available.

IRA as Conduit for Transfer from One Plan to Another

Finally, an IRA may be used as a conduit to carry out a tax-free transfer of cash or property from one corporate qualified plan to another. Basically, if the amount received from the qualified plan is transferred within 60 days to an IRA, the transfer is tax free, as described earlier. In addition, if the IRA plan contains no assets other than those attributable to the distribution from the qualified plan, then the amount in the IRA may subsequently be transferred tax free to another qualified plan. Similar provisions allow an IRA to be used as a conduit between two Section 403(b) annuity plans.

Employer-Sponsored IRAs

Although the IRA is viewed primarily as a device for facilitating individual retirement savings, an employer may sponsor an IRA for some or all employees. A labor union may also sponsor an IRA plan for its members. There is no requirement that employer-sponsored IRAs be available to all employees or be nondiscriminatory in coverage.

The contributions to the employer-sponsored IRA may be made as additional compensation or as a salary reduction. Any amount contributed by the employer to the IRA is taxable to the employee as additional compensation income. The employee is then eligible for the IRA tax deduction up to the 100 percent/$2,000 limitation. Because the amounts contributed are additional compensation, they are subject to FICA and FUTA taxes, therefore adding to employer costs. No federal income tax withholding is required if the employer believes that the employee will be entitled to the offsetting IRA tax deduction.

SIMPLIFIED EMPLOYEE PENSIONS

The simplified employee pension (SEP) is an expanded version of the employer-sponsored IRA, designed by Congress to make it easy and attractive for employers to adopt a retirement plan which, although not a qualified plan as such, has similar features. A SEP is designed much like an employer-sponsored IRA, but the deduction limits are much higher—instead of a $2,000 annual deduction limit, the limit on deductible contributions for each employee is the lesser of $30,000 or 15 percent of the employee's compensation. The price for this expanded deduction limit is that the employer loses discretion as to who must be covered; there is a coverage requirement that in some ways is more stringent than that for regular qualified plans.

Eligibility and Coverage

If the employer has a SEP plan, it must cover all employees who are at least 21 years of age and who have worked for the employer during three out of the preceding five calendar years. Part-time employment counts in determining this; there is no 1,000-hour definition of a year of service. However, contributions need not be made on behalf of employees whose compensation for the calendar year was less than $300 (as indexed for inflation; 2000: $450). The plan can exclude employees who are members of collective bargaining units if retirement benefits have been the subject of good-faith bargaining, and it can also exclude nonresident aliens. Employer contributions to a SEP can be made for employees over age 70½; these employees are not eligible for regular IRAs, as discussed earlier.

Contributions and Deductions

An employer need not contribute any particular amount to a SEP in a given year or even make any contribution at all. In this respect, a SEP is more flexible than any type of qualified plan, even a profit-sharing plan, which requires substantial and recurring employer contributions. However, any employer contribution that is made must be allocated to employees under a definite written formula. The formula may not discriminate in favor of highly compensated employees. In general, the formula must provide allocations as a uniform percentage of total compensation of each employee, taking only the first $150,000 (as indexed for inflation; 2000: $170,000) of compensation into account. The SEP allocation formula can be integrated with Social Security under the usual integration rules for qualified defined-contribution plans.

Each individual in a SEP maintains an IRA and employer contributions to the SEP are channeled to each employee's IRA. For tax purposes, the employer contributions are treated as if they are paid to the employee in cash and included in income and then contributed to the IRA. The Code provides a deduction to both the employer and to the employee for these amounts.

If the employer maintaining a SEP also has a regular qualified plan, contributions to the SEP may reduce the amount that can be deducted for contributions to the regular plan.

Other Requirements

Except for the contribution, allocation, and deduction provisions, the IRAs maintained as part of a SEP are the same as other IRAs and the rules discussed in the previous section apply to them as well. For example, the rules for taxation of distributions from SEP-IRAs are the same as those for other IRAs. As with regular IRAs, loans to participants from SEP-IRAs are not permitted.

Labor and IRS regulations contain certain reporting and disclosure provisions for SEPs. These are simplified if the employer uses the IRS prototype SEP contained on Form 5305-SEP. This form was designed to simplify the adoption of SEPs by employers; however, it uses a nonintegrated formula.

When Should an Employer Use a SEP?

The term *simplified* in the name of these plans is somewhat misleading; a SEP is not really much simpler than a regular qualified profit-sharing plan, especially where a qualified master or prototype plan is used. However, installation costs are minimal where the government Form 5305-SEP is used; administration costs are low because the annual report form (5500 series) need not be filed. Thus, SEPs are attractive for cases where administrative costs must be absolutely minimized, such as a one-person plan. In other specific situations, the special coverage rules for SEPs may be more attractive than the regular coverage rules. From an employee viewpoint, the complete portability of the SEP benefit is attractive.

STUDY QUESTIONS

1. Who is eligible to make deductible IRA contributions?

2. George and Mary Barke (marrieds filing jointly) have an adjusted gross income of $56,317. What is the amount of the deductible IRA contribution that they can make if they do not contribute toward a spousal IRA?

3. What are the advantages of Roth IRAs?

4. How are IRA distributions taxed?

5. What are the financial planning advantages associated with IRA rollovers?

6. What are the major similarities and differences between a SEP and a qualified profit-sharing plan?

CHAPTER 28

Executive Benefits and Nonqualified Deferred-Compensation Plans

The employee benefit plans discussed so far in this text usually are designed for relatively broad groups of employees. Some of the more tax-favored plans, such as qualified retirement plans, actually include specific nondiscriminatory coverage provisions. However, employers often wish to provide special or additional employee benefits to key employees.

In designing plans for executives and key employees, the first step is to identify the employer and employee objectives that the plan is to meet. Then, the plan must be designed to prevent—as far as possible—any undesirable tax or other legal consequences. Employer objectives for executive benefit plans usually include the attraction of appropriate key employees and the retention of such employees once they are hired. In particular, the employer may wish to prevent the employee from going to work for a competing organization. Key employees themselves are usually concerned about their high marginal income tax brackets and their need for savings and estate planning. They therefore favor benefit plans that provide them with tax-favored current compensation or a tax-favored savings medium. There are many types of plans that can be designed to meet employer or employee objectives of this type. In smaller organizations, key employees are often the owners of the business, so there is no difference between employer and employee objectives.

An important basic consideration for an employer in designing executive compensation is whether the amount paid is deductible by the employer as a business expense. Generally, the amount must be "reasonable" to be deducted. There is much tax litigation over the issue of reasonableness in this context. In addition, there is a specific annual deduction limit of $1 million on compensation for an employee. However, this $1 million limit applies only to publicly-held companies—those whose securities are traded on a securities exchange. Also, it applies only to the company's chief executive officer and the four highest-paid officers. In addition, there are exceptions for "performance-based" compensation.

Some common types of executive benefit plans will be listed here at the beginning of the chapter. In the rest of the chapter, some of these benefits will be discussed in more detail, particularly those involving design features that must be coordinated with tax and other laws.

EXECUTIVE BENEFIT CHECKLIST

1. *Nonqualifed Deferred-Compensation or Supplemental Retirement Plans.* A nonqualified deferred-compensation plan provides additional retirement or deferred-compensation benefits to key employees in addition to, or in place of, the amounts received under the employer's qualified plan, if any. There is a great deal of flexibility in the design of such plans, and many approaches have been used. (See later discussion.)
2. *Restricted Stock or Other Property.* Restricted property plans provide compensation to executives in the form of property, usually stock of the em-

ployer company, that is restricted in such a way as to help retain the services of the executives or provide an incentive for good executive performance. (See later discussion.)

3. *Stock Options.* Stock option plans are used for purposes similar to restricted stock plans; however, with an option plan, the employee is given an option to buy the stock at a stated price rather than an outright grant of the stock subject to restrictions. (See later discussion.)

4. *Life Insurance.* Life insurance is a valuable benefit for key employees. As discussed later, it can be provided in a variety of ways.

5. *Severance Pay.* Most employers have some form of severance pay policy for employees, often at a minimal level for rank-and-file employees. Executives, however, often negotiate favorable severance pay provisions as part of their compensation package. One particular type of contract regarded by Congress as abusive is the "golden parachute" contract, under which a company agrees to pay an executive large amounts of severance pay if the company changes ownership. Under Code Section 280G, tax deductions for golden parachute payments can be denied to the employer if the amount is excessive—generally, if it is at least three times the executive's average annual salary.

6. *Cash Bonus and Incentive Plans.* Executive compensation plans often include plans for cash bonuses paid currently or deferred for a relatively short period of time that are tied to company or executive performance. Most of these programs are based in some manner on growth in company earnings during the executive's tenure in office. Often the bonus or incentive award depends on the attainment of specified target earnings objectives. There are many design considerations for such plans, including eligibility for the plan, the amount of the award and the benefit formula, and the period of time over which executive performance will be assessed. All these design features must be tailored to the employer's specific situation. There are no special tax complications for these plans; generally, the compensation is taxable to the executive when received and deductible to the employer at the same time.

7. *Additional Medical Expense Benefits.* Additional health insurance is an attractive executive benefit, particularly where the company's basic plan has gaps in coverage.

8. *Disability Income Plans.* As with health insurance, the company may wish to provide a disability income (salary continuation) plan for executive employees to cover any gaps in or to supplement the company's broad-based disability income plan. If the additional coverage is provided through insurance owned by the company, the premium is fully deductible to the employer but benefits are taxable to the employee when paid, subject to a disability income tax credit that disappears for higher

income employees. If instead of relying on a company-provided plan, the executive purchases his or her own disability income insurance, the premium payments by the employee are nondeductible, but disability income payments are nontaxable. Because of this, many companies may prefer simply to provide extra compensation income to executives with the understanding that the executive will have the option of obtaining personally owned disability income insurance coverage.

9. *Loans to Executives.* A plan providing loans from company funds to executives on favorable terms may be attractive to executives. If the executives are owners of the company, such a program also provides a means of withdrawing corporate funds on a favorable basis, that is, without being taxed on the receipt of a dividend. While interest-free and bargain loans were once used for this purpose, Code Section 7872 now prescribes a minimum interest rate for such loans, which is basically the interest rate applicable during the same period for federal marketable securities of similar term. If the employee loan has a lower interest rate, the bargain element is taxed as if the employee had received that amount as cash compensation. The purpose of this Code provision is to treat as nearly as possible a bargain-rate loan as if it is a market-rate loan, in order to discourage bargain-rate loans.

Any employee loan should be a bona fide loan and should be evidenced by a formal written note with a fixed maturity date or a repayment schedule. The employee could be required to provide security for the loan, such as a home mortgage. Loan plans can be relatively unrestricted or can restrict executive loans to specific purposes, such as the purchase of a home or children's educational expenses.

Interest on the loan will generally be consumer interest that is nondeductible to the employee unless secured by a home mortgage. Interest could also be deductible as investment interest if the loan proceeds are used for investments.

10. *Other Fringe Benefits.* An infinite variety of perquisites and fringe benefits for executives is possible; for example, executive dining rooms, favorable expense account provisions, financial counseling and estate planning for executives, additional moving expense reimbursements, payment of professional association dues, and trips to professional seminars. The usefulness of these benefits depends entirely on individual facts and circumstances.

The decision whether to provide any of these benefits is often affected by their federal income tax treatment because executives tend to be in high marginal income tax brackets and prefer to receive extra compensation in tax-free form.

NONQUALIFIED DEFERRED-COMPENSATION PLANS

For qualified plans, Code Section 415, as discussed in Chapter 25, imposes limits on the benefits or contributions that can be provided to any one individual. Annual additions to a qualified defined-contribution plan are limited to the lesser of 25 percent of the employee's compensation or $30,000. Correspondingly, for a defined-benefit plan, the maximum projected annual benefit is the lesser of 100 percent of the employee's compensation or $90,000. For very highly paid executives, it may be desirable to provide additional retirement income in excess of these limits. Also, in some cases, an employer does not have a qualified plan because the employer does not want to provide the kind of broad retirement plan coverage required by the nondiscriminatory coverage requirements. Thus, a common form of executive benefit is the provision of retirement income or deferred compensation outside of a qualified plan. Plans that do this are generally referred to as *nonqualified deferred-compensation plans.* Many names have been coined by consulting firms and insurance companies to describe specific plans of this type—for example, *supplemental retirement plans, top-hat plans,* and the like. The design of nonqualified deferred-compensation plans is open-ended and almost any combination of features can be provided in one way or another.

Objectives for the Plan

The design of a nonqualified deferred-compensation plan will reflect the objectives of the person establishing it. A broad distinction can usually be made between plans designed to meet employer objectives and those designed primarily to meet employee objectives. The employer's objectives in instituting the plan are usually to provide an inducement for hiring key employees and then to provide additional inducements to the key employees to continue working for the employer—especially so that employees do not leave and go to work for a competitor. Employee objectives are usually to obtain an additional form of compensation at retirement or termination of employment, with tax on the additional amounts deferred, if possible, until the money is actually received.

Employer-Instituted Plan

Eligibility in an employer-instituted plan is usually confined to key executives or technical employees who are difficult to recruit and keep. The plan does not have to specify a class of employees to be covered; it can simply be adopted for specific individuals as the need arises. However, the need for fairness among a similarly situated group of executives often dictates that the plan cover a specified class of employees rather than individuals.

A plan instituted for employer objectives usually has some kind of forfeiture provision to discourage key employees from leaving. The plan may require that the employee forfeit all rights under the nonqualified deferred-compensation plan in the event of termination of employment prior to normal retirement age without the employer's consent. The employer might wish to soften this forfeiture provision somewhat by including graduated vesting similar to that required under a qualified plan. However, as long as the plan avoids the applicability of the ERISA vesting provisions discussed later, no particular vesting schedule is required and complete forfeiture can be provided for any reason. The plan might include additional forfeiture provisions, such as a forfeiture of any unpaid benefits, if the employee enters into competition with the employer or goes to work for a competitor. The courts have held that such covenants not to compete can be enforced by the employer, so long as the scope of the prohibited competition is reasonable in terms of the geographic area over which it applies and the period of time during which it is in effect.

Nonqualified deferred-compensation plans often require that the employee remain available for consulting services to the employer after retirement, with possible forfeiture of benefits if the employee does not comply. Actually, consulting services provisions can be beneficial to the employee, as they often provide a means for the employee to receive additional amounts from the employer after retirement in return for relatively nominal consulting services.

Employee-Option Nonqualified Deferred Compensation

Different objectives for a nonqualified deferred-compensation plan come from the employee's side. Employees with enough income to have substantial savings programs often seek tax-favored methods of saving. Additional amounts of tax-favored savings can be provided beyond the limits of a qualified plan through a salary-reduction arrangement, with the amount of the salary reduction paid to the employee after retirement instead of currently. This provides tax savings because income tax on the salary reduction is paid in the future instead of currently, a valuable benefit because of the time value of money. It is also possible that the employee may be in a lower marginal tax bracket after retirement.

The initial problem in designing a plan for this objective is to ensure that the employee is not taxed currently on the salary reduction that goes into the plan. The salary-reduction arrangement must avoid the constructive receipt doctrine, under which income is taxable to a taxpayer if it is credited to the taxpayer's account, set apart, or otherwise made available, even though it is not actually received. To avoid this doctrine, the amount set aside must be subject to substantial limitations. This can generally be accomplished if the salary-reduction agreement is made prior to the time the income is earned by the employee and if the employee's receipt of it is deferred for a period of time, such as to termination of employment or retirement, which constitutes a substantial limitation.

Plans designed to meet employee objectives generally will have generous provisions and, in particular, there will be few forfeiture provisions—usually 100 percent immediate vesting—unless the plan is formally funded.

Funded and Unfunded Plans

A nonqualified deferred-compensation plan can be either funded by the employer or unfunded. With a funded plan, the employer sets aside money or property to the employee's account in an irrevocable trust or through some other means that restricts access by the employer and the employer's creditors to the fund. With an unfunded plan, either there is no fund at all or the fund that is set up is accessible to the employer and its creditors at all times, so that it provides no particular security to the employee other than the knowledge that the fund exists.

It might appear desirable from the employee's point of view to have a funded plan. However, there are significant disadvantages: The amounts put into a funded plan generally are taxable to the employee at the time the employee's rights to the fund become nonforfeitable, or substantially vested, a concept to be discussed under "Compensation with Restricted Property." This may occur well in advance of the time these funds are actually received by the employee, thus producing a tax disadvantage. Also, funded plans are subject to the ERISA vesting and fiduciary requirements, as discussed later, and this is usually undesirable from the employer's point of view.

As a result of these disadvantages, nonqualified deferred-compensation plans generally are unfunded. The employee relies only on the employer's unsecured contractual obligation to pay the deferred compensation. Because such plans provide no real security to the employee, their value as an inducement may be minimal if the company is risky; employees will then probably opt for greater benefits in current cash or property rather than deferred compensation.

Informal Funding

To provide some assurance, the employer can informally fund the plan by setting money aside in some kind of separate account, with this arrangement known to the employee but with no formal legal rights on the part of the employee and with the amount in the fund therefore available to the employer's creditors. Life insurance policies on the employee's life (owned by and payable to the employer) are often used to provide this kind of informal funding. Life insurance is particularly useful for this purpose if the deferred-compensation plan provides a death benefit to the employee's designated beneficiary, because if the employee dies after only a few years of employment, the life insurance will make sufficient funds available immediately to pay the death benefit. Sometimes a trust is set up by the employer to finance the plan. If the trust assets are available to the employer's creditors, the arrangement is deemed unfunded by the IRS. This type of arrangement is sometimes referred to as a *rabbi trust* because an early IRS ruling on this issue involved a rabbi.

Form of Benefits

Most nonqualified deferred-compensation plans provide for benefit payments in installments beginning at retirement or termination of employment.

The five-year averaging provision available for qualified plan lump-sum benefits does not apply to nonqualified plans; benefits are taxable as ordinary income when received at the taxpayer's regular tax rates, assuming that the taxpayer has not already paid taxes on the amounts in prior years.

Nonqualified deferred-compensation plans often provide a death benefit, usually in the form of a benefit to a designated beneficiary in the amount the employee would have received if he or she had lived. If the plan uses life insurance as an informal funding medium, it usually also provides a flat-amount death benefit—usually related to the face amount of the life insurance policies—that is payable regardless of how much deferred compensation has accrued to the date of death. Death benefits are taxable as ordinary income to the beneficiary.

Employer's Tax Treatment

In a nonqualified deferred-compensation plan, the employer does not receive a tax deduction for deferred compensation until the year in which the employee must include the compensation in taxable income. This is the case even if the employer has put money aside through formal or informal funding of the plan in an earlier year. For an unfunded plan, the year of inclusion for the employee is the year in which the compensation is actually or constructively received. If the plan is formally funded, the employee includes the compensation in income in the year in which it becomes substantially vested.

Impact of ERISA and Other Regulatory Provisions

To retain design flexibility and keep administrative costs down, most deferred compensation plans are designed to avoid the fiduciary, vesting, and reporting and disclosure requirements of ERISA to the maximum extent possible. Generally, if the plan is unfunded and is maintained by an employer primarily for the purpose of providing deferred compensation for a select group of management or highly compensated employees, the plan will be exempt from all provisions of ERISA. However, if the plan does not come within this exemption, most of the provisions of ERISA become applicable, and the plan must comply with almost all of the ERISA provisions that apply to a qualified plan. The nonqualified plan could discriminate in participation, benefits or contributions, but for all other purposes—vesting, fiduciary, and reporting and disclosure—the plan would have to be designed like a qualified plan without the tax benefits for qualified plans. Consequently, most nonqualified deferred-compensation plans are designed to be unfunded and are limited to management or highly compensated employees.

COMPENSATION WITH RESTRICTED PROPERTY

An employee's compensation can be paid in either cash or noncash property. It is common for an executive's compensation to include payment in property, usually employer stock or securities, that is subject to some form of restriction at the time it is paid. The restriction on the property is usually designed to serve an employer goal, such as retaining a valued employee, and the restriction also can be designed to postpone taxability of the compensation to the employee and correspondingly postpone the employer's tax deduction.

Restricted stock or other restricted property is not an attractive benefit to an executive if the executive must pay income tax on the property when it is received, even though it is subject to restrictions. Therefore, most restricted property plans are designed around Code Section 83 that allows deferral of taxation to the employee if the restrictions meet certain requirements. Basically, the rules provide that an employee is not subject to tax on the value of restricted property until the year in which the property becomes *substantially vested*. Property is not considered substantially vested if it is subject to a *substantial risk of forfeiture* and not transferable by the employee free of the risk of forfeiture. As with most types of nonqualified compensation plans, the employer does not get a tax deduction until the year in which the property becomes substantially vested and includable in the employee's income.

The question whether there is a substantial risk of forfeiture depends on the facts and circumstances of each case. However, a substantial risk of forfeiture usually exists when the employee must return the property if a specified period of service for the employer is not completed—for example, five years of service. A forfeiture that results only from an unlikely event, such as the commission of a crime by the executive, probably would not constitute a substantial risk of forfeiture. Forfeitures as a result of failing to meet certain sales targets or going to work for a competitor could constitute substantial risks, depending on the facts and circumstances. If the employee is an owner of the company, the IRS is likely to be skeptical of any forfeiture provision in the plan, no matter how rigid it may appear on paper.

The nontransferability provision—the second half of the test—can be complied with in the case of the company stock by inscribing a statement on the share certificate to the effect that the shares are part of a restricted property plan. Thus, any prospective transferee is aware that the employee is not free to sell the shares to an outsider without restriction.

■ EXAMPLE

Suppose that executive Rita Bill is permitted to buy 500 shares of company stock at $10 per share in 2000, while the current market value is $100 per share. Rita must resell the shares to the company for $10 per share if she terminates employment with the company at any time during the next five years. The share certificates are also stamped with an appropriate statement to meet the nontransferability requirement. Rita pays no taxes on this arrangement until the restriction expires in 2005. If the unrestricted shares in 2005 have a market value of

continued

■ **EXAMPLE** (continued)

of $200 per share, Rita will have additional taxable compensation income for 2005 of $100,000, the market value of the shares, less $5,000, the amount Rita paid, or a net additional compensation income of $95,000. The company will get a tax deduction of $95,000 in 2005, but gets no deduction for 2000. Also, the allowance of the tax deduction to the company is, like all tax deductions for compensation paid, subject to the requirement that the total compensation package for the employee constitutes reasonable compensation for services rendered.

Many variations are possible in the design of restricted stock plans. The plan, for example, may provide that dividends on the restricted stock are payable to the executive during the restriction period; if so, these dividends are taxable currently to the executive as compensation income. The plan also might provide graduated vesting over a period of years, rather than full vesting at the end of a specified period like five years; this would mean that the executive would be taxed each year on the value of the property that became substantially vested that year.

In some plans, there are no forfeiture provisions; instead the stock is subject to other restrictions. For example, the employee may have a fully vested interest in the stock but may not be permitted to resell the stock without first offering it back to the company at a specified price. In that case, the value of stock to the executive would not be its market value, but would be a reduced value reflecting the restriction. Under the Internal Revenue Code, a restriction will be taken into account in valuing the property for tax purposes only if it is a *nonlapse restriction*—a restriction which by its terms will never lapse. The restriction in the example with a requirement of resale to the company at a fixed price would qualify as a nonlapse restriction. Other types of restrictions must be assessed on their own facts and circumstances, and the IRS tends to take a very limited view of what constitutes a nonlapse restriction.

Once an executive has become substantially vested in the restricted property and paid any tax on the compensation element involved, gain on a subsequent sale of the property is usually taxed as capital gain just as in the case of the sale of such property acquired by other means.

STOCK OPTION PLANS FOR EXECUTIVES (NONSTATUTORY)

A stock option is an offer to sell stock at a specified price at some time in the future or over a limited period of time with a specific termination date. Stock options have long been used for executive compensation to accomplish some of the same purposes as compensation with restricted stock. Over the years, Congress has designed special tax incentives to make certain types of stock option plans attractive. The type of tax-favored plan currently in effect is known as an *incentive stock option (ISO)* plan, which will be discussed separately. In this section, stock options in general—sometimes referred to as *non-statutory* or *nonqualified stock options*—will be discussed first.

Options to buy stock in the employer company are typically granted to executives as additional compensation at a favorable price, with the hope that the value of the stock will rise and make the option price a considerable bargain for the executive. If the stock price declines, the executive simply declines to exercise the option to buy the stock. This gives the executive a benefit whose potential value is tied to the fate of the company, but with no downside risk. This valuable incentive to the executive appears to cost the company very little, although this is somewhat misleading, as discussed below.

Stock options other than ISOs can be designed in any manner the employer and employee desire. Typically, a stock option runs for a period such as ten years, and is granted at a price equal to the fair market value of the stock on the date that it is granted.

■ **EXAMPLE**

Bill Kate is given an option in Year 1 to purchase up to 1,000 shares of stock at $50 per share, which is the current market price, with the option to be exercised over the next ten years. The plan may provide a waiting period before the option may be exercised, or it may provide that the option can be exercised only in successive installments—i.e., only 20 percent of the option can be exercised during the first two years, 40 percent over the first four years, and so on. The option has no value to Bill at the date of the grant because the option price was the same as the market price. Therefore, as of Year 1, there was no taxable income to Bill. Under the general tax rules in this situation, Bill will not be taxed until shares are actually purchased.

Suppose Bill purchases 400 shares in Year 4 for a total of $20,000. If the fair market value of the shares in Year 4 has risen to $40,000, the executive has $20,000 of ordinary income in Year 4. The company will get a tax deduction of $20,000 in Year 4, the same as the amount of Bill's compensation income, again assuming that Bill's compensation meets the reasonable compensation test for deductible compensation. However, the company gets no further deduction if Bill resells the stock and realizes a capital gain.

Options with an immediate value to the executive are sometimes used in executive compensation.

■ **EXAMPLE**

Suppose that the option had been granted at $40 per share, a bargain over the prevailing market price of $50 at the time of the grant. If the option has a determinable value and the option could be traded on an established market, the
continued

> ■ **EXAMPLE** (continued)
>
> value of the option is taxable as ordinary income to Bill at the time of the grant, with a corresponding deduction to the employer. If tax is payable at the grant of theoption, there is no further taxable compensation income when the option is exercised later. This can be an advantageous approach if the stock is expected to appreciate substantially in value, because the taxable compensation income at the time of the grant is relatively small, while the remainder of the gain on the overall deal will be taxed as capital gain only when the stock is sold.
>
> Suppose that Bill is granted an option for 500 shares of company stock at $40 per share in Year 1, the current market price being $50 per share. Bill has $5,000 of ordinary compensation income in Year 1, the year of the grant. In Year 4, Bill exercises the option and buys 400 shares for $16,000. There is no ordinary income tax to Bill at the time of the exercise in Year 4.

The stock option appears to be an almost ideal method of compensating executives, providing a valuable incentive-based compensation arrangement at practically no cost to the company. However, the company's cost is comparable to the cost of cash compensation. While it costs the company almost nothing to grant options and print stock certificates to provide shares when the options are exercised, the executive will exercise the option only when the stock has a substantial market value. If this is the case, the company could itself have sold the stock used in the option arrangement on the open market and received the full proceeds. However, the grant of an option does not result in a charge to the company's income statement, so this form of compensation can be attractive from an accounting point of view.

The tax rules applicable to nonstatutory stock options do not provide any particular tax advantage to the employer company in using stock option plans. Therefore, in designing a stock option plan the company must look for benefits to itself just as in the case of any other kind of executive compensation. Typically, stock option plans would be used where the executive has a strong desire to obtain an interest in the business, or where the executive has a direct impact on the company's profits and, therefore, its stock value.

INCENTIVE STOCK OPTIONS

The incentive stock option (ISO) is the current form of stock option plan eligible for special tax benefits, which are provided by Code Section 422. Under an ISO plan, the usual tax rules previously discussed do not apply. Instead, for stock purchased under an ISO plan, there is no taxation to the employee until the stock is sold. Employees do not realize any taxable income when they receive the option, even if the option has an ascertainable fair market value and, furthermore, there is no taxable income when the option is exercised. However, the difference between the option price and the fair market value at the time of exercise is a tax preference item that may be subject to the alternative minimum tax. Because there is no regular taxable income to the employee at either the grant or the exercise of the option, the corporation gets no deduction at any time.

Options under an ISO plan must generally be granted to employees within ten years of the plan's adoption or approval by the shareholders, and an option must be exercised by the employee within ten years after it is granted. The option price must equal or exceed the stock's fair market value at the time the option is granted. Any good-faith attempt to value stock will be acceptable if there is no readily established market.

ISO plans increase the tax benefit of stock options as a form of compensation by providing increased tax deferral and, therefore, represent an attractive executive benefit. However, they are most likely to be used in large corporations. If an option holder has stock with more than 10 percent of the total combined voting power of the employer corporation, taking certain stock attribution rules into account, there are additional restrictions on ISO plans that may make them unattractive for closely held corporations. In such cases, the option price must be at least 110 percent of the stock's fair market value at the time it is granted and the option must be exercised within five years after it is granted rather than ten. Also, an employee receives the maximum tax benefit from an ISO plan only when the stock is sold, and there may be no ready market for a stock of a closely held corporation. Furthermore, it may be undesirable to pass ownership of stock in a closely held corporation to outsiders. However, the plan may permit the employee to exercise an option and pay for the shares of stock with other stock of the employer.

The aggregate fair market value of stock for which an employee can be granted an option under an ISO plan during a single calendar year cannot exceed $100,000. There are carryover provisions if the employee does not use the full limit in any year.

LIFE INSURANCE FOR EXECUTIVES

Life insurance can be an important executive benefit. Life insurance is important to high income employees as a means of providing income security to their families during the early part of their careers. In later years, it can provide or augment the executive's estate to be left to family and other heirs, or it can help provide liquidity to the estate to meet estate taxes and other expenses. A number of methods with favorable tax consequences have been devised to provide life insurance to executives. Generally, the aim is to provide insurance in a way that minimizes the current year-to-year income tax cost of the plan to the employee, and also keeps the life insurance out of the employee's estate for federal estate tax purposes. Some of the methods used include the following:

- *Split-Dollar Plans*. In a split-dollar plan, cash-value life insurance is used, with the death benefit divided or split between the employer and the employee's designated beneficiary. The premium can be paid entirely by the employer or premium costs can be shared between employer and employee. The employer does not receive a tax deduction for its share of the premium payments. However, the plan is designed so that the employer is reimbursed for its premium payments by its share of the death benefit, which is received by the employer tax-free. Thus, the employer's cost for a split-dollar plan is the loss of the use of its share of the premium payments during the time in which the plan is in effect.

In Revenue Ruling 64-328 the IRS has held that the employee pays tax only on the term insurance cost of the portion of the death benefit payable to the employee's beneficiary, using the PS 58 table (Table 20-5 in Chapter 20) or the insurance company's term rates for valuation. From this is subtracted any amount paid by the employee toward the premium.

Many variations on the basic split-dollar approach are possible. For example, to avoid federal estate taxes, the plan is often designed so that the employee has no incidents of ownership in the policy. This can be done, for example, by having the policy applied for by a beneficiary such as a spouse or a family trust, with a split-dollar arrangement between the employer company and the policyholder. Although this arrangement may eliminate the federal estate tax in the employee's estate, it is still considered by the IRS to result in compensation income to the employee.

■ *Death Benefit Only (DBO) Plans.* A DBO plan is a form of deferred-compensation plan in which the benefits are paid only to a designated beneficiary upon the death of the employee. The purpose of this arrangement is to avoid federal estate taxes on the death benefit.

Under the federal estate tax law, a death benefit from a deferred-compensation plan is included in the employee's estate if the employee had a nonforfeitable right to receive benefits while living, even if the employee never actually received such benefits while alive. Thus, the DBO benefit is designed to be paid only at death. If there is a DBO plan, the employer's fringe benefit arrangements for the employee must also be designed carefully to make sure the DBO plan will accomplish its intended purpose. The IRS will lump other deferred-compensation plans—not including qualified plans—together with the DBO plan to determine if the company provides a lifetime benefit to the employee.

To provide a substantial death benefit even during the early years of the plan, DBO plans are usually funded informally with life insurance. That is, the employer owns insurance on the life of the employee, with the employer itself as beneficiary. At the death of the employee, the policy provides funds enabling the employer to pay the death benefit to the employee's beneficiary.

For income tax purposes, a DBO plan is treated the same as any other deferred-compensation plan—death benefits are taxable in full to the beneficiary as ordinary income when received.

■ *Group Term Life Insurance Plan.* Under Section 79, a group term life insurance plan can have a special class for executives and provide them with amounts of group term insurance relatively greater than the amounts provided for other employees. However, if the plan provides amounts of insurance that are higher multiples of compensation for key employees, it probably will be deemed discriminatory and, therefore, the tax exclusion for the value of the first $50,000 of insurance will be lost by key employees.

STUDY QUESTIONS

1. Briefly describe the present rules for interest-free and bargain loans made by a company to its executives.

2. What management objectives can be accomplished by using a nonqualified deferred-compensation plan for a selected group of executives?

3. What features does an executive typically want in his or her nonqualified deferred-compensation plan?

4. a. What is the usual form of benefit payments from a nonqualified deferred-compensation plan?
   b. How are these payments taxed?

5. When does the employer receive a tax deduction for nonqualified deferred-compensation payments made under an unfunded plan?

6. Why are nonqualified plans generally unfunded in the tax sense?

7. How can a nonqualified plan be informally funded (while remaining unfunded in the tax sense) to provide covered executives with some degree of benefit security?

8. Jim Franco purchased 100 shares of company stock at $5 per share. At the time of purchase, the market price for the shares was $50 per share. Jim must resell the shares back to the company for $5 per share if he terminates employment within three years of the purchase. The stock is nontransferable.
   a. Is there a tax impact on Jim when the shares are purchased? Explain.
   b. Will there be a tax impact on Jim if the stock is worth $100 per share when the restriction expires in three years? Explain.
   c. When will the company be allowed a tax deduction for the additional compensation to Jim?
   d. What amount will be deductible by the corporation?

9. In what ways does an incentive stock option differ from a nonstatutory stock option?

10. Describe a split-dollar plan by explaining the roles played by the employer and employee in order to achieve the intended benefits from the arrangement.

11. Explain DBO plans with respect to
    a. the primary purpose of the arrangement;
    b. how the plan is funded;
    c. the income tax impact to the beneficiary.

ADDITIONAL RESOURCES

PERIODICALS

WorldatWork Journal. Scottsdale, Ariz.: American Compensation Association. (quarterly)

Benefits Quarterly. Brookfield, Wis.: International Foundation of Employee Benefits Plans. (quarterly)

Best's Review. Oldwick, N.J.: A.M. Best Company, Inc. (monthly)

BNA Pension Reporter. Washington, D.C.: Bureau of National Affairs. (weekly)

Business Insurance. Chicago: Crain Communications, Inc. (weekly)

Employee Benefit Plan Review. Chicago: Charles D. Spencer & Assocs. (monthly)

Employee Benefits Journal. Brookfield, Wis.: International Foundation of Employee Benefits Plans. (quarterly)

Journal of Compensation and Benefits. Boston: Warren, Gorham & Lamont. (bimonthly)

Journal of Financial Service Professionals. Bryn Mawr, Pa.: Society of Financial Service Professionals. (bimonthly)

Journal of Pension Planning and Compliance. New York: Panel Publishers. (quarterly).

Life Insurance Fact Book. Washington, D.C.: American Council of Life Insurance. (annual)

Managed Care Week. Washington, D.C.: Atlantic Information Services. (weekly)

Medical Benefits. New York: Panel Publishers. (semimonthly)

National Underwriter (Property Casualty/Employee Benefits Edition). Chicago: National Underwriter Co. (weekly)

Pension Facts. Washington, D.C.: American Council of Life Insurance. (annual)

Pensions & Investments. Chicago: Crain Communications, Inc. (biweekly)

Pension World. Atlanta: Communication Channels, Inc. (monthly)

Personnel Administration. Alexandria, Va.: American Society for Personnel Administrators. (monthly)

Personnel Journal. Costa Mesa, Calif.: A. C. Craft, Inc. (monthly)

Social Security Bulletin. Washington, D.C.: U.S. Dept. of Health and Human Services. (monthly)

Social Security Manual. Cincinnati: The National Underwriter Company. (annual)

Source Book of Health Insurance Data. Washington, D.C.: Health Insurance Association of America. (annual)

Tax Facts on Life Insurance. Cincinnati: The National Underwriter Company. (annual)

LOOSE-LEAF SERVICES

Employee Benefit Handbook. Jeffrey D. Marmorsky, ed. Boston: Warren, Gorham & Lamont.

Employers Guide to Self-Insuring Health Benefits. Washington, D.C.: Thompson Publishing Group.

EBPR Research Reports. Chicago: Charles D. Spencer & Assocs.

Pension and Profit-Sharing Plans for Small and Medium-Size Businesses. New York: Panel Publishers, Inc.

Pension and Profit-Sharing Service. Englewood Cliffs, N.J.: Prentice-Hall.

Pension Plan Forms. Jacksonville, Fla.: Corbel & Company.

Pension Plan Guide. Chicago: Commerce Clearing House.

Pension Plan Service. Indianapolis, Ind.: Longman/R & R Newkirk.

Spencer's Retirement Plan Service. Chicago: Charles D. Spencer & Assocs.

BOOKS

Allen, Everett T., Jr.; Melone, Joseph J.; Rosenbloom, Jerry S.; and Van Derhei, Jack L. *Pension Planning.* 8th ed. Homewood, Ill.: Business One Irwin, 1997.

Beam, Burton T., Jr. *Group Benefits: Basic Concepts and Alternatives.* 8th ed. Bryn Mawr, Pa.: The American College, 2000.

Black, Ann. *New Era of Benefits Communication.* Brookfield, Wis.: International Foundation of Employee Benefit Plans, 1997.

Canan, Michael J. *Qualified Retirement and Other Employee Benefit Plans, Practitioner edition.* St. Paul: West Publishing Co., 1996.

Canan, Michael J. and Mitchell, William D. *Employee Fringe and Welfare Benefit Plans.* St. Paul: West Publishing Co., 2000.

Chandler, Darlene K. *The Group Life Insurance Handbook.* Cincinnati: The National Underwriter Co., 1997.

Douglas, Janet. *Integrated Disability Management.* Brookfield, Wis.: International Foundation of Employee Benefit Plans, 2000.

Employee Benefit Research Institute. Fundamentals of Employee Benefit Program. 5th ed. Washington, D.C.: Employee Benefit Research Institute, 1996.

Finkel, Madelon. *Health Care Cost Management.* 3rd ed. Brookfield, Wis.: International Foundation of Employee Benefits Plans, 1996.

Garner, John C. *Health Insurance Answer Book,* 5th ed. New York: Panel Publishers, 1998.

Golub, I. M; Combe, Cynthia; and Chevlowe, Roberta. *2000 COBRA Handbook.* New York: Panel Publishers, 2000.

Harker, Carlton. *Self-Funding of Health Care Benefits.* 4th ed. Brookfield, Wis.: International Foundation of Employee Benefit Plans, 1998.

Health Insurance Association of America. *Long-term Care: Knowing the Risk, Paying the Price.* Washington, D.C.: Health Insurance Association of America, 1997.

Health Insurance Association of America. *Managed Care: Integrating the Delivery and Financing of Health Care.* Washington, D.C.: Health Insurance Association of America, 1996.

Humo, Terry. *ERISA Health and Welfare Handbook.* 2d ed. Washington, D.C.: Thompson Publishing Group, 1999.

Johnson, Richard E. *Flexible Benefits—A How-To Guide,* 5th ed. Brookfield, Wis.: International Foundation of Employee Benefit Plans, 1996.

Knight, Wendy. *Managed Care: What It Is and How It Works.* Gaithersburg, Md.: Aspen Publishers, Inc., 1998.

Krass, Stephen J. *The Pension Answer Book.* New York: Panel Publishers, 2000.

Leimberg, Stephan R. and McFadden, John J. *Tools and Techniques of Employee Benefit and Retirement Planning.* 6th ed. Cincinnati: The National Underwriter Co., 1999.

Littell, David A.; and Tacchino, Kenn Beam. *The Practitioners Guide to Advanced Pension Topics.* 2d ed. Bryn Mawr, Pa.: The American College, 1999.

Life Office Management Association. *Intro to Managed Care.* Atlanta: Life Office Management Association, 1998.

McGill, Dan M. *Fundamentals of Private Pensions.* 7th ed. Philadelphia: University of Pennsylvania Press, 1996.

Oher, James M. *The Employee Assistance Handbook.* New York: John Wiley & Sons, Inc., 1999.

Podgurski, Walter B. *Payroll Deduction: The Selling of Voluntary Benefits.* Cincinnati: The National Underwriter Co., 1995.

Rejda, George M. *Social Insurance and Economic Security.* 6th ed. Englewood Cliffs, N.J.: Prentice-Hall, 1998.

Rosenbloom, Jerry S. Ed. *The Handbook of Employee Benefits.* 5th ed. New York: McGraw Hill, 2001.

Tacchino, Kenn Beam and Littell, David A. *Planning for Retirement Needs.* 3rd ed. Bryn Mawr, Pa.: The American College, 1999.

WEB SITES

Web sites on the Internet continue to come into existence and change locations. As a result, there is no substitute for searching the World Wide Web whenever information is needed about a specific topic. The general Web sites below contain information on many topics as well as numerous links to other Web sites. The other Web sites focus on more specific topics.

GENERAL WEB SITES

International Foundation of Employee Benefit Plans
http://www.lifebp.org
Benefits Link
http://www.benefits link.com

OTHER WEB SITES

American Accreditation HealthCare Commission/URAC
http://www.urac.org
American Association of Health Plans
http://www.aahp.org
American Association of Preferred Provider Organizations
http://www.aappo.org
American Society of Pension Actuaries
http://www.aspa.org

Blue Cross and Blue Shield Association
   http://www.bluecares.com
Department of Labor Pension and Welfare Benefits Administration
   http://www.dol.gov/dol/pwba
Equal Employment Opportunity Commission
   http://www.eeoc.gov
Health Care Financing Administration
   http://www.hcfa.gov
Health Insurance Association of America
   http://www.hiaa.org
National Association of Insurance Commissioners
   http://www.naic.org
National Committee for Quality Assurance
   http://www.ncqa.org
Pension Benefit Guaranty Corporation
   http://www.pbgc.gov
Profit Sharing 401k Council of America
   http://www.psca.org
Social Security Administration
   http://www.ssa.gov
Thomas (Library of Congress site for legislative information)
   http://thomas.loc.gov

INDEX